CHRISTOPHER MARLOWE — see Chronology on p. xxvi.

E. D. PENDRY was formerly Lecturer in English in the University of Bristol. He also taught in universities in Finland, Japan and the U.S.A., and at Birmingham University, where he was a Fellow of the Shakespeare Institute. His books included *The New Feminism of English Fiction: A Study in Contemporary Women-Novelists* (Tokyo, 1956), *Elizabethan Prisons and Prison Scenes* (Salzburg, 1974), and *Thomas Dekker* (1967)

J. C. MAXWELL was formerly Reader in English Literature in the University of Oxford, and a Fellow of Balliol College. He was previously Professor of English in the University of Newcastle upon Tyne. He edited a number of volumes in the Cambridge University Press 'New Shakespeare' series, and a parallel text of Wordsworth's *Prelude* (Penguin, 1971); he was also editor of *Notes and Queries*.

CHRISTOPHER MARLOWE

Complete Plays and Poems

Edited by
E. D. Pendry

Textual Adviser
J. C. Maxwell

J. M. Dent & Sons: London
EVERYMAN'S LIBRARY

© Textual editing and additional matter,
J. M. Dent & Sons Ltd, 1976
All rights reserved

Made in Great Britain by
Guernsey Press Co. Ltd, Guernsey, C.I. for
J. M. Dent & Sons Ltd
91 Clapham High Street, London SW4 7TA

Marlowe's *Plays and Poems* first published
in Everyman's Library in 1909
Present edition, completely revised, 1976
Reprinted in Everyman Paperback 1983
Last reprinted 1990

ISBN 0 460 87043 2

Contents

[v]

Introduction

Marlowe does not know why man is put here. But he is sure
that the arrangement does not work. Every one of his heroes
has high hopes of making something of himself and his life,
but comes to find that the world is not for him, nor he for
the world. This may seem well within the tradition of classical
tragedy, which affirms that the greatness of men and the rich-
ness of their experience lie as much in their agonies and defeats
as in their triumphs. But Marlowe's tragedy is not like that.
We think less well of his heroes at their ending, and the world
is a smaller and grimmer place. Nor are there Christian
consolations. Marlowe is in nothing more unchristian than in
flatly denying the worth of failure. To his eye his heroes die
in vain. They do not learn, we do not learn, from their mistakes; there is nothing to compensate for loss either here or
hereafter.

Yet his heroes are no puppets; they attract wonder, curiosity
and, more rarely, commiseration. We accept that they are all
gifted with a rich and forceful imaginative life from which
their actions spring. Images of the sun, moon and stars, of
meteors and storms, of distant places, of precious stones and
metals, of legendary and mythological doings—it is in images
of this kind that they have their keenest private sense of themselves, and that they confess their love. The imagery is like
that of Revelations. Yet there is no religious dimension to it;
and, although it is often beautiful in its vast reach and purity,
it has the remote and chilling beauty of hard surfaces reflecting
brilliant light, of a dead world without warmth and growth,
without humanity. For men so inspired, no mere worldly
activity can be a fulfilment.

This alienating imagination is a flaw common to all
Marlowe's heroes, and it takes various forms. But in every
case it is a flaw too radical to be likened to the 'tragic flaw'
of Shakespearean tragedy. Shakespeare's heroes have faults
appropriate to their virtues, but faults and virtues remain
distinct; and we are left only too keenly aware that in other
circumstances tragedy would have been averted. Othello's
love of Desdemona is not the same thing as his jealousy about
her, Macbeth's moral delicacy is not the same thing as his

violent nature. Marlowe's conception of such heroes would have been different—simpler, more predictable perhaps: an Othello with no other way of feeling tenderly and truly than through possessiveness, a Macbeth whose unrivalled military and political powers would be unlocked only through a usurped tyranny, the illness that (in Lady Macbeth's words) must inevitably attend ambition. For Marlowe, the flaws in qualities of undeniable greatness are so intimately associated with them as to be no less than intrinsic. So it is that Tamburlaine's leadership, Edward's emotional drive, Faustus's intellectual restlessness, Barabas's business acumen are at once admirable and contemptible. They must be accepted without qualm or qualification; their flaws go beyond the adventitious poignancy of what-might-have-been. Such heroes could have been no other than they are. And there are no other heroes but these.

Most of them steadily lose stature in the course of their plays, and it may seem that Marlowe intends us to change our minds completely about them by the close. Tamburlaine, we would then conclude, is simply a butcher, Faustus simply a charlatan. Though there is no denying Marlowe's disabused temper of mind, he has not met and mastered experience with straightforward cynicism. It is better to speak of the ambiguity of his plays, an ambiguity of his own in which he does not try to identify the alternatives of belief and disbelief in the grandeur of man that are open to us, and to insist on a choice being made between them, but rather, in a wry and bemused spirit, to observe the effect of the collision and confusion of possibilities.

When Doctor Johnson describes metaphysical imagery as '*discordia concors*; a combination of dissimilar images, or discovery of occult resemblances in things apparently unlike', we would, while we concur, attach more importance than Johnson would to the *concors* in the *discordia concors*: in other words, the reader of successful metaphysical imagery is aware at once of the implausibility and the justness of the combination of elements; the effect is rather that of finding vigorous objections fully met. Now Marlowe takes the opposite course in his imagery: that is to say, he combines elements that are *not* apparently unlike (or, to be more accurate, irreconcilable) in such a way as to produce a disturbing effect of incongruity, of objections unmet, of what might be termed occult dissimilarity. This may be readily illustrated from the detail of his verse. Sometimes a double meaning may seem to be well enough accommodated in a pun, as for instance in 'charg'd' in *1 Tamburlaine* I.i.46–8:

> Your grace hath taken order by Theridamas,
> Charg'd with a thousand horse, to apprehend
> And bring him captive to your highness' throne.

Yet here one may be slightly troubled with the sense that Theridamas himself is to be attacked. Similarly, in a famous passage in *Faustus* (V.i.100) the 'topless' towers of Ilium may be imagined as both lofty and roofless, though not with comfort. In *1 Tamburlaine* I.ii.249–51 there is a manifold ambiguity that may also seem ironical:

> Nor thee nor them, thrice-noble Tamburlaine,
> Shall want my heart to be with gladness pierc'd
> To do you honour and security.

The speaker, Theridamas, would not gladly entertain all the possibilities for his fate here. But there are passages in Marlowe where there is a more pronounced clash. In *Dido* III.iv.46–7 Aeneas speaks of

>   the purple sea
> From whence my radiant mother did descend

where Venus emerging from the sea and descending from Oceanus are confounded. In *Hero and Leander* I.169–70,

> When two are stripp'd, long ere the course begin
> We wish that one should lose, the other win

the sexual force of 'stripp'd' is unmistakable, and throws the entire image off tilter. The substitution of 'match' for 'course' would have made an easy concord.

The *concordia discors* may take the form of sudden changes of tone. There are famous examples of this, as when in *The Jew of Malta* the Friar greets the death of the saintly Abigail with the terse regret that she dies a virgin (III.vi.41), or when Tamburlaine turns from his splendid wooing-speech to Zenocrate with the no less terse 'women must be flattered' (I.ii.107). Such changes have often been considered undercutting. And it is true that Marlowe's discordancies are usually reductive rather than redemptive: one does not so readily recall instances (outside the fate of the heroes themselves) when the ignoble is unexpectedly thwarted. But even in the examples given above, Abigail's genuine conversion to Christianity, like the still more remarkable qualms of conscience felt by Bellamira and Pilia-

Borza, is a discordancy in Barabas's judgment of the world. So too, in *Edward II*, Mortimer is caught out, almost ludicrously, at his most self-confident. Cynicism does not stay on the rails. In the larger designs of the plays, critical controversy shows that it is possible to see Tamburlaine either as a hero or an ogre, Faustus either as a genius or a fool.

No doubt Marlowe might have removed some of the discordances of language in revision, but he could not have removed the great thematic discordances without establishing in his own philosophy a governing principle that it lacked. He characterizes his *concordia discors* most tellingly in Tamburlaine's famous speech of 'Nature, that fram'd us of four elements' (*1 Tamburlaine* II.vii.18), where the paradox of a cosmic design that contains incompatible or erratic parts is carried through to a conclusion that is itself disconcertingly off-key. Some readers, rather than allow room for such blatant incertitude in their conception of art, may prefer to find fault with Marlowe for it. At all events it may be agreed that this incertitude, ultimately moral and religious, is reflected in the form and style of his works, which, like the characters within them, give the impression of breaking down after the first two acts. In *Faustus*, though it has been argued that the tomfoolery in the later scenes of the play well expresses the triviality into which Faustus has sunk, the lack of any system in these scenes leads one to conclude that it is Marlowe as much as Faustus who has lost a clear sense of what he is doing.

But if one must speak of Marlowe's failing, one must urge in his defence that it is not for want of an alert intelligence and a lively concern for what is going on in his plays. Indeed there is a restless, unconfined energy in the very lack of order we have discussed. The detachment sometimes ascribed to Marlowe is difficult to deny, more difficult to define. It is the askance, inward-turned consciousness of a man who cares too much, for whom there is perplexity or despair at the heart of experience.

He may seem at some distance from his own heroes. Wilbur Sanders has suggested that in *The Massacre at Paris* and *The Jew of Malta* Marlowe traded on the lowest prejudices of his audience against the French and the Jews, but in the latter case adroitly betrayed the audience into condemning the shortcomings of Christians. It may be that these were not the only plays in which Marlowe deliberately and critically worked up commonplace notions and passions to which he had a less than full personal commitment. Tamburlaine may stand for

the political and military hero for whom Marlowe's con-
temporaries, writers and artists among them, seem to have
constantly hungered. And Faustus may be not the humanist's
but the illiterate's idea of a scholar, up to no good in the
middle of the night.

Whatever sympathy Marlowe feels for his heroes in themselves, and this is certainly not inconsiderable, he tends to lose
when they undertake worldly action, action which is, as he
shows, bound from the nature of the world to fail of its purpose.
So, for instance, Dido tries without any possibility of success
to force her own self-interested interpretation upon the pre-
diction of Aeneas's inevitable destiny as founder of Rome.
For Marlowe, tragedy is the lot of those whose wits have
deserted them.

This may be one reason why he is repelled by pity, the
concern we feel for the witless and the outwitted. One would
like to think that this goes deeper than intellectual arrogance,
not to mention shame for some soft centre of his own, and has
rather to do with a conviction on his part that pity, by imply-
ing as it does palliative relations between people, serves to
obscure the truth about the bitterness of such relations. In the
Prologue to *The Jew of Malta* Machevill scorns the downfall of
great men like Phalaris who end up (as Barabas does) the
victim of their own ingenuity:

> o' th' poor petty wits,
> Let me be envied and not pitied (26–7)

No failure, however much it is deplored, is the equal of any
success, however much it is resented. Barabas thinks the same
way:

> Rather had I, a Jew, be hated thus,
> Than pitied in a Christian poverty (I.i.112–13)

And he instructs Ithamore in pitilessness. In actual fact the
self-styled Christians are themselves to prove no less pitiless.
As in *Tamburlaine*, *Faustus* and *Hero and Leander*, pity is at best
an unfulfilled hope, at worst a dangerous delusion about the
soft terms on which man may live with man, and with God.
In *Edward II* there is the extended ill-treatment and assassination of the King, the most sustained and deliberate exploitation
of pathetic events: Marlowe actually went to Stow's *Annals* to
eke out what he had on the subject in Holinshed's *Chronicles*.
And yet one hesitates to speak of pathos or pity. Undoubtedly

Edward himself has a highly developed sense of his own pathos. But our sympathy for him lacks both particularity and warmth: our objection to his suffering is simply on general humanitarian grounds. The cold, cruel light of Lightborn's mockery in which Edward dies is shed from the centre of the play.

There are two related words which stand for much in Marlowe's mind: *resolution* and *dissolution*. He is by no means the only Elizabethan playwright for whom *resolution*, which the Guise in *The Massacre at Paris* calls 'honour's fairest aim' (ii.39), seems to mean the ruthless, deliberate pursuit of an often tainted self-interest. But for Marlowe it offers a promise of something hard and fast to believe in, a promise likewise of an artistic form. And it will remind him of its opposite, *dissolution*, the shedding of tears, pity, and the loss of form. Indeed the one word *resolve* is capable of bearing both senses at once, as when Zenocrate, appealing (with spirit) for pity, rains 'on the earth resolved pearl in showers' (*1 Tamburlaine* V.i.142: there is an ironic pun at II.vi.27). The combination of senses is Tamburlaine's dilemma in a nutshell. And Marlowe's.

If Marlowe remains in a quandary, unable to endorse either a constructive villainy or a destructive tenderness, he greets the antics of people caught up in such a quandary with a great deal of sardonic humour. Modern critics have come increasingly to recognize how widespread and extraordinary is the humour in Marlowe. It is easy enough to find in, say, the low comedy of *Faustus*, or in the indulgent ironies of *Hero and Leander*. Even in these the humour is aroused by circumstances that are in the end to prove very grave. Elsewhere we may find or suspect a flippant tone where the gravity of the circumstances is only too clearly present to the mind—as, for instance, when Edward complains that

> there in mire and puddle have I stood
> This ten days' space, and lest that I should sleep,
> One plays continually upon a drum (V.v.58–60)

That is a joke, of sorts. And Marlowe carries such humour everywhere. It is a contempt for the absurd strivings and conclusions of human beings, and for the *concordia discors* by which their worthiness and unworthiness may not be differentiated.

Marlowe's own heroes share his gamesomeness. They do not merely enjoy getting the better of others; there is more than a

[xii]

hint that they see their own exploits as lacking high seriousness. This is true even of Tamburlaine, who staggers Theridamas by remarking that a treacherous attack on Cosroe's twenty thousand men 'will prove a pretty jest, in faith' (*1 Tamburlaine* II.v.90), and whose macabre sense of humour it is that invents the cage for Bajazeth and the king-drawn chariot. And these latter examples show how far Marlowe will go in comedy, undeterred it seems by violence, suffering and death. Indeed it is largely because he is not deterred by such things as they really are that one hesitates to write off his humour as merely smart, the bitter knowingness a callow boy has wished himself into.

Marlowe's art greatly depends on bad taste, on the practical joke. The practical joke is a form of humiliation which is properly comic when it cuts down false pretensions, such as those of a Mycetes in kingship or those of a Leander in sexual adventure. But the humiliation is commonly physical, even violent, and it may be inflicted on true pretensions as well as false. In that case the vindictiveness behind it may be traced back to the deeply-felt personal inadequacy of the practical joker himself. So it seems to be with Marlowe: in humiliating his characters he is trying to free himself personally from fierce, immature emotions which are nevertheless still evident to us. This is clearest in passages treating of the humiliation inherent in sexual awareness. Here there is none of the easy-going, solicitous panderism which readers of erotica might expect of their authors:

> in his sportful hands an olive tree
> To hide those parts which men delight to see
> > > (*Edward II* I.i.63–4)

> And tumbling in the grass, he often stray'd
> Beyond the bounds of shame, in being bold
> To eye those parts which no eye should behold.
> > > (*Hero and Leander* I.406–8)

The exposure is indecent, an elegant act of violence. It shames us for our sexual nature to be looked at with so outwardly cold, so sadistic a curiosity. But the ridicule also reveals an inward-directed, secretive excitement; and words like 'sportful', 'delight' (like 'toy', 'wanton', 'frolic', 'dainty', 'dally' elsewhere) come from Marlowe's characteristic vocabulary of titillation, by which sexual feeling is at once aroused and demeaned (as it is in 'tumbling in the grass'). The following passage is also to be found in *Hero and Leander* (I.147–50):

> Jove slyly stealing from his sister's bed,
> To dally with Idalian Ganymede,
> Or for his love Europa bellowing loud,
> Or tumbling with the Rainbow in a cloud

Incest, paederasty, bestiality are recognized for what they are, but with a remorseless flippancy, and with a frisson of mincing sensuality that may disturb if it does not positively repel.

Tamburlaine is both traditional hero and iconoclast. He does superlatively well what has always been looked for in a leader: he wins his battles, he holds fast to an ideal of comradeship, he honours his followers with the spoils of war. Above all, as the Prologue promises us, he is gifted with great eloquence, 'Threat'ning the world with high astounding terms'. It is not the paltry Scythian but the King, Mycetes, who is the clown and the 'rhyming mother-wit' (see I.i.63–8, 104–5; II.ii.10–13, 57–8; II.iv.13–14).

Persia has fallen into a state of degeneracy. Cosroe, the King's brother, looks back with bitterness and the strong man's sentimentality to a period when Persia was to be feared by its neighbours, and leads an insurrection with the express purpose of making Persia great once again. A prefiguration of Tamburlaine himself, he wins much of his support from the very kind of men who would have been well represented in Marlowe's audience—discharged soldiers and gentlemen living idle in the capital 'Wanting both pay and martial discipline' (*1 Tamburlaine* I.i.147), Fortinbras's 'list of lawless resolutes' in *Hamlet*. Tamburlaine sweeps Cosroe away in his turn. To disappointed and neglected men such as Theridamas, who has never gained the promotion his talents merit, the baseborn Tamburlaine offers a new deal, a new hope and faith.

His followers may interpret his promises in their own way. To his immediate lieutenants, crowns and riches are the substantial prizes to dream of. But he would not inspire them as he does did he not appeal to them on other levels. The massive formations of marching and trotting troops he describes take on the character of heavenly bodies in their elemental power, beauty, discipline and order:

> Our quivering lances, shaking in the air,
> And bullets like Jove's dreadful thunderbolts

Enroll'd in flames and fiery smouldering mists,
Shall threat the gods more than Cyclopian wars;
And with our sun-bright armour, as we march,
We'll chase the stars from heaven, and dim their eyes
That stand and muse at our admired arms.

(*I Tamburlaine* II.iii.18–24)

By the application of sheer will and intellect, Tamburlaine seems to be founding a new order in the state, if not a new order in man's life and thought.

Marlowe draws together his complex characterization in one extraordinary emblem:

Of stature tall, and straightly fashioned
Like his desire, lift upwards and divine;
So large of limbs, his joints so strongly knit,
Such breadth of shoulders as might mainly bear
Old Atlas' burden; 'twixt his manly pitch
A pearl more worth than all the world is plac'd,
Wherein by curious sovereignty of art
Are fix'd his piercing instruments of sight,
Whose fiery circles bear encompassed
A heaven of heavenly bodies in their spheres,
That guides his steps and actions to the throne
Where honour sits invested royally

(*I Tamburlaine* II.i.7–18)

There may be promise of cosmic control here, but the head that is to exercise it is, amazingly, a pearl, and the eyes scientific instruments and celestial globes. Is it a robot, then, with a robot's dreams?

The inexorable fact that Tamburlaine's new order is founded exclusively on violence and bloodshed is slow to emerge, but it is given elaborate expression in the banquet 'all in scarlet' before the gates of Damascus. This is a scene of appalling barbarity. Power is equated with food in word and deed: Tamburlaine carves up the world with his dagger, and has a course of crowns served in to his lieutenants, while his invitation to Bajazeth to eat his own wife and himself suggests ironic and more terrible ways in which men may come to consume each other and themselves with their appetite for power. Men are reduced to caged animals and to meat.

Tamburlaine's treatment of Zenocrate is as dehumanizing as that of Bajazeth, since he seems intent on turning her, whether alive or dead, into some stiff and gaudily bedecked idol, to serve his own religion of self. But she remains human and experiences more conflict of mind than Tamburlaine himself. In her brief appearances she can be ironic, querulous, fretful with grief—her 'fortunes never mastered her griefs' (*1 Tamburlaine* V.i.414)—but above all as spokesman for pity in the play, baffled and desperate at Tamburlaine's mounting blood-thirstiness.

The whole of the final act of Part 1 is charged with concern about what happens to human feeling under Tamburlaine's leadership. Bajazeth and Zabina describe the new régime as diabolic, filling the world not with cold light (of which Zenocrate is so much a vessel) but with darkness and fire. Their fate is a timely warning, as Zenocrate recognizes, to the megalomaniac; but perhaps more significant is the fact that within their afflictions they discover or rediscover the value of their love for each other. Likewise Arabia dies speaking words of love, almost indeed the small talk of love.

Tamburlaine is himself aware of a crisis of values. His long soliloquy (which is sometimes, a little ineptly, called his hymn to beauty) stands at the centre of the two-part play, expressing with strain and obscurity a vain effort on Marlowe's part to make some sense of the countervailing forces he has found in his account of Tamburlaine's mind and deeds. It is at the very time that the Virgins of Damascus are massacred that Tamburlaine pauses to seek an answer to the question 'What is beauty, saith my sufferings, then?' (*1 Tamburlaine* V.i.160). At first sight he may seem to invoke a warrior code of virility against feminine pleas for mercy. But he warns us that there are forms of beauty that lie beyond words, and indeed what he means by 'beauty' becomes less and less clear, until he hovers on the brink of declaring, not just that the prizing of women's qualities is compatible with the prizing of men's, nor just that the warrior code is itself beautiful, but that the savagery that goes with it is beautiful also. The various possibilities are held loosely together when the play ends in wedding preparations, and Tamburlaine's career of conquest is made to appear in retrospect a courtship trial. Yet there is no real union to be celebrated. The wedding is another of Tamburlaine's crushing victories which one can enjoy for their fearful and resounding emptiness.

2 Tamburlaine is both more reckless and more jaundiced a work. Everywhere there is blood and fire, betrayals and death. And, as though in parody of Tamburlaine's earlier imagery of ordered and vigorous movement, the highest good that a

man can propose to himself or to anyone else is to hold a
procession. Indeed processions, with drums and trumpets
sounding, repeatedly march on to the stage. An emblematic
portrait of Tamburlaine markedly different from that in Part I
is now drawn by Theridamas: he treads

> fortune underneath his feet,
> And make the mighty god of arms his slave;
> On whom Death and the Fatal Sisters wait
> With naked swords and scarlet liveries;
> Before whom, mounted on a lion's back,
> Rhamnusia bears a helmet full of blood,
> And strows the way with brains of slaughtered men;
> By whose proud side the ugly Furies run,
> Hearkening when he shall bid them plague the world;
> Over whose zenith, cloth'd in windy air,
> And eagle's wings join'd to her feathered breast,
> Fame hovereth, sounding of her golden trump,
> That to the adverse poles of that straight line
> Which measureth the glorious frame of heaven
> The name of mighty Tamburlaine is spread.
>
> (*2 Tamburlaine* III.iv.52–77)

Here is yet another trumpeting, another procession, bringing
death and destruction as though these were the laws of nature
Tamburlaine has usurped, and made into a thing of terrible
beauty. And that former ordering, the creative element in the
art of war, becomes also (in III.ii) the solid, dreary technology
of bulwarks, rampires, cavalieros, counterforts, countermines,
high argins and covered ways, in which he instructs his sons,
and to which he can go in his frenzy of grief for Zenocrate and
find reassurance and self-control. The tender qualities for
which Zenocrate stood, on the other hand, have become as
debilitating as war has become brutalized, and with her death
and that of her ignoble son Calyphas are finally extinguished
and denied Tamburlaine in this life. Zenocrate seems to
comfort herself with the pious belief that there is a place without grief and fury hereafter. So much for love and patience—
and pity.

In this second part of the play, where Tamburlaine is seen
to be so powerless in the face of the very death which he had
supposed to be his loyal attendant, and his entire war-train
is made into a funeral procession by Zenocrate's hearse (death
replacing love as a challenge to his magnificence), his own
thoughts turn to what he is, what he has achieved, and how he

is to be perpetuated through his sons. It is in this way that Marlowe emphasizes the difference that will always remain between what a man is in his soul and that most questionable and imperfect thing that he becomes in body and action, just as a difference will always remain between what hovers in the restless head of a poet and what is digested into words. If Tamburlaine is defeated by any supernatural agency it is by Mahomet, Sigismund being defeated by Christ. But Marlowe writes less like one who believes God does or does not exist than one for whom God's existence is unimportant.

At the beginning of *The Jew of Malta* Barabas speaks in ecstatic imagery much like that of Tamburlaine—

> Bags of fiery opals, sapphires, amethysts,
> Jacinths, hard topaz, grass-green emeralds,
> Beauteous rubies, sparkling diamonds. (I.i.25–7)

In his mind's eye is the great mercantile vista of the Mediterranean and Near East, the mysterious Orient of the Elizabethans, with its delicacies of taste, touch and scent. These are not the outpourings of gross avarice, but of a lavish prodigality. Barabas himself tells us his is no 'vulgar trade': he scorns the riches that are to be counted, that enslave a man, wearying and troubling him, rather than ransoming him from captivity, liberating him. Riches are, in Tamburlaine's words, 'friends that help to wean my state' (*1 Tamburlaine* I.ii.29), the material means by which freedom is secured and power won; but, as again for Tamburlaine, they are the riches of the mind invested and ventured in the busy trade of life. On the one hand the counting-house is felt as an intensely private, even intimate and somewhat oppressive place of steel-barred coffers crammed full, of fingering and sweating; on the other, it is the centre of a windblown empire or an emporium to which men and ships and cargoes far and near are subject. In the opening scene Marlowe gives a remarkable impression of a man triumphantly integrated with his world—of, in fact, 'infinite riches in a little room'. If, as has been suggested, this famous phrase glances, blasphemously, at a traditional paradox of the incarnation, the almighty creator enclosed in the womb, so much the better for the purpose.

In the play as a whole there is a pulsation between the private and public characters of Barabas. Marlowe is no longer interested in leadership, but in the problem of the individual. The recurrence of the words 'one' and 'multitude' makes the essential point (see I.i.142, 155; I.ii.179, 308; at I.ii.97–100 there is an ironical allusion to Barabas's Christ-like state: see John xi.50). Barabas is of course an outsider: religion and race isolate him from the Christians, and wealth from his fellow Jews and merchants. Marlowe does not, however, ask us to identify with Barabas, who is deftly presented so as to give the unpleasant impression such as is made by members of any minority group, appearing at one time servile, at another arrogant, at one time secretive, at another demonstrative, and constantly discomfiting us with reminders that we do not know all the same things, or think of those we do in the same way. And at a deeper level we perceive that, like the Machevill of the Prologue, he weighs not men. He does not need us personally and does not like us; and, in common with the Christians of Malta, we feel much the same about him.

It is the damaging effect upon Barabas wrought by the degenerate society in which he lives that turns him into an out-and-out villain. The Order of the Knights of St John which governed Malta was expressly dedicated to the ideals of poverty, chastity and obedience, and one might well add hospitality. To Elizabethans, however, it was probably well known that their lives were scandalous, and their economy depended on piracy and the slave-trade. Marlowe makes much of their hypocrisy, which he may well regard as intellectually inferior to the downright dishonesty of the Jew:

> As good dissemble that thou never mean'st
> As first mean truth, and then dissemble it:
> A counterfeit profession is better
> Than unseen hypocrisy. (I.ii.289–92)

There is play elsewhere with that word 'profession', meaning as it does the code one claims to live by. The Knights cannot properly be called Machiavellian, because they are self-deceived: it is the essential feature of the Machiavellian that he sweeps away humbug and sentiment to get at the truth, however unpalatable. Only thus can one fully possess oneself.

The culture of Malta is shown to be corrupt in other ways. The sexual morals of the monasteries are a joke; the greed of the friars is shameless. Barabas adapts himself as readily to such social conditions as he has adapted himself to the conditions of trade: it is through his chicanery that the old and honourable duelling code (not to mention the love code) leads to the destruction of two young men, and the decent tradition of giving charity on St Jacques's Eve leads to the destruction of the nuns. No institution or practice is sound. A monstrous breach of hospitality is to be his masterpiece. One should thus make no simple distinction between the Jew and the Christians: Barabas becomes, if he has not always been, one of the things that is wrong with Malta. The biblical Barabbas was after all the thief preferred to Christ (Matt. xxvii.15–26).

The balcony scene is an important turning-point: here, feverish images of darkness and flying shapes, sleep, and death express that mood of anguish and despair in which, as other Elizabethan playwrights also tell us, with a cogency we have lost, the mind turns to evil. It is at the opposite extreme to the crystal clarity and far-reaching dimensions of joy.

When we next see Barabas, at the slave-market, his inner thoughts are represented by a succession of asides. These serve very well to portray an intelligence which so surpasses others in force and subtlety that its energies are not contained within social intercourse, but boil and bubble over. Its sense of its own reserved power, of the disparity between this and what only appears on the surface, is so enjoyed that it is felt as humour—wit and glee. Marlowe shows how reductive of moral value and sensibility this kind of self-possessed intellectuality can be. This is obvious in Barabas's unfeeling treatment of Abigail as though she were indeed no more than a jewel, one of his stock-in-trade. But his long list of the past atrocities he has committed, which has disconcerted critics, is a still better index of just how far the rot has gone: it no longer matters, to Barabas at least, whether any of the story is true or not.

If he depreciates society, he is himself depreciated. Ithamore has it right when he says he has 'the bravest, gravest, secret, subtle, bottle-nos'd knave to my master' (III.iii.9–10): it is a complex rather than inconsistent judgment. As G. K. Hunter and Eric Rothstein have noted, Barabas spirals downwards from the circle of Abigail and her two wooers to that of Ithamore and the two friars, and then to that of a pickpocket and courtezan. Then worse: 'prey for vultures and wild beasts' tossed over the city wall. The final scenes concentrate the issue: his decision to betray Malta as a whole brings on his own total destruction; in a quick succession of reversals he becomes first the betrayer of the Governor and then the Governor who is betrayed. He falls victim, like Phalaris in the Prologue, to his own ingenuity, dropping into 'a deep pit past recovery' (V.v.37), which may well be conceived, as Hunter suggests, in the tradition of the cauldron in hell reserved for Antichrist, but which is here both literally and figuratively prepared by the evil-doer for himself. Not that Marlowe is making a comfortable moral point: the intellect which is defeated in the play is a finer thing (there must remain with us that beauty, however tainted, of the opening soliloquy) than the intellects which triumph; and so much does Marlowe think as Barabas does, that the very destruction of his hero does not seem to matter more to him than that of the sick people groaning under walls mattered to Barabas—though, like that, it is good for a laugh.

There are some points of resemblance between the Jew and Faustus. Both are clever and imaginative men who choose evil in order to impose themselves upon society, and who are subsequently defeated. In Faustus's case, as in the Jew's, life has the appearance of farce not merely because it holds a reflection of the hero's degenerate thinking, but because life really is a farce. There is in fact no clear alternative to what they choose to do, and their sin and punishment is a measure of the world's quality as much as their own. It is particularly striking that Faustus never sees things as those critics do who condemn him for wasting his dearly-bought powers in trivial pastimes. He speaks late in the play of the famous 'wonders' he has done (V.ii.48), and when he deprecates 'the vain pleasure of four-and-twenty years' (V.ii.66: echoed in the B-text by Mephostophilis and the Bad Angel, who see any pleasure as reprehensible in itself), it is only in comparison with eternal joy and felicity. It is not that Faustus has failed in social responsibility; that he has not put the world to rights. His crime is not political, nor is it even moral: it is religious— he denies God, not man. And it is not a direct result of his denial of God that life becomes mere clownage: one can see from the incoherence of Faustus's high-sounding projects before signing his contract with the Devil that there never was much prospect of his achieving anything with much point to it. Sin is for him more a means of self-enjoyment than of things to do.

Faustus, besides (it may be) satisfying a popular expectation, may well embody (as in a different spirit does the unworldly Ramus in *The Massacre at Paris*) Marlowe's different conception and experience of what a scholar might be. This is a man whose life is predicated in books. His very temptation to sin is grounded in a textual misreading (in supposing or, with a very donnish skittishness, pretending that the Scripture rules out mercy), his fall takes the form of drafting a legal document (another 'petty case of paltry legacies'?), he is given forbidden books by Mephostophilis and Lucifer, he is cursed with bell, book and candle, and in his despair it is his books that he blames and would destroy. Like Marlowe's other heroes he is alienated: this time the alienation is that of the academic for whom questions of the most profound import have only a theoretical or (as we say) an academic interest; for whom disputes in heavenly matters of theology are no more than a sweet delight, a form of self-assertion. He has the scholar's rankling vanity. In conversation with Mephostophilis there is the authentic self-opinionated testiness. With this he finds himself able to contradict the devil and deny the existence of divine justice, just as later he will contradict Christ and deny the existence of divine mercy. But it is the dour, ecclesiastical Mephostophilis who is the real tutor on this Grand Tour.

If not a realist, Faustus is undoubtedly a sensualist: the play clearly remarks his fondness for food. The physicality of the level on which he largely lives is indicated by the dismemberment that is fitly meted out to him in both comic and serious forms. But his rich, if undisciplined, imagination is still very bookish. This is so in the visions of Alexander the Great and Helen, two figures from classical antiquity (like those of Homer and Amphion: II.ii.26–30) that suggest at once the resources of humanist learning and the ravages of time (which is about to ravage Faustus himself), and the comparative pettiness of the modern world (to which pettiness Faustus has contributed). It is partly through Faustus's conjuring up Helen that Marlowe is able to unsettle the easy impression that Faustus has done unreservedly wrong in selling his soul for such powers, and also perhaps to imply that it is not Faustus who wastes the world but the world Faustus. In comparison with such grand visions yielded by paganism, Christianity has little to offer beyond the grotesque Seven Deadly Sins. The choice really does seem to lie between a pagan Elysium and a Christian hell.

In 'the form of Faustus' fortunes, good or bad' one is tempted to see the lineaments of another life in which a gifted and arrogant young man moved from university to the world of entertainment and failed to fulfil himself there. The final epigraph in the printed text seems to identify Faustus's experiences with the writing of the play itself: *Terminat hora diem, terminat Author opus*, 'The hour ends the day, the author ends his work'.

The last speech is moving not because it springs from fear of death or fear of punishment, but because, in marked contrast to Faustus's early speeches in the play, it springs from fear of life. It is the utterance of someone who would rather dissolve, be no one, nothing. The vast prospect of eternity is appalling, but the consciousness of time passing and of the present moment in its intensity is no less so. In short, any human being, atheist or not, responds to such a speech, since it defines the anguish of what it is to be a soul poised for a span on the brink of infinity.

One sees how to read the speech by comparing it with Edward's in the deposition scene of *Edward II*, where he also faces the nightmare of self-knowledge, and would have time stop. In the two plays a tainted, ultimately sterile humanism is for both heroes the only apparent hope of escape from tedium or worse. Humanism is represented even by the homosexual relationship of the King and Gaveston. At the end of I.iv Mortimer Senior argues at some length that there are famous and worthy classical precedents for it; and elsewhere in this drab play the language comes alive through classical and neo-classical allusion when this relationship is at issue. Gaveston is associated with the arts (and with the pagan scholarship that goes to make of a man like Baldock a courtier rather than a curate). He is Italianate in his dress, and puts on Italian masques for the King's entertainment. Both he and the King enjoy the dramatic and the sub-dramatic: Mortimer scornfully recalls how Edward went to war

> But once; and then thy soldiers marched like players,
> With garish robes, not armour; and thyself,
> Bedaub'd with gold, rode laughing at the rest,
> Nodding and shaking of thy spangled crest,
> Where women's favours hung like labels down.
>
> (II.ii. 182–6)

And he takes great pleasure in tilts and tournaments, one of which he even remembers in his last minutes.

As with Barabas and Faustus, so with Edward: the distinction of his mind serves only to undermine his commonsense conception of what is important or real. He is histrionic even in his treatment of the kingship itself: he knows the aesthetic thrill of regality (in handing out titles, for instance), but little of the political responsibility supposed to go with it. It is never quite certain when he is putting on an act, whether it is in cursing his enemies, yearning for a contemplative life, or flirting with anger and sorrow (the stage direction in the deposition scene, ' *The King rageth*', indicates a set-piece). In his soliloquy in the first scene of the play (I.i.49–72)

Gaveston plans a programme of entertainment for Edward. There will be nothing but theatre. Day and night will be filled with hallucination and deception: the pliant king will be drawn many different ways, never allowed to rest, constantly beset and overwhelmed with fantastic things that never existed except in Gaveston's imaginings. Yet his creations have their own peculiar beauty, by which (as in *Hero and Leander*) lust is given sprightly, elegant shapes, and fancifulness invigorated with dirt, humour and pain. Both Edward and Gaveston are to meet Actaeon's violent end for their naughtiness.

It is clear that the humanism is tainted. Edward is effete and vicious. The relationship between the two men is discreditable. The assassination of Edward conveys too strong an impression of the guilty shame and secretiveness, the insinuations, the degradation and helplessness of violation, the physical violence, the grotesqueness and even the lewd hilarity of homosexuality. It may seem a punishment to fit the crime. Like Webster's Duchess of Malfi, Edward is systematically made to enact the life of the senses as it is held to be—squalid and maddening—in the traditional morality.

The political implications of his liaison are brought out early in the play with some formality. Gaveston confronts in turn the three estates of the realm—the common people as petitioners, the nobility and the Church—and, in abusing them all, he proves how dangerous a counsellor he is to have near the throne. As an upstart (like Baldock and the Spencers too) he may also seem disruptive of the social class-system.

The opposite camp is that of the barons led by young Mortimer. They appear martial, choleric, blunt men with the assurance of hereditary power. Gaveston jeers at them—

> Base leaden earls that glory in your birth,
> Go sit at home and eat your tenants' beef. (II.ii.74–5)

In the slang of another age, the barons play the 'hearties' to the 'arties' of Edward and Gaveston. They are at once disgusted and disturbed—angered and sexually excited—by the queers, as the laborious fluctuations in their behaviour shows. Mortimer, whose insistent virility is often figured in a sword, actually stabs Gaveston at Tynemouth in the presence of the King, and Lancaster proposes surprising the King and Gaveston unawares, as if, with the aim of some peeping Tom, to see them 'frolic'. Yet politically and sexually Mortimer's way is not much to be preferred. He turns out to be both regicide and adulterer; and even as the strong man who has asked 'what I

[xxiv]

list command, who dare control?' (V.iv.68) he must come to Edward's fatalism and answer

> There is a point, to which when men aspire,
> They tumble headlong down. (V.vi.60–1)

Marlowe has so designed the play that, against a background in which events seem grimly and narrowly to repeat themselves, our sympathies for the King grow as his fortunes decline, and our sympathies for the usurper diminish as his fortunes improve, so that, if there is a political moral, it must be that power corrupts whoever has it. The accession of a young, untried and vulnerable prince counterbalances this only if one knows him to be the great and glorious Edward III. Otherwise we are left with a sense only of loss. As in *The Massacre at Paris*, man is either thug or ponce: the sensibility is separated from the driving-force of the will. It is appropriate that decapitation, the severing of the mind from the body, is so often dwelt on in *Edward II*; and the whole play ends in a rich emblem, with the weeping boy-prince ceremonially placing Mortimer's severed head on the coffin of the dead King.

The poem *Hero and Leander* is very much after the style of the plays. Here as there Marlowe tells the story of an unmitigated disaster with great beauty and great humour. His plays may hardly prepare us for his shrewd understanding of the lovers and their struggle with forces that they do not control when they think they do, and do control when they think they do not. But such understanding comes from Marlowe's broader fascination with the embarrassments and shames that life lands men and women in; and in *Hero and Leander* there is at times a baroque voyeurism.

The tragedy of the poem lies most multifariously in the sea. The eventual drowning of Leander is kept in mind, no doubt, when marine imagery (often associated with destruction) is applied to Hero's dress and behaviour, but it is a fact that Venus herself was born of the sea, so a disastrous outcome may seem to be inherent in the passion of love itself. This is so while, with a Marlovian discordance, it is sexual feeling, gentle and lewd, earnest and whimsical, groping, tickling and caressing, that is the energy that fuels the poem, and no less the highly decorative imagery in it than the narrative itself. In the kiss of death there is both kiss and death.

The sea, 'father' of Venus, who appears personified as Neptune, falls in love with Leander. The homosexuality may have personally interested Marlowe as an attractive perversion; but in the poem itself it serves mainly to bring out more coldly the hectic beauty, the ruthlessness and the comic nastiness of the main love affair. Leander himself learns what it is to be the victim of an overbearing and insidious lust. There is no pity. It is hard not to believe that, given time, Marlowe would have concluded the poem with the death of Leander in a homosexual embrace. In this would have been the anguish, shame and rage experienced by Hero herself when there is no impediment to the marriage of true bodies.

The inset myth of Mercury and the milkmaid may suggest something of Marlowe's own thinking about the poem and, furthermore, about his whole work. The god of scholars and poets makes the mistake of seeking two paradises—the personal one to be imagined in love, and the social one to be imagined as within the scope of a broader destiny. Both are illusory and short-lived, and it is a world of murder, rape, war, lust and treachery that breaks in upon them, and gives its authority and rewards to the ignorant and the greedy. The scholar Leander might have consulted his self-interest in some better way than in loving. And the scholar Marlowe than in writing of it.

1975   E. D. Pendry

Marlowe's Life

A CHRONOLOGY OF DOCUMENTS

1564   26 February. Christofer, son of John Marlow, baptized at St George the Martyr, Canterbury [Register Book].

1579   14 January–December. Christopher Marley, scholar at King's School, Canterbury, receives his grant [Accounts of Treasurer of Canterbury Cathedral].

1580   December. Marlen first appears on the Buttery Book of Corpus Christi College, Cambridge.

1581   17 March. Chrōf. Marlen matriculated in *convictus secundus*, i.e. the middle rank of students [University Registry: Matriculation Book].

      24 March. Marlin listed among *pensionarii*, i.e. commoners [Corpus Christi Registrum Parvum].

      7–11 May. Marlin formally elected to tied scholarship established by Archbishop Parker [Registrum Parvum]; had received payments for it since January [Corpus Christi Audit Books].

      29 October. Merling at class in dialectic [Lansdowne MSS, British Library].

      From this year until Lent 1587. Marlin, Marly, etc. resident in Corpus Christi, with some absences in 1585 and 1586 [Audit Books, Buttery Book].

1584   Lent. Christopherus Marlin permitted to proceed to B.A. [University Registry: Supplicats, Grace Book].

1585   November. Christofer Marley witnesses will of Katherine Benchkyn of Canterbury [Canterbury Public Record Office].

1587   31 March. Christopherus Marley permitted to proceed to M.A. [Supplicats, Grace Book].

      29 June. Privy Council certify that it had been incorrectly rumoured that Christopher Morley had determined to go to Rheims to stay; and that he had on the contrary done the Queen good service, and should be furthered in his degree at the next Commencement: i.e. in July [Acts of Privy Council, Public Record Office].

      10 November. Election of successor to college scholarship [Registrum Parvum, College Order Book].

16 November. A shooting accident at a playhouse, possibly in performance of *Tamburlaine*. [See Preface to play.]

1588   29 March. Robert Greene refers to Tamburlaine. [See Preface to play.]

1589   18 September. Cristoferus Morley, gentleman of London, fights with William Bradley in Hog Lane, Parish of St Giles Without Cripplegate; Thomas Watson (the poet) intervenes, is attacked by Bradley and kills him in self-defence [Chancery Miscellanea, Public Record Office]. Thomas Watson, gentleman, and Cristoferus Marlowe, yeoman, both of Norton Folgate, Middlesex, are arrested by the Constable and committed to Newgate by the Lieutenant of the Tower on suspicion of murder [Middlesex Sessions Roll].

19 September. Inquest on Bradley [Chancery· Miscellanea].

1 October. Christophorus Marley of London, gentleman, released on bail of £40: Richardus Kytchine, gentleman of Clifford's Inn, and Humfridus Rowland, horner of East Smithfield, stand surety [Middlesex Sessions Roll].

3 December. Marlowe appears before justices (including Sir Roger Manwood) and is discharged [Middlesex Sessions Roll].

1590   14 August. *Tamburlaine* published.

1591   (Or before.) Thomas Kyd, the dramatist, writing in one room with Marlowe [Harleian MSS, British Library].

1592   9 May. Christopherus Marle, gentleman of London, bound over in £20 to keep the peace towards Allen Nicholls, Constable of Holywell Street, Shoreditch, and Nicholaus Helliott, Sub-Constable of the same [Middlesex Sessions Roll].

3 September. Robert Greene reproves a gifted fellow-playwright for his atheism and Machiavellian self-seeking [*Groatsworth of Wit*].

10 November. Dedication by C.M. to late Thomas Watson's *Amintae Gaudia*.

8 December. Henry Chettle admits two playwrights were offended by Greene's posthumous *Groatsworth of Wit*: one of them he reverences for his learning, but would rather not get to know [*Kind-Harts Dreame*].

14 December. Sir Roger Manwood dies: Christopher Marlo writes an epitaph [Oxinden Commonplace Book, Folger Library].

1593   12 May. Thomas Kyd arrested and heretical papers, which he attributes to Marlowe, discovered in his room [Harleian MSS].

18 May. Privy Council issue warrant for the arrest of Christofer Marlow, at the house of Mr Thomas Walsingham in Kent or elsewhere [Acts of the Privy Council].

20 May. Christofer Marley, gentleman of London, answers the warrant and is required to remain in daily attendance [Acts of the Privy Council].

30 May. Christoferus Morley killed in self-defence by Ingram Frizer, in the company of Robert Poley and Nicholas Skeres, at a house in Deptford Strand [Chancery Miscellanea].

1 June. Inquest held on Cristoferus Morley [Chancery Miscellanea].

1 June. Burial of Christopher Marlow, slain by Francis Frezer [Register of St Nicholas Church, Deptford].

After 1 June. Thomas Kyd writes to the Lord Keeper, Sir John Puckering, about Marlowe's monstrous opinions [Harleian MSS].

2 June. A note by Richard Baines about the horrible blasphemies of Christofer Marly or Morly [Harleian MSS].

15 June. A writ of certiorari issued to summon the case of Ingram Frizer into Chancery [Chancery Miscellanea].

28 June. Pardon issued to Frizer [Patent Rolls, Public Record Office].

Further Reading

REFERENCE

C. Crawford, *The Marlowe Concordance*, 5 vols (Louvain, 1911–32) in Bang's *Materialien zur Kunde des älteren englischen Dramas*, vols XXXIV, N.S. II, V, VI, VII.

MAJOR EDITIONS

The Works and Life of Christopher Marlowe, gen. ed. R. H. Case, 6 vols (1930–33): *The Life of Marlowe and The Tragedy of Dido, Queen of Carthage*, ed. C. F. Tucker Brooke (1930); *Tamburlaine the Great*, ed. U. M. Ellis-Fermor (1930, rev. 1951); *The Jew of Malta and The Massacre at Paris*, ed. H. S. Bennett (1931); *Poems*, ed. L. C. Martin (1931); *Doctor Faustus*, ed. F. S. Boas (1932); *Edward II*, ed. H. B. Charlton and R. D. Waller (1933, rev. F. N. Lees, 1955).
Marlowe's Doctor Faustus 1604–1616: Parallel Texts, ed. W. W. Greg (Oxford, 1950).
Doctor Faustus, ed. John D. Jump (1962).
Dido Queen of Carthage and The Massacre at Paris, ed. H. J. Oliver (1968).
The Poems, ed. Millar MacLure (1968).
The Complete Works of Christopher Marlowe, ed. Fredson Bowers, 2 vols (Cambridge, 1973). An old-spelling edition without literary notes.

LIFE AND THOUGHT

J. L. Hotson, *The Death of Christopher Marlowe* (1925).
F. S. Boas, *Christopher Marlowe: A Biographical and Critical Study* (Oxford, 1940, rev. 1953).
R. W. Battenhouse, *Marlowe's Tamburlaine: A Study in Renaissance Moral Philosophy* (Nashville, 1941, rev. 1964).
J. E. Bakeless, *The Tragicall History of Christopher Marlowe*, 2 vols (Cambridge, Mass., 1942).
P. H. Kocher, *Christopher Marlowe: A Study of his Thought, Learning, and Character* (Chapel Hill, N.C., 1946).
E. M. Waith, *The Herculean Hero* (1962).

CRITICISM: BOOKS

H. Levin, *The Overreacher: A Study of Christopher Marlowe* (Cambridge, Mass., 1952).

D. Cole. *Suffering and Evil in the Plays of Christopher Marlowe* (1962).

J. P. Brockbank, *Marlowe: Dr Faustus* (1962).

J. B. Steane, *Marlowe: A Critical Study* (Cambridge, 1964).

C. Leech, ed. *Marlowe: A Collection of Critical Essays* (Englewood Cliffs, N.J., 1964).

W. Sanders, *The Dramatist and the Received Idea: Studies in the Plays of Marlowe & Shakespeare* (Cambridge, 1968).

B. Morris, ed. *Christopher Marlowe* (1968).

J. Jump, ed. *Marlowe: Doctor Faustus* (1969).

C. G. Fanta, *Marlowe's 'Agonists': An Approach to the Ambiguity of His Plays* (Cambridge, Mass., 1970).

CRITICISM: ARTICLES

M. C. Bradbrook, *Themes and Conventions of Elizabethan Tragedy* (Cambridge, 1935), Ch. 6.

H. Gardner, 'The Second Part of *Tamburlaine the Great*', *Modern Language Review*, XXXVII (1942), 18–24.

G. I. Duthie, 'The Dramatic Structure of Marlowe's *Tamburlaine the Great*, Parts I and II', *English Studies (Essays and Studies)*, I (1948), 101–26.

M. M. Mahood, *Poetry and Humanism* (1950), Ch. 3.

N. C. Carpenter, 'Infinite Riches: A Note on Marlovian Unity', *Notes and Queries*, 3 Feb. 1951, 50–2.

C. S. Lewis, 'Hero and Leander', *Proceedings of the British Academy*, XXXVIII (1952); repr. in *Selected Literary Essays* (Cambridge, 1969), 58–73.

Robert Ornstein, 'The Comic Synthesis in *Doctor Faustus*', *English Literary History*, XXII (1955), 165–72.

J. C. Maxwell, 'The Plays of Christopher Marlowe', *The Age of Shakespeare*, ed. B. Ford (1955, rev. 1956), 162–78.

I. Ribner, 'Marlowe's *Edward II* and the Tudor History Play', *Journal of English Literary History*, XXII (1955), 243–53.

C. Leech, 'Marlowe's *Edward II*: Power and Suffering', *Critical Quarterly*, I (1959), 181–96.

I. Ribner, 'Marlowe's "Tragicke Glasse"', *Essays on Shakespeare and Elizabethan Drama in Honor of Hardin Craig*, ed. R. Hosley (Columbia, Miss., 1962), 91–114.

D. Bevington, *From Mankind to Marlowe* (Cambridge, Mass., 1962), Chs. 14–17.

Further Reading

G. K. Hunter, 'The Theology of Marlowe's *The Jew of Malta*', *Journal of the Warburg and Courtauld Institutes*, XXVII (1964), 211–40.

Arieh Sachs, 'The Religious Despair of *Doctor Faustus*', *Journal of English and Germanic Philology*, LXIII (1964), 625–47.

W. D. Smith, 'The Nature of Evil in *Doctor Faustus*', *Modern Language Review*, LX (1965), 171–5.

E. Rothstein, 'Structure as Meaning in *The Jew of Malta*', *Journal of English and Germanic Philology*, LXV (1966), 260–73.

T. McAlindon, 'Classical Mythology and Christian Tradition in Marlowe's *Doctor Faustus*', *Publications of the Modern Language Association*, LXXXI (1966), 214–23.

R. Ornstein, 'Marlowe and God: the Tragic Theology of Dr Faustus', *Publications of the Modern Language Association*, LXXXIII (1968), 1378–85.

W. D. Smith, 'The Substance of Meaning in *Tamburlaine*, Part I', *Studies in Philology*, LXVII (1970), 156–66.

A. L. French, 'The Philosophy of Dr Faustus', *Essays in Criticism*, XX (1970), 123–42.

J. Jensen, 'Heroic Convention and Doctor Faustus', *Essays in Criticism*, XXI (1971), 101–6.

William Keach, 'Marlowe's Hero as "Venus' Nun"', *English Literary Renaissance*, II (1972), 307–20.

J. Mills, 'The Courtship Ritual of Hero and Leander', *English Literary Renaissance*, II (1972), 298–306.

Note on the Text

The notes on individual works give only a brief account of the authority for the text. The notes on particular passages are restricted to giving the source for readings not recorded in the editions of Fredson Bowers (text or historical collation), Roma Gill (for the plays) or Stephen Orgel (for the poems and translations), and to noting a few places where the two editors disagree about the preferable reading. Where no earlier publication is recorded, a reading appears, to the best of our belief, for the first time in this edition.

Modernization. Modern spelling and punctuation are introduced throughout. Where a non-current spelling is retained, it is because it is judged to be a variant form rather than a mere spelling: thus, *supprise*, but not *murther* (except in rhyme); the border-line is inevitably arbitrary. The treatment of *'d* and *-ed* endings raises special problems. The past tense of *murder* may appear in the originals as *murdered*, *murderd* or *murdred*. These are here printed, respectively, as *murdered* (even where regular metre calls for two syllables, since the medial *e* can be slurred), *murder'd* and *murd'red*. Where the original offers a clearly unmetrical spelling (which is rare), it is corrected. Contrary to the usual practice of modern-spelling texts, which tend to normalize to *-ed* in prose, we follow the same practice for prose as for verse. We follow the normal practice of printing *-ied* rather than the *-i'd* that strict consistency would demand.

It is sometimes difficult to decide whether a place-name ending in *s*, followed by a noun, is possessive or adjectival. Since, in other place-names (except in the translation of Lucan) Marlowe prefers the adjectival form—'Carthage walls'—we have thought it more consistent to print 'Damascus walls', etc.; but not when another adjective intervenes: 'Avernus' darksome vaults'.

Stage Directions. Supplements, in square brackets, to those in the originals have been sparingly introduced, and a few errors corrected. Prefixes are normalized to names, but the titles sometimes used in the originals (e.g. 'Governor' in *The Jew of Malta*) are retained in entries, where there can be no ambiguity.

Tamburlaine. The only authority for both parts is the octavo of 1590 (O1), of which other early editions are mere reprints. The printer's copy was probably a fair copy, by Marlowe or a transcriber. Some of the very few obscure or confused passages may be the fault of Marlowe himself.

PART I. I.i.87 greater charge] Pendry; O1 greater
V.i.184 topmost] Deighton, *The Old Dramatists* (1896); O1 tempest [Pendry would retain O1's 'stopt the tempest'].
V.i.212 where we] Maxwell; O1 we

Edward II. The only authority is the quarto-form octavo of 1594 (Q1), of which other early editions are mere reprints. The printer's copy was probably a fair copy, by Marlowe or a transcriber.

I.i.22 fawn] Oxberry; Q1 fanne (which Pendry would retain).
IV.ii.20 shake off] Maxwell would prefer Tucker Brooke's 'share of'.

Dido. The only early edition is the quarto of 1594 (Q). The source may be holograph or a transcriber's fair copy.

III.iii.64 far-fet o'er] Q far fet to [Maxwell would prefer Broughton's 'forfeit to'.]
V.i.144 call] Maxwell; Q calles

The Massacre at Paris. The only early edition is an undated octavo (O), certainly not after 1603 and more probably of the mid 1590s. It has all the characteristics of a memorial reconstruction, and this is confirmed by the survival of a single leaf, now in the Folger Shakespeare Library, which gives a better text of sc. xix. This version, reproduced as an appendix, is clearly of playhouse origin, though it is not, as has sometimes been conjectured, in Marlowe's hand: see *The Times Literary Supplement*, 26 April 1974, pp. 446-7.

Dr Faustus. This is the one play which presents serious textual problems; little more can be attempted here than to indicate why a fully satisfactory restoration is impossible.

The first edition is a quarto of 1604 (A), which contains what corresponds to the following parts of the present text: Prologue; Acts I–II; Chorus 1; III.i.1–57; III.ii.57–104; III.iii; Chorus 2; IV.i,iv, vi. 1–32, 116–20; V.i, ii. 24–87, 134–91; Epilogue. All the rest appears for the first time in the

quarto of 1616 (B1), which also has a revised version of some
of the material in the A-text. Up to the edition of Sir Walter
Greg (1950), it was generally believed that the material
peculiar to B belonged to the additions for which Henslowe
recorded a payment to William Bird and Samuel Rowley on
22 November 1602. It is now clear that this older view was
right, and that Greg was wrong in believing that the B scenes
were also present in the original (in which he believed that
Rowley collaborated with Marlowe). If this were the whole
story, an editor might hope to get back to Marlowe's original
by taking the A-text as a basis. Unfortunately, where the two
texts run parallel, it is manifest that A is seriously corrupt, and
dependent on memorial reconstruction, and that B is more
faithful to the original. A further complication is that B,
though largely based on a manuscript superior to that from
which A was printed, was also, in part, printed from a 1611
reprint of A (A3), or, more probably, from a transcript of it,
with consultation of the superior manuscript. Faced with a
choice of evils, the present edition follows Fredson Bowers (see
his edition, ii, 142–5) in basing its text on B, but making use of
A to correct its errors, especially where B shows signs of
editorial tinkering, for example in the Prologue.

Prol. 18 delight's disputes] Maxwell; A delight disputes;
   B omits; Bowers, delight's dispute
I.i.36 Too servile] B; A The devill; Pendry conj. Too
   trivial
I.i.51 schemes] Logeman, *Faustus-Notes* (1897); A sceanes;
   B omits
III.i.173 synody] Maxwell; B synod
IV.i.72 like to a] Maxwell; B like; B2 like a

The Jew of Malta. The only early edition is the quarto of
1633 (Q). The long delay before publication, and the fact that
the quarto appeared with a dedicatory letter from Thomas
Heywood, have given rise to suspicions about the text, but
Heywood makes no claim to have revised it, and there is no
clear evidence that he did. Though it contains more trivial
errors than most of Marlowe's plays, Q offers a reasonably
good text, probably deriving from the prompt-book, or a
transcript of it.

I.i.51 all their] Maxwell, *Modern Language Review*, xlviii
   (1953); Q other
II.iii.99 Doth] Maxwell; Q Do [other edd. follow Dodsley
   (ed. Reed, 1780), in emending 'Turke' to 'Turks']

II.iii.170   that that] Maxwell; Q that

III.ii.34   disclose] Dodsley (ed. Collier); om.Q; Pendry conj. impart

IV.i.84   *Barnardine*] Dodsley (ed. Reed, 1780); Q 1 *Fryar* [=*Jacomo*]

V.i.86   sconce] Pendry; Q Truce

V.iii.5   Placed here by Craik (*New Mermaid* ed., 1966); Q after line 10.

Illustrissimae Heroinae . . ., from *Amintae Gaudia*, by Thomas Watson, 1592.

Hero and Leander. The only authority for Marlowe's poem is the quarto of 1598 (Q1). Q2, also 1598, added Chapman's continuation, and introduced the division into Sestiads, with Chapman's prefatory summaries. We have omitted the latter, but, for convenience of comparison with other editions, retain the division into two separately numerated parts of Marlowe's undivided text.

I.1   true-loves'] Martz (Introduction to Folger Facsimile, 1972); Q True-loues; edd. true love's

I.477   are] Pendry conj. jar

II.195   unkind] Maxwell; Q kind [but, apart from the metrical defect, the point is that the boy is not 'kind', i.e. does not yield to his lovers]

II.330   day-bright-bearing] Martin conj. (ed. of *Poems*, 1931), spelling 'day-bright bearing'; Q day bright-bearing

Ovid's Elegies. There are three undated octavo editions. O1 (of which O2 is a reprint) contains only I.i, ii, iii, v, xiii, xv; II.iv, x; III.vi, xiii. The rest were added in O3. There is evidence for some use of O1 by O3, but basically they are independent texts, each of which must be used to correct the errors of the other. A few variants suggest revision rather than mere error.

III.vi.41   Pylius' fire] Pendry; O1, O3 *Pilius* fire; Ovid has 'Pylius' only; possibly read 'Pylius sire' (Maxwell)

The Passionate Shepherd to his Love. First published, in a four-stanza version, in *The Passionate Pilgrim* (1599), which is also found in several manuscripts. The present text comes from *England's Helicon* (1600).

The First Book of Lucan. The only authority is a quarto-form octavo of 1600 (Q), which may have been printed from holograph.

413   roll] Maxwell; Q roul'd
624   pour'd] Maxwell; Q pearde

In Obitum . . . Manwood. Written on the verso of the title-page of a copy (now lost) of *Hero and Leander*, 1629, and published by J. P. Collier in the 'History of the English Stage' prefixed to *Works of William Shakespeare* (1844). The transcripts by Henry Oxinden (Folger Shakespeare Library) have no substantive variants.

The publishers note with regret the death of J. C. Maxwell during the preparation of this edition. He did, however, read the proofs and approve them for press, and the text is in the final form in which he wished to see it.

To Sola Thilén

Plays

Tamburlaine the Great

Tamburlaine the Great was entered to Richard Jones in the Stationers' Register on 14 August 1590 as '*The twooe commicall discourses of TOMBERLEIN the Cithian shepparde*'. The author is named neither here nor in the black-letter octavo, under Jones's imprint, that followed in the same year. The two parts were reprinted together by Jones in 1593 and 1597, and separately by Edward White in 1605 (Part I) and 1606 (Part II).

In his epistle to *Perimedes*, which was entered in the Stationers' Register on 29 March 1588, Robert Greene is scornful of a current tragic style which he describes as 'daring God out of heaven with that Atheist *Tamburlan*'; and he may be punning on Marlowe's name when he calls the practitioners of this style 'mad and scoffing poets, that have propheticall spirits as bred of *Merlins* race'. Marlowe's authorship of the plays is borne out when, in *The Arraignement of the Whole Creature* (1631), R[obert] H[enderson] calls to mind Tamburlaine's '*Coach drawne* with the Kings of *Asia*', and gives as his marginal reference '*Marlow* in his Poem'.

Greene's indication of date is not readily confirmed. A letter by Philip Gawdy of 16 November 1587 describes a mishap that occurred in a theatrical performance when the Admiral's Men tied one of their fellows to a post and made as if to shoot him to death, but killed members of the audience instead. Is this the scene in *2 Tamburlaine* where the Governor of Babylon is hung in chains and shot to death? It seems far from certain. On the other hand, borrowings from *The Faerie Queene*, which was entered in the Stationers' Register on 1 December 1589, and from Paul Ive's *Practise of Fortification* (1589) point to a later date. It is not impossible that the two parts of the play are more widely separated in time than is usually supposed, or that Marlowe revised his plays for publication.

Tamburlaine was a historical ruler contemporary with Henry IV. For the outline of his story Marlowe could have gone to Pedro Mexia's *Silva de Varia Leccion* (Seville, 1543), abridged in English by Thomas Fortescue in *The Foreste* (1571) and translated by George Whetstone in his *English Myrror* (1586), and to Petrus Perondinus, *Magni Tamerlanis Scytharum*

Imperatoris Vita (Florence, 1553). In Part II the circumstances of Sigismund's perfidy and defeat are based on those at the Battle of Varna (1444) described in *Antonii Bonfinii Rerum Ungaricarum Decades Tres* (Basle, 1543); the episode of Olympia and Theridamas derives from Ariosto. Marlowe's most considerable single inventions are of Zenocrate and her cowardly son Calyphas.

The 1590 title-page gives the Admiral's Men as the performing company, and Henslowe's Diary shows that the two plays were revived and frequently staged between 28 August 1594 and 13 November 1595. In his Prologue to *The Jew of Malta* which he revived about 1632, Thomas Heywood recalls that Edward Alleyn made himself famous with his playing the part of Tamburlaine. Inventories now lost which probably belonged to March 1598 list Tamburlaine's bridle, his coat with copper lace and his breeches of crimson velvet as amongst the properties of the Admiral's Men.

To the Gentlemen Readers, and others
that take pleasure in reading
Histories.

Gentlemen, and courteous readers whosoever: I have here published in print for your sakes the two tragical discourses of the Scythian shepherd Tamburlaine, that became so great a conqueror and so mighty a monarch. My hope is that they will be now no less acceptable unto you to read after your serious affairs and studies than they have been lately delightful for many of you to see when the same were showed in London upon stages. I have purposely omitted and left out some fond and frivolous gestures, digressing and, in my poor opinion, far unmeet for the matter, which I thought might seem more tedious unto the wise than any way else to be regarded. Though haply they have been of some vain-conceited fondlings greatly gaped at, what times they were showed upon the stage in their graced deformities, nevertheless now, to be mixtured in print with such matter of worth, it would prove a great disgrace to so honourable and stately a history. Great folly were it in me to commend unto your wisdoms either the eloquence of the author that writ them, or the worthiness of the matter itself. I therefore leave unto your learned censures both the one and the other; and myself, the poor printer of them, unto your most courteous and favourable protection. Which if you vouchsafe to accept, you shall evermore bind me to employ what travail and service I can to the advancing and pleasuring of your excellent degree.

Yours, most humble at commandment,

R[ichard] J[ones], Printer.

[DRAMATIS PERSONAE

The Prologue

Mycetes, King of Persia
Cosroe, his brother
Ceneus ⎫
Ortygius ⎪
Meander ⎬ Persian lords
Menaphon ⎪
Theridamas ⎭
Tamburlaine, a Scythian shepherd
Techelles ⎫
Usumcasane ⎬ his followers
Bajazeth, Emperor of the Turks
King of Argier
King of Fez
King of Morocco
Alcidamus, King of Arabia
Soldan of Egypt
Governor of Damascus
Agydas ⎫
Magnetes ⎬ Median lords
Capolin, an Egyptian
Philemus, a messenger
A Spy

Zenocrate, daughter of the Soldan
Anippe, her maid
Zabina, wife to Bajazeth
Ebea, her maid
Virgins of Damascus,
Messengers, Bassoes, Lords, Citizens, Moors, Soldiers,
Attendants]

Tamburlaine the Great
PART I

The Prologue

From jigging veins of rhyming mother-wits,
And such conceits as clownage keeps in pay,
We'll lead you to the stately tent of war,
Where you shall hear the Scythian Tamburlaine
Threat'ning the world with high astounding terms,
And scourging kingdoms with his conquering sword.
View but his picture in this tragic glass,
And then applaud his fortunes as you please.

Actus 1. Scaena 1.

[*Enter*] Mycetes, Cosroe, Meander, Theridamas, Ortygius,
Ceneus, [Menaphon,] *with others.*

MYCETES. Brother Cosroe, I find myself aggriev'd,
    Yet insufficient to express the same,
    For it requires a great and thund'ring speech.
    Good brother, tell the cause unto my lords;
    I know you have a better wit than I.
COSROE. Unhappy Persia, that in former age
    Hast been the seat of mighty conquerors,
    That in their prowess and their policies
    Have triumph'd over Afric and the bounds
    Of Europe where the sun dares scarce appear   10
    For freezing meteors and congealed cold,
    Now to be rul'd and govern'd by a man
    At whose birthday Cynthia with Saturn join'd,
    And Jove, the Sun, and Mercury denied
    To shed their influence in his fickle brain!
    Now Turks and Tartars shake their swords at thee,
    Meaning to mangle all thy provinces.
MYCETES. Brother, I see your meaning well enough,
    And through your planets I perceive you think
    I am not wise enough to be a king;   20
    But I refer me to my noblemen,
    That know my wit, and can be witnesses.
    I might command you to be slain for this;
    Meander, might I not?

MEANDER. Not for so small a fault, my sovereign lord.
MYCETES. I mean it not, but yet I know I might.
   Yet live, yea, live; Mycetes wills it so.
   Meander, thou my faithful counsellor,
   Declare the cause of my conceived grief,
   Which is, God knows, about that Tamburlaine,   30
   That like a fox in midst of harvest-time
   Doth prey upon my flocks of passengers,
   And, as I hear, doth mean to pull my plumes.
   Therefore 'tis good and meet for to be wise.
MEANDER. Oft have I heard your majesty complain
   Of Tamburlaine, that sturdy Scythian thief,
   That robs your merchants of Persepolis
   Trading by land unto the Western Isles,
   And in your confines with his lawless train
   Daily commits incivil outrages,   40
   Hoping (misled by dreaming prophecies)
   To reign in Asia, and with barbarous arms
   To make himself the monarch of the East.
   But ere he march in Asia, or display
   His vagrant ensign in the Persian fields,
   Your grace hath taken order by Theridamas,
   Charg'd with a thousand horse, to apprehend
   And bring him captive to your highness' throne.
MYCETES. Full true thou speak'st, and like thyself, my lord,
   Whom I may term a Damon for thy love.   50
   Therefore 'tis best, if so it like you all,
   To send my thousand horse incontinent
   To apprehend that paltry Scythian.
   How like you this, my honourable lords?
   Is it not a kingly resolution?
COSROE. It cannot choose, because it comes from you.
MYCETES. Then hear thy charge, valiant Theridamas,
   The chiefest captain of Mycetes' host,
   The hope of Persia, and the very legs
   Whereon our state doth lean as on a staff   60
   That holds us up and foils our neighbour foes:
   Thou shalt be leader of this thousand horse,
   Whose foaming gall with rage and high disdain
   Have sworn the death of wicked Tamburlaine.
   Go frowning forth, but come thou smiling home,
   As did Sir Paris with the Grecian dame.
   Return with speed, time passeth swift away,
   Our life is frail, and we may die today.

THERIDAMAS. Before the moon renew her borrowed light,
  Doubt not, my lord and gracious sovereign,   70
  But Tamburlaine and that Tartarian rout
  Shall either perish by our warlike hands,
  Or plead for mercy at your highness' feet.
MYCETES. Go, stout Theridamas, thy words are swords,
  And with thy looks thou conquerest all thy foes.
  I long to see thee back return from thence,
  That I may view these milk-white steeds of mine
  All loaden with the heads of killed men,
  And from their knees even to their hoofs below
  Besmear'd with blood that makes a dainty show.   80
THERIDAMAS. Then now, my lord, I humbly take my leave.
                                    Exit.
MYCETES. Theridamas, farewell ten thousand times.
  Ah, Menaphon, why stay'st thou thus behind,
  When other men press forward for renown?
  Go, Menaphon, go into Scythia,
  And foot by foot follow Theridamas.
COSROE. Nay, pray you, let him stay; a greater charge
  Fits Menaphon than warring with a thief.
  Create him prorex of Assyria,
  That he may win the Babylonians' hearts,   90
  Which will revolt from Persian government
  Unless they have a wiser king than you.
MYCETES. 'Unless they have a wiser king than you'?
  These are his words; Meander, set them down.
COSROE. And add this to them, that all Asia
  Lament to see the folly of their king.
MYCETES. Well, here I swear by this my royal seat—
COSROE. You may do well to kiss it then.
MYCETES. Emboss'd with silk as best beseems my state,
  To be reveng'd for these contemptuous words.   100
  O where is duty and allegiance now?
  Fled to the Caspian or the Ocean main?
  What, shall I call thee brother? No, a foe,
  Monster of nature, shame unto thy stock,
  That dar'st presume thy sovereign for to mock.
  Meander, come; I am abus'd, Meander.
      Exit [with Meander *and others]. Manent* Cosroe *and*
    Menaphon.
MENAPHON. How now, my lord! What, mated and amaz'd
  To hear the king thus threaten like himself?
COSROE. Ah, Menaphon, I pass not for his threats.

The plot is laid by Persian noblemen   110
And captains of the Median garrisons
To crown me emperor of Asia.
But this it is that doth excruciate
The very substance of my vexed soul,
To see our neighbours that were wont to quake
And tremble at the Persian monarch's name
Now sits and laughs our regiment to scorn;
And that which might resolve me into tears,
Men from the farthest equinoctial line
Have swarm'd in troops into the Eastern India,   120
Lading their ships with gold and precious stones,
And made their spoils from all our provinces.

MENAPHON. This should entreat your highness to rejoice,
Since fortune gives you opportunity
To gain the title of a conqueror
By curing of this maimed empery.
Afric and Europe bordering on your land,
And continent to your dominions,
How eas'ly may you with a mighty host
Pass into Graecia, as did Cyrus once,   130
And cause them to withdraw their forces home,
Lest you subdue the pride of Christendom!

COSROE. But, Menaphon, what means this trumpet's sound?

MENAPHON. Behold, my lord, Ortygius and the rest
Bringing the crown to make you emperor.

Enter Ortygius *and* Ceneus *bearing a crown, with others.*

ORTYGIUS. Magnificent and mighty prince Cosroe,
We, in the name of other Persian states
And commons of this mighty monarchy,
Present thee with th'imperial diadem.

CENEUS. The warlike soldiers and the gentlemen   140
That heretofore have fill'd Persepolis
With Afric captains taken in the field,
Whose ransom made them march in coats of gold,
With costly jewels hanging at their ears,
And shining stones upon their lofty crests,
Now living idle in the walled towns,
Wanting both pay and martial discipline,
Begin in troops to threaten civil war,
And openly exclaim against the king.
Therefore, to stay all sudden mutinies,   150
We will invest your highness emperor;
Whereat the soldiers will conceive more joy

[10]

Than did the Macedonians at the spoil
Of great Darius and his wealthy host.

COSROE. Well, since I see the state of Persia droop
And languish in my brother's government,
I willingly receive th'imperial crown,
And vow to wear it for my country's good,
In spite of them shall malice my estate.

ORTYGIUS. And, in assurance of desir'd success,   160
We here do crown thee monarch of the East,
Emperor of Asia and Persia,
Great lord of Media and Armenia,
Duke of Assyria and Albania,
Mesopotamia and of Parthia,
East India and the late-discovered isles,
Chief lord of all the wide vast Euxine Sea,
And of the ever-raging Caspian Lake.

ALL. Long live Cosroe, mighty emperor!

COSROE. And Jove may never let me longer live   170
Than I may seek to gratify your love,
And cause the soldiers that thus honour me
To triumph over many provinces;
By whose desires of discipline in arms
I doubt not shortly but to reign sole king,
And with the army of Theridamas,
Whither we presently will fly, my lords,
To rest secure against my brother's force.

ORTYGIUS. We knew, my lord, before we brought the crown,
Intending your investion so near   180
The residence of your despised brother,
The lords would not be too exasperate
To injure or suppress your worthy title;
Or if they would, there are in readiness
Ten thousand horse to carry you from hence
In spite of all suspected enemies.

COSROE. I know it well, my lord, and thank you all.

ORTYGIUS. Sound up the trumpets, then.

ALL.   God save the king!
                                                      Exeunt.

Actus 1. Scaena 2.

[*Enter*] Tamburlaine *leading* Zenocrate, Techelles, Usumcasane, [Agydas, Magnetes,] *other* Lords, *and* Soldiers
loaden with treasure.

TAMBURLAINE. Come, lady, let not this appal your thoughts;

The jewels and the treasure we have ta'en
Shall be reserv'd, and you in better state
Than if you were arriv'd in Syria,
Even in the circle of your father's arms,
The mighty Soldan of Egyptia.

ZENOCRATE. Ah, shepherd, pity my distressed plight
　(If, as thou seem'st, thou art so mean a man)
　And seek not to enrich thy followers
　By lawless rapine from a silly maid,　　　　　　10
　Who, travelling with these Median lords
　To Memphis, from my uncle's country of Media,
　Where all my youth I have been governed,
　Have pass'd the army of the mighty Turk,
　Bearing his privy signet and his hand
　To safe conduct us thorough Africa.

MAGNETES. And, since we have arrived in Scythia,
　Besides rich presents from the puissant Cham,
　We have his highness' letters to command
　Aid and assistance, if we stand in need.　　　　　20

TAMBURLAINE. But now you see these letters and commands
　Are countermanded by a greater man,
　And through my provinces you must expect
　Letters of conduct from my mightiness,
　If you intend to keep your treasure safe.
　But, since I love to live at liberty,
　As eas'ly may you get the Soldan's crown
　As any prizes out of my precinct;
　For they are friends that help to wean my state
　Till men and kingdoms help to strengthen it,　　　30
　And must maintain my life exempt from servitude.
　But tell me, madam, is your grace betroth'd?

ZENOCRATE. I am, my lord—for so you do import.

TAMBURLAINE. I am a lord, for so my deeds shall prove,
　And yet a shepherd by my parentage.
　But, lady, this fair face and heavenly hue
　Must grace his bed that conquers Asia
　And means to be a terror to the world,
　Measuring the limits of his empery
　By east and west, as Phoebus doth his course.　　　40
　Lie here, ye weeds that I disdain to wear.
　This complete armour and this curtle-axe
　Are adjuncts more beseeming Tamburlaine.
　And, madam, whatsoever you esteem
　Of this success, and loss unvalued,

Both may invest you empress of the East;
And these that seem but silly country swains
May have the leading of so great an host
As with their weight shall make the mountains quake,
Even as when windy exhalations,   50
Fighting for passage, tilt within the earth.

TECHELLES. As princely lions when they rouse themselves,
Stretching their paws, and threat'ning herds of beasts,
So in his armour looketh Tamburlaine.
Methinks I see kings kneeling at his feet,
And he with frowning brows and fiery looks
Spurning their crowns from off their captive heads.

USUMCASANE. And making thee and me, Techelles, kings,
That even to death will follow Tamburlaine.

TAMBURLAINE. Nobly resolv'd, sweet friends and followers. 60
These lords, perhaps, do scorn our estimates,
And think we prattle with distempered spirits:
But since they measure our deserts so mean
That in conceit bear empires on our spears,
Affecting thoughts co-equal with the clouds,
They shall be kept our forced followers
Till with their eyes they view us emperors.

ZENOCRATE. The gods, defenders of the innocent,
Will never prosper your intended drifts
That thus oppress poor friendless passengers.   70
Therefore at least admit us liberty,
Even as thou hop'st to be eternized
By living Asia's mighty emperor.

AGYDAS. I hope our lady's treasure and our own
May serve for ransom to our liberties.
Return our mules and empty camels back,
That we may travel into Syria,
Where her betrothed lord, Alcidamus,
Expects th'arrival of her highness' person.

MAGNETES. And wheresoever we repose ourselves,   80
We will report but well of Tamburlaine.

TAMBURLAINE. Disdains Zenocrate to live with me?
Or you, my lords, to be my followers?
Think you I weigh this treasure more than you?
Not all the gold in India's wealthy arms
Shall buy the meanest soldier in my train.
Zenocrate, lovelier than the love of Jove,
Brighter than is the silver Rhodope,
Fairer than whitest snow on Scythian hills,

Thy person is more worth to Tamburlaine   90
Than the possession of the Persian crown,
Which gracious stars have promis'd at my birth.
A hundred Tartars shall attend on thee,
Mounted on steeds swifter than Pegasus;
Thy garments shall be made of Median silk,
Enchas'd with precious jewels of mine own,
More rich and valurous than Zenocrate's;
With milk-white harts upon an ivory sled
Thou shalt be drawn amidst the frozen pools,
And scale the icy mountains' lofty tops,   100
Which with thy beauty will be soon resolv'd.
My martial prizes with five hundred men
Won on the fifty-headed Volga's waves,
Shall all we offer to Zenocrate,
And then myself to fair Zenocrate.

TECHELLES. What now? In love?

TAMBURLAINE. Techelles, women must be flattered:
But this is she with whom I am in love.
    Enter a Soldier.

SOLDIER. News, news!

TAMBURLAINE. How now, what's the matter?   110

SOLDIER. A thousand Persian horsemen are at hand,
Sent from the king to overcome us all.

TAMBURLAINE. How now, my lords of Egypt and Zenocrate!
Now must your jewels be restor'd again,
And I that triumph'd so be overcome?
How say you, lordings, is not this your hope?

AGYDAS. We hope yourself will willingly restore them.

TAMBURLAINE. Such hope, such fortune, have the thousand
    horse.
Soft ye, my lords and sweet Zenocrate.
You must be forced from me ere you go.   120
A thousand horsemen? We five hundred foot?
An odds too great for us to stand against.
But are they rich? And is their armour good?

SOLDIER. Their plumed helms are wrought with beaten gold,
Their swords enamell'd, and about their necks
Hangs massy chains of gold down to the waist;
In every part exceeding brave and rich.

TAMBURLAINE. Then shall we fight courageously with them?
Or look you I should play the orator?

TECHELLES. No, cowards and faint-hearted runaways   130
Look for orations when the foe is near:

Our swords shall play the orators for us.
USUMCASANE. Come, let us meet them at the mountain-foot,
    And with a sudden and an hot alarm
    Drive all their horses headlong down the hill.
TECHELLES. Come, let us march.
TAMBURLAINE. Stay, Techelles; ask a parley first.
    The Soldiers *enter.*
    Open the mails, yet guard the treasure sure.
    Lay out our golden wedges to the view,
    That their reflections may amaze the Persians;   140
    And look we friendly on them when they come.
    But if they offer word or violence,
    We'll fight, five hundred men-at-arms to one,
    Before we part with our possession;
    And 'gainst the general we will lift our swords,
    And either lanch his greedy thirsting throat,
    Or take him prisoner, and his chain shall serve
    For manacles till he be ransom'd home.
TECHELLES. I hear them come: shall we encounter them?
TAMBURLAINE. Keep all your standings, and not stir a foot: 150
    Myself will bide the danger of the brunt.
    Enter Theridamas, *with others.*
THERIDAMAS. Where is this Scythian Tamburlaine?
TAMBURLAINE. Whom seek'st thou, Persian? I am Tamburlaine.
THERIDAMAS. Tamburlaine?
    A Scythian shepherd so embellished
    With nature's pride and richest furniture?
    His looks do menace heaven and dare the gods;
    His fiery eyes are fix'd upon the earth,
    As if he now devis'd some stratagem,
    Or meant to pierce Avernus' darksome vaults   160
    And pull the triple-headed dog from hell.
TAMBURLAINE. Noble and mild this Persian seems to be,
    If outward habit judge the inward man.
TECHELLES. His deep affections make him passionate.
TAMBURLAINE. With what a majesty he rears his looks.
    In thee, thou valiant man of Persia,
    I see the folly of thy emperor.
    Art thou but captain of a thousand horse,
    That by characters graven in thy brows,
    And by thy martial face and stout aspect,   170
    Deserv'st to have the leading of an host?
    Forsake thy king, and do but join with me,
    And we will triumph over all the world.

I hold the Fates bound fast in iron chains,
And with my hand turn Fortune's wheel about;
And sooner shall the sun fall from his sphere
Than Tamburlaine be slain or overcome.
Draw forth thy sword, thou mighty man-at-arms,
Intending but to raze my charmed skin,
And Jove himself will stretch his hand from heaven   180
To ward the blow, and shield me safe from harm.
See how he rains down heaps of gold in showers,
As if he meant to give my soldiers pay;
And as a sure and grounded argument
That I shall be the monarch of the East,
He sends this Soldan's daughter rich and brave
To be my queen and portly emperess.
If thou wilt stay with me, renowmed man,
And lead thy thousand horse with my conduct,
Besides thy share of this Egyptian prize,   190
Those thousand horse shall sweat with martial spoil
Of conquered kingdoms and of cities sack'd.
Both we will walk upon the lofty cliffs,
And Christian merchants that with Russian stems
Plough up huge furrows in the Caspian Sea
Shall vail to us as lords of all the lake.
Both we will reign as consuls of the earth,
And mighty kings shall be our senators.
Jove sometime masked in a shepherd's weed,
And by those steps that he hath scal'd the heavens   200
May we become immortal like the gods.
Join with me now in this my mean estate
(I call it mean because, being yet obscure,
The nations far-remov'd admire me not)
And when my name and honour shall be spread
As far as Boreas claps his brazen wings,
Or fair Böotes sends his cheerful light,
Then shalt thou be competitor with me,
And sit with Tamburlaine in all his majesty.
THERIDAMAS. Not Hermes, prolocutor to the gods,   210
    Could use persuasions more pathetical.
TAMBURLAINE. Nor are Apollo's oracles more true
    Than thou shalt find my vaunts substantial.
TECHELLES. We are his friends, and if the Persian king
    Should offer present dukedoms to our state,
    We think it loss to make exchange for that
    We are assur'd of by our friend's success.

[16]

USUMCASANE. And kingdoms at the least we all expect,
Besides the honour in assured conquests,
Where kings shall crouch unto our conquering swords, 220
And hosts of soldiers stand amaz'd at us,
When with their fearful tongues they shall confess,
These are the men that all the world admires.

THERIDAMAS. What strong enchantments tice my yielding soul!
Are these resolved noble Scythians?
But shall I prove a traitor to my king?

TAMBURLAINE. No, but the trusty friend of Tamburlaine.

THERIDAMAS. Won with thy words and conquered with thy
    looks,
I yield myself, my men and horse to thee,
To be partaker of thy good or ill,   230
As long as life maintains Theridamas.

TAMBURLAINE. Theridamas my friend, take here my hand,
Which is as much as if I swore by heaven,
And call'd the gods to witness of my vow.
Thus shall my heart be still combin'd with thine
Until our bodies turn to elements,
And both our souls aspire celestial thrones.
Techelles and Casane, welcome him.

TECHELLES. Welcome, renowmed Persian, to us all.

USUMCASANE. Long may Theridamas remain with us.   240

TAMBURLAINE. These are my friends in whom I more rejoice
Than doth the King of Persia in his crown;
And, by the love of Pylades and Orestes,
Whose statues we adore in Scythia,
Thyself and them shall never part from me
Before I crown you kings in Asia.
Make much of them, gentle Theridamas,
And they will never leave thee till the death.

THERIDAMAS. Nor thee nor them, thrice-noble Tamburlaine,
Shall want my heart to be with gladness pierc'd   250
To do you honour and security.

TAMBURLAINE. A thousand thanks, worthy Theridamas.
And now, fair madam and my noble lords,
If you will willingly remain with me,
You shall have honours as your merits be;
Or else you shall be forc'd with slavery.

AGYDAS. We yield unto thee, happy Tamburlaine.

TAMBURLAINE. For you then, madam, I am out of doubt.

ZENOCRATE. I must be pleas'd perforce, wretched Zenocrate.

                                                    Exeunt.

Actus 2. Scaena 1.

[*Enter*] Cosroe, Menaphon, Ortygius, Ceneus, *with other* Soldiers.

COSROE. Thus far are we towards Theridamas,
  And valiant Tamburlaine, the man of fame,
  The man that in the forehead of his fortune
  Bears figures of renown and miracle.
  But tell me, that hast seen him, Menaphon,
  What stature wields he, and what personage?
MENAPHON. Of stature tall, and straightly fashioned
  Like his desire, lift upwards and divine;
  So large of limbs, his joints so strongly knit,
  Such breadth of shoulders as might mainly bear   10
  Old Atlas' burden; 'twixt his manly pitch
  A pearl more worth than all the world is plac'd,
  Wherein by curious sovereignty of art
  Are fix'd his piercing instruments of sight,
  Whose fiery circles bear encompassed
  A heaven of heavenly bodies in their spheres,
  That guides his steps and actions to the throne
  Where honour sits invested royally;
  Pale of complexion, wrought in him with passion,
  Thirsting with sovereignty, with love of arms;   20
  His lofty brows in folds do figure death,
  And in their smoothness amity and life;
  About them hangs a knot of amber hair,
  Wrapped in curls, as fierce Achilles' was,
  On which the breath of heaven delights to play,
  Making it dance with wanton majesty.
  His arms and fingers long and sinewy,
  Betokening valour and excess of strength;
  In every part proportioned like the man
  Should make the world subdu'd to Tamburlaine.   30
COSROE. Well hast thou portray'd in thy terms of life
  The face and personage of a wondrous man.
  Nature doth strive with Fortune and his stars
  To make him famous in accomplish'd worth;
  And well his merits show him to be made
  His fortune's master and the king of men,
  That could persuade, at such a sudden pinch,
  With reasons of his valour and his life,
  A thousand sworn and overmatching foes.
  Then when our powers in points of swords are join'd   40

[18]

And clos'd in compass of the killing bullet,
Though strait the passage and the port be made
That leads to palace of my brother's life,
Proud is his fortune if we pierce it not.
And when the princely Persian diadem
Shall overweigh his weary witless head,
And fall like mellowed fruit, with shakes of death,
In fair Persia noble Tamburlaine
Shall be my regent, and remain as King.
ORTYGIUS. In happy hour we have set the crown   50
Upon your kingly head, that seeks our honour
In joining with the man ordain'd by heaven
To further every action to the best.
CENEUS. He that with shepherds and a little spoil
Durst, in disdain of wrong and tyranny,
Defend his freedom 'gainst a monarchy,
What will he do supported by a king,
Leading a troop of gentlemen and lords,
And stuff'd with treasure for his highest thoughts?
COSROE. And such shall wait on worthy Tamburlaine.   60
Our army will be forty thousand strong,
When Tamburlaine and brave Theridamas
Have met us by the river Araris,
And all conjoin'd to meet the witless king
That now is marching near to Parthia,
And with unwilling soldiers faintly arm'd,
To seek revenge on me and Tamburlaine.
To whom, sweet Menaphon, direct me straight.
MENAPHON. I will, my lord.
                                                    Exeunt.

Actus 2. Scaena 2.
[*Enter*] Mycetes, Meander, *with other* Lords *and* Soldiers.
MYCETES. Come, my Meander, let us to this gear.
I tell you true, my heart is swoll'n with wrath
On this same thievish villain Tamburlaine,
And of that false Cosroe, my traitorous brother.
Would it not grieve a king to be so abus'd,
And have a thousand horsemen ta'en away?
And, which is worst, to have his diadem
Sought for by such scald knaves as love him not?
I think it would. Well then, by heavens I swear,
Aurora shall not peep out of her doors,   10
But I will have Cosroe by the head,
And kill proud Tamburlaine with point of sword.

Tell you the rest, Meander: I have said.

MEANDER. Then, having pass'd Armenian deserts now,
And pitch'd our tents under the Georgian hills,
Whose tops are covered with Tartarian thieves
That lie in ambush, waiting for a prey,
What should we do but bid them battle straight,
And rid the world of those detested troops?
Lest, if we let them linger here a while,   20
They gather strength by power of fresh supplies.
This country swarms with vile outrageous men
That live by rapine and by lawless spoil,
Fit soldiers for the wicked Tamburlaine;
And he that could with gifts and promises
Inveigle him that led a thousand horse,
And make him false his faith unto his king,
Will quickly win such as are like himself.
Therefore cheer up your minds; prepare to fight.
He that can take or slaughter Tamburlaine,   30
Shall rule the province of Albania.
Who brings that traitor's head Theridamas
Shall have a government in Media,
Beside the spoil of him and all his train.
But if Cosroe (as our spials say,
And as we know) remains with Tamburlaine,
His highness' pleasure is that he should live,
And be reclaim'd with princely lenity.
     [*Enter a* Spy.]

SPY. An hundred horsemen of my company,
Scouting abroad upon these champion plains,   40
Have view'd the army of the Scythians,
Which make report it far exceeds the king's.

MEANDER. Suppose they be in number infinite,
Yet being void of martial discipline,
All running headlong after greedy spoils,
And more regarding gain than victory,
Like to the cruel brothers of the earth,
Sprung of the teeth of dragons venomous,
Their careless swords shall lanch their fellows' throats
And make us triumph in their overthrow.   50

MYCETES. Was there such brethren, sweet Meander, say,
That sprung of teeth of dragons venomous?

MEANDER. So poets say, my lord.

MYCETES. And 'tis a pretty toy to be a poet.
Well, well, Meander, thou art deeply read,

And having thee, I have a jewel, sure.
Go on, my lord, and give your charge, I say;
Thy wit will make us conquerors today.

MEANDER. Then, noble soldiers, to entrap these thieves
That live confounded in disordered troops,   60
If wealth or riches may prevail with them,
We have our camels laden all with gold,
Which you that be but common soldiers
Shall fling in every corner of the field;
And while the base-born Tartars take it up,
You, fighting more for honour than for gold,
Shall massacre those greedy-minded slaves;
And when their scattered army is subdu'd,
And you march on their slaughtered carcasses,
Share equally the gold that bought their lives,   70
And live like gentlemen in Persia.
Strike up the drum, and march courageously:
Fortune herself doth sit upon our crests.

MYCETES. He tells you true, my masters, so he does.
Drums, why sound ye not when Meander speaks?   *Exeunt.*

Actus 2. Scaena 3.

[*Enter*] Cosroe, Tamburlaine, Theridamas, Techelles,
Usumcasane, Ortygius, *with others.*

COSROE. Now, worthy Tamburlaine, have I repos'd
In thy approved fortunes all my hope.
What think'st thou, man, shall come of our attempts?
For even as from assured oracle
I take thy doom for satisfaction.

TAMBURLAINE. And so mistake you not a whit, my lord.
For fates and oracles of heaven have sworn
To royalize the deeds of Tamburlaine,
And make them blest that share in his attempts.
And doubt you not but, if you favour me,   10
And let my fortunes and my valour sway
To some direction in your martial deeds,
The world will strive with hosts of men-at-arms
To swarm unto the ensign I support.
The host of Xerxes, which by fame is said
To drink the mighty Parthian Araris,
Was but a handful to that we will have.
Our quivering lances, shaking in the air,
And bullets like Jove's dreadful thunderbolts
Enroll'd in flames and fiery smouldering mists,   20

Shall threat the gods more than Cyclopian wars;
And with our sun-bright armour, as we march,
We'll chase the stars from heaven, and dim their eyes
That stand and muse at our admired arms.

THERIDAMAS. You see, my lord, what working words he hath;
But when you see his actions top his speech,
Your speech will stay, or so extol his worth
As I shall be commended and excus'd
For turning my poor charge to his direction.
And these his two renowmed friends, my lord,   30
Would make one thrust and strive to be retain'd
In such a great degree of amity.

TECHELLES. With duty and with amity we yield
Our utmost service to the fair Cosroe.

COSROE. Which I esteem as portion of my crown.
Usumcasane and Techelles both,
When she that rules in Rhamnus' golden gates,
And makes a passage for all prosperous arms,
Shall make me solely emperor of Asia,
Then shall your meeds and valours be advanc'd   40
To rooms of honour and nobility.

TAMBURLAINE. Then haste, Cosroe, to be king alone,
That I with these my friends and all my men
May triumph in our long-expected fate.
The king your brother is now hard at hand:
Meet with the fool, and rid your royal shoulders
Of such a burden as outweighs the sands
And all the craggy rocks of Caspia.
   [*Enter a* Messenger.]

MESSENGER. My lord, we have discovered the enemy
Ready to charge you with a mighty army.   50

COSROE. Come, Tamburlaine, now whet thy winged sword,
And lift thy lofty arm into the clouds,
That it may reach the King of Persia's crown,
And set it safe on my victorious head.

TAMBURLAINE. See where it is, the keenest curtle-axe
That e'er made passage thorough Persian arms.
These are the wings shall make it fly as swift
As doth the lightning or the breath of heaven,
And kill as sure as it swiftly flies.

COSROE. Thy words assure me of kind success.   60
Go, valiant soldier, go before and charge
The fainting army of that foolish king.

TAMBURLAINE. Usumcasane and Techelles, come;

We are enough to scare the enemy,
And more than needs to make an emperor.   [*Exeunt.*]

To the battle, and Mycetes *comes out alone with his crown in his hand, offering to hide it.*

MYCETES. Accurs'd be he that first invented war!
They knew not, ah, they knew not, simple men,
How those were hit by pelting cannon-shot
Stand staggering like a quivering aspen-leaf
Fearing the force of Boreas' boist'rous blasts.
In what a lamentable case were I,
If nature had not given me wisdom's lore!
For kings are clouts that every man shoots at,
Our crown the pin that thousands seek to cleave.
Therefore in policy I think it good   10
To hide it close; a goodly stratagem,
And far from any man that is a fool.
So shall not I be known; or if I be,
They cannot take away my crown from me.
Here will I hide it in this simple hole.
     Enter Tamburlaine.
TAMBURLAINE. What, fearful coward, straggling from the camp
When kings themselves are present in the field?
MYCETES. Thou liest.
TAMBURLAINE.   Base villain, dar'st thou give the lie?
MYCETES. Away, I am the king. Go, touch me not.
Thou break'st the law of arms unless thou kneel,   20
And cry me 'Mercy, noble king!'
TAMBURLAINE. Are you the witty King of Persia?
MYCETES. Ay, marry am I: have you any suit to me?
TAMBURLAINE. I would entreat you to speak but three wise
words.
MYCETES. So I can when I see my time.
TAMBURLAINE. Is this your crown?
MYCETES. Ay, didst thou ever see a fairer?
TAMBURLAINE. You will not sell it, will ye?
MYCETES. Such another word, and I will have thee executed.
Come, give it me.
TAMBURLAINE.   No, I took it prisoner.   30
MYCETES. You lie, I gave it you.
TAMBURLAINE.   Then 'tis mine.
MYCETES. No, I mean I let you keep it.
TAMBURLAINE. Well, I mean you shall have it again.

Here, take it for a while; I lend it thee
Till I may see thee hemm'd with armed men;
Then shalt thou see me pull it from thy head.
Thou art no match for mighty Tamburlaine.   [*Exit.*]
MYCETES. O gods, is this Tamburlaine the thief?
I marvel much he stole it not away.
                    Sound trumpets to the battle, and he runs in.

[*Actus 2. Scaena 5.*]

[*Enter*] Cosroe, Tamburlaine, Theridamas, Menaphon,
Meander, Ortygius, Techelles, Usumcasane, *with others.*
TAMBURLAINE. Hold thee, Cosroe; wear two imperial crowns.
Think thee invested now as royally,
Even by the mighty hand of Tamburlaine,
As if as many kings as could encompass thee
With greatest pomp had crown'd thee emperor.
COSROE. So do I, thrice-renowmed man-at-arms;
And none shall keep the crown but Tamburlaine.
Thee do I make my regent of Persia,
And general lieutenant of my armies.
Meander, you that were our brother's guide,   10
And chiefest counsellor in all his acts,
Since he is yielded to the stroke of war,
On your submission we with thanks excuse,
And give you equal place in our affairs.
MEANDER. Most happy emperor, in humblest terms
I vow my service to your majesty,
With utmost virtue of my faith and duty.
COSROE. Thanks good Meander. Then, Cosroe, reign,
And govern Persia in her former pomp.
Now send embassage to thy neighbour kings,   20
And let them know the Persian king is chang'd
From one that knew not what a king should do
To one that can command what 'longs thereto.
And now we will to fair Persepolis
With twenty thousand expert soldiers.
The lords and captains of my brother's camp
With little slaughter take Meander's course,
And gladly yield them to my gracious rule.
Ortygius and Menaphon, my trusty friends,
Now will I gratify your former good,   30
And grace your calling with a greater sway.
ORTYGIUS. And as we ever aim'd at your behoof,
And sought your state all honour it deserv'd,

[24]

So will we with our powers and our lives
Endeavour to preserve and prosper it.
COSROE. I will not thank thee, sweet Ortygius;
  Better replies shall prove my purposes.
  And now, Lord Tamburlaine, my brother's camp
  I leave to thee and to Theridamas,
  To follow me to fair Persepolis.   40
  Then will we march to all those Indian mines
  My witless brother to the Christians lost,
  And ransom them with fame and usury.
  And, till thou overtake me, Tamburlaine,
  Staying to order all the scattered troops,
  Farewell, lord regent and his happy friends.
  I long to sit upon my brother's throne.
MEANDER. Your majesty shall shortly have your wish,
  And ride in triumph through Persepolis.   *Exeunt.*
    Manent Tamburlaine, Techelles, Theridamas, Usum-
    casane.
TAMBURLAINE. And ride in triumph through Persepolis!   50
  Is it not brave to be a king, Techelles,
  Usumcasane and Theridamas?
  Is it not passing brave to be a king,
  And ride in triumph through Persepolis? .
TECHELLES. O my lord, 'tis sweet and full of pomp.
USUMCASANE. To be a king, is half to be a god.
THERIDAMAS. A god is not so glorious as a king:
  I think the pleasure they enjoy in heaven,
  Cannot compare with kingly joys in earth;
  To wear a crown enchas'd with pearl and gold,   60
  Whose virtues carry with it life and death;
  To ask and have, command and be obey'd;
  When looks breed love, with looks to gain the prize,
  Such power attractive shines in princes' eyes.
TAMBURLAINE. Why, say, Theridamas, wilt thou be a king?
THERIDAMAS. Nay, though I praise it, I can live without it.
TAMBURLAINE. What says my other friends, will you be kings?
TECHELLES. Ay, if I could, with all my heart, my lord.
TAMBURLAINE. Why, that's well said, Techelles; so would I,
  And so would you my masters, would you not?   70
USUMCASANE. What then, my lord?
TAMBURLAINE. Why then, Casane, shall we wish for aught
  The world affords in greatest novelty,
  And rest attemptless, faint, and destitute?
  Methinks we should not. I am strongly mov'd,

[25]

That if I should desire the Persian crown,
I could attain it with a wondrous ease;
And would not all our soldiers soon consent,
If we should aim at such a dignity?
THERIDAMAS. I know they would with our persuasions.   80
TAMBURLAINE. Why then, Theridamas, I'll first assay
To get the Persian kingdom to myself;
Then thou for Parthia; they for Scythia and Media;
And if I prosper, all shall be as sure
As if the Turk, the Pope, Afric, and Greece,
Came creeping to us with their crowns apiece.
TECHELLES. Then shall we send to this triumphing king,
And bid him battle for his novel crown?
USUMCASANE. Nay, quickly then, before his room be hot.
TAMBURLAINE. 'Twill prove a pretty jest, in faith, my friends. 90
THERIDAMAS. A jest to charge on twenty thousand men!
I judge the purchase more important far.
TAMBURLAINE. Judge by thyself, Theridamas, not me;
For presently Techelles here shall haste
To bid him battle ere he pass too far,
And lose more labour than the gain will quite.
Then shalt thou see the Scythian Tamburlaine
Make but a jest to win the Persian crown.
Techelles, take a thousand horse with thee,
And bid him turn him back to war with us   100
That only made him king to make us sport.
We will not steal upon him cowardly,
But give him warning and more warriors.
Haste thee, Techelles; we will follow thee.   [*Exit* Techelles.]
What saith Theridamas?
THERIDAMAS.   Go on, for me.   *Exeunt.*

Actus 2. Scaena 6.

[*Enter*] Cosroe, Meander, Ortygius, Menaphon, *with
other* Soldiers.
COSROE. What means this devilish shepherd to aspire
With such a giantly presumption,
To cast up hills against the face of heaven,
And dare the force of angry Jupiter?
But as he thrust them underneath the hills,
And press'd out fire from their burning jaws,
So will I send this monstrous slave to hell,
Where flames shall ever feed upon his soul.
MEANDER. Some powers divine, or else infernal, mix'd

Their angry seeds at his conception;
For he was never sprung of human race,
Since with the spirit of his fearful pride
He dares so doubtlessly resolve of rule,
And by profession be ambitious.

ORTYGIUS. What god, or fiend, or spirit of the earth,
Or monster turned to a manly shape,
Or of what mould or mettle he be made,
What star or state soever govern him,
Let us put on our meet encount'ring minds;
And in detesting such a devilish thief,   20
In love of honour and defence of right,
Be arm'd against the hate of such a foe,
Whether from earth or hell or heaven he grow.

COSROE. Nobly resolv'd, my good Ortygius;
And since we all have suck'd one wholesome air,
And with the same proportion of elements
Resolve, I hope we are resembled,
Vowing our loves to equal death and life;
Let's cheer our soldiers to encounter him,
That grievous image of ingratitude,   30
That fiery thirster after sovereignty,
And burn him in the fury of that flame
That none can quench but blood and empery.
Resolve, my lords and loving soldiers, now
To save your king and country from decay.
Then strike up, drum; and all the stars that make
The loathsome circle of my dated life,
Direct my weapon to his barbarous heart
That this opposeth him against the gods,
And scorns the powers that govern Persia.   40
                                              [*Exeunt.*]

[*Actus 2. Scaena 7.*]
Enter to the battle; and after the battle, enter Cosroe *wounded,*
Theridamas, Tamburlaine, Techelles, Usumcasane, *with*
others.

COSROE. Barbarous and bloody Tamburlaine,
Thus to deprive me of my crown and life!
Treacherous and false Theridamas,
Even at the morning of my happy state,
Scarce being seated in my royal throne,
To work my downfall and untimely end!

An uncouth pain torments my grieved soul
And death arrests the organ of my voice,
Who, ent'ring at the breach thy sword hath made,
Sacks every vein and artier of my heart.   10
Bloody and insatiate Tamburlaine!

TAMBURLAINE. The thirst of reign and sweetness of a crown,
   That caus'd the eldest son of heavenly Ops
   To thrust his doting father from his chair,
   And place himself in the imperial heaven,
   Mov'd me to manage arms against thy state.
   What better precedent than mighty Jove?
   Nature, that fram'd us of four elements
   Warring within our breasts for regiment,
   Doth teach us all to have aspiring minds.   20
   Our souls, whose faculties can comprehend
   The wondrous architecture of the world,
   And measure every wand'ring planet's course,
   Still climbing after knowledge infinite,
   And always moving as the restless spheres,
   Wills us to wear ourselves and never rest
   Until we reach the ripest fruit of all,
   That perfect bliss and sole felicity,
   The sweet fruition of an earthly crown.

THERIDAMAS. And that made me to join with Tamburlaine;   30
   For he is gross and like the massy earth
   That moves not upwards, nor by princely deeds
   Doth mean to soar above the highest sort.

TECHELLES. And that made us, the friends of Tamburlaine,
   To lift our swords against the Persian king.

USUMCASANE. For as, when Jove did thrust old Saturn down,
   Neptune and Dis gain'd each of them a crown,
   So do we hope to reign in Asia,
   If Tamburlaine be plac'd in Persia.

COSROE. The strangest men that ever nature made!   40
   I know not how to take their tyrannies.
   My bloodless body waxeth chill and cold,
   And with my blood my life slides through my wound;
   My soul begins to take her flight to hell,
   And summons all my senses to depart.
   The heat and moisture, which did feed each other,
   For want of nourishment to feed them both,
   Is dry and cold; and now doth ghastly Death
   With greedy talents gripe my bleeding heart,
   And like a harpy tires on my life.   50

[28]

Theridamas and Tamburlaine, I die,
And fearful vengeance light upon you both! [*Dies.*]
                    He takes the crown and puts it on.
TAMBURLAINE. Not all the curses which the Furies breathe
    Shall make me leave so rich a prize as this.
    Theridamas, Techelles, and the rest,
    Who think you now is King of Persia?
ALL. Tamburlaine! Tamburlaine!
TAMBURLAINE. Though Mars himself, the angry god of arms,
    And all the earthly potentates conspire
    To dispossess me of this diadem,   60
    Yet will I wear it in despite of them,
    As great commander of this eastern world,
    If you but say that Tamburlaine shall reign.
ALL. Long live Tamburlaine, and reign in Asia!
TAMBURLAINE. So; now it is more surer on my head
    Than if the gods had held a parliament,
    And all pronounc'd me King of Persia.   [*Exeunt.*]
                    Finis Actus 2.

                    Actus 3. Scaena 1.
    [*Enter*] Bajazeth, *the* Kings of Fez, Morocco, *and* Argier,
    with others, in great pomp.
BAJAZETH. Great kings of Barbary, and my portly bassoes,
    We hear the Tartars and the eastern thieves,
    Under the conduct of one Tamburlaine,
    Presume a bickering with your emperor,
    And think to rouse us from our dreadful siege
    Of the famous Grecian Constantinople.
    You know our army is invincible:
    As many circumcised Turks we have,
    And warlike bands of Christians renied,
    As hath the Ocean or the Terrene Sea   10
    Small drops of water, when the moon begins
    To join in one her semicircled horns.
    Yet would we not be brav'd with foreign power,
    Nor raise our siege before the Grecians yield,
    Or breathless lie before the city walls.
FEZ. Renowned emperor and mighty general,
    What if you sent the bassoes of your guard
    To charge him to remain in Asia,
    Or else to threaten death and deadly arms
    As from the mouth of mighty Bajazeth?   20

BAJAZETH. Hie thee, my basso, fast to Persia.
　Tell him thy lord, the Turkish emperor,
　Dread lord of Afric, Europe and Asia,
　Great king and conqueror of Graecia,
　The Ocean, Terrene, and the coal-black Sea,
　The high and highest monarch of the world,
　Wills and commands (for say not I entreat)
　Not once to set his foot in Africa,
　Or spread his colours in Graecia,
　Lest he incur the fury of my wrath.   30
　Tell him I am content to take a truce,
　Because I hear he bears a valiant mind;
　But if, presuming on his silly power,
　He be so mad to manage arms with me,
　Then stay thou with him; say I bid thee so.
　And if before the sun have measured heaven
　With triple circuit thou re-greet us not,
　We mean to take his morning's next arise
　For messenger he will not be reclaim'd,
　And mean to fetch thee in despite of him.   40
BASSO. Most great and puissant monarch of the earth,
　Your basso will accomplish your behest,
　And show your pleasure to the Persian,
　As fits the legate of the stately Turk.   *Exit* Basso.
ARGIER. They say he is the King of Persia;
　But if he dare attempt to stir your siege,
　'Twere requisite he should be ten times more,
　For all flesh quakes at your magnificence.
BAJAZETH. True, Argier, and tremble at my looks.
MOROCCO. The spring is hind'red by your smothering host, 50
　For neither rain can fall upon the earth,
　Nor sun reflex his virtuous beams thereon,
　The ground is mantled with such multitudes.
BAJAZETH. All this is true as holy Mahomet,
　And all the trees are blasted with our breaths.
FEZ. What thinks your greatness best to be achiev'd
　In pursuit of the city's overthrow?
BAJAZETH. I will the captive pioners of Argier
　Cut off the water that by leaden pipes
　Runs to the city from the mountain Carnon;   60
　Two thousand horse shall forage up and down,
　That no relief or succour come by land;
　And all the sea my galleys countermand.
　Then shall our footmen lie within the trench,

And with their cannons, mouth'd like Orcus gulf,
Batter the walls, and we will enter in;
And thus the Grecians shall be conquered.   *Exeunt.*

Actus 3. Scaena 2.
[*Enter*] Agydas, Zenocrate, Anippe, *with others.*
AGYDAS. Madam Zenocrate, may I presume
    To know the cause of these unquiet fits
    That work such trouble to your wonted rest?
    'Tis more than pity such a heavenly face
    Should by heart's sorrow wax so wan and pale,
    When your offensive rape by Tamburlaine
    (Which of your whole displeasures should be most)
    Hath seem'd to be digested long ago.
ZENOCRATE. Although it be digested long ago,
    As his exceeding favours have deserv'd,   10
    And might content the queen of heaven as well
    As it hath chang'd my first-conceiv'd disdain,
    Yet since a farther passion feeds my thoughts
    With ceaseless and disconsolate conceits,
    Which dyes my looks so lifeless as they are,
    And might, if my extremes had full events,
    Make me the ghastly counterfeit of death.
AGYDAS. Eternal heaven sooner be dissolv'd,
    And all that pierceth Phoebe's silver eye,
    Before such hap fall to Zenocrate!   20
ZENOCRATE. Ah, life and soul, still hover in his breast,
    And leave my body senseless as the earth,
    Or else unite you to his life and soul,
    That I may live and die with Tamburlaine.
                Enter Tamburlaine *with* Techelles *and others.*
AGYDAS. With Tamburlaine? Ah, fair Zenocrate,
    Let not a man so vile and barbarous,
    That holds you from your father in despite,
    And keeps you from the honours of a queen,
    Being suppos'd his worthless concubine,
    Be honoured with your love but for necessity.   30
    So now the mighty Soldan hears of you,
    Your highness needs not doubt but in short time
    He will with Tamburlaine's destruction
    Redeem you from this deadly servitude.
ZENOCRATE. Agydas, leave to wound me with these words,
    And speak of Tamburlaine as he deserves.
    The entertainment we have had of him

[31]

Is far from villainy or servitude,
And might in noble minds be counted princely.

AGYDAS. How can you fancy one that looks so fierce,   40
Only dispos'd to martial stratagems?
Who, when he shall embrace you in his arms,
Will tell how many thousand men he slew;
And when you look for amorous discourse,
Will rattle forth his facts of war and blood,
Too harsh a subject for your dainty ears.

ZENOCRATE. As looks the sun through Nilus' flowing stream,
Or when the morning holds him in her arms,
So looks my lordly love, fair Tamburlaine;
His talk much sweeter than the Muses' song   50
They sung for honour 'gainst Pierides,
Or when Minerva did with Neptune strive;
And higher would I rear my estimate
Than Juno, sister to the highest god,
If I were match'd with mighty Tamburlaine.

AGYDAS. Yet be not so inconstant in your love,
But let the young Arabian live in hope
After your rescue to enjoy his choice.
You see, though first the King of Persia,
Being a shepherd, seem'd to love you much,   60
Now in his majesty he leaves those looks,
Those words of favour, and those comfortings,
And gives no more than common courtesies.

ZENOCRATE. Thence rise the tears that so distain my cheeks,
Fearing his love through my unworthiness.

> Tamburlaine *goes to her, and takes her away lovingly by the*
> *hand, looking wrathfully on* Agydas, *and says nothing.*
>
> [*Exeunt. Manet* Agydas.]

AGYDAS. Betray'd by fortune and suspicious love,
Threat'ned with frowning wrath and jealousy,
Surpris'd with fear of hideous revenge,
I stand aghast; but most astonied
To see his choler shut in secret thoughts,   70
And wrapt in silence of his angry soul.
Upon his brows was portray'd ugly death,
And in his eyes the fury of his heart,
That shine as comets, menacing revenge,
And cast a pale complexion on his cheeks.
As when the seaman sees the Hyades
Gather an army of Cimmerian clouds
(Auster and Aquilon with winged steeds,

All sweating, tilt about the watery heavens,
With shivering spears enforcing thunder-claps,   80
And from their shields strike flames of lightening),
All fearful folds his sails, and sounds the main,
Lifting his prayers to the heavens for aid
Against the terror of the winds and waves:
So fares Agydas for the late-felt frowns
That sent a tempest to my daunted thoughts,
And makes my soul divine her overthrow.
    Enter Techelles *with a naked dagger* [*and* Usumcasane].
TECHELLES. See you, Agydas, how the king salutes you.
He bids you prophesy what it imports.
AGYDAS. I prophesied before and now I prove   90
The killing frowns of jealousy and love.
He needed not with words confirm my fear,
For words are vain where working tools present
The naked action of my threat'ned end.
It says, 'Agydas, thou shalt surely die,
And of extremities elect the least;
More honour and less pain it may procure,
To die by this resolved hand of thine
Than stay the torments he and heaven have sworn.'
Then haste, Agydas, and prevent the plagues   100
Which thy prolonged fates may draw on thee.
Go wander free from fear of tyrant's rage,
Removed from the torments and the hell
Wherewith he may excruciate thy soul;
And let Agydas by Agydas die,
And with this stab slumber eternally.
TECHELLES. Usumcasane, see how right the man
Hath hit the meaning of my lord the king.
USUMCASANE. Faith, and Techelles, it was manly done;
And since he was so wise and honourable,   110
Let us afford him now the bearing hence,
And crave his triple-worthy burial.
TECHELLES. Agreed, Casane; we will honour him.
                                [*Exeunt with body.*]

Actus 3. Scaena 3.
  [*Enter*] Tamburlaine, Techelles, Usumcasane, Theri-
damas, Basso, Zenocrate, [Anippe,] *with others.*
TAMBURLAINE. Basso, by this thy lord and master knows
I mean to meet him in Bithynia.
See how he comes! Tush, Turks are full of brags,

[33]

And menace more than they can well perform.
He meet me in the field and fetch thee hence!
Alas, poor Turk, his fortune is too weak
T'encounter with the strength of Tamburlaine.
View well my camp, and speak indifferently:
Do not my captains and my soldiers look
As if they meant to conquer Africa?　　　　　10
BASSO. Your men are valiant, but their number few,
　　And cannot terrify his mighty host.
　　My lord, the great commander of the world,
　　Besides fifteen contributory kings,
　　Hath now in arms ten thousand janizaries,
　　Mounted on lusty Mauritanian steeds,
　　Brought to the war by men of Tripoli;
　　Two hundred thousand footmen that have serv'd
　　In two set battles fought in Graecia;
　　And for the expedition of this war,　　　　20
　　If he think good, can from his garrisons
　　Withdraw as many more to follow him.
TECHELLES. The more he brings, the greater is the spoil;
　　For when they perish by our warlike hands,
　　We mean to seat our footmen on their steeds,
　　And rifle all those stately janizars.
TAMBURLAINE. But will those kings accompany your lord?
BASSO. Such as his highness please; but some must stay
　　To rule the provinces he late subdu'd.
TAMBURLAINE. Then fight courageously: their crowns are
　　yours;　　　　　30
　　This hand shall set them on your conquering heads
　　That made me emperor of Asia.
USUMCASANE. Let him bring millions infinite of men,
　　Unpeopling western Africa and Greece,
　　Yet we assure us of the victory.
THERIDAMAS. Even he, that in a trice vanquish'd two kings
　　More mighty than the Turkish emperor,
　　Shall rouse him out of Europe, and pursue
　　His scattered army till they yield or die.
TAMBURLAINE. Well said, Theridamas! Speak in that mood,　40
　　For *will* and *shall* best fitteth Tamburlaine,
　　Whose smiling stars give him assured hope
　　Of martial triumph ere he meet his foes.
　　I that am term'd the scourge and wrath of God,
　　The only fear and terror of the world,
　　Will first subdue the Turk, and then enlarge

Those Christian captives which you keep as slaves,
Burdening their bodies with your heavy chains,
And feeding them with thin and slender fare,
That naked row about the Terrene Sea,   50
And when they chance to breathe and rest a space,
Are punish'd with bastones so grievously
That they lie panting on the galley's side,
And strive for life at every stroke they give.
These are the cruel pirates of Argier,
That damned train, the scum of Africa,
Inhabited with straggling runagates,
That make quick havoc of the Christian blood.
But, as I live, that town shall curse the time
That Tamburlaine set foot in Africa.   60
    Enter Bajazeth *with his* Bassoes *and contributory Kings*
    [Zabina *and* Ebea].
BAJAZETH. Bassoes and janizaries of my guard,
    Attend upon the person of your lord,
    The greatest potentate of Africa.
TAMBURLAINE. Techelles and the rest, prepare your swords;
    I mean t'encounter with that Bajazeth.
BAJAZETH. Kings of Fez, Moroccus, and Argier,
    He calls me Bajazeth, whom you call lord.
    Note the presumption of this Scythian slave.
    I tell thee, villain, those that lead my horse
    Have to their names titles of dignity;   70
    And dar'st thou bluntly call me Bajazeth?
TAMBURLAINE. And know thou, Turk, that those which lead
        my horse
    Shall lead thee captive thorough Africa;
    And dar'st thou bluntly call me Tamburlaine?
BAJAZETH. By Mahomet my kinsman's sepulchre,
    And by the holy Alcoran I swear,
    He shall be made a chaste and lustless eunuch,
    And in my sarell tend my concubines;
    And all his captains that thus stoutly stand
    Shall draw the chariot of my emperess,   80
    Whom I have brought to see their overthrow.
TAMBURLAINE. By this my sword that conquer'd Persia,
    Thy fall shall make me famous through the world.
    I will not tell thee how I'll handle thee,
    But every common soldier of my camp
    Shall smile to see thy miserable state.
FEZ. What means the mighty Turkish emperor

To talk with one so base as Tamburlaine?
MOROCCO. Ye Moors and valiant men of Barbary,
    How can ye suffer these indignities?   90
ARGIER. Leave words, and let them feel your lances' points
    Which glided through the bowels of the Greeks.
BAJAZETH. Well said, my stout contributory kings!
    Your threefold army and my hugy host
    Shall swallow up these base-born Persians.
TECHELLES. Puissant, renowm'd, and mighty Tamburlaine,
    Why stay we thus prolonging all their lives?
THERIDAMAS. I long to see those crowns won by our swords,
    That we may reign as kings of Africa.
USUMCASANE. What coward would not fight for such a
    prize?   100
TAMBURLAINE. Fight all courageously, and be you kings:
    . I speak it, and my words are oracles.
BAJAZETH. Zabina, mother of three braver boys
    Than Hercules, that in his infancy
    Did pash the jaws of serpents venomous,
    Whose hands are made to gripe a warlike lance,
    Their shoulders broad, for complete armour fit,
    Their limbs more large and of a bigger size
    Than all the brats y-sprung from Typhon's loins,
    Who, when they come unto their father's age,   110
    Will batter turrets with their manly fists—
    Sit here upon this royal chair of state,
    And on thy head wear my imperial crown,
    Until I bring this sturdy Tamburlaine
    And all his captains bound in captive chains.
ZABINA. Such good success happen to Bajazeth!
TAMBURLAINE. Zenocrate, the loveliest maid alive,
    Fairer than rocks of pearl and precious stone,
    The only paragon of Tamburlaine;
    Whose eyes are brighter than the lamps of heaven,   120
    And speech more pleasant than sweet harmony;
    That with thy looks canst clear the darkened sky,
    And calm the rage of thund'ring Jupiter—
    Sit down by her, adorned with my crown,
    As if thou wert the empress of the world.
    Stir not, Zenocrate, until thou see
    Me march victoriously with all my men,
    Triumphing over him and these his kings,
    Which I will bring as vassals to thy feet.
    Till then, take thou my crown, vaunt of my worth,   130

And manage words with her, as we will arms.
ZENOCRATE. And may my love, the King of Persia,
    Return with victory and free from wound!
BAJAZETH. Now shalt thou feel the force of Turkish arms
    Which lately made all Europe quake for fear.
    I have of Turks, Arabians, Moors, and Jews,
    Enough to cover all Bithynia.
    Let thousands die: their slaughtered carcasses
    Shall serve for walls and bulwarks to the rest;
    And as the heads of Hydra, so my power,   140
    Subdu'd, shall stand as mighty as before.
    If they should yield their necks unto the sword,
    Thy soldiers' arms could not endure to strike
    So many blows as I have heads for thee.
    Thou know'st not, foolish-hardy Tamburlaine,
    What 'tis to meet me in the open field,
    That leave no ground for thee to march upon.
TAMBURLAINE. Our conquering swords shall marshal us the way
    We use to march upon the slaughtered foe,
    Trampling their bowels with our horses' hoofs,   150
    Brave horses bred on the white Tartarian hills.
    My camp is like to Julius Caesar's host,
    That never fought but had the victory;
    Nor in Pharsalia was there such hot war
    As these my followers willingly would have.
    Legions of spirits fleeting in the air
    Direct our bullets and our weapons' points,
    And make our strokes to wound the senseless air;
    And when she sees our bloody colours spread,
    Then Victory begins to take her flight,   160
    Resting herself upon my milk-white tent.
    But come, my lords, to weapons let us fall;
    The field is ours, the Turk, his wife, and all.
                                    Exit with his followers.
BAJAZETH. Come, kings and bassoes, let us glut our swords
    That thirst to drink the feeble Persians' blood.
                                    Exit with his followers.
ZABINA. Base concubine, must thou be plac'd by me
    That am the empress of the mighty Turk?
ZENOCRATE. Disdainful Turkess and unreverend boss,
    Call'st thou me concubine that am betroth'd
    Unto the great and mighty Tamburlaine?   170
ZABINA. To Tamburlaine, the great Tartarian thief?
ZENOCRATE. Thou wilt repent these lavish words of thine

When thy great basso-master and thyself
Must plead for mercy at his kingly feet,
And sue to me to be your advocate.
ZABINA. And sue to thee? I tell thee, shameless girl,
Thou shalt be laundress to my waiting-maid.
How lik'st thou her, Ebea? Will she serve?
EBEA. Madam, she thinks perhaps she is too fine;
But I shall turn her into other weeds,   180
And make her dainty fingers fall to work.
ZENOCRATE. Hear'st thou, Anippe, how thy drudge doth talk,
And how my slave, her mistress, menaceth?
Both for their sauciness shall be employ'd
To dress the common soldiers' meat and drink;
For we will scorn they should come near ourselves.
ANIPPE. Yet sometimes let your highness send for them
To do the work my chambermaid disdains.
                    They sound the battle within, and stay.
ZENOCRATE. Ye gods and powers that govern Persia,
And made my lordly love her worthy king,   190
Now strengthen him against the Turkish Bajazeth,
And let his foes, like flocks of fearful roes
Pursu'd by hunters, fly his angry looks,
That I may see him issue conqueror.
ZABINA. Now, Mahomet, solicit God himself,
And make him rain down murdering shot from heaven,
To dash the Scythians' brains, and strike them dead
That dare to manage arms with him
That offered jewels to thy sacred shrine
When first he warr'd against the Christians.   200
                    To the battle again.
ZENOCRATE. By this the Turks lie welt'ring in their blood,
And Tamburlaine is lord of Africa.
ZABINA. Thou art deceiv'd. I heard the trumpets sound
As when my emperor overthrew the Greeks,
And led them captive into Africa.
Straight will I use thee as thy pride deserves;
Prepare thyself to live and die my slave.
ZENOCRATE. If Mahomet should come from heaven and swear
My royal lord is slain or conquered,
Yet should he not persuade me otherwise   210
But that he lives and will be conqueror.
    Bajazeth *flies and he pursues him. The battle short, and they
    enter.* Bajazeth *is overcome.*
TAMBURLAINE. Now, king of bassoes, who is conqueror?

[38]

BAJAZETH. Thou, by the fortune of this damned foil.

TAMBURLAINE. Where are your stout contributory kings?

    Enter Techelles, Theridamas, *and* Usumcasane.

TECHELLES. We have their crowns; their bodies strow the field.

TAMBURLAINE. Each man a crown? Why, kingly fought, i'faith!

    Deliver them into my treasury.

ZENOCRATE. Now let me offer to my gracious lord

    His royal crown again so highly won.

TAMBURLAINE. Nay, take the Turkish crown from her, Zenocrate,   220

    And crown me Emperor of Africa.

ZABINA. No, Tamburlaine; though now thou gat the best,

    Thou shalt not yet be lord of Africa.

THERIDAMAS. Give her the crown, Turkess, you were best.

                He takes it from her, and gives it Zenocrate.

ZABINA. Injurious villains, thieves, runagates,

    How dare you thus abuse my majesty?

THERIDAMAS. Here, madam; you are empress, she is none.

TAMBURLAINE. Not now, Theridamas; her time is past:

    The pillars that have bolstered up those terms

    Are fall'n in clusters at my conquering feet.   230

ZABINA. Though he be prisoner, he may be ransomed.

TAMBURLAINE. Not all the world shall ransom Bajazeth.

BAJAZETH. Ah, fair Zabina, we have lost the field;

    And never had the Turkish emperor

    So great a foil by any foreign foe.

    Now will the Christian miscreants be glad,

    Ringing with joy their superstitious bells,

    And making bonfires for my overthrow.

    But ere I die, those foul idolaters

    Shall make me bonfires with their filthy bones;   240

    For though the glory of this day be lost,

    Afric and Greece have garrisons enough

    To make me sovereign of the earth again.

TAMBURLAINE. Those walled garrisons will I subdue,

    And write myself great lord of Africa.

    So from the East unto the furthest West

    Shall Tamburlaine extend his puissant arm.

    The galleys and those pilling brigandines

    That yearly sail to the Venetian gulf,

    And hover in the Straits for Christians' wrack,   250

    Shall lie at anchor in the Isle Asant,

    Until the Persian fleet and men-of-war,

Sailing along the oriental sea,
Have fetch'd about the Indian continent,
Even from Persepolis to Mexico,
And thence unto the Straits of Jubalter,
Where they shall meet and join their force in one,
Keeping in awe the Bay of Portingale,
And all the ocean by the British shore;
And by this means I'll win the world at last.   260

BAJAZETH. Yet set a ransom on me, Tamburlaine.

TAMBURLAINE. What, think'st thou Tamburlaine esteems thy
    gold?
I'll make the kings of India, ere I die,
Offer their mines to sue for peace to me,
And dig for treasure to appease my wrath.
Come, bind them both, and one lead in the Turk;
The Turkess let my love's maid lead away.   *They bind them.*

BAJAZETH. Ah, villains, dare ye touch my sacred arms?
O Mahomet! O sleepy Mahomet!

ZABINA. O cursed Mahomet, that mak'st us thus   270
The slaves to Scythians rude and barbarous!

TAMBURLAINE. Come, bring them in; and for this happy
    conquest
Triumph, and solemnize a martial feast.   *Exeunt.*
    Finis Actus tertii.

Actus 4. Scaena 1.

[*Enter*] Soldan *of Egypt with three or four* Lords, Capolin
[*and a* Messenger].

SOLDAN. Awake, ye men of Memphis. Hear the clang
Of Scythian trumpets; hear the basilisks,
That, roaring, shake Damascus turrets down!
The rogue of Volga holds Zenocrate,
The Soldan's daughter, for his concubine,
And with a troop of thieves and vagabonds
Hath spread his colours to our high disgrace,
While you faint-hearted base Egyptians
Lie slumbering on the flow'ry banks of Nile,
As crocodiles that unaffrighted rest   10
While thund'ring cannons rattle on their skins.

MESSENGER. Nay, mighty Soldan, did your greatness see
The frowning looks of fiery Tamburlaine,
That with his terror and imperious eyes
Commands the hearts of his associates,

It might amaze your royal majesty.

SOLDAN. Villain, I tell thee, were that Tamburlaine
As monstrous as Gorgon, prince of hell,
The Soldan would not start a foot from him.
But speak, what power hath he?

MESSENGER.   Mighty lord,   20
Three hundred thousand men in armour clad,
Upon their prancing steeds, disdainfully
With wanton paces trampling on the ground;
Five hundred thousand footmen threat'ning shot,
Shaking their swords, their spears, and iron bills,
Environing their standard round, that stood
As bristle-pointed as a thorny wood;
Their warlike engines and munition
Exceed the forces of their martial men.

SOLDAN. Nay, could their numbers countervail the stars,   30
Or ever-drizzling drops of April showers,
Or withered leaves that autumn shaketh down,
Yet would the Soldan by his conquering power
So scatter and consume them in his rage
That not a man should live to rue their fall.

CAPOLIN. So might your highness, had you time to sort
Your fighting men, and raise your royal host.
But Tamburlaine by expedition
Advantage takes of your unreadiness.

SOLDAN. Let him take all th'advantages he can.   40
Were all the world conspir'd to fight for him,
Nay, were he devil, as he is no man,
Yet in revenge of fair Zenocrate,
Whom he detaineth in despite of us,
This arm should send him down to Erebus
To shroud his shame in darkness of the night.

MESSENGER. Pleaseth your mightiness to understand,
His resolution far exceedeth all.
The first day when he pitcheth down his tents,
White is their hue, and on his silver crest   50
A snowy feather spangled white he bears,
To signify the mildness of his mind,
That satiate with spoil refuseth blood.
But when Aurora mounts the second time,
As red as scarlet is his furniture;
Then must his kindled wrath be quench'd with blood,
Not sparing any that can manage arms.
But if these threats move not submission,

Black are his colours, black pavilion;
His spear, his shield, his horse, his armour, plumes,   60
And jetty feathers menace death and hell;
Without respect of sex, degree, or age,
He razeth all his foes with fire and sword.
SOLDAN. Merciless villain, peasant ignorant
Of lawful arms or martial discipline!
Pillage and murder are his usual trades.
The slave usurps the glorious name of war.
See, Capolin, the fair Arabian king,
That hath been disappointed by this slave
Of my fair daughter and his princely love,   70
May have fresh warning to go war with us,
And he reveng'd for her disparagement.   [*Exeunt*]

Actus 4. Scaena 2.
[*Enter*] Tamburlaine, Techelles, Theridamas, Usum-
casane, Zenocrate, Anippe, *two* Moors *drawing* Bajazeth
in his cage, and his wife [Zabina] *following him.*
TAMBURLAINE. Bring out my footstool.
                            They take him out of the cage.
BAJAZETH. Ye holy priests of heavenly Mahomet,
That, sacrificing, slice and cut your flesh,
Staining his altars with your purple blood,
Make heaven to frown, and every fixed star
To suck up poison from the moorish fens,
And pour it in this glorious tyrant's throat.
TAMBURLAINE. The chiefest god, first mover of that sphere
Encas'd with thousands ever-shining lamps,
Will sooner burn the glorious frame of heaven   10
Than it should so conspire my overthrow.
But, villain, thou that wishest this to me,
Fall prostrate on the low disdainful earth,
And be the footstool of great Tamburlaine,
That I may rise into my royal throne.
BAJAZETH. First shalt thou rip my bowels with thy sword,
And sacrifice my heart to death and hell,
Before I yield to such a slavery.
TAMBURLAINE. Base villain, vassal, slave to Tamburlaine,
Unworthy to embrace or touch the ground   20
That bears the honour of my royal weight.
Stoop, villain, stoop. Stoop, for so he bids
That may command thee piecemeal to be torn,
Or scattered like the lofty cedar-trees

[42]

Struck with the voice of thund'ring Jupiter,
BAJAZETH. Then as I look down to the damned fiends,
　Fiends, look on me. And thou, dread god of hell,
　With ebon sceptre strike this hateful earth,
　And make it swallow both of us at once.
　　　　　　　　　　　　　He gets up upon him to his chair.
TAMBURLAINE. Now clear the triple region of the air,　　　30
　And let the majesty of heaven behold
　Their scourge and terror tread on emperors.
　Smile, stars that reign'd at my nativity,
　And dim the brightness of their neighbour lamps;
　Disdain to borrow light of Cynthia,
　For I, the chiefest lamp of all the earth,
　First rising in the east with mild aspect,
　But fixed now in the meridian line,
　Will send up fire to your turning spheres,
　And cause the sun to borrow light of you.　　　40
　My sword struck fire from his coat of steel
　Even in Bithynia, when I took this Turk;
　As when a fiery exhalation,
　Wrapt in the bowels of a freezing cloud,
　Fighting for passage, makes the welkin crack,
　And casts a flash of lightning to the earth.
　But ere I march to wealthy Persia,
　Or leave Damascus and th'Egyptian fields,
　As was the fame of Clymen's brain-sick son
　That almost brent the axle-tree of heaven,　　　50
　So shall our swords, our lances, and our shot
　Fill all the air with fiery meteors.
　Then when the sky shall wax as red as blood,
　It shall be said I made it red myself,
　To make me think of naught but blood and war.
ZABINA. Unworthy king, that by thy cruelty
　Unlawfully usurp'st the Persian seat,
　Dar'st thou, that never saw an emperor
　Before thou met my husband in the field,
　Being thy captive, thus abuse his state,　　　60
　Keeping his kingly body in a cage,
　That roofs of gold and sun-bright palaces
　Should have prepar'd to entertain his grace,
　And treading him beneath thy loathsome feet,
　Whose feet the kings of Africa have kiss'd?
TECHELLES. You must devise some torment worse, my lord,
　To make these captives rein their lavish tongues.

TAMBURLAINE. Zenocrate, look better to your slave.
ZENOCRATE. She is my handmaid's slave, and she shall look
   That these abuses flow not from her tongue.   70
   Chide her, Anippe.
ANIPPE. Let these be warnings for you then, my slave,
   How you abuse the person of the king;
   Or else I swear to have you whipp'd stark nak'd.
BAJAZETH. Great Tamburlaine, great in my overthrow,
   Ambitious pride shall make thee fall as low,
   For treading on the back of Bajazeth,
   That should be horsed on four mighty kings.
TAMBURLAINE. Thy names and titles and thy dignities
   Are fled from Bajazeth and remain with me,   80
   That will maintain it against a world of kings.
   Put him in again.
BAJAZETH. Is this a place for mighty Bajazeth?
   Confusion light on him that helps thee thus.
TAMBURLAINE. There whiles he lives shall Bajazeth be kept,
   And where I go be thus in triumph drawn;
   And thou, his wife, shall feed him with the scraps
   My servitors shall bring thee from my board,
   For he that gives him other food than this,
   Shall sit by him and starve to death himself: 90
   This is my mind, and I will have it so.
   Not all the kings and emperors of the earth,
   If they would lay their crowns before my feet,
   Shall ransom him, or take him from his cage.
   The ages that shall talk of Tamburlaine,
   Even from this day to Plato's wondrous year,
   Shall talk how I have handled Bajazeth.
   These Moors, that drew him from Bithynia
   To fair Damascus, where we now remain,
   Shall lead him with us whereso'er we go.   100
   Techelles, and my loving followers,
   Now may we see Damascus' lofty towers,
   Like to the shadows of Pyramides
   That with their beauties grac'd the Memphian fields.
   The golden stature of their feathered bird
   That spreads her wings upon the city walls
   Shall not defend it from our battering shot.
   The townsmen mask in silk and cloth of gold,
   And every house is as a treasury;
   The men, the treasure, and the town is ours.   110
THERIDAMAS. Your tents of white now pitch'd before the gates,

And gentle flags of amity display'd,
I doubt not but the governor will yield,
Offering Damascus to your majesty.
TAMBURLAINE. So shall he have his life, and all the rest.
But if he stay until the bloody flag
Be once advanc'd on my vermilion tent,
He dies, and those that kept us out so long;
And when they see me march in black array,
With mournful streamers hanging down their heads,   120
Were in that city all the world contain'd,
Not one should scape, but perish by our swords.
ZENOCRATE. Yet would you have some pity for my sake,
Because it is my country's and my father's.
TAMBURLAINE. Not for the world, Zenocrate, if I have sworn.
Come, bring in the Turk.   *Exeunt.*

Actus 4. Scaena 3.

[*Enter*] Soldan, Arabia, Capolin, *with streaming colours,*
and Soldiers.

SOLDAN. Methinks we march as Meleager did,
Environed with brave Argolian knights,
To chase the savage Calydonian boar;
Or Cephalus with lusty Theban youths
Against the wolf that angry Themis sent
To waste and spoil the sweet Aonian fields.
A monster of five hundred thousand heads,
Compact of rapine, piracy, and spoil,
The scum of men, the hate and scourge of God,
Raves in Egyptia, and annoyeth us.   10
My lord, it is the bloody Tamburlaine,
A sturdy felon and a base-bred thief,
By murder raised to the Persian crown,
That dares control us in our territories.
To tame the pride of this presumptuous beast,
Join your Arabians with the Soldan's power;
Let us unite our royal bands in one,
And hasten to remove Damascus siege.
It is a blemish to the majesty
And high estate of mighty emperors,   20
That such a base usurping vagabond
Should brave a king, or wear a princely crown.
ARABIA. Renowmed Soldan, have ye lately heard
The overthrow of mighty Bajazeth
About the confines of Bithynia?

The slavery wherewith he persecutes
The noble Turk and his great emperess?
SOLDAN. I have, and sorrow for his bad success.
    But, noble lord of great Arabia,
    Be so persuaded that the Soldan is   30
    No more dismay'd with tidings of his fall
    Than in the haven when the pilot stands,
    And views a stranger's ship rent in the winds,.
    And shivered against a craggy rock;
    Yet in compassion of his wretched state,
    A sacred vow to heaven and him I make,
    Confirming it with Ibis' holy name,
    That Tamburlaine shall rue the day, the hour,
    Wherein he wrought such ignominious wrong
    Unto the hallowed person of a prince,   40
    Or kept the fair Zenocrate so long,
    As concubine, I fear, to feed his lust.
ARABIA. Let grief and fury hasten on revenge;
    Let Tamburlaine for his offences feel
    Such plagues as heaven and we can pour on him.
    I long to break my spear upon his crest,
    And prove the weight of his victorious arm;
    For fame, I fear, hath been too prodigal
    In sounding through the world his partial praise.
SOLDAN. Capolin, hast thou survey'd our powers?   50
CAPOLIN. Great emperors of Egypt and Arabia,
    The number of your hosts united is:
    A hundred and fifty thousand horse,
    Two hundred thousand foot, brave men-at-arms,
    Courageous and full of hardiness,
    As frolic as the hunters in the chase
    Of savage beasts amid the desert woods.
ARABIA. My mind presageth fortunate success;
    And, Tamburlaine, my spirit doth foresee
    The utter ruin of thy men and thee.   60
SOLDAN. Then rear your standards; let your sounding drums
    Direct our soldiers to Damascus walls.
    Now, Tamburlaine, the mighty Soldan comes,
    And leads with him the great Arabian king,
    To dim thy baseness and obscurity,
    Famous for nothing but for theft and spoil;
    To raze and scatter thy inglorious crew
    Of Scythians and slavish Persians.   *Exeunt.*

Actus 4. Scaena 4.

The banquet, and to it cometh Tamburlaine *all in scarlet,*
Theridamas, Techelles, Usumcasane, *the Turk, with others.*

TAMBURLAINE. Now hang our bloody colours by Damascus,
Reflexing hues of blood upon their heads
While they walk quivering on their city walls,
Half-dead for fear before they feel my wrath.
Then let us freely banquet and carouse
Full bowls of wine unto the god of war,
That means to fill your helmets full of gold,
And make Damascus spoils as rich to you
As was to Jason Colchos' golden fleece.
And now Bajazeth, hast thou any stomach?   10
BAJAZETH. Ay, such a stomach, cruel Tamburlaine, as I could
willingly feed upon thy blood-raw heart.
TAMBURLAINE. Nay, thine own is easier to come by; pluck out
that, and 'twill serve thee and thy wife. Well, Zenocrate,
Techelles and the rest, fall to your victuals.
BAJAZETH. Fall to, and never may your meat digest.
Ye Furies, that can mask invisible,
Dive to the bottom of Avernus pool
And in your hands bring hellish poison up
And squeeze it in the cup of Tamburlaine;   20
Or winged snakes of Lerna, cast your stings
And leave your venoms in this tyrant's dish.
ZABINA. And may this banquet prove as ominous
As Procne's to th'adulterous Thracian king
That fed upon the substance of his child!
ZENOCRATE. My lord, how can you suffer these
Outrageous curses by these slaves of yours?
TAMBURLAINE. To let them see, divine Zenocrate,
I glory in the curses of my foes,
Having the power from the empyreal heaven   30
To turn them all upon their proper heads.
TECHELLES. I pray you give them leave, madam; this speech is
a goodly refreshing to them.
THERIDAMAS. But if his highness would let them be fed, it
would do them more good.
TAMBURLAINE. Sirrah, why fall you not to? Are you so daintily
brought up, you cannot eat your own flesh?
BAJAZETH. First, legions of devils shall tear thee in pieces.
USUMCASANE. Villain, knowest thou to whom thou speakest?

[47]

TAMBURLAINE. O let him alone. Here, eat, sir; take it from my
   sword's point, or I'll thrust it to thy heart.
                              He takes it and stamps upon it.
THERIDAMAS. He stamps it under his feet, my lord.   42
TAMBURLAINE. Take it up, villain, and eat it; or I will make
   thee slice the brawns of thy arms into carbonadoes and eat
   them.
USUMCASANE. Nay, 'twere better he kill'd his wife, and then
   she shall be sure not to be starv'd, and he be provided for
   a month's victual beforehand.
TAMBURLAINE. Here is my dagger. Dispatch her while she is
   fat, for if she live but a while longer she will fall into a
   consumption with fretting, and then she will not be worth
   the eating.   52
THERIDAMAS. Dost thou think that Mahomet will suffer this?
TECHELLES. 'Tis like he will, when he cannot let it.
TAMBURLAINE. Go to, fall to your meat. What, not a bit?
   Belike he hath not been watered today; give him some drink.
      They give him water to drink, and he flings it on the ground.
   Fast, and welcome, sir, while hunger make you eat. How
   now, Zenocrate, doth not the Turk and his wife make a
   goodly show at a banquet?
ZENOCRATE. Yes, my lord.   60
THERIDAMAS. Methinks 'tis a great deal better than a consort of
   music.
TAMBURLAINE. Yet music would do well to cheer up Zeno-
   crate. Pray thee, tell why art thou so sad? If thou wilt have
   a song, the Turk shall strain his voice. But why is it?
ZENOCRATE. My lord, to see my father's town besieg'd,
   The country wasted where myself was born,
   How can it but afflict my very soul?
   If any love remain in you, my lord,
   Or if my love unto your majesty   70
   May merit favour at your highness' hands,
   Then raise your siege from fair Damascus walls,
   And with my father take a friendly truce.
TAMBURLAINE. Zenocrate, were Egypt Jove's own land,
   Yet would I with my sword make Jove to stoop.
   I will confute those blind geographers
   That make a triple region in the world,
   Excluding regions which I mean to trace,
   And with this pen reduce them to a map,
   Calling the provinces, cities, and towns,   80
   After my name and thine, Zenocrate.

Here at Damascus will I make the point
That shall begin the perpendicular.
And wouldst thou have me buy thy father's love
With such a loss? Tell me, Zenocrate.

ZENOCRATE. Honour still wait on happy Tamburlaine;
     Yet give me leave to plead for him, my lord.

TAMBURLAINE. Content thyself; his person shall be safe,
     And all the friends of fair Zenocrate,
     If with their lives they will be pleas'd to yield,   90
     Or may be forc'd to make me emperor;
     For Egypt and Arabia must be mine.
     —Feed, you slave; thou mayst think thyself happy to be
     fed from my trencher.

BAJAZETH. My empty stomach, full of idle heat,
     Draws bloody humours from my feeble parts,
     Preserving life by hasting cruel death.
     My veins are pale, my sinews hard and dry,
     My joints benumb'd; unless I eat, I die.

ZABINA. Eat, Bajazeth. Let us live in spite of them, looking
     some happy power will pity and enlarge us.   101

TAMBURLAINE. Here, Turk, wilt thou have a clean trencher?

BAJAZETH. Ay, tyrant, and more meat.

TAMBURLAINE. Soft, sir, you must be dieted; too much eating
     will make you surfeit.

THERIDAMAS. So it would, my lord, specially having so small
     a walk and so little exercise.

     Enter a second course of crowns.

TAMBURLAINE. Theridamas, Techelles, and Casane, here are
     the cates you desire to finger, are they not?

THERIDAMAS. Ay, my lord, but none save kings must feed with
     these.   111

TECHELLES. 'Tis enough for us to see them, and for Tambur-
     laine only to enjoy them.

TAMBURLAINE. Well, here is now to the Soldan of Egypt, the
     King of Arabia, and the Governor of Damascus. Now take
     these three crowns, and pledge me, my contributory kings.
     I crown you here, Theridamas, King of Argier; Techelles,
     King of Fez; and Usumcasane, King of Moroccus. How say
     you to this, Turk? These are not your contributory kings.

BAJAZETH. Nor shall they long be thine, I warrant them. 120

TAMBURLAINE. Kings of Argier, Moroccus, and of Fez,
     You that have march'd with happy Tamburlaine
     As far as from the frozen plage of heaven
     Unto the wat'ry morning's ruddy bower,

And thence by land unto the torrid zone,
Deserve these titles I endow you with
By value and by magnanimity.
Your births shall be no blemish to your fame,
For virtue is the fount whence honour springs,
And they are worthy she investeth kings.   130
THERIDAMAS. And since your highness hath so well vouchsaf'd,
If we deserve them not with higher meeds
Than erst our states and actions have retain'd,
Take them away again, and make us slaves.
TAMBURLAINE. Well said, Theridamas. When holy Fates
Shall stablish me in strong Egyptia.
We mean to travel to th'antarctic pole,
Conquering the people underneath our feet,
And be renowm'd as never emperors were.
Zenocrate, I will not crown thee yet,   140
Until with greater honours I be grac'd.   [*Exeunt.*]
                Finis Actus Quarti.

                Actus 5. Scaena 1.
[*Enter*] *the* Governor of *Damascus with three or four* Citizens,
and four Virgins *with branches of laurel in their hands.*
GOVERNOR. Still doth this man, or rather god of war,
Batter our walls and beat our turrets down;
And to resist with longer stubbornness,
Or hope of rescue from the Soldan's power,
Were but to bring our wilful overthrow,
And make us desperate of our threat'ned lives.
We see his tents have now been altered
With terrors to the last and cruel'st hue.
His coal-black colours, everywhere advanc'd,
Threaten our city with a general spoil;   10
And if we should with common rites of arms
Offer our safeties to his clemency,
I fear the custom proper to his sword,
Which he observes as parcel of his fame,
Intending so to terrify the world,
By any innovation or remorse
Will never be dispens'd with till our deaths.
Therefore, for these our harmless virgins' sakes,
Whose honours and whose lives rely on him,
Let us have hope that their unspotted prayers,   20
Their blubbered cheeks, and hearty humble moans

Will melt this fury into some remorse,
And use us like a loving conqueror.
1 VIRGIN. If humble suits or imprecations
(Uttered with tears of wretchedness and blood
Shed from the heads and hearts of all our sex,
Some made your wives, and some your children)
Might have entreated your obdurate breasts
To entertain some care of our securities
Whiles only danger beat upon our walls,   30
These more than dangerous warrants of our death
Had never been erected as they be,
Nor you depend on such weak helps as we.
GOVERNOR. Well, lovely virgins, think our country's care,
Our love of honour, loath to be enthrall'd
To foreign powers and rough imperious yokes,
Would not with too much cowardice or fear,
Before all hope of rescue were denied,
Submit yourselves and us to servitude.
Therefore, in that your safeties and our own,   40
Your honours, liberties, and lives were weigh'd
In equal care and balance with our own,
Endure as we the malice of our stars,
The wrath of Tamburlaine and power of wars;
Or be the means the overweighing heavens
Have kept to qualify these hot extremes,
And bring us pardon in your cheerful looks.
2 VIRGIN. Then here, before the majesty of heaven
And holy patroness of Egyptia,
With knees and hearts submissive we entreat   50
Grace to our words and pity to our looks,
That this device may prove propitious,
And through the eyes and ears of Tamburlaine
Convey events of mercy to his heart;
Grant that these signs of victory we yield
May bind the temples of his conquering head,
To hide the folded furrows of his brows,
And shadow his displeased countenance
With happy looks of ruth and lenity.
Leave us, my lord, and loving countrymen: 60
What simple virgins may persuade, we will.
GOVERNOR. Farewell, sweet virgins, on whose safe return
Depends our city, liberty, and lives.

                              Exeunt. [*Manent* Virgins.]

[*Enter*] Tamburlaine, Techelles, Theridamas, Usumcasane, *with others*; Tamburlaine *all in black and very
melancholy.*

TAMBURLAINE. What, are the turtles fray'd out of their nests?
Alas, poor fools, must you be first shall feel
The sworn destruction of Damascus?
They know my custom; could they not as well
Have sent ye out when first my milk-white flags,
Through which sweet mercy threw her gentle beams,
Reflexing them on your disdainful eyes,   70
As now when fury and incensed hate
Flings slaughtering terror from my coal-black tents,
And tells for truth, submission comes too late?
VIRGIN. Most happy king and emperor of the earth,
Image of honour and nobility,
For whom the powers divine have made the world,
And on whose throne the holy Graces sit;
In whose sweet person is compris'd the sum
Of nature's skill and heavenly majesty;
Pity our plights. O, pity poor Damascus.   80
Pity old age, within whose silver hairs
Honour and reverence evermore have reign'd!
Pity the marriage-bed, where many a lord,
In prime and glory of his loving joy,
Embraceth now with tears of ruth and blood
The jealous body of his fearful wife,
Whose cheeks and hearts, so punish'd with conceit,
To think thy puissant never-stayed arm
Will part their bodies, and prevent their souls
From heavens of comfort yet their age might bear,   90
Now wax all pale and withered to the death,
As well for grief our ruthless governor
Have thus refus'd the mercy of thy hand
(Whose sceptre angels kiss and Furies dread)
As for their liberties, their loves, or lives.
O then for these, and such as we ourselves,
For us, for infants, and for all our bloods,
That never nourish'd thought against thy rule,
Pity, O pity, sacred emperor,
The prostrate service of this wretched town;   100
And take in sign thereof this gilded wreath,
Whereto each man of rule hath given his hand,
And wish'd, as worthy subjects, happy means
To be investers of thy royal brows

[52]

Even with the true Egyptian diadem.

TAMBURLAINE. Virgins, in vain ye labour to prevent
   That which mine honour swears shall be perform'd.
   Behold my sword; what see you at the point?

I VIRGIN. Nothing but fear and fatal steel, my lord.

TAMBURLAINE. Your fearful minds are thick and misty,
   then,   110
   For there sits Death; there sits imperious Death,
   Keeping his circuit by the slicing edge.
   But I am pleas'd you shall not see him there;
   He now is seated on my horsemen's spears,
   And on their points his fleshless body feeds.
   Techelles, straight go charge a few of them
   To charge these dames, and show my servant Death,
   Sitting in scarlet on their armed spears.

VIRGINS. O pity us.

TAMBURLAINE. Away with them, I say, and show them
   Death.   120
                                  They take them away.

I will not spare these proud Egyptians,
Nor change my martial observations
For all the wealth of Gihon's golden waves,
Or for the love of Venus, would she leave
The angry god of arms and lie with me.
They have refus'd the offer of their lives,
And know my customs are as peremptory
As wrathful planets, death, or destiny.
   Enter Techelles.
What, have your horsemen shown the virgins Death?

TECHELLES. They have, my lord, and on Damascus walls 130
   Have hoisted up their slaughtered carcasses,

TAMBURLAINE. A sight as baneful to their souls, I think,
   As are Thessalian drugs or mithridate.
   But go, my lords, put the rest to the sword.
                        Exeunt. [*Manet* Tamburlaine.]
Ah, fair Zenocrate, divine Zenocrate!
Fair is too foul an epithet for thee,
That in thy passion for thy country's love,
And fear to see thy kingly father's harm,
With hair dishevell'd wip'st thy watery cheeks,
And like to Flora in her morning's pride,   140
Shaking her silver tresses in the air,
Rain'st on the earth resolved pearl in showers,
And sprinklest sapphires on thy shining face,

Where Beauty, mother to the Muses, sits,
And comments volumes with her ivory pen,
Taking instructions from thy flowing eyes;
Eyes, when that Ebena steps to heaven,
In silence of thy solemn evening's walk,
Making the mantle of the richest night,
The moon, the planets, and the meteors, light;   150
There angels in their crystal armours fight
A doubtful battle with my tempted thoughts
For Egypt's freedom and the Soldan's life,
His life that so consumes Zenocrate,
Whose sorrows lay more siege unto my soul
Than all my army to Damascus walls;
And neither Persians' sovereign nor the Turk
Troubled my senses with conceit of foil
So much by much as doth Zenocrate.
What is beauty, saith my sufferings, then?   160
If all the pens that ever poets held
Had fed the feeling of their masters' thoughts,
And every sweetness that inspir'd their hearts,
Their minds, and muses on admired themes;
If all the heavenly quintessence they still
From their immortal flowers of poesy,
Wherein as in a mirror we perceive
The highest reaches of a human wit;
If these had made one poem's period,
And all combin'd in beauty's worthiness,   170
Yet should there hover in their restless heads
One thought, one grace, one wonder, at the least,
Which into words no virtue can digest.
But how unseemly is it for my sex,
My discipline of arms and chivalry,
My nature, and the terror of my name,
To harbour thoughts effeminate and faint!
Save only that in beauty's just applause,
With whose instinct the soul of man is touch'd,
And every warrior that is rapt with love   180
Of fame, of valour, and of victory,
Must needs have beauty beat on his conceits:
I thus conceiving and subduing both,
That which hath stoop'd the topmost of the gods,
Even from the fiery-spangled veil of heaven,
To feel the lovely warmth of shepherd's flames,
And march in cottages of strowed weeds,

Shall give the world to note, for all my birth,
That virtue solely is the sum of glory,
And fashions men with true nobility.　　　　　　190
Who's within there?
　　Enter two or three.
Hath Bajazeth been fed today?
ATTENDANT. Ay, my lord.
TAMBURLAINE. Bring him forth; and let us know if the town be
　　ransack'd.　　　　　　　　　　*[Exeunt* Attendants.]
　　Enter Techelles, Theridamas, Usumcasane, *and others.*
TECHELLES. The town is ours, my lord, and fresh supply
　　Of conquest and of spoil is offered us.
TAMBURLAINE. That's well, Techelles. What's the news?
TECHELLES. The Soldan and the Arabian king together
　　March on us with such eager violence
　　As if there were no way but one with us.　　　　200
TAMBURLAINE. No more there is not, I warrant thee, Techelles.
　　They bring in the Turk [Bajazeth *in his cage, and* Zabina].
THERIDAMAS. We know the victory is ours, my lord,
　　But let us save the reverend Soldan's life
　　For fair Zenocrate that so laments his state.
TAMBURLAINE. That will we chiefly see unto, Theridamas,
　　For sweet Zenocrate, whose worthiness
　　Deserves a conquest over every heart.
　　And now, my footstool, if I lose the field,
　　You hope of liberty and restitution?
　　Here let him stay, my masters, from the tents,　　210
　　Till we have made us ready for the field.
　　Pray for us, Bajazeth, where we are going.
　　　　　　　　Exeunt. [*Manent* Bajazeth *and* Zabina.]
BAJAZETH. Go, never to return with victory.
　　Millions of men encompass thee about,
　　And gore thy body with as many wounds!
　　Sharp forked arrows light upon thy horse!
　　Furies from the black Cocytus lake
　　Break up the earth, and with their firebrands
　　Enforce thee run upon the baneful pikes!
　　Volleys of shot pierce through thy charmed skin,　　220
　　And every bullet dipp'd in poisoned drugs!
　　Or roaring cannons sever all thy joints,
　　Making thee mount as high as eagles soar!
ZABINA. Let all the swords and lances in the field
　　Stick in his breast as in their proper rooms.
　　At every pore let blood come dropping forth,

That ling'ring pains may massacre his heart,
And madness send his damned soul to hell.
BAJAZETH. Ah, fair Zabina, we may curse his power,
The heavens may frown, the earth for anger quake;   230
But such a star hath influence in his sword
As rules the skies and countermands the gods
More than Cimmerian Styx or Destiny.
And then shall we in this detested guise,
With shame, with hunger, and with horror aye
Griping our bowels with retorqued thoughts,
And have no hope to end our ecstasies.
ZABINA. Then is there left no Mahomet, no God,
No fiend, no fortune, nor no hope of end
To our infamous, monstrous slaveries?   240
Gape earth, and let the fiends infernal view
A hell as hopeless and as full of fear
As are the blasted banks of Erebus,
Where shaking ghosts with ever-howling groans
Hover about the ugly ferryman
To get a passage to Elysium!
Why should we live? O wretches, beggars, slaves!
Why live we, Bajazeth, and build up nests
So high within the region of the air,
By living long in this oppression,   250
That all the world will see and laugh to scorn
The former triumphs of our mightiness
In this obscure infernal servitude?
BAJAZETH. O life more loathsome to my vexed thoughts
Than noisome parbreak of the Stygian snakes
Which fills the nooks of hell with standing air,
Infecting all the ghosts with cureless griefs!
O dreary engines of my loathed sight,
That sees my crown, my honour, and my name
Thrust under yoke and thraldom of a thief,   260
Why feed ye still on day's accursed beams,
And sink not quite into my tortur'd soul?
You see my wife, my queen and emperess,
Brought up and propped by the hand of Fame,
Queen of fifteen contributory queens,
Now thrown to rooms of black abjection,
Smear'd with blots of basest drudgery,
And villeiness to shame, disdain, and misery.
Accursed Bajazeth, whose words of ruth,
That would with pity cheer Zabina's heart,   270

And make our souls resolve in ceaseless tears,
Sharp hunger bites upon and gripes the root
From whence the issues of my thoughts do break!
O poor Zabina, O my queen, my queen,
Fetch me some water for my burning breast,
To cool and comfort me with longer date,
That in the short'ned sequel of my life,
I may pour forth my soul into thine arms
With words of love, whose moaning intercourse
Hath hitherto been stay'd with wrath and hate   280
Of our expressless bann'd inflictions.

ZABINA. Sweet Bajazeth, I will prolong thy life
As long as any blood or spark of breath
Can quench or cool the torments of my grief.   *She goes out.*

BAJAZETH. Now Bajazeth, abridge thy baneful days,
And beat thy brains out of thy conquer'd head,
Since other means are all forbidden me
That may be ministers of my decay.
O highest lamp of ever-living Jove,
Accursed day, infected with my griefs,   290
Hide now thy stained face in endless night,
And shut the windows of the lightsome heavens!
Let ugly darkness with her rusty coach,
Engirt with tempests wrapt in pitchy clouds,
Smother the earth with never-fading mists,
And let her horses from their nostrils breathe
Rebellious winds and dreadful thunder-claps,
That in this terror Tamburlaine may live,
And my pin'd soul, resolv'd in liquid air,
May still excruciate his tormented thoughts.   300
Then let the stony dart of senseless cold
Pierce through the centre of my withered heart,
And make a passage for my loathed life.
                    He brains himself against the cage.
    Enter Zabina.

ZABINA. What do mine eyes behold? My husband dead!
His skull all riven in twain, his brains dash'd out,
The brains of Bajazeth, my lord and sovereign!
O Bajazeth, my husband and my lord,
O Bajazeth, O Turk, O Emperor.   308
    Give him his liquor? Not I. Bring milk and fire, and my
blood I bring him again. Tear me in pieces. Give me the
sword with a ball of wild-fire upon it. Down with him!
Down with him! Go to my child; away, away, away! Ah,

save that infant, save him, save him! I, even I, speak to her.
The sun was down—streamers white, red, black, here, here,
here! Fling the meat in his face. Tamburlaine, Tamburlaine! Let the soldiers be buried. Hell, death, Tamburlaine,
hell! Make ready my coach, my chair, my jewels. I come,
I come, I come!

She runs against the cage and brains herself.
[*Enter*] Zenocrate *with* Anippe.

ZENOCRATE. Wretched Zenocrate, that liv'st to see
   Damascus walls dy'd with Egyptian blood,   320
   Thy father's subjects and thy countrymen;
   The streets strow'd with dissevered joints of men,
   And wounded bodies gasping yet for life;
   But most accurs'd, to see the sun-bright troop
   Of heavenly virgins and unspotted maids,
   Whose looks might make the angry god of arms
   To break his sword and mildly treat of love,
   On horsemen's lances to be hoisted up,
   And guiltlessly endure a cruel death.
   For every fell and stout Tartarian steed   330
   That stamp'd on others with their thund'ring hoofs,
   When all their riders charg'd their quivering spears,
   Began to check the ground and rein themselves,
   Gazing upon the beauty of their looks.
   Ah, Tamburlaine, wert thou the cause of this,
   That term'st Zenocrate thy dearest love?
   Whose lives were dearer to Zenocrate
   Than her own life, or aught save thine own love.
   But see, another bloody spectacle.
   Ah, wretched eyes, the enemies of my heart,   340
   How are ye glutted with these grievous objects,
   And tell my soul more tales of bleeding ruth!
   See, see, Anippe, if they breathe or no.
ANIPPE. No breath, nor sense, nor motion in them both.
   Ah, madam, this their slavery hath enforc'd,
   And ruthless cruelty of Tamburlaine.
ZENOCRATE. Earth, cast up fountains from thy entrails,
   And wet thy cheeks for their untimely deaths;
   Shake with their weight in sign of fear and grief.
   Blush, heaven, that gave them honour at their birth   350
   And let them die a death so barbarous.
   Those that are proud of fickle empery
   And place their chiefest good in earthly pomp,
   Behold the Turk and his great emperess.

Ah, Tamburlaine my love, sweet Tamburlaine,
That fights for sceptres and for slippery crowns,
Behold the Turk and his great emperess.
Thou that in conduct of thy happy stars
Sleep'st every night with conquest on thy brows,
And yet wouldst shun the wavering turns of war,   360
In fear and feeling of the like distress,
Behold the Turk and his great emperess.
Ah, mighty Jove and holy Mahomet,
Pardon my love, O pardon his contempt
Of earthly fortune and respect of pity;
And let not conquest ruthlessly pursu'd
Be equally against his life incens'd
In this great Turk and hapless emperess.
And pardon me that was not mov'd with ruth
To see them live so long in misery.   370
Ah, what may chance to thee, Zenocrate?
ANIPPE. Madam, content yourself, and be resolv'd,
Your love hath Fortune so at his command,
That she shall stay and turn her wheel no more,
As long as life maintains his mighty arm
That fights for honour to adorn your head.
   Enter [Philemus] *a messenger.*
ZENOCRATE. What other heavy news now brings Philemus?
PHILEMUS. Madam, your father and th'Arabian king,
The first affecter of your excellence,
Comes now as Turnus 'gainst Aeneas did,   380
Armed with lance into the Egyptian fields,
Ready for battle 'gainst my lord the King.
ZENOCRATE. Now shame and duty, love and fear presents
A thousand sorrows to my martyred soul.
Whom should I wish the fatal victory,
When my poor pleasures are divided thus,
And rack'd by duty from my cursed heart?
My father and my first-betrothed love
Must fight against my life and present love;
Wherein the change I use condemns my faith,   390
And makes my deeds infamous through the world.
But as the gods, to end the Troyans' toil,
Prevented Turnus of Lavinia,
And fatally enrich'd Aeneas' love,
So for a final issue to my griefs,
To pacify my country and my love,
Must Tamburlaine by their resistless powers,

With virtue of a gentle victory,
Conclude a league of honour to my hope;
Then as the powers divine have pre-ordain'd,   400
With happy safety of my father's life
Send like defence of fair Arabia.
    They sound to the battle. And Tamburlaine *enjoys the victory:
after,* Arabia *enters wounded.*

ARABIA. What cursed power guides the murdering hands
Of this infamous tyrant's soldiers,
That no escape may save their enemies,
Nor fortune keep themselves from victory?
Lie down, Arabia, wounded to the death,
And let Zenocrate's fair eyes behold
That, as for her thou bear'st these wretched arms,
Even so for her thou diest in these arms,   410
Leaving thy blood for witness of thy love.

ZENOCRATE. Too dear a witness for such love, my lord!
Behold Zenocrate, the cursed object
Whose fortunes never mastered her griefs;
Behold her wounded in conceit for thee,
As much as thy fair body is for me.

ARABIA. Then shall I die with full contented heart,
Having beheld divine Zenocrate,
Whose sight with joy would take away my life
As now it bringeth sweetness to my wound,   420
If I had not been wounded as I am.
Ah, that the deadly pangs I suffer now
Would lend an hour's licence to my tongue
To make discourse of some sweet accidents
Have chanc'd thy merits in this worthless bondage,
And that I might be privy to the state
Of thy deserv'd contentment and thy love.
But making now a virtue of thy sight,
To drive all sorrow from my fainting soul,
Since death denies me further cause of joy,   430
Depriv'd of care, my heart with comfort dies,
Since thy desired hand shall close mine eyes.

                                                           [Dies.]

    Enter Tamburlaine, *leading the* Soldan; Techelles, Theri-
damas, Usumcasane, *with others.*

TAMBURLAINE. Come, happy father of Zenocrate,
A title higher than thy Soldan's name.
Though my right hand have thus enthralled thee,
Thy princely daughter here shall set thee free;

She that hath calm'd the fury of my sword,
Which had ere this been bath'd in streams of blood
As vast and deep as Euphrates or Nile.

ZENOCRATE. O sight thrice-welcome to my joyful soul,   440
   To see the king my father issue safe
   From dangerous battle of my conquering love!

SOLDAN. Well met, my only dear Zenocrate,
   Though with the loss of Egypt and my crown.

TAMBURLAINE. 'Twas I, my lord, that gat the victory;
   And therefore grieve not at your overthrow.
   Since I shall render all into your hands,
   And add more strength to your dominions
   Than ever yet confirm'd th'Egyptian crown.
   The god of war resigns his room to me,   450
   Meaning to make me general of the world.
   Jove, viewing me in arms, looks pale and wan,
   Fearing my power should pull him from his throne.
   Where'er I come the Fatal Sisters sweat,
   And grisly Death, by running to and fro,
   To do their ceaseless homage to my sword;
   And here in Afric, where it seldom rains,
   Since I arriv'd with my triumphant host,
   Have swelling clouds, drawn from wide-gasping wounds,
   Been oft resolv'd in bloody purple showers,   460
   A meteor that might terrify the earth,
   And make it quake at every drop it drinks.
   Millions of souls sit on the banks of Styx,
   Waiting the back return of Charon's boat;
   Hell and Elysium swarm with ghosts of men
   That I have sent from sundry foughten fields
   To spread my fame through hell and up to heaven.
   And see, my lord, a sight of strange import,
   Emperors and kings lie breathless at my feet;
   The Turk and his great empress, as it seems,   470
   Left to themselves while we were at the fight,
   Have desperately despatch'd their slavish lives;
   With them Arabia, too, hath left his life:
   All sights of power to grace my victory.
   And such are objects fit for Tamburlaine,
   Wherein as in a mirror may be seen
   His honour, that consists in shedding blood
   When men presume to manage arms with him.

SOLDAN. Mighty hath God and Mahomet made thy hand
   Renowmed Tamburlaine, to whom all kings   480

Of force must yield their crowns and emperies;
And I am pleas'd with this my overthrow,
If, as beseems a person of thy state,
Thou hast with honour us'd Zenocrate.
TAMBURLAINE. Her state and person wants no pomp, you see;
And for all blot of foul inchastity,
I record heaven, her heavenly self is clear.
Then let me find no further time to grace
Her princely temples with the Persian crown;
But here these kings that on my fortunes wait,   490
And have been crown'd for proved worthiness
Even by this hand that shall establish them,
Shall now, adjoining all their hands with mine,
Invest her here my Queen of Persia.
What saith the noble Soldan, and Zenocrate?
SOLDAN. I yield with thanks and protestations
Of endless honour to thee for her love.
TAMBURLAINE. Then doubt I not but fair Zenocrate
Will soon consent to satisfy us both.
ZENOCRATE. Else should I much forget myself, my lord.   500
THERIDAMAS. Then let us set the crown upon her head
That long hath ling'red for so high a seat.
TÉCHELLES. My hand is ready to perform the deed,
For now her marriage-time shall work us rest.
USUMCASANE. And here's the crown, my lord; help set it on.
TAMBURLAINE. Then sit thou down, divine Zenocrate,
And here we crown thee Queen of Persia
And all the kingdoms and dominions
That late the power of Tamburlaine subdu'd:
As Juno, when the Giants were suppress'd   510
That darted mountains at her brother Jove,
So looks my love, shadowing in her brows
Triumphs and trophies for my victories;
Or as Latona's daughter bent to arms,
Adding more courage to my conquering mind.
To gratify the sweet Zenocrate,
Egyptians, Moors, and men of Asia,
From Barbary unto the Western Inde,
Shall pay a yearly tribute to thy sire;
And from the bounds of Afric to the banks   520
Of Ganges shall his mighty arm extend.
And now, my lords and loving followers,
That purchas'd kingdoms by your martial deeds,
Cast off your armour, put on scarlet robes,

Mount up your royal places of estate,
Environed with troops of noblemen,
And there make laws to rule your provinces.
Hang up your weapons on Alcides' post,
For Tamburlaine takes truce with all the world.
Thy first-betrothed love, Arabia,   530
Shall we with honour, as beseems, entomb
With this great Turk and his fair emperess.
Then, after all these solemn exequies,
We will our rites of marriage solemnize.   [*Exeunt.*]

Finis Actus Quinti et
Ultimi huius
Primae Partis.

[DRAMATIS PERSONAE

The Prologue

Tamburlaine, King of Persia
Calyphas
Amyras } his sons
Celebinus
Theridamas, King of Argier
Techelles, King of Fez
Usumcasane, King of Morocco
Orcanes, King of Natolia
King of Trebizon
King of Soria
King of Jerusalem
King of Amasia
Gazellus, Viceroy of Byron
Uribassa
Sigismund, King of Hungary
Frederick } lords of Hungary
Baldwin
Cullapine, son to Bajazeth and prisoner to Tamburlaine
Almeda, his keeper
The Captain of Balsera
His Son
Governor of Babylon
Maximus
Perdicas
A Captain
A Messenger

Zenocrate, wife to Tamburlaine
Olympia, wife to the Captain of Balsera

Lords, Citizens, Physicians, Soldiers, Pioners, Turkish
Concubines, Attendants]

[64]

Tamburlaine the Great
PART II

The Prologue
The general welcomes Tamburlaine receiv'd,
When he arrived last upon our stage,
Hath made our poet pen his second part,
Where death cuts off the progress of his pomp,
And murd'rous Fates throws all his triumphs down.
But what became of fair Zenocrate,
And with how many cities' sacrifice
He celebrated her sad funeral,
Himself in presence shall unfold at large.

Actus 1. Scaena 1.
[Enter] Orcanes *King of Natolia*, Gazellus *Viceroy of Byron*,
Uribassa, *and their train, with drums and trumpets.*

ORCANES. Egregious viceroys of these eastern parts,
　Plac'd by the issue of great Bajazeth,
　And sacred lord, the mighty Callapine,
　Who lives in Egypt prisoner to that slave
　Which kept his father in an iron cage,
　Now have we march'd from fair Natolia
　Two hundred leagues, and on Danubius banks
　Our warlike host in complete armour rest,
　Where Sigismund, the king of Hungary,
　Should meet our person to conclude a truce.　　　　　10
　What, shall we parle with the Christian?
　Or cross the stream, and meet him in the field?
GAZELLUS. King of Natolia, let us treat of peace:
　We all are glutted with the Christians' blood,
　And have a greater foe to fight against,
　Proud Tamburlaine, that now in Asia
　Near Guyron's head doth set his conquering feet,
　And means to fire Turkey as he goes:
　'Gainst him, my lord, must you address your power.
URIBASSA. Besides, King Sigismund hath brought from Christendom　　　　　20
　More than his camp of stout Hungarians:
　Slavonians, Almains, Rutters, Muffs, and Danes,

[65]

That with the halberd, lance, and murdering axe,
Will hazard that we might with surety hold.
ORCANES. Though from the shortest northren parallel,
    Vast Gruntland, compass'd with the frozen sea,
    Inhabited with tall and sturdy men,
    Giants as big as hugy Polypheme,
    Millions of soldiers cut the arctic line,
    Bringing the strength of Europe to these arms,   30
    Our Turkey blades shall glide through all their throats,
    And make this champion mead a bloody fen;
    Danubius stream, that runs to Trebizon,
    Shall carry wrapp'd within his scarlet waves,
    As martial presents to our friends at home,
    The slaughtered bodies of these Christians;
    The Terrene main wherein Danubius falls
    Shall by this battle be the Bloody Sea;
    The wand'ring sailors of proud Italy
    Shall meet those Christians fleeting with the tide,   40
    Beating in heaps against their argosies,
    And make fair Europe, mounted on her bull,
    Trapp'd with the wealth and riches of the world,
    Alight, and wear a woeful mourning weed.
GAZELLUS. Yet, stout Orcanes, prorex of the world,
    Since Tamburlaine hath must'red all his men,
    Marching from Cairo northward with his camp
    To Alexandria and the frontier towns,
    Meaning to make a conquest of our land,
    'Tis requisite to parle for a peace   50
    With Sigismund, the king of Hungary,
    And save our forces for the hot assaults
    Proud Tamburlaine intends Natolia.
ORCANES. Viceroy of Byron, wisely hast thou said.
    My realm, the centre of our empery,
    Once lost, all Turkey would be overthrown;
    And for that cause the Christians shall have peace.
    Slavonians, Almains, Rutters, Muffs, and Danes
    Fear not Orcanes, but great Tamburlaine—
    Nor he, but Fortune that hath made him great.   60
    We have revolted Grecians, Albanese,
    Sicilians, Jews, Arabians, Turks, and Moors,
    Natolians, Sorians, black Egyptians,
    Illyrians, Thracians, and Bithynians,
    Enough to swallow forceless Sigismund,
    Yet scarce enough t'encounter Tamburlaine.

He brings a world of people to the field:
From Scythia to the oriental plage
Of India, where raging Lantchidol
Beats on the regions with his boisterous blows,   70
That never seaman yet discovered,
All Asia is in arms with Tamburlaine;
Even from the midst of fiery Cancer's tropic
To Amazonia, under Capricorn,
And thence, as far as Archipelago,
All Afric is in arms with Tamburlaine.
Therefore, viceroys, the Christians must have peace.
    [*Enter*] Sigismund, Frederick, Baldwin, *and their train,*
    with drums and trumpets.
SIGISMUND. Orcanes, as our legates promis'd thee,
  We with our peers have cross'd Danubius stream
  To treat of friendly peace or deadly war.   80
  Take which thou wilt; for as the Romans us'd,
  I here present thee with a naked sword.
  Wilt thou have war, then shake this blade at me;
  If peace, restore it to my hands again,
  And I will sheathe it to confirm the same.
ORCANES. Stay, Sigismund. Forgett'st thou I am he
  That with the cannon shook Vienna walls
  And made it dance upon the continent
  As when the massy substance of the earth
  Quiver about the axle-tree of heaven?   90
  Forgett'st thou that I sent a shower of darts,
  Mingled with powdered shot and feathered steel,
  So thick upon the blink-ey'd burghers' heads,
  That thou thyself, then County Palatine,
  The King of Boheme, and the Austric Duke,
  Sent heralds out, which basely on their knees,
  In all your names desir'd a truce of me?
  Forgett'st thou that to have me raise my siege
  Waggons of gold were set before my tent,
  Stamp'd with the princely fowl that in her wings   100
  Carries the fearful thunderbolts of Jove?
  How canst thou think of this, and offer war?
SIGISMUND. Vienna was besieg'd, and I was there,
  Then County Palatine, but now a king;
  And what we did was in extremity.
  But now, Orcanes, view my royal host,
  That hides these plains, and seems as vast and wide
  As doth the desert of Arabia

To those that stand on Bagdet's lofty tower,
Or as the ocean to the traveller　　　　　110
That rests upon the snowy Appenines;
And tell me whether I should stoop so low
As treat of peace with the Natolian king.

GAZELLUS. Kings of Natolia and of Hungary,
We came from Turkey to confirm a league,
And not to dare each other to the field.
A friendly parle might become ye both.

FREDERICK. And we from Europe to the same intent,
Which if your general refuse or scorn,
Our tents are pitch'd, our men stand in array,　　　　　120
Ready to charge you ere you stir your feet.

ORCANES. So prest are we: but yet if Sigismund
Speak as a friend, and stand not upon terms,
Here is his sword; let peace be ratified
On these conditions specified before,
Drawn with advice of our ambassadors.

SIGISMUND. Then here I sheathe it, and give thee my hand,
Never to draw it out, or manage arms
Against thyself or thy confederates,
But whilst I live will be at truce with thee.　　　　　130

ORCANES. But, Sigismund confirm it with an oath,
And swear in sight of heaven and by thy Christ.

SIGISMUND. By Him that made the world and sav'd my soul,
The Son of God and issue of a maid,
Sweet Jesus Christ, I solemnly protest
And vow to keep this peace inviolable.

ORCANES. By sacred Mahomet, the friend of God,
Whose holy Alcoran remains with us,
Whose glorious body, when he left the world,
Clos'd in a coffin mounted up the air,　　　　　140
And hung on stately Mecca's temple roof,
I swear to keep this truce inviolable.
Of whose conditions and our solemn oaths,
Sign'd with our hands, each shall retain a scroll,
As memorable witness of our league.
Now, Sigismund, if any Christian king
Encroach upon the confines of thy realm,
Send word, Orcanes of Natolia
Confirm'd this league beyond Danubius stream,
And they will, trembling, sound a quick retreat;　　　　　150
So am I fear'd among all nations.

SIGISMUND. If any heathen potentate or king

Invade Natolia, Sigismund will send
 A hundred thousand horse train'd to the war,
 And back'd by stout lanciers of Germany,
 The strength and sinews of the imperial seat.
ORCANES. I thank thee, Sigismund; but when I war,
 All Asia Minor, Africa and Greece
 Follow my standard and my thund'ring drums.
 Come, let us go and banquet in our tents.   160
 I will despatch chief of my army hence
 To fair Natolia and to Trebizon,
 To stay my coming 'gainst proud Tamburlaine.
 Friend Sigismund, and peers of Hungary,
 Come banquet and carouse with us a while,
 And then depart we to our territories.   *Exeunt.*

Actus 1. Scaena 2.
[*Enter*] Callapine *with* Almeda *his keeper.*
CALLAPINE. Sweet Almeda, pity the ruthful plight
 Of Callapine, the son of Bajazeth,
 Born to be monarch of the western world,
 Yet here detain'd by cruel Tamburlaine.
ALMEDA. My lord, I pity it, and with my heart
 Wish your release; but he whose wrath is death,
 My sovereign lord, renowmed Tamburlaine,
 Forbids you further liberty than this.
CALLAPINE. Ah, were I now but half so eloquent
 To paint in words what I'll perform in deeds, 10
 I know thou wouldst depart from hence with me.
ALMEDA. Not for all Afric; therefore move me not.
CALLAPINE. Yet hear me speak, my gentle Almeda.
ALMEDA. No speech to that end, by your favour sir.
CALLAPINE. By Cairo runs—
ALMEDA. No talk of running, I tell you sir.
CALLAPINE. A little further, gentle Almeda.
ALMEDA. Well sir, what of this?
CALLAPINE. By Cairo runs to Alexandria bay
 Darote's stream, wherein at anchor lies   20
 A Turkish galley of my royal fleet,
 Waiting my coming to the river side,
 Hoping by some means I shall be releas'd;
 Which, when I come aboard, will hoist up sail,
 And soon put forth into the Terrene Sea,
 Where 'twixt the isles of Cyprus and of Crete,
 We quickly may in Turkish seas arrive.

Then shalt thou see a hundred kings and more,
Upon their knees, all bid me welcome home.
Amongst so many crowns of burnish'd gold,   30
Choose which thou wilt, all are at thy command.
A thousand galleys mann'd with Christian slaves
I freely give thee, which shall cut the Straits,
And bring armadoes from the coasts of Spain,
Fraughted with gold of rich America.
The Grecian virgins shall attend on thee,
Skilful in music and in amorous lays,
As fair as was Pygmalion's ivory girl,
Or lovely Io metamorphosed.
With naked negroes shall thy coach be drawn,   40
And as thou rid'st in triumph through the streets,
The pavement underneath thy chariot wheels
With Turkey carpets shall be covered,
And cloth of arras hung about the walls,
Fit objects for thy princely eye to pierce.
A hundred bassoes cloth'd in crimson silk
Shall ride before thee on Barbarian steeds;
And when thou go'st, a golden canopy
Enchas'd with precious stones, which shine as bright
As that fair veil that covers all the world   50
When Phoebus, leaping from his hemisphere,
Descendeth downward to th'Antipodes:
And more than this, for all I cannot tell.
ALMEDA. How far hence lies the galley, say you?
CALLAPINE. Sweet Almeda, scarce half a league from hence.
ALMEDA. But need we not be spied going aboard?
CALLAPINE. Betwixt the hollow hanging of a hill
    And crooked bending of a craggy rock,
    The sails wrapp'd up, the mast and tacklings down,
    She lies so close that none can find her out.   60
ALMEDA. I like that well. But tell me, my lord, if I should let
    you go, would you be as good as your word? Shall I be
    made a king for my labour?
CALLAPINE. As I am Callapine the emperor.
    And by the hand of Mahomet I swear,
    Thou shalt be crown'd a king, and be my mate.
ALMEDA. Then here I swear, as I am Almeda,
    Your keeper under Tamburlaine the Great
    (For that's the style and title I have yet)
    Although he sent a thousand armed men   70
    To intercept this haughty enterprise,

Yet would I venture to conduct your grace,
And die before I brought you back again.
CALLAPINE. Thanks, gentle Almeda. Then let us haste,
Lest time be past, and ling'ring let us both.
ALMEDA. When you will, my lord; I am ready.
CALLAPINE. Even straight. And farewell, cursed Tamburlaine.
Now go I to revenge my father's death.   *Exeunt.*

Actus 1. Scaena 3.
[*Enter*] Tamburlaine *with* Zenocrate, *and his three sons,*
Calyphas, Amyras, *and* Celebinus, *with drums and trumpets.*
TAMBURLAINE. Now, bright Zenocrate, the world's fair eye,
Whose beams illuminate the lamps of heaven,
Whose cheerful looks do clear the cloudy air
And clothe it in a crystal livery,
Now rest thee here on fair Larissa plains,
Where Egypt and the Turkish empire parts,
Between thy sons, that shall be emperors,
And every one commander of a world.
ZENOCRATE. Sweet Tamburlaine, when wilt thou leave these
      arms,
And save thy sacred person free from scathe   10
And dangerous chances of the wrathful war?
TAMBURLAINE. When heaven shall cease to move on both the
      poles,
And when the ground whereon my soldiers march
Shall rise aloft and touch the horned moon,
And not before, my sweet Zenocrate.
Sit up, and rest thee like a lovely queen.
So; now she sits in pomp and majesty,
When these my sons more precious in mine eyes
Than all the wealthy kingdoms I subdu'd,
Plac'd by her side, look on their mother's face.   20
But yet methinks their looks are amorous,
Not martial as the sons of Tamburlaine.
Water and air, being symboliz'd in one,
Argue their want of courage and of wit;
Their hair as white as milk and soft as down,
Which should be like the quills of porcupines,
As black as jet, and hard as iron or steel,
Bewrays they are too dainty for the wars.
Their fingers made to quaver on a lute,
Their arms to hang about a lady's neck,   30
Their legs to dance and caper in the air,

Would make me think them bastards, not my sons,
But that I know they issu'd from thy womb,
That never look'd on man but Tamburlaine.

ZENOCRATE. My gracious lord, they have their mother's looks,
But, when they list, their conquering father's heart.
This lovely boy, the youngest of the three,
Not long ago bestrid a Scythian steed,
Trotting the ring, and tilting at a glove,
Which when he tainted with his slender rod,   40
He rein'd him straight, and made him so curvet
As I cried out for fear he should have fall'n.

TAMBURLAINE. Well done, my boy! Thou shalt have shield and
    lance,
Armour of proof, horse, helm, and curtle-axe,
And I will teach thee how to charge thy foe,
And harmless run among the deadly pikes.
If thou wilt love the wars and follow me,
Thou shalt be made a king and reign with me,
Keeping in iron cages emperors.
If thou exceed thy elder brothers' worth,   50
And shine in complete virtue more than they,
Thou shalt be king before them, and thy seed
Shall issue crowned from their mother's womb.

CELEBINUS. Yes, father, you shall see me, if I live,
Have under me as many kings as you,
And march with such a multitude of men
As all the world shall tremble at their view.

TAMBURLAINE. These words assure me, boy, thou art my son.
When I am old and cannot manage arms,
Be thou the scourge and terror of the world.   60

AMYRAS. Why may not I, my lord, as well as he,
Be term'd the scourge and terror of the world?

TAMBURLAINE. Be all a scourge and terror to the world,
Or else you are not sons of Tamburlaine.

CALYPHAS. But while my brothers follow arms, my lord,
Let me accompany my gracious mother.
They are enough to conquer all the world,
And you have won enough for me to keep.

TAMBURLAINE. Bastardly boy, sprung from some coward's loins,
And not the issue of great Tamburlaine!   70
Of all the provinces I have subdu'd
Thou shalt not have a foot, unless thou bear
A mind courageous and invincible.
For he shall wear the crown of Persia

[72]

Whose head hath deepest scars, whose breast most wounds,
Which being wroth sends lightning from his eyes,
And in the furrows of his frowning brows
Harbours revenge, war, death, and cruelty;
For in a field, whose superficies
Is covered with a liquid purple veil,   80
And sprinkled with the brains of slaughtered men,
My royal chair of state shall be advanc'd;
And he that means to place himself therein,
Must armed wade up to the chin in blood.

ZENOCRATE. My lord, such speeches to our princely sons
Dismays their minds before they come to prove
The wounding troubles angry war affords.

CELEBINUS. No, madam, these are speeches fit for us;
For if his chair were in a sea of blood
I would prepare a ship and sail to it,   90
Ere I would lose the title of a king.

AMYRAS. And I would strive to swim through pools of blood,
Or make a bridge of murdered carcasses,
Whose arches should be fram'd with bones of Turks,
Ere I would lose the title of a king.

TAMBURLAINE. Well, lovely boys, you shall be emperors both,
Stretching your conquering arms from east to west.
And, sirrah, if you mean to wear a crown,
When we shall meet the Turkish deputy
And all his viceroys, snatch it from his head,   100
And cleave his pericranion with thy sword.

CALYPHAS. If any man will hold him, I will strike,
And cleave him to the channel with my sword.

TAMBURLAINE. Hold him, and cleave him too, or I'll cleave
   thee;
For we will march against them presently.
Theridamas, Techelles, and Casane
Promis'd to meet me on Larissa plains,
With hosts apiece against this Turkish crew;
For I have sworn by sacred Mahomet
To make it parcel of my empery.   110
The trumpets sound; Zenocrate, they come.
   Enter Theridamas, *and his train, with drums and trumpets.*
Welcome Theridamas, King of Argier.

THERIDAMAS. My lord, the great and mighty Tamburlaine,
Arch-monarch of the world, I offer here
My crown, myself, and all the power I have,
In all affection at thy kingly feet.

TAMBURLAINE. Thanks, good Theridamas.

THERIDAMAS. Under my colours march ten thousand Greeks,
And of Argier and Afric's frontier towns
Twice twenty thousand valiant men-at-arms,   120
All which have sworn to sack Natolia;
Five hundred brigandines are under sail,
Meet for your service on the sea, my lord,
That launching from Argier to Tripoli,
Will quickly ride before Natolia.
And batter down the castles on the shore.

TAMBURLAINE. Well said, Argier. Receive thy crown again.
    Enter Techelles *and* Usumcasane *together.*
Kings of Moroccus and of Fez, welcome.

USUMCASANE. Magnificent and peerless Tamburlaine,
I and my neighbour King of Fez have brought   130
To aid thee in this Turkish expedition,
A hundred thousand expert soldiers.
From Azamor to Tunis near the sea
Is Barbary unpeopled for thy sake,
And all the men in armour under me,
Which with my crown I gladly offer thee.

TAMBURLAINE. Thanks, King of Moroccus; take your crown
    again.

TECHELLES. And, mighty Tamburlaine, our earthly god,
Whose looks make this inferior world to quake,
I here present thee with the crown of Fez,   140
And with an host of Moors train'd to the war,
Whose coal-black faces make their foes retire
And quake for fear, as if infernal Jove,
Meaning to aid thee in these Turkish arms,
Should pierce the black circumference of hell,
With ugly Furies bearing fiery flags,
And millions of his strong tormenting spirits;
From strong Tesella unto Biledull
All Barbary is unpeopled for thy sake.

TAMBURLAINE. Thanks, King of Fez; take here thy crown again.
Your presence, loving friends and fellow kings,   151
Makes me to surfeit in conceiving joy.
If all the crystal gates of Jove's high court
Were opened wide, and I might enter in
To see the state and majesty of heaven,
It could not more delight me than your sight.
Now will we banquet on these plains a while,
And after march to Turkey with our camp,

In number more than are the drops that fall
When Boreas rents a thousand swelling clouds;   160
And proud Orcanes of Natolia
With all his viceroys shall be so afraid
That though the stones, as at Deucalion's flood,
Were turn'd to men, he should be overcome.
Such lavish will I make of Turkish blood
That Jove shall send his winged messenger
To bid me sheathe my sword and leave the field;
The sun, unable to sustain the sight,
Shall hide his head in Thetis' watery lap,
And leave his steeds to fair Böotes' charge;   170
For half the world shall perish in this fight.
But now, my friends, let me examine ye;
How have ye spent your absent time from me?

USUMCASANE. My lord, our men of Barbary have march'd
Four hundred miles with armour on their backs,
And lain in leaguer fifteen months and more;
For since we left you at the Soldan's court,
We have subdu'd the southern Guallatia,
And all the land unto the coast of Spain.
We kept the narrow Strait of Gibraltar,   180
And made Canaria call us kings and lords.
Yet never did they recreate themselves,
Or cease one day from war and hot alarms;
And therefore let them rest a while, my lord.

TAMBURLAINE. They shall, Casane, and 'tis time, i'faith.

TECHELLES. And I have march'd along the river Nile
To Machda, where the mighty Christian priest,
Call'd John the Great, sits in a milk-white robe,
Whose triple mitre I did take by force,
And made him swear obedience to my crown.   190
From thence unto Cazates did I march,
Where Amazonians met me in the field,
With whom, being women, I vouchsaf'd a league,
And with my power did march to Zanzibar,
The western part of Afric, where I view'd
The Ethiopian Sea, rivers and lakes,
But neither man nor child in all the land.
Therefore I took my course to Manico,
Where, unresisted, I remov'd my camp;
And by the coast of Byather at last   200
I came to Cubar, where the negroes dwell,
And conquering that, made haste to Nubia;

There, having sack'd Borno, the kingly seat,
I took the king and led him bound in chains
Unto Damasco, where I stay'd before.
TAMBURLAINE. Well done, Techelles! What saith Theridamas?
THERIDAMAS. I left the confines and the bounds of Afric,
And made a voyage into Europe,
Where by the river Tyros I subdu'd
Stoka, Padalia, and Codemia;   210
Then cross'd the sea and came to Oblia,
And Nigra Silva, where the devils dance,
Which in despite of them I set on fire.
From thence I cross'd the gulf call'd by the name
Mare Majore of th'inhabitants.
Yet shall my soldiers make no period
Until Natolia kneel before your feet.
TAMBURLAINE. Then will we triumph, banquet, and carouse;
Cooks shall have pensions to provide us cates,
And glut us with the dainties of the world;   220
Lachryma Christi and Calabrian wines
Shall common soldiers drink in quaffing bowls,
Ay, liquid gold, when we have conquer'd him,
Mingled with coral and with orient pearl.
Come, let us banquet and carouse the whiles.   *Exeunt.*
                    Finis Actus primi.

                    Actus 2. Scaena 1.
        [*Enter*] Sigismund, Frederick, Baldwin, *with their train.*
SIGISMUND. Now say, my lords of Buda and Bohemia,
What motion is it that inflames your thoughts,
And stirs your valours to such sudden arms?
FREDERICK. Your majesty remembers, I am sure,
What cruel slaughter of our Christian bloods
These heath'nish Turks and pagans lately made
Betwixt the city Zula and Danubius;
How through the midst of Varna and Bulgaria,
And almost to the very walls of Rome,
They have, not long since, massacred our camp.   10
It resteth now, then, that your majesty
Take all advantages of time and power,
And work revenge upon these infidels.
Your highness knows, for Tamburlaine's repair,
That strikes a terror to all Turkish hearts,
Natolia hath dismiss'd the greatest part

Of all his army, pitch'd against our power
Betwixt Cutheia and Orminius mount,
And sent them marching up to Belgasar,
Acantha, Antioch, and Caesarea,   20
To aid the kings of Soria and Jerusalem.
Now then, my lord, advantage take hereof,
And issue suddenly upon the rest,
That in the fortune of their overthrow,
We may discourage all the pagan troop
That dare attempt to war with Christians.

SIGISMUND. But calls not then your grace to memory
The league we lately made with King Orcanes,
Confirm'd by oath and articles of peace,
And calling Christ for record of our-truths?   30
This should be treachery and violence
Against the grace of our profession.

BALDWIN. No whit, my lord; for with such infidels
In whom no faith nor true religion rests
We are not bound to those accomplishments
The holy laws of Christendom enjoin;
But as the faith which they profanely plight
Is not by necessary policy
To be esteem'd assurance for ourselves,
So what we vow to them should not infringe   40
Our liberty of arms and victory.

SIGISMUND. Though I confess the oaths they undertake
Breed little strength to our security,
Yet those infirmities that thus defame
Their faiths, their honours, and their religion,
Should not give us presumption to the like.
Our faiths are sound, and must be consummate,
Religious, righteous, and inviolate.

FREDERICK. Assure your grace, 'tis superstition
To stand so strictly on dispensive faith;   50
And should we lose the opportunity
That God hath given to venge our Christians' death,
And scourge their foul blasphemous paganism,
As fell to Saul, to Balaam, and the rest
That would not kill and curse at God's command,
So surely will the vengeance of the Highest,
And jealous anger of His fearful arm,
Be pour'd with rigour on our sinful heads,
If we-neglect this offered victory.

SIGISMUND. Then arm, my lords, and issue suddenly,   60

[77]

Giving commandment to our general host
With expedition to assail the pagan,
And take the victory our God hath given.   *Exeunt*.

Actus 2. Scaena 2.
[*Enter*] Orcanes, Gazellus, Uribassa, *with their train*.
ORCANES. Gazellus, Uribassa and the rest,
　Now will we march from proud Orminius mount
　To fair Natolia, where our neighbour kings
　Expect our power and our royal presence,
　T'encounter with the cruel Tamburlaine,
　That nigh Larissa sways a mighty host,
　And with the thunder of his martial tools
　Makes earthquakes in the hearts of men and heaven.
GAZELLUS. And now come we to make his sinews shake
　With greater power than erst his pride hath felt.   10
　An hundred kings by scores will bid him arms,
　And hundred thousands subjects to each score:
　Which, if a shower of wounding thunderbolts
　Should break out of the bowels of the clouds,
　And fall as thick as hail upon our heads,
　In partial aid of that proud Scythian,
　Yet should our courages and steeled crests,
　And numbers more than infinite of men,
　Be able to withstand and conquer him.
URIBASSA. Methinks I see how glad the Christian king   20
　Is made for joy of your admitted truce,
　That could not but before be terrified
　With unacquainted power of our host.
　　Enter a Messenger.
MESSENGER. Arm, dread sovereign, and my noble lords.
　The treacherous army of the Christians,
　Taking advantage of your slender power,
　Comes marching on us, and determines straight
　To bid us battle for our dearest lives.
ORCANES. Traitors, villains, damned Christians!
　Have I not here the articles of peace   30
　And solemn covenants we have both confirm'd,
　He by his Christ, and I by Mahomet?
GAZELLUS. Hell and confusion light upon their heads
　That with such treason seek our overthrow,
　And care so little for their prophet Christ!
ORCANES. Can there be such deceit in Christians,
　Or treason in the fleshly heart of man,

[78]

Whose shape is figure of the highest God?
Then if there be a Christ, as Christians say,
But in their deeds deny him for their Christ;   40
If he be son to everliving Jove,
And hath the power of his outstretched arm;
If he be jealous of his name and honour
As is our holy prophet Mahomet,
Take here these papers as our sacrifice
And witness of thy servant's perjury.
Open, thou shining veil of Cynthia,
And make a passage from th'empyreal heaven,
That he that sits on high and never sleeps,
Nor in one place is circumscriptible,   50
But everywhere fills every continent
With strange infusion of his sacred vigour,
May in his endless power and purity
Behold and venge this traitor's perjury.
Thou Christ that art esteem'd omnipotent,
If thou wilt prove thyself a perfect God,
Worthy the worship of all faithful hearts,
Be now reveng'd upon this traitor's soul,
And make the power I have left behind
(Too little to defend our guiltless lives)   60
Sufficient to discomfort and confound
The trustless force of those false Christians!
To arms, my lords! On Christ still let us cry:
If there be Christ, we shall have victory.   [*Exeunt.*]

[*Actus 2. Scaena 3.*]
Sound to the battle; and Sigismund *comes out wounded.*
SIGISMUND. Discomfited is all the Christian host,
And God hath thundered vengeance from on high
For my accurs'd and hateful perjury.
O just and dreadful punisher of sin,
Let the dishonour of the pains I feel
In this my mortal well-deserved wound
End all my penance in my sudden death.
And let this death wherein to sin I die
Conceive a second life in endless mercy.
     Enter Orcanes, Gazellus, Uribassa, *with others.*
ORCANES. Now lie the Christians bathing in their bloods,   10
And Christ or Mahomet hath been my friend.
GAZELLUS. See here the perjur'd traitor Hungary,
Bloody and breathless for his villainy.

[79]

ORCANES. Now shall his barbarous body be a prey
  To beasts and fowls, and all the winds shall breathe
  Through shady leaves of every senseless tree
  Murmurs and hisses for his heinous sin.
  Now scalds his soul in the Tartarian streams,
  And feeds upon the baneful tree of hell,
  That Zoacum, that fruit of bitterness,   20
  That in the midst of fire is engraff'd,
  Yet flourisheth as Flora in her pride,
  With apples like the heads of damned fiends.
  The devils there in chains of quenchless flame
  Shall lead his soul through Orcus' burning gulf
  From pain to pain, whose change shall never end.
  What say'st thou yet, Gazellus, to his foil,
  Which we referr'd to justice of his Christ
  And to his power, which here appears as full
  As rays of Cynthia to the clearest sight?   30
GAZELLUS. 'Tis but the fortune of the wars, my lord,
  Whose power is often prov'd a miracle.
ORCANES. Yet in my thoughts shall Christ be honoured,
  Not doing Mahomet an injury,
  Whose power had share in this our victory;
  And since this miscreant hath disgrac'd his faith,
  And died a traitor both to heaven and earth,
  We will both watch and ward shall keep his trunk
  Amidst these plains for fowls to prey upon.
  Go, Uribassa, give it straight in charge.   40
URIBASSA. I will, my lord.   *Exit* Uribassa.
ORCANES. And now Gazellus, let us haste and meet
  Our army, and our brother of Jerusalem,
  Of Soria, Trebizon, and Amasia;
  And happily with full Natolian bowls
  Of Greekish wine now let us celebrate
  Our happy conquest and his angry fate.   *Exeunt.*

Actus 2. Scaena ultima [4].
  The arras is drawn, and Zenocrate *lies in her bed of state;*
  Tamburlaine *sitting by her; three* Physicians *about her bed,*
  tempering potions; Theridamas, Techelles, Usumcasane,
  and the three sons.
TAMBURLAINE. Black is the beauty of the brightest day;
  The golden ball of heaven's eternal fire
  That danc'd with glory on the silver waves
  Now wants the fuel that inflam'd his beams,

And all with faintness and for foul disgrace
He binds his temples with a frowning cloud,
Ready to darken earth with endless night.
Zenocrate, that gave him light and life,
Whose eyes shot fire from their ivory bowers,
And tempered every soul with lively heat,   10
Now by the malice of the angry skies,
Whose jealousy admits no second mate,
Draws in the comfort of her latest breath,
All dazzled with the hellish mists of death.
Now walk the angels on the walls of heaven,
As sentinels to warn th'immortal souls
To entertain divine Zenocrate.
Apollo, Cynthia, and the ceaseless lamps
That gently look'd upon this loathsome earth,
Shine downwards now no more, but deck the heavens   20
To entertain divine Zenocrate.
The crystal springs, whose taste illuminates
Refined eyes with an eternal sight,
Like tried silver runs through Paradise
To entertain divine Zenocrate.
The cherubins and holy seraphins
That sing and play before the King of Kings
Use all their voices and their instruments
To entertain divine Zenocrate.
And in this sweet and curious harmony,   30
The god that tunes this music to our souls
Holds out his hand in highest majesty
To entertain divine Zenocrate.
Then let some holy trance convey my thoughts
Up to the palace of th'empyreal heaven,
That this my life may be as short to me
As are the days of sweet Zenocrate.
Physicians, will no physic do her good?

PHYSICIAN. My lord, your majesty shall soon perceive;
And if she pass this fit, the worst is past.   40

TAMBURLAINE. Tell me, how fares my fair Zenocrate?

ZENOCRATES. I fare, my lord, as other empresses,
That, when this frail and transitory flesh
Hath suck'd the measure of that vital air
That feeds the body with his dated health,
Wanes with enforc'd and necessary change.

TAMBURLAINE. May never such a change transform my love,
In whose sweet being I repose my life;

[81]

Whose heavenly presence beautified with health,
Gives light to Phoebus and the fixed stars;   50
Whose absence makes the sun and moon as dark
As when, oppos'd in one diameter,
Their spheres are mounted on the serpent's head,
Or else descended to his winding train.
Live still, my love, and so conserve my life,
Or, dying, be the author of my death.
ZENOCRATE. Live still, my lord. O let my sovereign live,
And sooner let the fiery element
Dissolve, and make your kingdom in the sky,
Than this base earth should shroud your majesty;   60
For should I but suspect your death by mine,
The comfort of my future happiness,
And hope to meet your highness in the heavens,
Turn'd to despair, would break my wretched breast,
And fury would confound my present rest.
But let me die, my love; yet, let me die;
With love and patience let your true love die:
Your grief and fury hurts my second life.
Yet let me kiss my lord before I die,
And let me die with kissing of my lord.   70
But since my life is lengthened yet a while,
Let me take leave of these my loving sons,
And of my lords, whose true nobility
Have merited my latest memory.
Sweet sons, farewell. In death resemble me,
And in your lives your father's excellency.
Some music, and my fit will cease, my lord. *They call music.*
TAMBURLAINE. Proud fury and intolerable fit
That dares torment the body of my love,
And scourge the scourge of the immortal God!   80
Now are those spheres where Cupid us'd to sit,
Wounding the world with wonder and with love,
Sadly supplied with pale and ghastly death,
Whose darts do pierce the centre of my soul.
Her sacred beauty hath enchanted heaven,
And had she liv'd before the siege of Troy,
Helen, whose beauty summon'd Greece to arms,
And drew a thousand ships to Tenedos,
Had not been nam'd in Homer's Iliads:
Her name had been in every line he wrote.   90
Or had those wanton poets for whose birth
Old Rome was proud but gaz'd a while on her,

[82]

Nor Lesbia nor Corinna had been nam'd:
Zenocrate had been the argument
Of every epigram or elegy.   *The music sounds and she dies.*
What, is she dead? Techelles, draw thy sword,
And wound the earth, that it may cleave in twain,
And we descend into th'infernal vaults,
To hale the Fatal Sisters by the hair,
And throw them in the triple moat of hell,   100
For taking hence my fair Zenocrate.
Casane and Theridamas, to arms!
Raise cavalieros higher than the clouds,
And with the cannon break the frame of heaven;
Batter the shining palace of the sun,
And shiver all the starry firmament,
For amorous Jove hath snatch'd my love from hence,
Meaning to make her stately queen of heaven.
What god soever holds thee in his arms,
Giving thee nectar and ambrosia,   110
Behold me here, divine Zenocrate,
Raving, impatient, desperate and mad,
Breaking my steeled lance, with which I burst
The rusty beams of Janus' temple doors,
Letting out death and tyrannizing war,
To march with me under this bloody flag.
And if thou pitiest Tamburlaine the Great,
Come down from heaven and live with me again!
THERIDAMAS. Ah, good my lord, be patient; she is dead,
And all this raging cannot make her live.   120
If words might serve, our voice hath rent the air;
If tears, our eyes have watered all the earth;
If grief, our murdered hearts have strain'd forth blood.
Nothing prevails, for she is dead, my lord.
TAMBURLAINE. For she is dead? Thy words do pierce my soul.
Ah, sweet Theridamas, say so no more.
Though she be dead, yet let me think she lives,
And feed my mind that dies for want of her.
Where'er her soul be, thou shalt stay with me,
Embalm'd with cassia, ambergris, and myrrh,   130
Not lapp'd in lead, but in a sheet of gold,
And till I die thou shalt not be interr'd.
Then in as rich a tomb as Mausolus'
We both will rest, and have one epitaph
Writ in as many several languages
As I have conquered kingdoms with my sword.

This cursed town will I consume with fire,
Because this place bereft me of my love.
The houses, burnt, will look as if they mourn'd,
And here will I set up her stature,   140
And march about it with my mourning camp,
Drooping and pining for Zenocrate.   *The arras is drawn.*

Actus 3. Scaena 1.

Enter the Kings of Trebizon *and* Soria, *one bringing a sword and another a sceptre; next* Natolia *and* Jerusalem *with the imperial crown; after* Callapine, *and after him* [Almeda *and*] *other lords.* Orcanes *and* Jerusalem *crown him and the other give him the sceptre.*

ORCANES. Callapinus Cyricelibes, otherwise Cybelius, son and successive heir to the late mighty emperor Bajazeth, by the aid of God and his friend Mahomet, Emperor of Natolia, Jerusalem, Trebizon, Soria, Amasia, Thracia, Illyria, Carmonia, and all the hundred and thirty kingdoms late contributory to his mighty father. Long live Callapinus, Emperor of Turkey!

CALLAPINE. Thrice-worthy kings of Natolia and the rest,
I will requite your royal gratitudes
With all the benefits my empire yields;   10
And, were the sinews of th'imperial seat
So knit and strength'ned as when Bajazeth
My royal lord and father fill'd the throne,
Whose cursed fate hath so dismemb'red it,
Then should you see this thief of Scythia,
This proud usurping king of Persia,
Do us such honour and supremacy,
Bearing the vengeance of our father's wrongs,
As all the world should blot our dignities
Out of the book of base-born infamies.   20
And now I doubt not but your royal cares
Hath so provided for this cursed foe
That since the heir of mighty Bajazeth,
An emperor so honoured for his virtues,
Revives the spirits of true Turkish hearts,
In grievous memory of his father's shame,
We shall not need to nourish any doubt,
But that proud Fortune, who hath followed long
The martial sword of mighty Tamburlaine,
Will now retain her old inconstancy,   30

And raise our honours to as high a pitch
In this our strong and fortunate encounter;
For so hath heaven provided my escape
From all the cruelty my soul sustain'd,
By this my friendly keeper's happy means,
That Jove, surcharg'd with pity of our wrongs,
Will pour it down in showers on our heads,
Scourging the pride of cursed Tamburlaine.

ORCANES. I have a hundred thousand men in arms,
    Some that in conquest of the perjur'd Christian,   40
    Being a handful to a mighty host,
    Think them in number yet sufficient
    To drink the river Nile or Euphrates,
    And for their power enow to win the world.

JERUSALEM. And I as many from Jerusalem,
    Judaea, Gaza, and Scalonia's bounds,
    That on Mount Sinai, with their ensigns spread,
    Look like the parti-coloured clouds of heaven
    That show fair weather to the neighbour morn.

TREBIZON. And I as many bring from Trebizon,   50
    Chio, Famastro, and Amasia,
    All bordering on the Mare Major sea,
    Riso, Sancina, and the bordering towns
    That touch the end of famous Euphrates,
    Whose courages are kindled with the flames
    The cursed Scythian sets on all their towns,
    And vow to burn the villain's cruel heart.

SORIA. From Soria with seventy thousand strong,
    Ta'en from Aleppo, Soldino, Tripoli,
    And so unto my city of Damasco,   60
    I march to meet and aid my neighbour kings,
    All which will join against this Tamburlaine,
    And bring him captive to your highness' feet.

ORCANES. Our battle then in martial manner pitch'd,
    According to our ancient use, shall bear
    The figure of the semi-circled moon,
    Whose horns shall sprinkle through the tainted air
    The poisoned brains of this proud Scythian.

CALLAPINE. Well then, my noble lords, for this my friend
    That freed me from the bondage of my foe,   70
    I think it requisite and honourable
    To keep my promise and to make him king
    That is a gentleman, I know, at least.

ALMEDA. That's no matter, sir, for being a king; for Tamburlaine came up of nothing.

JERUSALEM. Your majesty may choose some 'pointed time,
Performing all your promise to the full;
'Tis naught for your majesty to give a kingdom.

CALLAPINE. Then will I shortly keep my promise, Almeda.

ALMEDA. Why, I thank your majesty.   *Exeunt.*

Actus 3. Scaena 2.

[*Enter*] Tamburlaine *with* Usumcasane, *and his three sons;
four bearing the hearse of* Zenocrate; *and the drums sounding
a doleful march; the town burning.*

TAMBURLAINE. So burn the turrets of this cursed town,
Flame to the highest region of the air,
And kindle heaps of exhalations,
That being fiery meteors, may presage
Death and destruction to th'inhabitants!
Over my zenith hang a blazing star,
That may endure till heaven be dissolv'd,
Fed with the fresh supply of earthly dregs,
Threat'ning a death and famine to this land!
Flying dragons, lightning, fearful thunder-claps,   10
Singe these fair plains, and make them seem as black
As is the island where the Furies mask,
Compass'd with Lethe, Styx, and Phlegethon,
Because my dear Zenocrate is dead!

CALYPHAS. This pillar plac'd in memory of her,
Where in Arabian, Hebrew, Greek, is writ,
*This town being burnt by Tamburlaine the Great
Forbids the world to build it up again.*

AMYRAS. And here this mournful streamer shall be plac'd,
Wrought with the Persian and Egyptian arms,   20
To signify she was a princess born,
And wife unto the monarch of the East.

CELEBINUS. And here this table as a register
Of all her virtues and perfections.

TAMBURLAINE. And here the picture of Zenocrate,
To show her beauty which the world admir'd;
Sweet picture of divine Zenocrate,
That hanging here will draw the gods from heaven,
And cause the stars fix'd in the southern arc,
Whose lovely faces never any view'd   30
That have not pass'd the centre's latitude,
As pilgrims travel to our hemisphere,
Only to gaze upon Zenocrate.

Thou shalt not beautify Larissa plains,
But keep within the circle of mine arms.
At every town and castle I besiege,
Thou shalt be set upon my royal tent;
And when I meet an army in the field,
Those looks will shed such influence in my camp
As if Bellona, goddess of the war,   40
Threw naked swords and sulphur-balls of fire
Upon the heads of all our enemies.
And now, my lords, advance your spears again.
Sorrow no more, my sweet Casane, now.
Boys, leave to mourn; this town shall ever mourn,
Being burnt to cinders for your mother's death.
CALYPHAS. If I had wept a sea of tears for her,
It would not ease the sorrow I sustain.
AMYRAS. As is that town, so is my heart consum'd
With grief and sorrow for my mother's death.   50
CELEBINUS. My mother's death hath mortified my mind,
And sorrow stops the passage of my speech.
TAMBURLAINE. But now, my boys, leave off, and list to me,
That mean to teach you rudiments of war.
I'll have you learn to sleep upon the ground,
March in your armour thorough watery fens,
Sustain the scorching heat and freezing cold,
Hunger and thirst, right adjuncts of the war,
And after this to scale a castle wall,
Besiege a fort, to undermine a town,   60
And make whole cities caper in the air.
Then next, the way to fortify your men;
In champion grounds what figure serves you best,
For which the quinque-angle form is meet,
Because the corners there may fall more flat
Whereas the fort may fittest be assail'd,
And sharpest where th'assault is desperate.
The ditches must be deep, the counterscarps
Narrow and steep, the walls made high and broad,
The bulwarks and the rampires large and strong,   70
With cavalieros and thick counterforts,
And room within to lodge six thousand men.
It must have privy ditches, countermines,
And secret issuings to defend the ditch;
It must have high argins and covered ways
To keep the bulwark fronts from battery,
And parapets to hide the musketeers,

[87]

Casemates to place the great artillery,
And store of ordnance, that from every flank
May scour the outward curtains of the fort,   80
Dismount the cannon of the adverse part,
Murder the foe, and save the walls from breach.
When this is learn'd for service on the land,
By plain and easy demonstration
I'll teach you how to make the water mount,
That you may dry-foot march through lakes and pools,
Deep rivers, havens, creeks, and little seas,
And make a fortress in the raging waves,
Fenc'd with the concave of a monstrous rock,
Invincible by nature of the place.   90
When this is done, then are ye soldiers,
And worthy sons of Tamburlaine the Great.

CALYPHAS. My lord, but this is dangerous to be done;
We may be slain or wounded ere we learn.

TAMBURLAINE. Villain, art thou the son of Tamburlaine,
And fear'st to die, or with a curtle-axe
To hew thy flesh and make a gaping wound?
Hast thou beheld a peal of ordnance strike
A ring of pikes, mingled with shot and horse,
Whose shattered limbs, being toss'd as high as heaven,   100
Hang in the air as thick as sunny motes,
And canst thou coward stand in fear of death?
Hast thou not seen my horsemen charge the foe,
Shot through the arms, cut overthwart the hands,
Dyeing their lances with their streaming blood,
And yet at night carouse within my tent,
Filling their empty veins with airy wine,
That, being concocted, turns to crimson blood,
And wilt thou shun the field for fear of wounds?
View me, thy father, that hath conquered kings,   110
And with his host march'd round about the earth,
Quite void of scars and clear from any wound,
That by the wars lost not a dram of blood,
And see him lance his flesh to teach you all. *He cuts his arm.*
A wound is nothing, be it ne'er so deep;
Blood is the god of war's rich livery.
Now look I like a soldier, and this wound
As great a grace and majesty to me,
As if a chair of gold enamelled,
Enchas'd with diamonds, sapphires, rubies,   120
And fairest pearl of wealthy India,

Were mounted here under a canopy,
And I sat down, cloth'd with the massy robe
That late adorn'd the Afric potentate
Whom I brought bound unto Damascus walls.
Come, boys, and with your fingers search my wound,
And in my blood wash all your hands at once,
While I sit smiling to behold the sight.
Now, my boys, what think you of a wound?

CALYPHAS. I know not what I should think of it; methinks 'tis
 a pitiful sight.   131

CELEBINUS. 'Tis nothing. Give me a wound, father.

AMYRAS. And me another, my lord.

TAMBURLAINE. Come, sirrah, give me your arm.

CELEBINUS. Here, father, cut it bravely as you did your own.

TAMBURLAINE. It shall suffice thou dar'st abide a wound.
My boy, thou shalt not lose a drop of blood
Before we meet the army of the Turk;
But then run desperate through the thickest throngs,
Dreadless of blows, of bloody wounds, and death; 140
And let the burning of Larissa walls,
My speech of war, and this my wound you see,
Teach you, my boys, to bear courageous minds,
Fit for the followers of great Tamburlaine.
Usumcasane now come, let us march
Towards Techelles and Theridamas
That we have sent before to fire the towns,
The towers and cities of these hateful Turks,
And hunt that coward faint-heart runaway,
With that accursed traitor Almeda,   150
Till fire and sword have found them at a bay.

USUMCASANE. I long to pierce his bowels with my sword
That hath betray'd my gracious sovereign,
That curs'd and damned traitor Almeda.

TAMBURLAINE. Then let us see if coward Callapine
Dare levy arms against our puissance,
That we may tread upon his captive neck,
And treble all his father's slaveries.   *Exeunt.*

Actus 3. Scaena 3.
[*Enter*] Techelles, Theridamas *and their train.*

THERIDAMAS. Thus have we march'd northward from Tam-
 burlaine,
Unto the frontier point of Soria;
And this is Balsera, their chiefest hold,

Wherein is all the treasure of the land.
TECHELLES. Then let us bring our light artillery,
    Minions, falc'nets, and sakers, to the trench,
    Filling the ditches with the walls' wide breach,
    And enter in to seize upon the gold.
    How say ye, soldiers, shall we not?
SOLDIERS. Yes, my lord, yes. Come, let's about it.   10
THERIDAMAS. But stay a while; summon a parle, drum.
    It may be they will yield it quietly,
    Knowing two kings, the friends to Tamburlaine,
    Stand at the walls with such a mighty power.
      Summon the battle. [*Enter above*] Captain *with his wife and* Son.
CAPTAIN. What require you, my masters?
THERIDAMAS. Captain, that thou yield up thy hold to us.
CAPTAIN. To you? Why, do you think me weary of it?
TECHELLES. Nay, captain, thou art weary of thy life,
    If thou withstand the friends of Tamburlaine.
THERIDAMAS. These pioners of Argier in Africa   20
    Even in the cannon's face shall raise a hill
    Of earth and faggots higher than thy fort,
    And over thy argins and covered ways
    Shall play upon the bulwarks of thy hold
    Volleys of ordnance, till the breach be made
    That with his ruin fills up all the trench;
    And when we enter in, not heaven itself
    Shall ransom thee, thy wife, and family.
TECHELLES. Captain, these Moors shall cut the leaden pipes
    That bring fresh water to thy men and thee;   30
    And lie in trench before thy castle walls,
    That no supply of victual shall come in,
    Nor any issue forth but they shall die;
    And therefore, captain, yield it quietly.
CAPTAIN. Were you that are the friends of Tamburlaine,
    Brothers to holy Mahomet himself,
    I would not yield it. Therefore do your worst:
    Raise mounts, batter, intrench, and undermine,
    Cut off the water, all convoys that can,   40
    Yet I am resolute: and so farewell.   [*Exeunt.*]
THERIDAMAS. Pioners, away, and where I stuck the stake,
    Intrench with those dimensions I prescrib'd.
    Cast up the earth towards the castle wall,
    Which, till it may defend you, labour low,
    And few or none shall perish by their shot.
PIONERS. We will, my lord.   *Exeunt.*

TECHELLES. A hundred horse shall scout about the plains
   To spy what force comes to relieve the hold.
   Both we, Theridamas, will intrench our men,
   And with the Jacob's staff measure the height   50
   And distance of the castle from the trench,
   That we may know if our artillery
   Will carry full point-blank unto their walls.
THERIDAMAS. Then see the bringing of our ordnance
   Along the trench into the battery,
   Where we will have gabions of six foot broad,
   To save our cannoneers from musket-shot;
   Betwixt which shall our ordnance thunder forth,
   And with the breach's fall, smoke, fire and dust,
   The crack, the echo, and the soldiers' cry,   60
   Make deaf the air and dim the crystal sky.
TECHELLES. Trumpets and drums, alarum presently!
   And, soldiers, play the men; the hold is yours.   *[Exeunt.]*

[Actus 3. Scaena 4.]
   Enter the Captain *with his wife and* Son.
OLYMPIA. Come, good my lord, and let us haste from hence
   Along the cave that leads beyond the foe;
   No hope is left to save this conquered hold.
CAPTAIN. A deadly bullet gliding through my side
   Lies heavy on my heart. I cannot live.
   I feel my liver pierc'd and all my veins
   That there begin and nourish every part
   Mangled and torn, and all my entrails bath'd
   In blood that straineth from their orifex.
   Farewell, sweet wife! Sweet son, farewell! I die.   10
OLYMPIA. Death, whither art thou gone, that both we live?
   Come back again, sweet Death, and strike us both.
   One minute end our days, and one sepulchre
   Contain our bodies! Death, why com'st thou not?
   Well, this must be the messenger for thee:
   Now ugly Death, stretch out thy sable wings,
   And carry both our souls where his remains.
   Tell me sweet boy, art thou content to die?
   These barbarous Scythians, full of cruelty,
   And Moors, in whom was never pity found,   20
   Will hew us piecemeal, put us to the wheel,
   Or else invent some torture worse than that;
   Therefore die by thy loving mother's hand,
   Who gently now will lance thy ivory throat,

And quickly rid thee both of pain and life.

SON. Mother, dispatch me, or I'll kill myself,
　　For think ye I can live and see him dead?
　　Give me your knife, good mother, or strike home:
　　The Scythians shall not tyrannize on me.
　　Sweet mother strike, that I may meet my father.　　30
　　　　　　　　　　　　　　　　She stabs him.

OLYMPIA. Ah, sacred Mahomet, if this be sin,
　　Entreat a pardon of the God of heaven,
　　And purge my soul before it come to thee.
　　　　Enter Theridamas, Techelles, *and all their train.*

THERIDAMAS. How now, madam, what are you doing?

OLYMPIA. Killing myself, as I have done my son,
　　Whose body with his father's I have burnt,
　　Lest cruel Scythians should dismember him.

TECHELLES. 'Twas bravely done, and like a soldier's wife.
　　Thou shalt with us to Tamburlaine the Great,
　　Who, when he hears how resolute thou wert,　　40
　　Will match thee with a viceroy or a king.

OLYMPIA. My lord deceas'd was dearer unto me
　　Than any viceroy, king, or emperor,
　　And for his sake here will I end my days.

THERIDAMAS. But, lady, go with us to Tamburlaine,
　　And thou shalt see a man greater than Mahomet,
　　In whose high looks is much more majesty,
　　Than from the concave superficies
　　Of Jove's vast palace, the empyreal orb,
　　Unto the shining bower where Cynthia sits,　　50
　　Like lovely Thetis, in a crystal robe;
　　That treadeth fortune underneath his feet,
　　And make the mighty god of arms his slave;
　　On whom Death and the Fatal Sisters wait
　　With naked swords and scarlet liveries;
　　Before whom, mounted on a lion's back,
　　Rhamnusia bears a helmet full of blood,
　　And strows the way with brains of slaughtered men;
　　By whose proud side the ugly Furies run,
　　Hearkening when he shall bid them plague the world;　　60
　　Over whose zenith, cloth'd in windy air,
　　And eagle's wings join'd to her feathered breast,
　　Fame hovereth, sounding of her golden trump,
　　That to the adverse poles of that straight line
　　Which measureth the glorious frame of heaven
　　The name of mighty Tamburlaine is spread;

And him, fair lady, shall thy eyes behold.
Come.

OLYMPIA. Take pity of a lady's ruthful tears,
   That humbly craves upon her knees to stay   70
   And cast her body in the burning flame
   That feeds upon her son's and husband's flesh.

TECHELLES. Madam, sooner shall fire consume us both
   Than scorch a face so beautiful as this,
   In frame of which Nature hath show'd more skill
   Than when she gave eternal chaos form,
   Drawing from it the shining lamps of heaven.

THERIDAMAS. Madam, I am so far in love with you
   That you must go with us: no remedy.

OLYMPIA. Then carry me, I care not, where you will,   80
   And let the end of this my fatal journey
   Be likewise end to my accursed life.

TECHELLES. No, madam, but the beginning of your joy;
   Come willingly therefore.

THERIDAMAS. Soldiers, now let us meet the general,
   Who by this time is at Natolia,
   Ready to charge the army of the Turk.
   The gold, the silver, and the pearl ye got
   Rifling this fort, divide in equal shares.
   This lady shall have twice so much again   90
   Out of the coffers of our treasury.   *Exeunt.*

Actus 3. Scaena 5.

[*Enter*] Callapine, Orcanes, Jerusalem, Trebizon, Soria,
Almeda, *with their train* [*and* Messenger].

MESSENGER. Renowmed emperor, mighty Callapine,
   God's great lieutenant over all the world,
   Here at Aleppo, with an host of men,
   Lies Tamburlaine, this king of Persia;
   In number more than are the quivering leaves
   Of Ida's forest, where your highness' hounds
   With open cry pursue the wounded stag;
   Who means to girt Natolia's walls with siege,
   Fire the town, and over-run the land.

CALLAPINE. My royal army is as great as his,   10
   That from the bounds of Phrygia to the sea
   Which washeth Cyprus with his brinish waves,
   Covers the hills, the valleys, and the plains.
   Viceroys and peers of Turkey, play the men;
   Whet all your swords to mangle Tamburlaine,

His sons, his captains, and his followers:
By Mahomet, not one of them shall live.
The field wherein this battle shall be fought
For ever term the Persians' sepulchre,
In memory of this our victory.   20
ORCANES. Now he that calls himself the scourge of Jove,
   The emperor of the world, and earthly god,
   Shall end the warlike progress he intends,
   And travel headlong to the lake of hell,
   Where legions of devils (knowing he must die
   Here in Natolia by your highness' hands)
   All brandishing their brands of quenchless fire,
   Stretching their monstrous paws, grin with their teeth,
   And guard the gates to entertain his soul.
CALLAPINE. Tell me, viceroys, the number of your men,   30
   And what our army royal is esteem'd.
JERUSALEM. From Palestina and Jerusalem,
   Of Hebrews three score thousand fighting men
   Are come, since last we show'd your majesty.
ORCANES. So from Arabia Desert, and the bounds
   Of that sweet land whose brave metropolis
   Re-edified the fair Semiramis,
   Came forty thousand warlike foot and horse,
   Since last we numb'red to your majesty.
TREBIZON. From Trebizon in Asia the Less,   40
   Naturaliz'd Turks and stout Bithynians
   Came to my bands full fifty thousand more,
   That, fighting, knows not what retreat doth mean,
   Nor e'er return but with the victory,
   Since last we numb'red to your majesty.
SORIA. Of Sorians from Halla is repair'd,
   And neighbour cities of your highness' land,
   Ten thousand horse, and thirty thousand foot,
   Since last we numb'red to your majesty;
   So that the army royal is esteem'd   50
   Six hundred thousand valiant fighting men.
CALLAPINE. Then welcome, Tamburlaine, unto thy death.
   Come puissant viceroys, let us to the field,
   The Persians' sepulchre, and sacrifice
   Mountains of breathless men to Mahomet,
   Who now with Jove opens the firmament
   To see the slaughter of our enemies.
      [*Enter*] Tamburlaine *with his three sons*, Usumcasane, *with
      other.*

TAMBURLAINE. How now, Casane! See, a knot of kings,
    Sitting as if they were a-telling riddles.
USUMCASANE. My lord, your presence makes them pale and
    wan: 60
    Poor souls, they look as if their deaths were near.
TAMBURLAINE. Why so he is, Casane: I am here.
    But yet I'll save their lives, and make them slaves.
    Ye petty kings of Turkey, I am come,
    As Hector did into the Grecian camp,
    To overdare the pride of Graecia,
    And set his warlike person to the view
    Of fierce Achilles, rival of his fame.
    I do you honour in the simile,
    For if I should, as Hector did Achilles   70
    (The worthiest knight that ever brandish'd sword),
    Challenge in combat any of you all,
    I see how fearfully ye would refuse,
    And fly my glove as from a scorpion.
ORCANES. Now thou art fearful of thy army's strength,
    Thou wouldst with overmatch of person fight.
    But shepherd's issue, base-born Tamburlaine,
    Think of thy end; this sword shall lance thy throat.
TAMBURLAINE. Villain, the shepherd's issue, at whose birth
    Heaven did afford a gracious aspect,   80
    And join'd those stars that shall be opposite
    Even till the dissolution of the world,
    And never meant to make a conqueror
    So famous as is mighty Tamburlaine,
    Shall so torment thee, and that Callapine
    That like a roguish runaway suborn'd
    That villain there, that slave, that Turkish dog,
    To false his service to his sovereign,
    As ye shall curse the birth of Tamburlaine.
CALLAPINE. Rail not, proud Scythian: I shall now revenge 90
    My father's vile abuses and mine own.
JERUSALEM. By Mahomet, he shall be tied in chains,
    Rowing with Christians in a brigandine
    About the Grecian isles to rob and spoil,
    And turn him to his ancient trade again.
    Methinks the slave should make a lusty thief.
CALLAPINE. Nay, when the battle ends, all we will meet,
    And sit in council to invent some pain
    That most may vex his body and his soul.
TAMBURLAINE. Sirrah Callapine, I'll hang a clog about your

neck for running away again: you shall not trouble me
thus to come and fetch you.   102
But as for you, viceroy, you shall have bits,
And harness'd like my horses, draw my coach,
And when ye stay, be lash'd with whips of wire.
I'll have you learn to feed on provender,
And in a stable lie upon the planks.

ORCANES. But, Tamburlaine, first thou shalt kneel to us,
And humbly crave a pardon for thy life.

TREBIZON. The common soldiers of our mighty host   110
Shall bring thee bound unto the general's tent.

SORIA. And all have jointly sworn thy cruel death,
Or bind thee in eternal torments' wrath.

TAMBURLAINE. Well, sirs, diet yourselves; you know I shall have
occasion shortly to journey you.

CELEBINUS. See, father, how Almeda the jailor looks upon us.

TAMBURLAINE. Villain, traitor, damned fugitive,
I'll make thee wish the earth had swallowed thee.
Seest thou not death within my wrathful looks?
Go villain, cast thee headlong from a rock,   120
Or rip thy bowels and rend out thy heart,
T'appease my wrath; or else I'll torture thee,
Searing thy hateful flesh with burning irons
And drops of scalding lead, while all thy joints
Be rack'd and beat asunder with the wheel;
For if thou liv'st, not any element
Shall shroud thee from the wrath of Tamburlaine.

CALLAPINE. Well, in despite of thee, he shall be king.
Come, Almeda; receive this crown of me.
I here invest thee King of Ariadan,   130
Bordering on Mare Rosso, near to Mecca.

ORCANES. What, take it, man.

ALMEDA. Good my lord, let me take it.

CALLAPINE. Dost thou ask him leave? Here, take it.

TAMBURLAINE. Go to, sirrah, take your crown, and make up
the half dozen.
So, sirrah, now you are a king you must give arms.

ORCANES. So he shall, and wear thy head in his scutcheon.

TAMBURLAINE. No, let him hang a bunch of keys on his
standard, to put him in remembrance he was a jailor;
that when I take him, I may knock out his brains with
them, and lock you in the stable, when you shall come
sweating from my chariot.   143

TREBIZON. Away! Let us to the field, that the villain may be slain.

[96]

TAMBURLAINE. Sirrah, prepare whips, and bring my chariot to
   my tent; for as soon as the battle is done, I'll ride in
   triumph through the camp.

   Enter Theridamas, Techelles, *and their train.*

How now, ye petty kings? Lo, here are bugs
Will make the hair stand upright on your heads,
And cast your crowns in slavery at their feet.   150
Welcome, Theridamas and Techelles both.
See ye this rout, and know ye this same king?

THERIDAMAS. Ay, my lord; he was Callapine's keeper.

TAMBURLAINE. Well, now you see he is a king. Look to him,
   Theridamas, when we are fighting, lest he hide his crown
   as the foolish king of Persia did.

SORIA. No, Tamburlaine; he shall not be put to that exigent, I
   warrant thee.

TAMBURLAINE. You know not, sir.
But now, my followers and my loving friends,   160
Fight as you ever did, like conquerors,
The glory of this happy day is yours.
My stern aspect shall make fair Victory,
Hovering betwixt our armies, light on me,
Loaden with laurel-wreaths to crown us all.

TECHELLES. I smile to think how, when this field is fought
And rich Natolia ours, our men shall sweat
With carrying pearl and treasure on their backs.

TAMBURLAINE. You shall be princes all immediately.
Come fight, ye Turks, or yield us victory.   170

ORCANES. No, we will meet thee, slavish Tamburlaine.

                                                    Exeunt.

                      Actus 4. Scaena 1.

   Alarm. Amyras *and* Celebinus *issue from the tent where*
   Calyphas *sits asleep.*

AMYRAS. Now in their glories shine the golden crowns
Of these proud Turks, much like so many suns
That half dismay the majesty of heaven.
Now brother, follow we our father's sword,
That flies with fury swifter than our thoughts,
And cuts down armies with his conquering wings.

CELEBINUS. Call forth our lazy brother from the tent,
For if my father miss him in the field,
Wrath, kindled in the furnace of his breast,
Will send a deadly lightning to his heart.   10

                         [97]

AMYRAS. Brother, ho! What, given so much to sleep
    You cannot leave it, when our enemies' drums
    And rattling cannons thunder in our ears
    Our proper ruin and our father's foil?
CALYPHAS. Away, ye fools, my father needs not me,
    Nor you, in faith, but that you will be thought
    More childish-valorous than manly-wise.
    If half our camp should sit and sleep with me,
    My father were enough to scare the foe.
    You do dishonour to his majesty   20
    To think our helps will do him any good.
AMYRAS. What, dar'st thou then be absent from the fight,
    Knowing my father hates thy cowardice,
    And oft hath warn'd thee to be still in field,
    When he himself amidst the thickest troops
    Beats down our foes, to flesh our taintless swords?
CALYPHAS. I know, sir, what it is to kill a man;
    It works remorse of conscience in me.
    I take no pleasure to be murderous,
    Nor care for blood when wine will quench my thirst.   30
CELEBINUS. O cowardly boy; fie, for shame, come forth.
    Thou dost dishonour manhood and thy house.
CALYPHAS. Go, go, tall stripling, fight you for us both,
    And take my other toward brother here,
    For person like to prove a second Mars.
    'Twill please my mind as well to hear both you
    Have won a heap of honour in the field,
    And left your slender carcasses behind,
    As if I lay with you for company.
AMYRAS. You will not go then?   40
CALYPHAS. You say true.
AMYRAS. Were all the lofty mounts of Zona Mundi
    That fill the midst of farthest Tartary
    Turn'd into pearl and proffered for my stay,
    I would not bide the fury of my father
    When, made a victor in these haughty arms,
    He comes and finds his sons have had no shares
    In all the honours he propos'd for us.
CALYPHAS. Take you the honour, I will take my ease;
    My wisdom shall excuse my cowardice.   50
    I go into the field before I need?
                        Alarm; and Amyras *and* Celebinus *run in.*
    The bullets fly at random where they list;
    And should I go and kill a thousand men,

[98]

I were as soon rewarded with a shot.
And sooner far than he that never fights;
And should I go and do nor harm nor good,
I might have harm, which all the good I have,
Join'd with my father's crown, would never cure.
I'll to cards. Perdicas!
   [*Enter* Perdicas.]

PERDICAS. Here my lord.   60

CALYPHAS. Come, thou and I will go to cards to drive away
   the time.

PERDICAS. Content, my lord; but what shall we play for?

CALYPHAS. Who shall kiss the fairest of the Turks' concubines
   first, when my father hath conquered them.

PERDICAS. Agreed, i'faith.   *They play.*

CALYPHAS. They say I am a coward, Perdicas, and I fear as
   little their taratantaras, their swords, or their cannons as
   I do a naked lady in a net of gold, and, for fear I should
   be afraid, would put it off and come to bed with me.   70

PERDICAS. Such a fear, my lord, would never make ye retire.

CALYPHAS. I would my father would let me be put in the front
   of such a battle once, to try my valour.   *Alarm.*
   What a coil they keep! I believe there will be some hurt
   done anon amongst them.

               [Calyphas *and* Perdicas *retire.*]
   Enter [*with soldiers*] Tamburlaine, Theridamas, Techelles,
   Usumcasane, Amyras, Celebinus, *leading the Turkish*
   Kings.

TAMBURLAINE. See now, ye slaves, my children stoops your
   pride,
And leads your glories sheep-like to the sword.
Bring them, my boys, and tell me if the wars
Be not a life that may illustrate gods,
And tickle not your spirits with desire   80
Still to be train'd in arms and chivalry?

AMYRAS. Shall we let go these kings again, my lord,
To gather greater numbers 'gainst our power,
That they may say, it is not chance doth this,
But matchless strength and magnanimity?

TAMBURLAINE. No, no, Amyras; tempt not fortune so;
Cherish thy valour still with fresh supplies,
And glut it not with stale and daunted foes.
But where's this coward villain, not my son,
But traitor to my name and majesty?   90
            He goes in and brings him out.

[99]

Image of sloth, and picture of a slave,
The obloquy and scorn of my renown,
How may my heart, thus fired with mine eyes,
Wounded with shame and kill'd with discontent,
Shroud any thought may hold my striving hands
From martial justice on thy wretched soul?

THERIDAMAS. Yet pardon him, I pray your majesty.

TECHELLES AND USUMCASANE. Let all of us entreat your highness'
pardon.

TAMBURLAINE. Stand up, ye base, unworthy soldiers.
Know ye not yet the argument of arms?   100

AMYRAS. Good my lord, let him be forgiven for once,
And we will force him to the field hereafter.

TAMBURLAINE. Stand up, my boys, and I will teach ye arms,
And what the jealousy of wars must do.
O Samarcanda, where I breathed first,
And joy'd the fire of this martial flesh,
Blush, blush, fair city, at thine honour's foil,
And shame of nature, which Jaertis stream
Embracing thee with deepest of his love,
Can never wash from thy distained brows.   110
Here, Jove, receive his fainting soul again,
A form not meet to give that subject essence
Whose matter is the flesh of Tamburlaine,
Wherein an incorporeal spirit moves,
Made of the mould whereof thyself consists,
Which makes me valiant, proud, ambitious,
Ready to levy power against thy throne,
That I might move the turning spheres of heaven;
For earth and all this airy region
Cannot contain the state of Tamburlaine. [*Stabs* Calyphas.]
By Mahomet, thy mighty friend, I swear,   121
In sending to my issue such a soul,
Created of the massy dregs of earth,
The scum and tartar of the elements,
Wherein was neither courage, strength or wit,
But folly, sloth, and damned idleness,
Thou hast procur'd a greater enemy
Than he that darted mountains at thy head,
Shaking the burden mighty Atlas bears,
Whereat thou trembling hidd'st thee in the air,   130
Cloth'd with a pitchy cloud for being seen.
And now, ye cank'red curs of Asia,
That will not see the strength of Tamburlaine

Although it shine as brightly as the sun,
Now you shall feel the strength of Tamburlaine,
And by the state of his supremacy
Approve the difference 'twixt himself and you.

ORCANES. Thou show'st the difference 'twixt ourselves and thee,
In this thy barbarous damned tyranny.

JERUSALEM. Thy victories are grown so violent　　　　140
That shortly heaven, fill'd with the meteors
Of blood and fire thy tyrannies have made,
Will pour down blood and fire on thy head,
Whose scalding drops will pierce thy seething brains,
And with our bloods revenge our bloods on thee.

TAMBURLAINE. Villains, these terrors and these tyrannies
(If tyrannies war's justice ye repute)
I execute, enjoin'd me from above,
To scourge the pride of such as Heaven abhors;
Nor am I made arch-monarch of the world,　　　　150
Crown'd and invested by the hand of Jove,
For deeds of bounty or nobility;
But since I exercise a greater name,
The scourge of God and terror of the world,
I must apply myself to fit those terms,
In war, in blood, in death, in cruelty,
And plague such peasants as resist in me
The power of heaven's eternal majesty.
Theridamas, Techelles, and Casane,
Ransack the tents and the pavilions　　　　160
Of these proud Turks, and take their concubines,
Making them bury this effeminate brat;
For not a common soldier shall defile
His manly fingers with so faint a boy.
Then bring those Turkish harlots to my tent,
And I'll dispose them as it likes me best.
Meanwhile, take him in.

SOLDIERS. We will, my lord. [*Exeunt with the body of* Calyphas.]

JERUSALEM. O damned monster, nay, a fiend of hell,
Whose cruelties are not so harsh as thine,　　　　170
Nor yet impos'd with such a bitter hate!

ORCANES. Revenge it, Rhadamanth and Aeacus,
And let your hates, extended in his pains,
Expel the hate wherewith he pains our souls.

TREBIZON. May never day give virtue to his eyes,
Whose sight, compos'd of fury and of fire,
Doth send such stern affections to his heart!

SORIA. May never spirit, vein or artier feed
    The cursed substance of that cruel heart;
    But, wanting moisture and remorseful blood,   180
    Dry up with anger, and consume with heat!
TAMBURLAINE. Well, bark, ye dogs; I'll bridle all your tongues,
    And bind them close with bits of burnish'd steel,
    Down to the channels of your hateful throats,
    And with the pains my rigour shall inflict,
    I'll make ye roar, that earth may echo forth
    The far-resounding torments ye sustain;
    As when an herd of lusty Cimbrian bulls
    Run mourning round about the females' miss,
    And stung with fury of their following,   190
    Fill all the air with troublous bellowing.
    I will, with engines never exercis'd,
    Conquer, sack, and utterly consume
    Your cities and your golden palaces,
    And with the flames that beat against the clouds
    Incense the heavens and make the stars to melt,
    As if they were the tears of Mahomet
    For hot consumption of his country's pride.
    And till by vision or by speech I hear
    Immortal Jove say 'Cease, my Tamburlaine',   200
    I will persist a terror to the world,
    Making the meteors that like armed men
    Are seen to march upon the towers of heaven
    Run tilting round about the firmament,
    And break their burning lances in the air,
    For honour of my wondrous victories.
    Come, bring them in to our pavilion.   *Exeunt.*

Actus 4. Scaena 2.

[*Enter*] Olympia *alone.*
OLYMPIA. Distress'd Olympia, whose weeping eyes
    Since thy arrival here beheld no sun,
    But, clos'd within the compass of a tent,
    Hath stain'd thy cheeks and made thee look like death,
    Devise some means to rid thee of thy life,
    Rather than yield to his detested suit
    Whose drift is only to dishonour thee;
    And since this earth, dew'd with thy brinish tears,
    Affords no herbs whose taste may poison thee,
    Nor yet this air, beat often with thy sighs,   10
    Contagious smells and vapours to infect thee,

Nor thy close cave a sword to murder thee,
Let this invention be the instrument.
 Enter Theridamas.

THERIDAMAS. Well met, Olympia. I sought thee in my tent,
 But when I saw the place obscure and dark,
 Which with thy beauty thou wast wont to light,
 Enrag'd, I ran about the fields for thee,
 Supposing amorous Jove had sent his son,
 The winged Hermes, to convey thee hence.
 But now I find thee, and that fear is past,   20
 Tell me, Olympia, wilt thou grant my suit?

OLYMPIA. My lord and husband's death, with my sweet son's,
 With whom I buried all affections
 Save grief and sorrow which torment my heart,
 Forbids my mind to entertain a thought
 That tends to love, but meditate on death,
 A fitter subject for a pensive soul.

THERIDAMAS. Olympia, pity him in whom thy looks
 Have greater operation and more force
 Than Cynthia's in the watery wilderness,   30
 For with thy view my joys are at the full,
 And ebb again as thou depart'st from me.

OLYMPIA. Ah, pity me, my lord, and draw your sword,
 Making a passage for my troubled soul,
 Which beats against this prison to get out,
 And meet my husband and my loving son.

THERIDAMAS. Nothing but still thy husband and thy son?
 Leave this, my love, and listen more to me;
 Thou shalt be stately queen of fair Argier,
 And, cloth'd in costly cloth of massy gold,   40
 Upon the marble turrets of my court
 Sit like to Venus in her chair of state,
 Commanding all thy princely eye desires;
 And I will cast off arms and sit with thee,
 Spending my life in sweet discourse of love.

OLYMPIA. No such discourse is pleasant in mine ears,
 But that where every period ends with death,
 And every line begins with death again.
 I cannot love, to be an emperess.

THERIDAMAS. Nay, lady, then if nothing will prevail,   50
 I'll use some other means to make you yield.
 Such is the sudden fury of my love,
 I must and will be pleas'd, and you shall yield:
 Come to the tent again.

OLYMPIA. Stay, good my lord; and, will you save my honour,
   I'll give your grace a present of such price
   As all the world cannot afford the like.
THERIDAMAS. What is it?
OLYMPIA. An ointment which a cunning alchemist
   Distilled from the purest balsamum   60
   And simplest extracts of all minerals,
   In which the essential form of marble stone,
   Tempered by science metaphysical,
   And spells of magic from the mouths of spirits,
   With which if you but 'noint your tender skin,
   Nor pistol, sword, nor lance, can pierce your flesh.
THERIDAMAS. Why, madam, think ye to mock me thus
      palpably?
OLYMPIA. To prove it, I will 'noint my naked throat,
   Which when you stab, look on your weapon's point,
   And you shall see't rebated with the blow.   70
THERIDAMAS. Why gave you not your husband some of it,
   If you lov'd him, and it so precious?
OLYMPIA. My purpose was, my lord, to spend it so,
   But was prevented by his sudden end;
   And for a present easy proof hereof,
   That I dissemble not, try it on me.
THERIDAMAS. I will, Olympia, and will keep it for
   The richest present of this eastern world.

                                    She 'noints her throat.

OLYMPIA. Now stab, my lord, and mark your weapon's point,
   That will be blunted if the blow be great.   80
THERIDAMAS. Here, then, Olympia.
   What, have I slain her? Villain, stab thyself.
   Cut off this arm that murdered my love,
   In whom the learned rabbis of this age
   Might find as many wondrous miracles
   As in the theoria of the world.
   Now hell is fairer than Elysium;
   A greater lamp than that bright eye of heaven,
   From whence the stars do borrow all their light,
   Wanders about the black circumference;   90
   And now the damned souls are free from pain,
   For every Fury gazeth on her looks.
   Infernal Dis is courting of my love,
   Inventing masques and stately shows for her,
   Opening the doors of his rich treasury
   To entertain this queen of chastity,

Whose body shall be tomb'd with all the pomp
The treasure of my kingdom may afford.

Exit, taking her away.

Actus 4. Scaena 3.

[*Enter*] Tamburlaine *drawn in his chariot by* Trebizon *and*
Soria *with bits in their mouths, reins in his left hand, in his*
right hand a whip, with which he scourgeth them. Techelles,
Theridamas, Usumcasane, Amyras, Celebinus, Natolia
and Jerusalem *led by with five or six common* Soldiers.

TAMBURLAINE. Holla, ye pampered jades of Asia!
What, can ye draw but twenty miles a day,
And have so proud a chariot at your heels,
And such a coachman as great Tamburlaine?
But from Asphaltis, where I conquer'd you,
To Byron here, where thus I honour you?
The horse that guide the golden eye of heaven,
And blow the morning from their nosterils,
Making their fiery gait above the clouds,
Are not so honoured in their governor   10
As you, ye slaves, in mighty Tamburlaine.
The headstrong jades of Thrace Alcides tam'd,
That King Aegeus fed with human flesh,
And made so wanton that they knew their strengths,
Were not subdu'd with valour more divine
Than you by this unconquered arm of mine.
To make you fierce, and fit my appetite,
You shall be fed with flesh as raw as blood,
And drink in pails the strongest muscadel.
If you can live with it, then live, and draw   20
My chariot swifter than the racking clouds;
If not, then die like beasts, and fit for naught
But perches for the black and fatal ravens.
Thus am I right the scourge of highest Jove;
And see the figure of my dignity
By which I hold my name and majesty.

AMYRAS. Let me have coach, my lord, that I may ride,
And thus be drawn with these two idle kings.

TAMBURLAINE. Thy youth forbids such ease, my kingly boy;
They shall tomorrow draw my chariot,   30
While these their fellow-kings may be refresh'd.

ORCANES. O thou that sway'st the region under earth,
And art a king as absolute as Jove,
Come as thou didst in fruitful Sicily,

[105]

Surveying all the glories of the land,
And as thou took'st the fair Proserpina,
Joying the fruit of Ceres' garden-plot,
For love, for honour, and to make her queen,
So for just hate, for shame, and to subdue
This proud contemner of thy dreadful power, 　　　40
Come once in fury and survey his pride,
Haling him headlong to the lowest hell.

THERIDAMAS. Your majesty must get some bits for these,
　To bridle their contemptuous cursing tongues,
　That like unruly never-broken jades,
　Break through the hedges of their hateful mouths,
　And pass their fixed bounds exceedingly.

TECHELLES. Nay, we will break the hedges of their mouths,
　And pull their kicking colts out of their pastures.

USUMCASANE. Your majesty already hath devis'd 　　　50
　A mean, as fit as may be, to restrain
　These coltish coach-horse tongues from blasphemy.

CELEBINUS. How like you that, sir king? Why speak you not?

JERUSALEM. Ah cruel brat, sprung from a tyrant's loins!
　How like his cursed father he begins
　To practise taunts and bitter tyrannies!

TAMBURLAINE. Ay, Turk, I tell thee, this same boy is he
　That must, advanc'd in higher pomp than this,
　Rifle the kingdoms I shall leave unsack'd,
　If Jove, esteeming me too good for earth, 　　　60
　Raise me to match the fair Aldebaran,
　Above the threefold astracism of heaven,
　Before I conquer all the triple world.
　Now fetch me out the Turkish concubines;
　I will prefer them for the funeral
　They have bestow'd on my abortive son.
　　　　　　　　　The Concubines *are brought in.*
　Where are my common soldiers now, that fought
　So lion-like upon Asphaltis plains?

SOLDIERS. Here, my lord.

TAMBURLAINE. Hold ye, tall soldiers, take ye queens apiece—
　I mean such queens as were kings' concubines. 　　　71
　Take them; divide them, and their jewels too,
　And let them equally serve all your turns.

SOLDIERS. We thank your majesty.

TAMBURLAINE. Brawl not, I warn you, for your lechery,
　For every man that so offends shall die.

ORCANES. Injurious tyrant, wilt thou so defame

The hateful fortunes of thy victory,
To exercise upon such guiltless dames
The violence of thy common soldiers' lust?   80
TAMBURLAINE. Live continent then, ye slaves, and meet not me
    With troops of harlots at your slothful heels.
CONCUBINES. O pity us, my lord, and save our honours.
TAMBULAINE. Are ye not gone, ye villains, with your spoils?
                            They run away with the Ladies.
JERUSALEM. O merciless, infernal cruelty!
TAMBURLAINE. Save your honours? 'Twere but time indeed,
    Lost long before you knew what honour meant.
THERIDAMAS. It seems they meant to conquer us, my lord,
    And make us jesting pageants for their trulls.
TAMBURLAINE. And now themselves shall make our pageant,
    And common soldiers jest with all their trulls.   91
    Let them take pleasure soundly in their spoils,
    Till we prepare our march to Babylon,
    Whither we next make expedition.
TECHELLES. Let us not be idle then, my lord,
    But presently be prest to conquer it.
TAMBURLAINE. We will, Techelles. Forward then, ye jades.
    Now crouch, ye kings of greatest Asia,
    And tremble when ye hear this scourge will come
    That whips down cities and controlleth crowns,   100
    Adding their wealth and treasure to my store.
    The Euxine Sea, north to Natolia;
    The Terrene, west; the Caspian, north-north-east;
    And on the south, Sinus Arabicus
    Shall all be loaden with the martial spoils
    We will convey with us to Persia.
    Then shall my native city Samarcanda,
    And crystal waves of fresh Jaertis stream,
    The pride and beauty of her princely seat,
    Be famous through the furthest continents;   110
    For there my palace royal shall be plac'd,
    Whose shining turrets shall dismay the heavens,
    And cast the fame of Ilion's tower to hell.
    Thorough the streets with troops of conquered kings
    I'll ride in golden armour like the sun,
    And in my helm a triple plume shall spring,
    Spangled with diamonds, dancing in the air,
    To note me emperor of the three-fold world:
    Like to an almond tree y-mounted high
    Upon the lofty and celestial mount   120

[107]

Of ever-green Selinus, quaintly deck'd
With blooms more white than Erycina's brows,
Whose tender blossoms tremble every one
At every little breath that thorough heaven is blown.
Then in my coach, like Saturn's royal son
Mounted his shining chariots gilt with fire,
And drawn with princely eagles through the path
Pav'd with bright crystal and enchas'd with stars
When all the gods stand gazing at his pomp,
So will I ride through Samarcanda streets,   130
Until my soul, dissevered from this flesh,
Shall mount the milk-white way, and meet him there.
To Babylon, my lords, to Babylon!   *Exeunt.*
              Finis Actus Quarti.

              Actus 5. Scaena 1.
    Enter the Governor *of Babylon upon the walls with* [Maximus
    and] *others.*

GOVERNOR. What saith Maximus?
MAXIMUS. My lord, the breach the enemy hath made
    Gives such assurance of our overthrow
    That little hope is left to save our lives,
    Or hold our city from the conqueror's hands.
    Then hang out flags, my lord, of humble truce,
    And satisfy the people's general prayers,
    That Tamburlaine's intolerable wrath
    May be suppress'd by our submission.
GOVERNOR. Villain, respects thou more thy slavish life   10
    Than honour of thy country or thy name?
    Is not my life and state as dear to me,
    The city and my native country's weal,
    As any thing of price with thy conceit?
    Have we not hope, for all our battered walls,
    To live secure and keep his forces out,
    When this our famous lake of Limnasphaltis
    Makes walls afresh with every thing that falls
    Into the liquid substance of his stream,
    More strong than are the gates of death or hell?   20
    What faintness should dismay our courages,
    When we are thus defenc'd against our foe,
    And have no terror but his threat'ning looks?
        Enter another [Citizen], *kneeling to the* Governor.

CITIZEN. My lord, if ever you did deed of ruth,
   And now will work a refuge to our lives,
   Offer submission, hang up flags of truce,
   That Tamburlaine may pity our distress
   And use us like a loving conqueror.
   Though this be held his last day's dreadful siege,
   Wherein he spareth neither man nor child,   30
   Yet are there Christians of Georgia here,
   Whose state he ever pitied and reliev'd,
   Will get his pardon, if your grace would send.
GOVERNOR. How is my soul environed,
   And this eterniz'd city Babylon
   Fill'd with a pack of faint-heart fugitives
   That thus entreat their shame and servitude!
     [*Enter a second* Citizen.]
2 CITIZEN. My lord, if ever you will win our hearts,
   Yield up the town, save our wives and children;
   For I will cast myself from off these walls,   40
   Or die some death of quickest violence,
   Before I bide the wrath of Tamburlaine.
GOVERNOR. Villains, cowards, traitors to our state,
   Fall to the earth, and pierce the pit of hell,
   That legions of tormenting spirits may vex
   Your slavish bosoms with continual pains.
   I care not, nor the town will never yield
   As long as any life is in my breast.
     Enter Theridamas *and* Techelles, *with other* Soldiers.
THERIDAMAS. Thou desperate governor of Babylon,
   To save thy life, and us a little labour,   50
   Yield speedily the city to our hands,
   Or else be sure thou shalt be forc'd with pains
   More exquisite than ever traitor felt.
GOVERNOR. Tyrant, I turn the traitor in thy throat,
   And will defend it in despite of thee.
   Call up the soldiers to defend these walls.
TECHELLES. Yield, foolish governor; we offer more
   Than ever yet we did to such proud slaves
   As durst resist us till our third day's siege.
   Thou seest us prest to give the last assault,   60
   And that shall bide no more regard of parley.
GOVERNOR. Assault and spare not; we will never yield.
     Alarm, and they scale the walls.
   Enter Tamburlaine [*drawn in his chariot by the Kings of*
Trebizon *and* Soria] *with* Usumcasane, Amyras, *and*

Celebinus, *with others; the two spare Kings* [Orcanes *of Natolia and* Jerusalem].

TAMBURLAINE. The stately buildings of fair Babylon,
  Whose lofty pillars, higher than the clouds,
  Were wont to guide the seaman in the deep,
  Being carried thither by the cannon's force
  Now fill the mouth of Limnasphaltis lake,
  And make a bridge unto the battered walls.
  Where Belus, Ninus, and great Alexander
  Have rode in triumph, triumphs Tamburlaine,   70
  Whose chariot wheels have burst th'Assyrians' bones,
  Drawn with these kings on heaps of carcasses.
  Now in the place where fair Semiramis,
  Courted by kings and peers of Asia,
  Hath trod the measures, do my soldiers march;
  And in the streets where brave Assyrian dames
  Have rid in pomp like rich Saturnia
  With furious words and frowning visages
  My horsemen brandish their unruly blades.
    Enter Theridamas *and* Techelles, *bringing the* Governor *of Babylon.*
  Who have ye there, my lord?   80
THERIDAMAS. The sturdy governor of Babylon,
  That made us all the labour for the town,
  And us'd such slender reck'ning of your majesty.
TAMBURLAINE. Go bind the villain. He shall hang in chains
  Upon the ruins of this conquered town.
  Sirrah, the view of our vermilion tents
  Which threat'ned more than if the region
  Next underneath the element of fire
  Were full of comets and of blazing stars,
  Whose flaming trains should reach down to the earth,   90
  Could not affright you; no, nor I myself,
  The wrathful messenger of mighty Jove,
  That with his sword hath quail'd all earthly kings,
  Could not persuade you to submission,
  But still the ports were shut. Villain, I say,
  Should I but touch the rusty gates of hell,
  The triple-headed Cerberus would howl,
  And wake black Jove to crouch and kneel to me;
  But I have sent volleys of shot to you,
  Yet could not enter till the breach was made.   100
GOVERNOR. Nor, if my body could have stopp'd the breach,
  Shouldst thou have ent'red, cruel Tamburlaine.

'Tis not thy bloody tents can make me yield,
Nor yet thyself, the anger of the Highest;
For though thy cannon shook the city walls,
My heart did never quake, or courage faint.
TAMBURLAINE. Well, now I'll make it quake. Go draw him up,
Hang him up in chains upon the city walls,
And let my soldiers shoot the slave to death.
GOVERNOR. Vilde monster, born of some infernal hag,   110
And sent from hell to tyrannize on earth,
Do all thy worst; nor death, nor Tamburlaine,
Torture, or pain, can daunt my dreadless mind.
TAMBURLAINE. Up with him, then! His body shall be scar'd.
GOVERNOR. But, Tamburlaine, in Limnasphaltis lake
There lies more gold than Babylon is worth,
Which when the city was besieg'd, I hid:
Save but my life, and I will give it thee.
TAMBURLAINE. Then, for all your valour, you would save your
life?
Whereabout lies it?   120
GOVERNOR. Under a hollow bank, right opposite
Against the western gate of Babylon.
TAMBURLAINE. Go thither some of you, and take his gold;
                        [Exeunt some Attendants.]
The rest forward with execution.
Away with him hence, let him speak no more.
I think I make your courage something quail.
        [Exeunt Attendants *with the* Governor *of Babylon.]*
When this is done, we'll march from Babylon,
And make our greatest haste to Persia.
These jades are broken winded and half-tir'd;
Unharness them, and let me have fresh horse.   130
So, now their best is done to honour me,
Take them and hang them both up presently.
TREBIZON. Vile tyrant! Barbarous bloody Tamburlaine!
TAMBURLAINE. Take them away, Theridamas; see them des-
patch'd.
THERIDAMAS. I will, my lord.
        [Exit with the Kings *of* Trebizon *and* Soria.]
TAMBURLAINE. Come, Asian viceroys, to your tasks a while,
And take such fortune as your fellows felt.
ORCANES. First let thy Scythian horse tear both our limbs,
Rather than we should draw thy chariot,
And like base slaves abject our princely minds   140
To vile and ignominious servitude.

JERUSALEM. Rather lend me thy weapon, Tamburlaine,
That I may sheathe it in this breast of mine.
A thousand deaths could not torment our hearts
More than the thought of this doth vex our souls.
AMYRAS. They will talk still, my lord, if you do not bridle them.
TAMBURLAINE. Bridle them, and let me to my coach.
                                        They bridle them.
[*The* Governor *of Babylon appears hanging in chains on the walls. Enter* Theridamas.]
AMYRAS. See now, my lord, how brave the captain hangs!
TAMBURLAINE. 'Tis brave indeed, my boy; well done!
    Shoot first my lord, and then the rest shall follow.   150
THERIDAMAS. Then have at him to begin withal.
                                    Theridamas shoots.
GOVERNOR. Yet save my life, and let this wound appease
    The mortal fury of great Tamburlaine.
TAMBURLAINE. No, though Asphaltis lake were liquid gold,
    And offer'd me as ransom for thy life,
    Yet shouldst thou die. Shoot at him all at once.   *They shoot.*
    So, now he hangs like Bagdet's governor,
    Having as many bullets in his flesh
    As there be breaches in her battered wall.
    Go now and bind the burghers hand and foot,   160
    And cast them headlong in the city's lake.
    Tartars and Persians shall inhabit there;
    And to command the city, I will build
    A citadel that all Assyria,
    Which hath been subject to the Persian king,
    Shall pay me tribute for in Babylon.
TECHELLES. What shall be done with their wives and children,
    my lord?
TAMBURLAINE. Techelles, drown them all, man, woman, and
    child;
    Leave not a Babylonian in the town.
TECHELLES. I will about it straight. Come soldiers.   170
                                            Exit.
TAMBURLAINE. Now Casane, where's the Turkish Alcoran,
    And all the heaps of superstitious books
    Found in the temples of that Mahomet
    Whom I have thought a god? They shall be burnt.
USUMCASANE. Here they are, my lord.
TAMBURLAINE. Well said! Let there be a fire presently.
    In vain, I see, men worship Mahomet.
    My sword hath sent millions of Turks to hell,

Slew all his priests, his kinsmen, and his friends,
And yet I live untouch'd by Mahomet.   180
There is a God, full of revenging wrath,
From whom the thunder and the lightning breaks,
Whose scourge I am, and him will I obey.
So, Casane, fling them in the fire.
Now Mahomet, if thou have any power,
Come down thyself and work a miracle.
Thou art not worthy to be worshipped
That suffers flames of fire to burn the writ
Wherein the sum of thy religion rests.
Why send'st thou not a furious whirlwind down,   190
To blow thy Alcoran up to thy throne
Where men report thou sitt'st by God himself,
Or vengeance on the head of Tamburlaine
That shakes his sword against thy majesty,
And spurns the abstracts of thy foolish laws?
Well, soldiers, Mahomet remains in hell;
He cannot hear the voice of Tamburlaine.
Seek out another godhead to adore:
The God that sits in heaven, if any god,
For he is God alone, and none but he.   200
    [*Enter* Techelles.]
TECHELLES. I have fulfill'd your highness' will, my lord.
Thousands of men drown'd in Asphaltis lake,
Have made the water swell above the banks,
And fishes, fed by human carcasses,
Amaz'd, swim up and down upon the waves,
As when they swallow asafoetida,
Which makes them fleet aloft and gasp for air.
TAMBURLAINE. Well then my friendly lords, what now remains,
But that we leave sufficient garrison,
And presently depart to Persia,   210
To triumph after all our victories?
THERIDAMAS. Ay good my lord, let us in haste to Persia;
And let this captain be remov'd the walls
To some high hill about the city here.
TAMBURLAINE. Let it be so; about it, soldiers.
But say, I feel myself distempered suddenly.
TECHELLES. What is it dares distemper Tamburlaine?
TAMBURLAINE. Something, Techelles, but I know not what.
But forth, ye vassals. Whatsoe'er it be,
Sickness or death can never conquer me.   220
                                                Exeunt.

Actus 5. Scaena 2.
Enter Callapine, Amasia, *with drums and trumpets.*

CALLAPINE. King of Amasia, now our mighty host
  Marcheth in Asia Major, where the streams
  Of Euphrates and Tigris swiftly runs;
  And here may we behold great Babylon,
  Circled about with Limnasphaltis lake,
  Where Tamburlaine with all his army lies,
  Which being faint and weary with the siege,
  We may lie ready to encounter him
  Before his host be full from Babylon,
  And so revenge our latest grievous loss,   10
  If God or Mahomet send any aid.
AMASIA. Doubt not, my lord, but we shall conquer him.
  The monster that hath drunk a sea of blood,
  And yet gapes still for more to quench his thirst,
  Our Turkish swords shall headlong send to hell;
  And that vile carcass, drawn by warlike kings,
  The fowls shall eat; for never sepulchre
  Shall grace that base-born tyrant Tamburlaine.
CALLAPINE. When I record my parents' slavish life,
  Their cruel death, mine own captivity,   20
  My viceroys' bondage under Tamburlaine,
  Methinks I could sustain a thousand deaths
  To be reveng'd of all his villainy.
  Ah, sacred Mahomet, thou that hast seen
  Millions of Turks perish by Tamburlaine,
  Kingdoms made waste, brave cities sack'd and burnt,
  And but one host is left to honour thee;
  Aid thy obedient servant Callapine,
  And make him after all these overthrows
  To triumph over cursed Tamburlaine.   30
AMASIA. Fear not my lord; I see great Mahomet,
  Clothed in purple clouds and on his head
  A chaplet brighter than Apollo's crown,
  Marching about the air with armed men,
  To join with you against this Tamburlaine.
  Renowmed general, mighty Callapine,
  Though God himself and holy Mahomet
  Should come in person to resist your power,
  Yet might your mighty host encounter all,
  And pull proud Tamburlaine upon his knees   40

To sue for mercy at your highness' feet.

CALLAPINE. Captain, the force of Tamburlaine is great,
His fortune greater, and the victories
Wherewith he hath so sore dismay'd the world
Are greatest to discourage all our drifts.
Yet, when the pride of Cynthia is at full,
She wanes again; and so shall his, I hope;
For we have here the chief selected men
Of twenty several kingdoms at the least.
Nor ploughman, priest, nor merchant, stays at home;   50
All Turkey is in arms with Callapine;
And never will we sunder camps and arms
Before himself or his be conquered.
This is the time that must eternize me
For conquering the tyrant of the world.
Come soldiers, let us lie in wait for him,
And if we find him absent from his camp,
Or that it be rejoin'd again at full,
Assail it, and be sure of victory.   *Exeunt.*

Actus 5. Scaena 3.
[*Enter*] Theridamas, Techelles, Usumcasane.
THERIDAMAS. Weep, heavens, and vanish into liquid tears.
Fall, stars that govern his nativity,
And summon all the shining lamps of heaven
To cast their bootless fires to the earth,
And shed their feeble influence in the air;
Muffle your beauties with eternal clouds,
For Hell and Darkness pitch their pitchy tents,
And Death, with armies of Cimmerian spirits,
Gives battle 'gainst the heart of Tamburlaine.
Now in defiance of that wonted love   10
Your sacred virtues pour'd upon his throne,
And made his state an honour to the heavens,
These cowards invisibly assail his soul,
And threaten conquest on our sovereign;
But if he die, your glories are disgrac'd,
Earth droops, and says that hell in heaven is plac'd.
TECHELLES. O then, ye powers that sway eternal seats,
And guide this massy substance of the earth,
If you retain desert of holiness,
As your supreme estates instruct our thoughts,   20
Be not inconstant, careless of your fame,
Bear not the burden of your enemies' joys,

Triumphing in his fall whom you advanc'd;
But as his birth, life, health, and majesty
Were strangely blest and governed by heaven,
So honour, heaven, till heaven dissolved be,
His birth, his life, his health, and majesty!

USUMCASANE. Blush, heaven, to lose the honour of thy name,
　To see thy footstool set upon thy head;
　And let no baseness in thy haughty breast　　　　　30
　Sustain a shame of such inexcellence,
　To see the devils mount in angels' thrones,
　And angels dive into the pools of hell.
　And though they think their painful date is out,
　And that their power is puissant as Jove's,
　Which makes them manage arms against thy state,
　Yet make them feel the strength of Tamburlaine,
　Thy instrument and note of majesty,
　Is greater far than they can thus subdue;
　For if he die, thy glory is disgrac'd,　　　　　40
　Earth droops, and says that hell in heaven is plac'd.
　　　[*Enter* Tamburlaine *drawn by captive kings*, Amyras,
　　　Celebinus, Physicians.]

TAMBURLAINE. What daring god torments my body thus,
　And seeks to conquer mighty Tamburlaine?
　Shall sickness prove me now to be a man,
　That have been term'd the terror of the world?
　Techelles and the rest, come, take your swords,
　And threaten him whose hand afflicts my soul.
　Come, let us march against the powers of heaven,
　And set black streamers in the firmament,
　To signify the slaughter of the gods.　　　　　50
　Ah, friends, what shall I do? I cannot stand.
　Come, carry me to war against the gods,
　That thus envy the health of Tamburlaine.

THERIDAMAS. Ah, good my lord, leave these impatient words
　Which add much danger to your malady.

TAMBURLAINE. Why, shall I sit and languish in this pain?
　No, strike the drums, and, in revenge of this,
　Come, let us charge our spears, and pierce his breast
　Whose shoulders bear the axis of the world,
　That if I perish, heaven and earth may fade.　　　　　60
　Theridamas, haste to the court of Jove;
　Will him to send Apollo hither straight
　To cure me, or I'll fetch him down myself.

TECHELLES. Sit still, my gracious lord; this grief will cease,

And cannot last, it is so violent.

TAMBURLAINE. Not last, Techelles? No, for I shall die.
See where my slave, the ugly monster Death,
Shaking and quivering, pale and wan for fear,
Stands aiming at me with his murdering dart,
Who flies away at every glance I give,   70
And when I look away, comes stealing on.
Villain, away, and hie thee to the field.
I and mine army come to load thy bark
With souls of thousand mangled carcasses.
Look where he goes. But see, he comes again,
Because I stay. Techelles, let us march,
And weary Death with bearing souls to hell.

PHYSICIAN. Pleaseth your majesty to drink this potion,
Which will abate the fury of your fit
And cause some milder spirits govern you.   80

TAMBURLAINE. Tell me, what think you of my sickness now?

PHYSICIAN. I view'd your urine, and the hypostasis,
Thick and obscure, doth make your danger great.
Your veins are full of accidental heat,
Whereby the moisture of your blood is dried.
The humidum and calor, which some hold
Is not a parcel of the elements,
But of a substance more divine and pure,
Is almost clean extinguished and spent;
Which, being the cause of life, imports your death.   90
Besides my lord, this day is critical,
Dangerous to those whose crisis is as yours.
Your artiers, which alongst the veins convey
The lively spirits which the heart engenders,
Are parch'd and void of spirit, that the soul,
Wanting those organons by which it moves,
Cannot endure, by argument of art.
Yet if your majesty may escape this day,
No doubt but you shall soon recover all.

TAMBURLAINE. Then will I comfort all my vital parts,   100
And live, in spite of death, above a day.   *Alarm within.*
[*Enter a* Messenger.]

MESSENGER. My lord, young Callapine, that lately fled from
your majesty, hath now gathered a fresh army, and, hearing
your absence in the field, offers to set upon us presently.

TAMBURLAINE. See, my physicians, now, how Jove hath sent
A present medicine to recure my pain.
My looks shall make them fly; and might I follow,

[117]

There should not one of all the villain's power
Live to give offer of another fight.
USUMCASANE. I joy, my lord, your highness is so strong,　110
That can endure so well your royal presence,
Which only will dismay the enemy.
TAMBURLAINE. I know it will, Casane. Draw, you slaves.
In spite of death, I will go show my face.
　　Alarm. Tamburlaine *goes in, and comes out again with all the*
　　rest.
Thus are the villains, cowards, fled for fear,
Like summer's vapours vanish'd by the sun;
And could I but a while pursue the field,
That Callapine should be my slave again.
But I perceive my martial strength is spent;
In vain I strive and rail against those powers　120
That mean t'invest me in a higher throne,
As much too high for this disdainful earth.
Give me a map; then let me see how much
Is left for me to conquer all the world,
That these my boys may finish all my wants.
　　　　　　　　　　　　　　　One brings a map.

Here I began to march towards Persia,
Along Armenia and the Caspian Sea,
And thence unto Bithynia, where I took
The Turk and his great empress prisoners;
Then march'd I into Egypt and Arabia;　130
And here, not far from Alexandria,
Whereas the Terrene and the Red Sea meet,
Being distant less than full a hundred leagues,
I meant to cut a channel to them both,
That men might quickly sail to India.
From thence to Nubia near Borno lake,
And so along the Ethiopian Sea,
Cutting the tropic line of Capricorn,
I conquered all as far as Zanzibar.
Then by the northern part of Africa,　140
I came at last to Graecia, and from thence
To Asia, where I stay against my will;
Which is from Scythia, where I first began,
Backward and forwards near five thousand leagues.
Look here, my boys; see, what a world of ground
Lies westward from the midst of Cancer's line
Unto the rising of this earthly globe,
Whereas the sun, declining from our sight,

Begins the day with our Antipodes.
And shall I die, and this unconquered?   150
Lo, here, my sons, are all the golden mines,
Inestimable drugs and precious stones,
More worth than Asia and the world beside;
And from th'Antarctic Pole eastward behold
As much more land, which never was descried,
Wherein are rocks of pearl that shine as bright
As all the lamps that beautify the sky.
And shall I die, and this unconquered?
Here, lovely boys; what death forbids my life,
That let your lives command in spite of death.   160
AMYRAS. Alas, my lord, how should our bleeding hearts,
Wounded and broken with your highness' grief,
Retain a thought of joy or spark of life?
Your soul gives essence to our wretched subjects,
Whose matter is incorporate in your flesh.
CELEBINUS. Your pains do pierce our souls; no hope survives,
For by your life we entertain our lives.
TAMBURLAINE. But, sons, this subject, not of force enough
To hold the fiery spirit it contains,
Must part, imparting his impressions   170
By equal portions into both your breasts;
My flesh, divided in your precious shapes,
Shall still retain my spirit, though I die,
And live in all your seeds immortally.
Then now remove me, that I may resign
My place and proper title to my son.
First, take my scourge and my imperial crown,
And mount my royal chariot of estate,
That I may see thee crown'd before I die.
Help me, my lords, to make my last remove.   180
THERIDAMAS. A woeful change, my lord, that daunts our
      thoughts
More than the ruin of our proper souls.
TAMBURLAINE. Sit up, my son, let me see how well
Thou wilt become thy father's majesty.   *They crown him.*
AMYRAS. With what a flinty bosom should I joy
The breath of life and burden of my soul,
If not resolv'd into resolved pains,
My body's mortified lineaments
Should exercise the motions of my heart,
Pierc'd with the joy of any dignity!   190
O father, if the unrelenting ears

Of death and hell be shut against my prayers,
And that the spiteful influence of heaven
Deny my soul fruition of her joy,
How should I step or stir my hateful feet
Against the inward powers of my heart,
Leading a life that only strives to die,
And plead in vain unpleasing sovereignty?

TAMBURLAINE. Let not thy love exceed thine honour, son,
  Nor bar thy mind that magnanimity   200
  That nobly must admit necessity.
  Sit up my boy, and with those silken reins
  Bridle the steeled stomachs of those jades.

THERIDAMAS. My lord, you must obey his majesty,
  Since fate commands and proud necessity.

AMYRAS. Heavens witness me with what a broken heart
  And damned spirit I ascend this seat,
  And send my soul, before my father die,
  His anguish and his burning agony.

TAMBURLAINE. Now fetch the hearse of fair Zenocrate;   210
  Let it be plac'd by this my fatal chair,
  And serve as parcel of my funeral.

USUMCASANE. Then feels your majesty no sovereign ease,
  Nor may our hearts, all drown'd in tears of blood,
  Joy any hope of your recovery?

TAMBURLAINE. Casane, no; the monarch of the earth,
  And eyeless monster that torments my soul,
  Cannot behold the tears ye shed for me,
  And therefore still augments his cruelty.

TECHELLES. Then let some god oppose his holy power   220
  Against the wrath and tyranny of Death,
  That his tear-thirsty and unquenched hate
  May be upon himself reverberate.   *They bring in the hearse.*

TAMBURLAINE. Now, eyes, enjoy your latest benefit,
  And when my soul hath virtue of your sight,
  Pierce through the coffin and the sheet of gold,
  And glut your longings with a heaven of joy.
  So, reign my son; scourge and control those slaves,
  Guiding thy chariot with thy father's hand.
  As precious is the charge thou undertak'st   230
  As that which Clymen's brain-sick son did guide,
  When wand'ring Phoebe's ivory cheeks were scorch'd,
  And all the earth, like Etna, breathing fire.
  Be warn'd by him, then; learn with awful eye
  To sway a throne as dangerous as his;

For if thy body thrive not full of thoughts
As pure and fiery as Phyteus' beams,
The nature of these proud rebelling jades
Will take occasion by the slenderest hair,
And draw thee piecemeal like Hippolytus   240
Through rocks more steep and sharp than Caspian cliffs.
The nature of thy chariot will not bear
A guide of baser temper than myself,
More than heaven's coach the pride of Phaeton.
Farewell, my boys! my dearest friends, farewell!
My body feels, my soul doth weep to see
Your sweet desires depriv'd my company,
For Tamburlaine, the scourge of God, must die.   [*Dies.*]
AMYRAS. Meet heaven and earth, and here let all things end,
For earth hath spent the pride of all her fruit,   250
And heaven consum'd his choicest living fire.
Let earth and heaven his timeless death deplore,
For both their worths will equal him no more.   [*Exeunt.*]

FINIS.

BOULEVARD BOOKSTORE
08/13/92   16:29   E   0   3690

CHESS!!!CHESS!!!CHESS!!!
AUGUST 22. 1992 RATED TOURNAMENT

BOULEVARD BOOKSTORE
08/13/92   16:36   E   0   3690
    1 @   9.95 0460870432 $ 9.95
              MARLOWE: COMPLET

SUBTOTAL	$	9.95
SALES TAX @ 7.00%	$	0.70
TOTAL	$	10.65
TENDER Cash	$	20.65
CHANGE	$	10.00

CHESS!!!CHESS!!!CHESS!!!
AUGUST 22. 1992 RATED TOURNAMENT

...RNAMENT

BOULEVARD BOOKSTORE
08/13/92   16:29   E   0   3690

CHESS!!!CHESS!!!CHESS!!!
AUGUST 22, 1992 RATED TOURNAMENT

BOULEVARD BOOKSTORE
08/13/92   16:36   E   0   3690

1 @ 9.95 0460870432	$		9.95

MARLOWE: COMPLET

SUBTOTAL	$	9.95
SALES TAX @ 7.00%	$	0.70
TOTAL	$	10.65
TENDER Cash	$	20.65
CHANGE	$	10.00

CHESS!!!CHESS!!!CHESS!!!
AUGUST 22, 1992 RATED TOURNAMENT

Edward II

Edward II was entered to William Jones in the Stationers' Register on 6 July 1593 as '*The troublesom Reign and Lamentable Death of EDWARD the SECOND, king of England, with the tragicall fall of proud MORTYMER*'. Jones published the first surviving (quarto-form) octavo in 1594, attributing the play to 'Chri. Marlow', and followed it with a reprint in 1598. On 16 December 1611 the copyright was assigned to Roger Barnes, who brought out an edition in 1612, and on 17 April 1617 to Henry Bell, who brought out an edition in 1622.

Marlowe's main source was Holinshed. To this he added the shaving-scene—which, if it comes from Stow's *Annales* (1592), gives a clue to the date of the play. The early title-pages state that the play was performed by Pembroke's Men (in the City of London, according to the first edition), but in the course of printing his edition Bell altered the title-page to read instead the late Queen's Majesty's Servants at the Red Bull. The latter performances would have been in King James's reign.

[DRAMATIS PERSONAE

King Edward II
Prince Edward, his son; later *King Edward III*
Edmund Earl of Kent, the King's brother
Piers de Gaveston
The Earls of
     Warwick
     Lancaster
     Pembroke
     Arundel
     Leicester
     Berkeley
Mortimer the elder
Mortimer the younger, his nephew
Spencer the elder
Spencer the younger, his son
Baldock
The Bishops of
     Coventry
     Canterbury
     Winchester
Beaumont
James, one of Pembroke's men
Levune
Sir John of Hainault
Rice ap Howell
Mayor of Bristol
Trussel
Gurney
Matrevis
Lightborn
Three Poor Men
Herald
Abbot
A Mower
Champion

Isabella, Queen to Edward II
Lady Margaret de Clare, betrothed to Gaveston

 Lords, Ladies, Messengers, Soldiers, Attendants, Monks]

Edward II

Enter Gaveston *reading on a letter that was brought him from
the King.*

GAVESTON. 'My father is deceas'd, come Gaveston,
And share the kingdom with thy dearest friend.'
Ah, words that make me surfeit with delight!
What greater bliss can hap to Gaveston
Than live and be the favourite of a king?
Sweet prince I come; these, these thy amorous lines
Might have enforc'd me to have swum from France,
And like Leander gasp'd upon the sand,
So thou wouldst smile and take me in thy arms.
The sight of London to my exil'd eyes   10
Is as Elysium to a new-come soul.
Not that I love the city or the men,
But that it harbours him I hold so dear,
The king, upon whose bosom let me die,
And with the world be still at enmity.
What need the arctic people love star-light
To whom the sun shines both by day and night?
Farewell base stooping to the lordly peers;
My knee shall bow to none but to the king.
As for the multitude, that are but sparks   20
Rak'd up in embers of their poverty,
Tanti! I'll fawn first on the wind,
That glanceth at my lips and flieth away.
But how now, what are these?
    Enter three Poor Men.
POOR MEN. Such as desire your worship's service.
GAVESTON. What canst thou do?
1 POOR MAN. I can ride.
GAVESTON. But I have no horses. What art thou?
2 POOR MAN. A traveller.
GAVESTON. Let me see, thou wouldst do well to wait at my
    trencher and tell me lies at dinner-time; and as I like your
    discoursing, I'll have you. And what art thou?   32
3 POOR MAN. A soldier, that hath serv'd against the Scot.
GAVESTON. Why, there are hospitals for such as you;

I have no war, and therefore, sir, be gone.

3 POOR MAN. Farewell, and perish by a soldier's hand,
That wouldst reward them with an hospital.

GAVESTON. Ay, ay. These words of his move me as much
As if a goose should play the porpentine,
And dart her plumes, thinking to pierce my breast.   40
But yet it is no pain to speak men fair;
I'll flatter these, and make them live in hope.
You know that I came lately out of France,
And yet I have not view'd my lord the king;
If I speed well, I'll entertain you all.

POOR MEN. We thank your worship.

GAVESTON. I have some business; leave me to myself.

POOR MEN. We will wait here about the court.   *Exeunt.*

GAVESTON. Do. These are not men for me;
I must have wanton poets, pleasant wits,   50
Musicians, that with touching of a string
May draw the pliant king which way I please;
Music and poetry is his delight:
Therefore I'll have Italian masques by night,
Sweet speeches, comedies, and pleasing shows;
And in the day, when he shall walk abroad,
Like sylvan nymphs my pages shall be clad;
My men like satyrs grazing on the lawns
Shall with their goat-feet dance an antic hay;
Sometime a lovely boy in Dian's shape,   60
With hair that gilds the water as it glides,
Crownets of pearl about his naked arms,
And in his sportful hands an olive tree
To hide those parts which men delight to see,
Shall bathe him in a spring; and there hard by,
One like Actaeon peeping through the grove,
Shall by the angry goddess be transform'd,
And running in the likeness of an hart,
By yelping hounds pull'd down, and seem to die.
Such things as these best please his majesty.   70
My lord! Here comes the king and the nobles
From the parliament; I'll stand aside.

Enter the King, Lancaster, Mortimer Senior, Mortimer
Junior, *Edmund Earl of* Kent, *Guy Earl of* Warwick, [*and*
Lords] *etc.*

EDWARD. Lancaster.

LANCASTER. My lord?

GAVESTON. That Earl of Lancaster do I abhor.

EDWARD. Will you not grant me this? [*Aside.*] In spite of them
    I'll have my will, and these two Mortimers
    That cross me thus shall know I am displeas'd.
MORTIMER SENIOR. If you love us, my lord, hate Gaveston.
GAVESTON. That villain Mortimer, I'll be his death.   80
MORTIMER. Mine uncle here, this earl, and I myself,
    Were sworn to your father at his death
    That he should ne'er return into the realm;
    And know, my lord, ere I will break my oath,
    This sword of mine that should offend your foes
    Shall sleep within the scabbard at thy need,
    And underneath thy banners march who will,
    For Mortimer will hang his armour up.
GAVESTON. *Mort Dieu!*
EDWARD. Well, Mortimer, I'll make thee rue these words; 90
    Beseems it thee to contradict thy king?
    Frownst thou thereat, aspiring Lancaster?
    The sword shall plane the furrows of thy brows,
    And hew these knees that now are grown so stiff.
    I will have Gaveston; and you shall know
    What danger 'tis to stand against your king.
GAVESTON. Well done, Ned.
LANCASTER. My lord, why do you thus incense your peers
    That naturally would love and honour you
    But for that base and obscure Gaveston?   100
    Four earldoms have I besides Lancaster—
    Derby, Salisbury, Lincoln, Leicester;
    These will I sell to give my soldiers pay
    Ere Gaveston shall stay within the realm.
    Therefore if he be come, expel him straight.
KENT. Barons and earls, your pride hath made me mute,
    But now I'll speak, and to the proof I hope.
    I do remember in my father's days,
    Lord Percy of the north, being highly mov'd,
    Brav'd Mowbery in presence of the king;   110
    For which, had not his highness lov'd him well,
    He should have lost his head; but with his look
    The undaunted spirit of Percy was appeas'd,
    And Mowbery and he were reconcil'd:
    Yet dare you brave the king unto his face.
    Brother, revenge it; and let these their heads
    Preach upon poles for trespass of their tongues.
WARWICK. O, our heads?
EDWARD. Ay, yours; and therefore I would wish you grant.

WARWICK. Bridle thy anger, gentle Mortimer.   120
MORTIMER. I cannot nor I will not; I must speak.
    Cousin, our hands I hope shall fence our heads,
    And strike off his that makes you threaten us.
    Come uncle, let us leave the brainsick king,
    And henceforth parley with our naked swords.
MORTIMER SENIOR. Wiltshire hath men enough to save our
    heads.
WARWICK. All Warwickshire will love him for my sake.
LANCASTER. And northward Gaveston hath many friends.
    Adieu my lord; and either change your mind,
    Or look to see the throne where you should sit   130
    To float in blood, and at thy wanton head
    The glozing head of thy base minion thrown.
                                Exeunt Nobiles.
EDWARD. I cannot brook these haughty menaces:
    Am I a king and must be overrul'd?
    Brother, display my ensigns in the field;
    I'll bandy with the barons and the earls,
    And either die or live with Gaveston.
GAVESTON. I can no longer keep me from my lord.
EDWARD. What, Gaveston, welcome! Kiss not my hand,
    Embrace me, Gaveston, as I do thee: 140
    Why shouldst thou kneel? Know'st thou not who I am?
    Thy friend, thy self, another Gaveston.
    Not Hylas was more mourn'd of Hercules
    Than thou hast been of me since thy exile.
GAVESTON. And since I went from hence, no soul in hell
    Hath felt more torment than poor Gaveston.
EDWARD. I know it. Brother, welcome home my friend.
    Now let the treacherous Mortimers conspire,
    And that high-minded Earl of Lancaster:
    I have my wish, in that I joy thy sight,   150
    And sooner shall the sea o'erwhelm my land
    Than bear the ship that shall transport thee hence.
    I here create thee Lord High Chamberlain,
    Chief Secretary to the state and me,
    Earl of Cornwall, King and Lord of Man.
GAVESTON. My lord, these titles far exceed my worth.
KENT. Brother, the least of these may well suffice
    For one of greater birth than Gaveston.
EDWARD. Cease, brother, for I cannot brook these words.
    Thy worth, sweet friend, is far above my gifts,   160
    Therefore to equal it, receive my heart.

If for these dignities thou be envied
I'll give thee more, for but to honour thee
Is Edward pleas'd with kingly regiment.
Fear'st thou thy person? Thou shalt have a guard.
Wants thou gold? Go to my treasury.
Wouldst thou be lov'd and fear'd? Receive my seal;
Save or condemn, and in our name command
Whatso thy mind affects or fancy likes.

GAVESTON. It shall suffice me to enjoy your love,   170
Which whiles I have, I think myself as great
As Caesar riding in the Roman street
With captive kings at his triumphant car.
     Enter the Bishop of Coventry.

EDWARD. Whither goes my lord of Coventry so fast?

COVENTRY. To celebrate your father's exequies.
But is that wicked Gaveston return'd?

EDWARD. Ay, priest; and lives to be reveng'd on thee
That wert the only cause of his exile.

GAVESTON. 'Tis true, and but for reverence of these robes
Thou shouldst not plod one foot beyond this place.   180

COVENTRY. I did no more than I was bound to do;
And, Gaveston, unless thou be reclaim'd,
As then I did incense the parliament,
So will I now, and thou shalt back to France.

GAVESTON. Saving your reverence, you must pardon me.

EDWARD. Throw off his golden mitre, rend his stole,
And in the channel christen him anew.

KENT. Ah, brother, lay not violent hands on him,
For he'll complain unto the See of Rome.

GAVESTON. Let him complain unto the See of Hell;   190
I'll be reveng'd on him for my exile.

EDWARD. No, spare his life, but seize upon his goods;
Be thou Lord Bishop and receive his rents,
And make him serve thee as thy chaplain;
I give him thee. Here, use him as thou wilt.

GAVESTON. He shall to prison, and there die in bolts.

EDWARD. Ay, to the Tower, the Fleet, or where thou wilt.

COVENTRY. For this offence be thou accurst of God.

EDWARD. Who's there? Convey this priest to the Tower.

COVENTRY. True, true!   [*Exit guarded.* |

EDWARD. But in the meantime, Gaveston, away
And take possession of his house and goods;
Come, follow me, and thou shalt have my guard
To see it done and bring thee safe again.

GAVESTON. What should a priest do with so fair a house?
  A prison may beseem his holiness.   [*Exeunt.*]

[*Scene ii.*]
Enter both the Mortimers, Warwick *and* Lancaster.
WARWICK. 'Tis true, the Bishop is in the Tower,
  And goods and body given to Gaveston.
LANCASTER. What, will they tyrannize upon the Church?
  Ah, wicked king, accursed Gaveston!
  This ground which is corrupted with their steps
  Shall be their timeless sepulchre, or mine.
MORTIMER. Well, let that peevish Frenchman guard him sure;
  Unless his breast be sword-proof he shall die.
MORTIMER SENIOR. How now, why droops the Earl of Lan-
  caster?
MORTIMER. Wherefore is Guy of Warwick discontent?   10
LANCASTER. That villain Gaveston is made an earl.
MORTIMER SENIOR. An earl!
WARWICK. Ay, and besides, Lord Chamberlain of the realm,
  And Secretary too, and Lord of Man.
MORTIMER SENIOR. We may not nor we will not suffer this.
MORTIMER. Why post we not from hence to levy men?
LANCASTER. 'My lord of Cornwall' now at every word;
  And happy is the man whom he vouchsafes,
  For vailing of his bonnet, one good look.
  Thus arm in arm the king and he doth march—   20
  Nay more, the guard upon his lordship waits,
  And all the court begins to flatter him.
WARWICK. Thus leaning on the shoulder of the king,
  He nods, and scorns, and smiles at those that pass.
MORTIMER SENIOR. Doth no man take exceptions at the slave?
LANCASTER. All stomach him, but none dare speak a word.
MORTIMER. Ah, that bewrays their baseness, Lancaster.
  Were all the earls and barons of my mind,
  We'll hale him from the bosom of the king,
  And at the court gate hang the peasant up,   30
  Who, swoln with venom of ambitious pride,
  Will be the ruin of the realm and us.
  Enter the Bishop of Canterbury [*with* Attendant].
WARWICK. Here comes my lord of Canterbury's grace.
LANCASTER. His countenance bewrays he is displeas'd.
CANTERBURY. First were his sacred garments rent and torn,
  Then laid they violent hands upon him, next
  Himself imprisoned and his goods asseiz'd;

This certify the Pope; away, take horse.   [*Exit* Attendant.]
LANCASTER. My lord, will you take arms against the king?
CANTERBURY. What need I? God himself is up in arms   40
  When violence is offered to the Church.
MORTIMER. Then will you join with us that be his peers
  To banish or behead that Gaveston?
CANTERBURY. What else my lords, for it concerns me near;
  The bishopric of Coventry is his.
    Enter the Queen.
MORTIMER. Madam, whither walks your majesty so fast?
ISABELLA. Unto the forest, gentle Mortimer,
  To live in grief and baleful discontent;
  For now my lord the king regards me not,
  But dotes upon the love of Gaveston.   50
  He claps his cheeks and hangs about his neck,
  Smiles in his face, and whispers in his ears;
  And when I come, he frowns, as who should say,
  'Go whither thou wilt, seeing I have Gaveston.'
MORTIMER SENIOR. Is it not strange that he is thus bewitch'd?
MORTIMER. Madam, return unto the court again:
  That sly inveigling Frenchman we'll exile,
  Or lose our lives; and yet ere that day come,
  The king shall lose his crown—for we have power,
  And courage too, to be reveng'd at full.   60
CANTERBURY. But yet lift not your swords against the king.
LANCASTER. No, but we'll lift Gaveston from hence.
WARWICK. And war must be the means, or he'll stay still.
ISABELLA. Then let him stay; for rather than my lord
  Shall be oppress'd by civil mutinies,
  I will endure a melancholy life,
  And let him frolic with his minion.
CANTERBURY. My lords, to ease all this but hear me speak:
  We and the rest that are his counsellors
  Will meet, and with a general consent   70
  Confirm his banishment with our hands and seals.
LANCASTER. What we confirm the king will frustrate.
MORTIMER. Then may we lawfully revolt from him.
WARWICK. But say, my lord, where shall this meeting be?
CANTERBURY. At the New Temple.
MORTIMER. Content.
CANTERBURY. And in the meantime I'll entreat you all
  To cross to Lambeth, and there stay with me.
LANCASTER. Come then, let's away.
MORTIMER. Madam, farewell.   80

ISABELLA. Farewell, sweet Mortimer; and for my sake
  Forbear to levy arms against the king.
MORTIMER. Ay, if words will serve; if not, I must.   [*Exeunt.*]

[*Scene iii.*]
Enter Gaveston *and the Earl of* Kent.
GAVESTON. Edmund, the mighty prince of Lancaster,
  That hath more earldoms than an ass can bear,
  And both the Mortimers—two goodly men—
  With Guy of Warwick, that redoubted knight,
  Are gone towards Lambeth; there let them remain.

                           Exeunt.

[*Scene iv.*]
Enter Nobiles [Lancaster, Warwick, Pembroke, Mortimer
Senior, Mortimer Junior, *Bishop of* Canterbury].
LANCASTER. Here is the form of Gaveston's exile:
  May it please your lordship to subscribe your name.
CANTERBURY. Give me the paper.
LANCASTER. Quick, quick, my lord; I long to write my name.
WARWICK. But I long more to see him banish'd hence.
MORTIMER. The name of Mortimer shall fright the king
  Unless he be declin'd from that base peasant.
    Enter the King *and* Gaveston [*and* Kent].
EDWARD. What, are you mov'd that Gaveston sits here?
  It is our pleasure; we will have it so.
LANCASTER. Your grace doth well to place him by your side,
  For nowhere else the new earl is so safe.   11
MORTIMER SENIOR. What man of noble birth can brook this
    sight?
Quam male conveniunt!
See what a scornful look the peasant casts.
PEMBROKE. Can kingly lions fawn on creeping ants?
WARWICK. Ignoble vassal that like Phaeton
  Aspir'st unto the guidance of the sun.
MORTIMER. Their downfall is at hand, their forces down;
  We will not thus be fac'd and over-peer'd.
EDWARD. Lay hands on that traitor Mortimer.   20
MORTIMER SENIOR. Lay hands on that traitor Gaveston.
                 [*They draw their swords.*]
KENT. Is this the duty that you owe your king?
WARWICK. We know our duties; let him know his peers.
                 [*They seize* Gaveston.]
EDWARD. Whither will you bear him? Stay, or ye shall die.

MORTIMER SENIOR. We are no traitors, therefore threaten not.

GAVESTON. No, threaten not, my lord, but pay them home.
Were I a king—

MORTIMER. Thou villain, wherefore talks thou of a king,
That hardly art a gentleman by birth?

EDWARD. Were he a peasant, being my minion,   30
I'll make the proudest of you stoop to him.

LANCASTER. My lord, you may not thus disparage us.
Away I say with hateful Gaveston.

MORTIMER SENIOR. And with the Earl of Kent that favours him.
                   [*Exeunt* Kent *and* Gaveston, *guarded.*]

EDWARD. Nay, then lay violent hands upon your king.
Here, Mortimer, sit thou in Edward's throne;
Warwick and Lancaster, wear you my crown.
Was ever king thus overrul'd as I?

LANCASTER. Learn then to rule us better, and the realm.

MORTIMER. What we have done, our heart-blood shall maintain.   40

WARWICK. Think you that we can brook this upstart pride?

EDWARD. Anger and wrathful fury stops my speech.

CANTERBURY. Why are you mov'd? Be patient, my lord,
And see what we your counsellors have done.

MORTIMER. My lords, now let us all be resolute,
And either have our wills or lose our lives.

EDWARD. Meet you for this, proud over-daring peers?
Ere my sweet Gaveston shall part from me,
This isle shall fleet upon the ocean
And wander to the unfrequented Inde.   50

CANTERBURY. You know that I am legate to the Pope;
On your allegiance to the See of Rome
Subscribe, as we have done, to his exile.

MORTIMER. Curse him if he refuse; and then may we
Depose him, and elect another king.

EDWARD. Ay, there it goes; but yet I will not yield.
Curse me; depose me; do the worst you can.

LANCASTER. Then linger not, my lord, but do it straight.

CANTERBURY. Remember how the Bishop was abus'd.
Either banish him that was the cause thereof,   60
Or I will presently discharge these lords
Of duty and allegiance due to thee.

EDWARD. It boots me not to threat; I must speak fair.
The legate of the Pope will be obey'd.
My lord, you shall be Chancellor of the realm;
Thou, Lancaster, High Admiral of our fleet;

Young Mortimer and his uncle shall be earls,
And you, Lord Warwick, President of the North,
And thou of Wales. If this content you not,
Make several kingdoms of this monarchy   70
And share it equally amongst you all,
So I may have some nook or corner left
To frolic with my dearest Gaveston.
CANTERBURY. Nothing shall alter us; we are resolv'd.
LANCASTER. Come, come, subscribe.
MORTIMER. Why should you love him whom the world hates so?
EDWARD. Because he loves me more than all the world.
    Ah, none but rude and savage-minded men
    Would seek the ruin of my Gaveston;
    You that be noble born should pity him.   80
WARWICK. You that are princely born should shake him off.
    For shame subscribe, and let the lown depart.
MORTIMER SENIOR. Urge him, my lord.
CANTERBURY. Are you content to banish him the realm?
EDWARD. I see I must, and therefore am content;
    Instead of ink I'll write it with my tears.
MORTIMER. The king is love-sick for his minion.
EDWARD. 'Tis done; and now accursed hand fall off.
LANCASTER. Give it me; I'll have it publish'd in the streets.
MORTIMER. I'll see him presently dispatch'd away.   90
CANTERBURY. Now is my heart at ease.
WARWICK.   And so is mine.
PEMBROKE. This will be good news to the common sort.
MORTIMER SENIOR. Be it or no, he shall not linger here.
                                    Exeunt Nobiles.
EDWARD. How fast they run to banish him I love;
    They would not stir, were it to do me good.
    Why should a king be subject to a priest?
    Proud Rome, that hatchest such imperial grooms,
    For these thy superstitious taper-lights
    Wherewith thy antichristian churches blaze,
    I'll fire thy crazed buildings, and enforce   100
    The papal towers to kiss the lowly ground;
    With slaughtered priests make Tiber's channel swell,
    And banks rais'd higher with their sepulchres.
    As for the peers that back the clergy thus,
    If I be king, not one of them shall live.
    Enter Gaveston.
GAVESTON. My lord, I hear it whispered everywhere
    That I am banish'd and must fly the land.

[134]

EDWARD. 'Tis true, sweet Gaveston—O were it false!
  The legate of the Pope will have it so,
  And thou must hence or I shall be depos'd.   110
  But I will reign to be reveng'd of them,
  And therefore, sweet friend, take it patiently.
  Live where thou wilt—I'll send thee gold enough;
  And long thou shalt not stay; or if thou dost
  I'll come to thee; my love shall ne'er decline.
GAVESTON. Is all my hope turn'd to this hell of grief?
EDWARD. Rend not my heart with thy too-piercing words.
  Thou from this land, I from my self am banish'd.
GAVESTON. To go from hence grieves not poor Gaveston,
  But to forsake you, in whose gracious looks   120
  The blessedness of Gaveston remains,
  For nowhere else seeks he felicity.
EDWARD. And only this torments my wretched soul,
  That whether I will or no thou must depart.
  Be Governor of Ireland in my stead,
  And there abide till fortune call thee home.
  Here, take my picture, and let me wear thine.
  O might I keep thee here, as I do this,
  Happy were I, but now most miserable.
GAVESTON. 'Tis something to be pitied of a king.   130
EDWARD. Thou shalt not hence; I'll hide thee, Gaveston.
GAVESTON. I shall be found, and then 'twill grieve me more.
EDWARD. Kind words and mutual talk makes our grief greater,
  Therefore with dumb embracement let us part.
  Stay, Gaveston—I cannot leave thee thus.
GAVESTON. For every look, my lord, drops down a tear.
  Seeing I must go, do not renew my sorrow.
EDWARD. The time is little that thou hast to stay,
  And therefore give me leave to look my fill.
  But come sweet friend, I'll bear thee on thy way.   140
GAVESTON. The peers will frown.
EDWARD. I pass not for their anger; come, let's go.
  O that we might as well return as go.
    Enter Queen Isabella.
ISABELLA. Whither goes my lord?
EDWARD. Fawn not on me, French strumpet; get thee gone.
ISABELLA. On whom but on my husband should I fawn?
GAVESTON. On Mortimer; with whom, ungentle queen—
  I say no more: judge you the rest, my lord.
ISABELLA. In saying this, thou wrongst me, Gaveston.
  Is't not enough that thou corrupts my lord,   150

And art a bawd to his affections,
But thou must call mine honour thus in question?
GAVESTON. I mean not so; your grace must pardon me.
EDWARD. Thou art too familiar with that Mortimer,
And by thy means is Gaveston exil'd;
But I would wish thee reconcile the lords,
Or thou shalt ne'er be reconcil'd to me.
ISABELLA. Your highness knows it lies not in my power.
EDWARD. Away then, touch me not; come, Gaveston.
ISABELLA. Villain, 'tis thou that robb'st me of my lord.   160
GAVESTON. Madam, 'tis you that rob me of my lord.
EDWARD. Speak not unto her, let her droop and pine.
ISABELLA. Wherein, my lord, have I deserv'd these words?
Witness the tears that Isabella sheds,
Witness this heart, that sighing for thee breaks,
How dear my lord is to poor Isabel.
EDWARD. And witness heaven how dear thou art to me.
There weep; for till my Gaveston be repeal'd,
Assure thyself, thou com'st not in my sight.

Exeunt Edward *and* Gaveston.

ISABELLA. O miserable and distressed queen!   170
Would when I left sweet France and was embark'd,
That charming Circes walking on the waves
Had chang'd my shape; or at the marriage-day
The cup of Hymen had been full of poison;
Or with those arms that twin'd about my neck
I had been stifl'd, and not liv'd to see
The king my lord thus to abandon me.
Like frantic Juno will I fill the earth
With ghastly murmur of my sighs and cries;
For never doted Jove on Ganymede   180
So much as he on cursed Gaveston.
But that will more exasperate his wrath;
I must entreat him, I must speak him fair,
And be a means to call home Gaveston;
And yet he'll ever dote on Gaveston,
And so am I for ever miserable.
Enter the Nobles to the Queen.
LANCASTER. Look where the sister of the King of France
Sits wringing of her hands and beats her breast.
WARWICK. The king I fear hath ill intreated her.
PEMBROKE. Hard is the heart that injures such a saint.   190
MORTIMER. I know 'tis 'long of Gaveston she weeps.
MORTIMER SENIOR. Why? He is gone.

MORTIMER.   Madam, how fares your grace?

ISABELLA. Ah, Mortimer, now breaks the king's hate forth,
And he confesseth that he loves me not.

MORTIMER. Cry quittance, madam, then; and love not him.

ISABELLA. No, rather will I die a thousand deaths;
And yet I love in vain, he'll ne'er love me.

LANCASTER. Fear ye not, madam; now his minion's gone
His wanton humour will be quickly left.

ISABELLA. O never, Lancaster. I am enjoin'd   200
To sue unto you all for his repeal:
This wills my lord, and this must I perform,
Or else be banish'd from his highness' presence.

LANCASTER. For his repeal? Madam, he comes not back
Unless the sea cast up his shipwrack body.

WARWICK. And to behold so sweet a sight as that
There's none here but would run his horse to death.

MORTIMER. But, madam, would you have us call him home?

ISABELLA. Ay, Mortimer, for till he be restor'd
The angry king hath banish'd me the court;   210
And therefore, as thou lov'st and tend'rest me,
Be thou my advocate unto these peers.

MORTIMER. What, would ye have me plead for Gaveston?

MORTIMER SENIOR. Plead for him he that will; I am resolv'd.

LANCASTER. And so am I my lord; dissuade the queen.

ISABELLA. O Lancaster, let him dissuade the king,
For 'tis against my will he should return.

WARWICK. Then speak not for him; let the peasant go.

ISABELLA. 'Tis for myself I speak, and not for him.

PEMBROKE. No speaking will prevail, and therefore cease. 220

MORTIMER. Fair queen, forbear to angle for the fish
Which, being caught, strikes him that takes it dead—
I mean that vile torpedo, Gaveston,
That now, I hope, floats on the Irish seas.

ISABELLA. Sweet Mortimer, sit down by me a while,
And I will tell thee reasons of such weight
As thou wilt soon subscribe to his repeal.

MORTIMER. It is impossible; but speak your mind.

ISABELLA. Then thus—but none shall hear it but ourselves.

LANCASTER. My lords, albeit the queen win Mortimer, 230
Will you be resolute and hold with me?

MORTIMER SENIOR. Not I against my nephew.

PEMBROKE. Fear not, the queen's words cannot alter him.

WARWICK. No? Do but mark how earnestly she pleads.

LANCASTER. And see how coldly his looks make denial.

WARWICK. She smiles; now for my life his mind is chang'd.

LANCASTER. I'll rather lose his friendship, I, than grant.

MORTIMER. Well, of necessity it must be so.

  My lords, that I abhor base Gaveston

  I hope your honours make no question;   240

  And therefore though I plead for his repeal,

  'Tis not for his sake, but for our avail—

  Nay, for the realm's behoof and for the king's.

LANCASTER. Fie Mortimer, dishonour not thyself.

  Can this be true, 'twas good to banish him?

  And is this true, to call him home again?

  Such reasons make white black, and dark night day.

MORTIMER. My lord of Lancaster, mark the respect.

LANCASTER. In no respect can contraries be true.

ISABELLA. Yet, good my lord, hear what he can allege.   250

WARWICK. All that he speaks is nothing. We are resolv'd.

MORTIMER. Do you not wish that Gaveston were dead?

PEMBROKE. I would he were.

MORTIMER. Why then, my lord, give me but leave to speak.

MORTIMER SENIOR. But, nephew, do not play the sophister.

MORTIMER. This which I urge is of a burning zeal

  To mend the king and do our country good.

  Know you not Gaveston hath store of gold

  Which may in Ireland purchase him such friends

  As he will front the mightiest of us all?   260

  And whereas he shall live and be belov'd,

  'Tis hard for us to work his overthrow.

WARWICK. Mark you but that, my lord of Lancaster?

MORTIMER. But were he here, detested as he is,

  How easily might some base slave be suborn'd

  To greet his lordship with a poniard;

  And none so much as blame the murderer,

  But rather praise him for that brave attempt,

  And in the chronicle enrol his name

  For purging of the realm of such a plague.   270

PEMBROKE. He saith true.

LANCASTER. Ay, but how chance this was not done before?

MORTIMER. Because, my lords, it was not thought upon.

  Nay more—when he shall know it lies in us

  To banish him, and then to call him home,

  'Twill make him vail the topflag of his pride,

  And fear to offend the meanest nobleman.

MORTIMER SENIOR. But how if he do not, nephew?

MORTIMER. Then may we with some colour rise in arms.

For howsoever we have borne it out,   280
'Tis treason to be up against the king;
So shall we have the people of our side,
Which for his father's sake lean to the king,
But cannot brook a night-grown mushrump,
Such a one as my lord of Cornwall is,
Should bear us down of the nobility;
And when the commons and the nobles join,
'Tis not the king can buckler Gaveston;
We'll pull him from the strongest hold he hath.
My lords, if to perform this I be slack,   290
Think me as base a groom as Gaveston.
LANCASTER. On that condition Lancaster will grant.
PEMBROKE. And so will Pembroke.
WARWICK.   And I.
MORTIMER SENIOR.   And I.
MORTIMER. In this I count me highly gratified,
And Mortimer will rest at your command.
ISABELLA. And when this favour Isabel forgets,
Then let her live abandon'd and forlorn.
But see, in happy time, my lord the king,
Having brought the Earl of Cornwall on his way,
Is new return'd; this news will glad him much,   300
Yet not so much as me; I love him more
Than he can Gaveston—would he lov'd me
But half so much, then were I treble blest.
        Enter King Edward *mourning* [*attended by* Beaumont].
EDWARD. He's gone, and for his absence thus I mourn.
Did never sorrow go so near my heart
As doth the want of my sweet Gaveston;
And could my crown's revenue bring him back
I would freely give it to his enemies,
And think I gain'd, having bought so dear a friend.
ISABELLA. Hark how he harps upon his minion.   310
EDWARD. My heart is as an anvil unto sorrow,
Which beats upon it like the Cyclops' hammers,
And with the noise turns up my giddy brain,
And makes me frantic for my Gaveston;
Ah, had some bloodless Fury rose from hell,
And with my kingly sceptre struck me dead,
When I was forc'd to leave my Gaveston!
LANCASTER. *Diablo!* What passions call you these?
ISABELLA. My gracious lord, I come to bring you news.
EDWARD. That you have parled with your Mortimer.   320

[139]

ISABELLA. That Gaveston, my lord, shall be repeal'd.

EDWARD. Repeal'd? The news is too sweet to be true.

ISABELLA. But will you love me, if you find it so?

EDWARD. If it be so, what will not Edward do?

ISABELLA. For Gaveston, but not for Isabel.

EDWARD. For thee, fair queen, if thou lov'st Gaveston;
  I'll hang a golden tongue about thy neck,
  Seeing thou hast pleaded with so good success.

ISABELLA. No other jewels hang about my neck
  Than these, my lord, nor let me have more wealth   330
  Than I may fetch from this rich treasury.
  O how a kiss revives poor Isabel.

EDWARD. Once more receive my hand; and let this be
  A second marriage 'twixt thyself and me.

ISABELLA. And may it prove more happy than the first.
  My gentle lord, bespeak these nobles fair
  That wait attendance for a gracious look,
  And on their knees salute your majesty.

EDWARD. Courageous Lancaster, embrace thy king,
  And as gross vapours perish by the sun,   340
  Even so let hatred with thy sovereign's smile:
  Live thou with me as my companion.

LANCASTER. This salutation overjoys my heart.

EDWARD. Warwick shall be my chiefest counsellor:
  These silver hairs will more adorn my court,
  Than gaudy silks or rich embroidery.
  Chide me, sweet Warwick, if I go astray.

WARWICK. Slay me, my lord, when I offend your grace.

EDWARD. In solemn triumphs and in public shows
  Pembroke shall bear the sword before the king.   350

PEMBROKE. And with this sword Pembroke will fight for you.

EDWARD. But wherefore walks young Mortimer aside?
  Be thou commander of our royal fleet,
  Or if that lofty office like thee not,
  I make thee here Lord Marshal of the realm.

MORTIMER. My lord, I'll marshal so your enemies
  As England shall be quiet and you safe.

EDWARD. And as for you, lord Mortimer of Chirk,
  Whose great achievements in our foreign war
  Deserves no common place nor mean reward,   360
  Be you the general of the levied troops
  That now are ready to assail the Scots.

MORTIMER SENIOR. In this your grace hath highly honoured me,
  For with my nature war doth best agree.

ISABELLA. Now is the King of England rich and strong,
  Having the love of his renowned peers.
EDWARD. Ay, Isabel, ne'er was my heart so light.
  Clerk of the crown, direct our warrant forth
  For Gaveston to Ireland; Beaumont, fly,
  As fast as Iris, or Jove's Mercury.   370
BEAUMONT. It shall be done, my gracious lord.   [*Exit.*]
EDWARD. Lord Mortimer, we leave you to your charge.
  Now let us in and feast it royally.
  Against our friend the Earl of Cornwall comes
  We'll have a general tilt and tournament,
  And then his marriage shall be solemniz'd;
  For wot you not that I have made him sure
  Unto our cousin, the Earl of Gloucester's heir?
LANCASTER. Such news we hear, my lord.
EDWARD. That day, if not for him, yet for my sake,   380
  Who in the triumph will be challenger,
  Spare for no cost; we will requite your love.
WARWICK. In this, or aught, your highness shall command us.
EDWARD. Thanks gentle Warwick. Come, let's in and revel.
                    Exeunt. Manent Mortimers.
MORTIMER SENIOR. Nephew, I must to Scotland; thou stay'st
      here.
  Leave now to oppose thyself against the king.
  Thou seest by nature he is mild and calm,
  And seeing his mind so dotes on Gaveston,
  Let him without controlment have his will.
  The mightiest kings have had their minions: 390
  Great Alexander lov'd Hephaestion;
  The conquering Hercules for Hylas wept;
  And for Patroclus stern Achilles droop'd;
  And not kings only, but the wisest men.
  The Roman Tully lov'd Octavius;
  Great Socrates, wild Alcibiades.
  Then let his grace, whose youth is flexible,
  And promiseth as much as we can wish,
  Freely enjoy that vain light-headed earl,
  For riper years will wean him from such toys.   400
MORTIMER. Uncle, his wanton humour grieves not me,
  But this I scorn, that one so basely born
  Should by his sovereign's favour grow so pert,
  And riot it with the treasure of the realm
  While soldiers mutiny for want of pay.
  He wears a lord's revenue on his back,

And Midas-like he jets it in the court
With base outlandish cullions at his heels,
Whose proud fantastic liveries make such show
As if that Proteus, god of shapes, appear'd.   410
I have not seen a dapper jack so brisk;
He wears a short Italian hooded cloak
Larded with pearl; and in his Tuscan cap
A jewel of more value than the crown.
Whiles other walk below, the king and he
From out a window laugh at such as we,
And flout our train, and jest at our attire.
Uncle, 'tis this that makes me impatient.
MORTIMER SENIOR. But nephew, now you see the king is
    chang'd.
MORTIMER. Then so am I, and live to do him service: 420
But whiles I have a sword, a hand, a heart,
I will not yield to any such upstart.
You know my mind; come, uncle, let's away.   *Exeunt*

[*Act II. Scene i.*]
  Enter Spencer *and* Baldock.
BALDOCK. Spencer,
  Seeing that our lord th'Earl of Gloucester's dead,
  Which of the nobles dost thou mean to serve?
SPENCER. Not Mortimer, nor any of his side,
  Because the king and he are enemies.
  Baldock, learn this of me: a factious lord
  Shall hardly do himself good, much less us;
  But he that hath the favour of a king
  May with one word advance us while we live.
  The liberal Earl of Cornwall is the man   10
  On whose good fortune Spencer's hope depends.
BALDOCK. What, mean you then to be his follower?
SPENCER. No, his companion, for he loves me well,
  And would have once preferr'd me to the king.
BALDOCK. But he is banish'd; there's small hope of him.
SPENCER. Ay, for a while; but, Baldock, mark the end:
  A friend of mine told me in secrecy
  That he's repeal'd, and sent for back again;
  And even now, a post came from the court
  With letters to our lady from the king,   20
  And as she read, she smil'd; which makes me think
  It is about her lover, Gaveston.

BALDOCK. 'Tis like enough, for since he was exil'd
    She neither walks abroad, nor comes in sight.
    But I had thought the match had been broke off,
    And that his banishment had chang'd her mind.
SPENCER. Our lady's first love is not wavering:
    My life for thine, she will have Gaveston.
BALDOCK. Then hope I by her means to be preferr'd,
    Having read unto her since she was a child.   30
SPENCER. Then, Baldock, you must cast the scholar off,
    And learn to court it like a gentleman.
    'Tis not a black coat and a little band,
    A velvet-cap'd cloak, fac'd before with serge,
    And smelling to a nosegay all the day,
    Or holding of a napkin in your hand,
    Or saying a long grace at a table's end,
    Or making low legs to a nobleman,
    Or looking downward, with your eyelids close,
    And saying 'truly, an't may please your honour',   40
    Can get you any favour with great men.
    You must be proud, bold, pleasant, resolute—
    And now and then, stab as occasion serves.
BALDOCK. Spencer, thou knowest I hate such formal toys,
    And use them but of mere hypocrisy.
    Mine old lord, whiles he liv'd, was so precise
    That he would take exceptions at my buttons,
    And, being like pins' heads, blame me for the bigness,
    Which made me curate-like in mine attire,
    Though inwardly licentious enough   50
    And apt for any kind of villainy.
    I am none of these common pedants, I,
    That cannot speak without '*propterea quod*'.
SPENCER. But one of those that saith '*quandoquidem*',
    And hath a special gift to form a verb.
BALDOCK. Leave off this jesting—here my lady comes.
    Enter the Lady [Margaret de Clare].
LADY MARGARET. The grief for his exile was not so much
    As is the joy of his returning home.
    This letter came from my sweet Gaveston.
    What needst thou, love, thus to excuse thyself?   60
    I know thou couldst not come and visit me.
    'I will not long be from thee, though I die':
    This argues the entire love of my lord;
    'When I forsake thee, death seize on my heart'.
    But rest thee here where Gaveston shall sleep.

Now to the letter of my lord the king.
He wills me to repair unto the court,
And meet my Gaveston; why do I stay,
Seeing that he talks thus of my marriage-day?
Who's there? Baldock? 70
See that my coach be ready, I must hence.
BALDOCK. It shall be done, madam. *Exit.*
LADY MARGARET. And meet me at the park pale presently.
Spencer, stay you and bear me company,
For I have joyful news to tell thee of:
My lord of Cornwall is a-coming over,
And will be at the court as soon as we.
SPENCER. I knew the king would have him home again.
LADY MARGARET. If all things sort out, as I hope they will,
Thy service, Spencer, shall be thought upon. 80
SPENCER. I humbly thank your ladyship.
LADY MARGARET. Come lead the way; I long till I am there.
[*Exeunt.*]

[*Scene ii.*]
Enter Edward, *the* Queen, Lancaster, Mortimer, Warwick,
Pembroke, Kent, Attendants.
EDWARD. The wind is good, I wonder why he stays.
I fear me he is wrack'd upon the sea.
ISABELLA. Look, Lancaster, how passionate he is,
And still his mind runs on his minion.
LANCASTER. My lord——
EDWARD. How now, what news? Is Gaveston arriv'd?
MORTIMER. Nothing but Gaveston! What means your grace?
You have matters of more weight to think upon;
The King of France sets foot in Normandy.
EDWARD. A trifle; we'll expel him when we please. 10
But tell me Mortimer, what's thy device
Against the stately triumph we decreed?
MORTIMER. A homely one, my lord, not worth the telling.
EDWARD. Prithee let me know it.
MORTIMER. But seeing you are so desirous, thus it is:
A lofty cedar tree fair flourishing,
On whose top branches kingly eagles perch,
And by the bark a canker creeps me up,
And gets unto the highest bough of all:
The motto: *Aeque tandem.* 20
EDWARD. And what is yours, my lord of Lancaster?
LANCASTER. My lord, mine's more obscure than Mortimer's.

Pliny reports, there is a flying fish
Which all the other fishes deadly hate,
And therefore being pursu'd, it takes the air;
No sooner is it up, but there's a fowl
That seizeth it: this fish, my lord, I bear;
The motto this: *Undique mors est.*

EDWARD. Proud Mortimer! Ungentle Lancaster!   30
Is this the love you bear your sovereign?
Is this the fruit your reconcilement bears?
Can you in words make show of amity,
And in your shields display your rancorous minds?
What call you this but private libelling
Against the Earl of Cornwall and my brother?

ISABELLA. Sweet husband, be content, they all love you.

EDWARD. They love me not that hate my Gaveston.
I am that cedar; shake me not too much.
And you the eagles; soar ye ne'er so high,
I have the jesses that will pull you down,   40
And *Aeque tandem* shall that canker cry
Unto the proudest peer of Britainy.
Though thou compar'st him to a flying fish,
And threat'nest death whether he rise or fall,
'Tis not the hugest monster of the sea
Nor foulest harpy that shall swallow him.

MORTIMER. If in his absence thus he favours him,
What will he do whenas he shall be present?

LANCASTER. That shall we see; look where his lordship comes.
     Enter Gaveston.

EDWARD. My Gaveston!   50
Welcome to Tynemouth, welcome to thy friend!
Thy absence made me droop and pine away,
For as the lovers of fair Danae,
When she was lock'd up in a brazen tower,
Desir'd her more, and wax'd outrageous,
So did it fare with me; and now thy sight
Is sweeter far than was thy parting hence
Bitter and irksome to my sobbing heart.

GAVESTON. Sweet lord and king, your speech preventeth mine,
Yet have I words left to express my joy: 60
The shepherd nipp'd with biting winter's rage
Frolics not more to see the painted spring
Than I do to behold your majesty.

EDWARD. Will none of you salute my Gaveston?

LANCASTER. Salute him? Yes: welcome Lord Chamberlain.

MORTIMER. Welcome is the good Earl of Cornwall.

WARWICK. Welcome Lord Governor of the Isle of Man.

PEMBROKE. Welcome Master Secretary.

KENT. Brother, do you hear them?

EDWARD. Still will these earls and barons use me thus?　70

GAVESTON. My lord, I cannot brook these injuries.

ISABELLA. Ay me, poor soul, when these begin to jar.

EDWARD. Return it to their throats; I'll be thy warrant.

GAVESTON. Base leaden earls that glory in your birth,
　Go sit at home and eat your tenants' beef,
　And come not here to scoff at Gaveston,
　Whose mounting thoughts did never creep so low
　As to bestow a look on such as you.

LANCASTER. Yet I disdain not to do this for you.
　　　　　　　　　　　　　　　　[Draws his sword.]

EDWARD. Treason, treason! Where's the traitor?　80

PEMBROKE. Here, here!

EDWARD. Convey hence Gaveston; they'll murder him.

GAVESTON. The life of thee shall salve this foul disgrace.

MORTIMER. Villain, thy life, unless I miss mine aim.
　　　　　　　　　　　　　　　　[Wounds Gaveston.]

ISABELLA. Ah, furious Mortimer, what hast thou done?

MORTIMER. No more than I would answer were he slain.
　　　　　　　　　　　[Exit Gaveston with Attendants.]

EDWARD. Yes, more than thou canst answer, though he live;
　Dear shall you both aby this riotous deed.
　Out of my presence! Come not near the court.

MORTIMER. I'll not be barr'd the court for Gaveston.　90

LANCASTER. We'll hale him by the ears unto the block.

EDWARD. Look to your own heads; his is sure enough.

WARWICK. Look to your own crown, if you back him thus.

KENT. Warwick, these words do ill beseem thy years.

EDWARD. Nay, all of them conspire to cross me thus;
　But if I live, I'll tread upon their heads
　That think with high looks thus to tread me down.
　Come Edmund let's away and levy men;
　'Tis war that must abate these barons' pride.
　　　　　　　　　　Exit the King [*with* Queen *and* Kent].

WARWICK. Let's to our castles, for the king is mov'd.　100

MORTIMER. Mov'd may he be, and perish in his wrath.

LANCASTER. Cousin, it is no dealing with him now;
　He means to make us stoop by force of arms,
　And therefore let us jointly here protest
　To prosecute that Gaveston to the death.

MORTIMER. By heaven, the abject villain shall not live.
WARWICK. I'll have his blood, or die in seeking it.
PEMBROKE. The like oath Pembroke takes.
LANCASTER. And so doth Lancaster.
  Now send our heralds to defy the king,   110
  And make the people swear to put him down.
    Enter a Post.
MORTIMER. Letters? From whence?
POST. From Scotland, my lord.
LANCASTER. Why how now, cousin, how fares all our friends?
MORTIMER [*reading letter*]. My uncle's taken prisoner by the
  Scots.
LANCASTER. We'll have him ransom'd, man; be of good cheer.
MORTIMER. They rate his ransom at five thousand pound.
  Who should defray the money but the king,
  Seeing he is taken prisoner in his wars?
  I'll to the king.   120
LANCASTER. Do cousin, and I'll bear thee company.
WARWICK. Meantime my lord of Pembroke and myself
  Will to Newcastle here, and gather head.
MORTIMER. About it then, and we will follow you.
LANCASTER. Be resolute and full of secrecy.
WARWICK. I warrant you.
        [*Exeunt. Manent* Mortimer *and* Lancaster.]
MORTIMER. Cousin, and if he will not ransom him,
  I'll thunder such a peal into his ears
  As never subject did unto his king.
LANCASTER. Content, I'll bear my part. Holla, who's there?
  [*Enter* Guard.]
MORTIMER. Ay, marry, such a guard as this doth well.
LANCASTER. Lead on the way.
GUARD. Whither will your lordships?
MORTIMER. Whither else but to the king?
GUARD. His highness is dispos'd to be alone.
LANCASTER. Why, so he may, but we will speak to him.
GUARD. You may not in, my lord.
MORTIMER. May we not?
  [*Enter* Edward *and* Kent.]
EDWARD. How now, what noise is this? Who have we there?
  Is't you?
MORTIMER. Nay, stay my lord, I come to bring you news; 140
  Mine uncle's taken prisoner by the Scots.
EDWARD. Then ransom him.
LANCASTER. 'Twas in your wars, you should ransom him.

MORTIMER. And you shall ransom him, or else——
KENT. What, Mortimer, you will not threaten him?
EDWARD. Quiet yourself; you shall have the broad seal
   To gather for him thoroughout the realm.
LANCASTER. Your minion Gaveston hath taught you this.
MORTIMER. My lord, the family of the Mortimers
   Are not so poor but, would they sell their land,   150
   Would levy men enough to anger you.
   We never beg, but use such prayers as these.
                     [*Lays hold of his sword.*]
EDWARD. Shall I still be haunted thus?
MORTIMER. Nay, now you are here alone, I'll speak my mind.
LANCASTER. And so will I, and then, my lord, farewell.
MORTIMER. The idle triumphs, masques, lascivious shows
   And prodigal gifts bestow'd on Gaveston,
   Have drawn thy treasure dry, and made thee weak,
   The murmuring commons overstretched hath.
LANCASTER. Look for rebellion, look to be depos'd: 160
   Thy garrisons are beaten out of France,
   And lame and poor lie groaning at the gates;
   The wild O'Neill, with swarms of Irish kerns,
   Lives uncontroll'd within the English Pale;
   Unto the walls of York the Scots made road,
   And unresisted drave away rich spoils.
MORTIMER. The haughty Dane commands the narrow seas,
   While in the harbour ride thy ships unrigg'd.
LANCASTER. What foreign prince sends thee ambassadors?
MORTIMER. Who loves thee but a sort of flatterers?   170
LANCASTER. Thy gentle queen, sole sister to Valois,
   Complains that thou hast left her all forlorn.
MORTIMER. Thy court is naked, being bereft of those
   That makes a king seem glorious to the world—
   I mean the peers, whom thou shouldst dearly love;
   Libels are cast against thee in the streets,
   Ballads and rhymes made of thy overthrow.
LANCASTER. The Northren borderers, seeing their houses burnt,
   Their wives and children slain, run up and down
   Cursing the name of thee and Gaveston.   180
MORTIMER. When wert thou in the field with banner spread?
   But once; and then thy soldiers marched like players,
   With garish robes, not armour; and thyself,
   Bedaub'd with gold, rode laughing at the rest,
   Nodding and shaking of thy spangled crest,
   Where women's favours hung like labels down.

LANCASTER. And thereof came it that the fleering Scots,
    To England's high disgrace, have made this jig:
        Maids of England, sore may you mourn
        For your lemans you have lost at Bannocks bourne.   190
                With a heave and a ho.
    What weeneth the King of England,
    So soon to have won Scotland?
              With a rombelow.
MORTIMER. Wigmore shall fly, to set my uncle free.
LANCASTER. And when 'tis gone, our swords shall purchase
    more.
    If ye be mov'd, revenge it as you can:
    Look next to see us with our ensigns spread.

                                    Exeunt Nobiles.

EDWARD. My swelling heart for very anger breaks.
    How oft have I been baited by these peers,   200
    And dare not be reveng'd, for their power is great?
    Yet shall the crowing of these cockerels
    Affright a lion? Edward, unfold thy paws,
    And let their life's blood slake thy fury's hunger;
    If I be cruel and grow tyrannous,
    Now let them thank themselves, and rue too late.
KENT. My lord, I see your love to Gaveston
    Will be the ruin of the realm and you,
    For now the wrathful nobles threaten wars;
    And therefore, brother, banish him for ever.   210
EDWARD. Art thou an enemy to my Gaveston?
KENT. Ay, and it grieves me that I favoured him.
EDWARD. Traitor, be gone; whine thou with Mortimer.
KENT. So will I, rather than with Gaveston.
EDWARD. Out of my sight, and trouble me no more.
KENT. No marvel though thou scorn thy noble peers,
    When I thy brother am rejected thus.   *Exit.*
EDWARD. Away!
    Poor Gaveston, that hast no friend but me,
    Do what they can, we'll live in Tynemouth here,   220
    And so I walk with him about the walls,
    What care I though the earls begirt us round?
    Here comes she that's cause of all these jars.

    Enter the Queen, *Ladies 3* [Margaret de Clare *and* Ladies
    in Waiting], Baldock *and* Spencer [*and* Gaveston].

ISABELLA. My lord, 'tis thought the earls are up in arms.
EDWARD. Ay, and 'tis likewise thought you favour him.
ISABELLA. Thus do you still suspect me without cause.

LADY MARGARET. Sweet uncle, speak more kindly to the queen.
GAVESTON. My lord, dissemble with her, speak her fair.
EDWARD. Pardon me, sweet, I forgot myself.
ISABELLA. Your pardon is quickly got of Isabel.   230
EDWARD. The younger Mortimer is grown so brave
    That to my face he threatens civil wars.
GAVESTON. Why do you not commit him to the Tower?
EDWARD. I dare not, for the people love him well.
GAVESTON. Why then, we'll have him privily made away.
EDWARD. Would Lancaster and he had both carous'd
    A bowl of poison to each other's health.
    But let them go, and tell me what are these?
LADY MARGARET. Two of my father's servants whilst he liv'd,
    May't please your grace to entertain them now.   240
EDWARD. Tell me, where wast thou born? What is thine arms?
BALDOCK. My name is Baldock, and my gentry
    I fetch'd from Oxford, not from heraldry.
EDWARD. The fitter art thou, Baldock, for my turn;
    Wait on me, and I'll see thou shalt not want.
BALDOCK. I humbly thank your majesty.
EDWARD. Knowest thou him, Gaveston?
GAVESTON.   Ay, my lord;
    His name is Spencer, he is well allied.
    For my sake let him wait upon your grace;
    Scarce shall you find a man of more desert.   250
EDWARD. Then, Spencer, wait upon me; for his sake
    I'll grace thee with a higher style ere long.
SPENCER. No greater titles happen unto me
    Than to be favoured of your majesty.
EDWARD. Cousin, this day shall be your marriage feast,
    And Gaveston, think that I love thee well
    To wed thee to our niece, the only heir
    Unto the Earl of Gloucester late deceas'd.
GAVESTON. I know, my lord, many will stomach me,
    But I respect neither their love nor hate.   260
EDWARD. The headstrong barons shall not limit me;
    He that I list to favour shall be great.
    Come, let's away; and when the marriage ends,
    Have at the rebels and their complices.   *Exeunt omnes.*

[*Scene iii.*]
Enter Lancaster, Mortimer, Warwick, Pembroke, Kent.
KENT. My lords, of love to this our native land
    I come to join with you and leave the king;

[150]

And in your quarrel and the realm's behoof
Will be the first that shall adventure life.
LANCASTER. I fear me you are sent of policy
    To undermine us with a show of love.
WARWICK. He is your brother, therefore have we cause
    To cast the worst, and doubt of your revolt.
KENT. Mine honour shall be hostage of my truth;
    If that will not suffice, farewell my lords.   10
MORTIMER. Stay, Edmund; never was Plantagenet
    False of his word and therefore trust we thee.
PEMBROKE. But what's the reason you should leave him now?
KENT. I have inform'd the Earl of Lancaster.
LANCASTER. And it sufficeth. Now, my lords, know this,
    That Gaveston is secretly arriv'd
    And here in Tynemouth frolics with the king.
    Let us with these our followers scale the walls,
    And suddenly surprise them unawares.
MORTIMER. I'll give the onset.
WARWICK.   And I'll follow thee.   20
MORTIMER. This tottered ensign of my ancestors
    Which swept the desert shore of that dead sea
    Whereof we got the name of Mortimer
    Will I advance upon this castle walls.
    Drums, strike alarum; raise them from their sport,
    And ring aloud the knell of Gaveston.
LANCASTER. None be so hardy as to touch the king;
    But neither spare you Gaveston nor his friends.   *Exeunt.*

[Scene iv.]
Enter the King *and* Spencer, *to them* Gaveston [*the* Queen,
    Margaret de Clare].
EDWARD. O tell me Spencer, where is Gaveston?
SPENCER. I fear me he is slain, my gracious lord.
EDWARD. No, here he comes; now let them spoil and kill.
    Fly, fly my lords, the earls have got the hold.
    Take shipping and away to Scarborough;
    Spencer and I will post away by land.
GAVESTON. O stay, my lord, they will not injure you.
EDWARD. I will not trust them. Gaveston, away!
GAVESTON. Farewell, my lord.
EDWARD. Lady, farewell.   10
LADY MARGARET. Farewell, sweet uncle, till we meet again.
EDWARD. Farewell, sweet Gaveston, and farewell, niece.
ISABELLA. No farewell to poor Isabel, thy queen?

EDWARD. Yes, yes, for Mortimer your lover's sake.
                         Exeunt omnes, manet Isabella.
ISABELLA. Heavens can witness, I love none but you.
    From my embracements thus he breaks away;
    O that mine arms could close this isle about,
    That I might pull him to me where I would;
    Or that these tears that drizzle from mine eyes
    Had power to mollify his stony heart,   20
    That when I had him we might never part.
        Enter the Barons. Alarums.
LANCASTER. I wonder how he scap'd?
MORTIMER.   Who's this? The queen!
ISABELLA. Ay, Mortimer, the miserable queen,
    Whose pining heart her inward sighs have blasted,
    And body with continual mourning wasted;
    These hands are tired with haling of my lord
    From Gaveston, from wicked Gaveston,
    And all in vain; for when I speak him fair,
    He turns away and smiles upon his minion.
MORTIMER. Cease to lament, and tell us where's the king.   30
ISABELLA. What would you with the king? Is't him you seek?
LANCASTER. No, madam, but that cursed Gaveston.
    Far be it from the thought of Lancaster
    To offer violence to his sovereign.
    We would but rid the realm of Gaveston;
    Tell us where he remains, and he shall die.
ISABELLA. He's gone by water unto Scarborough:
    Pursue him quickly, and he cannot scape;
    The king hath left him, and his train is small.
WARWICK. Forslow no time sweet Lancaster; let's march.   40
MORTIMER. How comes it that the king and he is parted?
ISABELLA. That this your army, going several ways,
    Might be of lesser force, and with the power
    That he intendeth presently to raise
    Be easily suppress'd; and therefore be gone.
MORTIMER. Here in the river rides a Flemish hoy;
    Let's all aboard and follow him amain.
LANCASTER. The wind that bears him hence will fill our sails;
    Come, come aboard; 'tis but an hour's sailing.
MORTIMER. Madam, stay you within this castle here.   50
ISABELLA. No, Mortimer, I'll to my lord the king.
MORTIMER. Nay, rather sail with us to Scarborough.
ISABELLA. You know the king is so suspicious
    As if he hear I have but talk'd with you

Mine honour will be call'd in question;
And therefore, gentle Mortimer, be gone.
MORTIMER. Madam, I cannot stay to answer you,
  But think of Mortimer as he deserves.

                          [Exeunt. Manet Isabella.]
ISABELLA. So well hast thou deserv'd, sweet Mortimer,
  As Isabel could live with thee for ever.   60
  In vain I look for love at Edward's hand,
  Whose eyes are fix'd on none but Gaveston.
  Yet once more I'll importune him with prayers;
  If he be strange and not regard my words,
  My son and I will over into France,
  And to the king my brother there complain
  How Gaveston hath robb'd me of his love.
  But yet I hope my sorrows will have end,
  And Gaveston this blessed day be slain.   *Exit.*

[*Scene v.*]

  Enter Gaveston *pursued.*
GAVESTON. Yet, lusty lords, I have escap'd your hands,
  Your threats, your larums, and your hot pursuits;
  And though divorced from King Edward's eyes,
  Yet liveth Piers of Gaveston unsurpris'd,
  Breathing, in hope (*malgrado* all your beards
  That muster rebels thus against your king)
  To see his royal sovereign once again.
    Enter the Nobles.
WARWICK. Upon him, soldiers; take away his weapons.
MORTIMER. Thou proud disturber of thy country's peace,
  Corrupter of thy king, cause of these broils,   10
  Base flatterer, yield, and were it not for shame,
  Shame and dishonour to a soldier's name,
  Upon my weapon's point here shouldst thou fall,
  And welter in thy gore.
LANCASTER.   Monster of men,
  That, like the Greekish strumpet, train'd to arms
  And bloody wars so many valiant knights,
  Look for no other fortune, wretch, than death.
  Kind Edward is not here to buckler thee.
WARWICK. Lancaster, why talkst thou to the slave?
  Go, soldiers, take him hence, for by my sword,   20
  His head shall off. Gaveston, short warning
  Shall serve thy turn: it is our country's cause
  That here severely we will execute

Upon thy person. Hang him at a bough.

GAVESTON. My lord——

WARWICK. Soldiers, have him away.
But, for thou wert the favourite of a king,
Thou shalt have so much honour at our hands.

GAVESTON. I thank you all, my lords. Then I perceive
That heading is one, and hanging is the other,   30
And death is all.

    Enter Earl of Arundel.

LANCASTER. How now, my lord of Arundel?

ARUNDEL. My lords, King Edward greets you all by me.

WARWICK. Arundel, say your message.

ARUNDEL.   His majesty,
Hearing that you had taken Gaveston,
Entreateth you by me, yet but he may
See him before he dies; for why, he says,
And sends you word, he knows that die he shall;
And if you gratify his grace so far,
He will be mindful of the courtesy.   40

WARWICK. How now?

GAVESTON.   Renowmed Edward, how thy name
Revives poor Gaveston.

WARWICK.   No, it needeth not.
Arundel, we will gratify the king
In other matters; he must pardon us in this.
Soldiers, away with him.

GAVESTON.   Why, my lord of Warwick,
Will not these delays beget my hopes?
I know it, lords, it is this life you aim at,
Yet grant King Edward this.

MORTIMER.   Shalt thou appoint
What we shall grant? Soldiers, away with him!
Thus we'll gratify the king: 50
We'll send his head by thee; let him bestow
His tears on that, for that is all he gets
Of Gaveston, or else his senseless trunk.

LANCASTER. Not so my lord, lest he bestow more cost
In burying him than he hath ever earned.

ARUNDEL. My lords, it is his majesty's request;
And in the honour of a king he swears
He will but talk with him and send him back.

WARWICK. When, can you tell? Arundel, no; we wot
He that the care of realm remits,   60
And drives his nobles to these exigents

For Gaveston, will, if he seize him once,
Violate any promise to possess him.
ARUNDEL. Then if you will not trust his grace in keep,
My lords, I will be pledge for his return.
MORTIMER. It is honourable in thee to offer this,
But, for we know thou art a noble gentleman,
We will not wrong thee so
To make away a true man for a thief.
GAVESTON. How mean'st thou, Mortimer? That is over-base.
MORTIMER. Away, base groom, robber of king's renowm,   71
Question with thy companions and thy mates.
PEMBROKE. My lord Mortimer, and you my lords each one,
To gratify the king's request therein,
Touching the sending of this Gaveston;
Because his majesty so earnestly
Desires to see the man before his death,
I will upon mine honour undertake
To carry him, and bring him back again;
Provided this, that you my lord of Arundel   80
Will join with me.
WARWICK.   Pembroke, what wilt thou do?
Cause yet more bloodshed? Is it not enough
That we have taken him, but must we now
Leave him on 'had I wist', and let him go?
PEMBROKE. My lords, I will not over-woo your honours,
But if you dare trust Pembroke with the prisoner,
Upon mine oath I will return him back.
ARUNDEL. My lord of Lancaster, what say you in this?
LANCASTER. Why, I say, let him go on Pembroke's word.
PEMBROKE. And you, lord Mortimer?   90
MORTIMER. How say you, my lord of Warwick?
WARWICK. Nay, do your pleasures; I know how 'twill prove.
PEMBROKE. Then give him me.
GAVESTON.   Sweet sovereign, yet I come
To see thee ere I die.
WARWICK [*aside*].   Yet not, perhaps,
If Warwick's wit and policy prevail.
MORTIMER. My lord of Pembroke, we deliver him you;
Return him on your honour. Sound away.   *Exeunt.*
    Manent Pembroke, [Arundel,] Gaveston, *and Pembroke's*
    Men [James *and three* Soldiers].
PEMBROKE. My lord, you shall go with me;
My house is not far hence, out of the way
A little, but our men shall go along.   100

We that have pretty wenches to our wives,
Sir, must not come so near and balk their lips.
ARUNDEL. 'Tis very kindly spoke, my lord of Pembroke:
Your honour hath an adamant of power
To draw a prince.
PEMBROKE.   So, my lord. Come hither, James.
I do commit this Gaveston to thee;
Be thou this night his keeper; in the morning
We will discharge thee of thy charge. Be gone.
GAVESTON. Unhappy Gaveston, whither goest thou now?
                                        Exit cum servis Pem.

HORSE-BOY. My lord, we'll quickly be at Cobham.   110
                                        Exeunt ambo.

[*Act III. Scene i.*]
    Enter Gaveston *mourning,* [James,] *and the Earl of Pem-
    broke's Men.*

GAVESTON. O treacherous Warwick, thus to wrong thy friend!
JAMES. I see it is your life these arms pursue.
GAVESTON. Weaponless must I fall, and die in bands.
    O, must this day be period of my life,
    Centre of all my bliss? And ye be men,
    Speed to the king.
    Enter Warwick *and his Company.*
WARWICK.   My lord of Pembroke's men,
Strive you no longer; I will have that Gaveston.
JAMES. Your lordship doth dishonour to yourself,
And wrong our lord, your honourable friend.
WARWICK. No, James, it is my country's cause I follow.   10
Go, take the villain; soldiers, come away,
We'll make quick work. Commend me to your master,
My friend, and tell him that I watch'd it well.
Come, let thy shadow parley with King Edward.
GAVESTON. Treacherous earl, shall I not see the king?
WARWICK. The king of heaven perhaps, no other king.
    Away.
                        Exeunt Warwick *and his Men, with* Gaveston.
                                Manent James *cum ceteris.*
JAMES. Come fellows, it booted not for us to strive.
We will in haste go certify our lord.   *Exeunt.*

[156]

[*Scene ii.*]

Enter *King* Edward *and* Spencer [*and* Baldock], *with*
Drums and Fifes.

EDWARD. I long to hear an answer from the barons
  Touching my friend, my dearest Gaveston.
  Ah, Spencer, not the riches of my realm
  Can ransom him; ah, he is mark'd to die.
  I know the malice of the younger Mortimer;
  Warwick I know is rough; and Lancaster
  Inexorable; and I shall never see
  My lovely Piers, my Gaveston, again.
  The barons overbear me with their pride.

SPENCER. Were I King Edward, England's sovereign,   10
  Son to the lovely Eleanor of Spain,
  Great Edward Longshanks' issue—would I bear
  These braves, this rage, and suffer uncontroll'd
  These barons thus to beard me in my land,
  In mine own realm? My lord, pardon my speech.
  Did you retain your father's magnanimity,
  Did you regard the honour of your name,
  You would not suffer thus your majesty
  Be counterbuff'd of your nobility.
  Strike off their heads, and let them preach on poles;   20
  No doubt such lessons they will teach the rest
  As by their preachments they will profit much,
  And learn obedience to their lawful king.

EDWARD. Yea, gentle Spencer, we have been too mild,
  Too kind to them; but now have drawn our sword,
  And if they send me not my Gaveston
  We'll steel it on their crest, and poll their tops.

BALDOCK. This haught resolve becomes your majesty,
  Not to be tied to their affection,
  As though your highness were a schoolboy still,   30
  And must be aw'd and govern'd like a child.

Enter Hugh Spencer *an old man, father to the young Spencer,*
with his truncheon and Soldiers.

SPENCER THE FATHER. Long live my sovereign, the noble
    Edward,
  In peace triumphant, fortunate in wars.

EDWARD. Welcome, old man. Com'st thou in Edward's aid?
  Then tell thy prince of whence and what thou art.

SPENCER THE FATHER. Lo, with a band of bowmen and of pikes,
  Brown bills and targeteers, four hundred strong,

Sworn to defend King Edward's royal right,
I come in person to your majesty;
Spencer, the father of Hugh Spencer there,   40
Bound to your highness everlastingly
For favours done in him unto us all.

E.)WARD. Thy father, Spencer?

SPENCER.   True, and it like your grace,
That pours in lieu of all your goodness shown,
His life, my lord, before your princely feet.

EDWARD. Welcome ten thousand times, old man, again.
Spencer, this love, this kindness to thy king,
Argues thy noble mind and disposition;
Spencer, I here create thee Earl of Wiltshire,
And daily will enrich thee with our favour,   50
That as the sunshine shall reflect o'er thee.
Beside, the more to manifest our love,
Because we hear lord Bruce doth sell his land,
And that the Mortimers are in hand withal,
Thou shalt have crowns of us, t'outbid the barons,
And, Spencer, spare them not but lay it on.
Soldiers, a largesse; and thrice welcome all.

SPENCER. My lord, here comes the queen.

  Enter the Queen *and her son, and* Levune *a Frenchman.*

EDWARD.   Madam, what news?

ISABELLA. News of dishonour, lord, and discontent:
Our friend Levune, faithful and full of trust,   60
Informeth us, by letters and by words,
That lord Valois our brother, King of France,
Because your highness hath been slack in homage,
Hath seized Normandy into his hands;
These be the letters, this the messenger.

EDWARD. Welcome, Levune. Tush, Sib, if this be all,
Valois and I will soon be friends again.
But to my Gaveston—shall I never see,
Never behold thee now? Madam, in this matter
We will employ you and your little son;   70
You shall go parley with the King of France.
Boy, see you bear you bravely to the king,
And do your message with a majesty.

PRINCE EDWARD. Commit not to my youth things of more
    weight
Than fits a prince so young as I to bear,
And fear not, lord and father, heaven's great beams
On Atlas' shoulder shall not lie more safe

Than shall your charge committed to my trust.

ISABELLA. Ah, boy, this towardness makes thy mother fear
    Thou art not mark'd to many days on earth.   80

EDWARD. Madam, we will that you with speed be shipp'd,
    And this our son; Levune shall follow you
    With all the haste we can dispatch him hence.
    Choose of our lords to bear you company,
    And go in peace; leave us in wars at home.

ISABELLA. Unnatural wars, where subjects brave their king:
    God end them once. My lord, I take my leave
    To make my preparation for France.

                    [*Exit* Queen *and* Prince Edward.]

    Enter Arundel.

EDWARD. What, lord Arundel, dost thou come alone?

ARUNDEL. Yea, my good lord, for Gaveston is dead.   90

EDWARD. Ah, traitors, have they put my friend to death?
    Tell me, Arundel, died he ere thou cam'st,
    Or didst thou see my friend to take his death?

ARUNDEL. Neither, my lord; for as he was surpris'd,
    Begirt with weapons, and with enemies round,
    I did your highness' message to them all,
    Demanding him of them, entreating rather,
    And said, upon the honour of my name,
    That I would undertake to carry him
    Unto your highness, and to bring him back.   100

EDWARD. And tell me, would the rebels deny me that?

SPENCER. Proud recreants!

EDWARD.   Yea, Spencer, traitors all.

ARUNDEL. I found them at the first inexorable;
    The Earl of Warwick would not bide the hearing,
    Mortimer hardly; Pembroke and Lancaster
    Spake least. And when they flatly had denied,
    Refusing to receive me pledge for him,
    The Earl of Pembroke mildly thus bespake:
    'My lords, because our sovereign sends for him
    And promiseth he shall be safe return'd,   110
    I will this undertake, to have him hence,
    And see him re-delivered to your hands.'

EDWARD. Well, and how fortunes that he came not?

SPENCER. Some treason or some villainy was cause.

ARUNDEL. The Earl of Warwick seiz'd him on his way.
    For being delivered unto Pembroke's men,
    Their lord rode home, thinking his prisoner safe;
    But ere he came, Warwick in ambush lay,

And bare him to his death, and in a trench
Strake off his head, and march'd unto the camp.   120
SPENCER. A bloody part, flatly against law of arms.
EDWARD. O, shall I speak, or shall I sigh and die?
SPENCER. My lord, refer your vengeance to the sword
    Upon these barons; hearten up your men.
    Let them not unreveng'd murder your friends.
    Advance your standard, Edward, in the field,
    And march to fire them from their starting-holes.
EDWARD (*kneels, and saith*). By earth, the common mother of us
    all,
    By heaven, and all the moving orbs thereof,
    By this right hand and by my father's sword,   130
    And all the honours 'longing to my crown,
    I will have heads and lives for him, as many
    As I have manors, castles, towns and towers.
    Treacherous Warwick, traitorous Mortimer,
    If I be England's king, in lakes of gore
    Your headless trunks, your bodies will I trail,
    That you may drink your fill, and quaff in blood,
    And stain my royal standard with the same;
    That so my bloody colours may suggest
    Remembrance of revenge immortally   140
    On your accursed traitorous progeny,
    You villains that have slain my Gaveston.
    And in this place of honour and of trust,
    Spencer, sweet Spencer, I adopt thee here,
    And merely of our love we do create thee
    Earl of Gloucester and Lord Chamberlain,
    Despite of times, despite of enemies.
SPENCER. My lord, here is a messenger from the barons
    Desires access unto your majesty.
EDWARD. Admit him near.   150
    Enter the Herald *from the barons, with his coat of arms.*
HERALD. Long live King Edward, England's lawful lord.
EDWARD. So wish not they, I wis, that sent thee hither;
    Thou com'st from Mortimer and his complices—
    A ranker rout of rebels never was.
    Well, say thy message.
HERALD. The barons, up in arms, by me salute
    Your highness with long life and happiness;
    And bid me say as plainer to your grace,
    That if without effusion of blood
    You will this grief have ease and remedy,   160

That from your princely person you remove
This Spencer, as a putrefying branch
That deads the royal vine, whose golden leaves
Empale your princely head, your diadem,
Whose brightness such pernicious upstarts dim;
Say they; and lovingly advise your grace
To cherish virtue and nobility,
And have old servitors in high esteem,
And shake off smooth dissembling flatterers.
This granted, they, their honours and their lives,   170
Are to your highness vow'd and consecrate.

SPENCER. Ah, traitors, will they still display their pride?

EDWARD. Away, tarry no answer but be gone.
Rebels, will they appoint their sovereign
His sports, his pleasures, and his company?
Yet ere thou go, see how I do divorce   *Embrace* Spencer.
Spencer from me. Now get thee to thy lords,
And tell them I will come to chastise them
For murdering Gaveston. Hie thee, get thee gone;
Edward with fire and sword follows at thy heels.   180
                             [*Exit* Herald.]
My lord, perceive you how these rebels swell?
Soldiers, good hearts, defend your sovereign's right,
For now, even now, we march to make them stoop.
Away.   *Exeunt.*

[Scene iii.]

Alarums, excursions, a great fight, and a retreat. Enter the
King, Spencer the Father, Spencer the Son, *and the*
Noblemen of the King's side.

EDWARD. Why do we sound retreat? Upon them, lords!
This day I shall pour vengeance with my sword
On those proud rebels that are up in arms,
And do confront and countermand their king.

SPENCER. I doubt it not, my lord; right will prevail.

SPENCER THE FATHER. 'Tis not amiss, my liege, for either part
To breathe awhile; our men, with sweat and dust
All chok'd well near, begin to faint for heat;
And this retire refresheth horse and man.

SPENCER. Here come the rebels.   10
Enter the Barons, Mortimer, Lancaster, Warwick, Pembroke, *cum ceteris.*

MORTIMER. Look, Lancaster, yonder is Edward
Among his flatterers.

LANCASTER.   And there let him be,
  Till he pay dearly for their company.
WARWICK. And shall, or Warwick's sword shall smite in vain.
EDWARD. What, rebels, do you shrink and sound retreat?
MORTIMER. No, Edward, no; thy flatterers faint and fly.
LANCASTER. Th'ad best betimes forsake them and their trains,
  For they'll betray thee, traitors as they are.
SPENCER. Traitor on thy face, rebellious Lancaster.
PEMBROKE. Away, base upstart; brav'st thou nobles thus?   20
SPENCER THE FATHER. A noble attempt and honourable deed
  Is it not, trow ye, to assemble aid
  And levy arms against your lawful king?
EDWARD. For which ere long, their heads shall satisfy
  T'appease the wrath of their offended king.
MORTIMER. Then Edward, thou wilt fight it to the last,
  And rather bathe thy sword in subjects' blood
  Than banish that pernicious company?
EDWARD. Ay, traitors all! Rather than thus be brav'd,
  Make England's civil towns huge heaps of stones   30
  And ploughs to go about our palace gates.
WARWICK. A desperate and unnatural resolution.
  Alarum to the fight!
  St George for England and the barons' right.
EDWARD. St George for England and King Edward's right.
                    [*Exeunt both parties different ways.*]
    [*Alarums.*] *Enter* Edward *with the Barons captives.*
EDWARD. Now, lusty lords, now, not by chance of war,
  But justice of the quarrel and the cause,
  Vail'd is your pride. Methinks you hang the heads,
  But we'll advance them, traitors; now 'tis time
  To be aveng'd on you for all your braves,   40
  And for the murder of my dearest friend,
  To whom right well you knew our soul was knit,
  Good Piers of Gaveston, my sweet favourite—
  Ah, rebels, recreants, you made him away.
KENT. Brother, in regard of thee and of thy land
  Did they remove that flatterer from thy throne.
EDWARD. So sir, you have spoke; away, avoid our presence.
                              [*Exit Kent.*]
  Accursed wretches, was't in regard of us,
  When we had sent our messenger to request
  He might be spar'd to come to speak with us,   50
  And Pembroke undertook for his return,
  That thou, proud Warwick, watch'd the prisoner,

Poor Piers, and headed him against law of arms?
For which thy head shall overlook the rest
As much as thou in rage out-went'st the rest.
WARWICK. Tyrant, I scorn thy threats and menaces;
'Tis but temporal that thou canst inflict.
LANCASTER. The worst is death, and better die to live,
Than live in infamy under such a king.
EDWARD. Away with them; my lord of Winchester,   60
These lusty leaders, Warwick and Lancaster,
I charge you roundly, off with both their heads.
Away.
WARWICK. Farewell, vain world.
LANCASTER.   Sweet Mortimer, farewell.
[*Exeunt* Warwick *and* Lancaster *with* Spencer the Father.]
MORTIMER. England, unkind to thy nobility,
Groan for this grief, behold how thou art maim'd.
EDWARD. Go take that haughty Mortimer to the Tower,
There see him safe bestow'd; and for the rest,
Do speedy execution on them all.
Be gone.   70
MORTIMER. What, Mortimer, can ragged stony walls
Immure thy virtue that aspires to heaven?
No, Edward, England's scourge, it may not be;
Mortimer's hope surmounts his fortune far.

                                        [*Exit, guarded.*]
EDWARD. Sound drums and trumpets, march with me, my
    friends;
Edward this day hath crown'd him king anew.   [*Exit.*]
                    Manent Spencer, Levune *and* Baldock.
SPENCER. Levune, the trust that we repose in thee
Begets the quiet of King Edward's land;
Therefore be gone in haste, and with advice
Bestow that treasure on the lords of France,   80
That therewithal enchanted, like the guard
That suffered Jove to pass in showers of gold
To Danae, all aid may be denied
To Isabel the queen, that now in France
Makes friends, to cross the seas with her young son,
And step into his father's regiment.
LEVUNE. That's it these barons and the subtle queen
Long levell'd at?
BALDOCK.   Yea, but Levune, thou seest
These barons lay their heads on blocks together;
What they intend, the hangman frustrates clean.   90

LEVUNE. Have you no doubts, my lords; I'll clap so close
    Among the lords of France with England's gold,
    That Isabel shall make her plaints in vain,
    And France shall be obdurate with her tears.
SPENCER. Then make for France amain; Levune, away,
    Proclaim King Edward's wars and victories.

Exeunt omnes.

[*Act IV. Scene i.*]
    Enter Edmund [*earl of* Kent].

KENT. Fair blows the wind for France; blow, gentle gale,
    Till Edmund be arriv'd for England's good.
    Nature, yield to my country's cause in this:
    A brother—no, a butcher of thy friends—
    Proud Edward, dost thou banish me thy presence?
    But I'll to France, and cheer the wronged queen,
    And certify what Edward's looseness is.
    Unnatural king, to slaughter noble men
    And cherish flatterers! Mortimer, I stay
    Thy sweet escape; stand gracious, gloomy night,   10
    To his device.
    Enter Mortimer *disguised.*
MORTIMER.   Holla, who walketh there?
    Is't you, my lord?
KENT.   Mortimer, 'tis I;
    But hath thy potion wrought so happily?
MORTIMER. It hath, my lord: the warders all asleep,
    I thank them, gave me leave to pass in peace.
    But hath your grace got shipping into France?
KENT. Fear it not.   *Exeunt.*

[*Scene ii.*]
    Enter the Queen *and her son.*

ISABELLA. Ah, boy, our friends do fail us all in France;
    The lords are cruel and the king unkind.
    What shall we do?
PRINCE EDWARD.   Madam, return to England,
    And please my father well, and then a fig
    For all my uncle's friendship here in France.
    I warrant you, I'll win his highness quickly;
    'A loves me better than a thousand Spencers.
ISABELLA. Ah, boy, thou art deceiv'd at least in this,
    To think that we can yet be tun'd together;

No, no, we jar too far. Unkind Valois,   10
Unhappy Isabel, when France rejects;
Whither, O whither dost thou bend thy steps?
    Enter Sir John of Hainault.

SIR JOHN. Madam, what cheer?

ISABELLA.   Ah, good Sir John of Hainault,
Never so cheerless, nor so far distress'd.

SIR JOHN. I hear, sweet lady, of the king's unkindness,
But droop not, madam; noble minds contemn
Despair. Will your grace with me to Hainault
And there stay time's advantage with your son?
How say you, my lord, will you go with your friends,
And shake off all our fortunes equally?   20

PRINCE EDWARD. So pleaseth the queen my mother, me it likes.
The King of England nor the court of France
Shall have me from my gracious mother's side
Till I be strong enough to break a staff;
And then have at the proudest Spencer's head.

SIR JOHN. Well said, my lord.

ISABELLA. Oh my sweet heart, how do I moan thy wrongs,
Yet triumph in the hope of thee, my joy.
Ah, sweet Sir John, even to the utmost verge
Of Europe, or the shore of Tanaïs   30
Will we with thee; to Hainault so we will.
The marquis is a noble gentleman;
His grace, I dare presume, will welcome me.
But who are these?
    Enter Edmund, [*earl of* Kent] *and* Mortimer.

KENT.   Madam, long may you live
Much happier than your friends in England do.

ISABELLA. Lord Edmund and lord Mortimer alive!
Welcome to France! The news was here, my lord,
That you were dead, or very near your death.

MORTIMER. Lady, the last was truest of the twain;
But Mortimer, reserv'd for better hap,   40
Hath shaken off the thraldom of the Tower
And lives t'advance your standard, good my lord.

PRINCE EDWARD. How mean you, and the king my father lives?
No, my lord Mortimer, not I, I trow.

ISABELLA. Not, son, why not? I would it were no worse;
But, gentle lords, friendless we are in France.

MORTIMER. Monsieur le Grand, a noble friend of yours,
Told us at our arrival all the news,
How hard the nobles, how unkind the king

Hath show'd himself. But, madam, right makes room   50
Where weapons want; and though a many friends
Are made away, as Warwick, Lancaster,
And others of our party and faction,
Yet have we friends, assure your grace, in England
Would cast up caps and clap their hands for joy,
To see us there appointed for our foes.

KENT. Would all were well, and Edward well reclaim'd,
  For England's honour, peace and quietness.

MORTIMER. But by the sword, my lord, it must be deserv'd;
  The king will ne'er forsake his flatterers.   60

SIR JOHN. My lords of England, sith the ungentle king
  Of France refuseth to give aid of arms
  To this distressed queen his sister here,
  Go you with her to Hainault; doubt ye not,
  We will find comfort, money, men and friends
  Ere long, to bid the English king a base.
  How say, young prince, what think you of the match?

PRINCE EDWARD. I think King Edward will out-run us all.

ISABELLA. Nay, son, not so; and you must not discourage
  Your friends that are so forward in your aid.   70

KENT. Sir John of Hainault, pardon us, I pray;
  These comforts that you give our woeful queen
  Bind us in kindness all at your command.

ISABELLA. Yea, gentle brother; and the God of Heaven
  Prosper your happy motion, good Sir John.

MORTIMER. This noble gentleman, forward in arms,
  Was born, I see, to be our anchor-hold.
  Sir John of Hainault, be it thy renown
  That England's queen and nobles in distress
  Have been by thee restor'd and comforted.

SIR JOHN. Madam, along, and you, my lord, with me,
  That England's peers may Hainault's welcome see.
                                           [*Exeunt.*]

[*Scene iii.*]
Enter the King, Arundel, *the two* Spencers, *with others.*

EDWARD. Thus after many threats of wrathful war,
  Triumpheth England's Edward with his friends;
  And triumph Edward with his friends uncontroll'd.
  My lord of Gloucester, do you hear the news?

SPENCER. What news, my lord?

EDWARD. Why, man, they say there is great execution
  Done through the realm; my lord of Arundel,

You have the note, have you not?
ARUNDEL. From the lieutenant of the Tower, my lord.
EDWARD. I pray let us see it. What have we there?   10
    Read it, Spencer.   Spencer *reads their names*.
    Why so; they bark'd apace a month ago,
    Now on my life they'll neither bark nor bite.
    Now sirs, the news from France: Gloucester, I trow
    The lords of France love England's gold so well
    As Isabella gets no aid from thence.
    What now remains? Have you proclaim'd, my lord,
    Reward for them can bring in Mortimer?
SPENCER. My lord, we have, and if he be in England
    'A will be had ere long, I doubt it not.   20
EDWARD. If, dost thou say? Spencer, as true as death
    He is in England's ground; our port-masters
    Are not so careless of their king's command.
      Enter a Post.
    How now, what news with thee? From whence come these?
POST. Letters, my lord, and tidings forth of France
    To you, my lord of Gloucester, from Levune.
EDWARD. Read.   Spencer *reads the letter*.
SPENCER. 'My duty to your honour premised, &c. I have
    according to instructions in that behalf, dealt with the King
    of France his lords, and effected that the queen, all dis-
    contented and discomforted, is gone; whither if you ask,
    with Sir John of Hainault, brother to the marquis, into
    Flanders; with them are gone lord Edmund and the lord
    Mortimer, having in their company divers of your nation,
    and others; and, as constant report goeth, they intend to
    give King Edward battle in England sooner than he can
    look for them. This is all the news of import.
                Your honour's in all service, Levune.'
EDWARD. Ah, villains, hath that Mortimer escap'd?
    With him is Edmund gone associate?   40
    And will Sir John of Hainault lead the round?
    Welcome, a God's name, madam, and your son;
    England shall welcome you and all your rout.
    Gallop apace, bright Phoebus, through the sky,
    And dusky night, in rusty iron car,
    Between you both, shorten the time, I pray,
    That I may see that most desired day
    When we may meet these traitors in the field.
    Ah, nothing grieves me but my little boy
    Is thus misled to countenance their ills.   50

Come, friends, to Bristow, there to make us strong;
And winds, as equal be to bring them in
As you injurious were to bear them forth.   [*Exeunt.*]

[*Scene iv.*]
Enter the Queen, *her son*, Edmund [*earl of* Kent], Mortimer
and Sir John.

ISABELLA. Now lords, our loving friends and countrymen,
    Welcome to England all; with prosperous winds
    Our kindest friends in Belgia have we left,
    To cope with friends at home. A heavy case,
    When force to force is knit, and sword and glaive
    In civil broils makes kin and countrymen
    Slaughter themselves in others, and their sides
    With their own weapons gor'd. But what's the help?
    Misgovern'd kings are cause of all this wrack;
    And Edward, thou art one among them all   10
    Whose looseness hath betray'd thy land to spoil,
    And made the channels overflow with blood;
    Of thine own people patron shouldst thou be,
    But thou——
MORTIMER. Nay, madam, if you be a warrior,
    You must not grow so passionate in speeches.
    Lords, sith that we are by sufferance of heaven
    Arriv'd and armed in this prince's right,
    Here for our country's cause swear we to him
    All homage, fealty and forwardness.   20
    And for the open wrongs and injuries
    Edward hath done to us, his queen and land,
    We come in arms to wreak it with the sword,
    That England's queen in peace may repossess
    Her dignities and honours; and withal
    We may remove these flatterers from the king,
    That havocs England's wealth and treasury.
SIR JOHN. Sound trumpets, my lord, and forward let us march;
    Edward will think we come to flatter him.
KENT. I would he never had been flattered more.   30
                                        [*Exeunt.*]

[*Scene v.*]
Enter the King, Baldock *and* Spencer *the son, flying about the
stage.*
SPENCER. Fly, fly, my lord, the queen is over-strong,
    Her friends do multiply and yours do fail.

Shape we our course to Ireland, there to breathe.
EDWARD. What, was I born to fly and run away,
    And leave the Mortimers conquerors behind?
    Give me my horse, and let's r'enforce our troops,
    And in this bed of honour die with fame.
BALDOCK. Oh no, my lord, this princely resolution
    Fits not the time; away, we are pursu'd.   [*Exeunt.*]
    [*Enter*] Edmund [*earl of* Kent] *alone with a sword and target.*
KENT. This way he fled, but I am come too late.   10
    Edward, alas, my heart relents for thee.
    Proud traitor Mortimer, why dost thou chase
    Thy lawful king, thy sovereign, with thy sword?
    Vilde wretch, and why hast thou of all unkind,
    Borne arms against thy brother and thy king?
    Rain showers of vengeance on my cursed head,
    Thou God, to whom in justice it belongs
    To punish this unnatural revolt.
    Edward, this Mortimer aims at thy life;
    O fly him then. But Edmund, calm this rage;   20
    Dissemble or thou diest; for Mortimer
    And Isabel do kiss while they conspire,
    And yet she bears a face of love, forsooth;
    Fie on that love that hatcheth death and hate!
    Edmund, away; Bristow to Longshanks' blood
    Is false. Be not found single for suspect;
    Proud Mortimer pries near into thy walks.
    Enter the Queen, Mortimer, *the young* Prince, *and* Sir John
    of Hainault.
ISABELLA. Successful battles gives the God of kings
    To them that fight in right and fear his wrath;
    Since then successfully we have prevail'd,   30
    Thanks be heaven's great architect, and you.
    Ere farther we proceed, my noble lords,
    We here create our well-beloved son,
    Of love and care unto his royal person,
    Lord Warden of the realm; and sith the fates
    Have made his father so infortunate,
    Deal you my lords in this, my loving lords,
    As to your wisdoms fittest seems in all.
KENT. Madam, without offence if I may ask,
    How will you deal with Edward in his fall?   40
PRINCE EDWARD. Tell me, good uncle, what Edward do you
    mean?
KENT. Nephew, your father; I dare not call him king.

MORTIMER. My lord of Kent, what needs these questions?
  'Tis not in her controlment, nor in ours;
  But as the realm and parliament shall please,
  So shall your brother be disposed of.
  [*Aside to the queen.*] I like not this relenting mood in Edmund,
  Madam; 'tis good to look to him betimes.
ISABELLA. My lord, the mayor of Bristow knows our mind?
MORTIMER. Yea, madam, and they scape not easily   50
  That fled the field.
ISABELLA.   Baldock is with the king;
  A goodly chancellor, is he not, my lord?
SIR JOHN. So are the Spencers, the father and the son.
KENT. This Edward is the ruin of the realm.
    Enter Rice ap Howell *and the* Mayor *of Bristow, with*
    Spencer the Father.
RICE AP HOWELL. God save Queen Isabel and her princely son!
  Madam, the mayor and citizens of Bristow,
  In sign of love and duty to this presence,
  Present by me this traitor to the state,
  Spencer, the father to that wanton Spencer
  That like the lawless Catiline of Rome   60
  Revell'd in England's wealth and treasury.
ISABELLA. We thank you all.
MORTIMER.   Your loving care in this
  Deserveth princely favours and rewards.
  But where's the king and the other Spencer fled?
RICE AP HOWELL. Spencer the son, created earl of Gloucester,
  Is with that smooth-tongu'd scholar Baldock gone,
  And shipp'd but late for Ireland with the king.
MORTIMER. Some whirlwind fetch them back or sink them all!
  They shall be started thence, I doubt it not.
PRINCE EDWARD. Shall I not see the king my father yet?   70
KENT [*aside*]. Unhappy Edward, chas'd from England's
  bounds.
SIR JOHN. Madam, what resteth, why stand ye in a muse?
ISABELLA. I rue my lord's ill fortune, but, alas,
  Care of my country call'd me to this war.
MORTIMER. Madam, have done with care and sad complaint;
  Your king hath wrong'd your country and himself,
  And we must seek to right it as we may.
  Meanwhile, have hence this rebel to the block;
  Your lordship cannot privilege your head.
SPENCER THE FATHER. Rebel is he that fights against his prince,
  So fought not they that fought in Edward's right.   81

MORTIMER. Take him away, he prates.

> [*Exit* Spencer the Father, *guarded.*]
>   You, Rice ap Howell,
Shall do good service to her majesty,
Being of countenance in your country here,
To follow these rebellious runagates.
We in meanwhile, madam, must take advice
How Baldock, Spencer, and their complices
May in their fall be followed to their end.

> *Exeunt omnes.*

[*Scene vi.*]
Enter the Abbot, Monks, Edward, Spencer *and* Baldock.

ABBOT. Have you no doubt, my lord, have you no fear;
As silent and as careful will we be
To keep your royal person safe with us,
Free from suspect and fell invasion
Of such as have your majesty in chase—
Yourself, and those your chosen company—
As danger of this stormy time requires.

EDWARD. Father, thy face should harbour no deceit.
O, hadst thou ever been a king, thy heart
Pierced deeply with sense of my distress,   10
Could not but take compassion of my state.
Stately and proud, in riches and in train,
Whilom I was, powerful and full of pomp;
But what is he, whom rule and empery
Have not in life or death made miserable?
Come Spencer, come Baldock, come sit down by me;
Make trial now of that philosophy
That in our famous nurseries of arts
Thou suck'dst from Plato and from Aristotle.
Father, this life contemplative is heaven—   20
O that I might this life in quiet lead!
But we alas are chas'd; and you, my friends,
Your lives and my dishonour they pursue.
Yet gentle monks, for treasure, gold nor fee,
Do you betray us and our company.

MONK. Your grace may sit secure, if none but we
Do wot of your abode.

SPENCER. Not one alive; but shrewdly I suspect
A gloomy fellow in a mead below.
'A gave a long look after us, my lord,   30
And all the land, I know, is up in arms,

[171]

Arms that pursue our lives with deadly hate.

BALDOCK. We were embark'd for Ireland, wretched we,
  With awkward winds and sore tempests driven
  To fall on shore, and here to pine in fear
  Of Mortimer and his confederates.

EDWARD. Mortimer, who talks of Mortimer?
  Who wounds me with the name of Mortimer,
  That bloody man? Good father, on thy lap
  Lay I this head, laden with mickle care.   40
  O might I never open these eyes again,
  Never again lift up this drooping head,
  O never more lift up this dying heart.

SPENCER. Look up, my lord. Baldock, this drowsiness
  Betides no good. Here even we are betray'd.

    Enter with Welsh hooks Rice ap Howell, *a* Mower, *and the*
    Earl *of* Leicester.

MOWER. Upon my life, those be the men ye seek.

RICE AP HOWELL. Fellow, enough. My lord, I pray be short,
  A fair commission warrants what we do.

LEICESTER. The queen's commission, urg'd by Mortimer;
  What cannot gallant Mortimer with the queen?   50
  Alas, see where he sits and hopes unseen
  T'escape their hands that seek to reave his life.
  Too true it is: *quem dies vidit veniens superbum,*
  Hunc dies vidit fugiens iacentem.
  But, Leicester, leave to grow so passionate.
  Spencer and Baldock, by no other names,
  I arrest you of high treason here;
  Stand not on titles, but obey th'arrest;
  'Tis in the name of Isabel the queen.
  My lord, why droop you thus?   60

EDWARD. O day, the last of all my bliss on earth,
  Centre of all misfortune! O my stars,
  Why do you lour unkindly on a king?
  Comes Leicester then in Isabella's name
  To take my life, my company, from me?
  Here man, rip up this panting breast of mine
  And take my heart in rescue of my friends.

RICE AP HOWELL. Away with them.

SPENCER.   It may become thee yet
  To let us take our farewell of his grace.

ABBOT. My heart with pity earns to see this sight,   70
  A king to bear these words and proud commands.

EDWARD. Spencer, ah, sweet Spencer; thus then must we part?

SPENCER. We must, my lord, so will the angry heavens.

EDWARD. Nay, so will hell and cruel Mortimer;
  The gentle heavens have not to do in this.

BALDOCK. My lord, it is in vain to grieve or storm;
  Here humbly of your grace we take our leaves;
  Our lots are cast. I fear me, so is thine.

EDWARD. In heaven we may, in earth never shall we meet.
  And Leicester say, what shall become of us?   80

LEICESTER. Your majesty must go to Killingworth.

EDWARD. Must! 'Tis somewhat hard when kings must go.

LEICESTER. Here is a litter ready for your grace
  That waits your pleasure; and the day grows old.

RICE AP HOWELL. As good be gone, as stay and be benighted.

EDWARD. A litter hast thou? Lay me in a hearse,
  And to the gates of hell convey me hence;
  Let Pluto's bells ring out my fatal knell,
  And hags howl for my death at Charon's shore,
  For friends hath Edward none, but these, and these,   90
  And these must die under a tyrant's sword.

RICE AP HOWELL. My lord, be going; care not for these,
  For we shall see them shorter by the heads.

EDWARD. Well, that shall be shall be; part we must,
  Sweet Spencer, gentle Baldock, part we must.
  Hence feigned weeds, unfeigned are my woes.
  Father, farewell. Leicester, thou stay'st for me
  And go I must. Life, farewell with my friends.

                          Exeunt Edward *and* Leicester.

SPENCER. O is he gone? Is noble Edward gone,
  Parted from hence, never to see us more?   100
  Rent sphere of heaven, and fire forsake thy orb,
  Earth melt to air, gone is my sovereign,
  Gone, gone, alas, never to make return.

BALDOCK. Spencer, I see our souls are fleeted hence,
  We are depriv'd the sunshine of our life.
  Make for a new life, man, throw up thy eyes,
  And heart and hand to heaven's immortal throne,
  Pay nature's debt with cheerful countenance;
  Reduce we all our lessons unto this:
  To die, sweet Spencer, therefore live we all;   110
  Spencer, all live to die, and rise to fall.

RICE AP HOWELL. Come, come, keep these preachments till
  you come to the place appointed. You, and such as you are,
  have made wise work in England. Will your lordships away?

MOWER. Your worship, I trust, will remember me?

RICE AP HOWELL. Remember thee, fellow? What else? Follow
   me to the town.   [*Exeunt.*]

[*Act V. Scene i.*]
Enter the King, Leicester, *with a Bishop* [*of* Winchester,]
for the crown [*and* Trussel].

LEICESTER. Be patient, good my lord, cease to lament;
   Imagine Killingworth Castle were your court,
   And that you lay for pleasure here a space,
   Not of compulsion or necessity.
EDWARD. Leicester, if gentle words might comfort me,
   Thy speeches long ago had eas'd my sorrows,
   For kind and loving hast thou always been.
   The griefs of private men are soon allay'd,
   But not of kings: the forest deer being struck
   Runs to an herb that closeth up the wounds,   10
   But when the imperial lion's flesh is gor'd
   He rends and tears it with his wrathful paw,
   And highly scorning that the lowly earth
   Should drink his blood, mounts up into the air:
   And so it fares with me, whose dauntless mind
   The ambitious Mortimer would seek to curb,
   And that unnatural queen, false Isabel,
   That thus hath pent and mew'd me in a prison;
   For such outrageous passions cloy my soul
   As with the wings of rancour and disdain   20
   Full often am I soaring up to heaven
   To plain me to the gods against them both.
   But when I call to mind I am a king,
   Methinks I should revenge me of the wrongs
   That Mortimer and Isabel have done.
   But what are kings, when regiment is gone,
   But perfect shadows in a sunshine day?
   My nobles rule, I bear the name of king;
   I wear the crown; but am controll'd by them,
   By Mortimer and my unconstant queen,   30
   Who spots my nuptial bed with infamy,
   Whilst I am lodg'd within this cave of care,
   Where sorrow at my elbow still attends
   To company my heart with sad laments,
   That bleeds within me for this strange exchange.
   But tell me, must I now resign my crown
   To make usurping Mortimer a king?

[174]

WINCHESTER. Your grace mistakes; it is for England's good,
And princely Edward's right we crave the crown.

EDWARD. No, 'tis for Mortimer, not Edward's head;   40
For he's a lamb encompassed by wolves
Which in a moment will abridge his life.
But if proud Mortimer do wear this crown,
Heavens turn it to a blaze of quenchless fire,
Or like the snaky wreath of Tisiphon
Engirt the temples of his hateful head;
So shall not England's vine be perished,
But Edward's name survive, though Edward dies.

LEICESTER. My lord, why waste you thus your time away?
They stay your answer: will you yield your crown?   50

EDWARD. Ah, Leicester, weigh how hardly I can brook
To lose my crown and kingdom without cause,
To give ambitious Mortimer my right,
That like a mountain overwhelms my bliss;
In which extreme my mind here murdered is.
But what the heavens appoint, I must obey.
Here, take my crown, the life of Edward too:
Two kings in England cannot reign at once.
But stay awhile, let me be king till night,
That I may gaze upon this glittering crown;   60
So shall my eyes receive their last content,
My head the latest honour due to it,
And jointly both yield up their wished right.
Continue ever, thou celestial sun,
Let never silent night possess this clime;
Stand still, you watches of the element,
All times and seasons, rest you at a stay,
That Edward may be still fair England's king.
But day's bright beams doth vanish fast away,
And needs I must resign my wished crown.   70
Inhuman creatures, nurs'd with tiger's milk,
Why gape you for your sovereign's overthrow—
My diadem, I mean, and guiltless life?
See, monsters, see, I'll wear my crown again!
What, fear you not the fury of your king?
But hapless Edward, thou art fondly led;
They pass not for thy frowns as late they did,
But seek to make a new elected king;
Which fills my mind with strange despairing thoughts;
Which thoughts are martyred with endless torments;   80
And in this torment, comfort find I none

[175]

But that I feel the crown upon my head.
And therefore let me wear it yet awhile.

TRUSSEL. My lord, the parliament must have present news,
And therefore say: will you resign or no?   *The King rageth.*

EDWARD. I'll not resign, but whilst I live—
Traitors, be gone, and join you with Mortimer.
Elect, conspire, install; do what you will,
Their blood and yours shall seal these treacheries.

WINCHESTER. This answer we'll return and so farewell.   90

LEICESTER. Call them again, my lord, and speak them fair,
For if they go the prince shall lose his right.

EDWARD. Call thou them back; I have no power to speak.

LEICESTER. My lord, the king is willing to resign.

WINCHESTER. If he be not, let him choose—

EDWARD. O would I might! But heavens and earth conspire
To make me miserable. Here, receive my crown.
Receive it? No, these innocent hands of mine
Shall not be guilty of so foul a crime.
He of you all that most desires my blood,   100
And will be called the murderer of a king,
Take it. What, are you mov'd? Pity you me?
Then send for unrelenting Mortimer
And Isabel, whose eyes being turn'd to steel
Will sooner sparkle fire than shed a tear.
Yet stay; for rather than I will look on them,
Here, here! Now, sweet God of Heaven,
Make me despise this transitory pomp,
And sit for aye enthronized in heaven.
Come death, and with thy fingers close my eyes,   110
Or if I live, let me forget myself.

WINCHESTER. My lord——

EDWARD. Call me not lord. Away, out of my sight!
Ah, pardon me, grief makes me lunatic.
Let not that Mortimer protect my son;
More safety is there in a tiger's jaws
Than his embracements. Bear this to the queen,
Wet with my tears, and dried again with sighs;
If with the sight thereof she be not mov'd,
Return it back, and dip it in my blood.   120
Commend me to my son, and bid him rule
Better than I. Yet how have I transgress'd,
Unless it be with too much clemency?

TRUSSEL. And thus, most humbly, do we take our leave.
                              [*Exeunt Bishop and* Trussel.]

EDWARD. Farewell. I know the next news that they bring
  Will be my death, and welcome shall it be;
  To wretched men death is felicity.
LEICESTER. Another post! What news brings he?
  Enter Berkeley.
EDWARD. Such news as I expect. Come, Berkeley, come,
  And tell thy message to my naked breast.   130
BERKELEY. My lord, think not a thought so villainous
  Can harbour in a man of noble birth.
  To do your highness service and devoir,
  And save you from your foes, Berkeley would die.
LEICESTER [*reading letter*]. My lord, the council of the queen
  commands
  That I resign my charge.
EDWARD. And who must keep me now? Must you, my lord?
BERKELEY. Ay, my most gracious lord, so 'tis decreed.
EDWARD [*taking the letter.*] By Mortimer, whose name is written
  here,
  Well may I rent his name that rends my heart.   140
  This poor revenge hath something eas'd my mind;
  So may his limbs be torn, as is this paper:
  Hear me, immortal Jove, and grant it too.
BERKELEY. Your grace must hence with me to Berkeley
  straight.
EDWARD. Whither you will; all places are alike,
  And every earth is fit for burial.
LEICESTER. Favour him, my lord, as much as lieth in you.
BERKELEY. Even so betide my soul as I use him.
EDWARD. Mine enemy hath pitied my estate,
  And that's the cause that I am now remov'd.   150
BERKELEY. And thinks your grace that Berkeley will be cruel?
EDWARD. I know not; but of this am I assur'd,
  That death ends all, and I can die but once.
  Leicester, farewell.
LEICESTER. Not yet, my lord; I'll bear you on your way.
                Exeunt omnes.

[*Scene ii.*]
  Enter Mortimer *and Queen* Isabel.
MORTIMER. Fair Isabel, now have we our desire.
  The proud corrupters of the light-brain'd king
  Have done their homage to the lofty gallows,
  And he himself lies in captivity.
  Be rul'd by me, and we will rule the realm.

In any case, take heed of childish fear,
For now we hold an old wolf by the ears
That if he slip will seize upon us both,
And gripe the sorer being grip'd himself.
Think therefore, madam, that imports us much   10
To erect your son with all the speed we may,
And that I be Protector over him;
For our behoof will bear the greater sway
Whenas a king's name shall be underwrit.

ISABELLA. Sweet Mortimer, the life of Isabel,
Be thou persuaded that I love thee well,
And therefore, so the prince my son be safe,
Whom I esteem as dear as these mine eyes,
Conclude against his father what thou wilt,
And I myself will willingly subscribe.   20

MORTIMER. First would I hear news that he were depos'd,
And then let me alone to handle him.
        Enter Messenger.
Letters, from whence?

MESSENGER.   From Killingworth, my lord.

ISABELLA. How fares my lord the king?

MESSENGER. In health, madam, but full of pensiveness.

ISABELLA. Alas, poor soul, would I could ease his grief.
        [*Enter the Bishop of* Winchester *with the crown.*]
Thanks, gentle Winchester. Sirra be gone.
                            [*Exit* Messenger.]

WINCHESTER. The king hath willingly resign'd his crown.

ISABELLA. O happy news; send for the prince my son.

WINCHESTER. Further, or this letter was seal'd, Lord Berkeley
    came,   30
So that he now is gone from Killingworth;
And we have heard that Edmund laid a plot
To set his brother free; no more but so.
The lord of Berkeley is so pitiful
As Leicester that had charge of him before.

ISABELLA. Then let some other be his guardian.

MORTIMER. Let me alone—here is the privy seal.
                        [*Exit Bishop of* Winchester.]
Who's there? Call hither Gurney and Matrevis.
To dash the heavy-headed Edmund's drift
Berkeley shall be discharg'd, the king remov'd,   40
And none but we shall know where he lieth.

ISABELLA. But, Mortimer, as long as he survives
What safety rests for us, or for my son?

MORTIMER. Speak, shall he presently be dispatch'd and die?
ISABELLA. I would he were, so it were not by my means.
      Enter Matrevis *and* Gurney.
MORTIMER. Enough.
   Matrevis, write a letter presently
   Unto the lord of Berkeley from ourself,
   That he resign the king to thee and Gurney;
   And when 'tis done we will subscribe our name.   50
MATREVIS. It shall be done, my lord.
MORTIMER.   Gurney.
GURNEY.   My lord?
MORTIMER. As thou intend'st to rise by Mortimer,
   Who now makes Fortune's wheel turn as he please,
   Seek all the means thou canst to make him droop,
   And neither give him kind word nor good look.
GURNEY. I warrant you, my lord.
MORTIMER. And this above the rest, because we hear
   That Edmund casts to work his liberty,
   Remove him still from place to place by night,
   Till at the last he come to Killingworth,   60
   And then from thence to Berkeley back again;
   And by the way, to make him fret the more,
   Speak curstly to him; and in any case
   Let no man comfort him, if he chance to weep,
   But amplify his grief with bitter words.
MATREVIS. Fear not, my lord, we'll do as you command.
MORTIMER. So now away, post thitherwards amain.
ISABELLA. Whither goes this letter? To my lord the king?
   Commend me humbly to his majesty
   And tell him that I labour all in vain   70
   To ease his grief and work his liberty;
   And bear him this, as witness of my love. [*Gives some token.*]
MATREVIS. I will, madam.   *Exeunt* Matrevis *and* Gurney.
                              Manent Isabel *and* Mortimer.
      Enter the young Prince *and the Earl of* Kent *talking with him.*
MORTIMER. Finely dissembled, do so still, sweet queen.
   Here comes the young prince, with the Earl of Kent.
ISABELLA. Something he whispers in his childish ears.
MORTIMER. If he have such access unto the prince
   Our plots and stratagems will soon be dash'd.
ISABELLA. Use Edmund friendly, as if all were well.
MORTIMER. How fares my honourable lord of Kent?   80
KENT. In health, sweet Mortimer. How fares your grace?
ISABELLA. Well, if my lord your brother were enlarg'd.

KENT. I hear of late he hath depos'd himself.

ISABELLA. The more my grief.

MORTIMER.   And mine.

KENT.   Ah, they do dissemble.

ISABELLA. Sweet son, come hither, I must talk with thee.

MORTIMER. Thou being his uncle and the next of blood
    Do look to be Protector over the prince?

KENT. Not I, my lord; who should protect the son
    But she that gave him life—I mean, the queen?

PRINCE EDWARD. Mother, persuade me not to wear the crown;
    Let him be king. I am too young to reign.   91

ISABELLA. But be content, seeing it his highness' pleasure.

PRINCE EDWARD. Let me but see him first, and then I will.

KENT. Ay, do, sweet nephew.

ISABELLA. Brother, you know it is impossible.

PRINCE EDWARD. Why, is he dead?

ISABELLA. No, God forbid!

KENT. I would these words proceeded from your heart.

MORTIMER. Inconstant Edmund, does thou favour him,
    That wast a cause of his imprisonment?   100

KENT. The more cause have I now to make amends.

MORTIMER. I tell thee 'tis not meet that one so false
    Should come about the person of a prince.
    My lord, he hath betray'd the king his brother,
    And therefore trust him not.

PRINCE EDWARD. But he repents, and sorrows for it now.

ISABELLA. Come, son, and go with this gentle lord and me.

PRINCE EDWARD. With you I will, but not with Mortimer.

MORTIMER. Why, youngling, 'sdain'st thou so of Mortimer?
    Then I will carry thee by force away.   110

PRINCE EDWARD. Help, uncle Kent, Mortimer will wrong me.

ISABELLA. Brother Edmund, strive not; we are his friends;
    Isabel is nearer than the Earl of Kent.

KENT. Sister, Edward is my charge; redeem him.

ISABELLA. Edward is my son and I will keep him.

KENT. Mortimer shall know that he hath wrong'd me.
    Hence will I haste to Killingworth castle,
    And rescue aged Edward from his foes
    To be reveng'd on Mortimer and thee.   *Exeunt omnes.*

[*Scene iii.*]

Enter Matrevis *and* Gurney *with the* King [*and* Soldiers].

MATREVIS. My lord, be not pensive, we are your friends.
    Men are ordain'd to live in misery;

Therefore come, dalliance dangereth our lives.

EDWARD. Friends, whither must unhappy Edward go?
  Will hateful Mortimer appoint no rest?
  Must I be vexed like the nightly bird
  Whose sight is loathsome to all winged fowls?
  When will the fury of his mind assuage?
  When will his heart be satisfied with blood?
  If mine will serve, unbowel straight this breast   10
  And give my heart to Isabel and him;
  It is the chiefest mark they level at.

GURNEY. Not so, my liege, the queen hath given this charge
  To keep your grace in safety;
  Your passions make your dolours to increase.

EDWARD. This usage makes my misery increase.
  But can my air of life continue long
  When all my senses are annoy'd with stench?
  Within a dungeon England's king is kept,
  Where I am starv'd for want of sustenance;   20
  My daily diet is heart-breaking sobs
  That almost rents the closet of my heart.
  Thus lives old Edward, not reliev'd by any;
  And so must die, though pitied by many.
  O water, gentle friends, to cool my thirst,
  And clear my body from foul excrements.

MATREVIS. Here's channel water, as our charge is given;
  Sit down, for we'll be barbers to your grace.

EDWARD. Traitors, away. What, will you murder me,
  Or choke your sovereign with puddle water?   30

GURNEY. No, but wash your face and shave away your beard,
  Lest you be known and so be rescued.

MATREVIS. Why strive you thus? Your labour is in vain.

EDWARD. The wren may strive against the lion's strength,
  But all in vain; so vainly do I strive
  To seek for mercy at a tyrant's hand.

      They wash him with puddle water, and shave his beard away.
  Immortal powers, that knows the painful cares
  That waits upon my poor distressed soul,
  O level all your looks upon these daring men,
  That wrongs their liege and sovereign, England's king.   40
  O Gaveston, it is for thee that I am wrong'd.
  For me, both thou and both the Spencers died;
  And for your sakes, a thousand wrongs I'll take.
  The Spencers' ghosts, wherever they remain,
  Wish well to mine; then tush, for them I'll die.

MATREVIS. 'Twixt theirs and yours shall be no enmity.
Come, come away; now put the torches out;
We'll enter in by darkness to Killingworth.
    Enter Edmund, [*Earl of* Kent].
GURNEY. How now, who comes there?
MATREVIS. Guard the king sure, it is the Earl of Kent.   50
EDWARD. O gentle brother, help to rescue me.
MATREVIS. Keep them asunder; thrust in the king.
KENT. Soldiers, let me but talk to him one word.
GURNEY. Lay hands upon the earl for this assault.
KENT. Lay down your weapons; traitors, yield the king.
MATREVIS. Edmund, yield thou thyself, or thou shalt die.
KENT. Base villains, wherefore do you gripe me thus?
GURNEY. Bind him, and so convey him to the court.
KENT. Where is the court but here? Here is the king,
And I will visit him; why stay you me?   60
MATREVIS. The court is where lord Mortimer remains,
Thither shall your honour go. And so farewell.
        Exeunt Matrevis *and* Gurney *with the* King.
KENT. O miserable is that commonweal
Where lords keep courts and kings are lock'd in prison!
SOLDIER. Wherefore stay we? On sirs, to the court.
KENT. Ay, lead me whither you will, even to my death,
Seeing that my brother cannot be releas'd.   *Exeunt omnes.*

[*Scene iv.*]
    Enter Mortimer *alone.*
MORTIMER. The king must die, or Mortimer goes down.
The commons now begin to pity him.
Yet he that is the cause of Edward's death
Is sure to pay for it when his son is of age;
And therefore will I do it cunningly.
This letter, written by a friend of ours,
Contains his death yet bids them save his life:
'*Edwardum occidere nolite timere, bonum est*';
Fear not to kill the king, 'tis good he die.
But read it thus, and that's another sense: 10
'*Edwardum occidere nolite, timere bonum est*';
Kill not the king, 'tis good to fear the worst.
Unpointed as it is, thus shall it go,
That, being dead, if it chance to be found,
Matrevis and the rest may bear the blame,
And we be quit that caus'd it to be done.
Within this room is lock'd the messenger

That shall convey it and perform the rest;
And by a secret token that he bears
Shall he be murdered when the deed is done.   20
Lightborn, come forth.
   [*Enter* Lightborn.]
Art thou as resolute as thou wast?

LIGHTBORN. What else; my lord? And far more resolute.

MORTIMER. And hast thou cast how to accomplish it?

LIGHTBORN. Ay, ay; and none shall know which way he died.

MORTIMER. But at his looks, Lightborn, thou wilt relent.

LIGHTBORN. Relent, ha, ha! I use much to relent.

MORTIMER. Well, do it bravely, and be secret.

LIGHTBORN. You shall not need to give instructions;
  'Tis not the first time I have kill'd a man.   30
  I learn'd in Naples how to poison flowers;
  To strangle with a lawn thrust through the throat;
  To pierce the windpipe with a needle's point;
  Or whilst one is asleep, to take a quill
  And blow a little powder in his ears,
  Or open his mouth and pour quicksilver down.
  But yet I have a braver way than these.

MORTIMER. What's that?

LIGHTBORN. Nay, you shall pardon me; none shall know my
  tricks.

MORTIMER. I care not how it is, so it be not spied.   40
  Deliver this to Gurney and Matrevis.
  At every ten miles' end thou hast a horse.
  Take this. [*Gives a token.*]
          Away, and never see me more.

LIGHTBORN. No?

MORTIMER. No,
Unless thou bring me news of Edward's death.

LIGHTBORN. That will I quickly do. Farewell, my lord.
                  [*Exit* Lightborn.]

MORTIMER. The prince I rule, the queen do I command,
  And with a lowly congé to the ground
  The proudest lords salute me as I pass.   50
  I seal, I cancel, I do what I will;
  Fear'd am I more than lov'd: let me be fear'd,
  And when I frown, make all the court look pale.
  I view the prince with Aristarchus' eyes,
  Whose looks were as a breeching to a boy.
  They thrust upon me the Protectorship,
  \nd sue to me for that that I desire:

While at the council-table, grave enough
And not unlike a bashful puritan,
First I complain of imbecility,   60
Saying it is *onus quam gravissimum*,
Till being interrupted by my friends,
Suscepi that *provinciam*, as they term it;
And, to conclude, I am Protector now.
Now all is sure: the queen and Mortimer
Shall rule the realm, the king, and none rule us.
Mine enemies will I plague, my friends advance,
And what I list command, who dare control?
Maior sum quam cui possit fortuna nocere.
And that this be the coronation day   70
It pleaseth me, and Isabel the queen.
The trumpets sound; I must go take my place.
    Enter the young King, *Bishop of* Canterbury, Champion,
    Nobles, Queen.

CANTERBURY. Long live King Edward, by the grace of God
  King of England and Lord of Ireland.

CHAMPION. If any Christian, heathen, Turk or Jew
  Dares but affirm that Edward's not true king,
  And will avouch his saying with the sword,
  I am the Champion that will combat him.

MORTIMER. None comes. Sound trumpets.

EDWARD III.   Champion, here's to thee.
                                       [*Drinks.*]

ISABELLA. Lord Mortimer, now take him to your charge. 80
    Enter Soldiers *with the Earl of* Kent *prisoner*.

MORTIMER. What traitor have we there, with blades and bills?

SOLDIER. Edmund the Earl of Kent.

EDWARD III.   What hath he done?

SOLDIER. 'A would have taken the king away perforce
  As we were bringing him to Killingworth.

MORTIMER. Did you attempt his rescue, Edmund? Speak.

KENT. Mortimer, I did. He is our king;
  And thou compell'st this prince to wear the crown.

MORTIMER. Strike off his head; he shall have martial law.

KENT. Strike off my head? Base traitor, I defy thee.

EDWARD III. My lord, he is my uncle, and shall live.   90

MORTIMER. My lord, he is your enemy, and shall die.

KENT. Stay, villains.

EDWARD III. Sweet mother, if I cannot pardon him,
  Entreat my lord Protector for his life.

ISABELLA. Son, be content, I dare not speak a word.

EDWARD III. Nor I, and yet methinks I should command.
  But seeing I cannot, I'll entreat for him:
  My lord, if you will let my uncle live,
  I will requite it when I come to age.
MORTIMER. 'Tis for your highness' good, and for the realm's.
  How often shall I bid you bear him hence?   101
KENT. Art thou king? Must I die at thy command?
MORTIMER. At our command. Once more, away with him.
KENT. Let me but stay and speak; I will not go.
  Either my brother or his son is king,
  And none of both them thirst for Edmund's blood;
  And therefore soldiers, whither will you hale me?
      They hale Edmund *away, and carry him to be beheaded.*
EDWARD III. What safety may I look for at his hands
  If that my uncle shall be murdered thus?
ISABELLA. Fear not, sweet boy, I'll guard thee from thy foes;
  Had Edmund liv'd, he would have sought thy death.   111
  Come son, we'll ride a-hunting in the park.
EDWARD III. And shall my uncle Edmund ride with us?
ISABELLA. He is a traitor; think not on him. Come. *Exeunt omnes.*

[*Scene v.*]
  Enter Matrevis *and* Gurney.
MATREVIS. Gurney, I wonder the king dies not,
  Being in a vault up to the knees in water,
  To which the channels of the castle run,
  From whence a damp continually ariseth,
  That were enough to poison any man,
  Much more a king brought up so tenderly.
GURNEY. And so do I, Matrevis; yesternight
  I opened but the door to throw him meat,
  And I was almost stifled with the savour.
MATREVIS. He hath a body able to endure   10
  More than we can inflict; and therefore now
  Let us assail his mind another while.
GURNEY. Send for him out thence and I will anger him.
MATREVIS. But stay, who's this?
  Enter Lightborn.
LIGHTBORN.   My lord Protector greets you.
GURNEY. What's here? I know not how to conster it.
MATREVIS. Gurney, it was left unpointed for the nonce:
  '*Edwardum occidere nolite timere*'—
  That's his meaning.
LIGHTBORN. Know you this token? I must have the king.

MATREVIS. Ay, stay awhile, thou shalt have answer straight.
    This villain's sent to make away the king.   21
GURNEY. I thought as much.
MATREVIS.   And when the murder's done,
    See how he must be handled for his labour:
    Pereat iste. Let him have the king,
    What else? Here is the keys, this is the lake;
    Do as you are commanded by my lord. .
LIGHTBORN. I know what I must do; get you away—
    Yet be not far off, I shall need your help.
    See that in the next room I have a fire,
    And get me a spit, and let it be red-hot.   30
MATREVIS. Very well.
GURNEY. Need you anything besides?
LIGHTBORN. What else? A table and a featherbed.
GURNEY. That's all?
LIGHTBORN. Ay, ay, so when I call you, bring it in.
MATREVIS. Fear not you that.
GURNEY. Here's a light to go into the dungeon.
                      [*Exeunt* Matrevis *and* Gurney.]
LIGHTBORN. So now must I about this gear; ne'er was there any
    So finely handled as this king shall be.
    Foh, here's a place indeed, with all my heart.   40
                    [Edward *discovered in prison.*]
EDWARD. Who's there? What light is that? Wherefore comes
    thou?
LIGHTBORN. To comfort you and bring you joyful news.
EDWARD. Small comfort finds poor Edward in thy looks;
    Villain, I know thou com'st to murder me.
LIGHTBORN. To murder you, my most gracious lord?
    Far is it from my heart to do you harm.
    The queen sent me, to see how you were us'd,
    For she relents at this your misery.
    And what eyes can refrain from shedding tears
    To see a king in this most piteous state?   50
EDWARD. Weep'st thou already? List awhile to me,
    And then thy heart, were it as Gurney's is,
    Or as Matrevis', hewn from the Caucasus,
    Yet will it melt ere I have done my tale.
    This dungeon where they keep me is the sink
    Wherein the filth of all the castle falls.
LIGHTBORN. O villains!
EDWARD. And there in mire and puddle have I stood
    This ten days' space, and lest that I should sleep,

One plays continually upon a drum;   60
They give me bread and water, being a king;
So that for want of sleep and sustenance
My mind's distempered and my body's numb'd,
And whether I have limbs or no, I know not.
O would my blood dropp'd out from every vein
As doth this water from my tattered robes;
Tell Isabel the queen, I look'd not thus
When for her sake I ran at tilt in France,
And there unhors'd the duke of Cleremont.
LIGHTBORN. O speak no more, my lord; this breaks my heart.
Lie on this bed and rest yourself awhile.   71
EDWARD. These looks of thine can harbour nought but death;
I see my tragedy written in thy brows.
Yet stay awhile, forbear thy bloody hand,
And let me see the stroke before it comes,
That even then when I shall lose my life
My mind may be more steadfast on my God.
LIGHTBORN. What means your highness to mistrust me thus?
EDWARD. What means thou to dissemble with me thus?
LIGHTBORN. These hands were never stain'd with innocent blood,
Nor shall they now be tainted with a king's.   81
EDWARD. Forgive my thought, for having such a thought.
One jewel have I left; receive thou this.
Still fear I, and I know not what's the cause,
But every joint shakes as I give it thee:
O, if thou harbour'st murder in thy heart,
Let this gift change thy mind, and save thy soul.
Know that I am a king——O, at that name
I feel a hell of grief. Where is my crown?
Gone, gone; and do I remain alive?   90
LIGHTBORN. You're overwatch'd, my lord; lie down and rest.
EDWARD. But that grief keeps me waking, I should sleep,
For not these ten days have these eyes' lids clos'd;
Now as I speak they fall: and yet with fear
Open again. O wherefore sits thou here?
LIGHTBORN. If you mistrust me I'll be gone, my lord.
EDWARD. No, no; for if thou mean'st to murder me
Thou wilt return again; and therefore stay.
LIGHTBORN. He sleeps.
EDWARD. O let me not die. Yet stay, O stay awhile.   100
LIGHTBORN. How now, my lord?
EDWARD. Something still buzzeth in mine ears,
And tells me, if I sleep I never wake;

This fear is that which makes me tremble thus,
And therefore tell me, wherefore art thou come?
LIGHTBORN. To rid thee of thy life. Matrevis, come.
    [*Enter* Matrevis.]
EDWARD. I am too weak and feeble to resist;
Assist me, sweet God, and receive my soul.
LIGHTBORN. Run for the table.
            [Matrevis *fetches in* Gurney, *with table and spit.*]
EDWARD. O spare me, or dispatch me in a trice.   110
LIGHTBORN. So, lay the table down and stamp on it,
But not too hard, lest that you bruise his body.
            [*They assault* Edward, *who screams and dies.*]
MATREVIS. I fear me that this cry will raise the town,
And therefore let us take horse and away.
LIGHTBORN. Tell me sirs, was it not bravely done?
GURNEY. Excellent well: take this for thy reward.
                  Then Gurney *stabs* Lightborn.
Come, let us cast the body in the moat,
And bear the king's to Mortimer our lord.
Away.   *Exeunt omnes.*

[*Scene vi.*]
   Enter Mortimer *and* Matrevis.
MORTIMER. Is't done, Matrevis, and the murderer dead?
MATREVIS. Ay, my good lord. I would it were undone.
MORTIMER. Matrevis, if thou now grow'st penitent,
I'll be thy ghostly father; therefore choose,
Whether thou wilt be secret in this,
Or else die by the hand of Mortimer.
MATREVIS. Gurney, my lord, is fled, and will I fear
Betray us both; therefore let me fly.
MORTIMER. Fly to the savages.
MATREVIS. I humbly thank your honour.   [*Exit.*]
MORTIMER. As for myself, I stand as Jove's huge tree,   11
And others are but shrubs compar'd to me;
All tremble at my name, and I fear none;
Let's see who dare impeach me for his death.
   Enter the Queen.
ISABELLA. Ah, Mortimer, the king my son hath news
His father's dead, and we have murdered him.
MORTIMER. What if we have? The king is yet a child.
ISABELLA. Ay, ay, but he tears his hair and wrings his hands,
And vows to be reveng'd upon us both;
Into the council-chamber he is gone,   20

To crave the aid and succour of his peers.
Ay me! See where he comes, and they with him;
Now, Mortimer, begins our tragedy.
   Enter the King *with the* Lords.

1 LORD. Fear not, my lord, know that you are a king.
EDWARD III. Villain!
MORTIMER. How now, my lord?
EDWARD III. Think not that I am frighted with thy words.
My father's murdered through thy treachery,
And thou shalt die, and on his mournful hearse
Thy hateful and accursed head shall lie,   30
To witness to the world that by thy means
His kingly body was too soon interr'd.
ISABELLA. Weep not, sweet son.
EDWARD III. Forbid not me to weep, he was my father;
And had you lov'd him half so well as I,
You could not bear his death thus patiently.
But you, I fear, conspir'd with Mortimer.
1 LORD. Why speak you not unto my lord the king?
MORTIMER. Because I think scorn to be accus'd.
Who is the man dare say I murdered him?   40
EDWARD III. Traitor, in me my loving father speaks,
And plainly saith, 'twas thou that murd'redst him.
MORTIMER. But hath your grace no other proof than this?
EDWARD III. Yes, if this be the hand of Mortimer.
MORTIMER. False Gurney hath betray'd me and himself.
ISABELLA. I fear'd as much; murder cannot be hid.
MORTIMER. 'Tis my hand. What gather you by this?
EDWARD III. That thither thou didst send a murderer.
MORTIMER. What murderer? Bring forth the man I sent.
EDWARD III. Ah, Mortimer, thou know'st that he is slain,   50
And so shalt thou be too. Why stays he here?
Bring him unto a hurdle, drag him forth,
Hang him, I say, and set his quarters up,
But bring his head back presently to me.
ISABELLA. For my sake, sweet son, pity Mortimer.
MORTIMER. Madam, entreat not; I will rather die
Than sue for life unto a paltry boy.
EDWARD III. Hence with the traitor, with the murderer.
MORTIMER. Base Fortune, now I see, that in thy wheel
There is a point, to which when men aspire,   60
They tumble headlong down; that point I touch'd,
And seeing there was no place to mount up higher,
Why should I grieve at my declining fall?

Farewell, fair queen, weep not for Mortimer,
That scorns the world, and as a traveller
Goes to discover countries yet unknown.
EDWARD III. What, suffer you the traitor to delay?
　　　　　　　　　　　　[*Exit* Mortimer *with first* Lord.]
ISABELLA. As thou receiv'dst thy life from me,
Spill not the blood of gentle Mortimer.
EDWARD III. This argues that you spilt my father's blood; 70
Else would you not entreat for Mortimer.
ISABELLA. I spill his blood? No!
EDWARD III. Ay, madam, you, for so the rumour runs.
ISABELLA. That rumour is untrue; for loving thee
Is this report rais'd on poor Isabel.
EDWARD III. I do not think her so unnatural.
2 LORD. My lord, I fear me it will prove too true.
EDWARD III. Mother, you are suspected for his death,
And therefore we commit you to the Tower
Till further trial may be made thereof.　　　　　　80
If you be guilty, though I be your son,
Think not to find me slack or pitiful.
ISABELLA. Nay, to my death, for too long have I liv'd
Whenas my son thinks to abridge my days.
EDWARD III. Away with her, her words enforce these tears,
And I shall pity her if she speak again.
ISABELLA. Shall I not mourn for my beloved lord,
And with the rest accompany him to his grave?
2 LORD. Thus, Madam, 'tis the king's will you shall hence.
ISABELLA. He hath forgotten me. Stay, I am his mother.　90
2 LORD. That boots not; therefore, gentle madam, go.
ISABELLA. Then come, sweet death, and rid me of this grief.
　　　　　　　　　　　　　　　[*Exit, attended.*]
　　[*Enter first* Lord.]
1 LORD. My lord, here is the head of Mortimer.
EDWARD III. Go fetch my father's hearse, where it shall lie,
And bring my funeral robes. Accursed head,
Could I have rul'd thee then, as I do now,
Thou hadst not hatch'd this monstrous treachery.
Here comes the hearse; help me to mourn, my lords.
　　[*Enter* Attendants *with the hearse and funeral robes.*]
Sweet father here, unto thy murdered ghost,
I offer up this wicked traitor's head;　　　　　　　100
And let these tears distilling from mine eyes
Be witness of my grief and innocency.　　[*Exeunt omnes.*]

FINIS.

[190]

Dido Queen of Carthage

Dido Queen of Carthage was published by Thomas Woodcock in 1594, naming 'Christopher Marlowe and Thomas Nash' as joint authors. There was no entry in the Stationers' Register except for the transfer of all the late Thomas Woodcock's (unspecified) books to Paul Linley on 9 February 1596, and the transfer of Linley's books, including '*the tragedie of DIDO*', to John Flasket on 26 June 1600, but these seem not to have led to editions. There is no certain indication of when it was written. Marlowe's source was Virgil's *Aeneid* Books I, II and IV; he invented the love of Anna for Iarbas, and the comedy of Jupiter and Ganymede, and Cupid and the Nurse. The title-page states that the play was performed by the Children of Her Majesty's Chapel, a court company. A play of Dido and Aeneas figures in Henslowe's Diary in 1598.

[DRAMATIS PERSONAE

Jupiter
Mercury, Hermes } Gods
Ganymede
Cupid

Venus } Goddesses
Juno

Aeneas
Ascanius, his son
Achates
Ilioneus } Trojans
Cloanthus
Sergestus
Iarbas, King of Gaetulia

Dido, Queen of Carthage
Anna, her sister
Nurse
        Trojan soldiers, Carthaginian lords, attendants]

Dido Queen of Carthage

Here the curtains draw; there is discovered Jupiter *dandling*
Ganymede *upon his knee, and* Mercury *lying asleep.*

JUPITER. Come, gentle Ganymede, and play with me;
  I love thee well, say Juno what she will.
GANYMEDE. I am much better for your worthless love
  That will not shield me from her shrewish blows.
  Today, whenas I fill'd into your cups
  And held the cloth of pleasance whiles you drank,
  She reach'd me such a rap for that I spill'd,
  As made the blood run down about mine ears.
JUPITER. What? Dares she strike the darling of my
    thoughts?
  By Saturn's soul, and this earth-threat'ning hair,   10
  That, shaken thrice, makes nature's buildings quake,
  I vow, if she but once frown on thee more,
  To hang her meteor-like 'twixt heaven and earth,
  And bind her hand and foot with golden cords,
  As once I did for harming Hercules.
GANYMEDE. Might I but see that pretty sport a-foot,
  O, how would I with Helen's brother laugh,
  And bring the gods to wonder at the game!
  Sweet Jupiter, if e'er I pleas'd thine eye,
  Or seemed fair, wall'd-in with eagle's wings,   20
  Grace my immortal beauty with this boon,
  And I will spend my time in thy bright arms.
JUPITER. What is't, sweet wag, I should deny thy youth?
  Whose face reflects such pleasure to mine eyes
  As I, exhal'd with thy fire-darting beams,
  Have oft driven back the horses of the night,
  Whenas they would have hal'd thee from my sight.
  Sit on my knee, and call for thy content,
  Control proud Fate, and cut the thread of Time.
  Why, are not all the gods at thy command,   30
  And heaven and earth the bounds of thy delight?
  Vulcan shall dance to make thee laughing sport,
  And my nine daughters sing when thou art sad;
  From Juno's bird I'll pluck her spotted pride,

To make thee fans wherewith to cool thy face;
And Venus' swans shall shed their silver down,
To sweeten out the slumbers of thy bed;
Hermes no more shall show the world his wings,
If that thy fancy in his feathers dwell,
But as this one I'll tear them all from him,   40
Do thou but say, 'their colour pleaseth me'.
Hold here, my little love; these linked gems
My Juno ware upon her marriage-day
Put thou about thy neck, my own sweet heart,
And trick thy arms and shoulders with my theft.

GANYMEDE. I would have a jewel for mine ear,
And a fine brooch to put in my hat,
And then I'll hug with you an hundred times.

JUPITER. And shall have, Ganymede, if thou wilt be my
    love.
    [*Enter* Venus.]

VENUS. Ay, this is it: you can sit toying there,   50
And playing with that female wanton boy,
Whiles my Aeneas wanders on the seas,
And rests a prey to every billow's pride.
Juno, false Juno, in her chariot's pomp,
Drawn through the heavens by steeds of Boreas' brood,
Made Hebe to direct her airy wheels
Into the windy country of the clouds;
Where, finding Aeolus entrench'd with storms,
And guarded with a thousand grisly ghosts,
She humbly did beseech him for our bane,   60
And charg'd him drown my son with all his train.
Then gan the winds break ope their brazen doors,
And all Aeolia to be up in arms.
Poor Troy must now be sack'd upon the sea,
And Neptune's waves be envious men of war;
Epeus' horse, to Etna's hill transform'd,
Prepared stands to wrack their wooden walls;
And Aeolus, like Agamemnon, sounds
The surges, his fierce soldiers, to the spoil.
See how the night, Ulysses-like, comes forth,   70
And intercepts the day, as Dolon erst.
Ay me! the stars suppris'd like Rhesus' steeds
Are drawn by darkness forth Astraeus' tents.
What shall I do to save thee, my sweet boy,
Whenas the waves do threat our crystal world,
And Proteus, raising hills of floods on high,

Intends ere long to sport him in the sky?
False Jupiter, reward'st thou virtue so?
What, is not piety exempt from woe?
Then die, Aeneas, in thine innocence,   80
Since that religion hath no recompense.
JUPITER. Content thee, Cytherea, in thy care,
Since thy Aeneas' wand'ring fate is firm,
Whose weary limbs shall shortly make repose
In those fair walls I promis'd him of yore.
But first in blood must his good fortune bud,
Before he be the lord of Turnus' town,
Or force her smile that hitherto hath frown'd.
Three winters shall he with the Rutiles war,
And in the end subdue them with his sword;   90
And full three summers likewise shall he waste
In managing those fierce barbarian minds;
Which once perform'd, poor Troy, so long suppress'd,
From forth her ashes shall advance her head,
And flourish once again, that erst was dead.
But bright Ascanius, beauty's better work,
Who with the sun divides one radiant shape,
Shall build his throne amidst those starry towers
That earth-born Atlas groaning underprops:
No bounds but heaven shall bound his empery,   100
Whose azured gates enchased with his name,
Shall make the morning haste her grey uprise
To feed her eyes with his engraven fame.
Thus in stout Hector's race three hundred years
The Roman sceptre royal shall remain,
Till that a princess-priest conceiv'd by Mars
Shall yield to dignity a double birth,
Who will eternish Troy in their attempts.
VENUS. How may I credit these thy flattering terms,
When yet both sea and sands beset their ships,   110
And Phoebus, as in Stygian pools, refrains
To taint his tresses in the Tyrrhene main?
JUPITER. I will take order for that presently.
Hermes, awake, and haste to Neptune's realm,
Whereas the Wind-god, warring now with fate,
Besiege the offspring of our kingly loins,
Charge him from me to turn his stormy powers,
And fetter them in Vulcan's sturdy brass,
That durst thus proudly wrong our kinsman's peace.
                                        [*Exit* Hermes.]

Venus, farewell; thy son shall be our care.   120
Come, Ganymede, we must about this gear.
                   Exeunt Jupiter *cum* Ganymede.
VENUS. Disquiet seas, lay down your swelling looks,
  And court Aeneas with your calmy cheer,
  Whose beauteous burden well might make you proud,
  Had not the heavens, conceiv'd with hell-born clouds,
  Veil'd his resplendent glory from your view.
  For my sake pity him, Oceanus,
  That erstwhile issued from thy wat'ry loins,
  And had my being from thy bubbling froth.
  Triton, I know, hath fill'd his trump with Troy,   130
  And therefore will take pity on his toil,
  And call both Thetis and Cymodoce
  To succour him in this extemity.
       Enter Aeneas *with* Ascanius, *with one or two more.*
  What, do I see my son now come on shore?
  Venus, how art thou compass'd with content,
  The while thine eyes attract their sought-for joys!
  Great Jupiter, still honour'd may'st thou be
  For this so friendly aid in time of need!
  Here in this bush disguised will I stand,
  Whiles my Aeneas spends himself in plaints,   140
  And heaven and earth with his unrest acquaints.
AENEAS. You sons of care, companions of my course,
  Priam's misfortune follows us by sea,
  And Helen's rape doth haunt us at the heels.
  How many dangers have we overpass'd!
  Both barking Scylla, and the sounding rocks,
  The Cyclops' shelves, and grim Cerania's seat
  Have you o'ergone, and yet remain alive.
  Pluck up your hearts, since Fate still rests our friend,
  And changing heavens may those good days return,   150
  Which Pergama did vaunt in all her pride.
ACHATES. Brave prince of Troy, thou only art our god,
  That by thy virtues free'st us from annoy,
  And makes our hopes survive to coming joys:
  Do thou but smile, and cloudy heaven will clear,
  Whose night and day descendeth from thy brows.
  Though we be now in extreme misery,
  And rest the map of weather-beaten woe,
  Yet shall the aged sun shed forth his hair,
  To make us live unto our former heat,   160
  And every beast the forest doth send forth

Bequeath her young ones to our scanted food.
ASCANIUS. Father, I faint; good father, give me meat.
AENEAS. Alas, sweet boy, thou must be still a while
    Till we have fire to dress the meat we kill'd.
    Gentle Achates, reach the tinder-box,
    That we may make a fire to warm us with,
    And roast our new-found victuals on this shore.
VENUS. See what strange arts necessity finds out.
    How near, my sweet Aeneas, art thou driven!   170
AENEAS. Hold, take this candle and go light a fire;
    You shall have leaves and windfall boughs enow,
    Near to these woods, to roast your meat withal.
    Ascanius, go and dry thy drenched limbs,
    Whiles I with my Achates rove abroad,
    To know what coast the wind hath driven us on,
    Or whether men or beasts inhabit it.

                     [*Exeunt* Ascanius *and others.*]

ACHATES. The air is pleasant, and the soil most fit
    For cities and society's supports;
    Yet much I marvel that I cannot find   180
    No steps of men imprinted in the earth.
VENUS. Now is the time for me to play my part.
    Ho, young men, saw you, as you came,
    Any of all my sisters wand'ring here,
    Having a quiver girded to her side,
    And clothed in a spotted leopard's skin?
AENEAS. I neither saw nor heard of any such.
    But what may I, fair virgin, call your name,
    Whose looks set forth no mortal form to view,
    Nor speech bewrays aught human in thy birth?   190
    Thou art a goddess that delud'st our eyes,
    And shrouds thy beauty in this borrow'd shape;
    But whether thou the Sun's bright sister be,
    Or one of chaste Diana's fellow nymphs,
    Live happy in the height of all content,
    And lighten our extremes with this one boon
    As to instruct us under what good heaven
    We breathe as now, and what this world is call'd
    On which by tempests' fury we are cast.
    Tell us, O tell us, that are ignorant;   200
    And this right hand shall make thy altars crack
    With mountain-heaps of milk-white sacrifice.
VENUS. Such honour, stranger, do I not affect.
    It is the use for Tyrian maids to wear

Their bow and quiver in this modest sort,
And suit themselves in purple for the nonce,
That they may trip more lightly o'er the lawnds,
And overtake the tusked boar in chase.
But for the land whereof thou dost inquire,
It is the Punic kingdom, rich and strong,   210
Adjoining on Agenor's stately town,
The kingly seat of southern Libya,
Whereas Sidonian Dido rules as queen.
But what are you that ask of me these things?
Whence may you come, or whither will you go?

AENEAS. Of Troy am I, Aeneas is my name,
Who, driven by war from forth my native world,
Put sails to sea to seek out Italy;
And my divine descent from sceptred Jove.
With twice twelve Phrygian ships I plough'd the deep, 220
And made that way my mother Venus led;
But of them all scarce seven do anchor safe,
And they so wrack'd and welt'red by the waves
As every tide tilts 'twixt their oaken sides,
And all of them, unburdened of their load,
Are ballassed with billows' wat'ry weight.
But hapless I, God wot, poor and unknown,
Do trace these Libyan deserts all despis'd,
Exil'd forth Europe and wide Asia both,
And have not any coverture but heaven.   230

VENUS. Fortune hath favour'd thee, whate'er thou be,
In sending thee unto this courteous coast.
A' God's name, on, and haste thee to the court,
Where Dido will receive ye with her smiles;
And for thy ships, which thou supposest lost,
Not one of them hath perish'd in the storm,
But are arrived safe not far from hence.
And so I leave thee to thy fortune's lot,
Wishing good luck unto thy wand'ring steps.   *Exit.*

AENEAS. Achates, 'tis my mother that is fled;   240
I know her by the movings of her feet.
Stay, gentle Venus, fly not from thy son.
Too cruel, why wilt thou forsake me thus,
Or in these shades deceiv'st mine eye so oft?
Why talk we not together hand in hand,
And tell our griefs in more familiar terms?
But thou art gone, and leav'st me here alone
To dull the air with my discoursive moan.   *Exeunt.*

[Scene ii.]

Enter Ilioneus *and* Cloanthus *[with* Iarbas *and* Sergestus*]*.

ILIONEUS. Follow, ye Trojans, follow this brave lord,
And plain to him the sum of your distress.

IARBAS. Why, what are you, or wherefore do you sue?

ILIONEUS. Wretches of Troy, envied of the winds,
That crave such favour at your honour's feet
As poor distressed misery may plead;
Save, save, O save our ships from cruel fire,
That do complain the wounds of thousand waves,
And spare our lives whom every spite pursues.
We come not, we, to wrong your Libyan gods,   10
Or steal your household Lares from their shrines;
Our hands are not prepar'd to lawless spoil,
Nor armed to offend in any kind;
Such force is far from our unweaponed thoughts,
Whose fading weal, of victory forsook,
Forbids all hope to harbour near our hearts.

IARBAS. But tell me, Trojans—Trojans if you be—
Unto what fruitful quarters were ye bound,
Before that Boreas buckled with your sails?

CLOANTHUS. There is a place, Hesperia term'd by us,   20
An ancient empire, famoused for arms,
And fertile in fair Ceres' furrowed wealth,
Which now we call Italia, of his name
That in such peace long time did rule the same.
Thither made we,
When suddenly gloomy Orion rose,
And led our ships into the shallow sands,
Whereas the southern wind with brackish breath
Dispers'd them all amongst the wrackful rocks.
From thence a few of us escap'd to land;   30
The rest, we fear, are folded in the floods.

IARBAS. Brave men-at-arms, abandon fruitless fears,
Since Carthage knows to entertain distress.

SERGESTUS. Ay, but the barbarous sort do threat our ships,
And will not let us lodge upon the sands;
In multitudes they swarm unto the shore,
And from the first earth interdict our feet.

IARBAS. Myself will see they shall not trouble ye:
Your men and you shall banquet in our court,
And every Trojan be as welcome here   40
As Jupiter to silly Baucis' house.

Come in with me; I'll bring you to my queen,
Who shall confirm my words with further deeds.
SERGESTUS. Thanks, gentle lord, for such unlook'd-for grace.
   Might we but once more see Aeneas' face,
   Then would we hope to quite such friendly turns
   As shall surpass the wonder of our speech.   [*Exeunt.*]

[*Act II. Scene i.*]
Enter Aeneas, Achates, *and* Ascanius [*and others*].
AENEAS. Where am I now? These should be Carthage walls.
ACHATES. Why stands my sweet Aeneas thus amaz'd?
AENEAS. O my Achates, Theban Niobe,
   Who for her sons' death wept out life and breath,
   And, dry with grief, was turn'd into a stone,
   Had not such passions in her head as I.
   Methinks that town there should be Troy, yon Ida's hill,
   There Xanthus' stream, because here's Priamus,
   And when I know it is not, then I die.
ACHATES. And in this humour is Achates too;   10
   I cannot choose but fall upon my knees,
   And kiss his hand. O where is Hecuba?
   Here she was wont to sit, but, saving air,
   Is nothing here; and what is this but stone?
AENEAS. O yet this stone doth make Aeneas weep.
   And would my prayers (as Pygmalion's did)
   Could give it life, that under his conduct
   We might sail back to Troy, and be reveng'd
   On these hard-hearted Grecians which rejoice
   That nothing now is left of Priamus.   20
   O, Priamus is left, and this is he.
   Come, come aboard; pursue the hateful Greeks.
ACHATES. What means Aeneas?
AENEAS. Achates, though mine eyes say this is stone,
   Yet thinks my mind that this is Priamus;
   And when my grieved heart sighs and says no,
   Then would it leap out to give Priam life.
   O were I not at all, so thou mightst be!
   Achates, see, King Priam wags his hand.
   He is alive; Troy is not overcome.   30
ACHATES. Thy mind, Aeneas, that would have it so,
   Deludes thy eyesight; Priamus is dead.
AENEAS. Ah, Troy is sack'd, and Priamus is dead.
   And why should poor Aeneas be alive?

ASCANIUS. Sweet father, leave to weep; this is not he,
    For were it Priam, he would smile on me.
ACHATES. Aeneas, see, here come the citizens.
    Leave to lament, lest they laugh at our fears.
      Enter Cloanthus, Sergestus, Ilioneus [*and others*].
AENEAS. Lords of this town, or whatsoever style
    Belongs unto your name, vouchsafe of ruth   40
    To tell us who inhabits this fair town,
    What kind of people, and who governs them;
    For we are strangers driven on this shore,
    And scarcely know within what clime we are.
ILIONEUS. I heard Aeneas' voice, but see him not,
    For none of these can be our general.
ACHATES. Like Ilioneus speaks this noble man,
    But Ilioneus goes not in such robes.
SERGESTUS. You are Achates, or I am deceiv'd.
ACHATES. Aeneas, see, Sergestus, or his ghost!   50
ILIONEUS. He names Aeneas; let us kiss his feet.
CLOANTHUS. It is our captain; see Ascanius.
SERGESTUS. Live long Aeneas and Ascanius!
AENEAS. Achates, speak, for I am overjoy'd.
ACHATES. O Ilioneus, art thou yet alive?
ILIONEUS. Blest be the time I see Achates' face!
CLOANTHUS. Why turns Aeneas from his trusty friends?
AENEAS. Sergestus, Ilioneus, and the rest,
    Your sight amaz'd me. O what destinies
    Have brought my sweet companions in such plight?   60
    O tell me, for I long to be resolv'd.
ILIONEUS. Lovely Aeneas, these are Carthage walls,
    And here Queen Dido wears th'imperial crown,
    Who for Troy's sake hath entertain'd us all,
    And clad us in these wealthy robes we wear.
    Oft hath she ask'd us under whom we serv'd;
    And when we told her, she would weep for grief,
    Thinking the sea had swallowed up thy ships;
    And now she sees thee, how will she rejoice!
SERGESTUS. See where her servitors pass through the hall, 70
    Bearing a banquet; Dido is not far.
ILIONEUS. Look where she comes. Aeneas, view her well.
AENEAS. Well may I view her, but she sees not me.
      Enter Dido [*with* Anna *and* Iarbas] *and her train.*
DIDO. What stranger art thou that dost eye me thus?
AENEAS. Sometime I was a Trojan, mighty queen,
    But Troy is not, what shall I say I am?

[201]

ILIONEUS. Renowmed Dido, 'tis our general,
    Warlike Aeneas.
DIDO. Warlike Aeneas, and in these base robes!
    Go fetch the garment which Sichaeus ware.   80
                     [*Exit an* Attendant.]
    Brave prince, welcome to Carthage and to me,
    Both happy that Aeneas **is** our guest.
    Sit in this chair and banquet with a queen;
    Aeneas is Aeneas, were he clad
    In weeds as bad as ever Irus ware.
AENEAS. This is no seat for one that's comfortless.
    May it please your grace to let Aeneas wait;
    For though my birth be great, my fortune's mean,
    Too mean to be companion to a queen.
DIDO. Thy fortune may be greater than thy birth.   90
    Sit down, Aeneas, sit in Dido's place,
    And if this be thy son, as I suppose,
    Here let him sit. Be merry, lovely child.
AENEAS. This place beseems me not; O pardon me!
DIDO. I'll have it so; Aeneas, be content.
ASCANIUS. Madam, you shall be my mother.
DIDO. And so I will, sweet child. Be merry, man;
    Here's to thy better fortune and good stars.
AENEAS. In all humility I thank your grace.
DIDO. Remember who thou art; speak like thyself: 100
    Humility belongs to common grooms.
AENEAS. And who so miserable as Aeneas is?
DIDO. Lies it in Dido's hands to make thee blest,
    Then be assur'd thou art not miserable.
AENEAS. O Priamus, O Troy, O Hecuba!
DIDO. May I entreat thee to discourse at large,
    And truly too, how Troy was overcome?
    For many tales go of that city's fall,
    And scarcely do agree upon one point.
    Some say Antenor did betray the town;   110
    Others report 'twas Sinon's perjury;
    But all in this, that Troy is overcome,
    And Priam dead; yet how, we hear no news.
AENEAS. A woeful tale bids Dido to unfold,
    Whose memory, like pale Death's stony mace,
    Beats forth my senses from this troubled soul,
    And makes Aeneas sink at Dido's feet.
DIDO. What, faints Aeneas to remember Troy,
    In whose defence he fought so valiantly?

Look up and speak.

AENEAS. Then speak, Aeneas, with Achilles' tongue;
And, Dido, and you Carthaginian peers,
Hear me; but yet with Myrmidons' harsh ears,
Daily inur'd to broils and massacres,
Lest you be mov'd too much with my sad tale.
The Grecian soldiers, tir'd with ten years' war,
Began to cry, 'Let us unto our ships,
Troy is invincible, why stay we here?'
With whose outcries Atrides being appall'd,
Summoned the captains to his princely tent,   130
Who, looking on the scars we Trojans gave,
Seeing the number of their men decreas'd,
And the remainder weak and out of heart,
Gave up their voices to dislodge the camp,
And so in troops all march'd to Tenedos;
Where when they came, Ulysses on the sand
Assay'd with honey words to turn them back;
And as he spoke, to further his intent
The winds did drive huge billows to the shore,
And heaven was dark'ned with tempestuous clouds.   140
Then he alleg'd the gods would have them stay,
And prophesied Troy should be overcome;
And therewithal he call'd false Sinon forth,
A man compact of craft and perjury,
Whose ticing tongue was made of Hermes' pipe,
To force an hundred watchful eyes to sleep;
And him, Epeus having made the horse,
With sacrificing wreaths upon his head,
Ulysses sent to our unhappy town;
Who, grovelling in the mire of Xanthus banks,   150
His hands bound at his back, and both his eyes
Turn'd up to heaven as one resolv'd to die,
Our Phrygian shepherds hal'd within the gates,
And brought unto the court of Priamus;
To whom he us'd action so pitiful,
Looks so remorseful, vows so forcible,
As therewithal the old man overcome,
Kiss'd him, embrac'd him, and unloos'd his bands,
And then—O Dido, pardon me!

DIDO. Nay, leave not here; resolve me of the rest.   160

AENEAS. O, th'enchanting words of that base slave
Made him to think Epeus' pine-tree horse
A sacrifice t'appease Minerva's wrath.

The rather for that one Laocöon,
Breaking a spear upon his hollow breast,
Was with two winged serpents stung to death.
Whereat aghast, we were commanded straight
With reverence to draw it into Troy,
In which unhappy work was I employ'd.
These hands did help to hale it to the gates,   170
Through which it could not enter, 'twas so huge.
O had it never ent'red, Troy had stood.
But Priamus, impatient of delay,
Enforc'd a wide breach in that rampir'd wall
Which thousand battering-rams could never pierce,
And so came in this fatal instrument,
At whose accursed feet, as overjoy'd,
We banqueted, till, overcome with wine,
Some surfeited, and others soundly slept.
Which Sinon viewing, caus'd the Greekish spies   180
To haste to Tenedos and tell the camp.
Then he unlock'd the horse; and suddenly
From out his entrails, Neoptolemus,
Setting his spear upon the ground, leapt forth,
And after him a thousand Grecians more,
In whose stern faces shin'd the quenchless fire
That after burnt the pride of Asia.
By this the camp was come unto the walls,
And through the breach did march into the streets,
Where, meeting with the rest, 'Kill, kill!' they cried.   190
Frighted with this confused noise, I rose,
And looking from a turret might behold
Young infants swimming in their parents' blood,
Headless carcasses pil'd up in heaps,
Virgins half-dead dragg'd by their golden hair
And with main force flung on a ring of pikes,
Old men with swords thrust through their aged sides,
Kneeling for mercy to a Greekish lad
Who with steel pole-axes dash'd out their brains.
Then buckled I mine armour, drew my sword,   200
And thinking to go down, came Hector's ghost,
With ashy visage, bluish sulphur eyes,
His arms torn from his shoulders, and his breast
Furrow'd with wounds, and, that which made me weep,
Thongs at his heels, by which Achilles' horse
Drew him in triumph through the Greekish camp,
Burst from the earth, crying 'Aeneas, fly!

Troy is a-fire, the Grecians have the town!'
DIDO. O Hector, who weeps not to hear thy name?
AENEAS. Yet flung I forth, and, desperate of my life,   210
  Ran in the thickest throngs, and with this sword
  Sent many of their savage ghosts to hell.
  At last came Pyrrhus, fell and full of ire,
  His harness dropping blood, and on his spear
  The mangled head of Priam's youngest son;
  And after him his band of Myrmidons,
  With balls of wild-fire in their murdering paws,
  Which made the funeral flame that burnt fair Troy:
  All which hemm'd me about, crying, 'This is he!'
DIDO. Ah, how could poor Aeneas scape their hands?   220
AENEAS. My mother Venus, jealous of my health,
  Convey'd me from their crooked nets and bands;
  So I escap'd the furious Pyrrhus' wrath,
  Who then ran to the palace of the king,
  And at Jove's altar finding Priamus,
  About whose withered neck hung Hecuba,
  Folding his hand in hers, and jointly both
  Beating their breasts and falling on the ground,
  He with his falchion's point rais'd up at once,
  And with Megaera's eyes, star'd in their face,   230
  Threat'ning a thousand deaths at every glance;
  To whom the aged king thus trembling spoke:
  'Achilles' son, remember what I was,
  Father of fifty sons, but they are slain;
  Lord of my fortune, but my fortune's turn'd;
  King of this city, but my Troy is fir'd;
  And now am neither father, lord, nor king:
  Yet who so wretched but desires to live?
  O let me live, great Neoptolemus.'
  Not mov'd at all, but smiling at his tears,   240
  This butcher, whilst his hands were yet held up,
  Treading upon his breast, struck off his hands.
DIDO. O end, Aeneas, I can hear no more.
AENEAS. At which the frantic queen leap'd on his face,
  And in his eyelids hanging by the nails,
  A little while prolong'd her husband's life.
  At last the soldiers pull'd her by the heels,
  And swung her howling in the empty air,
  Which sent an echo to the wounded king:
  Whereat he lifted up his bed-rid limbs,   250
  And would have grappl'd with Achilles' son,

Forgetting both his want of strength and hands;
Which he disdaining, whisk'd his sword about,
And with the wind thereof the king fell down.
Then from the navel to the throat at once
He ripp'd old Priam, at whose latter gasp
Jove's marble statue gan to bend the brow,
As loathing Pyrrhus for this wicked act.
Yet he, undaunted, took his father's flag,
And dipp'd it in the old king's chill-cold blood,   260
And then in triumph ran into the streets,
Through which he could not pass for slaught'red men;
So, leaning on his sword, he stood stone still,
Viewing the fire wherewith rich Ilion burnt.
By this I got my father on my back,
This young boy in mine arms, and by the hand
Led fair Creusa, my beloved wife;
When thou, Achates, with thy sword mad'st way,
And we were round environ'd with the Greeks.
O there I lost my wife, and had not we   270
Fought manfully, I had not told this tale.
Yet manhood would not serve; of force we fled;
And as we went unto our ships, thou know'st
We saw Cassandra sprawling in the streets,
Whom Ajax ravish'd in Diana's fane,
Her cheeks swoll'n with sighs, her hair all rent,
Whom I took up to bear unto our ships;
But suddenly the Grecians followed us,
And I, alas, was forc'd to let her lie.
Then got we to our ships and, being aboard,   280
Polyxena cried out, 'Aeneas, stay.
The Greeks pursue me; stay, and take me in.'
Mov'd with her voice, I leap'd into the sea,
Thinking to bear her on my back aboard,
For all our ships were launch'd into the deep,
And as I swum, she, standing on the shore,
Was by the cruel Myrmidons surpris'd
And after by that Pyrrhus sacrific'd.
DIDO. I die with melting ruth; Aeneas, leave.
ANNA. O, what became of aged Hecuba?   290
IARBAS. How got Aeneas to the fleet again?
DIDO. But how scap'd Helen, she that caus'd this war?
AENEAS. Achates, speak; sorrow hath tir'd me quite.
ACHATES. What happened to the queen we cannot show;
    We hear they led her captive into Greece.

[206]

As for Aeneas, he swum quickly back;
And Helena betray'd Deiphobus,
Her lover after Alexander died,
And so was reconcil'd to Menelaus.

DIDO. O, had that ticing strumpet ne'er been born! 300
Trojan, thy ruthful tale hath made me sad:
Come, let us think upon some pleasing sport,
To rid me from these melancholy thoughts.
   Exeunt omnes. Enter Venus [*with* Cupid] *at another door and*
   takes Ascanius *by the sleeve.*

VENUS. Fair child, stay thou with Dido's waiting maid;
I'll give thee sugar-almonds, sweet conserves,
A silver girdle, and a golden purse,
And this young prince shall be thy playfellow.

ASCANIUS. Are you Queen Dido's son?

CUPID. Ay, and my mother gave me this fine bow.

ASCANIUS. Shall I have such a quiver and a bow? 310

VENUS. Such bow, such quiver, and such golden shafts,
Will Dido give to sweet Ascanius.
For Dido's sake I take thee in my arms,
And stick these spangled feathers in thy hat.
Eat comfits in mine arms, and I will sing.
Now is he fast asleep, and in this grove,
Amongst green brakes, I'll lay Ascanius,
And strew him with sweet-smelling violets,
Blushing roses, purple hyacinth;
These milk-white doves shall be his centronels, 320
Who, if that any seek to do him hurt,
Will quickly fly to Cytherea's fist.
Now, Cupid, turn thee to Ascanius' shape,
And go to Dido, who instead of him
Will set thee on her lap and play with thee;
Then touch her white breast with this arrow head,
That she may dote upon Aeneas' love,
And by that means repair his broken ships,
Victual his soldiers, give him wealthy gifts,
And he at last depart to Italy, 330
Or else in Carthage make his kingly throne.

CUPID. I will, fair mother; and so play my part
As every touch shall wound Queen Dido's heart. [*Exit.*]

VENUS. Sleep, my sweet nephew, in these cooling shades,
Free from the murmur of these running streams,
The cry of beasts, the rattling of the winds,
Or whisking of these leaves; all shall be still,

[207]

And nothing interrupt thy quiet sleep
Till I return and take thee hence again.   *Exit.*

[*Act III. Scene i.*]
Enter Cupid *solus* [*disguised as Ascanius*].
CUPID. Now Cupid, cause the Carthaginian queen
To be enamour'd of thy brother's looks;
Convey this golden arrow in thy sleeve,
Lest she imagine thou art Venus' son;
And when she strokes thee softly on the head,
Then shall I touch her breast and conquer her.
        Enter Iarbas, Anna, *and* Dido.
IARBAS. How long, fair Dido, shall I pine for thee?
'Tis not enough that thou dost grant me love,
But that I may enjoy what I desire:
That love is childish which consists in words.   10
DIDO. Iarbas, know that thou, of all my wooers—
And yet have I had many mightier kings—
Hast had the greatest favours I could give.
I fear me, Dido hath been counted light
In being too familiar with Iarbas;
Albeit the gods do know no wanton thought
Had ever residence in Dido's breast.
IARBAS. But Dido is the favour I request.
DIDO. Fear not, Iarbas; Dido may be thine.
ANNA. Look, sister, how Aeneas' little son   20
Plays with your garments and embraceth you.
CUPID. No, Dido will not take me in her arms;
I shall not be her son, she loves me not.
DIDO. Weep not, sweet boy, thou shalt be Dido's son;
Sit in my lap, and let me hear thee sing.
No more, my child; now talk another while,
And tell me where learn'dst thou this pretty song.
CUPID. My cousin Helen taught it me in Troy.
DIDO. How lovely is Ascanius when he smiles!
CUPID. Will Dido let me hang about her neck?   30
DIDO. Ay, wag, and give thee leave to kiss her too.
CUPID. What will you give me? Now I'll have this fan.
DIDO. Take it, Ascanius, for thy father's sake.
IARBAS. Come, Dido, leave Ascanius; let us walk.
DIDO. Go thou away; Ascanius shall stay.
IARBAS. Ungentle queen, is this thy love to me?
DIDO. O stay, Iarbas, and I'll go with thee.

[208]

CUPID. And if my mother go, I'll follow her.
DIDO. Why stay'st thou here? Thou art no love of mine.
IARBAS. Iarbas, die, seeing she abandons thee.   40
DIDO. No, live, Iarbas. What hast thou deserv'd
    That I should say thou art no love of mine?
    Something thou hast deserv'd—Away, I say!
    Depart from Carthage, come not in my sight.
IARBAS. Am I not king of rich Gaetulia?
DIDO. Iarbas, pardon me, and stay a while.
CUPID. Mother, look here.
DIDO. What tell'st thou me of rich Gaetulia?
    Am not I queen of Libya? Then depart.
IARBAS. I go to feed the humour of my love,   50
    Yet not from Carthage for a thousand worlds.
DIDO. Iarbas!
IARBAS. Doth Dido call me back?
DIDO. No, but I charge thee never look on me.
IARBAS. Then pull out both mine eyes, or let me die.
                                            Exit Iarbas.
ANNA. Wherefore doth Dido bid Iarbas go?
DIDO. Because his loathsome sight offends mine eye,
    And in my thoughts is shrin'd another love.
    O Anna, didst thou know how sweet love were,
    Full soon wouldst thou abjure this single life.   60
ANNA. Poor soul, I know too well the sour of love:
    O that Iarbas could but fancy me!
DIDO. Is not Aeneas fair and beautiful?
ANNA. Yes, and Iarbas foul and favourless.
DIDO. Is he not eloquent in all his speech?
ANNA. Yes, and Iarbas rude and rustical.
DIDO. Name not Iarbas; but, sweet Anna, say,
    Is not Aeneas worthy Dido's love?
ANNA. O sister, were you empress of the world,
    Aeneas well deserves to be your love.   70
    So lovely is he that, where'er he goes,
    The people swarm to gaze him in the face.
DIDO. But tell them none shall gaze on him but I,
    Lest their gross eye-beams taint my lover's cheeks.
    Anna, good sister Anna, go for him,
    Lest with these sweet thoughts I melt clean away.
ANNA. Then sister, you'll abjure Iarbas' love?
DIDO. Yet must I hear that loathsome name again?
    Run for Aeneas, or I'll fly to him.   *Exit* Anna.
CUPID. You shall not hurt my father when he comes.   80

DIDO. No, for thy sake I'll love thy father well.
O dull-conceited Dido, that till now
Didst never think Aeneas beautiful!
But now, for quittance of this oversight,
I'll make me bracelets of his golden hair;
His glistering eyes shall be my looking-glass;
His lips an altar, where I'll offer up
As many kisses as the sea hath sands;
Instead of music I will hear him speak;
His looks shall be my only library;   90
And thou, Aeneas, Dido's treasury,
In whose fair bosom I will lock more wealth
Than twenty thousand Indias can afford.
O, here he comes. Love, love, give Dido leave
To be more modest than her thoughts admit,
Lest I be made a wonder to the world.
   [*Enter* Aeneas, Achates, Sergestus, Ilioneus, *and*
   Cloanthus.]
Achates, how doth Carthage please your lord?
ACHATES. That will Aeneas show your majesty.
DIDO. Aeneas, art thou there?
AENEAS. I understand your highness sent for me.   100
DIDO. No, but now thou art here, tell me, in sooth,
In what might Dido highly pleasure thee.
AENEAS. So much have I receiv'd at Dido's hands
As, without blushing, I can ask no more.
Yet, queen of Afric, are my ships unrigg'd,
My sails all rent in sunder with the wind,
My oars broken, and my tackling lost,
Yea, all my navy split with rocks and shelves;
Nor stern nor anchor have our maimed fleet;
Our masts the furious winds struck overboard: 110
Which piteous wants if Dido will supply,
We will account her author of our lives.
DIDO. Aeneas, I'll repair thy Trojan ships,
Conditionally that thou wilt stay with me,
And let Achates sail to Italy;
I'll give thee tackling made of rivell'd gold,
Wound on the barks of odoriferous trees;
Oars of massy ivory, full of holes,
Through which the water shall delight to play;
Thy anchors shall be hew'd from crystal rocks,   120
Which if thou lose shall shine above the waves;
The masts, whereon thy swelling sails shall hang,

Hollow pyramides of silver plate;
The sails of folded lawn, where shall be wrought
The wars of Troy, but not Troy's overthrow;
For ballace, empty Dido's treasury:
Take what ye will, but leave Aeneas here.
Achates, thou shalt be so meanly clad
As sea-born nymphs shall swarm about thy ships,
And wanton mermaids court thee with sweet songs,   130
Flinging in favours of more sovereign worth
Than Thetis hangs about Apollo's neck,
So that Aeneas may but stay with me.
AENEAS. Wherefore would Dido have Aeneas stay?
DIDO. To war against my bordering enemies.
Aeneas, think not Dido is in love;
For if that any man could conquer me,
I had been wedded ere Aeneas came.
See where the pictures of my suitors hang;
And are not these as fair as fair may be?   140
ACHATES. I saw this man at Troy ere Troy was sack'd.
SERGESTUS. I this in Greece when Paris stole fair Helen.
ILIONEUS. This man and I were at Olympus games.
SERGESTUS. I know this face; he is a Persian born:
I travell'd with him to Aetolia.
CLOANTHUS. And I in Athens with this gentleman,
Unless I be deceiv'd, disputed once.
DIDO. But speak, Aeneas; know you none of these?
AENEAS. No, madam; but it seems that these are kings.
DIDO. All these, and others which I never saw,   150
Have been most urgent suitors for my love;
Some came in person, others sent their legates,
Yet none obtain'd me. I am free from all;
And yet, God knows, entangled unto one.
This was an orator, and thought by words
To compass me, but yet he was deceiv'd;
And this a Spartan courtier vain and wild,
But his fantastic humours pleas'd not me;
This was Alcion, a musician,
But play'd he ne'er so sweet, I let him go;   160
This was the wealthy king of Thessaly,
But I had gold enough, and cast him off;
This Meleager's son, a warlike prince,
But weapons greed not with my tender years.
The rest are such as all the world well knows:
Yet here I swear, by heaven and him I love,

I was as far from love as they from hate.
AENEAS. O happy shall he be whom Dido loves!
DIDO. Then never say that thou art miserable,
Because it may be thou shalt be my love.   170
Yet boast not of it, for I love thee not—
And yet I hate thee not. O if I speak
I shall betray myself. Aeneas, speak.
We two will go a-hunting in the woods,
But not so much for thee—thou art but one—
As for Achates and his followers.   *Exeunt.*

[*Scene ii.*]
Enter Juno *to* Ascanius *asleep.*
JUNO. Here lies my hate, Aeneas' cursed brat,
The boy wherein false Destiny delights,
The heir of Fame, the favourite of the Fates,
That ugly imp that shall outwear my wrath,
And wrong my deity with high disgrace.
But I will take another order now,
And raze th'eternal register of Time.
Troy shall no more call him her second hope,
Nor Venus triumph in his tender youth;
For here, in spite of heaven, I'll murder him,   10
And feed infection with his let-out life.
Say, Paris, now shall Venus have the ball?
Say, vengeance, now shall her Ascanius die?
O no, God wot, I cannot watch my time,
Nor quit good turns with double fee down told.
Tut, I am simple, without mind to hurt,
And have no gall at all to grieve my foes.
But lustful Jove and his adulterous child
Shall find it written on confusion's front,
That only Juno rules in Rhamnus town.   20
   Enter Venus.
VENUS. What should this mean? My doves are back return'd,
Who warn me of such danger prest at hand
To harm my sweet Ascanius' lovely life.
Juno, my mortal foe, what make you here?
Avaunt, old witch, and trouble not my wits.
JUNO. Fie, Venus, that such causeless words of wrath
Should e'er defile so fair a mouth as thine!
Are not we both sprung of celestial race,
And banquet as two sisters with the gods?
Why is it then displeasure should disjoin   30

Whom kindred and acquaintance co-unites?
VENUS. Out, hateful hag! Thou wouldst have slain my son,
    Had not my doves discover'd thy intent.
    But I will tear thy eyes fro forth thy head,
    And feast the birds with their blood-shotten balls,
    If thou but lay thy fingers on my boy.
JUNO. Is this then all the thanks that I shall have
    For saving him from snakes' and serpents' stings,
    That would have kill'd him sleeping as he lay?
    What though I was offended with thy son,   40
    And wrought him mickle woe on sea and land,
    When, for the hate of Trojan Ganymede,
    That was advanced by my Hebe's shame,
    And Paris' judgement of the heavenly ball,
    I must'red all the winds unto his wrack,
    And urg'd each element to his annoy?
    Yet now I do repent me of his ruth,
    And wish that I had never wrong'd him so.
    Bootless I saw it was to war with fate,
    That hath so many unresisted friends: 50
    Wherefore I chang'd my counsel with the time,
    And planted love where envy erst had sprung.
VENUS. Sister of Jove, if that thy love be such
    As these thy protestations do paint forth,
    We two as friends one fortune will divide;
    Cupid shall lay his arrows in thy lap,
    And to a sceptre change his golden shafts;
    Fancy and modesty shall live as mates,
    And thy fair peacocks by my pigeons perch.
    Love my Aeneas, and desire is thine;   60
    The day, the night, my swans, my sweets, are thine.
JUNO. More than melodious are these words to me,
    That overcloy my soul with their content.
    Venus, sweet Venus, how may I deserve
    Such amorous favours at thy beauteous hand?
    But that thou mayst more easily perceive
    How highly I do prize this amity,
    Hark to a motion of eternal league,
    Which I will make in quittance of thy love.
    Thy son, thou know'st, with Dido now remains,   70
    And feeds his eyes with favours of her court;
    She likewise in admiring spends her time,
    And cannot talk nor think of aught but him;
    Why should not they, then, join in marriage,

[213]

And bring forth mighty kings to Carthage t˷wn,
Whom casualty of sea hath made such friends?
And, Venus, let there be a match confirm'd
Betwixt these two, whose loves are so alike;
And both our deities, conjoin'd in one,
Shall chain felicity unto their throne.   80

VENUS. Well could I like this reconcilement's means,
But much I fear my son will ne'er consent,
Whose armed soul, already on the sea,
Darts forth her light to Lavinia's shore.

JUNO. Fair queen of love, I will divorce these doubts,
And find the way to weary such fond thoughts.
This day they both a-hunting forth will ride
Into these woods, adjoining to these walls;
When, in the midst of all their gamesome sports,
I'll make the clouds dissolve their wat'ry works,   90
And drench Silvanus' dwellings with their showers.
Then in one cave the queen and he shall meet,
And interchangeably discourse their thoughts,
Whose short conclusion will seal up their hearts
Unto the purpose which we now propound.

VENUS. Sister, I see you savour of my wiles;
Be it as you will have it for this once.
Meantime, Ascanius shall be my charge,
Whom I will bear to Ida in mine arms,
And couch him in Adonis' purple down.   100
                                                        Exeunt.

[*Scene iii.*]

Enter Dido, Aeneas, Anna, Iarbas, Achates, [Cupid *as
Ascanius*] *and followers.*

DIDO. Aeneas, think not but I honour thee
That thus in person go with thee to hunt.
My princely robes thou see'st are laid aside,
Whose glittering pomp Diana's shrouds supplies;
All fellows now, dispos'd alike to sport;
The woods are wide, and we have store of game.
Fair Trojan, hold my golden bow a while,
Until I gird my quiver to my side.
Lords, go before; we two must talk alone.

IARBAS. Ungentle, can she wrong Iarbas so?   10
I'll die before a stranger have that grace.
'We two will talk alone'—what words be these?

DIDO. What makes Iarbas here of all the rest?

[214]

We could have gone without your company.
AENEAS. But love and duty led him on perhaps
   To press beyond acceptance to your sight.
IARBAS. Why, man of Troy, do I offend thine eyes?
   Or art thou griev'd thy betters press so nigh?
DIDO. How now, Gaetulian, are ye grown so brave,
   To challenge us with your comparisons?   20
   Peasant, go seek companions like thyself,
   And meddle not with any that I love.
   Aeneas, be not mov'd at what he says,
   For otherwhile he will be out of joint.
IARBAS. Women may wrong by privilege of love;
   But should that man of men, Dido except,
   Have taunted me in these opprobrious terms,
   I would have either drunk his dying blood,
   Or else I would have given my life in gage.
DIDO. Huntsmen, why pitch you not your toils apace,   30
   And rouse the light-foot deer from forth their lair?
ANNA. Sister, see, see Ascanius in his pomp,
   Bearing his hunt-spear bravely in his hand.
DIDO. Yea, little son, are you so forward now?
CUPID. Ay, mother; I shall one day be a man,
   And better able unto other arms;
   Meantime these wanton weapons serve my war,
   Which I will break betwixt a lion's jaws.
DIDO. What, dar'st thou look a lion in the face?
CUPID. Ay, and outface him too, do what he can.   40
ANNA. How like his father speaketh he in all!
AENEAS. And mought I live to see him sack rich Thebes,
   And load his spear with Grecian princes' heads,
   Then would I wish me with Anchises' tomb,
   And dead to honour that hath brought me up.
IARBAS. And might I live to see thee shipp'd away,
   And hoist aloft on Neptune's hideous hills,
   Then would I wish me in fair Dido's arms,
   And dead to scorn that hath pursu'd me so.
AENEAS. Stout friend Achates, dost thou know this wood? 50
ACHATES. As I remember, here you shot the deer
   That sav'd your famish'd soldiers' lives from death,
   When first you set your foot upon the shore;
   And here we met fair Venus, virgin-like,
   Bearing her bow and quiver at her back.
AENEAS. O, how these irksome labours now delight,
   And overjoy my thoughts with their escape!

Who would not undergo all kind of toil,
To be well stor'd with such a winter's tale?
DIDO. Aeneas, leave these dumps and let's away,   60
Some to the mountains, some unto the soil,
You to the valleys,—thou [*to* Iarbas] unto the house.
                    Exeunt omnes: manet [Iarbas].
IARBAS. Ay, this it is which wounds me to the death,
To see a Phrygian, far-fet o'er the sea,
Preferr'd before a man of majesty.
O love! O hate! O cruel women's hearts
That imitate the moon in every change,
And, like the planets, ever love to range!
What shall I do, thus wronged with disdain?
Revenge me on Aeneas, or on her?   70
On her? Fond man, that were to war 'gainst heaven,
And with one shaft provoke ten thousand darts.
This Trojan's end will be thy envy's aim,
Whose blood will reconcile thee to content,
And make love drunken with thy sweet desire.
But Dido, that now holdeth him so dear,
Will die with very tidings of his death;
But time will discontinue her content,
And mould her mind unto new fancy's shapes.
O God of heaven, turn the hand of Fate   80
Unto that happy day of my delight!
And then—what then? Iarbas shall but love:
So doth he now, though not with equal gain;
That resteth in the rival of thy pain,
Who ne'er will cease to soar till he be slain.   *Exit.*

                    [*Scene iv.*]
    The storm. Enter Aeneas *and* Dido *in the cave at several
    times.*
DIDO. Aeneas!
AENEAS. Dido!
DIDO. Tell me, dear love, how found you out this cave?
AENEAS. By chance, sweet queen, as Mars and Venus met.
DIDO. Why, that was in a net, where we are loose;
    And yet I am not free—O would I were!
AENEAS. Why, what is it that Dido may desire
    And not obtain, be it in human power?
DIDO. The thing that I will die before I ask,
    And yet desire to have before I die.   10
AENEAS. It is not aught Aeneas may achieve?

DIDO. Aeneas? No, although his eyes do pierce.
AENEAS. What, hath Iarbas ang'red her in aught?
  And will she be avenged on his life?
DIDO. Not ang'red me, except in ang'ring thee.
AENEAS. Who, then, of all so cruel may he be
  That should detain thy eye in his defects?
DIDO. The man that I do eye where'er I am,
  Whose amorous face, like Paean, sparkles fire,
  Whenas he butts his beams on Flora's bed.   20
  Prometheus hath put on Cupid's shape,
  And I must perish in his burning arms.
  Aeneas, O Aeneas, quench these flames!
AENEAS. What ails my queen? Is she fall'n sick of late?
DIDO. Not sick, my love; but sick I must conceal
  The torment that it boots me not reveal.
  And yet I'll speak, and yet I'll hold my peace;
  Do shame her worst, I will disclose my grief.
  Aeneas, thou art he—what did I say?
  Something it was that now I have forgot.   30
AENEAS. What means fair Dido by this doubtful speech?
DIDO. Nay, nothing; but Aeneas loves me not.
AENEAS. Aeneas' thoughts dare not ascend so high
  As Dido's heart, which monarchs might not scale.
DIDO. It was because I saw no king like thee,
  Whose golden crown might balance my content;
  But now that I have found what to affect,
  I follow one that loveth fame for me,
  And rather had seem fair in Sirens' eyes,
  Than to the Carthage queen that dies for him.   40
AENEAS. If that your majesty can look so low
  As my despised worths that shun all praise,
  With this my hand I give to you my heart,
  And love by all the gods of hospitality,
  By heaven and earth, and my fair brother's bow,
  By Paphos, Capys, and the purple sea
  From whence my radiant mother did descend,
  And by this sword that sav'd me from the Greeks,
  Never to leave these new-upreared walls,
  Whiles Dido lives and rules in Juno's town,   50
  Never to like or love any but her.
DIDO. What more than Delian music do I hear,
  That calls my soul from forth his living seat
  To move unto the measures of delight?
  Kind clouds, that sent forth such a courteous storm

As made disdain to fly to fancy's lap!
Stout love, in mine arms make thy Italy,
Whose crown and kingdom rests at thy command;
Sichaeus, not Aeneas, be thou call'd
The King of Carthage, not Anchises' son.   60
Hold, take these jewels at thy lover's hand,
These golden bracelets, and this wedding-ring,
Wherewith my husband woo'd me yet a maid,
And be thou King of Libya, by my gift.   *Exeunt to the cave.*

[*Act IV. Scene i.*]
Enter Achates, [Cupid *as*] *Ascanius,* Iarbas, *and* Anna.

ACHATES. Did ever men see such a sudden storm,
   Or day so clear so suddenly o'ercast?
IARBAS. I think some fell enchantress dwelleth here,
   That can call them forth whenas she please,
   And dive into black tempests' treasury,
   Whenas she means to mask the world with clouds.
ANNA. In all my life I never knew the like;
   It hail'd, it snow'd, it light'ned, all at once.
ACHATES. I think it was the devils' revelling night,
   There was such hurly-burly in the heavens;   10
   Doubtless Apollo's axle-tree is crack'd,
   Or aged Atlas' shoulder out of joint,
   The motion was so over-violent.
IARBAS. In all this coil, where have ye left the queen?
CUPID. Nay, where's my warlike father, can you tell?
ANNA. Behold, where both of them come forth the cave.
IARBAS. Come forth the cave? Can heaven endure this sight?
   Iarbas, curse that unrevenging Jove,
   Whose flinty darts slept in Typhoeus' den,
   Whiles these adulterers surfeited with sin.   20
   Nature, why mad'st me not some poisonous beast,
   That with the sharpness of my edged sting
   I might have stak'd them both unto the earth,
   Whilst they were sporting in this darksome cave?
      [*Enter* Aeneas *and* Dido.]
AENEAS. The air is clear, and southern winds are whist.
   Come, Dido, let us hasten to the town,
   Since gloomy Aeolus doth cease to frown.
DIDO. Achates and Ascanius, well met.
AENEAS. Fair Anna, how escap'd you from the shower?
ANNA. As others did, by running to the wood.   30

DIDO. But where were you, Iarbas, all this while?
IARBAS. Not with Aeneas in the ugly cave.
DIDO. I see Aeneas sticketh in your mind,
But I will soon put by that stumbling-block,
And quell those hopes that thus employ your cares.

Exeunt.

[*Scene ii.*]

Enter Iarbas *to sacrifice.*

IARBAS. Come, servants, come; bring forth the sacrifice,
That I may pacify that gloomy Jove
Whose empty altars have enlarg'd our ills.

[*Servants bring in the sacrifice, and then exeunt.*]

Eternal Jove, great master of the clouds,
Father of gladness and all frolic thoughts,
That with thy gloomy hand corrects the heaven
When airy creatures war amongst themselves;
Hear, hear, O hear Iarbas' plaining prayers,
Whose hideous echoes make the welkin howl,
And all the woods 'Eliza' to resound.   10
The woman that thou will'd us entertain,
Where, straying in our borders up and down,
She crav'd a hide of ground to build a town,
With whom we did divide both laws and land,
And all the fruits that plenty else sends forth,
Scorning our loves and royal marriage-rites,
Yields up her beauty to a stranger's bed;
Who, having wrought her shame, is straightway fled.
Now, if thou be'st a pitying god of power,
On whom ruth and compassion ever waits,   20
Redress these wrongs, and warn him to his ships
That now afflicts me with his flattering eyes.

Enter Anna.

ANNA. How now, Iarbas, at your prayers so hard?
IARBAS. Ay, Anna: is there aught you would with me?
ANNA. Nay, no such weighty business of import
But may be slack'd until another time;
Yet if you would partake with me the cause
Of this devotion that detaineth you,
I would be thankful for such courtesy.
IARBAS. Anna, against this Trojan do I pray,   30
Who seeks to rob me of thy sister's love,
And dive into her heart by coloured looks.
ANNA. Alas, poor king, that labours so in vain

[219]

For her that so delighteth in thy pain!
Be rul'd by me, and seek some other love,
Whose yielding heart may yield thee more relief.
IARBAS. Mine eye is fix'd where fancy cannot start;
O leave me, leave me to my silent thoughts,
That register the numbers of my ruth,
And I will either move the thoughtless flint,   40
Or drop out both mine eyes in drizzling tears,
Before my sorrow's tide have any stint.
ANNA. I will not leave Iarbas whom I love
In this delight of dying pensiveness.
Away with Dido! Anna be thy song;
Anna, that doth admire thee more than heaven.
IARBAS. I may nor will list to such loathsome change
That intercepts the course of my desire.
Servants, come fetch these empty vessels here;
For I will fly from these alluring eyes,   50
That do pursue my peace where'er it goes.   *Exit.*
ANNA. Iarbas, stay, loving Iarbas, stay,
For I have honey to present thee with.
Hard-hearted, wilt not deign to hear me speak?
I'll follow thee with outcries ne'ertheless,
And strew thy walks with my dishevell'd hair.   *Exit.*

[*Scene iii.*]

Enter Aeneas *alone*.

AENEAS. Carthage, my friendly host, adieu,
Since destiny doth call me from the shore:
Hermes this night descending in a dream
Hath summon'd me to fruitful Italy.
Jove wills it so; my mother wills it so;
Let my Phoenissa grant, and then I go.
Grant she or no, Aeneas must away;
Whose golden fortunes, clogg'd with courtly ease,
Cannot ascend to Fame's immortal house,
Or banquet in bright Honour's burnish'd hall,   10
Till he hath furrowed Neptune's glassy fields,
And cut a passage through his topless hills.
Achates, come forth; Sergestus, Ilioneus,
Cloanthus, haste away. Aeneas calls.
    Enter Achates, Cloanthus, Sergestus, *and* Ilioneus.
ACHATES. What wills our lord, or wherefore did he call?
AENEAS. The dreams, brave mates, that did beset my bed,
When sleep but newly had embrac'd the night,

Commands me leave these unrenowmed realms,
Whereas nobility abhors to stay,
And none but base Aeneas will abide.   20
Aboard, aboard, since Fates do bid aboard,
And slice the sea with sable-coloured ships,
On whom the nimble winds may all day wait,
And follow them, as footmen, through the deep.
Yet Dido casts her eyes like anchors out
To stay my fleet from loosing forth the bay:
'Come back, come back,' I hear her cry afar,
'And let me link thy body to my lips,
That, tied together by the striving tongues,
We may as one sail into Italy.'   30
ACHATES. Banish that ticing dame from forth your mouth,
And follow your foreseeing stars in all;
This is no life for men-at-arms to live,
Where dalliance doth consume a soldier's strength,
And wanton motions of alluring eyes
Effeminate our minds inur'd to war.
ILIONEUS. Why, let us build a city of our own,
And not stand lingering here for amorous looks.
Will Dido raise old Priam forth his grave,
And build the town again the Greeks did burn?   40
No, no, she cares not how we sink or swim,
So she may have Aeneas in her arms.
CLOANTHUS. To Italy, sweet friends, to Italy!
We will not stay a minute longer here.
AENEAS. Trojans, aboard, and I will follow you.

                  [*Exeunt all except* Aeneas.]

I fain would go, yet beauty calls me back.
To leave her so and not once say farewell
Were to transgress against all laws of love:
But if I use such ceremonious thanks
As parting friends accustom on the shore,   50
Her silver arms will coll me round about,
And tears of pearl cry, 'Stay, Aeneas, stay!'
Each word she says will then contain a crown,
And every speech be ended with a kiss.
I may not dure this female drudgery:
To sea, Aeneas! Find out Italy.   *Exit.*

[*Scene iv.*]

     Enter Dido *and* Anna.
DIDO. O Anna, run unto the water side.

[221]

They say Aeneas' men are going aboard,
It may be he will steal away with them.
Stay not to answer me; run, Anna, run.   [*Exit* Anna.]
O foolish Trojans that would steal from hence,
And not let Dido understand their drift!
I would have given Achates store of gold,
And Ilioneus gum and Libyan spice;
The common soldiers rich embroidered coats,
And silver whistles to control the winds,   10
Which Circes sent Sichaeus when he liv'd;
Unworthy are they of a queen's reward.
See where they come; how might I do to chide?
 Enter Anna, *with* Aeneas, Achates, Ilioneus, *and* Sergestus
 [*Carthaginian* Lord *and attendants*].
ANNA. 'Twas time to run; Aeneas had been gone,
 The sails were hoising up, and he aboard.
DIDO. Is this thy love to me?
AENEAS. O princely Dido, give me leave to speak.
 I went to take my farewell of Achates.
DIDO. How haps Achates bid me not farewell?
ACHATES. Because I fear'd your grace would keep me here. 20
DIDO. To rid thee of that doubt, aboard again:
 I charge thee put to sea and stay not here.
ACHATES. Then let Aeneas go aboard with us.
DIDO. Get you aboard; Aeneas means to stay.
AENEAS. The sea is rough, the winds blow to the shore.
DIDO. O false Aeneas! Now the sea is rough,
 But when you were aboard 'twas calm enough.
 Thou and Achates meant to sail away.
AENEAS. Hath not the Carthage queen mine only son?
 Thinks Dido I will go and leave him here?   30
DIDO. Aeneas, pardon me; for I forgot
 That young Ascanius lay with me this night.
 Love made me jealous, but to make amends,
 Wear the imperial crown of Libya,
 Sway thou the Punic sceptre in my stead,
 And punish me, Aeneas, for this crime.
AENEAS. This kiss shall be fair Dido's punishment.
DIDO. O, how a crown becomes Aeneas' head!
 Stay here, Aeneas, and command as king.
AENEAS. How vain am I to wear this diadem,   40
 And bear this golden sceptre in my hand!
 A burgonet of steel, and not a crown,
 A sword, and not a sceptre, fits Aeneas.

DIDO. O keep them still, and let me gaze my fill.
  Now looks Aeneas like immortal Jove.
  O where is Ganymede to hold his cup,
  And Mercury to fly for what he calls?
  Ten thousand Cupids hover in the air,
  And fan it in Aeneas' lovely face!
  O that the clouds were here wherein thou fled'st,   50
  That thou and I unseen might sport ourselves!
  Heaven, envious of our joys, is waxen pale,
  And when we whisper, then the stars fall down,
  To be partakers of our honey talk.
AENEAS. O Dido, patroness of all our lives,
  When I leave thee, death be my punishment.
  Swell, raging seas, frown, wayward Destinies.
  Blow, winds, threaten, ye rocks and sandy shelves.
  This is the harbour that Aeneas seeks:
  Let's see what tempests can annoy me now.   60
DIDO. Not all the world can take thee from mine arms.
  Aeneas may command as many Moors
  As in the sea are little water drops.
  And now, to make experience of my love,
  Fair sister Anna, lead my lover forth,
  And, seated on my jennet, let him ride
  As Dido's husband through the Punic streets;
  And will my guard, with Mauritanian darts,
  To wait upon him as their sovereign lord.
ANNA. What if the citizens repine thereat?   70
DIDO. Those that dislike what Dido gives in charge
  Command my guard to slay for their offence.
  Shall vulgar peasants storm at what I do?
  The ground is mine that gives them sustenance,
  The air wherein they breathe, the water, fire,
  All that they have, their lands, their goods, their lives;
  And I, the goddess of all these, command
  Aeneas ride as Carthaginian king.
ACHATES. Aeneas for his parentage deserves
  As large a kingdom as is Libya.   80
AENEAS. Ay, and unless the Destinies be false,
  I shall be planted in as rich a land.
DIDO. Speak of no other land; this land is thine;
  Dido is thine, henceforth I'll call thee lord.
  Do as I bid thee, sister; lead the way,
  And from a turret I'll behold my love.
AENEAS. Then here in me shall flourish Priam's race;

And thou and I, Achates, for revenge
For Troy, for Priam, for his fifty sons,
Our kinsmen's lives and thousand guiltless souls,   90
Will lead an host against the hateful Greeks,
And fire proud Lacedaemon o'er their heads.

Exeunt [all except Dido *and Carthaginian* Lord].

DIDO. Speaks not Aeneas like a conqueror?
O blessed tempests that did drive him in!
O happy sand that made him run aground!
Henceforth you shall be our Carthage gods.
Ay, but it may be he will leave my love,
And seek a foreign land call'd Italy.
O that I had a charm to keep the winds
Within the closure of a golden ball;   100
Or that the Tyrrhene sea were in mine arms,
That he might suffer shipwrack on my breast
As oft as he attempts to hoist up sail!
I must prevent him; wishing will not serve.
Go bid my nurse take young Ascanius,
And bear him in the country to her house;
Aeneas will not go without his son.
Yet lest he should, for I am full of fear,
Bring me his oars, his tackling, and his sails.

[Exit a Lord.]   110

What if I sink his ships? O he'll frown!
Better he frown than I should die for grief.
I cannot see him frown; it may not be.
Armies of foes resolv'd to win this town,
Or impious traitors vow'd to have my life,
Affright me not; only Aeneas' frown
Is that which terrifies poor Dido's heart;
Not bloody spears, appearing in the air,
Presage the downfall of my empery,
Nor blazing comets threatens Dido's death;
It is Aeneas' frown that ends my days.   120
If he forsake me not, I never die,
For in his looks I see eternity,
And he'll make me immortal with a kiss.

Enter a Lord [*with attendants carrying tackling, etc.*]

LORD. Your nurse is gone with young Ascanius,
And here's Aeneas' tackling, oars, and sails.

DIDO. Are these the sails that in despite of me
Pack'd with the winds to bear Aeneas hence?
I'll hang ye in the chamber where I lie;

Drive, if you can, my house to Italy.
I'll set the casement open, that the winds   130
May enter in, and once again conspire
Against the life of me, poor Carthage queen.
But, though he go, he stays in Carthage still;
And let rich Carthage fleet upon the seas,
So I may have Aeneas in mine arms.
Is this the wood that grew in Carthage plains,
And would be toiling in the wat'ry billows,
To rob their mistress of her Trojan guest?
O cursed tree, hadst thou but wit or sense,
To measure how I prize Aeneas' love,   140
Thou wouldst have leapt from out the sailors' hands,
And told me that Aeneas meant to go.
And yet I blame thee not; thou art but wood.
The water, which our poets term a nymph,
Why did it suffer thee to touch her breast,
And shrunk not back, knowing my love was there?
The water is an element, no nymph.
Why should I blame Aeneas for his flight?
O Dido, blame not him, but break his oars,
These were the instruments that launch'd him forth.   150
There's not so much as this base tackling too
But dares to heap up sorrow to my heart:
Was it not you that hoised up these sails?
Why burst you not, and they fell in the seas?
For this will Dido tie ye full of knots,
And shear ye all asunder with her hands.
Now serve to chastise shipboys for their faults;
Ye shall no more offend the Carthage queen.
Now let him hang my favours on his masts,
And see if those will serve instead of sails;   160
For tackling, let him take the chains of gold
Which I bestow'd upon his followers;
Instead of oars, let him use his hands,
And swim to Italy; I'll keep these sure.
Come, bear them in.   *Exeunt.*

[*Scene v.*]
Enter the Nurse, *with* Cupid *for Ascanius.*
NURSE. My lord Ascanius, ye must go with me.
CUPID. Whither must I go? I'll stay with my mother.
NURSE. No, thou shalt go with me unto my house.
    I have an orchard that hath store of plums,

Brown almonds, services, ripe figs, and dates,
Dewberries, apples, yellow oranges;
A garden where are beehives full of honey,
Musk-roses, and a thousand sort of flowers;
And in the midst doth run a silver stream,
Where thou shalt see the red-gill'd fishes leap,   10
White swans, and many lovely water-fowls.
Now speak, Ascanius, will ye go or no?
CUPID. Come, come, I'll go. How far hence is your house?
NURSE. But hereby, child; we shall get thither straight.
CUPID. Nurse, I am weary; will you carry me?
NURSE. Ay, so you'll dwell with me, and call me mother.
CUPID. So you'll love me, I care not if I do.
NURSE. That I might live to see this boy a man!
    How prettily he laughs! Go, ye wag,
    You'll be a twigger when you come to age.   20
    Say Dido what she will, I am not old;
    I'll be no more a widow; I am young,
    I'll have a husband, or else a lover.
CUPID. A husband, and no teeth!
NURSE. O what mean I to have such foolish thoughts!
    Foolish is love, a toy. O sacred love,
    If there be any heaven in earth, 'tis love,
    Especially in women of your years.
    Blush, blush for shame; why shouldst thou think of love?
    A grave, and not a lover, fits thy age.   30
    A grave? Why, I may live a hundred years:
    Fourscore is but a girl's age: love is sweet.
    My veins are withered, and my sinews dry:
    Why do I think of love, now I should die?
CUPID. Come, nurse.
NURSE. Well, if he come a-wooing, he shall speed:
    O, how unwise was I to say him nay!

                                                    Exeunt.

                            [*Act V. Scene i.*]
        Enter Aeneas, *with a paper in his hand, drawing the platform
        of the city; with him* Achates, [Sergestus,] Cloanthus, *and*
        Ilioneus.
    AENEAS. Triumph, my mates, our travels are at end;
        Here will Aeneas build a statelier Troy
        Than that which grim Atrides overthrew.
        Carthage shall vaunt her petty walls no more,

                            [226]

For I will grace them with a fairer frame,
And clad her in a crystal livery
Wherein the day may evermore delight;
From golden India Ganges will I fetch,
Whose wealthy streams may wait upon her towers,
And triple-wise entrench her round about;   10
The sun from Egypt shall rich odours bring,
Wherewith his burning beams, like labouring bees
That load their thighs with Hybla's honey's spoils,
Shall here unburden their exhaled sweets,
And plant our pleasant suburbs with her fumes.

ACHATES. What length or breadth shall this brave town
    contain?
AENEAS. Not past four thousand paces at the most.
ILIONEUS. But what shall it be call'd? Troy, as before?
AENEAS. That have I not determin'd with myself.
CLOANTHUS. Let it be term'd Aenea, by your name.   20
SERGESTUS. Rather Ascania, by your little son.
AENEAS. Nay, I will have it called Anchisaeon,
    Of my old father's name.
        Enter Hermes *with* Ascanius.
HERMES. Aeneas, stay; Jove's herald bids thee stay.
AENEAS. Whom do I see? Jove's winged messenger!
    Welcome to Carthage new-erected town.
HERMES. Why, cousin, stand you building cities here,
    And beautifying the empire of this queen,
    While Italy is clean out of thy mind?
    Too too forgetful of thine own affairs,   30
    Why wilt thou so betray thy son's good hap?
    The king of gods sent me from highest heaven,
    To sound this angry message in thine ears:
    Vain man, what monarchy expect'st thou here?
    Or with what thought sleep'st thou in Libya shore?
    If that all glory hath forsaken thee,
    And thou despise the praise of such attempts,
    Yet think upon Ascanius' prophecy,
    And young Iulus' more than thousand years,
    Whom I have brought from Ida, where he slept,   40
    And bore young Cupid unto Cyprus isle.
AENEAS. This was my mother that beguil'd the queen,
    And made me take my brother for my son.
    No marvel, Dido, though thou be in love,
    That daily dandlest Cupid in thy arms.
    Welcome, sweet child: where hast thou been this long?

ASCANIUS. Eating sweet comfits with Queen Dido's maid,
  Who ever since hath lull'd me in her arms.
AENEAS. Sergestus, bear him hence unto our ships,
  Lest Dido, spying him, keep him for a pledge.   50
                        [*Exit* Sergestus *with* Ascanius.]
HERMES. Spend'st thou thy time about this little boy,
  And giv'st not ear unto the charge I bring?
  I tell thee, thou must straight to Italy,
  Or else abide the wrath of frowning Jove.   [*Exit.*]
AENEAS. How should I put into the raging deep,
  Who have no sails nor tackling for my ships?
  What, would the gods have me, Deucalion-like,
  Float up and down where'er the billows drive?
  Though she repair'd my fleet and gave me ships,
  Yet hath she ta'en away my oars and masts,   60
  And let me neither sail nor stern aboard.
    Enter to them Iarbas.
IARBAS. How now, Aeneas, sad? What means these dumps?
AENEAS. Iarbas, I am clean besides myself;
  Jove hath heap'd upon me such a desperate charge,
  Which neither art nor reason may achieve,
  Nor I devise by what means to contrive.
IARBAS. As how, I pray? May I entreat you tell?
AENEAS. With speed he bids me sail to Italy,
  Whenas I want both rigging for my fleet,
  And also furniture for these my men.   70
IARBAS. If that be all, then cheer thy drooping looks,
  For I will furnish thee with such supplies;
  Let some of those thy followers go with me,
  And they shall have what thing soe'er thou need'st.
AENEAS. Thanks, good Iarbas, for thy friendly aid.
  Achates and the rest shall wait on thee,
  Whilst I rest thankful for this courtesy.
                  Exeunt Iarbas *and Aeneas' train.*
  Now will I haste unto Lavinian shore,
  And raise a new foundation to old Troy.
  Witness the gods, and witness heaven and earth,   80
  How loath I am to leave these Libyan bounds,
  But that eternal Jupiter commands!
    Enter Dido [*with attendants*] *to Aeneas.*
DIDO. I fear I saw Aeneas' little son
  Led by Achates to the Trojan fleet;
  If it be so, his father means to fly.
  But here he is; now, Dido, try thy wit.

Aeneas, wherefore go thy men aboard?
Why are thy ships new rigg'd? Or to what end,
Launch'd from the haven, lie they in the road?
Pardon me though I ask; love makes me ask.   90
AENEAS. O pardon me if I resolve thee why.
Aeneas will not feign with his dear love.
I must from hence: this day, swift Mercury,
When I was laying a platform for these walls,
Sent from his father Jove, appear'd to me,
And in his name rebuk'd me bitterly
For lingering here, neglecting Italy.
DIDO. But yet Aeneas will not leave his love.
AENEAS. I am commanded by immortal Jove
To leave this town and pass to Italy;   100
And therefore must of force.
DIDO. These words proceed not from Aeneas' heart.
AENEAS. Not from my heart, for I can hardly go;
And yet I may not stay. Dido, farewell.
DIDO. Farewell? Is this the mends for Dido's love?
Do Trojans use to quit their lovers thus?
Fare well may Dido, so Aeneas stay;
I die, if my Aeneas say farewell.
AENEAS. Then let me go, and never say farewell.
DIDO. 'Let me go'; 'farewell'; 'I must from hence'.   110
These words are poison to poor Dido's soul:
O speak like my Aeneas, like my love!
Why look'st thou toward the sea? The time hath been
When Dido's beauty chain'd thine eyes to her.
Am I less fair than when thou saw'st me first?
O then, Aeneas, 'tis for grief of thee.
Say thou wilt stay in Carthage with thy queen,
And Dido's beauty will return again.
Aeneas, say, how canst thou take thy leave?
Wilt thou kiss Dido? O, thy lips have sworn   120
To stay with Dido. Canst thou take her hand?
Thy hand and mine have plighted mutual faith;
Therefore, unkind Aeneas, must thou say,
'Then let me go, and never say farewell'?
AENEAS. O Queen of Carthage, were thou ugly-black,
Aeneas could not choose but hold thee dear.
Yet must he not gainsay the gods' behest.
DIDO. The gods? What gods be those that seek my death?
Wherein have I offended Jupiter,
That he should take Aeneas from mine arms?   130

O no! The gods weigh not what lovers do:
It is Aeneas calls Aeneas hence,
And woeful Dido, by these blubb'red cheeks,
By this right hand, and by our spousal rites,
Desires Aeneas to remain with her.
Si bene quid de te merui, fuit aut tibi quidquam
Dulce meum, miserere domus labentis, et istam
Oro, si quis adhuc precibus locus, exue mentem.
AENEAS. *Desine meque tuis incendere teque querelis;*
   Italiam non sponte sequor.   140
DIDO. Hast thou forgot how many neighbour kings
   Were up in arms, for making thee my love?
   How Carthage did rebel, Iarbas storm,
   And all the world call me a second Helen
   For being entangled by a stranger's looks?
   So thou wouldst prove as true as Paris did,
   Would, as fair Troy was, Carthage might be sack'd,
   And I be call'd a second Helena!
   Had I a son by thee the grief were less,
   That I might see Aeneas in his face.   150
   Now if thou go'st, what canst thou leave behind
   But rather will augment than ease my woe?
AENEAS. In vain, my love, thou spend'st thy fainting breath:
   If words might move me, I were overcome.
DIDO. And wilt thou not be mov'd with Dido's words?
   Thy mother was no goddess, perjur'd man,
   Nor Dardanus the author of thy stock;
   But thou art sprung from Scythian Caucasus,
   And tigers from Hyrcania gave thee suck.
   Ah, foolish Dido, to forbear this long!   160
   Wast thou not wrack'd upon this Libyan shore,
   And cam'st to Dido like a fisher swain?
   Repair'd not I thy ships, made thee a king,
   And all thy needy followers noblemen?
   O serpent, that came creeping from the shore,
   And I for pity harbour'd in my bosom,
   Wilt thou now slay me with thy venomed sting,
   And hiss at Dido for preserving thee?
   Go, go and spare not; seek out Italy;
   I hope that that which love forbids me do,   170
   The rocks and sea-gulfs will perform at large,
   And thou shalt perish in the billows' ways,
   To whom poor Dido doth bequeath revenge.
   Ay, traitor, and the waves shall cast thee up,

Where thou and false Achates first set foot;
Which if it chance, I'll give ye burial,
And weep upon your lifeless carcasses,
Though thou nor he will pity me a whit.
Why star'st thou in my face? If thou wilt stay,
Leap in mine arms, mine arms are open wide;   180
If not, turn from me, and I'll turn from thee;
For though thou hast the heart to say farewell,
I have not power to stay thee.   [*Exit* Aeneas.]
                Is he gone?
Ay, but he'll come again, he cannot go;
He loves me too too well to serve me so:
Yet he that in my sight would not relent,
Will, being absent, be obdurate still.
By this is he got to the water-side;
And see, the sailors take him by the hand,
But he shrinks back; and now, rememb'ring me,   190
Returns amain: welcome, welcome, my love!
But where's Aeneas? Ah, he's gone, he's gone!
    [*Enter* Anna.]
ANNA. What means my sister thus to rave and cry?
DIDO. O Anna, my Aeneas is aboard,
And, leaving me, will sail to Italy!
Once didst thou go, and he came back again:
Now bring him back, and thou shalt be a queen,
And I will live a private life with him.
ANNA. Wicked Aeneas!
DIDO. Call him not wicked, sister; speak him fair,   200
And look upon him with a mermaid's eye;
Tell him, I never vow'd at Aulis gulf
The desolation of his native Troy,
Nor sent a thousand ships unto the walls,
Nor ever violated faith to him.
Request him gently, Anna, to return:
I crave but this, he stay a tide or two,
That I may learn to bear it patiently;
If he depart thus suddenly, I die.
Run, Anna, run; stay not to answer me.   210
ANNA. I go, fair sister: heavens grant good success!   *Exit.*
    Enter the Nurse.
NURSE. O Dido, your little son Ascanius
Is gone. He lay with me last night,
And in the morning he was stol'n from me:
I think some fairies have beguiled me.

DIDO. O cursed hag and false dissembling wretch,
That slay'st me with thy harsh and hellish tale.
Thou for some petty gift hast let him go,
And I am thus deluded of my boy.
Away with her to prison presently,   220
Traitoress too keen and cursed sorceress!
NURSE. I know not what you mean by treason, I;
I am as true as any one of yours.

                          Exeunt the Nurse [*and* Attendants].

DIDO. Away with her! Suffer her not to speak.
My sister comes: I like not her sad looks.
    Enter Anna.
ANNA. Before I came, Aeneas was aboard,
And spying me, hois'd up the sails amain;
But I cried out, 'Aeneas, false Aeneas, stay!'
Then gan he wag his hand, which yet held up,
Made me suppose he would have heard me speak.   230
Then gan they drive into the ocean,
Which when I view'd, I cried, 'Aeneas, stay!
Dido, fair Dido wills Aeneas stay!'
Yet he, whose heart of adamant or flint
My tears nor plaints could mollify a whit.
Then carelessly I rent my hair for grief,
Which seen to all, though he beheld me not,
They gan to move him to redress my ruth,
And stay a while to hear what I could say;
But he, clapp'd under hatches, sail'd away.   240
DIDO. O Anna, Anna, I will follow him!
ANNA. How can ye go when he hath all your fleet?
DIDO. I'll frame me wings of wax like Icarus,
And o'er his ships will soar unto the sun,
That they may melt and I fall in his arms;
Or else I'll make a prayer unto the waves,
That I may swim to him, like Triton's niece.
O Anna, fetch Arion's harp,
That I may tice a dolphin to the shore,
And ride upon his back unto my love.   250
Look, sister, look, lovely Aeneas' ships!
See, see, the billows heave him up to heaven,
And now down falls the keels into the deep.
O sister, sister, take away the rocks,
They'll break his ships, O Proteus, Neptune, Jove,
Save, save Aeneas, Dido's liefest love.
Now is he come on shore, safe without hurt;

But see, Achates wills him put to sea,
And all the sailors merry-make for joy;
But he, rememb'ring me, shrinks back again.   260
See where he comes. Welcome, welcome, my love!
ANNA. Ah, sister, leave these idle fantasies.
Sweet sister, cease; remember who you are.
DIDO. Dido I am, unless I be deceiv'd,
And must I rave thus for a runagate?
Must I make ships for him to sail away?
Nothing can bear me to him but a ship,
And he hath all my fleet. What shall I do,
But die in fury of this oversight?
Ay, I must be the murderer of myself: 270
No, but I am not; yet I will be straight.
Anna, be glad; now have I found a mean
To rid me from these thoughts of lunacy:
Not far from hence
There is a woman famoused for arts,
Daughter unto the nymphs Hesperides,
Who will'd me sacrifice his ticing relics.
Go, Anna, bid my servants bring me fire.   *Exit* Anna.
     Enter Iarbas.
IARBAS. How long will Dido mourn a stranger's flight
That hath dishonour'd her and Carthage both?   280
How long shall I with grief consume my days,
And reap no guerdon for my truest love?
     [*Enter attendants with wood and torches.*]
DIDO. Iarbas, talk not of Aeneas. Let him go.
Lay to thy hands, and help me make a fire
That shall consume all that this stranger left;
For I intend a private sacrifice,
To cure my mind that melts for unkind love.
IARBAS. But afterwards will Dido grant me love?
DIDO. Ay, ay, Iarbas; after this is done,
None in the world shall have my love but thou.   290
So, leave me now; let none approach this place.
                                        Exit Iarbas.
Now, Dido, with these relics burn thyself,
And make Aeneas famous through the world
For perjury and slaughter of a queen.
Here lie the sword that in the darksome cave
He drew, and swore by to be true to me:
Thou shalt burn first; thy crime is worse than his.
Here lie the garment which I cloth'd him in

[233]

When first he came on shore; perish thou too.
These letters, lines, and perjur'd papers all   300
Shall burn to cinders in this precious flame.
And now ye gods that guide the starry frame
And order all things at your high dispose,
Grant, though the traitors land in Italy,
They may be still tormented with unrest;
And from mine ashes let a conqueror rise,
That may revenge this treason to a queen
By ploughing up his countries with the sword:
Betwixt this land and that be never league;
Litora litoribus contraria, fluctibus undas   310
Imprecor, arma armis; pugnent ipsique nepotes!
Live, false Aeneas. Truest Dido dies;
Sic, sic iuvat ire sub umbras.   [*Throws herself into the flames.*]
   Enter Anna.

ANNA. O help, Iarbas, Dido in these flames
   Hath burnt herself. Ay me, unhappy me!
   Enter Iarbas *running.*

IARBAS. Cursed Iarbas, die to expiate
   The grief that tires upon thine inward soul.
   Dido, I come to thee. Ay me, Aeneas!   [*Kills himself.*]

ANNA. What can my tears or cries prevail me now?
   Dido is dead, Iarbas slain, Iarbas my dear love.   320
   O sweet Iarbas, Anna's sole delight,
   What fatal Destiny envies me thus,
   To see my sweet Iarbas slay himself?
   But Anna now shall honour thee in death,
   And mix her blood with thine; this shall I do,
   That gods and men may pity this my death,
   And rue our ends, senseless of life or breath.
   Now, sweet Iarbas, stay; I come to thee.   [*Kills herself.*]

FINIS.

The Massacre at Paris

The Massacre at Paris was published by Edward White in an undated and unregistered octavo, attributing the authorship to 'Christopher Marlow'. This is the only early edition, though a manuscript fragment survives from a different, longer text. The date of composition must be after the death of Henry III on 2 August 1589, and possibly that of Pope Sixtus V on 27 August 1590, and before the first recorded performance of January 1593. Marlowe was in fact dramatizing very recent history, of which there were accounts to be had in pamphlets as well, no doubt, as by word of mouth. His source for the early scenes is Ernest Varamund, *A true and plaine report of the Furious outrages of Fraunce* (1573, 1574).

White's title-page states that the play was performed by the Admiral's Men. Henslowe's Diary records performances of 'the tragedey of the gvyes' at the Rose Theatre in January 1593, and by the Admiral's Men some ten times in 1594. William Bird alias Borne (who was later to help provide additions to *Faustus*) borrowed twelve shillings on 19 November 1598 to embroider his hat for 'the gwisse', and twenty shillings on 27 November to buy a pair of silk stockings 'to playe the gwisse in'. On 3 November 1601 Henslowe put up £3 for 'stamell cllath for A clocke for the gwisse' (coarse red woollen cloth for a cloak) and thirty shillings for 'fuschen and lynynge for the clockes for the masaker of france' (i.e. fustian); and there are further expenses 'for mackeynge of sewtes for the gwesse' in November. On 18 January 1602 Henslowe bought the play-book from Edward Alleyn, his son-in-law, on behalf of the company. This might be thought to indicate that the text was not then available in print, were it not that the printed text we have is some kind of surreptitious copy.

Charles IX, King of France
Duke of Anjou, his brother; later *King Henry III*
Duke of Guise
Cardinal of Lorraine } brothers to the Duke of Guise
Duke of Dumaine
Son to the Duke of Guise
Gonzago } followers of the Duke of Guise
Retes
Mountsorell
Epernoun
Joyeux } minions of Anjou
Mugeroun
King of Navarre, later *King Henry IV*
Prince of Condé
Lord High Admiral
The Admiral's Man
Pleshé } friends of Navarre
Bartus
Cossin, Captain of the Guard
Loreine
Seroune } victims in the Massacre
Ramus
Taleus, friend to Ramus

Catherine, Queen-Mother of France
Joan, Old Queen of Navarre, mother to Navarre
Margaret, Queen of Navarre, daughter to Catherine, wife to
  Navarre
Duchess of Guise
Wife to Seroune
Maid to the Duchess of Guise

Apothecary
Two Lords of Poland
Cutpurse
Friar
Surgeon
The English Agent
Three Murderers

Protestants, Schoolmasters,
Soldiers, Attendants, Messengers]

The Massacre at Paris

[Scene i.]
Enter Charles *the French King,* [Catherine] *the Queen-Mother, the King of* Navarre, *the Prince of* Condé, *the* Lord High Admiral, *and* [Margaret] *the Queen of Navarre, with others.*

CHARLES. Prince of Navarre, my honourable brother,
Prince Condé, and my good Lord Admiral,
I wish this union and religious league,
Knit in these hands, thus join'd in nuptial rites,
May not dissolve till death dissolve our lives,
And that the native sparks of princely love,
That kindled first this motion in our hearts,
May still be fuell'd in our progeny.
NAVARRE. The many favours which your grace hath shown,
From time to time, but specially in this,   10
Shall bind me ever to your highness' will,
In what Queen-Mother or your grace commands.
CATHERINE. Thanks, son Navarre; you see we love you well,
That link you in marriage with our daughter here;
And, as you know, our difference in religion
Might be a means to cross you in your love.
CHARLES. Well, Madam, let that rest.
And now, my lords, the marriage-rites perform'd,
We think it good to go and consummate
The rest with hearing of a holy mass.   20
Sister, I think yourself will bear us company.
MARGARET. I will, my good lord.
CHARLES. The rest that will not go, my lords, may stay.
Come, mother,
Let us go to honour this solemnity.
CATHERINE. Which I'll dissolve with blood and cruelty.
Exeunt the King, Queen-Mother *and the* Queen of Navarre
[*with others*]. *And manent* Navarre, *the Prince of* Condé, *and
the* Lord High Admiral.
NAVARRE. Prince Condé and my good Lord Admiral,
Now Guise may storm, but do us little hurt,
Having the King, Queen-Mother on our sides
To stop the malice of his envious heart   30
That seeks to murder all the Protestants.

Have you not heard of late how he decreed,
If that the King had given consent thereto,
That all the Protestants that are in Paris
Should have been murdered the other night?
ADMIRAL. My lord, I marvel that th'aspiring Guise
  Dares once adventure without the king's consent
  To meddle or attempt such dangerous things.
CONDÉ. My lord, you need not marvel at the Guise,
  For what he doth the Pope will ratify,   40
  In murder, mischief, or in tyranny.
NAVARRE. But He that sits and rules above the clouds
  Doth hear and see the prayers of the just,
  And will revenge the blood of innocents
  That Guise hath slain by treason of his heart,
  And brought by murder to their timeless ends.
ADMIRAL. My lord, but did you mark the Cardinal,
  The Guise's brother, and the Duke Dumaine,
  How they did storm at these your nuptial rites,
  Because the house of Bourbon now comes in,   50
  And joins your linnage to the crown of France?
NAVARRE. And that's the cause that Guise so frowns at us,
  And beats his brains to catch us in his trap,
  Which he hath pitch'd within his deadly toil.
  Come, my lords, let's go to the church, and pray
  That God may still defend the right of France,
  And make his gospel flourish in this land.   *Exeunt.*

[*Scene ii.*]
Enter the Duke of Guise.

GUISE. If ever Hymen lour'd at marriage-rites,
  And had his altars deck'd with dusky lights;
  If ever sun stain'd heaven with bloody clouds,
  And made it look with terror on the world;
  If ever day were turn'd to ugly night,
  And night made semblance of the hue of hell;
  This day, this hour, this fatal night,
  Shall fully show the fury of them all.
  Apothecary!
    Enter the Apothecary.
APOTHECARY. My lord?   10
GUISE. Now shall I prove and guerdon to the full
  The love thou bear'st unto the house of Guise.
  Where are those perfumed gloves which I sent
  To be poisoned? Hast thou done them? Speak;

Will every savour breed a pang of death?
APOTHECARY. See where they be, my good lord,
  And he that smells but to them, dies.
GUISE. Then thou remainest resolute?
APOTHECARY. I am, my lord, in what your grace commands,
  Till death.   20
GUISE. Thanks, my good friend, I will requite thy love.
  Go then, present them to the Queen Navarre:
  For she is that huge blemish in our eye,
  That makes these upstart heresies in France.
  Be gone my friend, present them to her straight.
                                   Exit Apothecary.

Soldier!
    Enter a Soldier.
SOLDIER. My lord?
GUISE. Now come thou forth, and play thy tragic part.
  Stand in some window opening near the street,
  And when thou see'st the Admiral ride by,   30
  Discharge thy musket and perform his death,
  And then I'll guerdon thee with store of crowns.
SOLDIER. I will, my lord.   *Exit* Soldier.
GUISE. Now, Guise, begins those deep-engend'red thoughts
  To burst abroad those never-dying flames
  Which cannot be extinguish'd but by blood.
  Oft have I levell'd, and at last have learn'd
  That peril is the chiefest way to happiness,
  And resolution honour's fairest aim.
  What glory is there in a common good   40
  That hangs for every peasant to achieve?
  That like I best that flies beyond my reach.
  Set me to scale the high Pyramides,
  And thereon set the diadem of France,
  I'll either rend it with my nails to naught,
  Or mount the top with my aspiring wings,
  Although my downfall be the deepest hell.
  For this I wake, when others think I sleep;
  For this I wait, that scorns attendance else;
  For this, my quenchless thirst whereon I build,   50
  Hath often pleaded kindred to the king;
  For this, this head, this heart, this hand and sword,
  Contrives, imagines, and fully executes,
  Matters of import aimed at by many,
  Yet understood by none.
  For this, hath heaven engend'red me of earth;

For this, this earth sustains my body's weight,
And with this weight I'll counterpoise a crown,
Or with seditions weary all the world.
For this, from Spain the stately Catholic   60
Sends Indian gold to coin me French écus;
For this, have I a largess from the Pope,
A pension and dispensation too;
And by that privilege to work upon,
My policy hath fram'd religion.
Religion: *O Diabole!*
Fie, I am asham'd, however that I seem,
To think a word of such a simple sound
Of so great matter should be made the ground.
The gentle king, whose pleasure uncontroll'd   70
Weak'neth his body and will waste his realm,
If I repair not what he ruinates,
Him as a child I daily win with words,
So that for proof he barely bears the name;
I execute, and he sustains the blame.
The Mother Queen works wonders for my sake,
And in my love entombs the hope of France,
Rifling the bowels of her treasury,
To supply my wants and necessity.
Paris hath full five hundred colleges,   80
As monasteries, priories, abbeys, and halls,
Wherein are thirty thousand able men,
Besides a thousand sturdy student Catholics;
And more—of my knowledge, in one cloister keeps
Five hundred fat Franciscan friars and priests.
All this and more, if more may be compris'd,
To bring the will of our desires to end.
Then, Guise,
Since thou hast all the cards within thy hands,
To shuffle or cut, take this as surest thing,   90
That, right or wrong, thou deal thyself a king.
Ay, but Navarre, Navarre—'tis but a nook of France,
Sufficient yet for such a petty king,
That with a rabblement of his heretics
Blinds Europe's eyes, and troubleth our estate.
Him will we—(*Pointing to his sword.*)
But first let's follow those in France
That hinder our possession to the crown.
As Caesar to his soldiers, so say I:
Those that hate me will I learn to loathe.   100

Give me a look that when I bend the brows
Pale death may walk in furrows of my face;
A hand that with a grasp may gripe the world;
An ear to hear what my detractors say;
A royal seat, a sceptre, and a crown,
That those which do behold, they may become
As men that stand and gaze against the sun.
The plot is laid, and things shall come to pass
Where resolution strives for victory.   *Exit.*

[*Scene iii.*]
Enter the King of Navarre *and Queen* [Margaret] *and his
Mother Queen* [Joan], *the Prince of* Condé, *the* Admiral, *and
the* Apothecary *with the gloves, and gives them to the Old
Queen.*

APOTHECARY. Madam,
  I beseech your grace to accept this simple gift.
JOAN. Thanks, my good friend. Hold, take thou this reward.
APOTHECARY. I humbly thank your majesty.
                               Exit Apothecary.
JOAN. Methinks the gloves have a very strong perfume,
  The scent whereof doth make my head to ache.
NAVARRE. Doth not your grace know the man that gave
    them you?
JOAN. Not well, but do remember such a man.
ADMIRAL. Your grace was ill-advis'd to take them, then,
  Considering of these dangerous times.   10
JOAN. Help, son Navarre, I am poisoned.
MARGARET. The heavens forbid your highness such mishap.
NAVARRE. The late suspicion of the Duke of Guise
  Might well have mov'd your highness to beware
  How you did meddle with such dangerous gifts.
MARGARET. Too late it is, my lord, if that be true,
  To blame her highness; but I hope it be
  Only some natural passion makes her sick.
JOAN. O, no, sweet Margaret,
  The fatal poison works within my head;   20
  My brain-pan breaks, my heart doth faint; I die.   *She dies.*
NAVARRE. My mother poisoned here before my face!
  O gracious God, what times are these?
  O grant, sweet God, my days may end with hers,
  That I with her may die and live again.
MARGARET. Let not this heavy chance, my dearest lord
  (For whose effects my soul is massacred)

[241]

Infect thy gracious breast with fresh supply
To aggravate our sudden misery.

ADMIRAL. Come, my lords, let us bear her body hence,   30
And see it honoured with just solemnity.

As they are going, the Soldier *dischargeth his musket at the*
Lord Admiral.

CONDÉ. What, are you hurt, my Lord High Admiral?

ADMIRAL. Ay, my good lord, shot through the arm.

NAVARRE. We are betray'd. Come, my lords, and let us go tell
the king of this.

ADMIRAL. These are the cursed Guisians, that do seek our
death.

O, fatal was this marriage to us all.

They bear away the Queen and go out.

[*Scene iv.*]

Enter the King, Queen-Mother, *Duke of* Guise, *Duke* Anjou,
Duke Dumaine [,Cossin, *and* Attendants].

CATHERINE. My noble son, and princely Duke of Guise,
Now have we got the fatal, straggling deer
Within the compass of a deadly toil,
And as we late decreed we may perform.

CHARLES. Madam, it will be noted through the world
An action bloody and tyrannical—
Chiefly since under safety of our word
They justly challenge their protection.
Besides, my heart relents that noble men,
Only corrupted in religion,   10
Ladies of honour, knights, and gentlemen,
Should for their conscience taste such ruthless ends.

ANJOU. Though gentle minds should pity others' pains,
Yet will the wisest note their proper griefs,
And rather seek to scourge their enemies
Than be themselves base subjects to the whip.

GUISE. Methinks, my lord, Anjou hath well advis'd
Your highness to consider of the thing,
And rather choose to seek your country's good
Than pity or relieve these upstart heretics.   20 ·

CATHERINE. I hope these reasons may serve my princely son
To have some care for fear of enemies.

CHARLES. Well, madam, I refer it to your majesty,
And to my nephew here, the Duke of Guise:
What you determine, I will ratify.

CATHERINE. Thanks to my princely son. Then tell me, Guise,

What order will you set down for the massacre?
GUISE. Thus, madam.
They that shall be actors in this massacre
Shall wear white crosses on their burgonets,   30
And tie white linen scarfs about their arms;
He that wants these, and is suspected of heresy,
Shall die, be he king or emperor. Then I'll have
A peal of ordnance shot from the tower, at which
They all shall issue out, and set the streets;
And then, the watchword being given, a bell shall ring,
Which when they hear, they shall begin to kill,
And never cease until that bell shall cease;
Then breathe a while.
        Enter the Admiral's Man.
CHARLES. How now, fellow, what news?   40
MAN. And it please your grace, the Lord High Admiral,
Riding the streets, was traitorously shot;
And most humbly entreats your majesty
To visit him sick in his bed.
CHARLES. Messenger, tell him I will see him straight.
                                        Exit Messenger.
What shall we do now with the Admiral?
CATHERINE. Your majesty were best go visit him,
And make a show as if all were well.
CHARLES. Content; I will go visit the Admiral.
GUISE. And I will go take order for his death.   50
                                        Exit Guise.

[Scene v.]
        Enter the Admiral *in his bed.*
CHARLES. How fares it with my Lord High Admiral?
Hath he been hurt with villains in the street?
I vow and swear, as I am King of France,
To find and to repay the man with death,
With death delay'd and torments never us'd,
That durst presume, for hope of any gain,
To hurt the noble man their sovereign loves.
ADMIRAL. Ah, my good lord, these are the Guisians,
That seek to massacre our guiltless lives.
CHARLES. Assure yourself, my good Lord Admiral,   10
I deeply sorrow for your treacherous wrong,
And that I am not more secure myself
Than I am careful you should be preserv'd.
Cossin, take twenty of our strongest guard,

And under your direction see they keep
All treacherous violence from our noble friend,
Repaying all attempts with present death
Upon the cursed breakers of our peace.
And so be patient, good Lord Admiral,
And every hour I will visit you.   20
ADMIRAL. I humbly thank your royal majesty.   *Exeunt omnes.*

[*Scene vi.*]

Enter Guise, Anjou, Dumaine, Gonzago, Retes, Mountsorrell, *and* Soldiers *to the massacre.*

GUISE. Anjou, Dumaine, Gonzago, Retes, swear
By the argent crosses in your burgonets
To kill all that you suspect of heresy.
DUMAINE. I swear by this to be unmerciful.
ANJOU. I am disguis'd, and none knows who I am,
And therefore mean to murder all I meet.
GONZAGO. And so will I.
RETES. And I.
GUISE. Away, then, break into the Admiral's house.
RETES. Ay, let the Admiral be first dispatch'd.   10
GUISE. The Admiral,
Chief standard-bearer to the Lutherans,
Shall in the entrance of this massacre
Be murdered in his bed.
Gonzago, conduct them thither, and then
Beset his house, that not a man may live.
ANJOU. That charge is mine. Switzers, keep you the streets;
And at each corner shall the King's guard stand.
GONZAGO. Come, sirs, follow me.
                    Exit Gonzago *and others with him.*
ANJOU. Cossin, the captain of the Admiral's guard,   20
Plac'd by my brother, will betray his lord.
Now, Guise, shall Catholics flourish once again;
The head being off, the members cannot stand.
RETES. But look, my lord, there's some in the Admiral's house.
    Enter [Gonzago *and others*] *into the* Admiral's *house; and he
    in his bed.*
ANJOU. In lucky time: come, let us keep this lane,
And slay his servants that shall issue out.
GONZAGO. Where is the Admiral?
ADMIRAL. O, let me pray before I die.
GONZAGO. Then pray unto our Lady; kiss this cross. *Stab him.*
ADMIRAL. O God, forgive my sins.   30

GUISE. Gonzago, what, is he dead?
GONZAGO. Ay, my lord.
GUISE. Then throw him down.
                    [*The body of the* Admiral *is thrown down.*]
ANJOU. Now, cousin, view him well;
   It may be it is some other, and he escap'd.
GUISE. Cousin, 'tis he, I know him by his look.
   See where my soldier shot him through the arm;
   He miss'd him near, but we have struck him now.
   Ah, base Shatillian and degenerate,
   Chief standard-bearer to the Lutherans,   40
   Thus in despite of thy religion
   The Duke of Guise stamps on thy lifeless bulk.
ANJOU. Away with him, cut off his head and hands,
   And send them for a present to the Pope;
   And when this just revenge is finished,
   Unto Mount Faucon will we drag his corse,
   And he that living hated so the cross,
   Shall, being dead, be hang'd thereon in chains.
GUISE. Anjou, Gonzago, Retes, if that you three
   Will be as resolute as I and Dumaine,   50
   There shall not a Huguenot breathe in France.
ANJOU. I swear by this cross, we'll not be partial,
   But slay as many as we can come near.
GUISE. Mountsorrell, go shoot the ordnance off,
   That they which have already set the street
   May know their watchword; then toll the bell,
   And so let's forward to the massacre.
MOUNTSORRELL. I will, my lord.   *Exit.*
GUISE. And now, my lords, let us closely to our business.
ANJOU. Anjou will follow thee.   60
DUMAINE. And so will Dumaine.
                    The ordnance being shot off, the bell tolls.
GUISE. Come, then, let's away.   *Exeunt.*

                    [*Scene vii.*]
   The Guise *enters again, with all the rest, with their swords
   drawn, chasing the* Protestants.
GUISE. *Tue, tue, tue.*
   Let none escape. Murder the Huguenots.
ANJOU. Kill them. Kill them.   *Exeunt.*
   Enter Loreine, *running;* Guise *and the rest pursuing him.*
GUISE. Loreine, Loreine, follow Loreine.—Sirrah,
   Are you a preacher of these heresies?

                    [245]

LOREINE. I am a preacher of the word of God,
   And thou a traitor to thy soul and him.
GUISE. Dearly beloved brother, thus 'tis written.
                                              He stabs him.
ANJOU. Stay, my lord, let me begin the psalm.
GUISE. Come, drag him away, and throw him in a ditch.   10
                                              Exeunt.

[*Scene viii.*]
   Enter Mountsorrell, *and knocks at* Seroune's *door.*
SEROUNE'S WIFE [*within*]. Who is that which knocks there?
MOUNTSORRELL. Mountsorrell, from the Duke of Guise.
SEROUNE'S WIFE. Husband, come down; here's one would speak
   with you from the Duke of Guise.
   Enter Seroune.
SEROUNE. To speak with me, from such a man as he?
MOUNTSORRELL. Ay, ay, for this, Seroune; and thou shalt ha't.
                                              Showing his dagger.
SEROUNE. O'let me pray before I take my death.
MOUNTSORRELL. Dispatch then, quickly.
SEROUNE. O Christ my Saviour!
MOUNTSORRELL. Christ, villain?   10
   Why, dar'st thou presume to call on Christ,
   Without the intercession of some saint?
   Sanctus Jacobus, he's my saint; pray to him.
SEROUNE. O, let me pray unto my God.
MOUNTSORRELL. Then take this with you.   *Stab him.*
                                              Exit.

[*Scene ix.*]
   Enter Ramus *in his study.*
RAMUS. What fearful cries comes from the river Seine,
   That frights poor Ramus sitting at his book?
   I fear the Guisians have pass'd the bridge,
   And mean once more to menace me.
   Enter Taleus.
TALEUS. Fly, Ramus, fly, if thou wilt save thy life.
RAMUS. Tell me, Taleus, wherefore should I fly?
TALEUS. The Guisians are
   Hard at thy door, and mean to murder us.
   Hark, hark, they come. I'll leap out at the window.
RAMUS. Sweet Taleus, stay.   10
   Enter Gonzago *and* Retes.
GONZAGO. Who goes there?

[246]

RETES. 'Tis Taleus, Ramus' bedfellow.

GONZAGO. What art thou?

TALEUS. I am as Ramus is, a Christian.

RETES. O let him go; he is a Catholic.   *Exit* Taleus.

GONZAGO. Come, Ramus, more gold, or thou shalt have the stab.

RAMUS. Alas, I am a scholar, how should I have gold?
    All that I have is but my stipend from the king,
    Which is no sooner receiv'd but it is spent.
      Enter the Guise *and* Anjou [*with* Dumaine, Mountsorrell,
      and Soldiers].

ANJOU. Who have you there?   20

RETES. 'Tis Ramus, the king's Professor of Logic.

GUISE. Stab him.

RAMUS. O good my lord,
    Wherein hath Ramus been so offensious?

GUISE. Marry, sir, in having a smack in all,
    And yet didst never sound anything to the depth.
    Was it not thou that scoff'dst the *Organon*,
    And said it was a heap of vanities?
    He that will be a flat dichotomist,
    And seen in nothing but epitomes,   30
    Is in your judgement thought a learned man;
    And he, forsooth, must go and preach in Germany,
    Excepting against doctors' axioms,
    And *ipse dixi* with this quiddity,
    Argumentum testimonii est inartificiale.
    To contradict which, I say; Ramus shall die.
    How answer you that? Your *nego argumentum*
    Cannot serve, sirrah. Kill him.

RAMUS. O, good my lord, let me but speak a word.

ANJOU. Well, say on.   40

RAMUS. Not for my life do I desire this pause,
    But in my latter hour to purge myself,
    In that I know the things that I have wrote,
    Which, as I hear, one Scheckius takes it ill,
    Because my places, being but three, contains all his.
    I knew the *Organon* to be confus'd,
    And I reduc'd it into better form:
    And this for Aristotle will I say,
    That he that despiseth him can ne'er
    Be good in logic or philosophy;   50
    And that's because the blockish Sorbonnists
    Attribute as much unto their works
    As to the service of the eternal God.

GUISE. Why suffer you that peasant to declaim?
　　Stab him, I say, and send him to his friends in hell.
ANJOU. Ne'er was there collier's son so full of pride. *Kill him.*
GUISE. My lord of Anjou, there are a hundred Protestants
　　Which we have chas'd into the river Seine
　　That swim about and so preserve their lives.
　　How may we do? I fear me they will live.   60
DUAMINE. Go place some men upon the bridge
　　With bows and darts to shoot at them they see,
　　And sink them in the river as they swim.
GUISE. 'Tis well advis'd, Dumaine; go see it straight be done.
　　　　　　　　　　　　　　　　　　　　[*Exit* Dumaine.]
　　And in the meantime, my lord, could we devise
　　To get those pedants from the King Navarre
　　That are tutors to him and the Prince of Condé—
ANJOU. For that, let me alone; cousin, stay you here,
　　And when you see me in, then follow hard.
　　　　He knocketh, and enter the King of Navarre *and Prince of*
　　　　Condé, *with their* Schoolmasters.
　　How now, my lords, how fare you?   70
NAVARRE. My lord, they say
　　That all the Protestants are massacred.
ANJOU. Ay, so they are; but yet, what remedy?
　　I have done what I could to stay this broil.
NAVARRE. But yet, my lord, the report doth run
　　That you were one that made this massacre.
ANJOU. Who, I? You are deceiv'd; I rose but now.
　　　　Guise [*with* Gonzago, Retes, Mountsorrell, *and* Soldiers]
　　　　comes forward.
GUISE. Murder the Huguenots, take those pedants hence.
NAVARRE. Thou traitor, Guise, lay off thy bloody hands.
CONDÉ. Come, let us go tell the King.   80
　　　　　　　　　　　Exeunt [Condé *and* Navarre].
GUISE. Come sirs,
　　I'll whip you to death with my poniard's point.
　　　　　　　　　　　　　　　　He kills them.
ANJOU. Away with them both.
　　　　　　　　Exit Anjou [*with* Soldiers *carrying the bodies*].
GUISE. And now, sirs, for this night let our fury stay.
　　Yet will we not that the massacre shall end.
　　Gonzago, post you to Orleans,
　　Retes to Dieppe, Mountsorrell unto Rouen,
　　And spare not one that you suspect of heresy.
　　And now stay that bell, that to the devil's matins rings.

Now every man put off his burgonet,   90
And so convey him closely to his bed.   *Exeunt.*

[*Scene x.*]
Enter Anjou, *with two* Lords *of Poland.*
ANJOU. My lords of Poland, I must needs confess
The offer of your Prince Electors far
Beyond the reach of my deserts;
For Poland is, as I have been inform'd,
A martial people, worthy such a king
As hath sufficient counsel in himself
To lighten doubts and frustrate subtle foes;
And such a king whom practice long hath taught
To please himself with manage of the wars,
The greatest wars within our Christian bounds,   10
I mean our wars against the Muscovites,
And on the other side against the Turk,
Rich princes both, and mighty emperors.
Yet, by my brother Charles, our King of France,
And by his grace's council, it is thought
That if I undertake to wear the crown
Of Poland, it may prejudice their hope
Of my inheritance to the crown of France;
For if th'Almighty take my brother hence,
By due descent the regal seat is mine.   20
With Poland, therefore, must I covenant thus:
That if, by death of Charles, the diadem
Of France be cast on me, then with your leaves
I may retire me to my native home.
If your commission serve to warrant this,
I thankfully shall undertake the charge
Of you and yours, and carefully maintain
The wealth and safety of your kingdom's right.
1 LORD. All this and more your highness shall command
For Poland's crown and kingly diadem.   30
ANJOU. Then come, my lords, let's go.   *Exeunt.*

[*Scene xi.*]
Enter two, with the Admiral's *body.*
1. Now, sirrah, what shall we do with the Admiral?
2. Why, let us burn him for an heretic.
1. O no, his body will infect the fire, and the fire the air, and
    so we shall be poisoned with him.
2. What shall we do, then?

1. Let's throw him into the river.
2. O, 'twill corrupt the water, and the water the fish, and by
   the fish ourselves, when we eat them.
1. Then throw him into the ditch.
2. No, no, to decide all doubts, be rul'd by me: let's hang him
   here upon this tree.   11
1. Agreed.   *They hang him* [*and exeunt*].
   Enter the Duke of Guise, Queen-Mother *and the* Cardinal
   [*of Lorraine*] [*with* Attendants].
GUISE. Now, madam, how like you our lusty Admiral?
CATHERINE. Believe me, Guise, he becomes the place so well
   As I could long ere this have wish'd him there.
   But come, let's walk aside; th'air's not very sweet.
GUISE. No, by my faith, madam.
   Sirs, take him away, and throw him in some ditch.
                              [Attendants] *carry away the dead body*.
   And now, madam, as I understand,
   There are a hundred Huguenots and more   20
   Which in the woods do hold their synagogue,
   And daily meet about this time of day;
   And thither will I, to put them to the sword.
CATHERINE. Do so, sweet Guise, let us delay no time;
   For if these stragglers gather head again,
   And disperse themselves throughout the realm of France,
   It will be hard for us to work their deaths.
   Be gone, delay no time, sweet Guise.
GUISE. Madam,   29
   I go as whirlwinds rage before a storm.   *Exit* Guise.
CATHERINE. My lord of Lorraine, have you mark'd of late
   How Charles our son begins for to lament
   For the late night's work which my lord of Guise
   Did make in Paris amongst the Huguenots?
CARDINAL. Madam, I have heard him solemnly vow,
   With the rebellious King of Navarre,
   For to revenge their deaths upon us all.
CATHERINE. Ay, but my lord, let me alone for that,
   For Catherine must have her will in France.
   As I do live, so surely shall he die,   40
   And Henry then shall wear the diadem;
   And if he grudge or cross his mother's will,
   I'll disinherit him and all the rest;
   For I'll rule France, but they shall wear the crown,
   And if they storm, I then may pull them down.
   Come, my lord, let us go.   *Exeunt*.

[*Scene xii.*]
Enter five or six Protestants, *with books, and kneel together.*
Enter also the Guise [*and others*].

GUISE. Down with the Huguenots! Murder them!

I PROTESTANT. O Monsieur de Guise, hear me but speak.

GUISE. No, villain, that tongue of thine
That hath blasphem'd the holy Church of Rome
Shall drive no plaints into the Guise's ears,
To make the justice of my heart relent.
Tue, tue, tue, let none escape.   *Kill them.*
So, drag them away.   *Exeunt.*

[*Scene xiii.*]
Enter the King of France, Navarre *and* Epernoun *staying
him; enter* Queen-Mother, *and the* Cardinal [*with* Pleshé
and Attendants].

CHARLES. O let me stay and rest me here a while.
A griping pain hath seiz'd upon my heart;
A sudden pang, the messenger of death.

CATHERINE. O say not so. Thou kill'st thy mother's heart.

CHARLES. I must say so; pain forceth me complain.

NAVARRE. Comfort yourself, my lord, and have no doubt
But God will sure restore you to your health.

CHARLES. O no, my loving brother of Navarre!
I have deserv'd a scourge, I must confess;
Yet is their patience of another sort   10
Than to misdo the welfare of their king:
God grant my nearest friends may prove no worse!
O, hold me up, my sight begins to fail,
My sinews shrink, my brains turn upside down;
My heart doth break, I faint and die.   *He dies.*

CATHERINE. What, art thou dead? Sweet son, speak to thy
mother!
O no, his soul is fled from out his breast,
And he nor hears nor sees us what we do.
My lords, what resteth there now for to be done,
But that we presently dispatch ambassadors   20
To Poland, to call Henry back again
To wear his brother's crown and dignity?
Epernoun, go see it presently be done,
And bid him come without delay to us.

EPERNOUN. Madam, I will.   *Exit* Epernoun.

CATHERINE. And now, my lords, after these funerals be done,

We will, with all the speed we can, provide
For Henry's coronation from Polony.
Come, let us take his body hence.
                                    All go out but Navarre *and* Pleshé.

NAVARRE. And now, Navarre, whilst that these broils do
 last,   30
My opportunity may serve me fit
To steal from France, and hie me to my home,
For here's no safety in the realm for me;
And now that Henry is call'd from Poland,
It is my due, by just succession;
And therefore, as speedily as I can perform,
I'll muster up an army secretly,
For fear that Guise, join'd with the King of Spain,
Might seem to cross me in mine enterprise.
But God, that always doth defend the right,   40
Will show his mercy and preserve us still.

PLESHÉ. The virtues of our true religion
Cannot but march with many graces more,
Whose army shall discomfort all your foes,
And, at the length, in Pampelonia crown
(In spite of Spain, and all the popish power,
That holds it from your highness wrongfully)
Your majesty her rightful lord and sovereign.

NAVARRE. Truth, Pleshé; and God so prosper me in all
As I intend to labour for the truth   50
And true profession of his holy word.
Come, Pleshé, let's away whilst time doth serve.   *Exeunt.*

[Scene xiv.]

Sound trumpets within, and then all cry 'vive le roi' *two or three times.*
 Enter Henry [Anjou] *crowned,* Queen[-Mother], Cardinal,
 Duke of Guise, Epernoun, *the King's Minions with others,*
 and the Cutpurse.

ALL. *Vive le roi, Vive le roi!*   *Sound trumpets.*

CATHERINE. Welcome from Poland, Henry, once again,
Welcome to France, thy father's royal seat.
Here hast thou a country void of fears,
A warlike people to maintain thy right,
A watchful senate for ordaining laws,
A loving mother to preserve thy state,
And all things that a king may wish besides;
All this and more hath Henry with his crown.

CARDINAL. And long may Henry enjoy all this, and more! 10
ALL. *Vive le roi, Vive le roi!* *Sound trumpets.*
HENRY. Thanks to you all. The guider of all crowns
  Grant that our deeds may well deserve your loves!
  And so they shall, if fortune speed my will,
  And yield your thoughts to height of my deserts.
  What says our minions? Think they Henry's heart
  Will not both harbour love and majesty?
  Put off that fear, they are already join'd:
  No person, place, or time, or circumstance,
  Shall slack my love's affection from his bent. 20
  As now you are, so shall you still persist,
  Removeless from the favours of your king.
MUGEROUN. We know that noble minds change not their
    thoughts
  For wearing of a crown, in that your grace
  Hath worn the Poland diadem before
  You were invested in the crown of France.
HENRY. I tell thee, Mugeroun, we will be friends,
  And fellows too, whatever storms arise.
MUGEROUN. Then may it please your majesty to give me leave
  To punish those that do profane this holy feast. 30
    He cuts off the Cutpurse's *ear, for cutting of the gold buttons*
    off his cloak.
HENRY. How mean'st thou that?
CUTPURSE. O Lord, mine ear!
MUGEROUN. Come sir, give me my buttons, and here's your ear.
GUISE. Sirrah, take him away.
HENRY. Hands off, good fellow; I will be his bail
  For this offence. Go, sirrah, work no more
  Till this our coronation-day be past.
  And now,
  Our solemn rites of coronation done,
  What now remains but for a while to feast, 40
  And spend some days in barriers, tourney, tilt,
  And like disports, such as do fit the court?
  Let's go, my lords; our dinner stays for us.
    Go out all but the Queen[-Mother] *and the* Cardinal.
CATHERINE. My Lord Cardinal of Lorraine, tell me,
  How likes your grace my son's pleasantness?
  His mind, you see, runs on his minions,
  And all his heaven is to delight himself;
  And whilst he sleeps securely thus in ease,
  Thy brother Guise and we may now provide

To plant ourselves with such authority   50
As not a man may live without our leaves.
Then shall the Catholic faith of Rome
Flourish in France, and none deny the same.
CARDINAL. Madam, as in secrecy I was told,
My brother Guise hath gathered a power of men,
Which, as he saith, to kill the Puritans;
But 'tis the house of Bourbon that he means.
Now, madam, must you insinuate with the king,
And tell him that 'tis for his country's good,
And common profit of religion.   60
CATHERINE. Tush, man, let me alone with him,
To work the way to bring this thing to pass;
And if he do deny what I do say,
I'll dispatch him with his brother presently,
And then shall Monsieur wear the diadem.
Tush, all shall die unless I have my will,
For while she lives Catherine will be queen.
Come my lord, let us go seek the Guise,
And then determine of this enterprise.   *Exeunt.*

[*Scene xv.*]
Enter the Duchess *of Guise and her* Maid.
DUCHESS. Go fetch me pen and ink—
MAID. I will, madam.   *Exit* Maid.
DUCHESS. That I may write unto my dearest lord.
Sweet Mugeroun, 'tis he that hath my heart,
And Guise usurps it 'cause I am his wife.
Fain would I find some means to speak with him,
But cannot, and therefore am enforc'd to write,
That he may come and meet me in some place
Where we may one enjoy the other's sight.
    Enter the Maid, *with ink and paper.*
So, set it down and leave me to myself.   10
                                              She writes.

O would to God this quill that here doth write
Had late been pluck'd from out fair Cupid's wing,
That it might print these lines within his heart!
    Enter the Guise.
GUISE. What, all alone, my love? And writing too?
I prithee, say to whom thou writes.
DUCHESS. To such a one, my lord, as when she reads my lines
Will laugh, I fear me, at their good array.
GUISE. I pray thee, let me see.

DUCHESS. O no, my lord; a woman only must
  Partake the secrets of my heart.   20
GUISE. But, madam, I must see.   *He takes it.*
  Are these your secrets that no man must know?
DUCHESS. O pardon me, my lord.
GUISE. Thou trothless and unjust, what lines are these?
  Am I grown old, or is thy lust grown young,
  Or hath my love been so obscur'd in thee,
  That others needs to comment on my text?
  Is all my love forgot which held thee dear,
  Ay, dearer than the apple of mine eye?
  Is Guise's glory but a cloudy mist,   30
  In sight and judgement of thy lustful eye?
  Mort Dieu! Were't not the fruit within thy womb,
  Of whose increase I set some longing hope,
  This wrathful hand should strike thee to the heart.
  Hence, strumpet, hide thy head for shame,
  And fly my presence, if thou look to live.   *Exit* [Duchess].
  O wicked sex, perjured and unjust,
  Now do I see that from the very first
  Her eyes and looks sow'd seeds of perjury.
  But villain he to whom these lines should go   40
  Shall buy her love even with his dearest blood.   *Exit.*

[Scene xvi.]
  Enter the King of Navarre, Pleshé *and* Bartus, *and their*
  train, with drums and trumpets.
NAVARRE. My lords, sith in a quarrel just and right
  We undertake to manage these our wars
  Against the proud disturbers of the faith,
  I mean the Guise, the Pope, and King of Spain,
  Who set themselves to tread us under foot,
  And rent our true religion from this land;
  But for you know our quarrel is no more
  But to defend their strange inventions,
  Which they will put us to with sword and fire,
  We must with resolute minds resolve to fight,   10
  In honour of our God and country's good.
  Spain is the council-chamber of the Pope,
  Spain is the place where he makes peace and war:
  And Guise for Spain hath now incens'd the king
  To send his power to meet us in the field.
BARTUS. Then in this bloody brunt they may behold
  The sole endeavour of your princely care,

To plant the true succession of the faith
In spite of Spain and all his heresies.
NAVARRE. The power of vengeance now encamps itself   20
Upon the haughty mountains of my breast;
Plays with her gory colours of revenge,
Whom I respect as leaves of boasting green
That change their colour when the winter comes,
When I shall vaunt as victor in revenge.
    Enter a Messenger.
How now, sirrah, what news?
MESSENGER. My lord, as by our scouts we understand,
A mighty army comes from France with speed,
Which are already mustered in the land,
And means to meet your highness in the field.   30
NAVARRE. In God's name, let them come.
This is the Guise that hath incens'd the king
To levy arms and make these civil broils.
But canst thou tell who is their general?
MESSENGER. Not yet, my lord, for thereon do they stay;
But, as report doth go, the Duke of Joyeux
Hath made great suit unto the king therefore.
NAVARRE. It will not countervail his pains, I hope.
I would the Guise in his stead might have come.
But he doth lurk within his drowsy couch,   40
And makes his footstool on security:
So he be safe, he cares not what becomes
Of king or country; no, not for them both.
But come, my lords, let us away with speed,
And place ourselves in order for the fight.   *Exeunt.*

[*Scene xvii.*]
    Enter the King of France, *Duke of* Guise, Epernoun *and*
    Duke Joyeux.
HENRY. My sweet Joyeux, I make thee general
Of all my army, now in readiness
To march against the rebellious king Navarre.
At thy request I am content thou go,
Although my love to thee can hardly suffer,
Regarding still the danger of thy life.
JOYEUX. Thanks to your majesty; and so I take my leave.
Farewell to my lord of Guise, and Epernoun.
GUISE. Health and hearty farewell to my lord Joyeux.
    Exit Joyeux.
HENRY. So kindly, cousin of Guise, you and your wife   10

Do both salute our lovely minions.

He makes horns at the Guise.

Remember you the letter, gentle sir,
Which your wife writ to my dear minion
And her chosen friend?

GUISE. How now, my lord, faith, this is more than need.
Am I thus to be jested at and scorn'd?
'Tis more than kingly or imperious;
And sure, if all the proudest kings
In Christendom should bear me such derision,
They should know how I scorn'd them and their mocks.   20
I love your minions? Dote on them yourself;
I know none else but holds them in disgrace;
And here by all the saints in heaven I swear,
That villain for whom I bear this deep disgrace,
Even for your words that have incens'd me so,
Shall buy that strumpet's favour with his blood,
Whether he have dishonoured me or no.
Par la mort Dieu, il mourra!   *Exit.*

HENRY. Believe me, this jest bites sore.

EPERNOUN. My lord, 'twere good to make them friends,   30
For his oaths are seldom spent in vain.

Enter Mugeroun.

HENRY. How now, Mugeroun, met'st thou not the Guise at the
door?

MUGEROUN. Not I, my lord. What if I had?

HENRY. Marry, if thou hadst, thou mightst have had the stab.
For he hath solemnly sworn thy death.

MUGEROUN. I may be stabb'd, and live till he be dead.
But wherefore bears he me such deadly hate?

HENRY. Because his wife bears thee such kindly love.

MUGEROUN. If that be all, the next time that I meet her
I'll make her shake off love with her heels.   40
But which way is he gone? I'll go make a walk
On purpose from the court to meet with him.   *Exit.*

HENRY. I like not this. Come Epernoun,
Let's go seek the duke and make them friends.   *Exeunt.*

[*Scene xviii.*]

Alarms within. The Duke Joyeux *slain. Enter the King of*
Navarre [*with* Bartus] *and his train.*

NAVARRE. The duke is slain and all his power dispers'd,
And we are grac'd with wreaths of victory.
Thus God, we see, doth ever guide the right,

To make his glory great upon the earth.
BARTUS. The terror of this happy victory,
   I hope will make the king surcease his hate,
   And either never manage army more,
   Or else employ them in some better cause.
NAVARRE. How many noble men have lost their lives
   In prosecution of these cruel arms,   10
   Is ruth and almost death to call to mind.
   But God, we know, will always put them down
   That lift themselves against the perfect truth;
   Which I'll maintain so long as life doth last,
   And with the Queen of England join my force
   To beat the papal monarch from our lands,
   And keep those relics from our countries' coasts.
   Come my lords, now that this storm is overpast,
   Let us away with triumph to our tents.   *Exeunt.*

[*Scene xix.*]
   Enter a Soldier.
SOLDIER. Sir, to you sir, that dares make the duke a cuckold,
   and use a counterfeit key to his privy-chamber door; and
   although you take out nothing but your own, yet you put in
   that which displeaseth him and so forestall his market, and
   set up your standing where you should not; and whereas he
   is your landlord, you will take upon you to be his, and till
   the ground that he himself should occupy, which is his own
   free land—if it be not too free, there's the question. And
   though I come not to take possession (as I would I might),
   yet I mean to keep you out—which I will, if this gear hold.
   What, are ye come so soon? Have at ye, sir.   11
   Enter Mugeroun. *He shoots at him and kills him.*
   Enter the Guise.
GUISE. Hold thee, tall soldier; take thee this and fly.
                                          Exit Soldier.
   Lie there, the king's delight and Guise's scorn.
   Revenge it, Henry, as thou list or dare;
   I did it only in despite of thee.   *Take him away.*

[*Scene xx.*]
   Enter the King *and* Epernoun [*and the Duke of* Guise].
HENRY. My lord of Guise, we understand
   That you have gathered a power of men:
   What your intent is yet we cannot learn,
   But we presume it is not for our good.

GUISE. Why, I am no traitor to the crown of France;
    What I have done, 'tis for the Gospel sake.
EPERNOUN. Nay, for the Pope's sake, and thine own benefit.
    What peer in France but thou, aspiring Guise,
    Durst be in arms without the king's consent?
    I challenge thee for treason in the cause.   10
GUISE. Ah, base Epernoun, were not his highness here,
    Thou shouldst perceive the Duke of Guise is mov'd.
HENRY. Be patient, Guise, and threat not Epernoun,
    Lest thou perceive the King of France be mov'd.
GUISE. Why, I am a prince of the Valois's line,
    Therefore an enemy to the Bourbonites;
    I am a juror in the Holy League,
    And therefore hated of the Protestants:
    What should I do but stand upon my guard?
    And, being able, I'll keep an host in pay.   20
EPERNOUN. Thou able to maintain an host in pay
    That liv'st by foreign exhibition?
    The Pope and King of Spain are thy good friends,
    Else all France knows how poor a duke thou art.
HENRY. Ay, those are they that feed him with their gold,
    To countermand our will and check our friends.
GUISE. My lord, to speak more plainly, thus it is:
    Being animated by religious zeal,
    I mean to muster all the power I can,
    To overthrow those sectious Puritans.   30
    And know, my lord, the Pope will sell his triple crown,
    Ay, and the Catholic Philip, King of Spain,
    Ere I shall want, will cause his Indians
    To rip the golden bowels of America.
    Navarre, that cloaks them underneath his wings,
    Shall feel the house of Lorraine is his foe.
    Your highness needs not fear mine army's force;
    'Tis for your safety, and your enemies' wrack.
HENRY. Guise, wear our crown, and be thou King of France,
    And as dictator make or war or peace,   40
    Whilst I cry *placet* like a senator.
    I cannot brook thy haughty insolence.
    Dismiss thy camp, or else by our edict
    Be thou proclaim'd a traitor throughout France.
GUISE. The choice is hard; I must dissemble.
    My lord, in token of my true humility,
    And simple meaning to your majesty,
    I kiss your grace's hand, and take my leave,

Intending to dislodge my camp with speed.

HENRY. Then farewell, Guise; the king and thou are friends.   50

Exit Guise.

EPERNOUN. But trust him not, my lord; for had your highness
　Seen with what a pomp he ent'red Paris,
　And how the citizens with gifts and shows
　Did entertain him,
　And promised to be at his command—
　Nay, they fear'd not to speak in the streets,
　That the Guise durst stand in arms against the king,
　For not effecting of his holiness' will.

HENRY. Did they of Paris entertain him so?
　Then means he present treason to our state.   60
　Well, let me alone. Who's within there?

　　Enter one with a pen and ink.

　Make a discharge of all my council straight,
　And I'll subscribe my name, and seal it straight.
　My head shall be my council, they are false;
　And, Epernoun, I will be rul'd by thee.

EPERNOUN. My lord,
　I think for safety of your royal person,
　It would be good the Guise were made away,
　And so to quite your grace of all suspect.

HENRY. First let us set our hand and seal to this,   70
　And then I'll tell thee what I mean to do.   *He writes.*
　So, convey this to the council presently.   *Exit one.*
　And Epernoun, though I seem mild and calm,
　Think not but I am tragical within.
　I'll secretly convey me unto Blois;
　For now that Paris takes the Guise's part,
　Here is no staying for the King of France,
　Unless he mean to be betray'd and die.
　But as I live, so sure the Guise shall die.   *Exeunt.*

[*Scene xxi.*]

Enter the King of Navarre, *reading of a letter, and* Bartus.

NAVARRE. My lord, I am advertised from France
　That the Guise hath taken arms against the king,
　And that Paris is revolted from his grace.

BARTUS. Then hath your grace fit opportunity
　To show your love unto the King of France,
　Offering him aid against his enemies,
　Which cannot but be thankfully receiv'd.

NAVARRE. Bartus, it shall be so. Post then to France,

And there salute his highness in our name;
Assure him all the aid we can provide   10
Against the Guisians and their complices.
Bartus, be gone: commend me to his grace,
And tell him, ere it be long, I'll visit him.
BARTUS. I will, my lord.   *Exit.*
NAVARRE. Pleshé!
    Enter Pleshé.
PLESHÉ. My lord!
NAVARRE. Pleshé, go muster up our men with speed,
  And let them march away to France amain,
  For we must aid the king against the Guise.
  Be gone, I say; 'tis time that we were there.   20
PLESHÉ. I go, my lord.   *[Exit.]*
NAVARRE. That wicked Guise, I fear me much, will be
  The ruin of that famous realm of France,
  For his aspiring thoughts aim at the crown,
  And takes his vantage on religion,
  To plant the Pope and popelings in the realm,
  And bind it wholly to the See of Rome.
  But, if that God do prosper mine attempts,
  And send us safely to arrive in France,
  We'll beat him back, and drive him to his death   30
  That basely seeks the ruin of his realm.   *Exit.*

[Scene xxii.]
  Enter the Captain of the Guard [Cossin], *and three* Murderers.
COSSIN. Come on, sirs. What, are you resolutely bent,
  Hating the life and honour of the Guise?
  What, will you not fear, when you see him come?
1 MURDERER. Fear him, said you? Tush, were he here, we
  would kill him presently.
2 MURDERER. O that his heart were leaping in my hand!
3 MURDERER. But when will he come, that we may murder him?
COSSIN. Well, then I see you are resolute.
1 MURDERER. Let us alone, I warrant you.
COSSIN. Then, sirs, take your standings within this chamber,
  for anon the Guise will come.   11
ALL 3 MURDERERS. You will give us our money?
COSSIN. Ay, ay, fear not. Stand close: so, be resolute.
            [The Murderers *conceal themselves.]*
Now falls the star whose influence governs France,
Whose light was deadly to the Protestants:
Now must he fall and perish in his height.

Enter the King *and* Epernoun.

HENRY. Now, captain of my guard, are these murderers ready?
COSSIN. They be, my good lord.
HENRY. But are they resolute, and arm'd to kill,
  Hating the life and honour of the Guise?   20
COSSIN. I warrant ye, my lord.
HENRY. Then come, proud Guise, and here disgorge thy breast,
  Surcharg'd with surfeit of ambitious thoughts;
  Breathe out that life wherein my death was hid,
  And end thy endless treasons with thy death.
    Enter the Guise *and knocketh.*
GUISE. *Holà*, varlet, *hé!* Epernoun! Where is the king?
EPERNOUN. Mounted his royal cabinet.
GUISE. I prithee tell him that the Guise is here.
EPERNOUN. And please your grace, the Duke of Guise doth crave
  Access unto your highness.   30
HENRY. Let him come in.
  Come, Guise, and see thy traitorous guile outreach'd,
  And perish in the pit thou mad'st for me.
             The Guise *comes to the* King.
GUISE. Good morrow to your majesty.
HENRY. Good morrow to my loving cousin of Guise.
  How fares it this morning with your excellence?
GUISE. I heard your majesty was scarcely pleas'd
  That in the court I bare so great a train.
HENRY. They were to blame that said I was displeas'd;
  And you, good cousin, to imagine it.   40
  'Twere hard with me if I should doubt my kin,
  Or be suspicious of my dearest friends.
  Cousin, assure you I am resolute,
  Whatsoever any whisper in mine ears,
  Not to suspect disloyalty in thee:
  And so, sweet coz, farewell.
          Exit King [*with* Epernoun *and Captain*].
GUISE. So;
  Now sues the king for favour to the Guise,
  And all his minions stoop when I command.
  Why, this 'tis to have an army in the field.   50
  Now by the holy sacrament I swear,
  As ancient Romans over their captive lords,
  So will I triumph over this wanton king,
  And he shall follow my proud chariot's wheels.
  Now do I but begin to look about,
  And all my former time was spent in vain.

Hold, sword,
For in thee is the Duke of Guise's hope.
    Enter one of the Murderers.
Villain, why dost thou look so ghastly? Speak.
3 MURDERER. O pardon me, my lord of Guise.   60
GUISE. Pardon thee? Why, what hast thou done?
3 MURDERER. O my lord, I am one of them that is set to murder
    you.
GUISE. To murder me, villain?
3 MURDERER. Ay, my lord: the rest have ta'en their standings
    in the next room; therefore, good my lord, go not forth.
GUISE. Yet Caesar shall go forth.
    Let mean conceits and baser men fear death:
    Tut, they are peasants. I am Duke of Guise;
    And princes with their looks engender fear.   70
1 MURDERER [*within*]. Stand close, he is coming; I know him
    by his voice.
GUISE. As pale as ashes! Nay then 'tis time to look about.
    [*Enter First and Second* Murderers.]
1 AND 2 MURDERERS. Down with him, down with him!
                                                They stab him.
GUISE. O, I have my death's wound. Give me leave to speak.
2 MURDERER. Then pray to God, and ask forgiveness of the king.
GUISE. Trouble me not. I ne'er offended Him,
    Nor will I ask forgiveness of the king.
    O that I have not power to stay my life,
    Nor immortality to be reveng'd!   80
    To die by peasants, what a grief is this!
    Ah, Sixtus, be reveng'd upon the king.
    Philip and Parma, I am slain for you.
    Pope, excommunicate, Philip, depose,
    The wicked branch of curs'd Valois his line.
    Vive la messe! Perish Huguenots!
    Thus Caesar did go forth, and thus he died.   *He dies.*
    Enter Captain of the Guard.
COSSIN. What, have you done?
    Then stay a while, and I'll go call the king.
    But see where he comes.   90
    [*Enter King* Henry, Epernoun, *and* Attendants.]
    My lord, see where the Guise is slain.
HENRY. Ah, this sweet sight is physic to my soul.
    Go fetch his son for to behold his death.
                                        [*Exit an* Attendant.]
    Surcharg'd with guilt of thousand massacres,

Monsieur of Lorraine, sink away to hell.
And in remembrance of those bloody broils
To which thou didst allure me, being alive,
And here in presence of you all, I swear
I ne'er was King of France until this hour.
This is the traitor that hath spent my gold   100
In making foreign wars and civil broils.
Did he not draw a sort of English priests
From Douai to the seminary at Rheims,
To hatch forth treason 'gainst their natural queen?
Did he not cause the King of Spain's huge fleet
To threaten England, and to menace me?
Did he not injure Monsieur that's deceas'd?
Hath he not made me in the Pope's defence
To spend the treasure that should strength my land
In civil broils between Navarre and me?   110
Tush, to be short, he meant to make me monk,
Or else to murder me, and so be king.
Let Christian princes that shall hear of this
(As all the world shall know our Guise is dead)
Rest satisfied with this: that here I swear,
Ne'er was there King of France so yok'd as I.

EPERNOUN. My lord, here is his son.
      Enter the Guise's *Son.*

HENRY. Boy, look where your father lies.

GUISE'S SON. My father slain; who hath done this deed?

HENRY. Sirrah, 'twas I that slew him; and will slay   120
      Thee too, and thou prove such a traitor.

GUISE'S SON. Art thou king, and hast done this bloody deed?
      I'll be reveng'd.   *He offereth to throw his dagger.*

HENRY. Away to prison with him. I'll clip his wings
      Or e'er he pass my hands. Away with him.
                              Exit Boy [*guarded*].

But what availeth that this traitor's dead,
When Duke Dumaine, his brother, is alive,
And that young cardinal that is grown so proud?
Go to the governor of Orleans,
And will him, in my name, to kill the duke.   130
Get you away, and strangle the cardinal.
            [*Exeunt Captain of the Guard and* Murderers.]
These two will make one entire Duke of Guise,
Especially with our old mother's help.

EPERNOUN. My lord, see where she comes, as if she droop'd
      To hear these news.

HENRY. And let her droop; my heart is light enough.
 Enter Queen-Mother.
 Mother, how like you this device of mine?
 I slew the Guise, because I would be king.
CATHERINE. King, why, so thou wert before:
 Pray God thou be a king now this is done.   140
HENRY. Nay, he was king, and countermanded me,
 But now I will be king, and rule myself,
 And make the Guisians stoop that are alive.
CATHERINE. I cannot speak for grief. When thou wast born,
 I would that I had murdered thee, my son.
 My son? Thou art a changeling, not my son.
 I curse thee, and exclaim thee miscreant,
 Traitor to God and to the realm of France.
HENRY. Cry out, exclaim, howl till thy throat be hoarse.
 The Guise is slain, and I rejoice therefore.   150
 And now will I to arms; come, Epernoun,
 And let her grieve her heart out if she will.
         Exit the King *and* Epernoun.
CATHERINE. Away, leave me alone to meditate.
          [*Exeunt* Attendants.]
 Sweet Guise, would he had died, so thou wert here!
 To whom shall I bewray my secrets now,
 Or who will help to build religion?
 The Protestants will glory and insult;
 Wicked Navarre will get the crown of France;
 The Popedom cannot stand; all goes to wrack,
 And all for thee, my Guise; what may I do?   160
 But sorrow seize upon my toiling soul,
 For since the Guise is dead, I will not live.   *Exit.*

       [*Scene xxiii.*]
    Enter two dragging in the Cardinal.
CARDINAL. Murder me not, I am a cardinal.
1 MURDERER. Wert thou the Pope, thou mightst not 'scape
 from us.
CARDINAL. What, will you file your hands with churchmen's
 blood?
2 MURDERER. Shed your blood? O Lord, no, for we intend to
 strangle you.
CARDINAL. Then there is no remedy but I must die?
1 MURDERER. No remedy; therefore prepare yourself.
CARDINAL. Yet lives my brother Duke Dumaine, and many moe,
 To revenge our deaths upon that cursed king,

Upon whose heart may all the Furies gripe,
And with their paws drench his black soul in hell!　　10
1 MURDERER. Yours, my Lord Cardinal, you should have said.
　　　　　　　　　　　　　　Now they strangle him.
So, pluck amain.
He is hard-hearted, therefore pull with violence.
Come, take him away.　　　　　　　　　*Exeunt.*

[*Scene xxiv.*]
　Enter Duke Dumaine *reading of a letter, with others.*
DUMAINE. My noble brother murdered by the king!
　O, what may I do for to revenge thy death?
　The king's alone, it cannot satisfy.
　Sweet Duke of Guise, our prop to lean upon,
　Now thou art dead, here is no stay for us.
　I am thy brother, and I'll revenge thy death,
　And root Valois his line from forth of France,
　And beat proud Bourbon to his native home,
　That basely seeks to join with such a king,
　Whose murderous thoughts will be his overthrow.　　10
　He will'd the governor of Orleans, in his name,
　That I with speed should have been put to death;
　But that's prevented, for to end his life,
　And all those traitors to the Church of Rome
　That durst attempt to murder noble Guise.
　　　Enter the Friar.
FRIAR. My lord, I come to bring you news that your brother
　the Cardinal of Lorraine, by the king's consent, is lately
　strangled unto death.
DUMAINE. My brother cardinal slain, and I alive?
　O words of power to kill a thousand men!　　20
　Come, let us away and levy men;
　'Tis war that must assuage this tyrant's pride.
FRIAR. My lord, hear me but speak.
　I am a friar of the order of the Jacobins,
　That for my conscience' sake will kill the king.
DUMAINE. But what doth move thee above the rest to do the
　deed?
FRIAR. O my lord, I have been a great sinner in my days, and
　the deed is meritorious.
DUMAINE. But how wilt thou get opportunity?　　30
FRIAR. Tush, my lord, let me alone for that.
DUMAINE. Friar, come with me;
　We will go talk more of this within.　　　　*Exeunt.*

[266]

[*Scene xxv.*]
Sound drum and trumpets; and enter the King of France, *and*
Navarre, Epernoun, Bartus, Pleshé, *and* Soldiers [*and*
Attendants].

HENRY. Brother of Navarre, I sorrow much
    That ever I was prov'd your enemy,
    And that the sweet and princely mind you bear
    Was ever troubled with injurious wars.
    I vow, as I am lawful King of France,
    To recompense your reconciled love
    With all the honours and affections
    That ever I vouchsaf'd my dearest friends.

NAVARRE. It is enough if that Navarre may be
    Esteemed faithful to the King of France,   10
    Whose service he may still command till death.

HENRY. Thanks to my kingly brother of Navarre.
    Then here we'll lie before Lutetia walls,
    Girting this strumpet city with our siege,
    Till, surfeiting with our afflicting arms,
    She cast her hateful stomach to the earth.
        Enter a Messenger.

MESSENGER. And it please your majesty, here is a friar of the
    order of the Jacobins, sent from the President of Paris,
    that craves access unto your grace.

HENRY. Let him come in.   20
        Enter Friar, *with a letter.*

EPERNOUN. I like not this friar's look:
    'Twere not amiss, my lord, if he were search'd.

HENRY. Sweet Epernoun, our friars are holy men,
    And will not offer violence to their king
    For all the wealth and treasure of the world.
    Friar, thou dost acknowledge me thy king?

FRIAR. Ay, my good lord, and will die therein.

HENRY. Then come thou near, and tell what news thou bring'st.

FRIAR. My lord,
    The President of Paris greets your grace,   30
    And sends his duty by these speedy lines,
    Humbly craving your gracious reply.

HENRY. I'll read them, friar, and then I'll answer thee.

FRIAR. *Sancte Jacobe*, now have mercy upon me.
        He stabs the King with a knife as he readeth the letter, and
        then the King getteth the knife and kills him.

EPERNOUN. O my lord, let him live a while.

HENRY. No, let the villain die, and feel in hell
    Just torments for his treachery.
NAVARRE. What, is your highness hurt?
HENRY. Yes, Navarre; but not to death, I hope.   39
NAVARRE. God shield your grace from such a sudden death!
    Go call a surgeon hither straight.   [*Exit an* Attendant.]
HENRY. What irreligious pagans' parts be these
    Of such as hold them of the holy church?
    Take hence that damned villain from my sight.
               [Attendants *carry out the* Friar's *body*.]
EPERNOUN. Ah, had your highness let him live,
    We might have punish'd him to his deserts.
HENRY. Sweet Epernoun, all rebels under heaven
    Shall take example by his punishment
    How they bear arms against their sovereign.
    Go call the English agent hither straight: 50
               [*Exit an* Attendant.]
    I'll send my sister England news of this,
    And give her warning of her treacherous foes.
    [*Enter a* Surgeon.]
NAVARRE. Pleaseth your grace to let the surgeon search your
    wound?
HENRY. The wound, I warrant ye, is deep, my lord.
    Search, surgeon, and resolve me what thou see'st.
               The Surgeon *searcheth*.

    Enter the English Agent.
    Agent for England, send thy mistress word
    What this detested Jacobin hath done.
    Tell her, for all this, that I hope to live;
    Which if I do, the papal monarch goes
    To wrack, and antichristian kingdom falls.   60
    These bloody hands shall tear his triple crown,
    And fire accursed Rome about his ears;
    I'll fire his crazed buildings, and enforce
    The papal towers to kiss the lowly earth.
    Navarre, give me thy hand: I here do swear
    To ruinate that wicked Church of Rome
    That hatcheth up such bloody practices;
    And here protest eternal love to thee,
    And to the Queen of England specially,
    Whom God hath bless'd for hating papistry.   70
NAVARRE. These words revive my thoughts, and comforts me,
    To see your highness in this virtuous mind.
HENRY. Tell me, surgeon, shall I live?

SURGEON. Alas, my lord, the wound is dangerous,
For you are stricken with a poisoned knife.
HENRY. A poisoned knife? What, shall the French king die
Wounded and poisoned both at once?
EPERNOUN. O, that that damned villain were alive again,
That we might torture him with some new-found death!
BARTUS. He died a death too good: 80
The devil of hell torture his wicked soul!
HENRY. Ah, curse him not, sith he is dead.
O, the fatal poison works within my breast.
Tell me, surgeon, and flatter not, may I live?
SURGEON. Alas, my lord, your highness cannot live.
NAVARRE. Surgeon, why say'st thou so? The king may live.
HENRY. O no, Navarre, thou must be King of France!
NAVARRE. Long may you live, and still be King of France.
EPERNOUN. Or else die Epernoun!
HENRY. Sweet Epernoun, thy king must die. My lords,   90
Fight in the quarrel of this valiant prince,
For he is your lawful king, and my next heir;
Valois's line ends in my tragedy.
Now let the house of Bourbon wear the crown;
And may it never end in blood, as mine hath done!
Weep not, sweet Navarre, but revenge my death.
Ah, Epernoun, is this thy love to me?
Henry thy king wipes off these childish tears,
And bids thee whet thy sword on Sixtus' bones,
That it may keenly slice the Catholics.   100
He loves me not that sheds most tears,
But he that makes most lavish of his blood.
Fire Paris, where these treacherous rebels lurk.
I die, Navarre; come bear me to my sepulchre.
Salute the Queen of England in my name,
And tell her, Henry dies her faithful friend.   *He dies.*
NAVARRE. Come, lords, take up the body of the king,
That we may see it honourably interr'd:
And then I vow for to revenge his death
As Rome and all those popish prelates there   110
Shall curse the time that e'er Navarre was king,
And rul'd in France by Henry's fatal death.
They march out with the body of the King lying on four men's shoulders, with a dead march, drawing weapons on the ground.

FINIS.

APPENDIX

[Manuscript version of Scene xix.]

Enter a Soldier *with a musket.*

SOLDIER. Now sir, to you that dares make a duke a cuckold,
and use a counterfeit key to his privy chamber—though you
take out none but your own treasure, yet you put in that
displeases him, and fill up his room that he should occupy;
herein, sir, you forestall the market, and set up your standing where you should not. But you will say, you leave him
room enough besides: that's no answer; he's to have the
choice of his own freeland—if it be not too free, there's the
question. Now sir, where he is your landlord, you take upon
you to be his, and will needs enter by default. What though
you were once in possession, yet coming upon you once
unawares he fray'd you out again; therefore your entry is
mere intrusion. This is against the law, sir. And though I
come not to keep possession (as I would I might), yet I come
to keep you out, sir. You are welcome, sir. Have at you!   15
 Enter Minion [Mugeroun]. *He kills him.*
MUGEROUN. Traitorous Guise! Ah, thou hast murdered me.
 Enter Guise.
GUISE. Hold thee, tall soldier, take thee this and fly.
            Exit [Soldier].

Thus fall, imperfect exhalation,
Which our great sun of France could not effect
A fiery meteor in the firmament.   20
Lie there, the king's delight and Guise's scorn!
Revenge it Henry, if thou list or dar'st;
I did it only in despite of thee.
Fondly hast thou incens'd the Guise's soul
That of itself was hot enough to work
Thy just digestion with extremest shame.
The army I have gathered now shall aim
More at thy end than extirpation.
And when thou think'st I have forgotten this,
And that thou most reposest on my faith,   30
Then will I wake thee from thy foolish dream
And let thee see thyself my prisoner.   *Exit.*

[270]

Doctor Faustus

Doctor Faustus was entered to Thomas Busshell in the Stationers' Register on 7 January 1601 as '*the plaie of Doctor FAUSTUS*', and on 13 September 1610 '*The tragicall history of the horrible life and Death of Doctor FFAUSTUS, written by C.M:*' was assigned by Busshell to John Wright. Busshell published his edition in 1604 and Wright followed this in 1609 and 1611, but published his own distinct text in another series of reprints in 1616, 1619, 1620, 1624, 1628 and 1631. The play appears with further additions in 1663. Title-pages give the author as 'Ch. Marl.'.

Marlowe's source was *The historie of the damnable life, and deserved death of Doctor John Faustus* (1592), a translation by P.F. from the German of 1587. The title-page of the one surviving English edition indicates that it was not the first; and the record of a copyright dispute in the Stationers' Company raises the possibility that the lost first edition came out in May of the same year. The Prince of Parma, who died on the night of 2–3 December 1592, is spoken of as though alive at I.i.93 of the play. But there is no conclusive evidence against any date from 1588 to 1592.

On 22 November 1602, before the appearance of the play in print, Henslowe paid £4 to 'wᵐ Burde & Samwell Rowle' (William Bird alias Borne, and Samuel Rowley) for 'ther adicyones in docter fostes', which at such a fee are likely to have been extensive. Both men were established actors in the Admiral's Men and active in Henslowe's business dealings. Bird had played the part of the Guise in *The Massacre at Paris*. He had collaborated with Rowley in another play the year before; but that seems to be the sum of his writing for the stage. Rowley, however, wrote other plays on his own. *When You See Me, You Know Me*, a history play printed in 1605, is a touchstone of his style.

The first title-page of *Faustus* states that it was performed by the Earl of Nottingham's Men, i.e. the Admiral's Men. Henslowe records the receipts at some twenty-four performances between 30 September 1594 and 5 January 1597: these would have been by the Admiral's Men at the Rose, with Edward Alleyn in the lead. An inventory of props for the

Admiral's Men taken on 10 March 1598 includes 'j dragon in fostes'. A list of playing apparel, perhaps from about 1602, includes 'faustus Jerkin his clok' (i.e. cloak). A contemporary, Samuel Rowlands, describes Alleyn in the part dressed in a surplice with a cross on his breast; the title-page woodcut of the 1616 quarto shows Faustus in academic garb raising Mephostophilis as a dragon. The play may have been staged at the old Theatre before it was abandoned (by 1598), and perhaps also at the obscure playhouse the Belsavage, which was probably closed during Queen Elizabeth's reign. Tales were told in the seventeenth century of performances at both these playhouses and at others when the actors were terrified, and chastened, to discover that the real Devil was present amongst them.

[DRAMATIS PERSONAE

Chorus

Dr John Faustus
Wagner, his servant
Valdes ⎫
Cornelius ⎭ magicians
Three Scholars
Old Man

Pope Adrian
Raymond, King of Hungary
Bruno, the rival Pope
Cardinals of France and Padua
Archbishop of Rheims

Charles V, Emperor of Germany
Martino ⎫
Frederick ⎬ knights at court
Benvolio ⎭
Duke of Saxony

Duke of Vanholt
Duchess of Vanholt

Robin
Dick
Vintner
Horse-courser
Carter
Hostess

Good Angel
Bad Angel (Spirit)
Mephostophilis
Lucifer
Belzebub
Spirits presenting The Seven Deadly Sins
                Alexander the Great
                Alexander's Paramour
                Darius, King of Persia
                Helen of Troy

Devils, Cupids, Bishops, Monks, Friars, Soldiers, Attendants,
a Piper]

[274]

Doctor Faustus

Enter Chorus.

Not marching now in fields of Thrasimene,
Where Mars did mate the warlike Carthagens,
Nor sporting in the dalliance of love
In courts of kings where state is overturn'd,
Nor in the pomp of proud audacious deeds,
Intends our muse to vaunt his heavenly verse.
Only this, gentlemen: we must perform
The form of Faustus' fortunes, good or bad.
To patient judgements we appeal our plaud,
And speak for Faustus in his infancy.   10
Now is he born, his parents base of stock,
In Germany, within a town called Rhode.
At riper years to Wittenberg he went,
Whereas his kinsmen chiefly brought him up.
So much he profits in divinity,
The fruitful plot of scholarism grac'd,
That shortly he was grac'd with doctor's name,
Excelling all whose sweet delight's disputes
In th'heavenly matters of theology.
Till swol'n with cunning, of a self-conceit,   20
His waxen wings did mount above his reach,
And melting, heavens conspir'd his overthrow.
For falling to a devilish exercise,
And glutted now with learning's golden gifts,
He surfeits upon cursed necromancy;
Nothing so sweet as magic is to him,
Which he prefers before his chiefest bliss:
And this the man that in his study sits.   *Exit.*

[*Act I. Scene i.*]

Faustus in his study.

FAUSTUS. Settle thy studies, Faustus, and begin
To sound the depth of that thou wilt profess.
Having commenc'd, be a divine in show,
Yet level at the end of every art

And live and die in Aristotle's works.
Sweet Analytics, 'tis thou hast ravish'd me.
Bene disserere est finis logices.
Is to dispute well logic's chiefest end?
Affords this art no greater miracle?
Then read no more, thou hast attain'd that end.   10
A greater subject fitteth Faustus' wit:
Bid *on kai me on* farewell; Galen, come.
Seeing, *ubi desinit philosophus, ibi incipit medicus.*
Be a physician, Faustus, heap up gold,
And be eterniz'd for some wondrous cure.
Summum bonum medicinae sanitas:
The end of physic is our body's health.
Why, Faustus, hast thou not attain'd that end?
Is not thy common talk sound aphorisms?
Are not thy bills hung up as monuments   20
Whereby whole cities have escap'd the plague
And thousand desperate maladies been cur'd?
Yet art thou still but Faustus, and a man.
Couldst thou make men to live eternally,
Or, being dead, raise them to life again,
Then this profession were to be esteem'd.
Physic, farewell. Where is Justinian?
Si una eademque res legatur duobus,
Alter rem, alter valorem rei—etc.,
A petty case of paltry legacies.   30
Exhaereditare filium non potest pater, nisi—
Such is the subject of the Institute
And universal body of the law.
This study fits a mercenary drudge
Who aims at nothing but external trash,
Too servile and illiberal for me.
When all is done, divinity is best.
Jerome's Bible, Faustus, view it well.
Stipendium peccati mors est. Ha, *Stipendium, etc.,*
The reward of sin is death. That's hard.   40
Si peccasse negamus, fallimur, et nulla est in nobis veritas.
If we say that we have no sin we deceive ourselves, and there
is no truth in us.
Why then, belike,
We must sin, and so consequently die.
Ay, we must die an everlasting death.
What doctrine call you this? *Che sera, sera.*
What will be, shall be. Divinity, adieu!

These metaphysics of magicians
And necromantic books are heavenly;   50
Lines, circles, schemes, letters and characters:
Ay, these are those that Faustus most desires.
O what a world of profit and delight,
Of power, of honour, and omnipotence,
Is promis'd to the studious artisan!
All things that move between the quiet poles
Shall be at my command. Emperors and kings
Are but obey'd in their several provinces,
Nor can they raise the wind or rend the clouds.
But his dominion that exceeds in this   60
Stretcheth as far as doth the mind of man:
A sound magician is a demi-god.
Here, Faustus, try thy brains to get a deity.
    Enter Wagner.
Wagner, commend me to my dearest friends,
The German Valdes and Cornelius.
Request them earnestly to visit me.
WAGNER. I will sir.   *Exit.*
FAUSTUS. Their conference will be a greater help to me
    Than all my labours, plod I ne'er so fast.
        Enter the Angel *and* Spirit.
GOOD ANGEL. O Faustus, lay that damned book aside,   70
    And gaze not on it lest it tempt thy soul,
    And heap God's heavy wrath upon thy head.
    Read, read the scriptures: that is blasphemy.
BAD ANGEL. Go forward, Faustus, in that famous art
    Wherein all nature's treasury is contain'd.
    Be thou on earth as Jove is in the sky,
    Lord and commander of these elements.   *Exeunt* Angels.
FAUSTUS. How am I glutted with conceit of this!
    Shall I make spirits fetch me what I please,
    Resolve me of all ambiguities,   80
    Perform what desperate enterprise I will?
    I'll have them fly to India for gold,
    Ransack the ocean for orient pearl,
    And search all corners of the new-found world
    For pleasant fruits and princely delicates;
    I'll have them read me strange philosophy,
    And tell the secrets of all foreign kings;
    I'll have them wall all Germany with brass,
    And make swift Rhine circle fair Wittenberg;
    I'll have them fill the public schools with silk,   90

Wherewith the students shall be bravely clad;
I'll levy soldiers with the coin they bring,
And chase the Prince of Parma from our land,
And reign sole king of all our provinces.
Yea, stranger engines for the brunt of war
Than was the fiery keel at Antwerp bridge
I'll make my servile spirits to invent.
Come, German Valdes and Cornelius,
And make me blest with your sage conference.
    Enter Valdes *and* Cornelius.
Valdes, sweet Valdes and Cornelius,   100
Know that your words have won me at the last
To practise magic and concealed arts.
Yet not your words only but mine own fantasy
That will receive no object for my head,
But ruminates on necromantic skill.
Philosophy is odious and obscure,
Both law and physic are for petty wits;
Divinity is basest of the three,
Unpleasant, harsh, contemptible and vilde.
'Tis magic, magic that hath ravish'd me.   110
Then, gentle friends, aid me in this attempt,
And I, that have with concise syllogisms
Gravell'd the pastors of the German church
And made the flow'ring pride of Wittenberg
Swarm to my problems as th'infernal spirits
On sweet Musaeus when he came to hell,
Will be as cunning as Agrippa was,
Whose shadows made all Europe honour him.
VALDES. Faustus, these books, thy wit and our experience
Shall make all nations to canonize us.   120
As Indian Moors obey their Spanish lords,
So shall the spirits of every element
Be always serviceable to us three.
Like lions shall they guard us when we please,
Like Almain rutters with their horsemen's staves,
Or Lapland giants trotting by our sides;
Sometimes like women or unwedded maids,
Shadowing more beauty in their airy brows
Than has the white breasts of the Queen of Love.
From Venice shall they drag huge argosies,   130
And from America the golden fleece
That yearly stuffs old Philip's treasury,
If learned Faustus will be resolute.

FAUSTUS. Valdes, as resolute am I in this
  As thou to live, therefore object it not.
CORNELIUS. The miracles that magic will perform
  Will make thee vow to study nothing else.
  He that is grounded in astrology,
  Enrich'd with tongues, well seen in minerals,
  Hath all the principles magic doth require.   140
  Then doubt not, Faustus, but to be renowm'd,
  And more frequented for this mystery
  Than heretofore the Delphian oracle.
  The spirits tell me they can dry the sea,
  And fetch the treasure of all foreign wracks,
  Yea, all the wealth that our forefathers hid
  Within the massy entrails of the earth
  Then tell me, Faustus, what shall we three want?
FAUSTUS. Nothing, Cornelius. O, this cheers my soul.
  Come, show me some demonstrations magical,   150
  That I may conjure in some lusty grove,
  And have these joys in full possession.
VALDES. Then haste thee to some solitary grove,
  And bear wise Bacon's and Abanus' works,
  The Hebrew Psalter and New Testament;
  And whatsoever else is requisite
  We will inform thee ere our conference cease.
CORNELIUS. Valdes, first let him know the words of art,
  And then, all other ceremonies learn'd,
  Faustus may try his cunning by himself.   160
VALDES. First I'll instruct thee in the rudiments,
  And then wilt thou be perfecter than I.
FAUSTUS. Then come and dine with me, and after meat
  We'll canvass every quiddity thereof,
  For ere I sleep, I'll try what I can do.
  This night I'll conjure, though I die therefore.   *Exeunt omnes.*

[Scene ii.]
  Enter two Scholars.
1 SCHOLAR. I wonder what's become of Faustus, that was wont
  to make our schools ring with *sic probo.*
  Enter Wagner.
2 SCHOLAR. That shall we presently know. Here comes his boy.
1 SCHOLAR. How now, sirrah, where's thy master?
WAGNER. God in heaven knows.
2 SCHOLAR. Why, dost not thou know then?
WAGNER. Yes, I know, but that follows not.

1 SCHOLAR. Go to, sirrah, leave your jesting and tell us where
  he is.

WAGNER. That follows not by force of argument, which you,
  being licentiates, should stand upon; therefore acknowledge
  your error and be attentive.   12

2 SCHOLAR. Then you will not tell us?

WAGNER. You are deceiv'd, for I will tell you. Yet if you were
  not dunces, you would never ask me such a question. For is
  he not *corpus naturale*? And is not that *mobile*? Then wherefore should you ask me such a question? But that I am by
  nature phlegmatic, slow to wrath and prone to lechery (to
  love, I would say), it were not for you to come within forty
  foot of the place of execution, although I do not doubt but
  to see you both hang'd the next sessions. Thus having
  triumphed over you, I will set my countenance like a
  precisian, and begin to speak thus: Truly, my dear brethren,
  my master is within at dinner with Valdes and Cornelius,
  as this wine, if it could speak, would inform your worships.
  And so the Lord bless you, preserve you and keep you, my
  dear brethren.   *Exit.*

1 SCHOLAR. O Faustus, then I fear that which I have long
    suspected
  That thou art fall'n into that damned art   30
  For which they two are infamous through the world.

2 SCHOLAR. Were he a stranger, not allied to me,
  The danger of his soul would make me mourn.
  But come, let us go and inform the Rector;
  It may be his grave counsel may reclaim him.

1 SCHOLAR. I fear me nothing will reclaim him now.

2 SCHOLAR. Yet let us see what we can do.   *Exeunt.*

[*Scene iii.*]
Thunder. Enter Lucifer *and four Devils* [*above*]. Faustus *to
them with this speech.*

FAUSTUS. Now that the gloomy shadow of the night,
  Longing to view Orion's drizzling look,
  Leaps from th'antarctic world unto the sky,
  And dims the welkin with her pitchy breath,
  Faustus, begin thine incantations
  And try if devils will obey thy hest,
  Seeing thou hast pray'd and sacrific'd to them.
  Within this circle is Jehovah's name
  Forward and backward anagrammatiz'd:
  Th'abbreviated names of holy saints,   10

Figures of every adjunct to the heavens,
And characters of signs and erring stars
By which the spirits are enforc'd to rise.
Then fear not, Faustus, to be resolute
And try the utmost magic can perform.   *Thunder.*
Sint mihi dei Acherontis propitii; valeat numen triplex Jehovae;
ignei, aerii, aquatici, terreni spiritus salvete! Orientis princeps,
Belzebub inferni ardentis monarcha, et Demogorgon, propitiamus
vos, ut appareat, et surgat, Mephostophilis.   *Dragon.*
Quid tu moraris? Per Jehovam, Gehennam, et consecratam aquam
quam nunc spargo, signumque crucis quod nunc facio, et per vota
nostra, ipse nunc surgat nobis dicatus Mephostophilis.   22
     Enter a Devil.
I charge thee to return and change thy shape,
Thou art too ugly to attend on me.
Go, and return an old Franciscan friar,
That holy shape becomes a devil best.   *Exit Devil.*
I see there's virtue in my heavenly words.
Who would not be proficient in this art?
How pliant is this Mephostophilis,
Full of obedience and humility,   30
Such is the force of magic and my spells.
Now, Faustus, thou art conjurer laureate,
That canst command great Mephostophilis.
Quin redis, Mephostophilis, fratris imagine?
     Enter Mephostophilis.
MEPHOSTOPHILIS. Now, Faustus, what wouldst thou have me do?
FAUSTUS. I charge thee wait upon me whilst I live,
To do whatever Faustus shall command,
Be it to make the moon drop from her sphere,
Or the ocean to overwhelm the world.
MEPHOSTOPHILIS. I am a servant to great Lucifer,   40
And may not follow thee without his leave;
No more than he commands must we perform.
FAUSTUS. Did not he charge thee to appear to me?
MEPHOSTOPHILIS. No, I came now hither of mine own accord.
FAUSTUS. Did not my conjuring speeches raise thee? Speak.
MEPHOSTOPHILIS. That was the cause, but yet *per accidens*;
For when we hear one rack the name of God,
Abjure the scriptures and his saviour Christ,
We fly in hope to get his glorious soul;
Nor will we come unless he use such means   50
Whereby he is in danger to be damn'd.
Therefore the shortest cut for conjuring

Is stoutly to abjure the Trinity
And pray devoutly to the prince of hell.

FAUSTUS. So Faustus hath already done, and holds this principle:
There is no chief but only Belzebub,
To whom Faustus doth dedicate himself.
This word 'damnation' terrifies not him,
For he confounds hell in Elysium.
His ghost be with the old philosophers.   60
But leaving these vain trifles of men's souls,
Tell me, what is that Lucifer, thy lord?

MEPHOSTOPHILIS. Arch-regent and commander of all spirits.

FAUSTUS. Was not that Lucifer an angel once?

MEPHOSTOPHILIS. Yes, Faustus, and most dearly lov'd of God.

FAUSTUS. How comes it then that he is prince of devils?

MEPHOSTOPHILIS. O, by aspiring pride and insolence,
For which God threw him from the face of heaven.

FAUSTUS. And what are you that live with Lucifer?

MEPHOSTOPHILIS. Unhappy spirits that fell with Lucifer,   70
Conspir'd against our God with Lucifer,
And are for ever damn'd with Lucifer.

FAUSTUS. Where are you damn'd?

MEPHOSTOPHILIS. In hell.

FAUSTUS. How comes it then that thou art out of hell?

MEPHOSTOPHILIS. Why, this is hell, nor am I out of it.
Think'st thou that I who saw the face of God
And tasted the eternal joys of heaven
Am not tormented with ten thousand hells
In being depriv'd of everlasting bliss?   80
O Faustus, leave these frivolous demands,
Which strike a terror to my fainting soul.

FAUSTUS. What, is great Mephostophilis so passionate
For being deprived of the joys of heaven?
Learn thou of Faustus manly fortitude,
And scorn those joys thou never shalt possess.
Go, bear these tidings to great Lucifer:
Seeing Faustus hath incurr'd eternal death
By desperate thoughts against Jove's deity.
Say he surrenders up to him his soul,   90
So he will spare him four and twenty years,
Letting him live in all voluptuousness,
Having thee ever to attend on me,
To give me whatsoever I shall ask,
To tell me whatsoever I demand,
To slay mine enemies and aid my friends,

And always be obedient to my will.
Go, and return to mighty Lucifer,
And meet me in my study at midnight,
And then resolve me of thy master's mind.   100
MEPHOSTOPHILIS. I will, Faustus.   *Exit.*
FAUSTUS. Had I as many souls as there be stars,
    I'd give them all for Mephostophilis.
    By him I'll be great emperor of the world,
    And make a bridge thorough the moving air
    To pass the ocean with a band of men;
    I'll join the hills that bind the Afric shore,
    And make that country continent to Spain,
    And both contributory to my crown.
    The Emperor shall not live but by my leave,   110
    Nor any potentate of Germany.
    Now that I have obtain'd what I desire
    I'll live in speculation of this art
    Till Mephostophilis return again.   *Exit.*
                        [*Exeunt* Lucifer *and Devils.*]

                        [*Scene iv.*]
        Enter Wagner *and the Clown* [Robin].
WAGNER. Come hither, sirrah boy.
ROBIN. Boy? O disgrace to my person! Zounds, boy in your
    face! You have seen many boys with such pickadevants, I
    am sure.
WAGNER. Sirrah, hast thou no comings in?
ROBIN. Yes, and goings out too, you may see, sir.
WAGNER. Alas, poor slave, see how poverty jests in his naked-
    ness. I know the villain's out of service and so hungry that
    he would give his soul to the devil for a shoulder of mutton,
    though it were blood-raw.   10
ROBIN. Not so neither. I had need to have it well roasted, and
    good sauce to it, if I pay so dear, I can tell you.
WAGNER. Sirrah, wilt thou be my man and wait on me? And I
    will make thee go like *Qui mihi discipulus.*
ROBIN. What, in verse?
WAGNER. No, slave, in beaten silk and stavesacre.
ROBIN. Stavesacre? That's good to kill vermin; then belike if
    I serve you I shall be lousy.
WAGNER. Why, so thou shalt be whether thou dost it or no;
    for, sirrah, if thou dost not presently bind thyself to me for
    seven years, I'll turn all the lice about thee into familiars
    and make them tear thee in pieces.   22

                        [283]

ROBIN. Nay sir, you may save yourself a labour, for they are as
familiar with me as if they paid for their meat and drink, I
can tell you.

WAGNER. Well sirrah, leave your jesting and take these guilders.

ROBIN. Yes, marry sir, and I thank you too.

WAGNER. So, now thou art to be at an hour's warning, when-
soever and wheresoever the devil shall fetch thee.

ROBIN. Here, take your guilders, I'll none of 'em.   30

WAGNER. Not I, thou art press'd; prepare thyself, for I will
presently raise up two devils to carry thee away. Banio!
Belcher!

ROBIN. Belcher? And Belcher come here, I'll belch him. I am
not afraid of a devil.

Enter two Devils, *and the Clown runs up and down crying.*

WAGNER. How now, sir, will you serve me now?

ROBIN. Ay, good Wagner; take away the devil then.

WAGNER. Spirits, away.   *Exeunt [Devils].*
                    Now, sirrah, follow me.

ROBIN. I will, sir. But hark you, master, will you teach me this
conjuring occupation?   40

WAGNER. Ay sirrah, I'll teach thee to turn thyself to a dog, or a
cat, or a mouse, or a rat, or anything.

ROBIN. A dog, or a cat, or a mouse, or a rat? O brave Wagner.

WAGNER. Villain, call me Master Wagner, and see that you
walk attentively, and let your right eye be always diametrally
fixed upon my left heel, that thou may'st *quasi vestigiis
nostris insistere.*

ROBIN. Well sir, I warrant you.   *Exeunt.*

[*Act II. Scene i.*]

Enter Faustus *in his study.*

FAUSTUS. Now, Faustus, must thou needs be damn'd,
And canst thou not be sav'd.
What boots it then to think on God or heaven?
Away with such vain fancies, and despair;
Despair in God, and trust in Belzebub.
Now go not backward; no, Faustus, be resolute.
Why waver'st thou? O something soundeth in mine ears,
'Abjure this magic, turn to God again.'
Ay, and Faustus will turn to God again.
To God? He loves thee not.   10
The God thou serv'st is thine own appetite,
Wherein is fix'd the love of Belzebub.

To him I'll build an altar and a church,
And offer lukewarm blood of new-born babes.
    Enter the two Angels.
BAD ANGEL. Go forward, Faustus, in that famous art.
GOOD ANGEL. Sweet Faustus, leave that execrable art.
FAUSTUS. Contrition, prayer, repentance, what of these?
GOOD ANGEL. O they are means to bring thee unto heaven.
BAD ANGEL. Rather illusions, fruits of lunacy,
    That make them foolish that do use them most.   20
GOOD ANGEL. Sweet Faustus, think of heaven and heavenly
    things.
BAD ANGEL. No, Faustus, think of honour and of wealth.
                                        Exeunt Angels.
FAUSTUS. Wealth!
    Why, the signory of Emden shall be mine.
    When Mephostophilis shall stand by me,
    What God can hurt me? Faustus, thou art safe:
    Cast no more doubts. Mephostophilis, come,
    And bring glad tidings from great Lucifer.
    Is't not midnight? Come, Mephostophilis!
    Veni, veni, Mephostophile.   30
        Enter Mephostophilis.
    Now tell me what saith Lucifer thy lord.
MEPHOSTOPHILIS. That I shall wait on Faustus whilst he lives,
    So he will buy my service with his soul.
FAUSTUS. Already Faustus hath hazarded that for thee.
MEPHOSTOPHILIS. But now thou must bequeath it solemnly,
    And write a deed of gift with thine own blood,
    For that security craves Lucifer.
    If thou deny it, I must back to hell.
FAUSTUS. Stay, Mephostophilis, and tell me
    What good will my soul do thy lord?   40
MEPHOSTOPHILIS. Enlarge his kingdom.
FAUSTUS. Is that the reason why he tempts us thus?
MEPHOSTOPHILIS. *Solamen miseris socios habuisse doloris.*
FAUSTUS. Why, have you any pain that torture other?
MEPHOSTOPHILIS. As great as have the human souls of men.
    But tell me, Faustus, shall I have thy soul?
    And I will be thy slave and wait on thee,
    And give thee more than thou hast wit to ask.
FAUSTUS. Ay, Mephostophilis, I'll give it him.
MEPHOSTOPHILIS. Then, Faustus, stab thy arm courageously,
    And bind thy soul, that at some certain day   51
    Great Lucifer may claim it as his own,

And then be thou as great as Lucifer.

FAUSTUS. Lo, Mephostophilis, for love of thee
Faustus hath cut his arm, and with his proper blood
Assures his soul to be great Lucifer's,
Chief lord and regent of perpetual night.
View here this blood that trickles from mine arm,
And let it be propitious for my wish.

MEPHOSTOPHILIS. But, Faustus,   60
Write it in manner of a deed of gift.

FAUSTUS. Ay, so I will. But, Mephostophilis,
My blood congeals and I can write no more.

MEPHOSTOPHILIS. I'll fetch thee fire to dissolve it straight.

Exit.

FAUSTUS. What might the staying of my blood portend?
Is it unwilling I should write this bill?
Why streams it not that I may write afresh?
'Faustus gives to thee his soul': ah, there it stay'd.
Why shouldst thou not? Is not thy soul thine own?
Then write again: 'Faustus gives to thee his soul.'   70

Enter Mephostophilis *with the chafer of fire.*

MEPHOSTOPHILIS. See, Faustus, here is fire; set it on.

FAUSTUS. So, now the blood begins to clear again;
Now will I make an end immediately.

MEPHOSTOPHILIS. What will not I do to obtain his soul?

FAUSTUS. *Consummatum est*: this bill is ended,
And Faustus hath bequeath'd his soul to Lucifer.
But what is this inscription on mine arm?
Homo fuge: whither should I flie?
If unto God, he'll throw me down to hell.
My senses are deceiv'd: here's nothing writ!   80
O yes, I see it plain. Even here is writ
Homo fuge: yet shall not Faustus fly.

MEPHOSTOPHILIS. I'll fetch him somewhat to delight his mind.

Exit.

Enter Devils, giving crowns and rich apparel to Faustus; *they dance and then depart. Enter* Mephostophilis.

FAUSTUS. What means this show? Speak, Mephostophilis.

MEPHOSTOPHILIS. Nothing, Faustus, but to delight thy mind,
And let thee see what magic can perform.

FAUSTUS. But may I raise such spirits when I please?

MEPHOSTOPHILIS. Ay, Faustus, and do greater things than these.

FAUSTUS. Then, Mephostophilis, receive this scroll,
A deed of gift, of body and of soul: 90
But yet conditionally that thou perform

All covenants and articles between us both.

MEPHOSTOPHILIS. Faustus, I swear by hell and Lucifer
   To effect all promises between us made.

FAUSTUS. Then hear me read it, Mephostophilis.
   On these conditions following:
   'First, that Faustus may be a spirit in form and sub-
stance.
   'Secondly, that Mephostophilis shall be his servant, and
at his command.   100
   'Thirdly, that Mephostophilis shall do for him and bring
him whatsoever.
   'Fourthly, that he shall be in his chamber or house invisible.
   'Lastly, that he shall appear to the said John Faustus at
all times, in what form or shape soever he please.
   'I, John Faustus of Wittenberg, doctor, by these presents,
do give both body and soul to Lucifer, Prince of the East,
and his minister Mephostophilis, and furthermore grant
unto them that, four-and-twenty years being expired, the
articles above written inviolate, full power to fetch or carry
the said John Faustus, body and soul, flesh, blood or goods,
into their habitation wheresoever.   113
   By me John Faustus.'

MEPHOSTOPHILIS. Speak, Faustus, do you deliver this as your
   deed?

FAUSTUS. Ay, take it, and the devil give thee good of it.

MEPHOSTOPHILIS. So, now, Faustus, ask me what thou wilt.

FAUSTUS. First I will question with thee about hell.
   Tell me, where is the place that men call hell?

MEPHOSTOPHILIS. Under the heavens.   120

FAUSTUS. Ay, so are all things else; but whereabouts?

MEPHOSTOPHILIS. Within the bowels of these elements,
   Where we are tortur'd and remain for ever.
   Hell hath no limits, nor is circumscrib'd
   In one self place, but where we are is hell,
   And where hell is, there must we ever be.
   And to be short, when all the world dissolves
   And every creature shall be purified,
   All places shall be hell that is not heaven.

FAUSTUS. I think hell's a fable.   130

MEPHOSTOPHILIS. Ay, think so still, till experience change thy
   mind.

FAUSTUS. Why, dost thou think that Faustus shall be damn'd?

MEPHOSTOPHILIS. Ay, of necessity, for here's the scroll

In which thou hast given thy soul to Lucifer.

FAUSTUS. Ay, and body too, but what of that?
Think'st thou that Faustus is so fond to imagine
That after this life there is any pain?
Tush, these are trifles and mere old wives' tales.

MEPHOSTOPHILIS. But I am an instance to prove the contrary,
For I tell thee I am damn'd, and now in hell.   140

FAUSTUS. Nay, and this be hell, I'll willingly be damn'd.
What, sleeping, eating, walking and disputing?
But leaving this, let me have a wife, the fairest maid in
Germany, for I am wanton and lascivious, and cannot live
without a wife.

MEPHOSTOPHILIS. Well, Faustus, thou shalt have a wife.

He fetches in a woman devil.

FAUSTUS. What sight is this?

MEPHOSTOPHILIS. Now, Faustus, wilt thou have a wife?

FAUSTUS. Here's a hot whore indeed; no. I'll no wife.

MEPHOSTOPHILIS. Marriage is but a ceremonial toy,   150
And if thou lov'st me, think no more of it.
I'll cull thee out the fairest courtesans
And bring them every morning to thy bed:
She whom thine eye shall like, thy heart shall have,
Were she as chaste as was Penelope,
As wise as Saba, or as beautiful
As was bright Lucifer before his fall.
Hold, take this book, peruse it thoroughly:
The iterating of these lines brings gold,
The framing of this circle on the ground   160
Brings thunder, whirlwinds, storm and lightning.
Pronounce this thrice devoutly to thyself
And men in harness shall appear to thee,
Ready to execute what thou command'st.

FAUSTUS. Thanks, Mephostophilis, for this sweet book.
This will I keepe as chary as my life.
Yet fain would I have a book wherein I might behold all
spells and incantations, that I might raise up spirits when
I please.

MEPHOSTOPHILIS. Here they are in this book.

There turn to them.

FAUSTUS. Now would I have a book where I might see all
characters and planets of the heavens, that I might know
their motions and dispositions.   173

MEPHOSTOPHILIS. Here they are too.   *Turn to them.*

FAUSTUS. Nay, let me have one book more, and then I have

done, wherein I might see all plants, herbs and trees that
grow upon the earth.
MEPHOSTOPHILIS. Here they be.
FAUSTUS. O thou art deceived.
MEPHOSTOPHILIS. Tut, I warrant thee.   *Turn to them.*
                                              Exeunt.

[*Scene ii.*]
Enter Faustus *in his study, and* Mephostophilis.

FAUSTUS. When I behold the heavens then I repent,
    And curse thee, wicked Mephostophilis,
    Because thou hast depriv'd me of those joys.
MEPHOSTOPHILIS. 'Twas thine own seeking, Faustus, thank
    thyself.
    But think'st thou heaven is such a glorious thing?
    I tell thee, Faustus, it is not half so fair
    As thou or any man that breathes on earth.
FAUSTUS. How prov'st thou that?
MEPHOSTOPHILIS. 'Twas made for man; then he's more
    excellent.
FAUSTUS. If heaven was made for man, 'twas made for me. 10
    I will renounce this magic and repent.
        Enter the two Angels.
GOOD ANGEL. Faustus, repent; yet God will pity thee.
BAD ANGEL. Thou art a spirit; God cannot pity thee.
FAUSTUS. Who buzzeth in mine ears I am a spirit?
    Be I a devil, yet God may pity me;
    Yea, God will pity me if I repent.
BAD ANGEL. Ay, but Faustus never shall repent.
                                          Exeunt Angels.
FAUSTUS. My heart is hard'ned; I cannot repent.
    Scarce can I name salvation, faith or heaven,
    But fearful echoes thunder in mine ears   20
    'Faustus, thou art damn'd'; then swords and knives,
    Poison, guns, halters and envenom'd steel
    Are laid before me to dispatch myself.
    And long ere this I should have done the deed,
    Had not sweet pleasure conquer'd deep despair.
    Have not I made blind Homer sing to me
    Of Alexander's love and Oenon's death?
    And hath not he that built the walls of Thebes
    With ravishing sound of his melodious harp
    Made music with my Mephostophilis?   30
    Why should I die then, or basely despair?

[289]

I am resolv'd, Faustus shall not repent.
Come, Mephostophilis, let us dispute again,
And reason of divine astrology.
Speak, are there many spheres above the moon?
Are all celestial bodies but one globe,
As is the substance of this centric earth?

MEPHOSTOPHILIS. As are the elements, such are the heavens,
Even from the moon unto the empyreal orb,
Mutually folded in each other's spheres,   40
And jointly move upon one axle-tree,
Whose termine is term'd the world's wide pole.
Nor are the names of Saturn, Mars or Jupiter
Feign'd, but are erring stars.

FAUSTUS. But have they all one motion, both *situ et tempore*?

MEPHOSTOPHILIS. All move from east to west in four and twenty
hours upon the poles of the world, but differ in their motions
upon the poles of the zodiac.

FAUSTUS. These slender questions Wagner can decide.
Hath Mephostophilis no greater skill?   50
Who knows not the double motion of the planets,
That the first is finish'd in a natural day,
    The second thus: Saturn in thirty years, Jupiter in
twelve, Mars in four, the Sun, Venus and Mercury in a
year, the moon in twenty-eight days. These are freshmen's
suppositions. But tell me, hath every sphere a dominion or
intelligentia?

MEPHOSTOPHILIS. Ay.

FAUSTUS. How many heavens or spheres are there?

MEPHOSTOPHILIS. Nine, the seven planets, the firmament, and
the empyreal heaven.   61

FAUSTUS. But is there not *coelum igneum*, and *cristallinum*?

MEPHOSTOPHILIS. No, Faustus, they be but fables.

FAUSTUS. Resolve me then in this one question. Why are not
conjunctions, oppositions, aspects, eclipses, all at one time,
but in some years we have more, in some less?

MEPHOSTOPHILIS. *Per inaequalem motum respectu totius.*

FAUSTUS. Well, I am answer'd. Now tell me, who made the
world?

MEPHOSTOPHILIS. I will not.   70

FAUSTUS. Sweet Mephostophilis, tell me.

MEPHOSTOPHILIS. Move me not, Faustus.

FAUSTUS. Villain, have not I bound thee to tell me anything?

MEPHOSTOPHILIS. Ay, that is not against our kingdom:
This is. Thou art damn'd, think thou of hell.

FAUSTUS. Think, Faustus, upon God, that made the world.

MEPHOSTOPHILIS. Remember this—   *Exit.*

FAUSTUS. Ay, go, accursed spirit, to ugly hell.
'Tis thou hast damn'd distressed Faustus' soul.
Is't not too late?   80
     Enter the two Angels.

BAD ANGEL. Too late.

GOOD ANGEL. Never too late, if Faustus will repent.

BAD ANGEL. If thou repent, devils will tear thee in pieces.

GOOD ANGEL. Repent, and they shall never raze thy skin.
                   Exeunt Angels.

FAUSTUS. O Christ my saviour, my saviour,
    Help to save distressed Faustus' soul.
     Enter Lucifer, Belzebub, *and* Mephostophilis.

LUCIFER. Christ cannot save thy soul, for he is just;
    There's none but I have interest in the same.

FAUSTUS. O what art thou that look'st so terribly?

LUCIFER. I am Lucifer, and this is my companion prince in hell.

FAUSTUS. O Faustus, they are come to fetch thy soul.   91

BELZEBUB. We are come to tell thee thou dost injure us.

LUCIFER. Thou call'st on Christ contrary to thy promise.

BELZEBUB. Thou shouldst not think on God.

LUCIFER. Think of the devil.

BELZEBUB. And his dam too.

FAUSTUS. Nor will I henceforth. Pardon me in this,
    And Faustus vows never to look to heaven,
    Never to name God or to pray to him,
    To burn his scriptures, slay his ministers,   100
    And make my spirits pull his churches down.

LUCIFER. So shalt thou show thyself an obedient servant,
    And we will highly gratify thee for it.

BELZEBUB. Faustus, we are come from hell in person to show
thee some pastime. Sit down and thou shalt behold the
Seven Deadly Sins appear to thee in their own proper
shapes and likeness.

FAUSTUS. That sight will be as pleasant to me as Paradise was to
Adam the first day of his creation.

LUCIFER. Talk not of Paradise or Creation, but mark the show.
Go, Mephostophilis, fetch them in.   111
     Enter the Seven Deadly Sins.

BELZEBUB. Now, Faustus, question them of their names and
dispositions.

FAUSTUS. That shall I soon. What art thou, the first?

PRIDE. I am Pride. I disdain to have any parents. I am like to

Ovid's flea, I can creep into every corner of a wench; sometimes like a periwig I sit upon her brow; next, like a necklace I hang about her neck; then, like a fan of feathers, I kiss her lips; and then, turning myself to a wrought smock, do what I list. But fie, what a smell is here! I'll not speak a word more for a king's ransom, unless the ground be perfum'd and cover'd with cloth of arras.   122

FAUSTUS. Thou art a proud knave indeed. What art thou, the second?

COVETOUSNESS. I am Covetousness, begotten of an old churl in a leather bag; and might I now obtain my wish, this house, you and all, should turn to gold, that I might lock you safe into my chest. O my sweet gold!

FAUSTUS. And what art thou, the third?   129

ENVY. I am Envy, begotten of a chimney-sweeper and an oyster-wife. I cannot read and therefore wish all books burn'd. I am lean with seeing others eat: O that there would come a famine over all the world, that all might die, and I live alone; then thou shouldst see how fat I'd be. But must thou sit and I stand? Come down, with a vengeance.

FAUSTUS. Out, envious wretch. But what art thou, the fourth?

WRATH. I am Wrath. I had neither father nor mother. I leapt out of a lion's mouth when I was scarce an hour old, and ever since have run up and down the world with these case of rapiers, wounding myself when I could get none to fight withal. I was born in hell, and look to it, for some of you shall be my father.   142

FAUSTUS. And what art thou, the fifth?

GLUTTONY. I am Gluttony. My parents are all dead, and the devil a penny they have left me, but a small pension, and that buys me thirty meals a day and ten bevers: a small trifle to suffice nature. I come of a royal pedigree: my father was a gammon of bacon and my mother was a hogshead of claret wine. My godfathers were these: Peter Pickled-herring and Martin Martlemas-beef. But my godmother, O, she was an ancient gentlewoman, and well-beloved in every good town and city; her name was Mistress Margery March-beer. Now, Faustus, thou hast heard all my progeny, wilt thou bid me to supper?   154

FAUSTUS. Not I.

GLUTTONY. Then the devil choke thee.

FAUSTUS. Choke thyself, Glutton. What art thou, the sixth?

SLOTH. Hey ho, I am Sloth. I was begotten on a sunny bank, where I have lain ever since, and you have done me great

injury to bring me from thence. Let me be carried thither
again by Gluttony and Lechery. Hey ho! I'll not speak
another word.   162

FAUSTUS. And what are you, Mistress Minx, the seventh and
last?

LECHERY. Who, I, sir? I am one that loves an inch of raw
mutton better than an ell of fried stockfish, and the first
letter of my name begins with Lechery.

LUCIFER. Away to hell, away. On, piper!

Exeunt the Seven Sins.

FAUSTUS. O how this sight doth delight my soul!

LUCIFER. Tut, Faustus, in hell is all manner of delight.   170

FAUSTUS. O might I see hell and return again safe, how happy
were I then.

LUCIFER. Faustus, thou shalt; at midnight I will send for thee.
Meanwhile, peruse this book and view it throughly, and
thou shalt turn thyself into what shape thou wilt.

FAUSTUS. Thanks, mighty Lucifer; this will I keep as chary as
my life.

LUCIFER. Now, Faustus, farewell.

FAUSTUS. Farewell, great Lucifer. Come, Mephostophilis.

Exeunt omnes, several ways.

[*Scene iii.*]

Enter the Clown [Robin].

ROBIN. What, Dick, look to the horses there till I come again.
I have gotten one of Doctor Faustus' conjuring books, and
now we'll have such knavery as't passes.

Enter Dick.

DICK. What, Robin, you must come away and walk the horses.

ROBIN. I walk the horses? I scorn't, 'faith. I have other matters
in hand. Let the horses walk themselves and they will.
A per se a, t.h.e. the, o per se o, deny orgon, gorgon. Keep further
from me, O thou illiterate and unlearned hostler.

DICK. 'Snails, what hast thou got there? A book? Why, thou
canst not tell ne'er a word on't.   10

ROBIN. That thou shalt see presently. Keep out of the circle,
I say, lest I send you into the hostry with a vengeance.

DICK. That's like, 'faith. You had best leave your foolery, for
an my master come, he'll conjure you, 'faith.

ROBIN. My master conjure me? I'll tell thee what, an my master
come here, I'll clap as fair a pair of horns on's head as e'er
thou sawest in thy life.

DICK. Thou need'st not do that, for my mistress hath done it.

ROBIN. Ay, there be of us here, that have waded as deep into
　　matters as other men, if they were disposed to talk.　　20
DICK. A plague take you! I thought you did not sneak up and
　　down after her for nothing. But I prithee tell me, in good
　　sadness, Robin, is that a conjuring book?
ROBIN. Do but speak what thou'lt have me to do, and I'll do't.
　　If thou'lt dance naked, put off thy clothes and I'll conjure
　　thee about presently. Or if thou'lt go but to the tavern with
　　me, I'll give thee white wine, red wine, claret wine, sack,
　　muscadine, malmsey and whippincrust, hold, belly, hold,
　　and we'll not pay one penny for it.
DICK. O brave, prithee, let's to it presently, for I am as dry as
　　a dog.　　　　　　　　　　　　　　　　　　　　31
ROBIN. Come, then, let's away.　　　　　　　　　*Exeunt.*

[*Chorus 1.*]

　Enter the Chorus.
Learned Faustus,
To find the secrets of astronomy
Graven in the book of Jove's high firmament,
Did mount him up to scale Olympus top,
Where, sitting in a chariot burning bright
Drawn by the strength of yoked dragons' necks,
He views the clouds, the planets, and the stars,
The tropics, zones, and quarters of the sky,
From the bright circle of the horned moon,
Even to the height of *Primum Mobile.*　　　　　　10
And whirling round with this circumference
Within the concave compass of the pole,
From east to west his dragons swiftly glide,
And in eight days did bring him home again.
Not long he stay'd within his quiet house
To rest his bones after his weary toil,
But new exploits do hale him out again,
And mounted then upon a dragon's back,
That with his wings did part the subtle air,
He now is gone to prove cosmography,　　　　　　20
That measures coasts and kingdoms of the earth;
And as I guess will first arrive at Rome,
To see the Pope and manner of his court,
And take some part of holy Peter's feast,
The which this day is highly solemniz'd.

　　　　　　　　　　　　　　　　　　　Exit.

[*Act III. Scene i.*]

Enter Faustus *and* Mephostophilis.

FAUSTUS. Having now, my good Mephostophilis,
Pass'd with delight the stately town of Trier,
Environed round with airy mountain tops,
With walls of flint, and deep-entrenched lakes,
Not to be won by any conquering prince;
From Paris next, coasting the realm of France,
We saw the river Main fall into Rhine,
Whose banks are set with groves of fruitful vines;
Then up to Naples, rich Campania,
Whose buildings fair and gorgeous to the eye,   10
The streets straight forth and pav'd with finest brick,
Quarters the town in four equivalents.
There saw we learned Maro's golden tomb,
The way he cut, an English mile in length,
Thorough a rock of stone in one night's space.
From thence to Venice, Padua and the rest,
In midst of which a sumptuous temple stands,
That threats the stars with her aspiring top,
Whose frame is pav'd with sundry-coloured stones,
And roof'd aloft with curious work in gold.   20
Thus hitherto hath Faustus spent his time.
But tell me now, what resting place is this?
Hast thou, as erst I did command,
Conducted me within the walls of Rome?
MEPHOSTOPHILIS. I have, my Faustus, and for proof thereof
This is the goodly palace of the Pope;
And 'cause we are no common guests
I choose his privy chamber for our use.
FAUSTUS. I hope his Holiness will bid us welcome.
MEPHOSTOPHILIS. All's one, for we'll be bold with his venison.
But now, my Faustus, that thou may'st perceive   31
What Rome contains for to delight thine eyes,
Know that this city stands upon seven hills
That underprop the groundwork of the same;
Just through the midst runs flowing Tiber's stream,
With winding banks that cut it in two parts,
Over the which four stately bridges lean,
That make safe passage to each part of Rome.
Upon the bridge called Ponte Angelo
Erected is a castle passing strong,   40
Where thou shalt see such store of ordinance

As that the double cannons forg'd of brass
Do match the number of the days contain'd
Within the compass of one complete year;
Beside the gates, and high pyramides
That Julius Caesar brought from Africa.

FAUSTUS. Now by the kingdoms of infernal rule,
Of Styx, of Acheron, and the fiery lake
Of ever-burning Phlegethon, I swear
That I do long to see the monuments   50
And situation of bright-splendent Rome.
Come, therefore, let's away.

MEPHOSTOPHILIS. Nay, stay, my Faustus. I know you'd see the
    Pope,
And take some part of holy Peter's feast,
The which in state and high solemnity
This day is held through Rome and Italy
In honour of the Pope's triumphant victory.

FAUSTUS. Sweet Mephostophilis, thou pleasest me.
Whilst I am here on earth let me be cloy'd
With all things that delight the heart of man.   60
My four-and-twenty years of liberty
I'll spend in pleasure and in dalliance,
That Faustus' name, whilst this bright frame doth stand,
May be admired through the furthest land.

MEPHOSTOPHILIS. 'Tis well said, Faustus. Come then, stand by
    me,
And thou shalt see them come immediately.

FAUSTUS. Nay, stay, my gentle Mephostophilis,
And grant me my request, and then I go.
Thou know'st within the compass of eight days
We view'd the face of heaven, of earth and hell;   70
So high our dragons soar'd into the air,
That, looking down, the earth appear'd to me
No bigger than my hand in quantity.
There did we view the kingdoms of the world,
And what might please mine eye I there beheld.
Then in this show let me an actor be,
That this proud Pope may Faustus' cunning see.

MEPHOSTOPHILIS. Let it be so, my Faustus, but first stay
And view their triumphs as they pass this way.
And then devise what best contents thy mind   80
By cunning in thine art to cross the Pope,
Or dash the pride of this solemnity,
To make his monks and abbots stand like apes,

And point like antics at his triple crown,
To beat the beads about the friars' pates,
Or clap huge horns upon the cardinals' heads,
Or any villainy thou canst devise,
And I'll perform it, Faustus. Hark, they come.
This day shall make thee be admir'd in Rome.

> *Enter the* Cardinals *and* Bishops, *some bearing crosiers, some the pillars;* Monks *and* Friars *singing their procession. Then the* Pope *and* Raymond *King of Hungary with* Bruno *led in chains.*

POPE. Cast down our footstool.
RAYMOND.   Saxon Bruno, stoop,   90
  Whilst on thy back his Holiness ascends
  Saint Peter's chair and state pontifical.
BRUNO. Proud Lucifer, that state belongs to me:
  But thus I fall to Peter, not to thee.
POPE. To me and Peter shalt thou grovelling lie,
  And crouch before the papal dignity.
  Sound trumpets then, for thus Saint Peter's heir
  From Bruno's back ascends Saint Peter's chair.

>   *A flourish while he ascends.*

  Thus, as the gods creep on with feet of wool
  Long ere with iron hands they punish men,   100
  So shall our sleeping vengeance now arise,
  And smite with death thy hated enterprise.
  Lord cardinals of France and Padua,
  Go forthwith to our holy consistory,
  And read amongst the statutes decretal,
  What by the holy council held at Trent
  The sacred synod hath decreed for him
  That doth assume the papal government,
  Without election and a true consent.
  Away, and bring us word with speed.   110
I CARDINAL. We go, my lord.

>   *Exeunt* Cardinals.

POPE. Lord Raymond.
FAUSTUS. Go, haste thee, gentle Mephostophilis,
  Follow the cardinals to the consistory,
  And as they turn their superstitious books,
  Strike them with sloth and drowsy idleness,
  And make them sleep so sound that in their shapes
  Thyself and I may parley with this Pope,
  This proud confronter of the Emperor,
  And in despite of all his holiness   120

Restore this Bruno to his liberty
And bear him to the states of Germany.
MEPHOSTOPHILIS. Faustus, I go.
FAUSTUS.   Dispatch it soon.
The Pope shall curse that Faustus came to Rome.
                    Exeunt Faustus *and* Mephostophilis.
BRUNO. Pope Adrian, let me have some right of law;
I was elected by the Emperor.
POPE. We will depose the Emperor for that deed,
And curse the people that submit to him.
Both he and thou shalt stand excommunicate,
And interdict from Church's privilege   130
And all society of holy men.
He grows too proud in his authority,
Lifting his lofty head above the clouds
And like a steeple overpeers the Church.
But we'll pull down his haughty insolence,
And as Pope Alexander, our progenitor,
Trod on the neck of German Frederick,
Adding this golden sentence to our praise,
That Peter's heirs should tread on emperors
And walk upon the dreadful adder's back,   140
Treading the lion and the dragon down,
And fearless spurn the killing basilisk,
So will we quell that haughty schismatic,
And by authority apostolical
Depose him from his regal government.
BRUNO. Pope Julius swore to princely Sigismund,
For him and the succeeding popes of Rome,
To hold the emperors their lawful lords.
POPE. Pope Julius did abuse the Church's rites,
And therefore none of his decrees can stand.   150
Is not all power on earth bestow'd on us?
And therefore though we would we cannot err.
Behold this silver belt, whereto is fix'd
Seven golden keys fast seal'd with seven seals,
In token of our seven-fold power from heaven,
To bind or loose, lock fast, condemn or judge,
Resign or seal, or whatso pleaseth us.
Then he and thou and all the world shall stoop,
Or be assured of our dreadful curse,
To light as heavy as the pains of hell.   160
     Enter Faustus *and* Mephostophilis, *like the cardinals.*
MEPHOSTOPHILIS. Now tell me, Faustus, are we not fitted well?

FAUSTUS. Yes, Mephostophilis, and two such cardinals
  Ne'er served a holy pope as we shall do.
  But whilst they sleep within the consistory,
  Let us salute his reverend Fatherhood.
RAYMOND. Behold, my lord, the cardinals are return'd.
POPE. Welcome, grave fathers, answer presently:
  What have our holy council there decreed
  Concerning Bruno and the Emperor,
  In quittance of their late conspiracy   170
  Against our state and papal dignity?
FAUSTUS. Most sacred patron of the Church of Rome,
  By full consent of all the synody
  Of priests and prelates, it is thus decreed:
  That Bruno and the German Emperor
  Be held as lollards and bold schismatics
  And proud disturbers of the Church's peace.
  And if that Bruno by his own assent,
  Without enforcement of the German peers,
  Did seek to wear the triple diadem   180
  And by your death to climb Saint Peter's chair,
  The statutes decretal have thus decreed:
  He shall be straight condemn'd of heresy
  And on a pile of faggots burnt to death.
POPE. It is enough. Here, take him to your charge,
  And bear him straight to Ponte Angelo,
  And in the strongest tower enclose him fast.
  Tomorrow, sitting in our consistory
  With all our college of grave cardinals,
  We will determine of his life or death.   190
  Here, take his triple crown along with you,
  And leave it in the Church's treasury.
  Make haste again, my good lord cardinals,
  And take our blessing apostolical.
MEPHOSTOPHILIS. So, so, was never devil thus bless'd before.
FAUSTUS. Away, sweet Mephostophilis, be gone:
  The cardinals will be plagu'd for this anon.
        Exeunt Faustus *and* Mephostophilis [*with* Bruno].
POPE. Go presently and bring a banquet forth
  That we may solemnize Saint Peter's feast,
  And with Lord Raymond, King of Hungary,   200
  Drink to our late and happy victory.   *Exeunt.*

[*Scene ii.*]
A sennet while the banquet is brought in; and then enter Faustus
and Mephostophilis *in their own shapes.*

MEPHOSTOPHILIS. Now, Faustus, come prepare thyself for mirth;
The sleepy cardinals are hard at hand
To censure Bruno, that is posted hence,
And on a proud-pac'd steed as swift as thought
Flies o'er the Alps to fruitful Germany,
There to salute the woeful Emperor.

FAUSTUS. The Pope will curse them for their sloth today
That slept both Bruno and his crown away.
But now, that Faustus may delight his mind,
And by their folly make some merriment,   10
Sweet Mephostophilis, so charm me here
That I may walk invisible to all,
And do whate'er I please unseen of any.

MEPHOSTOPHILIS. Faustus, thou shalt. Then kneel down
    presently:
            Whilst on thy head I lay my hand,
            And charm thee with this magic wand.
            First wear this girdle, then appear
            Invisible to all are here.
            The planets seven, the gloomy air,
            Hell, and the Furies' forked hair,   20
            Pluto's blue fire and Hecat's tree,
            With magic spells so compass thee
            That no eye may thy body see.
So, Faustus, now for all their holiness,
Do what thou wilt, thou shalt not be discern'd.

FAUSTUS. Thanks, Mephostophilis. Now, friars, take heed
Lest Faustus make your shaven crowns to bleed.

MEPHOSTOPHILIS. Faustus, no more; see where the cardinals
    come.
        Enter Pope *and all the* Lords. *Enter the* Cardinals *with a book.*

POPE. Welcome, lord cardinals. Come, sit down.
Lord Raymond, take your seat. Friars, attend,   30
And see that all things be in readiness
As best beseems this solemn festival.

I CARDINAL. First, may it please your sacred holiness
To view the sentence of the reverend synod
Concerning Bruno and the Emperor?

POPE. What needs this question? Did I not tell you
Tomorrow we would sit i'th'consistory

And there determine of his punishment?
You brought us word even now, it was decreed
That Bruno and the cursed Emperor   40
Were by the holy Council both condemn'd
For loathed lollards and base schismatics.
Then wherefore would you have me view that book?
1 CARDINAL. Your grace mistakes. You gave us no such charge.
RAYMOND. Deny it not; we all are witnesses
    That Bruno here was late delivered you,
    With his rich triple crown to be reserv'd
    And put into the Church's treasury.
BOTH CARDINALS. By holy Paul, we saw them not.
POPE. By Peter, you shall die   50
    Unless you bring them forth immediately.
    Hale them to prison, lade their limbs with gyves.
    False prelates, for this hateful treachery,
    Curs'd be your souls to hellish misery.

                              [*Exit* Cardinals, *guarded.*]
FAUSTUS. So, they are safe. Now Faustus, to the feast;
    The Pope had never such a frolic guest.
POPE. Lord Archbishop of Rheims, sit down with us.
ARCHBISHOP. I thank your holiness.
FAUSTUS. Fall to; the devil choke you an you spare.
POPE. Who's that spoke? Friars, look about.   60
    Lord Raymond, pray fall to. I am beholding
    To the Bishop of Milan for this so rare a present.
FAUSTUS. I thank you, sir.   *Snatch it.*
POPE. How now? Who snatch'd the meat from me?
    Villains, why speak you not?
    My good Lord Archbishop, here's a most dainty dish
    Was sent me from a cardinal in France.
FAUSTUS. I'll have that too.   [*Snatch it.*]
POPE. What lollards do attend our holiness
    That we receive such great indignity? Fetch me some wine.
FAUSTUS. Ay, pray do, for Faustus is a-dry.   71
POPE. Lord Raymond, I drink unto your grace.
FAUSTUS. I pledge your grace.   [*Snatch it.*]
POPE. My wine gone too? Ye lubbers, look about
    And find the man that doth this villainy,
    Or by our sanctitude you all shall die.
    I pray, my lords, have patience at this troublesome banquet.
ARCHBISHOP. Please it your holiness, I think it be some ghost
    crept out of purgatory, and now is come unto your holiness
    for his pardon.   80

[301]

POPE. It may be so.
Go, then, command our priests to sing a dirge
To lay the fury of this same troublesome ghost.
The Pope *crosseth himself.*

FAUSTUS. How now?
Must every bit be spiced with a cross?
Nay then, take that.   Faustus *hits him a box of the ear.*

POPE. O I am slain. Help me, my lords.
O come and help to bear my body hence.
Damn'd be this soul for ever for this deed.
Exeunt the Pope *and his train.*

MEPHOSTOPHILIS. Now, Faustus, what will you do now? For I
can tell you, you'll be curs'd with bell, book and candle.

FAUSTUS. Bell, book and candle, candle, book and bell,   92
Forward and backward, to curse Faustus to hell.
Enter the Friars *with bell, book and candle, for the dirge.*

FRIAR. Come, brethren, let's about our business with good
devotion.   *Sing this.*
Cursed be he that stole his holiness' meat from the table.
Maledicat Dominus!
Cursed be he that struck his holiness a blow on the face.
Maledicat Dominus!
Cursed be he that took Friar Sandelo a blow on the pate.
Maledicat Dominus!   101
Cursed be he that disturbeth our holy dirge.
Maledicat Dominus!
Cursed be he that took away his holiness' wine.
Maledicat Dominus!
Beat the Friars, *fling fireworks among them, and exeunt* [*omnes*].

[*Scene iii.*]
Enter Clown [Robin] *and Dick, with a cup.*

DICK. Sirrah Robin, we were best look that your devil can
answer the stealing of this same cup, for the vintner's boy
follows us at the hard heels.

ROBIN. 'Tis no matter, let him come; an he follow us, I'll so
conjure him as he was never conjur'd in his life, I warrant
him. Let me see the cup.
Enter Vintner.

DICK. Here 'tis. Yonder he comes. Now Robin, now or never
show thy cunning.

VINTNER. O, are you here? I am glad I have found you. You are
a couple of fine companions. Pray where's the cup you stole
from the tavern?   11

ROBIN. How, how? We steal a cup? Take heed of what you say; we look not like cup-stealers, I can tell you.

VINTNER. Never deny't, for I know you have it, and I'll search you.

ROBIN. Search me? Ay, and spare not. [*Aside*]. Hold the cup, Dick. Come, come, search me, search me.

[Vintner searches him.]

VINTNER. Come on sirrah, let me search you now.

DICK. Ay, ay, do, do. [*Aside*.] Hold the cup, Robin. I fear not your searching; we scorn to steal your cups, I can tell you.

[Vintner searches him.]

VINTNER. Never outface me for the matter, for sure the cup is between you two.   22

ROBIN. Nay, there you lie; 'tis beyond us both.

VINTNER. A plague take you, I thought 'twas your knavery to take it away. Come, give it me again.

ROBIN. Ay, much! When, can you tell? Dick, make me a circle, and stand close at my back, and stir not for thy life. Vintner, you shall have your cup back anon. Say nothing, Dick. *O per se o; Demogorgon, Belcher and Mephostophilis!*
Enter Mephostophilis.

MEPHOSTOPHILIS. You princely legions of infernal rule,   30
How am I vexed by these villains' charms!
From Constantinople have they brought me now,
Only for pleasure of these damned slaves.   [*Exit* Vintner.]

ROBIN. By lady sir, you have had a shrewd journey of it. Will it please you to take a shoulder of mutton to supper, and a tester in your purse, and go back again?

DICK. Ay, I pray you heartily, sir, for we called you but in jest, I promise you.

MEPHOSTOPHILIS. To purge the rashness of this cursed deed
First, be thou turned to this ugly shape,   40
For apish deeds transformed to an ape.

ROBIN. O brave, an ape! I pray sir, let me have the carrying of him about to show some tricks.

MEPHOSTOPHILIS. And so thou shalt: be thou transformed to a dog, and carry him upon thy back. Away, be gone!   41

ROBIN. A dog? That's excellent: let the maids look well to their porridge-pots, for I'll into the kitchen presently. Come, Dick, come.   *Exeunt the two Clowns.*

MEPHOSTOPHILIS. Now with the flames of ever-burning fire
I'll wing myself and forthwith fly amain   50
Unto my Faustus to the great Turk's court.

Exit.

[*Chorus 2.*]

Enter Chorus.

When Faustus had with pleasure ta'en the view
Of rarest things and royal courts of kings,
He stay'd his course and so returned home,
Where such as bare his absence but with grief—
I mean his friends and near'st companions—
Did gratulate his safety with kind words;
And in their conference of what befell
Touching his journey through the world and air,
They put forth questions of astrology
Which Faustus answer'd with such learned skill   10
As they admir'd and wond'red at his wit.
Now is his fame spread forth in every land:
Amongst the rest, the Emperor is one,
Carolus the Fifth, at whose palace now
Faustus is feasted 'mongst his noblemen.
What there he did in trial of his art,
I leave untold: your eyes shall see perform'd.   *Exit.*

[*Act IV. Scene i.*]

Enter Martino *and* Frederick *at several doors.*

MARTINO. What ho, officers, gentlemen,
   Hie to the presence to attend the Emperor.
   Good Frederick, see the rooms be voided straight,
   His majesty is coming to the hall;
   Go back, and see the state in readiness.
FREDERICK. But where is Bruno, our elected Pope,
   That on a fury's back came post from Rome?
   Will not his grace consort the Emperor?
MARTINO. O yes, and with him comes the German conjurer,
   The learned Faustus, fame of Wittenberg,   10
   The wonder of the world for magic art;
   And he intends to show great Carolus
   The race of all his stout progenitors,
   And bring in presence of his majesty
   The royal shapes and warlike semblances
   Of Alexander and his beauteous paramour.
FREDERICK. Where is Benvolio?
MARTINO. Fast asleep, I warrant you.
   He took his rouse with stoups of Rhenish wine
   So kindly yesternight to Bruno's health   20

[304]

That all this day the sluggard keeps his bed.

FREDERICK. See, see, his window's ope. We'll call to him.

MARTINO. What ho, Benvolio?

    Enter Benvolio *above at a window in his nightcap, buttoning.*

BENVOLIO. What a devil ail you two?

MARTINO. Speak softly, sir, lest the devil hear you;
  For Faustus at the court is late arriv'd,
  And at his heels a thousand furies wait
  To accomplish whatsoever the doctor please.

BENVOLIO. What of this?

MARTINO. Come, leave thy chamber first, and thou shalt see
  This conjurer perform such rare exploits   31
  Before the Pope and royal Emperor
  As never yet was seen in Germany.

BENVOLIO. Has not the Pope enough of conjuring yet?
  He was upon the devil's back late enough,
  And if he be so far in love with him,
  I would he would post with him to Rome again.

FREDERICK. Speak, wilt thou come and see this sport?

BENVOLIO.   Not I.

MARTINO. Wilt thou stand in thy window and see it, then?

BENVOLIO. Ay, and I fall not asleep i'th'meantime.   40

MARTINO. The Emperor is at hand, who comes to see
  What wonders by black spells may compass'd be.

BENVOLIO. Well, go you attend the Emperor. I am content for
this once to thrust my head out at a window, for they say if
a man be drunk overnight the devil cannot hurt him in the
morning. If that be true, I have a charm in my head shall
control him as well as the conjurer, I warrant you.

    A sennet. [*Enter*] *Charles the German* Emperor, Bruno, [*Duke
    of*] Saxony, Faustus, Mephostophilis, *and* Attendants.

EMPEROR. Wonder of men, renown'd magician,
  Thrice-learned Faustus, welcome to our court.
  This deed of thine, in setting Bruno free   50
  From his and our professed enemy,
  Shall add more excellence unto thine art
  Than if by powerful necromantic spells
  Thou couldst command the world's obedience.
  For ever be belov'd of Carolus;
  And if this Bruno thou hast late redeem'd,
  In peace possess the triple diadem
  And sit in Peter's chair, despite of chance,
  Thou shalt be famous through all Italy,
  And honour'd of the German Emperor.   60

FAUSTUS. These gracious words, most royal Carolus,
    Shall make poor Faustus to his utmost power
    Both love and serve the German Emperor,
    And lay his life at holy Bruno's feet.
    For proof whereof, if so your grace be pleas'd,
    The doctor stands prepar'd by power of art
    To cast his magic charms that shall pierce through
    The ebon gates of ever-burning hell,
    And hale the stubborn furies from their caves,
    To compass whatsoe'er your grace commands.   70

BENVOLIO. Blood, he speaks terribly. But for all that, I do not
    greatly believe him; he looks as like to a conjurer as the
    Pope to a costermonger.

EMPEROR. Then, Faustus, as thou late didst promise us,
    We would behold that famous conqueror,
    Great Alexander, and his paramour,
    In their true shapes and state majestical,
    That we may wonder at their excellence.

FAUSTUS. Your majesty shall see them presently.
    Mephostophilis, away.   80
    And with a solemn noise of trumpets' sound,
    Present before this royal Emperor
    Great Alexander and his beauteous paramour.

MEPHOSTOPHILIS. Faustus, I will.   [*Exit.*]

BENVOLIO. Well, master doctor, an your devils come not away
    quickly, you shall have me asleep presently. Zounds, I could
    eat myself for anger, to think I have been such an ass all this
    while, to stand gaping after the devil's governor, and can see
    nothing.

FAUSTUS. I'll make you feel something anon, if my art fail me
    not.   91
    My lord, I must forewarn your majesty
    That when my spirits present the royal shapes
    Of Alexander and his paramour,
    Your grace demand no questions of the king,
    But in dumb silence let them come and go.

EMPEROR. Be it as Faustus please, we are content.

BENVOLIO. Ay, ay, and I am content too. And thou bring
    Alexander and his paramour before the Emperor, I'll be
    Actaeon and turn myself to a stag.   100

FAUSTUS. And I'll play Diana, and send you the horns presently.
    Sennet. Enter at one door the Emperor Alexander, *at the other*
    Darius; *they meet;* Darius *is thrown down;* Alexander *kills*
    him, takes off his crown, and, offering to go out, his Paramour

meets him; he embraceth her and sets Darius' *crown upon her head, and coming back, both salute the* Emperor, *who, leaving his state, offers to embrace them, which* Faustus *seeing, suddenly stays him. Then trumpets cease and music sounds.*

My gracious lord, you do forget yourself;
These are but shadows, not substantial.

EMPEROR. O pardon me, my thoughts are so ravished
With sight of this renowned emperor
That in mine arms I would have compass'd him.
But, Faustus, since I may not speak to them
To satisfy my longing thoughts at full,
Let me this tell thee: I have heard it said
That this fair lady, whilst she liv'd on earth,   110
Had on her neck a little wart or mole;
How may I prove that saying to be true?

FAUSTUS. Your majesty may boldly go and see.

EMPEROR. Faustus, I see it plain,
And in this sight thou better pleasest me
Than if I gain'd another monarchy.

FAUSTUS. Away, be gone.   *Exit Show.*
    See, see, my gracious lord, what strange beast is yon, that
thrusts his head out at window?

EMPEROR. O wondrous sight! See, Duke of Saxony,   120
Two spreading horns most strangely fastened
Upon the head of young Benvolio.

SAXONY. What, is he asleep or dead?

FAUSTUS. He sleeps, my lord, but dreams not of his horns.

EMPEROR. This sport is excellent. We'll call and wake him.
    What ho, Benvolio!

BENVOLIO. A plague upon you! Let me sleep awhile.

EMPEROR. I blame thee not to sleep much, having such a head
of thine own.

SAXONY. Look up, Benvolio, 'tis the Emperor calls.   130

BENVOLIO. The Emperor? Where? O, zounds, my head!

EMPEROR. Nay, and thy horns hold, 'tis no matter for thy head,
for that's arm'd sufficiently.

FAUSTUS. Why, how now, sir knight? What, hang'd by the
horns? This is most horrible. Fie, fie, pull in your head for
shame, let not all the world wonder at you.

BENVOLIO. Zounds, doctor, is this your villainy?

FAUSTUS. O say not so, sir. The doctor has no skill,
No art, no cunning, to present these lords
Or bring before this royal Emperor   140
The mighty monarch, warlike Alexander.

If Faustus do it, you are straight resolv'd
In bold Actaeon's shape to turn a stag.
And therefore, my lord, so please your majesty,
I'll raise a kennel of hounds shall hunt him so
As all his footmanship shall scarce prevail
To keep his carcass from their bloody fangs.
Ho, Belimoth, Argiron, Asteroth!

BENVOLIO. Hold, hold! Zounds, he'll raise up a kennel of
devils, I think, anon. Good my lord, entreat for me. 'Sblood,
I am never able to endure these torments.   151

EMPEROR. Then, good master doctor,
Let me entreat you to remove his horns:
He has done penance now sufficiently.

FAUSTUS. My gracious lord, not so much for injury done to
me, as to delight your majesty with some mirth, hath
Faustus justly requited this injurious knight; which being all
I desire, I am content to remove his horns. Mephostophilis,
transform him. And hereafter, sir, look you speak well of
scholars.   160

BENVOLIO. Speak well of ye? 'Sblood, and scholars be such
cuckold-makers to clap horns of honest men's heads o' this
order, I'll ne'er trust smooth faces and small ruffs more.
But an I be not reveng'd for this, would I might be turn'd
to a gaping oyster and drink nothing but salt water.

EMPEROR. Come, Faustus, while the Emperor lives,
In recompense of this thy high desert,
Thou shalt command the state of Germany,
And live belov'd of mighty Carolus.   *Exeunt omnes.*

[*Scene ii.*]
Enter Benvolio, Martino, Frederick, *and* Soldiers.

MARTINO. Nay, sweet Benvolio, let us sway thy thoughts
From this attempt against the conjurer.

BENVOLIO. Away, you love me not to urge me thus.
Shall I let slip so great an injury,
When every servile groom jests at my wrongs,
And in their rustic gambols proudly say
'Benvolio's head was grac'd with horns today'?
O may these eyelids never close again
Till with my sword I have that conjurer slain.
If you will aid me in this enterprise,   10
Then draw your weapons and be resolute;
If not, depart: here will Benvolio die,
But Faustus' death shall quit my infamy.

FREDERICK. Nay, we will stay with thee, betide what may,
  And kill that doctor if he come this way.
BENVOLIO. Then, gentle Frederick, hie thee to the grove,
  And place our servants and our followers
  Close in an ambush there behind the trees.
  By this, I know, the conjurer is near:
  I saw him kneel and kiss the Emperor's hand,   20
  And take his leave, laden with rich rewards.
  Then soldiers, boldly fight; if Faustus die,
  Take you the wealth, leave us the victory.
FREDERICK. Come, soldiers, follow me unto the grove.
  Who kills him shall have gold and endless love.
                              Exit Frederick *with the* Soldiers.
BENVOLIO. My head is lighter than it was by th'horns,
  But yet my heart more ponderous than my head,
  And pants until I see that conjurer dead.
MARTINO. Where shall we place ourselves, Benvolio?
BENVOLIO. Here will we stay to bide the first assault.   30
  O were that damned hell-hound but in place,
  Thou soon shouldst see me quit my foul disgrace.
    Enter Frederick.
FREDERICK. Close, close! The conjurer is at hand,
  And all alone comes walking in his gown.
  Be ready then, and strike the peasant down.
BENVOLIO. Mine be that honour, then; now sword, strike home.
  For horns he gave, I'll have his head anon.
    Enter Faustus *with the false head.*
MARTINO. See, see, he comes.
BENVOLIO.   No words. This blow ends all.
  Hell take his soul; his body thus must fall.
FAUSTUS. O!   40
FREDERICK. Groan you, master doctor?
BENVOLIO. Break may his heart with groans! Dear Frederick, see,
  Thus will I end his griefs immediately.
MARTINO. Strike with a willing hand; his head is off.
BENVOLIO. The devil's dead; the Furies now may laugh.
FREDERICK. Was this that stern aspect, that awful frown,
  Made the grim monarch of infernal spirits
  Tremble and quake at his commanding charms?
MARTINO. Was this that damned head, whose heart conspir'd
  Benvolio's shame before the Emperor?   50
BENEVOLIO. Ay, that's the head, and here the body lies,
  Justly rewarded for his villainies.
FREDERICK. Come, let's devise how we may add more shame

[309]

To the black scandal of his hated name.

BENVOLIO. First, on his head, in quittance of my wrongs,
  I'll nail huge forked horns, and let them hang
  Within the window where he yok'd me first,
  That all the world may see my just revenge.

MARTINO. What use shall we put his beard to?

BENEVOLIO. We'll sell it to a chimney-sweeper; it will wear out
  ten birchen brooms, I warrant you.   61

FREDERICK. What shall his eyes do?

BENVOLIO. We'll put out his eyes, and they shall serve for
  buttons to his lips, to keep his tongue from catching cold.

MARTINO. An excellent policy. And now, sirs, having divided
  him, what shall the body do?   [*Faustus stands up.*]

BENVOLIO. Zounds, the devil's alive again.

FREDERICK. Give him his head, for God's sake.

FAUSTUS. Nay, keep it. Faustus will have heads and hands,
  Ay, all your hearts to recompense this deed.   70
  Knew you not, traitors, I was limited
  For four-and-twenty years to breathe on earth?
  And had you cut my body with your swords,
  Or hew'd this flesh and bones as small as sand,
  Yet in a minute had my spirit return'd,
  And I had breath'd a man made free from harm.
  But wherefore do I dally my revenge?
  Asteroth, Belimoth, Mephostophilis!
    Enter Mephostophilis *and other Devils.*
  Go, horse these traitors on your fiery backs,
  And mount aloft with them as high as heaven;   80
  Thence pitch them headlong to the lowest hell.
  Yet stay, the world shall see their misery,
  And hell shall after plague their treachery.
  Go, Belimoth, and take this caitiff hence,
  And hurl him in some lake of mud and dirt.
  Take thou this other, drag him through the woods
  Amongst the pricking thorns and sharpest briars,
  Whilst with my gentle Mephostophilis
  This traitor flies unto some steepy rock,
  That rolling down may break the villain's bones   90
  As he intended to dismember me.
  Fly hence, dispatch my charge immediately.

FREDERICK. Pity us, gentle Faustus; save our lives.

FAUSTUS. Away.

FREDERICK.   He must needs go that the devil drives.
                 Exeunt Spirits with the Knights.

Enter the ambushed Soldiers.

1 SOLDIER. Come, sirs, prepare yourselves in readiness.
  Make haste to help these noble gentlemen.
  I heard them parley with the conjurer.
2 SOLDIER. See where he comes; dispatch and kill the slave.
FAUSTUS. What's here? An ambush to betray my life.
  Then, Faustus, try thy skill. Base peasants, stand.   100
  For lo, these trees remove at my command,
  And stand as bulwarks twixt yourselves and me,
  To shield me from your hated treachery.
  Yet, to encounter this your weak attempt,
  Behold an army comes incontinent.

  Faustus *strikes the door, and enter a Devil playing on a drum;*
  after him another bearing an ensign; and divers with weapons;
  Mephostophilis *with fireworks. They set upon the* Soldiers *and*
  drive them out.

                                  [*Exeunt omnes.*]

[*Scene iii.*]

Enter at several doors Benvolio, Frederick, *and* Martino, *their*
heads and faces bloody and besmear'd with mud and dirt, all
having horns on their heads.

MARTINO. What ho, Benvolio!
BENVOLIO.   Here, what, Frederick, ho!
FREDERICK. O help me, gentle friend; where is Martino?
MARTINO. Dear Frederick, here,
  Half smother'd in a lake of mud and dirt,
  Through which the furies dragg'd me by the heels.
FREDERICK. Martino, see, Benvolio's horns again.
MARTINO. O misery! How now, Benvolio?
BENVOLIO. Defend me, heaven, shall I be haunted still?
MARTINO. Nay, fear not, man; we have no power to kill.
BENVOLIO. My friends transformed thus: O hellish spite!   10
  Your heads are all set with horns.
FREDERICK.   You hit it right:
  It is your own you mean; feel on your head.
BENVOLIO. Zounds, horns again!
MARTINO.   Nay, chafe not, man, we all are sped.
BENVOLIO. What devil attends this damn'd magician,
  That, spite of spite, our wrongs are doubled?
FREDERICK. What may we do, that we may hide our shames?
BENVOLIO. If we should follow him to work revenge,
  He'd join long asses' ears to these huge horns,
  And make us laughing stocks to all the world.

MARTINO. What shall we then do, dear Benvolio? 20
BENVOLIO. I have a castle joining near these woods,
 And thither we'll repair and live obscure,
 Till time shall alter these our brutish shapes.
 Sith black disgrace hath thus eclips'd our fame,
 We'll rather die with grief, than live with shame.

          Exeunt omnes.

[*Scene iv.*]
 Enter Faustus *and the* Horse-courser *and* Mephostophilis.

HORSE-COURSER. I beseech your worship accept of these forty
 dollars.
FAUSTUS. Friend, thou canst not buy so good a horse for so
 small a price; I have no great need to sell him, but if thou
 likest him for ten dollars more, take him, because I see thou
 hast a good mind to him.
HORSE-COURSER. I beseech you sir, accept of this. I am a very
 poor man, and have lost very much of late by horse-flesh,
 and this bargain will set me up again. 9
FAUSTUS. Well, I will not stand with thee, give me the money.
 Now sirrah, I must tell you, that you may ride him o'er
 hedge and ditch, and spare him not; but, do you hear, in
 any case, ride him not into the water.
HORSE-COURSER. How sir, not into the water? Why, will he not
 drink of all waters?
FAUSTUS. Yes, he will drink of all waters, but ride him not into
 the water; o'er hedge and ditch or where thou wilt, but not
 into the water. Go bid the ostler deliver him unto you, and
 remember what I say.
HORSE-COURSER. I warrant you, sir. O joyful day! Now am I a
 made man for ever. 21

              Exit.

FAUSTUS. What art thou, Faustus, but a man condemn'd to die?
 Thy fatal time draws to a final end.
 Despair doth drive distrust into my thoughts;
 Confound these passions with a quiet sleep.
 Tush, Christ did call the thief upon the cross,
 Then rest thee, Faustus, quiet in conceit. *He sits to sleep.*
  Enter the Horse-courser, *wet.*
HORSE-COURSER. O what a cozening doctor was this! I, riding
 my horse into the water, thinking some hidden mystery had
 been in the horse, I had nothing under me but a little straw,
 and had much ado to escape drowning. Well, I'll go rouse
 him, and make him give me my forty dollars again. Ho,

sirrah doctor, you cozening scab! Master doctor, awake, and
rise, and give me my money again, for your horse is turned
to a bottle of hay. Master doctor! *He pulls off his leg.*
Alas, I am undone; what shall I do? I have pull'd off his
leg.   37

FAUSTUS. O help, help! The villain hath murder'd me.

HORSE-COURSER. Murder or not murder, now he has but one
leg I'll outrun him, and cast this leg into some ditch or
other.   41
                                                   [Exit.]

FAUSTUS. Stop him, stop him, stop him—ha, ha, ha! Faustus
hath his leg again, and the horse-courser a bundle of hay
for his forty dollars.

Enter Wagner.

How now, Wagner, what news with thee?

WAGNER. If it please you, the Duke of Vanholt doth earnestly
entreat your company, and hath sent some of his men to
attend you with provision fit for your journey.   48

FAUSTUS. The Duke of Vanholt's an honourable gentleman,
and one to whom I must be no niggard of my cunning.
Come, away.   *Exeunt.*

[Scene v.]

Enter Clown [Robin], Dick, Horse-courser, *and a* Carter.

CARTER. Come, my masters, I'll bring you to the best beer in
Europe. What ho, hostess. Where be these whores?

Enter Hostess.

HOSTESS. How now, what lack you? What, my old guests,
welcome.

ROBIN. Sirrah Dick, dost thou know why I stand so mute?

DICK. No, Robin, why is't?

ROBIN. I am eighteen pence on the score; but say nothing, see
if she have forgotten me.

HOSTESS. Who's this, that stands so solemnly by himself? What,
my old guest?   10

ROBIN. Oh, hostess, how do you? I hope my score stands still.

HOSTESS. Ay, there's no doubt of that, for methinks you make
no haste to wipe it out.

DICK. Why, hostess, I say, fetch us some beer.

HOSTESS. You shall presently. Look up into th'hall there, ho!
                                                    Exit.

DICK. Come, sirs, what shall we do now till mine hostess comes?

CARTER. Marry, sir, I'll tell you the bravest tale how a conjurer
served me. You know Doctor Fauster?

HORSE-COURSER. Ay, a plague take him. Here's some on's have cause to know him. Did he conjure thee too?   20

CARTER. I'll tell you how he serv'd me. As I was going to Wittenberg t'other day, with a load of hay, he met me and asked me what he should give me for as much hay as he could eat. Now, sir, I, thinking that a little would serve his turn, bade him take as much as he would for three-farthings. So he presently gave me my money and fell to eating; and, as I am a cursen man, he never left eating till he had eat up all my load of hay.

ALL. O monstrous, eat a whole load of hay!

ROBIN. Yes, yes, that may be, for I have heard of one that has eat a load of logs.   31

HORSE-COURSER. Now, sirs, you shall hear how villainously he serv'd me. I went to him yesterday to buy a horse of him, and he would by no means sell him under forty dollars. So, sir, because I knew him to be such a horse as would run over hedge and ditch and never tire, I gave him his money. So when I had my horse, Doctor Fauster bade me ride him night and day and spare him no time. 'But,' quoth he, 'in any case ride him not into the water.' Now, sir, I thinking the horse had some quality that he would not have me know of, what did I but rid him into a great river, and when I came just in the midst, my horse vanish'd away, and I sat straddling upon a bottle of hay.   43

ALL. O brave doctor!

HORSE-COURSER. But you shall hear how bravely I serv'd him for it: I went me home to his house, and there I found him asleep. I kept a-hallowing and whooping in his ears, but all could not wake him. I, seeing that, took him by the leg and never rested pulling, till I had pull'd me his leg quite off, and now 'tis at home in mine hostry.   50

ROBIN. And has the doctor but one leg, then? That's excellent, for one of his devils turned me into the likeness of an ape's face.

CARTER. Some more drink, hostess.

ROBIN. Hark you, we'll into another room and drink a while, and then we'll go seek out the doctor.   *Exeunt omnes.*

[*Scene vi.*]

Enter the Duke of Vanholt, *his* Duchess, [Servants,] Faustus *and* Mephostophilis.

DUKE. Thanks, master doctor, for these pleasant sights; nor know I how sufficiently to recompense your great deserts in

erecting that enchanted castle in the air, the sight whereof
so delighted me as nothing in the world could please me
more.

FAUSTUS. I do think myself, my good lord, highly recompensed
in that it pleaseth your grace to think but well of that which
Faustus hath performed. But, gracious lady, it may be that
you have taken no pleasure in those sights; therefore, I pray
you tell me, what is the thing you most desire to have: be
it in the world, it shall be yours. I have heard that great-
bellied women do long for things are rare and dainty.   12

DUCHESS. True, master doctor, and since I find you so kind, I
will make known unto you what my heart desires to have;
and were it now summer, as it is January, a dead time of
the winter, I would request no better meat than a dish of
ripe grapes.

FAUSTUS. This is but a small matter; go, Mephostophilis, away.
                                    Exit Mephostophilis.
Madame, I will do more than this for your content.
    Enter Mephostophilis *again with the grapes.*
Here, now taste ye these; they should be good, for they come
from a far country, I can tell you.   21

DUKE. This makes me wonder more than all the rest, that at this
time of the year, when every tree is barren of his fruit, from
whence you had these ripe grapes.

FAUSTUS. Please it your grace, the year is divided into two
circles over the whole world, so that when it is winter with
us, in the contrary circle it is likewise summer with them, as
in India, Saba and such countries that lie far east, where they
have fruit twice a year. From whence, by means of a swift
spirit that I have, I had these grapes brought as you see.   30

DUCHESS. And trust me, they are the sweetest grapes that e'er
I tasted.   *The Clowns bounce at the gate within.*

DUKE. What rude disturbers have we at the gate?
Go, pacify their fury. Set it ope,
And then demand of them what they would have.
        They knock again and call out to talk with Faustus.

SERVANT. Why, how now, masters, what a coil is there? What
is the reason you disturb the duke?

DICK. We have no reason for it, therefore a fig for him.

SERVANT. Why, saucy varlets, dare you be so bold?

HORSE-COURSER. I hope, sir, we have wit enough to be more
bold than welcome.   41

SERVANT. It appears so. Pray be bold elsewhere, and trouble not
the duke.

DUKE. What would they have?

SERVANT. They all cry out to speak with Doctor Faustus.

CARTER. Ay, and we will speak with him.

DUKE. Will you, sir? Commit the rascals.

DICK. Commit with us: he were as good commit with his father
as commit with us.

FAUSTUS. I do beseech your grace let them come in.   50
They are good subject for a merriment.

DUKE. Do as thou wilt, Faustus; I give thee leave.

FAUSTUS. I thank your grace.
> *Enter the Clown* [Robin], Dick, Carter, *and* Horse-courser.
>   Why, how now, my good friends?
Faith, you are too outrageous, but come near;
I have procur'd your pardons. Welcome all.

ROBIN. Nay, sir, we will be welcome for our money, and we will
pay for what we take. What ho! Give's half-a-dozen of beer
here, and be hang'd.

FAUSTUS. Nay, hark you, can you tell me where you are?

CARTER. Ay, marry can I; we are under heaven.   60

SERVANT. Ay, but, sir sauce-box, know you in what place?

HORSE-COURSER. Ay, ay, the house is good enough to drink in.
Zounds, fill us some beer or we'll break all the barrels in the
house and dash out all your brains with your bottles.

FAUSTUS. Be not so furious; come, you shall have beer.
My lord, beseech you give me leave awhile.
I'll gage my credit, 'twill content your grace.

DUKE. With all my heart, kind doctor, please thyself;
Our servants and our court's at thy command.   69

FAUSTUS. I humbly thank your grace. Then fetch some beer.

HORSE-COURSER. Ay, marry, there spake a doctor indeed, and,
'faith, I'll drink a health to thy wooden leg for that word.

FAUSTUS. My wooden leg? What dost thou mean by that?

CARTER. Ha, ha, ha! Dost hear him, Dick? He has forgot
his leg.

HORSE-COURSER. Ay, ay, he does not stand much upon that.

FAUSTUS. No, 'faith, not much upon a wooden leg.

CARTER. Good Lord, that flesh and blood should be so frail
with your worship! Do not you remember a horse-courser
you sold a horse to?   80

FAUSTUS. Yes, I remember I sold one a horse.

CARTER. And do you remember you bid he should not ride
into the water?

FAUSTUS. Yes, I do very well remember that.

CARTER. And do you remember nothing of your leg?

[316]

FAUSTUS. No, in good sooth.

CARTER. Then I pray remember your curtsy.

FAUSTUS. I thank you, sir.

CARTER. 'Tis not so much worth; I pray you, tell me one thing.

FAUSTUS. What's that? 90

CARTER. Be both your legs bedfellows every night together?

FAUSTUS. Wouldst thou make a colossus of me, that thou askest
me such questions?

CARTER. No, truly, sir; I would make nothing of you, but I
would fain know that.

    Enter Hostess *with drink.*

FAUSTUS. Then I assure thee certainly they are.

CARTER. I thank you, I am fully satisfied.

FAUSTUS. But wherefore dost thou ask?

CARTER. For nothing, sir; but methinks you should have a
wooden bedfellow of one of 'em. 100

HORSE-COURSER. Why, do you hear, sir, did not I pull off one
of your legs when you were asleep?

FAUSTUS. But I have it again now I am awake. Look you here,
sir.

ALL. O horrible! Had the doctor three legs?

CARTER. Do you remember, sir, how you cozened me and eat
up my load of—   Faustus *charms him dumb.*

DICK. Do you remember how you made me wear an ape's—

HORSE-COURSER. You whoreson conjuring scab, do you
remember how you cozened me with a ho— 110

ROBIN. Ha' you forgotten me? You think to carry it away with
your hey-pass and re-pass. Do you remember the dog's fa—
    Exeunt Clowns.

HOSTESS. Who pays for the ale? Hear you, master doctor, now
you have sent away my guests, I pray who shall pay me for
my a—   *Exit* Hostess.

DUCHESS. My lord,
We are much beholding to this learned man.

DUKE. So are we, madam, which we will recompense
With all the love and kindness that we may.
His artful sport drives all sad thoughts away. 120
    Exeunt.

[*Act V. Scene i.*]

Thunder and lightning. Enter Devils *with cover'd dishes.*
Mephostophilis *leads them into* Faustus' *study. Then enter*
Wagner.

WAGNER. I think my master means to die shortly.
  He hath made his will, and given me his wealth,
  His house, his goods, and store of golden plate,
  Besides two thousand ducats ready coin'd.
  And yet methinks, if that death were near,
  He would not banquet and carouse and swill
  Amongst the students, as even now he doth,
  Who are at supper with such belly-cheer
  As Wagner ne'er beheld in all his life.
  See where they come; belike the feast is ended.   10
                                         Exit.

  Enter Faustus, Mephostophilis, *and two or three* Scholars.
1 SCHOLAR. Master Doctor Faustus, since our conference about
  fair ladies, which was the beautifullest in all the world, we
  have determin'd with ourselves that Helen of Greece was
  the admirablest lady that ever lived. Therefore master
  doctor, if you will do us so much favour as to let us see
  that peerless dame of Greece, whom all the world admires
  for majesty, we should think ourselves much beholding unto
  you.
FAUSTUS. Gentlemen,
  For that I know your friendship is unfeign'd,   20
  And Faustus' custom is not to deny
  The just requests of those that wish him well,
  You shall behold that peerless dame of Greece,
  No otherways for pomp and majesty
  Than when Sir Paris cross'd the seas with her,
  And brought the spoils to rich Dardania.
  Be silent then, for danger is in words.
    Music sounds. Mephostophilis *brings in* Helen; *she passeth*
    over the stage.
2 SCHOLAR. Too simple is my wit to tell her praise
  Whom all the world admires for majesty.
3 SCHOLAR. No marvel though the angry Greeks pursu'd   30
  With ten years war the rape of such a queen,
  Whose heavenly beauty passeth all compare.
1 SCHOLAR. Since we have seen the pride of nature's works
  And only paragon of excellence,
  Let us depart; and for this glorious deed

Happy and blest be Faustus evermore.
   Enter an Old Man.
FAUSTUS. Gentlemen, farewell: the same wish I to you.
                                        Exeunt Scholars.
OLD MAN. O gentle Faustus, leave this damned art,
   This magic, that will charm thy soul to hell,
   And quite bereave thee of salvation.   40
   Though thou hast now offended like a man,
   Do not persever in it like a devil.
   Yet, yet, thou hast an amiable soul,
   If sin by custom grow not into nature:
   Then, Faustus, will repentance come too late,
   Then thou art banish'd from the sight of heaven;
   No mortal can express the pains of hell.
   It may be this my exhortation
   Seems harsh and all unpleasant; let it not,
   For, gentle son, I speak it not in wrath,   50
   Or envy of thee, but in tender love,
   And pity of thy future misery;
   And so have hope that this my kind rebuke,
   Checking thy body, may amend thy soul.
FAUSTUS. Where art thou, Faustus? Wretch, what hast thou
      done?
   Damn'd art thou, Faustus, damn'd: despair and die.
   Hell claims his right, and with a roaring voice
   Says 'Faustus, come, thine hour is almost come',
                     Mephostophilis *gives him a dagger.*
   And Faustus now will come to do thee right.
OLD MAN. O stay, good Faustus, stay thy desperate steps. 60
   I see an angel hover o'er thy head,
   And with a vial full of precious grace
   Offers to pour the same into thy soul.
   Then call for mercy and avoid despair.
FAUSTUS. O friend, I feel thy words
   To comfort my distressed soul.
   Leave me awhile to ponder on my sins.
OLD MAN. Faustus, I leave thee, but with grief of heart,
   Fearing the ruin of thy hapless soul.   *Exit.*
FAUSTUS. Accursed Faustus, where is mercy now?   70
   I do repent, and yet I do despair.
   Hell strives with grace for conquest in my breast;
   What shall I do to shun the snares of death?
MEPHOSTOPHILIS. Thou traitor, Faustus, I arrest thy soul
   For disobedience to my sovereign lord.

Revolt, or I'll in piecemeal tear thy flesh.
FAUSTUS. I do repent I e'er offended him.
　Sweet Mephostophilis, entreat thy lord
　To pardon my unjust presumption,
　And with my blood again I will confirm   80
　The former vow I made to Lucifer.
MEPHOSTOPHILIS. Do it then, Faustus, with unfeigned heart,
　Lest greater dangers do attend thy drift.
FAUSTUS. Torment, sweet friend, that base and crooked age
　That durst dissuade me from thy Lucifer,
　With greatest torments that our hell affords.
MEPHOSTOPHILIS. His faith is great: I cannot touch his soul;
　But what I may afflict his body with
　I will attempt, which is but little worth.
FAUSTUS. One thing, good servant, let me crave of thee,   90
　To glut the longing of my heart's desire,
　That I may have unto my paramour
　That heavenly Helen which I saw of late,
　Whose sweet embracings may extinguish clear
　Those thoughts that do dissuade me from my vow,
　And keep mine oath I made to Lucifer.
MEPHOSTOPHILIS. This, or what else my Faustus shall desire,
　Shall be perform'd in twinkling of an eye.
　　Enter Helen *again, passing over between two Cupids.*
FAUSTUS. Was this the face that launch'd a thousand ships,
　And burnt the topless towers of Ilium?   100
　Sweet Helen, make me immortal with a kiss:
　Her lips suck forth my soul, see where it flies.
　Come, Helen, come, give me my soul again.
　Here will I dwell, for heaven is in these lips,
　And all is dross that is not Helena.
　　Enter Old Man.
　I will be Paris, and for love of thee
　Instead of Troy shall Wittenberg be sack'd,
　And I will combat with weak Menelaus,
　And wear thy colours on my plumed crest.
　Yea, I will wound Achilles in the heel,   110
　And then return to Helen for a kiss.
　O, thou art fairer than the evening's air,
　Clad in the beauty of a thousand stars.
　Brighter art thou than flaming Jupiter,
　When he appear'd to hapless Semele:
　More lovely than the monarch of the sky,
　In wanton Arethusa's azur'd arms,

And none but thou shalt be my paramour.
                   Exeunt [Faustus *and* Helen].
OLD MAN. Accursed Faustus, miserable man,
    That from thy soul exclud'st the grace of heaven,   120
    And fliest the throne of his tribunal seat.
    Enter the Devils.
Satan begins to sift me with his pride,
As in this furnace God shall try my faith.
My faith, vile hell, shall triumph over thee.
Ambitious fiends, see how the heavens smiles
At your repulse, and laughs your state to scorn.
Hence, hell, for hence I fly unto my God.   *Exeunt.*

[*Scene ii.*]
   Thunder. Enter Lucifer, Belzebub, *and* Mephostophilis
[*above*].
LUCIFER. Thus from infernal Dis do we ascend
    To view the subjects of our monarchy,
    Those souls which sin seals the black sons of hell,
    'Mong which as chief, Faustus, we come to thee,
    Bringing with us lasting damnation
    To wait upon thy soul; the time is come
    Which makes it forfeit.
MEPHOSTOPHILIS.   And this gloomy night,
    Here in this room will wretched Faustus be.
BELZEBUB. And here we'll stay,
    To mark him how he doth demean himself.   10
MEPHOSTOPHILIS. How should he, but in desperate lunacy?
    Fond worldling, now his heart-blood dries with grief,
    His conscience kills it, and his labouring brain
    Begets a world of idle fantasies
    To overreach the devil, but all in vain:
    His store of pleasures must be sauc'd with pain.
    He and his servant Wagner are at hand.
    Both come from drawing Faustus' latest will.
    See where they come.
    Enter Faustus *and* Wagner.
FAUSTUS. Say, Wagner, thou hast perus'd my will: 20
    How dost thou like it?
WAGNER.   Sir, so wondrous well
    As in all humble duty I do yield
    My life and lasting service for your love.
    Enter the Scholars.

FAUSTUS. Gramercies, Wagner. Welcome, gentlemen.

[*Exit* Wagner.]

1 SCHOLAR. Now, worthy Faustus, methinks your looks are
chang'd.

FAUSTUS. Ah, gentlemen!

2 SCHOLAR. What ails Faustus?

FAUSTUS. Ah, my sweet chamber-fellow, had I liv'd with thee,
then had I lived still, but now must die eternally. Look, sirs,
comes he not, comes he not?   31

1 SCHOLAR. O my dear Faustus, what imports this fear?

2 SCHOLAR. Is all our pleasure turn'd to melancholy?

3 SCHOLAR. He is not well with being over-solitary.

2 SCHOLAR. If it be so, we'll have physicians, and Faustus shall
be cur'd.

3 SCHOLAR. 'Tis but a surfeit, sir, fear nothing.

FAUSTUS. A surfeit of deadly sin, that hath damn'd both body
and soul.

2 SCHOLAR. Yet, Faustus, look up to heaven, and remember
God's mercy is infinite.   41

FAUSTUS. But Faustus' offence can ne'er be pardoned; the
serpent that tempted Eve may be saved, but not Faustus.
O gentlemen, hear with patience and tremble not at my
speeches. Though my heart pants and quivers to remember
that I have been a student here these thirty years—O would
I had never seen Wittenberg, never read book! And what
wonders I have done all Germany can witness, yea all the
world—for which Faustus hath lost both Germany and the
world, yea heaven itself, heaven, the seat of God, the throne
of the blessed, the kingdom of joy; and must remain in hell
for ever. Hell, ah hell for ever! Sweet friends, what shall
become of Faustus, being in hell for ever?   53

2 SCHOLAR. Yet, Faustus, call on God.

FAUSTUS. On God, whom Faustus hath abjur'd? On God,
whom Faustus hath blasphem'd? Ah my God—I would
weep, but the devil draws in my tears. Gush forth blood
instead of tears, yea, life and soul! O, he stays my tongue.
I would lift up my hands, but see, they hold them, they
hold them.   60

ALL. Who, Faustus?

FAUSTUS. Why, Lucifer and Mephostophilis. Ah gentlemen, I
gave them my soul for my cunning.

ALL. God forbid.

FAUSTUS. God forbade it indeed, but Faustus hath done it.
For the vain pleasure of four-and-twenty years hath Faustus

lost eternal joy and felicity. I writ them a bill with mine own blood; the date is expired; this is the time, and he will fetch me.

1 SCHOLAR. Why did not Faustus tell us of this before, that divines might have pray'd for thee?   71

FAUSTUS. Oft have I thought to have done so, but the devil threat'ned to tear me in pieces if I nam'd God, to fetch me body and soul if I once gave ear to divinity; and now 'tis too late. Gentlemen, away, lest you perish with me.

2 SCHOLAR. O what may we do to save Faustus?

FAUSTUS. Talk not of me, but save yourselves and depart.

3 SCHOLAR. God will strengthen me. I will stay with Faustus.

1 SCHOLAR. Tempt not God, sweet friend, but let us into the next room and pray for him.   80

FAUSTUS. Ay, pray for me, pray for me. And what noise soever you hear, come not unto me, for nothing can rescue me.

2 SCHOLAR. Pray thou, and we will pray, that God may have mercy upon thee.

FAUSTUS. Gentlemen, farewell. If I live till morning, I'll visit you. If not, Faustus is gone to hell.

ALL. Faustus, farewell.   *Exeunt* Scholars.

MEPHOSTOPHILIS. Ay, Faustus, now thou hast no hope of heaven,
  Therefore despair, think only upon hell,
  For that must be thy mansion, there to dwell.   90

FAUSTUS. O thou bewitching fiend, 'twas thy temptation
  Hath robb'd me of eternal happiness.

MEPHOSTOPHILIS. I do confess it, Faustus, and rejoice.
  'Twas I that, when thou wert i'the way to heaven,
  Damm'd up thy passage; when thou took'st the book
  To view the scriptures, then I turn'd the leaves
  And led thine eye.
  What, weep'st thou? 'Tis too late, despair. Farewell.
  Fools that will laugh on earth, must weep in hell.   *Exit.*
    Enter the Good *and the* Bad Angel *at several doors.*

GOOD ANGEL. O Faustus, if thou hadst given ear to me   100
  Innumerable joys had followed thee.
  But thou didst love the world.

BAD ANGEL.   Gave ear to me,
  And now must taste hell's pains perpetually.

GOOD ANGEL. O what will all thy riches, pleasures, pomps,
  Avail thee now?

BAD ANGEL.   Nothing but vex thee more,
  To want in hell, that had on earth such store.

Music while the throne descends.

GOOD ANGEL. O thou hast lost celestial happiness,
   Pleasures unspeakable, bliss without end.
   Hadst thou affected sweet divinity,
   Hell, or the devil, had had no power on thee.   110
   Hadst thou kept on that way, Faustus, behold
   In what resplendent glory thou hadst set
   In yonder throne, like those bright shining saints,
   And triumph'd over hell. That hast thou lost,
   And now, poor soul, must thy good angel leave thee:
   The jaws of hell are open to receive thee.

                      Exit [the throne ascends].
                          Hell is discovered.

BAD ANGEL. Now, Faustus, let thine eyes with horror stare
   Into that vast perpetual torture-house.
   There are the furies tossing damned souls
   On burning forks; there bodies boil in lead;   120
   There are live quarters broiling on the coals
   That ne'er can die; this ever-burning chair
   Is for o'er-tortur'd souls to rest them in;
   These, that are fed with sops of flaming fire,
   Were gluttons, and loved only delicates,
   And laugh'd to see the poor starve at their gates.
   But yet all these are nothing: thou shalt see
   Ten thousand tortures that more horrid be.

FAUSTUS. O I have seen enough to torture me.

BAD ANGEL. Nay, thou must feel them, taste the smart of all:
   He that loves pleasure must for pleasure fall.   131
   And so I leave thee, Faustus, till anon:
   Then wilt thou tumble in confusion.

                      Exit [Hell is concealed].
                        The clock strikes eleven.

FAUSTUS. Ah Faustus,
   Now hast thou but one bare hour to live,
   And then thou must be damn'd perpetually.
   Stand still, you ever-moving spheres of heaven,
   That time may cease and midnight never come.
   Fair nature's eye, rise, rise again, and make
   Perpetual day; or let this hour be but   140
   A year, a month, a week, a natural day,
   That Faustus may repent and save his soul.
   O lente, lente, currite noctis equi!
   The stars move still, time runs, the clock will strike.
   The devil will come, and Faustus must be damn'd.

O I'll leap up to my God; who pulls me down?
See, see, where Christ's blood streams in the firmament.
One drop would save my soul, half a drop. Ah, my Christ.
Rend not my heart for naming of my Christ;
Yet will I call on him. O spare me, Lucifer.   150
Where is it now? 'Tis gone: and see where God
Stretcheth out his arm and bends his ireful brows.
Mountains and hills, come, come, and fall on me,
And hide me from the heavy wrath of God.
No, no!
Then will I headlong run into the earth.
Earth, gape. O no, it will not harbour me.
You stars that reign'd at my nativity,
Whose influence hath allotted death and hell,
Now draw up Faustus like a foggy mist   160
Into the entrails of yon labouring cloud,
That when you vomit forth into the air
My limbs may issue from your smoky mouths,
So that my soul may but ascend to heaven.

The watch strikes.

Ah, half the hour is past, 'twill all be past anon.
O God,
If thou wilt not have mercy on my soul,
Yet for Christ's sake whose blood hath ransom'd me
Impose some end to my incessant pain:
Let Faustus live in hell a thousand years,   170
A hundred thousand, and at last be sav'd.
No end is limited to damned souls.
Why wert thou not a creature wanting soul?
Or why is this immortal that thou hast?
Ah, Pythagoras' *metempsychosis*, were that true,
This soul should fly from me, and I be chang'd
Unto some brutish beast. All beasts are happy,
For when they die
Their souls are soon dissolv'd in elements,
But mine must live still to be plagu'd in hell.   180
Curs'd be the parents that engend'red me!
No, Faustus, curse thyself, curse Lucifer,
That hath depriv'd thee of the joys of heaven.

The clock striketh twelve.

It strikes, it strikes; now body turn to air,
Or Lucifer will bear thee quick to hell.

Thunder and lightning.

O soul, be chang'd to little water drops

[325]

And fall into the ocean, ne'er be found.
                              Thunder, and enter the Devils.
My God, my God, look not so fierce on me.
Adders and serpents, let me breathe awhile.
Ugly hell, gape not; come not, Lucifer.   190
I'll burn my books. Ah, Mephostophilis!   *Exeunt with him.*

                              [*Scene iii.*]
    Enter the Scholars.
1 SCHOLAR. Come gentlemen, let us go visit Faustus,
    For such a dreadful night was never seen
    Since first the world's creation did begin.
    Such fearful shrieks and cries were never heard;
    Pray heaven the doctor have escap'd the danger.
2 SCHOLAR. O help us, heaven! See, here are Faustus' limbs,
    All torn asunder by the hand of death.
3 SCHOLAR. The devils whom Faustus serv'd have torn him thus;
    For 'twixt the hours of twelve and one, methought
    I heard him shriek and call aloud for help,   10
    At which self time the house seem'd all on fire
    With dreadful horror of these damned fiends.
2 SCHOLAR. Well, gentlemen, though Faustus' end be such
    As every Christian heart laments to think on,
    Yet, for he was a scholar once admir'd
    For wondrous knowledge in our German schools,
    We'll give his mangled limbs due burial,
    And all the students cloth'd in mourning black
    Shall wait upon his heavy funeral.   *Exeunt.*

                              [*Epilogue*]
    Enter Chorus.
Cut is the branch that might have grown full straight,
And burned is Apollo's laurel bough
That sometime grew within this learned man.
Faustus is gone: regard his hellish fall,
Whose fiendful fortune may exhort the wise
Only to wonder at unlawful things,
Whose deepness doth entice such forward wits
To practise more than heavenly power permits.   [*Exit.*]

        Terminat hora diem, terminat Author opus.

            FINIS.

            [326]

The Jew of Malta

The Jew of Malta was entered in the Stationers' Register on 17 May 1594 to Nicholas Ling and Thomas Millington as '*the famouse tragedie of the Riche Jewe of Malta*' and on 20 November 1632 to Nicholas Vavasour. The earliest extant quarto, printed by John Beale for Nicholas Vavasour, was published in 1633, together with epistle, prologues and epilogues added by the playwright Thomas Heywood, who had recently revived the play at the Court and, in public, at the Cockpit playhouse. 'Christopher Marlo' is the author.

The date of composition lies between the death of the Duke of Guise (mentioned in Marlowe's Prologue) on 23 December 1588, and the performance of the play recorded by Henslowe on 26 February 1592. The portrait of a 'cross-biting' cutpurse would have been especially topical after the success of Robert Greene's underworld pamphlet, *A Notable Discovery of Coosnage*, entered in the Stationers' Register on 13 December 1591. No source for the plot has been discovered. There was a famous siege of Malta in 1565 by the Turks, but it was not successful.

Between 26 February 1592 and 21 June 1596 Strange's Men and other companies performed the play no fewer than thirty-six times. Preparations were being made for a revival on 19 May 1601. An inventory of props for the Admiral's Men now lost, dated 10 March 1598, lists the 'cauderm for the Jewe'. William Rowley's *A Search for Money* (1609) refers to the great size of the Jew of Malta's false nose.

THE EPISTLE DEDICATORY

TO MY WORTHY FRIEND, MR THOMAS
HAMMON, OF GRAYS INN, &c.

This play, composed by so worthy an author as Mr Marlowe, and the part of the Jew presented by so unimitable an actor as Mr Alleyn, being in this later age commended to the stage; as I usher'd it unto the Court, and presented it to the Cock-pit, with these Prologues and Epilogues here inserted, so now being newly brought to the press, I was loath it should be published without the ornament of an Epistle; making choice of you unto whom to devote it; than whom (of all those gentlemen and acquaintance within the compass of my long knowledge) there is none more able to tax ignorance, or attribute right to merit. Sir, you have been pleased to grace some of mine own works with your courteous patronage: I hope this will not be the worse accepted, because commended by me; over whom none can claim more power or privilege than yourself. I had no better a New Year's gift to present you with; receive it therefore as a continuance of the inviolable obligement, by which he rests still engaged; who, as he ever hath, shall always remain,

Tuissimus,
Tho. Heywood

THE PROLOGUE SPOKEN AT COURT

Gracious and great, that we so boldly dare
('Mongst other plays that now in fashion are)
To present this, writ many years agone,
And in that age thought second unto none,
We humbly crave your pardon. We pursue
The story of a rich and famous Jew
Who liv'd in Malta: you shall find him still,
In all his projects, a sound Machevill;
And that's his character. He that hath pass'd
So many censures is now come at last   10
To have your princely ears: grace you him; then
You crown the action, and renown the pen.

EPILOGUE

It is our fear (dread Sovereign) we have bin
Too tedious; neither can't be less than sin
To wrong your princely patience. If we have,
(Thus low dejected) we your pardon crave;
And if aught here offend your ear or sight,
We only act and speak what others write.

THE PROLOGUE TO THE STAGE
AT THE COCK-PIT

We know not how our play may pass this stage,
But by the best of *poets in that age
The Malta Jew had being and was made;
And he then by the best of †actors play'd:
In *Hero and Leander* one did gain
A lasting memory; in Tamburlaine,
This Jew, with others many, th'other wan
The attribute of peerless, being a man
Whom we may rank with (doing no one wrong)
Proteus for shapes, and Roscius for a tongue,   10
So could he speak, so vary; nor is't hate
To merit in ‡him who doth personate
Our Jew this day; nor is it his ambition
To exceed or equal, being of condition
More modest: this is all that he intends
(And that too, at the urgence of some friends)
To prove his best, and, if none here gainsay it,
The part he hath studied, and intends to play it.

EPILOGUE

In graving with Pygmalion to contend,
Or painting with Apelles, doubtless the end
Must be disgrace; our actor did not so:
He only aim'd to go, but not out-go.
Nor think that this day any prize was play'd;
Here were no bets at all, no wagers laid;
All the ambition that his mind doth swell
Is but to hear from you (by me) 'twas well.

* Marlowe.   † Alleyn.   ‡ Perkins.

[331]

[DRAMATIS PERSONAE

Machevill, the Prologue

Barabas, the Jew
Ferneze, Governor of Malta
Calymath, son to the Emperor of Turkey
Don Mathias
Don Lodowick, the Governor's son
Martin del Bosco, the Spanish Vice-Admiral
Ithamore, a Turkish slave
Jacomo } friars
Barnardine
Pilia-Borza
Two Merchants
Three Jews

Abigail, daughter to Barabas
Katharine, mother to Mathias
Bellamira, a courtesan
Abbess

Nuns, Knights, Officers, Bassoes, Turks, Guard, Slaves,
Messenger, Carpenters, Attendants]

The Jew of Malta

[THE PROLOGUE]

Machevill

Albeit the world think Machevill is dead,
Yet was his soul but flown beyond the Alps,
And now the Guise is dead, is come from France
To view this land, and frolic with his friends.
To some perhaps my name is odious;
But such as love me, guard me from their tongues,
And let them know that I am Machevill,
And weigh not men, and therefore not men's words.
Admir'd I am of those that hate me most.
Though some speak openly against my books,   10
Yet will they read me, and thereby attain
To Peter's chair; and when they cast me off,
Are poison'd by my climbing followers.
I count religion but a childish toy,
And hold there is no sin but ignorance.
Birds of the air will tell of murders past.
I am asham'd to hear such fooleries.
Many will talk of title to a crown:
What right had Caesar to the empire?
Might first made kings, and laws were then most sure   20
When like the Draco's they were writ in blood.
Hence comes it, that a strong-built citadel
Commands much more than letters can import:
Which maxim had but Phalaris observ'd,
H'ad never bellowed in a brazen bull
Of great ones' envy; o'th'poor petty wits,
Let me be envied and not pitied.
But whither am I bound? I come not, I,
To read a lecture here in Britanie,
But to present the tragedy of a Jew   30
Who smiles to see how full his bags are cramm'd;
Which money was not got without my means.
I crave but this: grace him as he deserves,
And let him not be entertain'd the worse
Because he favours me.   [*Exit.*]

[*Actus Primus. Scaena 1.*]
Enter Barabas *in his Counting-house, with heaps of gold before him.*

BARABAS. So that of thus much that return was made;
And of the third part of the Persian ships
There was the venture summ'd and satisfied.
As for those Samnites, and the men of Uz,
That bought my Spanish oils and wines of Greece,
Here have I purs'd their paltry silverlings.
Fie, what a trouble 'tis to count this trash!
Well fare the Arabians who so richly pay
The things they traffic for with wedge of gold,
Whereof a man may easily in a day   10
Tell that which may maintain him all his life.
The needy groom that never fing'red groat,
Would make a miracle of thus much coin;
But he whose steel-barr'd coffers are cramm'd full,
And all his life-time hath been tired,
Wearying his fingers' ends with telling it,
Would in his age be loath to labour so,
And for a pound to sweat himself to death.
Give me the merchants of the Indian mines
That trade in metal of the purest mould;   20
The wealthy Moor that in the eastern rocks
Without control can pick his riches up,
And in his house heap pearl like pebble stones,
Receive them free, and sell them by the weight;
Bags of fiery opals, sapphires, amethysts,
Jacinths, hard topaz, grass-green emeralds,
Beauteous rubies, sparkling diamonds,
And seld-seen costly stones of so great price
As one of them, indifferently rated,
And of a carat of this quantity,   30
May serve in peril of calamity
To ransom great kings from captivity.
This is the ware wherein consists my wealth;
And thus methinks should men of judgement frame
Their means of traffic from the vulgar trade,
And as their wealth increaseth, so inclose
Infinite riches in a little room.
But now how stands the wind?
Into what corner peers my halcyon's bill?
Ha, to the east? Yes. See how stands the vanes?   40

[334]

East and by south: why then I hope my ships
I sent for Egypt and the bordering isles
Are gotten up by Nilus' winding banks;
Mine argosy from Alexandria,
Loaden with spice and silks, now under sail,
Are smoothly gliding down by Candy shore
To Malta, through our Mediterranean sea.
But who comes here?

Enter a Merchant.

How now?

MERCHANT. Barabas, thy ships are safe,
Riding in Malta road; and all the merchants   50
With all their merchandise are safe arriv'd,
And have sent me to know whether yourself
Will come and custom them.
BARABAS. The ships are safe thou say'st, and richly fraught?
MERCHANT. They are.
BARABAS.   Why then, go bid them come ashore,
And bring with them their bills of entry:
I hope our credit in the custom-house
Will serve as well as I were present there.
Go send 'em three-score camels, thirty mules,
And twenty waggons to bring up the ware.   60
But art thou master in a ship of mine,
And is thy credit not enough for that?
MERCHANT. The very custom barely comes to more
Than many merchants of the town are worth,
And therefore far exceeds my credit, sir.
BARABAS. Go tell 'em the Jew of Malta sent thee, man:
Tush, who amongst 'em knows not Barabas?
MERCHANT. I go.
BARABAS.   So then, there's somewhat come.
Sirrah, which of my ships art thou master of?
MERCHANT. Of the Speranza, sir.
BARABAS.   And saw'st thou not   70
Mine argosy at Alexandria?
Thou couldst not come from Egypt, or by Caire,
But at the entry there into the sea,
Where Nilus pays his tribute to the main,
Thou needs must sail by Alexandria.
MERCHANT. I neither saw them nor inquir'd of them;
But this we heard some of our seamen say,
They wond'red how you durst with so much wealth
Trust such a crazed vessel, and so far.

BARABAS. Tush, they are wise. I know her and her strength.
  But go, go thou thy ways, discharge thy ship,   81
  And bid my factor bring his loading in.   [*Exit* Merchant.]
  And yet I wonder at this argosy.
    Enter a second Merchant.
2 MERCHANT. Thine argosy from Alexandria,
  Know, Barabas, doth ride in Malta road,
  Laden with riches, and exceeding store
  Of Persian silks, of gold, and orient pearl.
BARABAS. How chance you came not with those other ships
  That sail'd by Egypt?
2 MERCHANT.   Sir, we saw 'em not.
BARABAS. Belike they coasted round by Candy shore   90
  About their oils or other businesses.
  But 'twas ill done of you to come so far
  Without the aid or conduct of their ships.
2 MERCHANT. Sir, we were wafted by a Spanish fleet
  That never left us till within a league,
  That had the galleys of the Turk in chase.
BARABAS. O, they were going up to Sicily. Well, go
  And bid the merchants and my men dispatch,
  And come ashore, and see the fraught discharg'd.
2 MERCHANT. I go.   100
                                  Exit.

BARABAS. Thus trolls our fortune in by land and sea,
  And thus are we on every side enrich'd.
  These are the blessings promis'd to the Jews,
  And herein was old Abram's happiness.
  What more may heaven do for earthly man
  Than thus to pour out plenty in their laps,
  Ripping the bowels of the earth for them,
  Making the seas their servants, and the winds
  To drive their substance with successful blasts?
  Who hateth me but for my happiness?   110
  Or who is honour'd now but for his wealth?
  Rather had I, a Jew, be hated thus,
  Than pitied in a Christian poverty;
  For I can see no fruits in all their faith,
  But malice, falsehood, and excessive pride,
  Which methinks fits not their profession.
  Haply some hapless man hath conscience,
  And for his conscience lives in beggary.
  They say we are a scatter'd nation:
  I cannot tell; but we have scambled up   120

More wealth by far than those that brag of faith.
There's Kirriah Jairim, the great Jew of Greece,
Obed in Bairseth, Nones in Portugal,
Myself in Malta, some in Italy,
Many in France, and wealthy every one;
Ay, wealthier far than any Christian.
I must confess we come not to be kings:
That's not our fault: alas, our number's few,
And crowns come either by succession,
Or urg'd by force; and nothing violent,   130
Oft have I heard tell, can be permanent.
Give us a peaceful rule; make Christians kings,
That thirst so much for principality.
I have no charge, nor many children,
But one sole daughter, whom I hold as dear
As Agamemnon did his Iphigen;
And all I have is hers. But who comes here?
    Enter three Jews.
1 JEW. Tush, tell not me 'twas done of policy.
2 JEW. Come therefore, let us go to Barabas,
For he can counsel best in these affairs.   140
And here he comes.
BARABAS.   Why, how now, countrymen?
Why flock you thus to me in multitudes?
What accident's betided to the Jews?
1 JEW. A fleet of warlike galleys, Barabas,
Are come from Turkey, and lie in our road:
And they this day sit in the council-house
To entertain them and their embassy.
BARABAS. Why, let 'em come, so they come not to war;
Or let 'em war, so we be conquerors.
   (*Aside.*) Nay, let 'em combat, conquer, and kill all,   150
So they spare me, my daughter, and my wealth.
1 JEW. Were it for confirmation of a league
They would not come in warlike manner thus.
2 JEW. I fear their coming will afflict us all.
BARABAS. Fond men, what dream you of their multitudes?
What need they treat of peace that are in league?
The Turks and those of Malta are in league:
Tut, tut, there is some other matter in't.
1 JEW. Why, Barabas, they come for peace or war.
BARABAS. Haply for neither, but to pass along   160
Towards Venice by the Adriatic sea,
With whom they have attempted many times,

But never could effect their stratagem.
3 JEW. And very wisely said; it may be so.
2 JEW. But there's a meeting in the senate-house,
    And all the Jews in Malta must be there.
BARABAS. Umh; all the Jews in Malta must be there?
    Ay, like enough; why then, let every man
    Provide him, and be there for fashion-sake.
    If anything shall there concern our state,   170
    Assure yourselves I'll look unto (*Aside.*) myself.
1 JEW. I know you will. Well, brethren, let us go.
2 JEW. Let's take our leaves. Farewell, good Barabas.
BARABAS. Do so. Farewell, Zaareth; farewell, Temainte.
                                    [*Exeunt* Jews.]

And Barabas, now search this secret out.
Summon thy senses, call thy wits together:
These silly men mistake the matter clean.
Long to the Turk did Malta contribute;
Which tribute all in policy, I fear,
The Turks have let increase to such a sum   180
As all the wealth of Malta cannot pay;
And now by that advantage thinks, belike,
To seize upon the town. Ay, that he seeks.
Howe'er the world go, I'll make sure for one,
And seek in time to intercept the worst,
Warily guarding that which I ha' got.
Ego mihimet sum semper proximus.
Why, let 'em enter. Let 'em take the town.   [*Exit.*]

              [*Scaena 2.*]
    Enter [Ferneze, *the*] *Governor of Malta,* Knights [*and*
    Officers*], *met by* Bassoes *of the Turk* [*and*] Calymath.
FERNEZE. Now, bassoes, what demand you at our hands?
BASSO. Know, knights of Malta, that we came from Rhodes,
    From Cyprus, Candy, and those other isles
    That lie betwixt the Mediterranean seas.
FERNEZE. What's Cyprus, Candy, and those other isles
    To us or Malta? What at our hands demand ye?
CALYMATH. The ten years' tribute that remains unpaid.
FERNEZE. Alas, my lord, the sum is over-great.
    I hope your highness will consider us.
CALYMATH. I wish, grave Governor, 'twere in my power   10
    To favour you; but 'tis my father's cause,
    Wherein I may not, nay, I dare not dally.
FERNEZE. Then give us leave, great Selim-Calymath.

CALYMATH. Stand all aside, and let the knights determine,
And send to keep our galleys under sail,
For happily we shall not tarry here.
Now Governor, how are you resolv'd?
FERNEZE. Thus: since your hard conditions are such
That you will needs have ten years' tribute past,
We may have time to make collection   20
Amongst the inhabitants of Malta for't.
BASSO. That's more than is in our commission.
CALYMATH. What, Callapine, a little courtesy.
Let's know their time, perhaps it is not long;
And 'tis more kingly to obtain by peace
Than to enforce conditions by constraint.
What respite ask you, Governor?
FERNEZE.   But a month.
CALYMATH. We grant a month, but see you keep your promise.
Now launch our galleys back again to sea,
Where we'll attend the respite you have ta'en,   30
And for the money send our messenger.
Farewell, great Governor and brave knights of Malta.
Exeunt [Turks].
FERNEZE. And all good fortune wait on Calymath.
Go one and call those Jews of Malta hither:
Were they not summon'd to appear today?
OFFICER. They were, my lord; and here they come.
Enter Barabas *and three* Jews.
1 KNIGHT. Have you determin'd what to say to them?
FERNEZE. Yes, give me leave; and, Hebrews, now come near.
From the Emperor of Turkey is arriv'd
Great Selim-Calymath, his highness' son,
To levy of us ten years' tribute past: 40
Now, then, here know that it concerneth us—
BARABAS. Then, good my lord, to keep your quiet still,
Your lordship shall do well to let them have it.
FERNEZE. Soft, Barabas, there's more 'longs to't than so.
To what this ten years' tribute will amount,
That we have cast, but cannot compass it
By reason of the wars, that robb'd our store;
And therefore are we to request your aid.
BARABAS. Alas, my lord, we are no soldiers;   50
And what's our aid against so great a prince?
1 KNIGHT. Tut, Jew, we know thou art no soldier:
Thou art a merchant and a money'd man,
And 'tis thy money, Barabas, we seek.

BARABAS. How, my lord, my money?

FERNEZE.   Thine and the rest.
  For, to be short, amongst you 't must be had.

1 JEW. Alas, my lord, the most of us are poor.

FERNEZE. Then let the rich increase your portions.

BARABAS. Are strangers with your tribute to be tax'd?

2 KNIGHT. Have strangers leave with us to get their wealth?   60
  Then let them with us contribute.

BARABAS. How, equally?

FERNEZE.   No, Jew, like infidels;
  For through our sufferance of your hateful lives
  Who stand accursed in the sight of heaven
  These taxes and afflictions are befall'n,
  And therefore thus we are determined.
  Read there the articles of our decrees.

OFFICER. 'First, the tribute-money of the Turks shall all be
  levied amongst the Jews, and each of them to pay one half
  of his estate.'   70

BARABAS. How, half his estate? I hope you mean not mine.

FERNEZE. Read on.

OFFICER. 'Secondly, he that denies to pay, shall straight become
  a Christian.'

BARABAS. How, a Christian? Hum, what's here to do?

OFFICER. 'Lastly, he that denies this, shall absolutely lose all
  he has.'

ALL 3 JEWS. O my lord, we will give half.

BARABAS. O earth-metall'd villains, and no Hebrews born!
  And will you basely thus submit yourselves   80
  To leave your goods to their arbitrement?

FERNEZE. Why, Barabas, wilt thou be christened?

BARABAS. No, Governor, I will be no convertite.

FERNEZE. Then pay thy half.

BARABAS. Why, know you what you did by this device?
  Half of my substance is a city's wealth.
  Governor, it was not got so easily;
  Nor will I part so slightly therewithal.

FERNEZE. Sir, half is the penalty of our decree.
  Either pay that, or we will seize on all.   90

BARABAS. *Corpo di Dio*, stay, you shall have half;
  Let me be us'd but as my brethren are.

FERNEZE. No, Jew, thou hast denied the articles,
  And now it cannot be recall'd.   [*Exeunt* Officers.]

BARABAS. Will you then steal my goods?
  Is theft the ground of your religion?

FERNEZE. No, Jew, we take particularly thine
    To save the ruin of a multitude.
    And better one want for a common good
    Than many perish for a private man.   100
    Yet, Barabas, we will not banish thee,
    But here in Malta, where thou got'st thy wealth,
    Live still; and if thou canst, get more.
BARABAS. Christians, what or how can I multiply?
    Of naught is nothing made.
1 KNIGHT. From naught at first thou cam'st to little wealth,
    From little unto more, from more to most.
    If your first curse fall heavy on thy head,
    And make thee poor and scorn'd of all the world,
    'Tis not our fault, but thy inherent sin.   110
BARABAS. What, bring you Scripture to confirm your wrongs?
    Preach me not out of my possessions.
    Some Jews are wicked, as all Christians are;
    But say the tribe that I descended of
    Were all in general cast away for sin,
    Shall I be tried by their transgression?
    The man that dealeth righteously shall live;
    And which of you can charge me otherwise?
FERNEZE. Out, wretched Barabas,
    Sham'st thou not thus to justify thyself,   120
    As if we knew not thy profession?
    If thou rely upon thy righteousness,
    Be patient, and thy riches will increase.
    Excess of wealth is cause of covetousness;
    And covetousness, O, 'tis a monstrous sin!
BARABAS. Ay, but theft is worse. Tush, take not from me then,
    For that is theft; and if you rob me thus
    I must be forc'd to steal, and compass more.
1 KNIGHT. Grave Governor, list not to his exclaims.
    Convert his mansion to a nunnery;   130
    His house will harbour many holy nuns.
FERNEZE. It shall be so.
        Enter Officers.
                        Now, officers, have you done?
1 OFFICER. Ay, my lord. We have seiz'd upon the goods
    And wares of Barabas, which, being valu'd,
    Amount to more than all the wealth in Malta;
    And of the other we have seized half.
FERNEZE. Then we'll take order for the residue.
BARABAS. Well then, my lord, say, are you satisfied?

[341]

You have my goods, my money, and my wealth,
My ships, my store, and all that I enjoy'd;   140
And having all, you can request no more,
Unless your unrelenting flinty hearts
Suppress all pity in your stony breasts
And now shall move you to bereave my life.
FERENZE. No, Barabas, to stain our hands with blood
Is far from us and our profession.
BARABAS. Why, I esteem the injury far less,
To take the lives of miserable men
Than be the causers of their misery.
You have my wealth, the labour of my life,   150
The comfort of mine age, my children's hope;
And therefore ne'er distinguish of the wrong.
FERNEZE. Content thee, Barabas; thou hast naught but right.
BARABAS. Your extreme right does me exceeding wrong:
But take it to you i'the devil's name.
FERNEZE. Come, let us in, and gather of these goods
The money for this tribute of the Turk.
1 KNIGHT. 'Tis necessary that be look'd unto;
For if we break our day, we break the league,
And that will prove but simple policy.   160
                    Exeunt. [*Manent* Barabas *and the three* Jews.]
BARABAS. Ay, policy! That's their profession,
And not simplicity, as they suggest.
The plagues of Egypt and the curse of heaven,
Earth's barrenness and all men's hatred,
Inflict upon them, thou great *Primus Motor.*
And here upon my knees, striking the earth,
I ban their souls to everlasting pains,
And extreme tortures of the fiery deep,
That thus have dealt with me in my distress.
1 JEW. O yet be patient, gentle Barabas.   170
BARABAS. O silly brethren, born to see this day,
Why stand you thus unmov'd with my laments?
Why weep you not to think upon my wrongs?
Why pine not I, and die in this distress?
1 JEW. Why, Barabas, as hardly can we brook
The cruel handling of ourselves in this:
Thou seest they have taken half our goods.
BARABAS. Why did you yield to their extortion?
You were a multitude, and I but one;
And of me only have they taken all.   180
1 JEW. Yet brother Barabas, remember Job.

BARABAS. What tell you me of Job? I wot his wealth
  Was written thus: he had seven thousand sheep,
  Three thousand camels, and two hundred yoke
  Of labouring oxen, and five hundred
  She-asses; but for every one of those,
  Had they been valued at indifferent rate,
  I had at home, and in mine argosy,
  And other ships that came from Egypt last,
  As much as would have bought his beasts and him,   190
  And yet have kept enough to live upon;
  So that not he but I may curse the day,
  Thy fatal birthday, forlorn Barabas;
  And henceforth wish for an eternal night,
  That clouds of darkness may enclose my flesh,
  And hide these extreme sorrows from mine eyes.
  For only I have toil'd to inherit here
  The months of vanity and loss of time,
  And painful nights have been appointed me.
2 JEW. Good Barabas, be patient.   200
BARABAS. Ay, I pray leave me in my patience.
  You, that were ne'er possess'd of wealth, are pleas'd with
    want.
  But give him liberty at least to mourn
  That in a field amidst his enemies
  Doth see his soldiers slain, himself disarm'd,
  And knows no means of his recovery.
  Ay, let me sorrow for this sudden chance;
  'Tis in the trouble of my spirit I speak:
  Great injuries are not so soon forgot.
1 JEW. Come, let us leave him in his ireful mood,   210
  Our words will but increase his ecstasy.
2 JEW. On, then: but, trust me, 'tis a misery
  To see a man in such affliction.
  Farewell Barabas.   *Exeunt.*
BARABAS.   Ay, fare you well.
  See the simplicity of these base slaves,
  Who, for the villains have no wit themselves,
  Think me to be a senseless lump of clay.
  That will with every water wash to dirt.
  No, Barabas is born to better chance,
  And fram'd of finer mould than common men   220
  That measure naught but by the present time.
  A reaching thought will search his deepest wits,
  And cast with cunning for the time to come;

For evils are apt to happen every day.
But whither wends my beauteous Abigail?
  Enter Abigail, *the Jew's daughter.*
O, what has made my lovely daughter sad?
What, woman, moan not for a little loss;
Thy father has enough in store for thee.

ABIGAIL. Not for myself, but aged Barabas,
  Father, for thee lamenteth Abigail.   230
  But I will learn to leave these fruitless tears,
  And urg'd thereto with my afflictions,
  With fierce exclaims run to the senate-house,
  And in the senate reprehend them all,
  And rent their hearts with tearing of my hair,
  Till they reduce the wrongs done to my father.

BARABAS. No, Abigail, things past recovery
  Are hardly cur'd with exclamations.
  Be silent, daughter; sufferance breeds ease,
  And time may yield us an occasion,   240
  Which on the sudden cannot serve the turn.
  Besides, my girl, think me not all so fond
  As negligently to forgo so much
  Without provision for thyself and me.
  Ten thousand portagues, besides great pearls,
  Rich costly jewels, and stones infinite,
  Fearing the worst of this before it fell,
  I closely hid.

ABIGAIL.   Where, father?

BARABAS.   In my house, my girl.

ABIGAIL. Then shall they ne'er be seen of Barabas;
  For they have seiz'd upon thy house and wares. 250

BARABAS. But they will give me leave once more, I trow,
  To go into my house.

ABIGAIL.   That may they not,
  For there I left the Governor placing nuns,
  Displacing me; and of thy house they mean
  To make a nunnery, where none but their own sect
  Must enter in, men generally barr'd.

BARABAS. My gold, my gold, and all my wealth is gone.
  You partial heavens, have I deserv'd this plague?
  What, will you thus oppose me, luckless stars,
  To make me desperate in my poverty? 260
  And knowing me impatient in distress,
  Think me so mad as I will hang myself,
  That I may vanish o'er the earth in air,

And leave no memory that e'er I was?
No, I will live; nor loathe I this my life:
And since you leave me in the ocean thus
To sink or swim, and put me to my shifts,
I'll rouse my senses, and awake myself.
Daughter, I have it: thou perceiv'st the plight
Wherein these Christians have oppressed me: 270
Be rul'd by me, for in extremity
We ought to make bar of no policy.

ABIGAIL. Father, whate'er it be, to injure them
That have so manifestly wronged us,
What will not Abigail attempt?

BARABAS.   Why, so.
Then thus: thou told'st me they have turn'd my house
Into a nunnery, and some nuns are there?

ABIGAIL. I did.

BARABAS.   Then, Abigail, there must my girl
Entreat the abbess to be entertain'd.

ABIGAIL. How, as a nun?

BARABAS.   Ay, daughter; for religion   280
Hides many mischiefs from suspicion.

ABIGAIL. Ay, but, father, they will suspect me there.

BARABAS. Let 'em suspect, but be thou so precise
As they may think it done of holiness.
Entreat 'em fair, and give them friendly speech,
And seem to them as if thy sins were great,
Till thou hast gotten to be entertain'd.

ABIGAIL. Thus, father, shall I much dissemble.

BARABAS.   Tush,
As good dissemble that thou never mean'st
As first mean truth, and then dissemble it: 290
A counterfeit profession is better
Than unseen hypocrisy.

ABIGAIL. Well, father, say I be entertain'd,
What then shall follow?

BARABAS.   This shall follow then.
There have I hid, close underneath the plank
That runs along the upper-chamber floor,
The gold and jewels which I kept for thee.
But here they come; be cunning, Abigail.

ABIGAIL. Then, father, go with me.

BARABAS. No, Abigail, in this   300
It is not necessary I be seen;
For I will seem offended with thee for't.

Be close, my girl, for this must fetch my gold.
   [*Enter* Jacomo, Barnardine, Abbess, *and a* Nun.]
JACOMO. Sisters,
  We now are almost at the new-made nunnery.
ABBESS. The better; for we love not to be seen.
  'Tis thirty winters long since some of us
  Did stray so far amongst the multitude.
JACOMO. But, madam, this house
  And waters of this new-made nunnery   310
  Will much delight you.
ABBESS. It may be so. But who comes here?
ABIGAIL. Grave abbess, and you happy virgins' guide,
  Pity the state of a distressed maid.
ABBESS. What art thou, daughter?
ABIGAIL. The hopeless daughter of a hapless Jew,
  The Jew of Malta, wretched Barabas,
  Sometime the owner of a goodly house,
  Which they have now turn'd to a nunnery.
ABBESS. Well, daughter, say, what is thy suit with us? 320
ABIGAIL. Fearing the afflictions which my father feels
  Proceed from sin or want of faith in us,
  I'd pass away my life in penitence
  And be a novice in your nunnery,
  To make atonement for my labouring soul.
JACOMO. No doubt, brother, but this proceedeth of the spirit.
BARNARDINE. Ay, and of a moving spirit too, brother: but come,
  let us entreat she may be entertain'd.
ABBESS. Well, daughter, we admit you for a nun.
ABIGAIL. First let me as a novice learn to frame 330
  My solitary life to your strait laws,
  And let me lodge where I was wont to lie.
  I do not doubt, by your divine precepts
  And mine own industry, but to profit much.
BARABAS (*aside*). As much, I hope, as all I hid is worth.
ABBESS. Come, daughter, follow us.
BARABAS.   Why, how now, Abigail,
  What mak'st thou amongst these hateful Christians?
JACOMO. Hinder her not, thou man of little faith,
  For she has mortified herself.
BARABAS.   How, mortified?
JACOMO. And is admitted to the sisterhood. 340
BARABAS. Child of perdition, and thy father's shame,
  What wilt thou do among these hateful fiends?
  I charge thee on my blessing that thou leave

These devils and their damned heresy.
ABIGAIL. Father, give me—
BARABAS.   Nay, back, Abigail—

Whispers to her.

And think upon the jewels and the gold;
The board is marked thus that covers it.
Away, accursed, from thy father's sight!
JACOMO. Barabas, although thou art in misbelief,
And wilt not see thine own afflictions,   350
Yet let thy daughter be no longer blind.
BARABAS. Blind, friar, I reck not thy persuasions.
[*Aside.*] The board is marked thus † that covers it.
For I had rather die than see her thus.
Wilt thou forsake me too in my distress,
Seduced daughter? (*Aside to her.*) Go, forget not—
Becomes it Jews to be so credulous?
(*Aside to her.*) Tomorrow early I'll be at the door—
No, come not at me; if thou wilt be damn'd,
Forget me, see me not, and so be gone.   360
(*Aside.*) Farewell, remember tomorrow morning.
Out, out, thou wretch.   *Exeunt [at different doors].*
      Enter Mathias.
MATHIAS. Who's this? Fair Abigail, the rich Jew's daughter
Become a nun? Her father's sudden fall
Has humbled her and brought her down to this.
Tut, she were fitter for a tale of love
Than to be tired out with orisons;
And better would she far become a bed
Embraced in a friendly lover's arms,
Than rise at midnight to a solemn mass.   370
      Enter Lodowick.
LODOWICK. Why, how now, Don Mathias, in a dump?
MATHIAS. Believe me, noble Lodowick, I have seen
The strangest sight, in my opinion,
That ever I beheld.
LODOWICK.   What was't, I prithee?
MATHIAS. A fair young maid, scarce fourteen years of age,
The sweetest flower in Cytherea's field,
Cropp'd from the pleasures of the fruitful earth,
And strangely metamorphos'd nun.
LODOWICK. But say, what was she?
MATHIAS.   Why, the rich Jew's daughter.
LODOWICK. What, Barabas, whose goods were lately seiz'd?
Is she so fair?

MATHIAS.   And matchless beautiful;   381
   As had you seen her, 'twould have mov'd your heart,
   Though countermur'd with walls of brass, to love,
   Or at the least, to pity.
LODOWICK. And if she be so fair as you report,
   'Twere time well spent to go and visit her.
   How say you? Shall we?
MATHIAS. I must and will, sir, there's no remedy.
LODOWICK. And so will I too, or it shall go hard.
   Farewell, Mathias.
MATHIAS.   Farewell, Lodowick.   *Exeunt.*

Actus Secundus. [*Scaena 1.*]
   Enter Barabas *with a light.*
BARABAS. Thus like the sad presaging raven that tolls
   The sick man's passport in her hollow beak,
   And in the shadow of the silent night
   Doth shake contagion from her sable wings,
   Vex'd and tormented runs poor Barabas
   With fatal curses towards these Christians.
   The incertain pleasures of swift-footed time
   Have ta'en their flight, and left me in despair;
   And of my former riches rests no more
   But bare remembrance, like a soldier's scar,   10
   That has no further comfort for his maim.
   O Thou, that with a fiery pillar led'st
   The sons of Israel through the dismal shades,
   Light Abraham's offspring, and direct the hand
   Of Abigail this night; or let the day
   Turn to eternal darkness after this.
   No sleep can fasten on my watchful eyes,
   Nor quiet enter my distemper'd thoughts,
   Till I have answer of my Abigail.
   Enter Abigail *above.*
ABIGAIL. Now have I happily espied a time   20
   To search the plank my father did appoint;
   And here behold, unseen, where I have found
   The gold, the pearls, and jewels, which he hid.
BARABAS. Now I remember those old women's words
   Who in my wealth would tell me winter's tales
   And speak of spirits and ghosts that glide by night
   About the place where treasure hath been hid.
   And now methinks that I am one of those;

For whilst I live, here lives my soul's sole hope,
And when I die, here shall my spirit walk.   30
ABIGAIL. Now that my father's fortune were so good
As but to be about this happy place!
'Tis not so happy: yet, when we parted last,
He said he would attend me in the morn.
Then, gentle Sleep, where'er his body rests,
Give charge to Morpheus that he may dream
A golden dream, and of the sudden walk,
Come and receive the treasure I have found.
BARABAS. *Bien para todos mi ganado no es;*
As good go on as sit so sadly thus.   40
But stay, what star shines yonder in the east?
The loadstar of my life, if Abigail.
Who's there?
ABIGAIL.   Who's that?
BARABAS.   Peace, Abigail, 'tis I.
ABIGAIL. Then, father, here receive thy happiness.
BARABAS. Hast thou't?
ABIGAIL.   Here. (*Throws down bags.*) Hast thou't?
There's more, and more, and more.
BARABAS.   O my girl,
My gold, my fortune, my felicity,
Strength to my soul, death to mine enemy.
Welcome the first beginner of my bliss.
O Abigail, Abigail, that I had thee here too!   50
Then my desires were fully satisfied:
But I will practise thy enlargement thence.
O girl! O gold! O beauty! O my bliss!   *Hugs his bags.*
ABIGAIL. Father, it draweth towards midnight now,
And 'bout this time the nuns begin to wake.
To shun suspicion, therefore, let us part.
BARABAS. Farewell my joy, and by my fingers take
A kiss from him that sends it from his soul.
Now Phoebus ope the eyelids of the day,
And for the raven wake the morning lark,   60
That I may hover with her in the air,
Singing o'er these as she does o'er her young:
Hermoso placer de los dineros.   *Exeunt.*

[Scaena 2.]

Enter Governor, Martin del Bosco, *the* Knights [*and*
Officers].
FERNEZE. Now, Captain, tell us whither thou art bound?

Whence is thy ship that anchors in our road?
And why thou cam'st ashore without our leave?
BOSCO. Governor of Malta, hither am I bound;
My ship, the Flying Dragon, is of Spain,
And so am I, del Bosco is my name,
Vice-Admiral unto the Catholic king.
I KNIGHT. 'Tis true, my lord, therefore entreat him well.
BOSCO. Our fraught is Grecians, Turks, and Afric Moors;
For late upon the coast of Corsica,   10
Because we vail'd not to the Turkish fleet,
Their creeping galleys had us in the chase;
But suddenly the wind began to rise,
And then we luff'd and tack'd, and fought at ease.
Some have we fir'd, and many have we sunk;
But one amongst the rest became our prize:
The captain's slain; the rest remain our slaves,
Of whom we would make sale in Malta here.
FERNEZE. Martin del Bosco, I have heard of thee.
Welcome to Malta, and to all of us;   20
But to admit a sale of these thy Turks,
We may not, nay we dare not give consent,
By reason of a tributary league.
I KNIGHT. Del Bosco, as thou lov'st and honour'st us,
Persuade our governor against the Turk.
This truce we have is but in hope of gold,
And with that sum he craves might we wage war.
BOSCO. Will Knights of Malta be in league with Turks,
And buy it basely too for sums of gold?
My lord, remember that, to Europe's shame,   30
The Christian Isle of Rhodes, from whence you came,
Was lately lost, and you were stated here
To be at deadly enmity with Turks.
FERNEZE. Captain, we know it, but our force is small.
BOSCO. What is the sum that Calymath requires?
FERNEZE. A hundred thousand crowns.
BOSCO. My lord and king hath title to this isle,
And he means quickly to expel you hence.
Therefore be rul'd by me, and keep the gold:
I'll write unto his majesty for aid,   40
And not depart until I see you free.
FERNEZE. On this condition shall thy Turks be sold.
Go, officers, and set them straight in show.
                             [*Exeunt* Officers.]
Bosco, thou shalt be Malta's general;

We and our warlike knights will follow thee
Against these barbarous misbelieving Turks.
BOSCO. So shall you imitate those you succeed;
  For when their hideous force environ'd Rhodes,
  Small though the number was that kept the town,
  They fought it out, and not a man surviv'd   50
  To bring the hapless news to Christendom.
FERNEZE. So will we fight it out. Come, let's away.
  Proud-daring Calymath, instead of gold,
  We'll send thee bullets wrapp'd in smoke and fire.
  Claim tribute where thou wilt, we are resolv'd:
  Honour is bought with blood, and not with gold.   *Exeunt.*

[*Scaena 3.*]
  Enter Officers *with* Slaves.
1 OFFICER. This is the market-place, here let 'em stand:
  Fear not their sale, for they'll be quickly bought.
2 OFFICER. Every one's price is written on his back,
  And so much must they yield, or not be sold.
1 OFFICER. Here comes the Jew; had not his goods been seiz'd,
  He'd give us present money for them all.
  Enter Barabas.
BARABAS. In spite of these swine-eating Christians
  (Unchosen nation, never circumcis'd,
  Such as, poor villains, were ne'er thought upon
  Till Titus and Vespasian conquer'd us),   10
  Am I become as wealthy as I was.
  They hop'd my daughter would ha' been a nun;
  But she's at home, and I have bought a house
  As great and fair as is the Governor's;
  And there in spite of Malta will I dwell,
  Having Ferneze's hand, whose heart I'll have;
  Ay, and his son's too, or it shall go hard.
  I am not of the tribe of Levi, I,
  That can so soon forget an injury.
  We Jews can fawn like spaniels when we please,   20
  And when we grin we bite; yet are our looks
  As innocent and harmless as a lamb's.
  I learn'd in Florence how to kiss my hand,
  Heave up my shoulders when they call me dog,
  And duck as low as any bare-foot friar,
  Hoping to see them starve upon a stall,
  Or else be gather'd for in our synagogue,
  That, when the offering-basin comes to me,

Even for charity I may spit into't.
Here comes Don Lodowick, the Governor's son,   30
One that I love for his good father's sake.
    Enter Lodowick.
LODOWICK. I hear the wealthy Jew walked this way.
    I'll seek him out, and so insinuate
    That I may have a sight of Abigail,
    For Don Mathias tells me she is fair.
BARABAS. Now will I show myself to have more of the serpent
    than the dove; that is, more knave than fool.
LODOWICK. Yond' walks the Jew: now for fair Abigail.
BARABAS. Ay, ay, no doubt but she's at your command.
LODOWICK. Barabas, thou know'st I am the Governor's son.
BARABAS. I would you were his father too, sir; that's all the
    harm I wish you. The slave looks like a hog's cheek new
    sing'd.   43
LODOWICK. Whither walk'st thou, Barabas?
BARABAS. No further. 'Tis a custom held with us,
    That when we speak with Gentiles like to you,
    We turn into the air to purge ourselves:
    For unto us the promise doth belong.
LODOWICK. Well, Barabas, canst help me to a diamond?
BARABAS. O, sir, your father had my diamonds.   50
    Yet I have one left that will serve your turn—
    (*Aside.*) I mean my daughter; but ere he shall have her
    I'll sacrifice her on a pile of wood:
    I ha' the poison of the city for him,
    And the white leprosy.
LODOWICK. What sparkle does it give without a foil?
BARABAS. The diamond that I talk of ne'er was foil'd—
    But when he touches it it will be foil'd—
    Lord Lodowick, it sparkles bright and fair.
LODOWICK. Is it square or pointed, pray let me know?   60
BARABAS. Pointed it is, good sir, (*Aside.*) but not for you.
LODOWICK. I like it much the better.
BARABAS.   So do I too.
LODOWICK. How shows it by night?
BARABAS.   Outshines Cynthia's rays:
    (*Aside.*) You'll like it better far a-nights than days.
LODOWICK. And what's the price?
BARABAS [*Aside*].   Your life, and if you have it.
    O my lord,
    We will not jar about the price: come to my house,
    And I will give't your honour (*Aside.*) with a vengeance.

[352]

LODOWICK. No, Barabas, I will deserve it first.

BARABAS. Good sir,   70
  Your father has deserv'd it at my hands,
  Who of mere charity and Christian ruth,
  To bring me to religious purity,
  And as it were in catechizing sort,
  To make me mindful of my mortal sins,
  Against my will, and whether I would or no,
  Seiz'd all I had, and thrust me out-a-doors,
  And made my house a place for nuns most chaste.

LODOWICK. No doubt your soul shall reap the fruit of it.

BARABAS. Ay, but, my lord, the harvest is far off.   80
  And yet I know the prayers of those nuns
  And holy friars, having money for their pains,
  Are wondrous; (*Aside.*) and indeed do no man good;
  And, seeing they are not idle, but still doing,
  'Tis likely they in time may reap some fruit,
  I mean, in fullness of perfection.

LODOWICK. Good Barabas, glance not at our holy nuns.

BARABAS. No, but I do it through a burning zeal—
  (*Aside.*) Hoping ere long to set the house a-fire;
  For, though they do a while increase and multiply,   90
  I'll have a saying to that nunnery—
  As for the diamond, sir, I told you of,
  Come home, and there's no price shall make us part,
  Even for your honourable father's sake—
  (*Aside.*) It shall go hard but I will see your death—
  But now I must be gone to buy a slave.

LODOWICK. And, Barabas, I'll bear thee company.

BARABAS. Come, then; here's the market-place. What's the
  price of this slave? Two hundred crowns? Doth the Turk
  weigh so much?   100

1 OFFICER. Sir, that's his price.

BARABAS. What, can he steal, that you demand so much?
  Belike he has some new trick for a purse;
  And if he has, he is worth three hundred plats,
  So that, being bought, the town seal might be got
  To keep him for his lifetime from the gallows.
  The sessions-day is critical to thieves,
  And few or none scape but by being purg'd.

LODOWICK. Rat'st thou this Moor but at two hundred plats?

1 OFFICER. No more, my lord.   110

BARABAS. Why should this Turk be dearer than that Moor?

1 OFFICER. Because he is young, and has more qualities.

BARABAS. What, hast the philosopher's stone? And thou hast,
   break my head with it, I'll forgive thee.

SLAVE. No sir; I can cut and shave.

BARABAS. Let me see, sirrah, are you not an old shaver?

SLAVE. Alas, sir, I am a very youth.

BARABAS. A youth? I'll buy you, and marry you to Lady
   Vanity, if you do well.

SLAVE. I will serve you, sir.   120

BARABAS. Some wicked trick or other. It may be, under colour
   of shaving, thou'lt cut my throat for my goods. Tell me,
   hast thou thy health well?

SLAVE. Ay, passing well.

BARABAS. So much the worse; I must have one that's sickly,
   and't be but for sparing victuals. 'Tis not a stone of beef a
   day will maintain you in these chops; let me see one that's
   somewhat leaner.

1 OFFICER. Here's a leaner; how like you him?

BARABAS. Where was thou born?   130

ITHAMORE. In Thrace; brought up in Arabia.

BARABAS. So much the better; thou art for my turn.
   An hundred crowns? I'll have him; there's the coin.

1 OFFICER. Then mark him, sir, and take him hence.

BARABAS. Ay, mark him, you were best; for this is he
   That by my help shall do much villainy.
   My lord, farewell. Come, sirrah, you are mine.
   As for the diamond, it shall be yours;
   I pray, sir, be no stranger at my house,
   All that I have shall be at your command.   140
      Enter Mathias [*and* Katharine], *his mother.*

MATHIAS. What makes the Jew and Lodowick so private?
   I fear me 'tis about fair Abigail.

BARABAS. Yonder comes Don Mathias; let us stay:
   He loves my daughter, and she holds him dear;
   But I have sworn to frustrate both their hopes,
   And be reveng'd upon the—Governor.   [*Exit* Lodowick.]

KATHARINE. This Moor is comeliest, is he not? Speak, son.

MATHIAS. No, this is the better, mother, view this well.

BARABAS. Seem not to know me here before your mother,
   Lest she mistrust the match that is in hand.   150
   When you have brought her home, come to my house;
   Think of me as thy father. Son, farewell.

MATHIAS. But wherefore talk'd Don Lodowick with you?

BARABAS. Tush, man, we talk'd of diamonds, not of Abigail.

KATHARINE. Tell me, Mathias, is not that the Jew?

BARABAS. As for the comment on the Maccabees,
  I have it, sir, and 'tis at your command.
MATHIAS. Yes, madam, and my talk with him was about the
  borrowing of a book or two.
KATHARINE. Converse not with him; he is cast off from heaven.
  Thou hast thy crowns, fellow. Come, let's away.   161
MATHIAS. Sirrah Jew, remember the book.
BARABAS. Marry will I, sir.

               Exeunt [Katharine *and* Mathias, *with a* Slave].

I OFFICER. Come, I have made a reasonable market; let's away.
                 [*Exeunt* Officers *with* Slaves.]
BARABAS. Now let me know thy name, and therewithal
  Thy birth, condition, and profession.
ITHAMORE. Faith, sir, my birth is but mean, my name's
  Ithamore, my profession what you please.
BARABAS. Hast thou no trade? Then listen to my words,
  And I will teach that that shall stick by thee.   170
  First be thou void of these affections:
  Compassion, love, vain hope, and heartless fear;
  Be mov'd at nothing, see thou pity none,
  But to thyself smile when the Christians moan.
ITHAMORE. O, brave, master, I worship your nose for this.
BARABAS. As for myself, I walk abroad a-nights,
  And kill sick people groaning under walls;
  Sometimes I go about and poison wells;
  And now and then, to cherish Christian thieves,
  I am content to lose some of my crowns,   180
  That I may, walking in my gallery,
  See 'em go pinion'd along by my door.
  Being young, I studied physic, and began
  To practise first upon the Italian;
  There I enrich'd the priests with burials,
  And always kept the sexton's arms in ure
  With digging graves and ringing dead men's knells.
  And after that, was I an engineer,
  And in the wars 'twixt France and Germany,
  Under pretence of helping Charles the Fifth,   190
  Slew friend and enemy with my stratagems.
  Then after that was I an usurer,
  And with extorting, cozening, forfeiting,
  And tricks belonging unto brokery,
  I fill'd the gaols with bankrouts in a year,
  And with young orphans planted hospitals,
  And every moon made some or other mad,

And now and then one hang himself for grief,
Pinning upon his breast a long great scroll
How I with interest tormented him.   200
But mark how I am blest for plaguing them:
I have as much coin as will buy the town.
But tell me now, how hast thou spent thy time?

ITHAMORE. Faith, master,
In setting Christian villages on fire,
Chaining of eunuchs, binding galley-slaves.
One time I was an hostler in an inn,
And in the night time secretly would I steal
To travellers' chambers, and there cut their throats;
Once at Jerusalem, where the pilgrims kneel'd,   210
I strewed powder on the marble stones,
And therewithal their knees would rankle so
That I have laugh'd a-good to see the cripples
Go limping home to Christendom on stilts.

BARABAS. Why, this is something: make account of me
As of thy fellow; we are villains both:
Both circumcised, we hate Christians both.
Be true and secret, thou shalt want no gold.
But stand aside, here comes Don Lodowick.
    Enter Lodowick.

LODOWICK. O, Barabas, well met.   220
Where is the diamond you told me of?

BARABAS. I have it for you, sir: please you walk in with me—
What ho, Abigail; open the door, I say.
    Enter Abigail.

ABIGAIL. In good time, father; here are letters come
From Ormus, and the post stays here within.

BARABAS. Give me the letters. Daughter, do you hear?
Entertain Lodowick, the Governor's son,
With all the courtesy you can afford,
Provided that you keep your maidenhead.
Use him as if he were a (*Aside.*) Philistine;   230
Dissemble, swear, protest, vow to love him:
He is not of the seed of Abraham.
I am a little busy, sir; pray pardon me.
Abigail, bid him welcome for my sake.

ABIGAIL. For your sake and his own he's welcome hither.

BARABAS. Daughter, a word more: kiss him, speak him fair,
And like a cunning Jew so cast about
That ye be both made sure ere you come out.

ABIGAIL. O father, Don Mathias is my love.

[356]

BARABAS. I know it: yet, I say, make love to him;   240
 Do, it is requisite it should be so.
 Nay on my life, it is my factor's hand;
 But go you in, I'll think upon the account.
       [*Exeunt* Abigail *and* Lodowick.]
 The account is made, for Lodovico dies.
 My factor sends me word a merchant's fled
 That owes me for a hundred tun of wine:
 I weigh it thus much; I have wealth enough;
 For now by this has he kiss'd Abigail,
 And she vows love to him, and he to her.
 And sure as heaven rain'd manna for the Jews,   250
 So sure shall he and Don Mathias die:
 His father was my chiefest enemy.
  Enter Mathias.
 Whither goes Don Mathias? Stay a while.
MATHIAS. Whither but to my fair love Abigail?
BARABAS. Thou know'st, and heaven can witness it is true,
 That I intend my daughter shall be thine.
MATHIAS. Ay, Barabas, or else thou wrong'st me much.
BARABAS. O, heaven forbid I should have such a thought!
 Pardon me though I weep: the Governor's son
 Will, whether I will or no, have Abigail;   260
 He sends her letters, bracelets, jewels, rings.
MATHIAS. Does she receive them?
BARABAS. She? No, Mathias, no, but sends them back,
 And when he comes, she locks herself up fast;
 Yet through the key-hole will he talk to her,
 While she runs to the window looking out
 When you should come and hale him from the door.
MATHIAS. O treacherous Lodowick!
BARABAS. Even now, as I came home, he slipp'd me in,
 And I am sure he is with Abigail.   270
MATHIAS. I'll rouse him thence.
BARABAS. Not for all Malta; therefore sheathe your sword.
 If you love me, no quarrels in my house;
 But steal you in, and seem to see him not:
 I'll give him such a warning ere he goes
 As he shall have small hopes of Abigail.
 Away, for here they come.
  Enter Lodowick, Abigail.
MATHIAS. What, hand in hand; I cannot suffer this.
BARABAS. Mathias, as thou lov'st me, not a word.
MATHIAS. Well, let it pass. Another time shall serve.   *Exit.*

LODOWICK. Barabas, is not that the widow's son?   281
BARABAS. Ay, and take heed, for he hath sworn your death.
LODOWICK. My death? What, is the base-born peasant mad?
BARABAS. No, no; but happily he stands in fear
  Of that which you, I think, ne'er dream upon,
  My daughter here, a paltry silly girl.
LODOWICK. Why, loves she Don Mathias?
BARABAS. Doth she not with her smiling answer you?
ABIGAIL [*aside*]. He has my heart; I smile against my will.
LODOWICK. Barabas, thou know'st I have lov'd thy daughter
  long.   290
BARABAS. And so has she done you, even from a child.
LODOWICK. And now I can no longer hold my mind.
BARABAS. Nor I the affection that I bear to you.
LODOWICK. This is thy diamond. Tell me, shall I have it?
BARABAS. Win it, and wear it; it is yet unfoil'd.
  O but I know your lordship would disdain
  To marry with the daughter of a Jew:
  And yet I'll give her many a golden cross,
  With Christian posies round about the ring.
LODOWICK. 'Tis not thy wealth, but her that I esteem;   300
  Yet crave I thy consent.
BARABAS. And mine you have; yet let me talk to her.
  (*Aside.*) This offspring of Cain, this Jebusite
  That never tasted of the Passover
  Nor e'er shall see the land of Canaan
  Nor our Messias that is yet to come,
  This gentle maggot, Lodowick I mean,
  Must be deluded: let him have thy hand,
  But keep thy heart till Don Mathias comes.
ABIGAIL. What, shall I be betroth'd to Lodowick?   310
BARABAS. It's no sin to deceive a Christian;
  For they themselves hold it a principle,
  Faith is not to be held with heretics:
  But all are heretics that are not Jews.
  This follows well, and therefore, daughter, fear not.
  I have entreated her, and she will grant.
LODOWICK. Then gentle Abigail, plight thy faith to me.
ABIGAIL. I cannot choose, seeing my father bids:
  Nothing but death shall part my love and me.
LODOWICK. Now have I that for which my soul hath long'd.
BARABAS (*aside*). So have not I; but yet I hope I shall.   321
ABIGAIL. O wretched Abigail, what hast thou done?
LODOWICK. Why on the sudden is your colour chang'd?

ABIGAIL. I know not: but farewell, I must be gone.

BARABAS. Stay her, but let her not speak one word more.

LODOWICK. Mute o' the sudden! Here's a sudden change.

BARABAS. O muse not at it; 'tis the Hebrews' guise
That maidens new-betroth'd should weep a while.
Trouble her not; sweet Lodowick, depart;
She is thy wife, and thou shalt be mine heir.   330

LODOWICK. O, is't the custom? Then I am resolv'd:
But rather let the brightsome heavens be dim,
And nature's beauty choke with stifling clouds,
Than my fair Abigail should frown on me.
There comes the villain; now I'll be reveng'd.
    Enter Mathias.

BARABAS. Be quiet, Lodowick; it is enough
That I have made thee sure to Abigail.

LODOWICK. Well, let him go.   *Exit.*

BARABAS. Well, but for me, as you went in at doors
You had been stabb'd: but not a word on't now.   340
Here must no speeches pass, nor swords be drawn.

MATHIAS. Suffer me, Barabas, but to follow him.

BARABAS. No; so shall I, if any hurt be done,
Be made an accessary of your deeds.
Revenge it on him when you meet him next.

MATHIAS. For this I'll have his heart.

BARABAS. Do so. Lo, here I give thee Abigail.

MATHIAS. What greater gift can poor Mathias have?
Shall Lodowick rob me of so fair a love?
My life is not so dear as Abigail.   350

BARABAS. My heart misgives me that to cross your love
He's with your mother; therefore after him.

MATHIAS. What, is he gone unto my mother?

BARABAS. Nay, if you will, stay till she comes herself.

MATHIAS. I cannot stay; for, if my mother come,
She'll die with grief.   *Exit.*

ABIGAIL. I cannot take my leave of him for tears.
Father, why have you thus incens'd them both?

BARABAS. What's that to thee?

ABIGAIL.   I'll make 'em friends again.

BARABAS. You'll make 'em friends? Are there not Jews enow in
    Malta,   360
But thou must dote upon a Christian?

ABIGAIL. I will have Don Mathias; he is my love.

BARABAS. Yes, you shall have him. Go, put her in.

ITHAMORE. Ay, I'll put her in.   [*Exit* Abigail.]

BARABAS. Now tell me, Ithamore, how lik'st thou this?
ITHAMORE. Faith, master, I think by this
  You purchase both their lives: is it not so?
BARABAS. True, and it shall be cunningly perform'd.
ITHAMORE. O, master, that I might have a hand in this.
BARABAS. Ay, so thou shalt: 'tis thou must do the deed.   370
  Take this, and bear it to Mathias straight,
  And tell him that it comes from Lodowick.
ITHAMORE. 'Tis poison'd, is it not?
BARABAS. No, no; and yet it might be done that way.
  It is a challenge feign'd from Lodowick,
ITHAMORE. Fear not, I'll so set his heart a-fire,
  That he shall verily think it comes from him.
BARABAS. I cannot choose but like thy readiness;
  Yet be not rash, but do it cunningly.
ITHAMORE. As I behave myself in this, employ me hereafter.
                                    Exit.
BARABAS. Away, then.   381
  So, now will I go in to Lodowick,
  And like a cunning spirit feign some lie,
  Till I have set 'em both at enmity.   *Exit.*

Actus Tertius. [*Scaena 1.*]
  Enter [Bellamira] *a courtesan.*
BELLAMIRA. Since this town was besieg'd, my gain grows cold:
  The time has been, that but for one bare night
  A hundred ducats have been freely given;
  But now against my will I must be chaste;
  And yet I know my beauty doth not fail.
  From Venice merchants, and from Padua
  Were wont to come rare-witted gentlemen,
  Scholars I mean, learned and liberal;
  And now, save Pilia-Borza, comes there none,
  And he is very seldom from my house;   10
  And here he comes.
    Enter Pilia-Borza.
PILIA-BORZA. Hold thee, wench, there's something for thee to
  spend.
BELLAMIRA. 'Tis silver; I disdain it.
PILIA-BORZA. Ay, but the Jew has gold,
  And I will have it, or it shall go hard.
BELLAMIRA. Tell me, how cam'st thou by this?
PILIA-BORZA. Faith, walking the back lanes through the

gardens, I chanc'd to cast mine eye up to the Jew's counting-house, where I saw some bags of money, and in the night I clamber'd up with my hooks; and as I was taking my choice, I heard a rumbling in the house; so I took only this, and run my way. But here's the Jew's man.   22
    Enter Ithamore.

BELLAMIRA. Hide the bag.

PILIA-BORZA. Look not towards him, let's away. Zoons, what a looking thou keep'st, thou'lt betray's anon.

                [*Exeunt* Bellamira *and* Pilia-Borza.]

ITHAMORE. O the sweetest face that ever I beheld! I know she is a courtesan by her attire: now would I give a hundred of the Jew's crowns that I had such a concubine.
Well, I have deliver'd the challenge in such sort,
As meet they will, and fighting die; brave sport.   *Exit.*

[*Scaena 2.*]
    Enter Mathias.

MATHIAS. This is the place; now Abigail shall see
Whether Mathias holds her dear or no.
    Enter Lodowick *reading.*

LODOWICK. What, dares the villain write in such base terms?

MATHIAS. I did it; and revenge it if thou dar'st.   *Fight.*
    Enter Barabas *above.*

BARABAS. O bravely fought! and yet they thrust not home.
Now Lodovico, now Mathias; so!   [*Both fall.*]
So now they have show'd themselves to be tall fellows.

[VOICES] *within.* Part 'em, part 'em.

BARABAS. Ay, part 'em now they are dead. Farewell, farewell.
                            Exit.

    Enter Governor, Katharine [*and* Attendants].

FERNEZE. What sight is this? My Lodovico slain!   10
These arms of mine shall be thy sepulchre.

KATHARINE. Who is this? My son Mathias slain!

FERNEZE. O Lodowick, hadst thou perish'd by the Turk,
Wretched Ferneze might have veng'd thy death.

KATHARINE. Thy son slew mine, and I'll revenge his death.

FERNEZE. Look, Katharine, look, thy son gave mine these wounds.

KATHARINE. O leave to grieve me, I am griev'd enough.

FERNEZE. O that my sighs could turn to lively breath,
And these my tears to blood, that he might live.

KATHARINE. Who made them enemies?   20

FERNEZE. I know not, and that grieves me most of all.

KATHARINE. My son lov'd thine.

FERNEZE.   And so did Lodowick him.

KATHARINE. Lend me that weapon that did kill my son,
And it shall murder me.

FERNEZE. Nay, madam, stay; that weapon was my son's,
And on that rather should Ferneze die.

KATHARINE. Hold, let's inquire the causers of their deaths,
That we may venge their blood upon their heads.

FERNEZE. Then take them up, and let them be interr'd
Within one sacred monument of stone,   30
Upon which altar I will offer up
My daily sacrifice of sighs and tears,
And with my prayers pierce impartial heavens,
Till they disclose the causers of our smarts,
Which forc'd their hands divide united hearts.
Come, Katharine, our losses equal are;
Then of true grief let us take equal share.   *Exeunt.*

[Scaena 3.]

Enter Ithamore.

ITHAMORE. Why, was there ever seen such villainy,
So neatly plotted, and so well perform'd?
Both held in hand, and flatly both beguil'd.

Enter Abigail.

ABIGAIL. Why, how now, Ithamore, why laugh'st thou so?

ITHAMORE. O mistress, ha, ha, ha!

ABIGAIL. Why, what ail'st thou?

ITHAMORE. O, my master!

ABIGAIL. Ha?

ITHAMORE. O mistress, I have the bravest, gravest, secret,
subtle, bottle-nos'd knave to my master, that ever gentleman
had.   11

ABIGAIL. Say, knave, why rail'st upon my father thus?

ITHAMORE. O, my master has the bravest policy.

ABIGAIL. Wherein?

ITHAMORE. Why, know you not?

ABIGAIL. Why, no.

ITHAMORE. Know you not of Mathias' and Don Lodowick's
disaster?

ABIGAIL. No, what was it?

ITHAMORE. Why, the devil invented a challenge, my master writ
it, and I carried it, first to Lodowick, and *imprimis* to
Mathias: 22
And then they met, and as the story says,

In doleful wise they ended both their days.

ABIGAIL. And was my father furtherer of their deaths?

ITHAMORE. Am I Ithamore?

ABIGAIL. Yes.

ITHAMORE. So sure did your father write, and I carry the
    challenge.   30

ABIGAIL. Well, Ithamore, let me request thee this:
    Go to the new-made nunnery, and inquire
    For any of the friars of Saint Jacques,
    And say, I pray them come and speak with me.

ITHAMORE. I pray, mistress, will you answer me to one question?

ABIGAIL. Well, sirrah, what is't?

ITHAMORE. A very feeling one: have not the nuns fine sport
    with the friars now and then?

ABIGAIL. Go to, Sirrah Sauce, is this your question? Get ye
    gone.

ITHAMORE. I will forsooth, mistress.   *Exit.*

ABIGAIL. Hard-hearted father, unkind Barabas,   41
    Was this the pursuit of thy policy,
    To make me show them favour severally,
    That by my favour they should both be slain?
    Admit thou lov'dst not Lodowick for his sire,
    Yet Don Mathias ne'er offended thee.
    But thou wert set upon extreme revenge,
    Because the Prior dispossess'd thee once,
    And couldst not venge it but upon his son;
    Nor on his son but by Mathias' means;   50
    Nor on Mathias but by murdering me.
    But I perceive there is no love on earth,
    Pity in Jews, nor piety in Turks.
    But here comes cursed Ithamore with the friar.

    Enter Ithamore, *Friar* [Jacomo].

JACOMO. *Virgo, salve.*

ITHAMORE. When, duck you?

ABIGAIL. Welcome, grave friar. Ithamore, be gone.

                                 Exit [Ithamore].

    Know, holy sir, I am bold to solicit thee.

JACOMO. Wherein?

ABIGAIL. To get me be admitted for a nun.   60

JACOMO. Why Abigail, it is not yet long since
    That I did labour thy admission,
    And then thou didst not like that holy life.

ABIGAIL. Then were my thoughts so frail and unconfirm'd
    And I was chain'd to follies of the world;

But now experience, purchased with grief,
Has made me see the difference of things.
My sinful soul, alas, hath pac'd too long
The fatal labyrinth of misbelief,
Far from the sun that gives eternal life.   70
JACOMO. Who taught thee this?
ABIGAIL.   The abbess of the house,
Whose zealous admonition I embrace.
O therefore, Jacomo, let me be one,
Although unworthy, of that sisterhood.
JACOMO. Abigail, I will; but see thou change no more,
For that will be most heavy to thy soul.
ABIGAIL. That was my father's fault.
JACOMO.   Thy father's, how?
ABIGAIL. Nay, you shall pardon me. O Barabas,
Though thou deservest hardly at my hands,
Yet never shall these lips bewray thy life.   80
JACOMO. Come, shall we go?
ABIGAIL.   My duty waits on you.   *Exeunt.*

[*Scaena 4.*]
Enter Barabas *reading a letter.*
BARABAS. What, Abigail become a nun again?
False and unkind! What, hast thou lost thy father?
And, all unknown and unconstrain'd of me,
Art thou again got to the nunnery?
Now here she writes, and wills me to repent:
Repentance? *Spurca!* What pretendeth this?
I fear she knows ('tis so) of my device
In Don Mathias' and Lodovico's deaths:
If so, 'tis time that it be seen into;
For she that varies from me in belief   10
Gives great presumption that she loves me not;
Or loving, doth dislike of something done.
But who comes here?
     [*Enter* Ithamore.]
     O Ithamore, come near;
Come near, my love; come near, thy master's life,
My trusty servant, nay, my second self;
For I have now no hope but even in thee,
And on that hope my happiness is built.
When saw'st thou Abigail?
ITHAMORE. Today.
BARABAS. With whom?   20

ITHAMORE. A friar.

BARABAS. A friar? False villain, he hath done the deed.

ITHAMORE. How, sir?

BARABAS. Why, made mine Abigail a nun.

ITHAMORE. That's no lie, for she sent me for him.

BARABAS. O unhappy day!
  False, credulous, inconstant Abigail!
  But let 'em go: and, Ithamore, from hence
  Ne'er shall she grieve me more with her disgrace;
  Ne'er shall she live to inherit aught of mine,   30
  Be bless'd of me, nor come within my gates,
  But perish underneath my bitter curse,
  Like Cain by Adam for his brother's death.

ITHAMORE. O master—

BARABAS. Ithamore, entreat not for her. I am mov'd,
  And she is hateful to my soul and me:
  And, 'less thou yield to this that I intreat,
  I cannot think but that thou hat'st my life.

ITHAMORE. Who, I, master? Why, I'll run to some rock, and
  throw myself headlong into the sea; why, I'll do anything
  for your sweet sake.   41

BARABAS. O trusty Ithamore; no servant, but my friend.
  I here adopt thee for mine only heir:
  All that I have is thine when I am dead;
  And whilst I live, use half; spend as myself.
  Here, take my keys—I'll give 'em thee anon.
  Go buy thee garments; but thou shalt not want.
  Only know this, that thus thou art to do:
  But first go fetch me in the pot of rice
  That for our supper stands upon the fire.   50

ITHAMORE. I hold my head, my master's hungry; I go, sir.
                                                          Exit.

BARABAS. Thus every villain ambles after wealth,
  Although he ne'er be richer than in hope.
  But husht!
      Enter Ithamore *with the pot.*

ITHAMORE. Here 'tis, master.

BARABAS. Well said, Ithamore. What, hast thou brought the
  ladle with thee too?

ITHAMORE. Yes, sir; the proverb says, he that eats with the
  devil had need of a long spoon; I have brought you a
  ladle.   60

BARABAS. Very well, Ithamore, then now be secret;
  And for thy sake, whom I so dearly love,

[365]

Now shalt thou see the death of Abigail,
That thou mayst freely live to be my heir.

ITHAMORE. Why, master, will you poison her with a mess of
rice-porridge? That will preserve life, make her round and
plump, and batten more than you are aware.

BARABAS. Ay but, Ithamore, seest thou this?
It is a precious powder that I bought
Of an Italian in Ancona once, 70
Whose operation is to bind, infect,
And poison deeply, yet not appear
In forty hours after it is ta'en.

ITHAMORE. How, master?

BARABAS. Thus, Ithamore:
This even they use in Malta here ('tis call'd
Saint Jacques' Even) and then, I say, they use
To send their alms unto the nunneries:
Among the rest bear this, and set it there;
There's a dark entry where they take it in, 80
Where they must neither see the messenger
Nor make inquiry who hath sent it them.

ITHAMORE. How so?

BARABAS. Belike there is some ceremony in't.
There, Ithamore, must thou go place this pot:
Stay, let me spice it first.

ITHAMORE. Pray do, and let me help you, master. Pray let me
taste first.

BARABAS. Prithee, do; what say'st thou now?

ITHAMORE. Troth, master, I'm loath such a pot of pottage
should be spoil'd. 91

BARABAS. Peace, Ithamore, 'tis better so than spar'd.
Assure thyself thou shalt have broth by the eye.
My purse, my coffer, and myself is thine.

ITHAMORE. Well, master, I go.

BARABAS. Stay, first let me stir it, Ithamore.
As fatal be it to her as the draught
Of which great Alexander drunk and died;
And with her let it work like Borgia's wine,
Whereof his sire the Pope was poisoned. 100
In few, the blood of Hydra, Lerna's bane,
The juice of hebon, and Cocytus' breath,
And all the poisons of the Stygian pool,
Break from the fiery kingdom; and in this
Vomit your venom, and envenom her
That like a fiend hath left her father thus!

ITHAMORE. What a blessing has he given't! Was ever pot of
    rice-porridge so sauc'd? What shall I do with it?
BARABAS. O my sweet Ithamore, go set it down;
    And come again as soon as thou hast done,   110
    For I have other business for thee.
ITHAMORE. Here's a drench to poison a whole stable of Flanders
    mares: I'll carry't to the nuns with a powder.
BARABAS. And the horse-pestilence to boot. Away.
ITHAMORE. I am gone:
    Pay me my wages, for my work is done.   *Exit.*
BARABAS. I'll pay thee with a vengeance, Ithamore.   *Exit.*

[*Scaena 5.*]
Enter Governor, Bosco, Knights [*meeting a*] Basso.

FERNEZE. Welcome, great Basso; how fares Calymath?
    What wind drives you thus into Malta road?
BASSO. The wind that bloweth all the world besides,
    Desire of gold.
FERNEZE.   Desire of gold, great sir?
    That's to be gotten in the Western Inde:
    In Malta are no golden minerals.
BASSO. To you of Malta thus saith Calymath:
    The time you took for respite is at hand
    For the performance of your promise pass'd,
    And for the tribute money I am sent.   10
FERNEZE. Basso, in brief, shalt have no tribute here,
    Nor shall the heathens live upon our spoil:
    First will we raze the city walls ourselves,
    Lay waste the island, hew the temples down,
    And, shipping of our goods to Sicily,
    Open an entrance for the wasteful sea,
    Whose billows, beating the resistless banks,
    Shall overflow it with their refluence.
BASSO. Well, Governor, since thou hast broke the league
    By flat denial of the promis'd tribute,   20
    Talk not of razing down your city walls,
    You shall not need trouble yourselves so far,
    For Selim-Calymath shall come himself,
    And with brass bullets batter down your towers,
    And turn proud Malta to a wilderness,
    For these intolerable wrongs of yours:
    And so farewell.   [*Exit.*]
FERNEZE. Farewell.
    And now, you men of Malta, look about,

And let's provide to welcome Calymath.   30
Close your portcullis, charge your basilisks,
And as you profitably take up arms,
So now courageously encounter them;
For by this answer broken is the league,
And naught is to be look'd for now but wars,
And naught to us more welcome is than wars.   *Exeunt.*

[*Scaena 6.*]
        Enter two Friars [Jacomo *and* Barnardine].

JACOMO. O brother, brother, all the nuns are sick,
    And physic will not help them; they must die.
BARNARDINE. The abbess sent for me to be confess'd.
    O what a sad confession will there be!
JACOMO. And so did fair Maria send for me.
    I'll to her lodging; hereabouts she lies.   *Exit.*
        Enter Abigail.
BARNARDINE. What, all dead save only Abigail?
ABIGAIL. And I shall die too, for I feel death coming.
    Where is the friar that convers'd with me?
BARNARDINE. O he is gone to see the other nuns.   10
ABIGAIL. I sent for him, but seeing you are come,
    Be you my ghostly father: and first know,
    That in this house I liv'd religiously,
    Chaste, and devout, much sorrowing for my sins;
    But ere I came—
BARNARDINE. What then?
ABIGAIL. I did offend high heaven so grievously
    As I am almost desperate for my sins;
    And one offence torments me more than all.
    You knew Mathias and Don Lodowick?   20
BARNARDINE. Yes, what of them?
ABIGAIL. My father did contract me to 'em both;
    First to Don Lodowick: him I never lov'd;
    Mathias was the man that I held dear,
    And for his sake did I become a nun.
BARNARDINE. So: say how was their end?
ABIGAIL. Both, jealous of my love, envied each other;
    And by my father's practice, which is there
    Set down at large, the gallants were both slain.
                                            [*Gives a paper.*]
BARNARDINE. O monstrous villainy!   30
ABIGAIL. To work my peace, this I confess to thee.
    Reveal it not, for then my father dies.

[368]

BARNARDINE. Know that confession must not be reveal'd;
  The canon law forbids it, and the priest
  That makes it known, being degraded first,
  Shall be condemn'd, and then sent to the fire.
ABIGAIL. So I have heard; pray therefore keep it .close.
  Death seizeth on my heart: ah, gentle friar,
  Convert my father that he may be sav'd,
  And witness that I die a Christian.   40
                                              [*Dies.*]

BARNARDINE. Ay, and a virgin too; that grieves me most.
  But I must to the Jew, and exclaim on him,
  And make him stand in fear of me.
    Enter first Friar [Jacomo].
JACOMO. O brother, all the nuns are dead; let's bury them.
BARNARDINE. First help to bury this; then go with me,
  And help me to exclaim against the Jew.
JACOMO. Why, what has he done?
BARNARDINE. A thing that makes me tremble to unfold.
JACOMO. What, has he crucified a child?
BARNARDINE. No, but a worse thing: 'twas told me in shrift.
  Thou know'st 'tis death and if it be reveal'd.   51
  Come, let's away.   *Exeunt.*

              Actus Quartus. [*Scaena 1.*]
    Enter Barabas, Ithamore. *Bells within.*
BARABAS. There is no music to a Christian's knell.
  How sweet the bells ring now the nuns are dead
  That sound at other times like tinkers' pans!
  I was afraid the poison had not wrought,
  Or though it wrought, it would have done no good,
  For every year they swell, and yet they live;
  Now all are dead, not one remains alive.
ITHAMORE. That's brave, master; but think you it will not be
  known?
BARABAS. How can it, if we two be secret?
ITHAMORE. For my part, fear you not.   10
BARABAS. I'd cut thy throat, if I did.
ITHAMORE. And reason too.
  But here's a royal monast'ry hard by;
  Good master, let me poison all the monks.
BARABAS. Thou shalt not need, for now the nuns are dead
  They'll die with grief.
ITHAMORE. Do you not sorrow for your daughter's death?

BARABAS. No, but I grieve because she liv'd so long;
An Hebrew born, and would become a Christian:
Cazzo diabole!   20
ITHAMORE. Look, look, master, here come two religious cater-
    pillars.
    Enter the two Friars.
BARABAS. I smelt 'em ere they came.
ITHAMORE. God-a-mercy, nose; come, let's be gone.
BARNARDINE. Stay, wicked Jew; repent, I say, and stay.
JACOMO. Thou hast offended, therefore must be damn'd.
BARABAS. I fear they know we sent the poison'd broth.
ITHAMORE. And so do I, master; therefore speak 'em fair.
BARNARDINE. Barabas, thou hast—
JACOMO. Ay, that thou hast—
BARABAS. True, I have money; what though I have?   30
BARNARDINE. Thou art a—
JACOMO. Ay, that thou art, a—
BARABAS. What needs all this? I know I am a Jew.
BARNARDINE. Thy daughter—
JACOMO. Ay, thy daughter—
BARABAS. O, speak not of her, then I die with grief.
BARNARDINE. Remember that—
JACOMO. Ay, remember that—
BARABAS. I must needs say that I have been a great usurer.
BARNARDINE. Thou hast committed—   40
BARABAS. Fornication? But that was in another country, and
    besides the wench is dead.
BARNARDINE. Ay, but Barabas, remember Mathias and Don
    Lodowick.
BARABAS. Why, what of them?
BARNARDINE. I will not say that by a forged challenge they met.
BARABAS (*aside*). She has confess'd, and we are both undone,
    My bosom inmate, but I must dissemble.
    O holy friars, the burden of my sins
    Lie heavy on my soul; then pray you tell me,
    Is't not too late now to turn Christian?   50
    I have been zealous in the Jewish faith,
    Hard-hearted to the poor, a covetous wretch,
    That would for lucre's sake have sold my soul.
    A hundred for a hundred I have ta'en;
    And now for store of wealth may I compare
    With all the Jews in Malta: but what is wealth?
    I am a Jew, and therefore am I lost.
    Would penance serve for this my sin,

I could afford to whip myself to death.
ITHAMORE. And so could I; but penance will not serve.   60
BARABAS. To fast, to pray, and wear a shirt of hair,
    And on my knees creep to Jerusalem.
    Cellars of wine, and sollars full of wheat,
    Warehouses stuff'd with spices and with drugs,
    Whole chests of gold in bullion and in coin,
    Besides I know not how much weight in pearl,
    Orient and round, have I within my house;
    At Alexandria, merchandise unsold;
    But yesterday two ships went from this town,
    Their voyage will be worth ten thousand crowns.   70
    In Florence, Venice, Antwerp, London, Seville,
    Frankfort, Lubeck, Moscow, and where not,
    Have I debts owing; and in most of these
    Great sums of money lying in the banco.
    All this I'll give to some religious house,
    So I may be baptiz'd and live therein.
JACOMO. O good Barabas, come to our house.
BARNARDINE. O no, good Barabas, come to our house.
    And Barabas, you know—
BARABAS. I know that I have highly sinn'd: 80
    You shall convert me, you shall have all my wealth.
JACOMO. O Barabas, their laws are strict.
BARABAS. I know they are; and I will be with you.
BARNARDINE. They wear no shirts, and they go barefoot too.
BARABAS. Then 'tis not for me; and I am resolv'd
    You shall confess me, and have all my goods.
JACOMO. Good Barabas, come to me.
BARABAS [*to* Barnardine]. You see I answer him, and yet he
        stays;
    Rid him away, and go you home with me.
JACOMO. I'll be with you tonight.   90
BARABAS. Come to my house at one o'clock this night.
JACOMO. You hear your answer, and you may be gone.
BARNARDINE. Why go, get you away.
JACOMO. I will not go for thee.
BARNARDINE. Not? Then I'll make thee, rogue.
JACOMO. How, dost call me rogue?   *Fight.*
ITHAMORE. Part 'em, master, part 'em.
BARABAS. This is mere frailty, brethren, be content.
    Friar Barnardine, go you with Ithamore.
    You know my mind; let me alone with him.   100
JACOMO. Why does he go to thy house? Let him be gone.

[371]

BARABAS. I'll give him something, and so stop his mouth.
                              Exit [Ithamore *with* Barnardine].
   I never heard of any man but he
   Malign'd the order of the Jacobins;
   But do you think that I believe his words?
   Why, brother, you converted Abigail;
   And I am bound in charity to requite it,
   And so I will. O Jacomo, fail not, but come.
JACOMO. But Barabas, who shall be your godfathers?
   For presently you shall be shriv'd.   110
BARABAS. Marry, the Turk shall be one of my godfathers,
   But not a word to any of your covent.
JACOMO. I warrant thee, Barabas.   *Exit.*
BARABAS. So, now the fear is past, and I am safe;
   For he that shriv'd her is within my house.
   What if I murder'd him ere Jacomo comes?
   Now I have such a plot for both their lives
   As never Jew nor Christian knew the like:
   One turn'd my daughter, therefore he shall die;
   The other knows enough to have my life,   120
   Therefore 'tis not requisite he should live.
   But are not both these wise men, to suppose
   That I will leave my house, my goods, and all,
   To fast and be well whipp'd? I'll none of that.
   Now Friar Barnardine, I come to you;
   I'll feast you, lodge you, give you fair words,
   And after that, I and my trusty Turk—
   No more but so: it must and shall be done.
    Enter Ithamore.
   Ithamore, tell me, is the friar asleep?
ITHAMORE. Yes; and I know not what the reason is,   130
   Do what I can, he will not strip himself,
   Nor go to bed, but sleeps in his own clothes.
   I fear me he mistrusts what we intend.
BARABAS. No, 'tis an order which the friars use:
   Yet if he knew our meanings, could he scape?
ITHAMORE. No, none can hear him, cry he ne'er so loud.
BARABAS. Why, true; therefore did I place him there:
   The other chambers open towards the street.
ITHAMORE. You loiter, master; wherefore stay we thus?
   O how I long to see him shake his heels!   140
BARABAS. Come on, sirrah, off with your girdle; make a
   handsome noose. Friar, awake.
BARNARDINE. What, do you mean to strangle me?

ITHAMORE. Yes, 'cause you use to confess.

BARABAS. Blame not us, but the proverb: Confess and be hang'd. Pull hard.

BARNARDINE. What, will you have my life?

BARABAS. Pull hard, I say. You would have had my goods.

ITHAMORE. Ay, and our lives too, therefore pull amain.
'Tis neatly done, sir; here's no print at all.   150

BARABAS. Then is it as it should be. Take him up.

ITHAMORE. Nay, master, be rul'd by me a little. So, let him lean upon his staff. Excellent! He stands as if he were begging of bacon.

BARABAS. Who would not think but that this friar liv'd? What time o'night is't now, sweet Ithamore?

ITHAMORE. Towards one.

BARABAS. Then will not Jacomo be long from hence.   *Exeunt.*
     Enter Jacomo.

JACOMO. This is the hour wherein I shall proceed.
O happy hour, wherein I shall convert   160
An infidel, and bring his gold into our treasury!
But soft, is not this Barnardine? It is;
And understanding I should come this way,
Stands here o'purpose, meaning me some wrong,
And intercept my going to the Jew.
Barnardine—
Wilt thou not speak? Thou think'st I see thee not.
Away, I'd wish thee, and let me go by:
No, wilt thou not? Nay then, I'll force my way;
And see, a staff stands ready for the purpose.   170
As thou lik'st that, stop me another time.
                                        Strike him, he falls.
     Enter Barabas [*and* Ithamore].

BARABAS. Why, how now, Jacomo, what hast thou done?

JACOMO. Why, stricken him that would have struck at me.

BARABAS. Who is it? Barnardine? Now, out, alas, he is slain.

ITHAMORE. Ay, master, he's slain; look how his brains drop out on's nose.

JACOMO. Good sirs, I have done't: but nobody knows it but you two; I may escape.

BARABAS. So might my man and I hang with you for company.

ITHAMORE. No, let us bear him to the magistrates.   180

JACOMO. Good Barabas, let me go.

BARABAS. No, pardon me, the law must have his course.
I must be forc'd to give in evidence
That being importun'd by this Barnardine

To be a Christian, I shut him out,
And there he sate. Now I, to keep my word,
And give my goods and substance to your house,
Was up thus early, with intent to go
Unto your friary, because you stay'd.

ITHAMORE. Fie upon 'em! Master, will you turn Christian,
    when holy friars turn devils and murder one another? 191

BARABAS. No, for this example I'll remain a Jew.
    Heaven bless me! What, a friar a murderer?
    When shall you see a Jew commit the like?

ITHAMORE. Why, a Turk could ha' done no more.

BARABAS. Tomorrow is the sessions; you shall to it.
    Come Ithamore, let's help to take him hence.

JACOMO. Villains, I am a sacred person; touch me not.

BARABAS. The law shall touch you, we'll but lead you, we.
    'Las, I could weep at your calamity.   200
    Take in the staff too, for that must be shown:
    Law wills that each particular be known.   *Exeunt.*

[*Scaena 2.*]
Enter Courtesan *and* Pilia-Borza.

BELLAMIRA. Pilia-Borza, didst thou meet with Ithamore?

PILIA-BORZA. I did.

BELLAMIRA. And didst thou deliver my letter?

PILIA-BORZA. I did.

BELLAMIRA. And what think'st thou? Will he come?

PILIA-BORZA. I think so, and yet I cannot tell; for at the reading
    of the letter, he look'd like a man of another world.

BELLAMIRA. Why so?

PILIA-BORZA. That such a base slave as he should be saluted
    by such a tall man as I am, from such a beautiful dame as
    you.   11

BELLAMIRA. And what said he?

PILIA-BORZA. Not a wise word; only gave me a nod, as who
    should say, 'Is it even so?'; and so I left him, being driven
    to a non-plus at the critical aspect of my terrible counten-
    ance.

BELLAMIRA. And where didst meet him?

PILIA-BORZA. Upon mine own freehold, within forty foot of the
    gallows, conning his neck-verse, I take it, looking of a friar's
    execution; whom I saluted with an old hempen proverb,
    Hodie tibi, cras mihi, and so I left him to the mercy of
    the hangman; but the exercise being done, see where he
    comes.   23

Enter Ithamore.

ITHAMORE. I never knew a man take his death so patiently as
this friar. He was ready to leap off ere the halter was about
his neck; and when the hangman had put on his hempen
tippet, he made such haste to his prayers as if he had had
another cure to serve. Well, go whither he will, I'll be none
of his followers in haste. And now I think on't, going to the
execution, a fellow met me with a muschatoes like a raven's
wing, and a dagger with a hilt like a warming pan; and he
gave me a letter from one Madam Bellamira, saluting me in
such sort as if he had meant to make clean my boots with
his lips. The effect was, that I should come to her house. I
wonder what the reason is; it may be she sees more in me
than I can find in myself; for she writes further, that she
loves me ever since she saw me, and who would not requite
such love? Here's her house; and here she comes. And now
would I were gone! I am not worthy to look upon her.

PILIA-BORZA. This is the gentleman you writ to.   40

ITHAMORE. Gentleman? He flouts me: what gentry can be in a
poor Turk of tenpence? I'll be gone.

BELLAMIRA. Is't not a sweet-faced youth, Pilia?

ITHAMORE. Again, sweet youth; did not you, sir, bring the
sweet youth a letter?

PILIA-BORZA. I did, sir, and from this gentlewoman, who, as
myself and the rest of the family, stand or fall at your service.

BELLAMIRA. Though woman's modesty should hale me back,
I can withhold no longer; welcome, sweet love.

ITHAMORE. Now am I clean, or rather foully, out of the way.

BELLAMIRA. Whither so soon?   51

ITHAMORE. I'll go steal some money from my master to make
me handsome. Pray pardon me; I must go see a ship discharg'd.

BELLAMIRA. Canst thou be so unkind to leave me thus?

PILIA-BORZA. And ye did but know how she loves you, sir.

ITHAMORE. Nay, I care not how much she loves me. Sweet
Allamira, would I had my master's wealth for thy sake!

PILIA-BORZA. And you can have it, sir, and if you please.   59

ITHAMORE. If 'twere above ground, I could and would have it;
but he hides and buries it up as partridges do their eggs,
under the earth.

PILIA-BORZA. And is't not possible to find it out?

ITHAMORE. By no means possible.

BELLAMIRA [*aside to* Pilia-Borza]. What shall we do with this
base villain, then?

PILIA-BORZA. Let me alone; do but you speak him fair:—
   But you know some secrets of the Jew, which, if they were
   reveal'd, would do him harm.
ITHAMORE. Ay, and such as—go to, no more! I'll make him
   send me half he has, and glad he scapes so too. Pen and ink:
   I'll write unto him; we'll have money straight.   71
PILIA-BORZA. Send for a hundred crowns at least.
ITHAMORE. Ten hundred thousand crowns.   *He writes.*
   'Master Barabas—'
PILIA-BORZA. Write not so submissively, but threat'ning him.
ITHAMORE. 'Sirrah Barabas, send me a hundred crowns.'
PILIA-BORZA. Put in two hundred at least.
ITHAMORE. 'I charge thee send me three hundred by this
   bearer, and this shall be your warrant: if you do not—no
   more but so.'   80
PILIA-BORZA. Tell him you will confess.
ITHAMORE. 'Otherwise I'll confess all.' Vanish, and return in a
   twinkle.
PILIA-BORZA. Let me alone; I'll use him in his kind.   [*Exit.*]
ITHAMORE. Hang him, Jew!
BELLAMIRA. Now, gentle Ithamore, lie in my lap.
   Where are my maids? Provide a running banquet;
   Send to the merchant, bid him bring me silks;
   Shall Ithamore my love go in such rags?
ITHAMORE. And bid the jeweller come hither too.   90
BELLAMIRA. I have no husband, sweet; I'll marry thee.
ITHAMORE. Content: but we will leave this paltry land,
   And sail from hence to Greece, to lovely Greece.
   I'll be thy Jason, thou my golden fleece;
   Where painted carpets o'er the meads are hurl'd,
   And Bacchus' vineyards overspread the world;
   Where woods and forests go in goodly green;
   I'll be Adonis, thou shalt be Love's Queen;
   The meads, the orchards, and the primrose-lanes,
   Instead of sedge and reed, bear sugar-canes: 100
   Thou in those groves, by Dis above,
   Shalt live with me and be my love.
BELLAMIRA. Whither will I not go with gentle Ithamore?
      Enter Pilia-Borza.
ITHAMORE. How now? Hast thou the gold?
PILIA-BORZA. Yes.
ITHAMORE. But came it freely? Did the cow give down her milk
   freely?
PILIA-BORZA. At reading of the letter, he star'd and stamp'd,

[376]

and turn'd aside. I took him by the beard, and look'd upon
him thus; told him he were best to send it. Then he hugg'd
and embrac'd me.   111
ITHAMORE. Rather for fear than love.
PILIA-BORZA. Then like a Jew he laugh'd and jeer'd, and told
me he lov'd me for your sake, and said what a faithful
servant you had been.
ITHAMORE. The more villain he to keep me thus: here's goodly
'parel, is there not?
PILIA-BORZA. To conclude, he gave me ten crowns.
ITHAMORE. But ten? I'll not leave him worth a grey groat.
Give me a ream of paper: we'll have a kingdom of gold
for't.   121
PILIA-BORZA. Write for five hundred crowns.
ITHAMORE. 'Sirrah Jew, as you love your life, send me five
hundred crowns, and give the bearer a hundred.' Tell him
I must have't.
PILIA-BORZA. I warrant your worship shall have't.
ITHAMORE. And if he ask why I demand so much, tell him I
scorn to write a line under a hundred crowns.
PILIA-BORZA. You'd make a rich poet, sir. I am gone.   *Exit.*
ITHAMORE. Take thou the money; spend it for my sake.   130
BELLAMIRA. 'Tis not thy money, but thyself I weigh.
Thus Bellamira esteems of gold;   [*Throw it aside.*]
                    But thus of thee. *Kiss him.*
ITHAMORE. That kiss again; she runs division of my lips. What
an eye she casts on me! It twinkles like a star.
BELLAMIRA. Come, my dear love, let's in and sleep together.
ITHAMORE. O, that ten thousand nights were put in one, that
we might sleep seven years together afore we wake!
BELLAMIRA. Come, amorous wag, first banquet, and then sleep.
                                                    [*Exeunt.*]

[*Scaena 3.*]
Enter Barabas, *reading a letter.*
BARABAS. 'Barabas, send me three hundred crowns'—
Plain Barabas! O that wicked courtesan!
He was not wont to call me Barabas—
'Or else I will confess'—ay, there it goes:
But, if I get him, *coupe de gorge* for that.
He sent a shaggy, totter'd, staring slave,
That when he speaks, draws out his grizzly beard,
And winds it twice or thrice about his ear;
Whose face has been a grindstone for men's swords;

His hands are hack'd, some fingers cut quite off,   10
Who when he speaks, grunts like a hog, and looks
Like one that is employ'd in catzery
And cross-biting; such a rogue
As is the husband to a hundred whores:
And I by him must send three hundred crowns!
Well, my hope is, he will not stay there still;
And when he comes—O, that he were but here!
      Enter Pilia-Borza.
PILIA-BORZA. Jew, I must ha' more gold.
BARABAS. Why, want'st thou any of thy tale?
PILIA-BORZA. No, but three hundred will not serve his turn.
BARABAS. Not serve his turn, sir?   21
PILIA-BORZA. No, sir; and therefore I must have five hundred
      more.
BARABAS. I'll rather—
PILIA-BORZA. O, good words, sir, and send it you were best;
      see, there's his letter.
BARABAS. Might he not as well come as send? Pray, bid him
      come and fetch it: what he writes for you, ye shall have
      straight.
PILIA-BORZA. Ay, and the rest too, or else—   30
BARABAS [*aside*]. I must make this villain away—Please you
      dine with me, sir, and you shall be most heartily (*Aside.*)
      poison'd.
PILIA-BORZA. No, God-a-mercy; shall I have these crowns?
BARABAS. I cannot do it; I have lost my keys.
PILIA-BORZA. O, if that be all, I can pick ope your locks.
BARABAS. Or climb up to my counting-house window: you
      know my meaning.
PILIA-BORZA. I know enough, and therefore talk not to me of
      your counting-house. The gold, or know, Jew, it is in my
      power to hang thee.   41
BARABAS. I am betray'd.
      'Tis not five hundred crowns that I esteem;
      I am not mov'd at that: this angers me,
      That he who knows I love him as myself
      Should write in this imperious vein. Why sir,
      You know I have no child, and unto whom
      Should I leave all, but unto Ithamore?
PILIA-BORZA. Here's many words, but no crowns: the crowns!
BARABAS. Commend me to him, sir, most humbly,   50
      And unto your good mistress as unknown.
PILIA-BORZA. Speak, shall I have 'em, sir?

BARABAS. Sir, here they are.
  [*Aside.*] O, that I should part with so much gold!—
  Here, take 'em, fellow, with as good a will—
  [*Aside.*] As I would see thee hang'd.—O, love stops my
    breath!
  Never lov'd man servant as I do Ithamore.
PILIA-BORZA. I know it, sir.
BARABAS. Pray when, sir, shall I see you at my house?
PILIA-BORZA. Soon enough to your cost, sir. Fare you well. 60
                                 Exit.
BARABAS. Nay to thine own cost, villain, if thou com'st.
  Was ever Jew tormented as I am?
  To have a shag-rag knave to come convey
  Three hundred crowns, and then five hundred crowns!
  Well, I must seek a means to rid 'em all,
  And presently; for in his villainy
  He will tell all he knows, and I shall die for't.
  I have it:
  I will in some disguise go see the slave,
  And how the villain revels with my gold.   *Exit.*

[*Scaena 4.*]
Enter Courtesan, Ithamore, Pilia-Borza.
BELLAMIRA. I'll pledge thee, love, and therefore drink it off.
ITHAMORE. Say'st thou me so? Have at it! And, do you hear?
                              [*Whispers to her.*]
BELLAMIRA. Go to, it shall be so.
ITHAMORE. Of that condition I will drink it up: here's to thee.
BELLAMIRA. Nay, I'll have all or none.
ITHAMORE. There, if thou lov'st me, do not leave a drop.
BELLAMIRA. Love thee? Fill me three glasses.
ITHAMORE. Three and fifty dozen: I'll pledge thee.
PILIA-BORZA. Knavely spoke, and like a knight-at-arms.
ITHAMORE. Hey, *Rivo Castiliano!* A man's a man.   10
BELLAMIRA. Now to the Jew.
ITHAMORE. Ha, to the Jew; and send me money you were best.
PILIA-BORZA. What wouldst thou do, if he should send thee
  none?
ITHAMORE. Do? nothing. But I know what I know: he's a
  murderer.
BELLAMIRA. I had not thought he had been so brave a man.
ITHAMORE. You knew Mathias and the Governor's son: he
  and I kill'd 'em both, and yet never touch'd 'em.
PILIA-BORZA. O bravely done!   20

ITHAMORE. I carried the broth that poison'd the nuns; and he and I, snicle hand to fast, strangled a friar.

BELLAMIRA. You two alone?

ITHAMORE. We two; and 'twas never known, nor never shall be for me.

PILIA-BORZA [*aside to* Bellamira]. This shall with me unto the Governor.

BELLAMIRA [*aside to* Pilia-Borza]. And fit it should: but first let's ha' more gold.

Come, gentle Ithamore, lie in my lap.

ITHAMORE. Love me little, love me long: let music rumble,
Whilst I in thy incony lap do tumble.   30

    Enter Barabas *with a lute, disguised.*

BELLAMIRA. A French musician! Come, let's hear your skill.

BARABAS. Must tuna my lute for sound, twang twang first.

ITHAMORE. Wilt drink, Frenchman? Here's to thee with a—pox on this drunken hiccup!

BARABAS. Gramercy, monsieur.

BELLAMIRA. Prithee, Pilia-Borza, bid the fiddler give me the posy in his hat there.

PILIA-BORZA. Sirrah, you must give my mistress your posy.

BARABAS. *A votre commandement, madame.*

BELLAMIRA. How sweet, my Ithamore, the flowers smell!   40

ITHAMORE. Like thy breath, sweetheart; no violet like 'em.

PILIA-BORZA. Foh! Methinks they stink like a hollyhock.

BARABAS [*aside*]. So, now I am reveng'd upon 'em all.
The scent thereof was death; I poison'd it.

ITHAMORE. Play, fiddler, or I'll cut your cat's guts into chitter-lings.

BARABAS. *Pardonnez moi*, be no in tune yet; so, now, now all be in.

ITHAMORE. Give him a crown, and fill me out more wine.

PILIA-BORZA. There's two crowns for thee; play.   50

BARABAS (*aside*). How liberally the villain gives me mine own gold!   [*He plays.*]

PILIA-BORZA. Methinks he fingers very well.

BARABAS (*aside*). So did you when you stole my gold.

PILIA-BORZA. How swift he runs!

BARABAS (*aside*). You run swifter when you threw my gold out of my window.

BELLAMIRA. Musician, hast been in Malta long?

BARABAS. Two, three, four month, madam.

ITHAMORE. Dost not know a Jew, one Barabas?   60

BARABAS. Very mush, monsieur, you no be his man?

PILIA-BORZA. His man?

ITHAMORE. .I scorn the peasant: tell him so.

BARABAS [aside]. He knows it already.

ITHAMORE. 'Tis a strange thing of that Jew: he lives upon pickled grasshoppers and sauc'd mushrumps.

BARABAS (aside). What a slave's this! The Governor feeds not as I do.

ITHAMORE. He never put on clean shirt since he was circumcis'd.

BARABAS (aside). O rascal! I change myself twice a day.   70

ITHAMORE. The hat he wears, Judas left under the elder when he hang'd himself.

BARABAS (aside). 'Twas sent me for a present from the Great Cham.

PILIA-BORZA. A masty slave he is. Whither now, fiddler?

BARABAS. *Pardonnez moi, monsieur*; me be no well.   *Exit.*

PILIA-BORZA. Farewell, fiddler. One letter more to the Jew.

BELLAMIRA. Prithee sweet love, one more, and write it sharp.

ITHAMORE. No, I'll send by word of mouth now. Bid him deliver thee a thousand crowns, by the same token that the nuns lov'd rice, that Friar Barnardine slept in his own clothes; any of 'em will do it.   82

PILIA-BORZA. Let me alone to urge it now I know the meaning.

ITHAMORE. The meaning has a meaning. Come, let's in:
To undo a Jew is charity, and not sin.   *Exeunt.*

Actus Quintus. [*Scaena 1.*]
Enter Governor, Knights, Martin del Bosco [*and* Officers].

FERENZE. Now, gentlemen, betake you to your arms,
And see that Malta be well fortified;
And it behoves you to be resolute,
For Calymath, having hover'd here so long,
Will win the town, or die before the walls.

1 KNIGHT. And die he shall, for we will never yield.
Enter Courtesan, Pilia-Borza.

BELLAMIRA. O bring us to the Governor.

FERNEZE. Away with her, she is a courtesan.

BELLAMIRA. Whate'er I am, yet, Governor, hear me speak.
I bring thee news by whom thy son was slain: 10
Mathias did it not; it was the Jew.

PILIA-BORZA. Who, besides the slaughter of these gentlemen,
Poison'd his own daughter and the nuns,
Strangled a friar, and I know not what
Mischief beside.

FERNEZE.   Had we but proof of this—

BELLAMIRA. Strong proof, my lord: his man's now at my
    lodging
That was his agent; he'll confess it all.

FERNEZE. Go fetch him straight.   [*Exeunt* Officers.]
                        I always fear'd that Jew.
    Enter [Officers *with*] Barabas *and* Ithamore.

BARABAS. I'll go alone; dogs, do not hale me thus.

ITHAMORE. Nor me neither; I cannot outrun you, constable. O,
    my belly!   21

BARABAS. One dram of powder more had made all sure:
What a damn'd slave was I!

FERNEZE. Make fires, heat irons, let the rack be fetch'd.

I KNIGHT. Nay, stay, my lord; 't may be he will confess.

BARABAS. Confess; what mean you, lords? Who should confess?

FERNEZE. Thou and thy Turk; 'twas you that slew my son.

ITHAMORE. Guilty, my lord, I confess. Your son and Mathias
    were both contracted unto Abigail: 'a forg'd a counterfeit
    challenge.   30

BARABAS. Who carried that challenge?

ITHAMORE. I carried it, I confess; but who writ it? Marry, even
    he that strangled Barnardine, poison'd the nuns and his own
    daughter.

FERNEZE. Away with him, his sight is death to me.

BARABAS. For what? You men of Malta, hear me speak.
She is a courtesan, and he a thief,
And he my bondman; let me have law,
For none of this can prejudice my life.

FERNEZE. Once more, away with him; you shall have law.

BARABAS. Devils, do your worst. I'll live in spite of you.   41
As these have spoke, so be it to their souls!—
I hope the poison'd flowers will work anon.
    [*Exeunt* Officers *with* Barabas *and* Ithamore; Bellamira,
    and Pilia-Borza.]
    Enter Katharine.

KATHARINE. Was my Mathias murder'd by the Jew?
Ferneze, 'twas thy son that murder'd him.

FERNEZE. Be patient, gentle madam; it was he;
He forg'd the daring challenge made them fight.

KATHARINE. Where is the Jew? Where is that murderer?

FERNEZE. In prison, till the law has pass'd on him.
    Enter Officer.

OFFICER. My lord, the courtesan and her man are dead;   50
So is the Turk and Barabas the Jew.

FERNEZE. Dead?

OFFICER.   Dead, my lord, and here they bring his body.

BOSCO. This sudden death of his is very strange.

   [*Enter* Officers, *carrying* Barabas *as dead.*]

FERNEZE. Wonder not at it, sir; the heavens are just.
   Their deaths were like their lives; then think not of 'em.
   Since they are dead, let them be buried.
   For the Jew's body, throw that o'er the walls,
   To be a prey for vultures and wild beasts.
   So, now away and fortify the town.

                                 Exeunt. [*Manet* Barabas.]

BARABAS. What, all alone? Well fare, sleepy drink!   60
   I'll be reveng'd on this accursed town;
   For by my means Calymath shall enter in.
   I'll help to slay their children and their wives,
   To fire the churches, pull their houses down,
   Take my goods too, and seize upon my lands.
   I hope to see the Governor a slave,
   And, rowing in a galley, whipp'd to death.
   Enter Calymath, Bassoes, Turks.

CALYMATH. Whom have we there? A spy?

BARABAS. Yes, my good lord, one that can spy a place   70
   Where you may enter, and surprise the town.
   My name is Barabas; I am a Jew.

CALYMATH. Art thou that Jew whose goods we heard were sold
   For tribute money?

BARABAS.   The very same, my lord:
   And since that time they have hir'd a slave, my man,
   To accuse me of a thousand villainies.
   I was imprisoned, but scap'd their hands.

CALYMATH. Didst break prison?

BARABAS. No, no:
   I drank of poppy and cold mandrake juice;   80
   And being asleep, belike they thought me dead,
   And threw me o'er the walls: so, or how else,
   The Jew is here, and rests at your command.

CALYMATH. 'Twas bravely done. But tell me, Barabas,
   Canst thou, as thou report'st, make Malta ours?

BARABAS. Fear not, my lord, for here, against the sconce,
   The rock is hollow, and of purpose digg'd
   To make a passage for the running streams
   And common channels of the city.
   Now, whilst you give assault unto the walls,   90
   I'll lead five hundred soldiers through the vault,

And rise with them i'th'middle of the town,
Open the gates for you to enter in,
And by this means the city is your own.

CALYMATH. If this be true, I'll make thee Governor.

BARABAS. And if it be not true, then let me die.

CALYMATH. Thou'st doom'd thyself. Assault it presently.

Exeunt.

[*Scaena 2.*]

Alarms. Enter Turks, Barabas; Governor *and* Knights
prisoners.

CALYMATH. Now vail your pride, you captive Christians,
And kneel for mercy to your conquering foe.
Now where's the hope you had of haughty Spain?
Ferneze, speak; had it not been much better
To keep thy promise than be thus surpris'd?

FERNEZE. What should I say? We are captives, and must yield.

CALYMATH. Ay, villains, you must yield, and under Turkish
yokes
Shall groaning bear the burden of our ire.
And Barabas, as erst we promis'd thee,
For thy desert we make thee Governor;   10
Use them at thy discretion.

BARABAS.   Thanks, my lord.

FERNEZE. O fatal day, to fall into the hands
Of such a traitor and unhallowed Jew!
What greater misery could heaven inflict?

CALYMATH. 'Tis our command; and, Barabas, we give,
To guard thy person, these our janizaries:
Intreat them well, as we have used thee.
And now, brave bassoes, come; we'll walk about
The ruin'd town, and see the wrack we made.
Farewell brave Jew, farewell great Barabas.   20

Exeunt [Calymath *and* Bassoes].

BARABAS. May all good fortune follow Calymath!
And now, as entrance to our safety,
To prison with the Governor and these
Captains, his consorts and confederates.

FERNEZE. O villain, heaven will be reveng'd on thee.

Exeunt. [*Manet* Barabas].

BARABAS. Away, no more; let him not trouble me.
Thus hast thou gotten, by thy policy,
No simple place, no small authority:
I now am Governor of Malta; true.

[384]

But Malta hates me, and in hating me
My life's in danger; and what boots it thee,   30
Poor Barabas, to be the Governor,
Whenas thy life shall be at their command?
No, Barabas, this must be look'd into;
And, since by wrong thou got'st authority,
Maintain it bravely by firm policy;
At least, unprofitably lose it not.
For he that liveth in authority,
And neither gets him friends nor fills his bags,
Lives like the ass that Aesop speaketh of
That labours with a load of bread and wine   40
And leaves it off to snap on thistle-tops.
But Barabas will be more circumspect.
Begin betimes; Occasion's bald behind:
Slip not thine opportunity, for fear too late
Thou seek'st for much, but canst not compass it.
Within here!

      Enter [Governor] *with a* Guard.

FERNEZE.   My lord?
BARABAS.   Ay, 'lord'; thus slaves will learn.
Now, Governor—stand by there, wait within.

                           [*Exeunt* Guard.]

This is the reason that I sent for thee:
Thou seest thy life and Malta's happiness
Are at my arbitrement; and Barabas   50
At his discretion may dispose of both.
Now tell me, Governor, and plainly too,
What think'st thou shall become of it and thee?
FERNEZE. This, Barabas: since things are in thy power,
I see no reason but of Malta's wrack,
Nor hope of thee but extreme cruelty.
Nor fear I death, nor will I flatter thee.
BARABAS. Governor, good words, be not so furious.
'Tis not thy life which can avail me aught;
Yet you do live, and live, for me, you shall.   60
And as for Malta's ruin, think you not
'Twere slender policy for Barabas
To dispossess himself of such a place?
For sith, as once you said, within this isle,
In Malta here, that I have got my goods,
And in this city still have had success,
And now at length am grown your Governor,
Yourselves shall see it shall not be forgot;

For as a friend not known but in distress,
I'll rear up Malta now remediless.   70
FERNEZE. Will Barabas recover Malta's loss?
Will Barabas be good to Christians?
BARABAS. What wilt thou give me, Governor, to procure
A dissolution of the slavish bands
Wherein the Turk hath yok'd your land and you?
What will you give me if I render you
The life of Calymath, surprise his men,
And in an out-house of the city shut
His soldiers, till I have consum'd 'em all with fire?
What will you give him that procureth this?   80
FERNEZE. Do but bring this to pass which thou pretendest,
Deal truly with us as thou intimatest,
And I will send amongst the citizens,
And by my letters privately procure
Great sums of money for thy recompense:
Nay more, do this, and live thou Governor still.
BARABAS. Nay, do thou this, Ferneze, and be free.
Governor, I enlarge thee. Live with me;
Go walk about the city, see thy friends.
Tush, send not letters to 'em; go thy self,   90
And let me see what money thou canst make.
Here is my hand that I'll set Malta free.
And thus we cast it: to a solemn feast
I will invite young Selim-Calymath,
Where be thou present, only to perform
One stratagem that I'll impart to thee,
Wherein no danger shall betide thy life,
And I will warrant Malta free for ever.
FERNEZE. Here is my hand; believe me, Barabas,
I will be there, and do as thou desirest.   100
When is the time?
BARABAS.   Governor, presently.
For Calymath, when he hath view'd the town,
Will take his leave and sail toward Ottoman.
FERNEZE. Then will I, Barabas, about this coin,
And bring it with me to thee in the evening.
BARABAS. Do so, but fail not. Now farewell, Ferneze.
                                        [*Exit* Ferneze.]

And thus far roundly goes the business:
Thus loving neither, will I live with both,
Making a profit of my policy;
And he from whom my most advantage comes,   110

Shall be my friend.
This is the life we Jews are us'd to lead;
And reason too, for Christians do the like.
Well, now about effecting this device:
First, to surprise great Selim's soldiers,
And then to make provision for the feast,
That at one instant all things may be done.
My policy detests prevention.
To what event my secret purpose drives,   119
I know; and they shall witness with their lives.   *Exit.*

[Scaena 3.]

Enter Calymath, Bassoes.

CALYMATH. Thus have we view'd the city, seen the sack,
And caus'd the ruins to be new repair'd
Which with our bombards' shot and basilisk
We rent in sunder at our entry,
Two lofty turrets that command the town.
And now I see the situation,
And how secure this conquer'd island stands,
Environ'd with the Mediterranean sea,
Strong countermur'd with other petty isles
And toward Calabria, back'd by Sicily   10
Where Syracusian Dionysius reign'd,
I wonder how it could be conquer'd thus.
    Enter a Messenger.

MESSENGER. From Barabas, Malta's Governor, I bring
A message unto mighty Calymath:
Hearing his sovereign was bound for sea,
To sail to Turkey, to great Ottoman,
He humbly would entreat your majesty
To come and see his homely citadel,
And banquet with him ere thou leav'st the isle.

CALYMATH. To banquet with him in his citadel?   20
I fear me, messenger, to feast my train
Within a town of war so lately pillag'd,
Will be too costly and too troublesome;
Yet would I gladly visit Barabas,
For well has Barabas deserv'd of us.

MESSENGER. Selim, for that, thus saith the Governor:
That he hath in store a pearl so big,
So precious, and withal so orient,
As, be it valued but indifferently,
The price thereof will serve to entertain   30

Selim and all his soldiers for a month.
Therefore he humbly would entreat your highness
Not to depart till he has feasted you.
CALYMATH. I cannot feast my men in Malta walls,
    Except he place his tables in the streets.
MESSENGER. Know, Selim, that there is a monastery
    Which standeth as an out-house to the town;
    There will he banquet them, but thee at home,
    With all thy bassoes and brave followers.
CALYMATH. Well, tell the Governor we grant his suit;   40
    We'll in this summer evening feast with him.
MESSENGER. I shall, my lord.   *Exit.*
CALYMATH. And now, bold bassoes, let us to our tents,
    And meditate how we may grace us best
    To solemnize our Governor's great feast.   *Exeunt.*

[*Scaena 4.*]
Enter Governor, Knights, del Bosco.
FERNEZE. In this, my countrymen, be rul'd by me:
    Have special care that no man sally forth
    Till you shall hear a culverin discharg'd
    By him that bears the linstock, kindled thus;
    Then issue out and come to rescue me,
    For happily I shall be in distress,
    Or you released of this servitude.
1 KNIGHT. Rather than thus to live as Turkish thralls
    What will we not adventure?
FERNEZE. On, then; be gone.
KNIGHTS.   Farewell, grave Governor. [*Exeunt.*]

[*Scaena 5.*]
Enter [Barabas] *with a hammer, above, very busy* [*and*
Carpenters].
BARABAS. How stand the cords? How hang these hinges, fast?
    Are all the cranes and pulleys sure?
CARPENTER.   All fast.
BARABAS. Leave nothing loose, all levell'd to my mind.
    Why, now I see that you have art indeed.
    There, carpenters, divide that gold amongst you.
    Go, swill in bowls of sack and muscadine;
    Down to the cellar, taste of all my wines.
CARPENTER. We shall, my lord, and thank you.   *Exeunt.*
BARABAS. And if you like them, drink your fill and die;
    For so I live, perish may all the world.   10

Now Selim-Calymath, return me word
That thou wilt come, and I am satisfied.
    Enter Messenger.
Now, sirrah; what, will he come?

MESSENGER. He will; and has commanded all his men
To come ashore, and march through Malta streets,
That thou mayst feast them in thy citadel.

BARABAS. Then now are all things as my wish would have 'em;
There wanteth nothing but the Governor's pelf;
And see, he brings it.
    Enter Governor.

                        Now, Governor, the sum.   20

FERNEZE. With free consent, a hundred thousand pounds.

BARABAS. Pounds say'st thou, Governor? Well, since it is no
    more,
I'll satisfy myself with that; nay, keep it still,
For if I keep not promise, trust not me.
And Governor, now partake my policy:
First, for his army, they are sent before,
Enter'd the monastery, and underneath
In several places are field-pieces pitch'd,
Bombards, whole barrels full of gunpowder,
That on the sudden shall dissever it   30
And batter all the stones about their ears,
Whence none can possibly escape alive.
Now as for Calymath and his consorts,
Here have I made a dainty gallery,
The floor whereof, this cable being cut,
Doth fall asunder, so that it doth sink
Into a deep pit past recovery.
Here, hold that knife; and when thou seest he comes,
And with his bassoes shall be blithely set,
A warning-piece shall be shot off from the tower,   40
To give thee knowledge when to cut the cord,
And fire the house. Say, will not this be brave?

FERNEZE. O, excellent! Here, hold thee, Barabas;
I trust thy word; take what I promis'd thee.

BARABAS. No, Governor, I'll satisfy thee first.
Thou shalt not live in doubt of anything.
Stand close, for here they come.   [Ferneze *retires.*]
                      Why, is not this
A kingly kind of trade, to purchase towns
By treachery, and sell 'em by deceit?
Now tell me, worldlings, underneath the sun   50

If greater falsehood ever has been done.
   Enter Calymath *and* Bassoes.
CALYMATH. Come, my companion bassoes: see, I pray,
   How busy Barabas is there above
   To entertain us in his gallery.
   Let us salute him. Save thee, Barabas.
BARABAS. Welcome, great Calymath.
FERNEZE. How the slave jeers at him!
BARABAS. Will't please thee, mighty Selim-Calymath,
   To ascend our homely stairs?
CALYMATH.   Ay, Barabas.
   Come, bassoes, ascend.   60
FERNEZE [*coming forward*]. Stay, Calymath;
   For I will show thee greater courtesy
   Than Barabas would have afforded thee.
KNIGHT [*within*]. Sound a charge there!
   A charge, the cable cut. A cauldron discovered [into which
   Barabas *falls*].
   [*Enter* Knights *and* del Bosco.]
CALYMATH. How now, what means this?
BARABAS. Help, help me, Christians, help.
FERNEZE. See, Calymath, this was devis'd for thee.
CALYMATH. Treason, treason! Bassoes, fly.
FERNEZE. No, Selim, do not fly.
   See his end first, and fly then if thou canst.   70
BARABAS. O help me, Selim, help me, Christians.
   Governor, why stand you all so pitiless?
FERNEZE. Should I in pity of thy plaints or thee,
   Accursed Barabas, base Jew, relent?
   No, thus I'll see thy treachery repaid,
   But wish thou hadst behav'd thee otherwise.
BARABAS. You will not help me, then?
FERNEZE.   No, villain, no.
BARABAS. And villains, know you cannot help me now.
   Then, Barabas, breathe forth thy latest fate,
   And in the fury of thy torments strive   80
   To end thy life with resolution.
   Know, Governor, 'twas I that slew thy son;
   I fram'd the challenge that did make them meet.
   Know, Calymath, I aim'd thy overthrow;
   And had I but escap'd this stratagem,
   I would have brought confusion on you all,
   Damn'd Christians, dogs, and Turkish infidels.
   But now begins the extremity of heat

To pinch me with intolerable pangs.
Die life, fly soul, tongue curse thy fill, and die.   90
                                    [*Dies.*]

CALYMATH. Tell me, you Christians, what doth this portend?
FERNEZE. This train he laid to have entrapp'd thy life.
Now, Selim, note the unhallowed deeds of Jews:
Thus he determin'd to have handled thee,
But I have rather chose to save thy life.
CALYMATH. Was this the banquet he prepar'd for us?
Let's hence, lest further mischief be pretended.
FERNEZE. Nay, Selim, stay, for since we have thee here,
We will not let thee part so suddenly.
Besides, if we should let thee go, all's one,   100
For with thy galleys couldst thou not get hence,
Without fresh men to rig and furnish them.
CALYMATH. Tush, Governor, take thou no care for that.
My men are all aboard,
And do attend my coming there by this.
FERNEZE. Why, heard'st thou not the trumpet sound a charge?
CALYMATH. Yes, what of that?
FERNEZE.   Why, then the house was fir'd,
Blown up, and all thy soldiers massacred.
CALYMATH. O monstrous treason!
FERNEZE.   A Jew's courtesy.
For he that did by treason work our fall   110
By treason hath delivered thee to us.
Know therefore, till thy father hath made good
The ruins done to Malta and to us,
Thou canst not part; for Malta shall be freed,
Or Selim ne'er return to Ottoman.
CALYMATH. Nay rather, Christians, let me go to Turkey,
In person there to mediate your peace.
To keep me here will naught advantage you.
FERNEZE. Content thee, Calymath, here thou must stay,
And live in Malta prisoner; for come all the world   120
To rescue thee, so will we guard us now
As sooner shall they drink the ocean dry
Than conquer Malta, or endanger us.
So march away; and let due praise be given,
Neither to Fate nor Fortune, but to Heaven.

                                         [*Exeunt.*]

FINIS.

Poems, etc.

Illustrissimae Heroinae Mariae Penbrokiae

Thomas Watson's *Amintae Gaudia* (1592) was entered on the Stationers' Register on 10 November 1592, some two months after his death. The Latin dedicatory epistle to Mary, Countess of Pembroke, is signed 'C.M.'. Marlowe was a friend of Watson's.

Illustrissimae Heroinae Omnibus
et Animi et Corporis Dotibus Ornatissimae,
Mariae Penbrokiae Comitissae

Laurigera stirpe prognata Delia, Sidnaei vatis Apollinei genuina soror, alma litteratum parens, ad cuius immaculatos amplexus confugit virtus, barbariei et ignorantiae impetu violata, ut olim a Threicio tyranno Philomela; poetarum nostri temporis, ingeniorumque omnium felicissime pullulantium, Musa; Dia proles, quae iam rudi calamo spiritus infundis elati furoris, quibus ipse misellus plus mihi videor praestare posse quam cruda nostra indoles proferre solet: dignare posthumo huic Amyntae ut tuo adoptivo filio patrocinari; eoque magis quod moribundus pater illius tutelam humillime tibi legaverat. Et licet illustre nomen tuum non solum apud nos, sed exteras etiam nationes, latius propagatum est quam aut unquam possit aeruginosa Temporis vetustate aboleri, aut mortalium encomiis augeri—quomodo enim quicquam possit esse infinito plus?—multorum tamen camenis, quasi siderum diademate redimita Ariadne, noli hunc purum Phoebi sacerdotem, stellam alteram coronae tuae largientem, aspernari; sed animi candore quem sator hominum atque deorum Iupiter praenobili familiae tuae quasi haereditarium alligavit accipe et tuere. Sic nos, quorum opes tenuissimae littorea sunt Myrtus Veneris Nymphaeque Peneiae semper virens coma, prima quaque poematis pagina, te Musarum dominam in auxilium invocabimus. Tua denique virtus, quae virtutem ipsam, ipsam quoque aeternitatem superabit.

Honoris tui studiosissimus, C.M.

To the most illustrious lady,
endowed with all gifts both of mind and of body,
Mary, Countess of Pembroke

Delia, sprung from a laurel-crowned race, true sister of Sidney the bard of Apollo, generous parent of letters, in whose blameless embraces virtue, assailed by the blows of barbarism and ignorance, has taken refuge, as once Philomela from the Thracian tyrant; muse of the poets of our age, and of all its most happily flourishing wits; offspring of the gods, you who imbue my yet rude quill with the spirit of a lofty rage; by whose aid, wretch as I am, I believe that I can achieve more than my unripe natural talents are accustomed to bring forth: deign to be patroness to this posthumous Amyntas as to your adopted son; the more so that the father, on his death-bed, in all humility named you as his guardian. And though your illustrious name is too widely published, not only in this land but also among other nations, ever to be destroyed by the rust of long ages, or to be increased by the praise of mortals—for how can anything be more than infinite?—yet, adorned as you are with the verses of many, as Ariadne with a diadem of stars, do not scorn this pure priest of Phoebus when he bestows another star on your crown; but accept and protect it, with the generosity which Jove, the father of men and of gods, has linked with your most noble family as a hereditary gift. So shall I, whose scanty riches are but the shore-myrtle of Venus and the evergreen tresses of the Peneian nymph [Daphne], call you to my aid on the first page of every poem, as mistress of the Muses. In short, your virtue, which surpasses virtue itself, will likewise surpass eternity itself.

Most zealous to do you honour, C.M.

Hero and Leander

Hero and Leander was entered to John Wolf in the Stationers' Register on 28 September 1593 as '*HERO and LEANDER* beinge an amorous poem devised by CHRISTOPHER MARLOW'. A (quarto-form) octavo published by Edward Blount (who contributed the dedicatory epistle) appeared in 1598. On 2 March of the same year Blount assigned his rights to Paul Linley, whose own (quarto-form) octavo of 1598 reprints Blount's, but adds George Chapman's completion of the poem. Linley's rights were assigned on 26 June 1600 to John Flasket, who published his edition the same year. Other editions followed thick and fast in 1606, 1609, 1613, 1617, 1622, 1629, 1637.

The date of composition is uncertain. Henry Petowe, who published his own inept continuation of the poem in 1598, is a very unreliable authority for the belief that Marlowe was working on *Hero and Leander* at the time of his death.

A poem in Greek by Musaeus, a fifth-century Alexandrian, is the ultimate source, though Marlowe may well have used an intermediate Latin translation, such as that in the parallel-text edition of Marcus Musurus. Marlowe treated Musaeus with great freedom, adding such significant new features as Leander's ingenuousness, Hero's shame, and the importunity of Neptune. Ovid's *Heroides* XVIII and XIX, which are also about Hero and Leander, cannot properly be called sources.

To the Right Worshipful,
Sir Thomas Walsingham, Knight.

Sir: we think not ourselves discharged of the duty we owe
to our friend when we have brought the breathless body to
the earth; for albeit the eye there taketh his ever farewell
of that beloved object, yet the impression of the man that
hath been dear unto us, living an after life in our memory,
there putteth us in mind of farther obsequies due unto the
deceased. And namely, of the performance of whatsoever
we may judge shall make to his living credit, and to the
effecting of his determinations prevented by the stroke of
death. By these meditations (as by an intellectual will)   10
I suppose myself executor to the unhappily deceased
author of this poem, upon whom knowing that in his life-
time you bestowed many kind favours, entertaining the
parts of reckoning and worth which you found in him,
with good countenance and liberal affection: I cannot but
see so far into the will of him dead, but whatsoever issue
of his brain should chance to come abroad, that the first
breath it should take might be the gentle air of your liking;
for since his self had been accustomed thereunto, it would
prove more agreeable and thriving to his right children   20
than any other foster countenance whatsoever. At this
time seeing that this unfinished tragedy happens under my
hands to be imprinted, of a double duty, the one to yourself, the other to the deceased, I present the same to your
most favourable allowance, off'ring my utmost self now
and ever to be ready, at your worship's disposing.

Edward Blount

Hero and Leander

I

On Hellespont guilty of true-loves' blood,
In view and opposite two cities stood,
Sea-borderers, disjoin'd by Neptune's might:
The one Abydos, the other Sestos hight.
At Sestos Hero dwelt; Hero the fair,
Whom young Apollo courted for her hair,
And off'red as a dower his burning throne,
Where she should sit for men to gaze upon.
The outside of her garments were of lawn,
The lining purple silk, with gilt stars drawn;   10
Her wide sleeves green, and bordered with a grove,
Where Venus in her naked glory strove
To please the careless and disdainful eyes
Of proud Adonis that before her lies.
Her kirtle blue, whereon was many a stain
Made with the blood of wretched lovers slain.
Upon her head she ware a myrtle wreath,
From whence her veil reach'd to the ground beneath.
Her veil was artificial flowers and leaves
Whose workmanship both man and beast deceives.   20
Many would praise the sweet smell as she pass'd,
When 'twas the odour which her breath forth cast;
And there for honey bees have sought in vain,
And, beat from thence, have lighted there again.
About her neck hung chains of pebble-stone,
Which light'ned by her neck, like diamonds shone.
She ware no gloves, for neither sun nor wind
Would burn or parch her hands, but to her mind
Or warm or cool them, for they took delight
To play upon those hands, they were so white.   30
Buskins of shells all silvered used she,
And branch'd with blushing coral to the knee,
Where sparrows perch'd, of hollow pearl and gold,
Such as the world would wonder to behold.
Those with sweet water oft her handmaid fills,
Which as she went would chirrup through the bills.

Some say for her the fairest Cupid pin'd,
And looking in her face, was strooken blind.
But this is true, so like was one the other,
As he imagin'd Hero was his mother,   40
And oftentimes into her bosom flew,
About her naked neck his bare arms threw,
And laid his childish head upon her breast,
And with still panting rock'd, there took his rest.
So lovely fair was Hero, Venus' nun,
As Nature wept, thinking she was undone,
Because she took more from her than she left,
And of such wondrous beauty her bereft;
Therefore, in sign her treasure suff'red wrack,
Since Hero's time hath half the world been black.   50
Amorous Leander, beautiful and young
(Whose tragedy divine Musaeus sung)
Dwelt at Abydos; since him dwelt there none
For whom succeeding times make greater moan.
His dangling tresses that were never shorn,
Had they been cut, and unto Colchos borne,
Would have allur'd the vent'rous youth of Greece
To hazard more than for the Golden Fleece.
Fair Cynthia wish'd his arms might be her sphere;
Grief makes her pale because she moves not there.   60
His body was as straight as Circes' wand;
Jove might have sipp'd out nectar from his hand.
Even as delicious meat is to the taste,
So was his neck in touching, and surpass'd
The white of Pelops' shoulder. I could tell ye
How smooth his breast was, and how white his belly,
And whose immortal fingers did imprint
That heavenly path with many a curious dint
That runs along his back, but my rude pen
Can hardly blazon forth the loves of men,   70
Much less of powerful gods; let it suffice
That my slack muse sings of Leander's eyes,
Those orient cheeks and lips, exceeding his
That leapt into the water for a kiss
Of his own shadow, and despising many,
Died ere he could enjoy the love of any.
Had wild Hippolytus Leander seen,
Enamoured of his beauty had he been;
His presence made the rudest peasant melt,
That in the vast uplandish country dwelt.   80

The barbarous Thracian soldier, mov'd with nought,
Was mov'd with him, and for his favour sought.
Some swore he was a maid in man's attire,
For in his looks were all that men desire,
A pleasant smiling cheek, a speaking eye,
A brow for love to banquet royally;
And such as knew he was a man would say,
'Leander, thou art made for amorous play:
Why art thou not in love, and lov'd of all?
Though thou be fair, yet be not thine own thrall.'   90
    The men of wealthy Sestos, every year,
For his sake whom their goddess held so dear,
Rose-cheek'd Adonis, kept a solemn feast.
Thither resorted many a wand'ring guest
To meet their loves; such as had none at all
Came lovers home from this great festival.
For every street like to a firmament
Glistered with breathing stars, who where they went
Frighted the melancholy earth, which deem'd
Eternal heaven to burn, for so it seem'd   100
As if another Phaethon had got
The guidance of the sun's rich chariot.
But far above the loveliest Hero shin'd,
And stole away th'enchanted gazer's mind;
For like sea-nymphs' inveigling harmony,
So was her beauty to the standers by.
Nor that night-wand'ring, pale and wat'ry star,
When yawning dragons draw her thirling car
From Latmus mount up to the gloomy sky,
Where crown'd with blazing light and majesty   110
She proudly sits, more overrules the flood
Than she the hearts of those that near her stood.
Even as, when gaudy nymphs pursue the chase,
Wretched Ixion's shaggy-footed race,
Incens'd with savage heat, gallop amain
From steep pine-bearing mountains to the plain,
So ran the people forth to gaze upon her,
And all that view'd her were enamour'd on her.
And as in fury of a dreadful fight,
Their fellows being slain or put to flight,   120
Poor soldiers stand with fear of death dead-strooken,
So at her presence all surpris'd and tooken
Await the sentence of her scornful eyes;
He whom she favours lives, the other dies.

There might you see one sigh, another rage,
And some (their violent passions to assuage)
Compile sharp satires, but alas too late,
For faithful love will never turn to hate.
And many seeing great princes were denied,
Pin'd as they went, and thinking on her died.   130
On this feast day, O cursed day and hour,
Went Hero thorough Sestos, from her tower
To Venus' temple, where unhappily,
As after chanc'd, they did each other spy.
So fair a church as this had Venus none;
The walls were of discoloured jasper stone,
Wherein was Proteus carved, and o'erhead
A lively vine of green sea-agate spread;
Where by one hand light-headed Bacchus hung,
And with the other, wine from grapes outwrung.   140
Of crystal shining fair the pavement was;
The town of Sestos call'd it Venus' glass.
There might you see the gods in sundry shapes,
Committing heady riots, incest, rapes:
For know that underneath this radiant floor
Was Danae's statue in a brazen tower,
Jove slyly stealing from his sister's bed,
To dally with Idalian Ganymede,
Or for his love Europa bellowing loud,
Or tumbling with the Rainbow in a cloud;   150
Blood-quaffing Mars, heaving the iron net
Which limping Vulcan and his Cyclops set;
Love kindling fire, to burn such towns as Troy;
Silvanus weeping for the lovely boy
That now is turn'd into a cypress tree,
Under whose shade the wood-gods love to be.
And in the midst a silver altar stood;
There Hero sacrificing turtles' blood,
Vail'd to the ground, vailing her eyelids close,
And modestly they opened as she rose.   160
Thence flew Love's arrow with the golden head,
And thus Leander was enamoured.
Stone still he stood, and evermore he gazed,
Till with the fire that from his count'nance blazed
Relenting Hero's gentle heart was strook:
Such force and virtue hath an amorous look.
    It lies not in our power to love or hate,
For will in us is overrul'd by fate.

[404]

When two are stripp'd, long ere the course begin
We wish that one should lose, the other win; 170
And one especially do we affect
Of two gold ingots like in each respect.
The reason no man knows: let it suffice,
What we behold is censur'd by our eyes.
Where both deliberate, the love is slight;
Who ever lov'd, that lov'd not at first sight?
He kneel'd, but unto her devoutly pray'd;
Chaste Hero to herself thus softly said:
'Were I the saint he worships, I would hear him',
And as she spake those words, came somewhat near him. 180
He started up, she blush'd as one asham'd;
Wherewith Leander much more was inflam'd.
He touch'd her hand, in touching it she trembled:
Love deeply grounded hardly is dissembled.
These lovers parled by the touch of hands;
True love is mute, and oft amazed stands.
Thus while dumb signs their yielding hearts entangled,
The air with sparks of living fire was spangled,
And Night, deep-drench'd in misty Acheron,
Heav'd up her head, and half the world upon 190
Breath'd darkness forth (dark night is Cupid's day).
And now begins Leander to display
Love's holy fire, with words, with sighs and tears,
Which like sweet music ent'red Hero's ears,
And yet at every word she turn'd aside,
And always cut him off as he replied.
At last, like to a bold sharp sophister,
With cheerful hope thus he accosted her.
'Fair creature, let me speak without offence,
I would my rude words had the influence 200
To lead thy thoughts, as thy fair looks do mine,
Then shouldst thou be his prisoner who is thine.
Be not unkind and fair; misshapen stuff
Are of behaviour boisterous and rough.
O shun me not, but hear me ere you go,
God knows I cannot force love, as you do.
My words shall be as spotless as my youth,
Full of simplicity and naked truth.
This sacrifice (whose sweet perfume descending
From Venus' altar to your footsteps bending) 210
Doth testify that you exceed her far
To whom you offer, and whose nun you are.

[405]

Why should you worship her? Her you surpass
As much as sparkling diamonds flaring glass.
A diamond set in lead his worth retains;
A heavenly nymph, belov'd of human swains,
Receives no blemish, but oft-times more grace,
Which makes me hope, although I am but base,
Base in respect of thee, divine and pure,
Dutiful service may thy love procure;   220
And I in duty will excel all other,
As thou in beauty dost exceed Love's mother.
Nor heaven, nor thou, were made to gaze upon;
As heaven preserves all things, so save thou one.
A stately builded ship, well-rigg'd and tall,
The ocean maketh more majestical:
Why vowest thou then to live in Sestos here,
Who on Love's seas more glorious wouldst appear?
Like untun'd golden strings all women are,
Which long time lie untouch'd will harshly jar.   230
Vessels of brass oft handled brightly shine;
What difference betwixt the richest mine
And basest mould but use? For both, not us'd,
Are of like worth. Then treasure is abus'd
When misers keep it; being put to loan,
In time it will return us two for one.
Rich robes themselves and others do adorn;
Neither themselves nor others, if not worn.
Who builds a palace and rams up the gate,
Shall see it ruinous and desolate.   240
Ah, simple Hero, learn thyself to cherish;
Lone women like to empty houses perish.
Less sins the poor rich man that starves himself
In heaping up a mass of drossy pelf
Than such as you: his golden earth remains,
Which, after his decease, some other gains;
But this fair gem, sweet in the loss alone,
When you fleet hence, can be bequeath'd to none.
Or if it could, down from th'enamell'd sky
All heaven would come to claim this legacy,   250
And with intestine broils the world destroy,
And quite confound nature's sweet harmony.
Well therefore by the gods decreed it is,
We human creatures should enjoy that bliss.
One is no number; maids are nothing, then,
Without the sweet society of men.

Wilt thou live single still? One shalt thou be,
Though never-singling Hymen couple thee.
Wild savages that drink of running springs
Think water far excels all earthly things: 260
But they that daily taste neat wine, despise it.
Virginity, albeit some highly prize it,
Compar'd with marriage, had you tried them both,
Differs as much as wine and water doth.
Base bullion for the stamp's sake we allow,
Even so for men's impression do we you.
By which alone, our reverend fathers say,
Women receive perfection every way.
This idol which you term virginity
Is neither essence subject to the eye,   270
No, nor to any one exterior sense,
Nor hath it any place of residence,
Nor is't of earth or mould celestial,
Or capable of any form at all.
Of that which hath no being, do not boast;
Things that are not at all, are never lost.
Men foolishly do call it virtuous:
What virtue is it that is born with us?
Much less can honour be ascrib'd thereto;
Honour is purchas'd by the deeds we do.   280
Believe me, Hero, honour is not won
Until some honourable deed be done.
Seek you for chastity, immortal fame,
And know that some have wrong'd Diana's name?
Whose name is it, if she be false or not,
So she be fair, but some vile tongues will blot?
But you are fair (ay me) so wondrous fair,
So young, so gentle, and so debonair,
As Greece will think, if thus you live alone,
Some one or other keeps you as his own.   290
Then, Hero, hate me not, nor from me fly,
To follow swiftly blasting infamy.
Perhaps thy sacred priesthood makes thee loth,
Tell me, to whom mad'st thou that heedless oath?'
   'To Venus', answered she, and as she spake,
Forth from those two tralucent cisterns brake
A stream of liquid pearl, which down her face
Made milk-white paths, whereon the gods might trace
To Jove's high court. He thus replied: 'The rites
In which love's beauteous empress most delights,   300

Are banquets, Doric music, midnight revel,
Plays, masques, and all that stern age counteth evil.
Thee as a holy idiot doth she scorn,
For thou in vowing chastity hast sworn
To rob her name and honour, and thereby
Commit'st a sin far worse than perjury,
Even sacrilege against her deity,
Through regular and formal purity.
To expiate which sin, kiss and shake hands,
Such sacrifice as this Venus demands.'   310
    Thereat she smil'd, and did deny him so
As put thereby yet might he hope for mo.
Which makes him quickly reinforce his speech,
And her in humble manner thus beseech:
   'Though neither gods nor men may thee deserve,
Yet for her sake whom you have vow'd to serve,
Abandon fruitless cold virginity,
The gentle queen of love's sole enemy.
Then shall you most resemble Venus' nun
When Venus' sweet rites are perform'd and done.   320
Flint-breasted Pallas joys in single life,
But Pallas and your mistress are at strife.
Love, Hero, then, and be not tyrannous,
But heal the heart that thou hast wounded thus,
Nor stain thy youthful years with avarice;
Fair fools delight to be accounted nice.
The richest corn dies if it be not reap'd;
Beauty alone is lost, too warily kept.'
These arguments he us'd, and many more,
Wherewith she yielded that was won before.   330
Hero's looks yielded, but her words made war;
Women are won when they begin to jar.
Thus having swallow'd Cupid's golden hook,
The more she striv'd, the deeper was she strook.
Yet evilly feigning anger, strove she still,
And would be thought to grant against her will.
So having paus'd a while, at last she said:
'Who taught thee rhetoric to deceive a maid?
Ay me, such words as these should I abhor,
And yet I like them for the orator.'   340
    With that, Leander stoop'd to have embrac'd her,
But from his spreading arms away she cast her,
And thus bespake him: 'Gentle youth, forbear
To touch the sacred garments which I wear.

Upon a rock, and underneath a hill,
Far from the town (where all is whist and still,
Save that the sea, playing on yellow sand,
Sends forth a rattling murmur to the land,
Whose sound allures the golden Morpheus
In silence of the night to visit us)   350
My turret stands, and there God knows I play
With Venus' swans and sparrows all the day.
A dwarfish beldam bears me company,
That hops about the chamber where I lie,
And spends the night (that might be better spent)
In vain discourse and apish merriment.
Come thither.' As she spake this, her tongue tripp'd,
For unawares 'Come thither' from her slipp'd,
And suddenly her former colour chang'd,
And here and there her eyes through anger rang'd.   360
And like a planet, moving several ways
At one self instant, she poor soul assays,
Loving, not to love at all, and every part
Strove to resist the motions of her heart.
And hands so pure, so innocent, nay such
As might have made heaven stoop to have a touch,
Did she uphold to Venus, and again
Vow'd spotless chastity, but all in vain.
Cupid beats down her prayers with his wings,
Her vows above the empty air he flings;   370
All deep enrag'd, his sinewy bow he bent,
And shot a shaft that burning from him went,
Wherewith she strooken looked so dolefully
As made Love sigh to see his tyranny.
And as she wept, her tears to pearl he turn'd,
And wound them on his arm, and for her mourn'd.
Then towards the palace of the Destinies
Laden with languishment and grief he flies,
And to those stern nymphs humbly made request
Both might enjoy each other, and be blest.   380
But with a ghastly dreadful countenance,
Threat'ning a thousand deaths at every glance,
They answered Love, nor would vouchsafe so much
As one poor word, their hate to him was such.
Hearken awhile, and I will tell you why.
   Heaven's winged herald, Jove-born Mercury,
The self-same day that he asleep had laid
Enchanted Argus, spied a country maid,

Whose careless hair, instead of pearl t'adorn it,
Glist'red with dew, as one that seem'd to scorn it.   390
Her breath as fragrant as the morning rose,
Her mind pure, and her tongue untaught to glose,
Yet proud she was (for lofty pride that dwells
In tow'red courts is oft in shepherds' cells),
And too too well the fair vermilion knew,
And silver tincture of her cheeks, that drew
The love of every swain. On her this god
Enamoured was, and with his snaky rod
Did charm her nimble feet, and made her stay,
The while upon a hillock down he lay,   400
And sweetly on his pipe began to play,
And with smooth speech her fancy to assay,
Till in his twining arms he lock'd her fast,
And then he woo'd with kisses, and at last,
As shepherds do, her on the ground he laid,
And tumbling in the grass, he often stray'd
Beyond the bounds of shame, in being bold
To eye those parts which no eye should behold.
And like an insolent commanding lover,
Boasting his parentage, would needs discover   410
The way to new Elysium; but she,
Whose only dower was her chastity,
Having striv'n in vain, was now about to cry,
And crave the help of shepherds that were nigh.
Herewith he stay'd his fury, and began
To give her leave to rise; away she ran,
After went Mercury, who us'd such cunning,
As she, to hear his tale, left off her running.
Maids are not won by brutish force and might,
But speeches full of pleasure and delight.   420
And knowing Hermes courted her, was glad
That she such loveliness and beauty had
As could provoke his liking, yet was mute,
And neither would deny nor grant his suit.
Still vow'd he love; she, wanting no excuse
To feed him with delays, as women use,
Or thirsting after immortality—
All women are ambitious naturally—
Impos'd upon her lover such a task
As he ought not perform, nor yet she ask.   430
A draught of flowing nectar she requested
Wherewith the king of gods and men is feasted.

He, ready to accomplish what she will'd,
Stole some from Hebe (Hebe Jove's cup fill'd)
And gave it to his simple rustic love;
Which being known (as what is hid from Jove?)
He inly storm'd, and wax'd more furious
Than for the fire filch'd by Prometheus,
And thrusts him down from heaven; he wand'ring here,
In mournful terms, with sad and heavy cheer,   440
Complain'd to Cupid. Cupid for his sake,
To be reveng'd on Jove did undertake,
And those on whom heaven, earth, and hell relies,
I mean the adamantine Destinies,
He wounds with love, and forc'd them equally
To dote upon deceitful Mercury.
They off'red him the deadly fatal knife
That shears the slender threads of human life;
At his fair feathered feet the engines laid
Which th'earth from ugly Chaos' den upweigh'd.   450
These he regarded not, but did entreat
That Jove, usurper of his father's seat,
Might presently be banish'd into hell,
And aged Saturn in Olympus dwell.
They granted what he crav'd, and once again
Saturn and Ops began their golden reign.
Murder, rape, war, lust and treachery
Were with Jove clos'd in Stygian empery.
But long this blessed time continued not:
As soon as he his wished purpose got,   460
He reckless of his promise did despise
The love of th'everlasting Destinies.
They seeing it both Love and him abhorr'd,
And Jupiter unto his place restor'd.
And but that Learning, in despite of Fate,
Will mount aloft, and enter heaven gate,
And to the seat of Jove itself advance,
Hermes had slept in hell with Ignorance.
Yet as a punishment they added this,
That he and Poverty should always kiss.   470
And to this day is every scholar poor;
Gross gold from them runs headlong to the boor.
Likewise the angry Sisters, thus deluded,
To venge themselves on Hermes, have concluded
That Midas' brood shall sit in honour's chair,
To which the Muses' sons are only heir:

And fruitful wits that in aspiring are
Shall discontent run into regions far.
And few great lords in virtuous deeds shall joy,
But be surpris'd with every garish toy,   480
And still enrich the lofty servile clown,
Who with encroaching guile keeps learning down.
Then muse not Cupid's suit no better sped,
Seeing in their loves the Fates were injur'd.

II

By this, sad Hero, with love unacquainted,
Viewing Leander's face, fell down and fainted.
He kiss'd her, and breath'd life into her lips,
Wherewith, as one displeas'd, away she trips.
Yet as she went, full often look'd behind,
And many poor excuses did she find
To linger by the way, and once she stay'd,
And would have turn'd again, but was afraid,
In off'ring parley, to be counted light.
So on she goes, and in her idle flight   10
Her painted fan of curled plumes let fall,
Thinking to train Leander therewithal.
He being a novice, knew not what she meant,
But stay'd, and after her a letter sent,
Which joyful Hero answer'd in such sort
As he had hope to scale the beauteous fort
Wherein the liberal Graces lock'd their wealth,
And therefore to her tower he got by stealth.
Wide open stood the door, he need not climb,
And she herself before the pointed time   20
Had spread the board, with roses strew'd the room,
And oft look'd out, and mus'd he did not come.
At last he came; O who can tell the greeting
These greedy lovers had at their first meeting?
He ask'd, she gave, and nothing was denied;
Both to each other quickly were affied.
Look how their hands, so were their hearts united,
And what he did she willingly requited.
(Sweet are the kisses, the embracements sweet,
When like desires and affections meet,
For from the earth to heaven is Cupid rais'd,   30
Where fancy is in equal balance pais'd.)
Yet she this rashness suddenly repented,
And turn'd aside, and to herself lamented,
As if her name and honour had been wrong'd
By being possess'd of him for whom she long'd;

[413]

Ay, and she wish'd, albeit not from her heart,
That he would leave her turret and depart.
The mirthful god of amorous pleasure smil'd
To see how he this captive nymph beguil'd; 40
For hitherto he did but fan the fire,
And kept it down that it might mount the higher.
Now wax'd she jealous, lest his love abated,
Fearing her own thoughts made her to be hated.
Therefore unto him hastily she goes,
And, like light Salmacis, her body throws
Upon his bosom, where with yielding eyes
She offers up herself a sacrifice
To slake his anger, if he were displeas'd.
O what god would not therewith be appeas'd? 50
Like Aesop's cock, this jewel he enjoyed,
And as a brother with his sister toyed,
Supposing nothing else was to be done,
Now he her favour and good will had won.
But know you not that creatures wanting sense
By nature have a mutual appetence,
And wanting organs to advance a step,
Mov'd by love's force, unto each other leap?
Much more in subjects having intellect
Some hidden influence breeds like effect. 60
Albeit Leander, rude in love, and raw,
Long dallying with Hero, nothing saw
That might delight him more, yet he suspected
Some amorous rites or other were neglected.
Therefore unto his body hers he clung;
She, fearing on the rushes to be flung,
Striv'd with redoubled strength; the more she strived,
The more a gentle pleasing heat revived,
Which taught him all that elder lovers know.
And now the same 'gan so to scorch and glow, 70
As in plain terms (yet cunningly) he crav'd it;
Love always makes those eloquent that have it.
She, with a kind of granting, put him by it,
And ever as he thought himself most nigh it,
Like to the tree of Tantalus she fled,
And, seeming lavish, sav'd her maidenhead.
Ne'er king more sought to keep his diadem,
Than Hero this inestimable gem.
Above our life we love a steadfast friend,
Yet when a token of great worth we send, 80

We often kiss it, often look thereon,
And stay the messenger that would be gone:
No marvel, then, though Hero would not yield
So soon to part from that she dearly held.
Jewels being lost are found again, this never;
'Tis lost but once, and once lost, lost for ever.
  Now had the Morn espied her lover's steeds,
Whereat she starts, puts on her purple weeds,
And red for anger that he stay'd so long,
All headlong throws herself the clouds among.   90
And now Leander, fearing to be miss'd,
Embrac'd her suddenly, took leave, and kiss'd.
Long was he taking leave, and loth to go,
And kiss'd again, as lovers use to do.
Sad Hero wrung him by the hand and wept,
Saying, 'Let your vows and promises be kept.'
Then standing at the door she turn'd about,
As loth to see Leander going out.
And now the sun that through th'horizon peeps,
As pitying these lovers, downward creeps,   100
So that in silence of the cloudy night,
Though it was morning, did he take his flight.
But what the secret trusty night conceal'd,
Leander's amorous habit soon reveal'd.
With Cupid's myrtle was his bonnet crown'd,
About his arms the purple riband wound
Wherewith she wreath'd her largely spreading hair;
Nor could the youth abstain, but he must wear
The sacred ring wherewith she was endow'd
When first religious chastity she vow'd;   110
Which made his love through Sestos to be known,
And thence unto Abydos sooner blown
Than he could sail; for incorporeal Fame,
Whose weight consists in nothing but her name,
Is swifter than the wind, whose tardy plumes
Are reeking water, and dull earthly fumes.
Home when he came, he seem'd not to be there,
But like exiled air thrust from his sphere,
Set in a foreign place; and straight from thence,
Alcides-like, by mighty violence,   120
He would have chas'd away the swelling main
That him from her unjustly did detain.
Like as the sun in a diameter
Fires and inflames objects removed far

And heateth kindly, shining lat'rally,
So beauty sweetly quickens when 'tis nigh,
But being separated and removed,
Burns where it cherish'd, murders where it loved.
Therefore even as an index to a book,
So to his mind was young Leander's look.   130
O none but gods have power their love to hide,
Affection by the count'nance is descried.
The light of hidden fire itself discovers,
And love that is conceal'd betrays poor lovers.
His secret flame apparently was seen,
Leander's father knew where he had been,
And for the same mildly rebuk'd his son,
Thinking to quench the sparkles new begun.
But love, resisted once, grows passionate,
And nothing more than counsel lovers hate.   140
For as a hot proud horse highly disdains
To have his head controll'd, but breaks the reins,
Spits forth the ringled bit, and with his hooves
Checks the submissive ground, so he that loves,
The more he is restrain'd, the worse he fares.
What is it now but mad Leander dares?
'O Hero, Hero!' thus he cried full oft,
And then he got him to a rock aloft,
Where having spied her tower, long stared he on't,
And prayed the narrow toiling Hellespont   150
To part in twain, that he might come and go,
But still the rising billows answered 'No.'
With that he stripp'd him to the ivory skin,
And crying, 'Love, I come', leapt lively in.
Whereat the sapphire-visag'd god grew proud,
And made his cap'ring Triton sound aloud,
Imagining that Ganymede, displeas'd,
Had left the heavens; therefore on him he seiz'd.
Leander striv'd, the waves about him wound,
And pull'd him to the bottom, where the ground   160
Was strew'd with pearl, and in low coral groves
Sweet singing mermaids sported with their loves
On heaps of heavy gold, and took great pleasure
To spurn in careless sort the shipwrack treasure.
For here the stately azure palace stood
Where kingly Neptune and his train abode.
The lusty god embrac'd him, call'd him love,
And swore he never should return to Jove.

But when he knew it was not Ganymede,
For under water he was almost dead,   170
He heav'd him up, and looking on his face,
Beat down the bold waves with his triple mace,
Which mounted up, intending to have kiss'd him,
And fell in drops like tears because they miss'd him.
Leander being up, began to swim,
And, looking back, saw Neptune follow him;
Whereat aghast, the poor soul 'gan to cry,
'O let me visit Hero ere I die.'
The god put Helle's bracelet on his arm,
And swore the sea should never do him harm.   180
He clapp'd his plump cheeks, with his tresses play'd,
And smiling wantonly, his love bewray'd.
He watch'd his arms, and as they open'd wide
At every stroke, betwixt them would he slide
And steal a kiss, and then run out and dance,
And as he turn'd, cast many a lustful glance,
And throw him gaudy toys to please his eye,
And dive into the water, and there pry
Upon his breast, his thighs, and every limb,
And up again, and close beside him swim,   190
And talk of love. Leander made reply,
'You are deceiv'd, I am no woman, I.'
Thereat smil'd Neptune, and then told a tale,
How that a shepherd, sitting in a vale,.
Play'd with a boy so fair and unkind
As for his love both earth and heaven pin'd;
That of the cooling river durst not drink,
Lest water-nymphs should pull him from the brink;
And when he sported in the fragrant lawns,
Goat-footed satyrs and up-staring fauns   200
Would steal him thence. Ere half this tale was done,
'Ay me,' Leander cried, 'th'enamoured sun,
That now should shine on Thetis' glassy bower,
Descends upon my radiant Hero's tower.
O that these tardy arms of mine were wings!'
And as he spake, upon the waves he springs.
Neptune was angry that he gave no ear,
And in his heart revenging malice bare;
He flung at him his mace, but as it went,
He call'd it in, for love made him repent.   210
The mace returning back, his own hand hit,
As meaning to be veng'd for darting it.

When this fresh-bleeding wound Leander view'd,
His colour went and came, as if he ru'd
The grief which Neptune felt. In gentle breasts
Relenting thoughts, remorse and pity rests.
And who have hard hearts and obdurate minds
But vicious, harebrain'd, and illit'rate hinds?
The god, seeing him with pity to be moved,
Thereon concluded that he was beloved.   220
(Love is too full of faith, too credulous,
With folly and false hope deluding us.)
Wherefore Leander's fancy to surprise,
To the rich Ocean for gifts he flies.
'Tis wisdom to give much, a gift prevails
When deep-persuading oratory fails.
   By this, Leander, being near the land,
Cast down his weary feet, and felt the sand.
Breathless albeit he were, he rested not
Till to the solitary tower he got,   230
And knock'd and call'd, at which celestial noise
The longing heart of Hero much more joys
Than nymphs and shepherds when the timbrel rings,
Or crooked dolphin when the sailor sings.
She stay'd not for her robes, but straight arose,
And drunk with gladness to the door she goes,
Where seeing a naked man she screech'd for fear—
Such sights as this to tender maids are rare—
And ran into the dark herself to hide;
Rich jewels in the dark are soonest spied.   240
Unto her was he led, or rather drawn,
By those white limbs, which sparkled through the lawn.
The nearer that he came, the more she fled,
And seeking refuge, slipp'd into her bed.
Whereon Leander sitting thus began,
Through numbing cold all feeble, faint and wan:
'If not for love, yet, love, for pity sake,
Me in thy bed and maiden bosom take;
At least vouchsafe these arms some little room,
Who, hoping to embrace thee, cheerly swum.   250
This head was beat with many a churlish billow,
And therefore let it rest upon thy pillow.'
Herewith affrighted Hero shrunk away,
And in her lukewarm place Leander lay,
Whose lively heat, like fire from heaven fet,
Would animate gross clay, and higher set

The drooping thoughts of base-declining souls
Than dreary Mars carousing nectar bowls.
His hands he cast upon her like a snare;
She, overcome with shame and sallow fear,   260
Like chaste Diana when Actaeon spied her,
Being suddenly betray'd, div'd down to hide her.
And as her silver body downward went,
With both her hands she made the bed a tent,
And in her own mind thought herself secure,
O'ercast with dim and darksome coverture.
And now she lets him whisper in her ear,
Flatter, entreat, promise, protest and swear;
Yet ever as he greedily assay'd
To touch those dainties, she the harpy play'd,   270
And every limb did as a soldier stout
Defend the fort, and keep the foeman out.
For though the rising iv'ry mount he scal'd,
Which is with azure circling lines empal'd,
Much like a globe (a globe may I term this,
By which love sails to regions full of bliss),
Yet there with Sisyphus he toil'd in vain,
Till gentle parley did the truce obtain.
Wherein Leander on her quivering breast
Breathless spoke something, and sigh'd out the rest; 280
Which so prevail'd as he with small ado
Enclos'd her in his arms and kiss'd her too.
And every kiss to her was as a charm,
And to Leander as a fresh alarm,
So that the truce was broke, and she alas
(Poor silly maiden) at his mercy was.
Love is not full of pity (as men say)
But deaf and cruel where he means to prey.
Even as a bird, which in our hands we wring,
Forth plungeth, and oft flutters with her wing,   290
She trembling strove; this strife of hers (like that
Which made the world) another world begat
Of unknown joy. Treason was in her thought,
And cunningly to yield herself she sought.
Seeming not won, yet won she was at length;
In such wars women use but half their strength.
Leander now, like Theban Hercules,
Ent'red the orchard of th'Hesperides,
Whose fruit none rightly can describe but he
That pulls or shakes it from the golden tree.   300

And now she wish'd this night were never done,
And sigh'd to think upon th'approaching sun,
For much it griev'd her that the bright daylight
Should know the pleasure of this blessed night,
And them like Mars and Erycine display'd,
Both in each other's arms chain'd as they laid.
Again she knew not how to frame her look,
Or speak to him who in a moment took
That which so long so charily she kept,
And fain by stealth away she would have crept,   310
And to some corner secretly have gone,
Leaving Leander in the bed alone.
But as her naked feet were whipping out,
He on the sudden cling'd her so about
That mermaid-like unto the floor she slid;
One half appear'd, the other half was hid.
Thus near the bed she blushing stood upright,
And from her countenance behold ye might
A kind of twilight break, which through the hair,
As from an orient cloud, glimps'd here and there.   320
And round about the chamber this false morn
Brought forth the day before the day was born.
So Hero's ruddy cheek Hero betray'd,
And her all naked to his sight display'd,
Whence his admiring eyes more pleasure took
Than Dis on heaps of gold fixing his look.
By this Apollo's golden harp began
To sound forth music to the Ocean,
Which watchful Hesperus no sooner heard,
But he the day-bright-bearing car prepar'd,   330
And ran before, as harbinger of light,
And with his flaring beams mock'd ugly Night,
Till she, o'ercome with anguish, shame and rage,
Dang'd down to hell her loathsome carriage.

Desunt nonnulla

Ovid's Elegies

Marlowe's translations of Ovid's *Amores* appear only in company with Sir John Davies's *Epigrams* and in undated and unregistered editions purporting to be printed in 'Middlebourgh' (in Holland). It has been conjectured that two of these editions, entitled *Epigrammes and Elegies by J.D. and C.M.*, and containing only a selection of the Elegies, may have been printed by Robert Waldegrave, the Edinburgh printer, in about 1598 and 1599. 'Davyes Epigrams, with Marlowes Elegys' were amongst satirical books burned by order of the Church of England in June 1599. The full three books of elegies are first published in *All Ovids Elegies: 3 Bookes. By C.M. Epigrams by J.D.* in two editions, probably in London, about 1600. Further editions follow about 1630 and 1640.

There is no external evidence as to the date of composition. For his Latin text Marlowe may have gone to an edition printed in Basle in 1568.

Ovid's Elegies

P. Ovidii Nasonis Amorum, Liber Primus

ELEGIA I

Quemadmodum a Cupidine pro bellis amores scribere coactus sit

We which were Ovid's five books now are three,
For these before the rest preferreth he;
If reading five thou plain'st of tediousness,
Two ta'en away, thy labour will be less.
  With Muse uprear'd I meant to sing of arms,
Choosing a subject fit for fierce alarms.
Both verses were alike till Love (men say)
Began to smile and took one foot away.
Rash boy, who gave thee power to change a line?
We are the Muses' prophets, none of thine.   10
What if thy mother take Diana's bow?
Shall Dian fan when Love begins to glow?
In woody groves is't meet that Ceres reign,
And quiver-bearing Dian till the plain?
Who'll set the fair-tress'd Sun in battle ray,
While Mars doth take the Aonian harp to play?
Great are thy kingdoms, over-strong and large,
Ambitious imp, why seek'st thou further charge?
Are all things thine? the Muses' Tempe thine?
Then scarce can Phoebus say, 'This harp is mine.'   20
When in this work's first verse I trod aloft,
Love slack'd my muse, and made my numbers soft.
I have no mistress nor no favourite,
Being fittest matter for a wanton wit.
Thus I complain'd, but Love unlock'd his quiver,
Took out the shaft, ordain'd my heart to shiver,
And bent his sinewy bow upon his knee,
Saying, 'Poet, here's a work beseeming thee.'
O woe is me, he never shoots but hits;
I burn, Love in my idle bosom sits.   30
Let my first verse be six, my last five feet;
Farewell stern war, for blunter poets meet.
Elegian muse, that warblest amorous lays,
Girt my shine brow with sea-bank myrtle sprays.

[423]

ELEGIA II

Quod primo amore correptus, in triumphum duci se a Cupidine patiatur
  What makes my bed seem hard seeing it is soft?
Or why slips down the coverlet so oft?
Although the nights be long, I sleep not though,
My sides are sore with tumbling to and fro.
Were Love the cause, it's like I should descry him,
Or lies he close, and shoots where none can spy him?
'Twas so, he struck me with a slender dart,
'Tis cruel Love turmoils my captive heart.
Yielding or struggling do we give him might;
Let's yield, a burden eas'ly borne is light.   10
I saw a brandish'd fire increase in strength,
Which being not shak'd, I saw it die at length.
Young oxen newly yok'd are beaten more
Than oxen which have drawn the plough before;
And rough jades' mouths with stubborn bits are torn,
But manag'd horses' heads are lightly borne.
Unwilling lovers love doth more torment
Than such as in their bondage feel content.
Lo, I confess, I am thy captive, I,
And hold my conquered hands for thee to tie.   20
What needs thou war? I sue to thee for grace;
With arms to conquer armless men is base.
Yoke Venus' doves, put myrtle on thy hair,
Vulcan will give thee chariots rich and fair;
The people thee applauding, thou shalt stand,
Guiding the harmless pigeons with thy hand;
Young men and women shalt thou lead as thrall,
So will thy triumph seem magnifical.
I, lately caught, will have a new-made wound,
And captive-like be manacled and bound;   30
Good Meaning, Shame, and such as seek love's wrack
Shall follow thee, their hands tied at their back.
Thee all shall fear and worship as a king,
Io triumphing shall thy people sing.
Smooth Speeches, Fear and Rage shall by thee ride,
Which troops have always been on Cupid's side;
Thou with these soldiers conquerest gods and men,
Take these away, where is thine honour then?
Thy mother shall from heaven applaud this show,
And on their faces heaps of roses strow.   40
With beauty of thy wings thy fair hair gilded,
Ride, golden Love, in chariots richly builded.

Unless I err, full many shalt thou burn,
And give wounds infinite at every turn.
In spite of thee, forth will thine arrows fly,
A scorching flame burns all the standers by.
So, having conquer'd Inde, was Bacchus' hue;
Thee pompous birds, and him two tigers drew.
Then seeing I grace thy show in following thee,
Forbear to hurt thyself in spoiling me.
Behold thy kinsman's Caesar's prosperous bands,   50
Who guards the conquered with his conquering hands.

ELEGIA III
Ad amicam
   I ask but right: let her that caught me late
Either love, or cause that I may never hate.
I ask too much, would she but let me love her;
Love knows with such like prayers I daily move her.
Accept him that will serve thee all his youth,
Accept him that will love with spotless truth.
If lofty titles cannot make me thine
That am descended but of knightly line
(Soon may you plough the little land I have;
I gladly grant my parents given to save),   10
Apollo, Bacchus and the Muses may,
And Cupid, who hath mark'd me for thy prey,
My spotless life, which but to gods gives place,
Naked simplicity, and modest grace.
I love but one, and her I love change never,
If men have faith, I'll live with thee for ever.
The years that fatal destiny shall give
I'll live with thee, and die, or thou shalt grieve.
Be thou the happy subject of my books,
That I may write things worthy thy fair looks.   20
By verses horned Io got her name,
And she to whom in shape of swan Jove came,
And she that on a feign'd bull swam to land,
Griping his false horns with her virgin hand.
So likewise we will through the world be rung,
And with my name shall thine be always sung.

ELEGIA IV
*Amicam, qua arte, quibusve nutibus in cena, praesente viro uti debeat,
admonet*
   Thy husband to a banquet goes with me,

Pray God it may his latest supper be.
Shall I sit gazing as a bashful guest,
While others touch the damsel I love best?
Wilt, lying under him, his bosom clip?
About thy neck shall he at pleasure skip?
Marvel not though the fair bride did incite
The drunken Centaurs to a sudden fight;
I am no half-horse, nor in woods I dwell,
Yet scarce my hands from thee contain I well.   10
But how thou shouldst behave thyself now know,
Nor let the winds away my warnings blow.
Before thy husband come, though I not see
What may be done, yet there before him be.
Lie with him gently, when his limbs he spread
Upon the bed, but on my foot first tread.
View me, my becks and speaking countenance;
Take and receive each secret amorous glance.
Words without voice shall on my eyebrows sit,
Lines thou shalt read in wine by my hand writ.   20
When our lascivious toys come in thy mind,
Thy rosy cheeks be to thy thumb inclin'd.
If aught of me thou speak'st in inward thought,
Let thy soft finger to thy ear be brought.
When I (my light) do or say aught that please thee,
Turn round thy gold ring, as it were to ease thee.
Strike on the board like them that pray for evil
When thou dost wish thy husband at the devil.
What wine he fills thee, wisely will him drink;
Ask thou the boy what thou enough dost think.   30
When thou hast tasted, I will take the cup,
And where thou drink'st, on that part I will sup.
If he gives thee what first himself did taste,
Even in his face his offered gobbets cast.
Let not thy neck by his vile arms be press'd,
Nor lean thy soft head on his boist'rous breast.
Thy bosom's roseate buds let him not finger,
Chiefly on thy lips let not his lips linger.
If thou givest kisses, I shall all disclose,
Say they are mine and hands on thee impose.
Yet this I'll see, but if thy gown aught cover,   40
Suspicious fear in all my veins will hover.
Mingle not thighs nor to his leg join thine,
Nor thy soft foot with his hard foot combine.
I have been wanton, therefore am perplex'd,

And with mistrust of the like measure vex'd.
I and my wench oft under clothes did lurk,
When pleasure mov'd us to our sweetest work.
Do not thou so, but throw thy mantle hence,
Lest I should think thee guilty of offence.   50
Entreat thy husband drink, but do not kiss,
And while he drinks, to add more do not miss;
If he lies down with wine and sleep oppress'd,
The thing and place shall counsel us the rest.
When to go homewards we rise all along,
Have care to walk in middle of the throng;
There will I find thee or be found by thee,
There touch whatever thou canst touch of me.
Ay me, I warn what profits some few hours,
But we must part when heav'n with black night lours. 60
At night thy husband clips thee; I will weep
And to the doors sight of thyself keep.
Then will he kiss thee, and not only kiss,
But force thee give him my stol'n honey bliss.
Constrain'd against thy will, give it the peasant;
Forbear sweet words, and be your sport unpleasant.
To him I pray it no delight may bring,
Or if it do, to thee no joy thence spring;
But though this night thy fortune be to try it,
To me tomorrow constantly deny it.   70

ELEGIA V
Corinnae concubitus
   In summer's heat, and mid-time of the day,
To rest my limbs upon a bed I lay; ·
One window shut, the other open stood,
Which gave such light as twinkles in a wood
Like twilight glimpse at setting of the sun,
Or night being past, and yet not day begun.
Such light to shamefast maidens must be shown,
Where they may sport and seem to be unknown.
Then came Corinna in a long loose gown,
Her white neck hid with tresses hanging down,   10
Resembling fair Semiramis going to bed,
Or Lais of a thousand wooers sped.
I snatch'd her gown; being thin, the harm was small,
Yet striv'd she to be covered therewithal,
And striving thus as one that would be cast,
Betray'd herself, and yielded at the last.

[427]

Stark naked as she stood before mine eye,
Not one wen in her body could I spy.
What arms and shoulders did I touch and see,
How apt her breasts were to be press'd by me!　　　20
How smooth a belly under her waist saw I,
How large a leg, and what a lusty thigh!
To leave the rest, all lik'd me passing well;
I cling'd her naked body, down she fell.
Judge you the rest: being tir'd she bade me kiss;
Jove send me more such afternoons as this.

ELEGIA VI
Ad Janitorem, ut fores sibi aperiat
　Unworthy porter, bound in chains full sore,
On moved hooks set ope the churlish door.
Little I ask, a little entrance make;
The gate half-ope my bent side in will take.
Long love my body to such use makes slender,
And to get out doth like apt members render.
He shows me how unheard to pass the watch,
And guides my feet lest stumbling falls they catch.
But in times past I fear'd vain shades, and night,
Wond'ring if any walked without light.　　　10
Love hearing it laugh'd with his tender mother,
And smiling said, 'Be thou as bold as other.'
Forthwith Love came: no dark night-flying sprite,
Nor hands prepar'd to slaughter, me affright.
Thee fear I too much, only thee I flatter,
Thy lightning can my life in pieces batter.
Why enviest me? this hostile den unbar,
See how the gates with my tears wat'red are.
When thou stood'st naked, ready to be beat,
For thee I did thy mistress fair entreat;　　　20
But what entreats for thee sometimes took place
(O mischief) now for me obtain small grace.
Gratis thou mayst be free, give like for like,
Night goes away: the door's bar backward strike.
Strike, so again hard chains shall bind thee never,
Nor servile water shalt thou drink for ever.
Hard-hearted porter, dost and wilt not hear?
With stiff oak propp'd the gate doth still appear.
Such rampir'd gates besieged cities aid,
In midst of peace why art of arms afraid?　　　30
Exclud'st a lover, how would'st use a foe?

Strike back the bar, night fast away doth go.
With arms or armed men I come not guarded,
I am alone, were furious Love discarded.
Although I would, I cannot him cashier
Before I be divided from my gear.
See Love with me, wine moderate in my brain,
And on my hairs a crown of flowers remain.
Who fears these arms? who will not go to meet them?
Night runs away; with open entrance greet them.   40
Art careless? or is't sleep forbids thee hear,
Giving the winds my words running in thine ear?
Well I remember when I first did hire thee
Watching till after midnight did not tire thee;
But now perchance thy wench with thee doth rest—
Ah, how thy lot is above my lot blest!
Though it be so, shut me not out therefore;
Night goes away, I pray thee ope the door.
Err we? or do the turned hinges sound,
And opening doors with creaking noise abound?   50
We err: a strong blast seem'd the gates to ope;
Ay me, how high that gale did lift my hope!
If, Boreas, bears Oreithyia's rape in mind,
Come break these deaf doors with thy boisterous wind.
Silent the city is: night's dewy host
March fast away; the bar strike from the post,
Or I more stern than fire or sword will turn
And with my brand these gorgeous houses burn.
Night, love, and wine to all extremes persuade;
Night shameless, wine and love are fearless made.   60
All have I spent: no threats or prayers move thee;
O harder than the doors thou guard'st I prove thee.
No pretty wench's keeper mayst thou be:
The careful prison is more meet for thee.
Now frosty night her flight begins to take,
And crowing cocks poor souls to work awake;
But thou my crown, from sad hairs ta'en away,
On this hard threshold till the morning lay,
That when my mistress there beholds thee cast,
She may perceive how we the time did waste.   70
Whate'er thou art, farewell; be like me pain'd,
Careless, farewell, with my fault not distain'd!
And farewell cruel posts, rough threshold's block,
And doors conjoin'd with an hard iron lock.

ELEGIA VII

Ad pacandam amicam, quam verberaverat

Bind fast my hands, they have deserved chains,
While rage is absent, take some friend the pains;
For rage against my wench mov'd my rash arm,
My mistress weeps whom my mad hand did harm.
I might have then my parents dear misus'd,
Or holy gods with cruel strokes abus'd.
Why, Ajax, master of the seven-fold shield,
Butcher'd the flocks he found in spacious field,
And he who on his mother veng'd his sire
Against the Destinies durst sharp darts require.   10
Could I therefore her comely tresses tear?
Yet was she graced with her ruffled hair.
So fair she was, Atalanta she resembled,
Before whose bow th'Arcadian wild beasts trembled;
Such Ariadne was, when she bewails
Her perjur'd Theseus' flying vows and sails;
So, chaste Minerva, did Cassandra fall,
Deflow'r'd except, within thy temple wall.
That I was mad and barbarous all men cried,
She nothing said, pale fear her tongue had tied;   20
But secretly her looks with checks did trounce me,
Her tears, she silent, guilty did pronounce me.
Would of mine arms my shoulders had been scanted,
Better I could part of myself have wanted.
To mine own self have I had strength so furious,
And to myself could I be so injurious?
Slaughter and mischief's instruments, no better,
Deserved chains these cursed hands shall fetter.
Punish'd I am, if I a Roman beat;
Over my mistress is my right more great?   30
Tydides left worst signs of villainy,
He first a goddess struck; another I.
Yet he harm'd less; whom I profess'd to love
I harm'd; a foe did Diomede's anger move.
Go now, thou conqueror, glorious triumphs raise,
Pay vows to Jove, engirt thy hairs with bays,
And let the troops which shall thy chariot follow
'*Io*, a strong man conquer'd this wench', hollow.
Let the sad captive foremost with locks spread,
On her white neck but for hurt cheeks be led;   40
Meeter it were her lips were blue with kissing,
And on her neck a wanton's mark not missing.

But though I like a swelling flood was driven,
And like a prey unto blind anger given,
Was't not enough the fearful wench to chide,
Nor thunder in rough threatings' haughty pride,
Nor shamefully her coat pull o'er her crown,
Which to her waist her girdle still kept down?
But cruelly her tresses having rent,
My nails to scratch her lovely cheeks I bent.   50
Sighing she stood, her bloodless white looks showed
Like marble from the Parian mountains hewed;
Her half-dead joints and trembling limbs I saw,
Like poplar leaves blown with a stormy flaw,
Or slender ears with gentle Zephyr shaken,
Or waters' tops with the warm south wind taken.
And down her cheeks the trickling tears did flow
Like water gushing from consuming snow.
Then first I did perceive I had offended,
My blood the tears were that from her descended.   60
Before her feet thrice prostrate down I fell,
My feared hands thrice back she did repel.
But doubt thou not (revenge doth grief appease)
With thy sharp nails upon my face to seize;
Bescratch mine eyes, spare not my locks to break
(Anger will help thy hands though ne'er so weak),
And lest the sad signs of my crime remain,
Put in their place thy kembed hairs again.

ELEGIA VIII
Execratur lenam, quae puellam suam meretricia arte instituebat
   There is—whoe'er will know a bawd aright,
Give ear—there is an old trot, Dipsas hight.
Her name comes from the thing: she being wise
Sees not the Morn on rosy horses rise,
She magic arts and Thessale charms doth know,
And makes large streams back to their fountains flow;
She knows with grass, with threads on wrong wheels spun,
And what with mares' rank humour may be done.
When she will, clouds the dark'ned heav'n obscure;
When she will, day shines everywhere most pure.   10
If I have faith, I saw the stars drop blood,
The purple moon with sanguine visage stood.
Her I suspect among night's spirits to fly,
And her old body in birds' plumes to lie.
Fame saith as I suspect, and in her eyes

Two eyeballs shine and double light thence flies.
Great-grandsires from their ancient graves she chides,
And with long charms the solid earth divides.
She draws chaste women to incontinence,
Nor doth her tongue want harmful eloquence.   20
By chance I heard her talk; these words she said,
While closely hid betwixt two doors I laid:
'Mistress, thou knowest thou hast a blest youth pleas'd,
He stay'd and on thy looks his gazes seiz'd.
And why shouldst not please? none thy face exceeds;
Ay me, thy body hath no worthy weeds.
As thou art fair, would thou wert fortunate!
Wert thou rich, poor should not be my state.
Th'opposed star of Mars hath done thee harm;
Now Mars is gone, Venus thy side doth warm,   30
And brings good fortune: a rich lover plants
His love on thee, and can supply thy wants.
Such is his form as may with thine compare,
Would he not buy thee, thou for him shouldst care.'
She blush'd. 'Red shame becomes white cheeks, but this,
If feign'd, doth well; if true, it doth amiss.
When on thy lap thine eyes thou dost deject,
Each one according to his gifts respect.
Perhaps the Sabines rude, when Tatius reign'd,
To yield their love to more than one disdain'd;   40
Now Mars doth rage abroad without all pity,
And Venus rules in her Aeneas' city.
Fair women play, she's chaste whom none will have,
Or, but for bashfulness, herself would crave.
Shake off these wrinkles that thy front assault,
Wrinkles in beauty is a grievous fault.
Penelope in bows her youths' strength tried,
Of horn the bow was that approv'd their side.
Time flying slides hence closely, and deceives us,
And with swift horses the swift year soon leaves us.   50
Brass shines with use; good garments would be worn;
Houses not dwelt in are with filth forlorn.
Beauty not exercis'd with age is spent,
Nor one or two men are sufficient.
Many to rob is more sure, and less hateful,
From dog-kept flocks come preys to wolves most grateful.
Behold, what gives the poet but new verses?
And thereof many thousand he rehearses.
The poet's god, array'd in robes of gold,

Of his gilt harp the well-tun'd strings doth hold.   60
Let Homer yield to such as presents bring;
(Trust me) to give, it is a witty thing.
Nor, so thou mayst obtain a wealthy prize,
The vain name of inferior slaves despise.
Nor let the arms of ancient lines beguile thee;
Poor lover, with thy grandsires I exile thee.
Who seeks, for being fair, a night to have,
What he will give, with greater instance crave.
Make a small price, while thou thy nets dost lay,
Lest they should fly; being ta'en, the tyrant play.   70
Dissemble so as lov'd he may be thought,
And take heed lest he gets that love for nought.
Deny him oft; feign now thy head doth ache:
And Isis now will show what scuse to make.
Receive him soon, lest patient use he gain,
Or lest his love oft beaten back should wane.
To beggars shut, to bringers ope thy gate;
Let him within hear barr'd-out lovers prate.
And as first wrong'd the wronged sometimes banish,
Thy fault with his fault so repuls'd will vanish.   80
But never give a spacious time to ire,
Anger delay'd doth oft to hate retire.
And let thine eyes constrained learn to weep,
That this or that man may thy cheeks moist keep.
Nor, if thou cozen'st one, dread to forswear,
Venus to mock'd men lends a senseless ear.
Servants fit for thy purpose thou must hire,
To teach thy lover what thy thoughts desire.
Let them ask somewhat; many asking little,
Within a while great heaps grow of a tittle.   90
And sister, nurse, and mother spare him not,
By many hands great wealth is quickly got.
When causes fail thee to require a gift,
By keeping of thy birth make but a shift.
Beware lest he unrivall'd loves secure;
Take strife away, love doth not well endure.
On all the bed men's tumbling let him view,
And thy neck with lascivious marks made blue;
Chiefly show him the gifts which others send;
If he gives nothing, let him from thee wend.   100
When thou hast so much as he gives no more,
Pray him to lend what thou mayst ne'er restore.
Let thy tongue flatter, while thy mind harm works,

Under sweet honey deadly poison lurks.
If this thou dost, to me by long use known,
Nor let my words be with the winds hence blown,
Oft thou wilt say, "live well"; thou wilt pray oft
That my dead bones may in their grave lie soft.'
As thus she spake, my shadow me betray'd,
With much ado my hands I scarcely stay'd;   110
But her blear eyes, bald scalp's thin hoary fleeces,
And rivell'd cheeks I would have pull'd a-pieces.
The gods send thee no house, a poor old age,
Perpetual thirst, and winter's lasting rage.

ELEGIA IX
Ad Atticum, amantem non oportere desidiosum esse, sicuti nec militem
  All lovers war, and Cupid hath his tent,
Attic, all lovers are to war far sent.
What age fits Mars, with Venus doth agree,
'Tis shame for eld in war or love to be.
What years in soldiers captains do require,
Those in their lovers pretty maids desire.
Both of them watch: each on the hard earth sleeps;
His mistress' doors this, that his captain's keeps.
Soldiers must travel far; the wench forth send,
Her valiant lover follows without end.   10
Mounts, and rain-doubled floods he passeth over,
And treads the deserts snowy heaps do cover.
Going to sea, east winds he doth not chide,
Nor to hoist sail attends fit time and tide.
Who but a soldier or a lover is bold
To suffer storm-mix'd snows with night's sharp cold?
One as a spy doth to his enemies go,
The other eyes his rival as his foe.
He cities great, this thresholds lies before;
This breaks town gates, but he his mistress' door.   20
Oft to invade the sleeping foe 'tis good,
And arm'd to shed unarmed people's blood.
So the fierce troops of Thracian Rhesus fell,
And captive horses bade their lord farewell.
Sooth, lovers watch till sleep the husband charms,
Who slumb'ring, they rise up in swelling arms.
The keeper's hands and corps-du-gard to pass,
The soldier's, and poor lover's work e'er was.
Doubtful is war and love: the vanquish'd rise,
And who thou never think'st should fall, down lies.   30

Therefore whoe'er love slothfulness doth call,
Let him surcease: love tries wit best of all.
Achilles burn'd, Briseis being ta'en away;
Trojans, destroy the Greek wealth while you may;
Hector to arms went from his wife's embraces,
And on Andromache his helmet laces.
Great Agamemnon was, men say, amazed,
On Priam's loose-tress'd daughter when he gazed.
Mars in the deed the blacksmith's net did stable,
In heaven was never more notorious fable.   40
Myself was dull and faint, to sloth inclin'd,
Pleasure and ease had mollified my mind;
A fair maid's care expell'd this sluggishness,
And to her tents will'd me myself address.
Since mayst thou see me watch and night-wars move:
He that will not grow slothful, let him love.

ELEGIA X
Ad puellam, ne pro amore praemia poscat
   Such as the cause was of two husbands' war,
Whom Trojan ships fetch'd from Europa far;
Such as was Leda, whom the god deluded
In snow-white plumes of a false swan included;
Such as Amymone through the dry fields strayed,
When on her head a water pitcher layed:
Such wert thou, and I fear'd the bull and eagle,
And whate'er love made Jove should thee inveigle.
Now all fear with my mind's hot love abates,
No more this beauty mine eyes captivates.   10
Ask'st why I change? because thou crav'st reward:
This cause hath thee from pleasing me debarr'd.
While thou wert plain, I lov'd thy mind and face,
Now inward faults thy outward form disgrace.
Love is a naked boy, his years sans stain,
And hath no clothes, but open doth remain.
Will you for gain have Cupid sell himself?
He hath no bosom where to hide base pelf.
Love and Love's son are with fierce arms to odds;
To serve for pay beseems not wanton gods.   20
The whore stands to be bought for each man's money,
And seeks vilde wealth by selling of her coney,
Yet greedy bawd's command she curseth still,
And doth, constrain'd, what you do of good will.
Take from irrational beasts a precedent;

'Tis shame their wits should be more excellent.
The mare asks not the horse, the cow the bull,
Nor the mild ewe gifts from the ram doth pull;
Only a woman gets spoils from a man,
Farms out herself on nights for what she can,   30
And lets what both delight, what both desire,
Making her joy according to her hire.
The sport being such as both alike sweet try it,
Why should one sell it and the other buy it?
Why should I lose and thou gain by the pleasure
Which man and woman reap in equal measure?
Knights of the post of perjuries make sale,
The unjust judge for bribes becomes a stale.
'Tis shame sold tongues the guilty should defend,
Or great wealth from a judgement seat ascend;   40
'Tis shame to grow rich by bed merchandise,
Or prostitute thy beauty for bad prize.
Thanks worthily are due for things unbought,
For beds ill-hir'd we are indebted nought.
The hirer payeth all, his rent discharg'd,
From further duty he rests then enlarg'd.
Fair dames forbear rewards for nights to crave,
Ill-gotten goods good end will never have.
The Sabine gauntlets were too dearly won
That unto death did press the holy nun.   50
The son slew her that forth to meet him went,
And a rich necklace caus'd that punishment.
Yet think no scorn to ask a wealthy churl;
He wants no gifts into thy lap to hurl.
Take clust'red grapes from an o'er-laden vine,
May bounteous loam Alcinous' fruit resign.
Let poor men show their service, faith, and care;
All for their mistress, what they have, prepare.
In verse to praise kind wenches 'tis my part,
And whom I like eternize by mine art.   60
Garments do wear, jewels and gold do waste,
The fame that verse gives doth for ever last.
To give I love, but to be ask'd disdain;
Leave asking, and I'll give what I refrain.

ELEGIA XI
Napen alloquitur, ut paratas tabellas ad Corinnam perferat
    In skilful gathering ruffled hairs in order,
Nape, free-born, whose cunning hath no border,

Thy service for night's scapes is known commodious,
And to give signs dull wit to thee is odious.
Corinna clips me oft by thy persuasion,
Never to harm me made thy faith evasion.
Receive these lines, them to thy mistress carry,
Be sedulous, let no stay cause thee tarry.
Nor flint nor iron are in thy soft breast,
But pure simplicity in thee doth rest.   10
And 'tis suppos'd Love's bow hath wounded thee,
Defend the ensigns of thy war in me.
If what I do she asks, say 'hope for night';
The rest my hand doth in my letters write.
Time passeth while I speak, give her my writ,
But see that forthwith she peruseth it.
I charge thee mark her eyes and front in reading,
By speechless looks we guess at things succeeding.
Straight being read, will her to write much back,
I hate fair paper should writ matter lack.   20
Let her make verses, and some blotted letter
On the last edge to stay mine eyes the better.
What need she tire her hand to hold the quill?
Let this word, 'Come', alone the tables fill.
Then with triumphant laurel will I grace them,
And in the midst of Venus' temple place them,
Subscribing that to her I consecrate
My faithful tables, being vile maple late.

ELEGIA XII

Tabellas quas miserat execratur, quod amica noctem negabat
  Bewail my chance: the sad book is returned,
This day denial hath my sport adjourned.
Presages are not vain; when she departed,
Nape by stumbling on the threshold started.
Going out again, pass forth the door more wisely,
And somewhat higher bear thy foot precisely.
Hence, luckless tables, funeral wood, be flying,
And thou the wax stuff'd full with notes denying,
Which I think gather'd from cold hemlock's flower,
Wherein bad honey Corsic bees did pour.   10
Yet as if mix'd with red lead thou wert ruddy,
That colour rightly did appear so bloody,
As evil wood thrown in the highways lie,
Be broke with wheels of chariots passing by,
And him that hew'd you out for needful uses

[437]

I'll prove had hands impure with all abuses.
Poor wretches on the tree themselves did strangle;
There sat the hangman for men's necks to angle.
To hoarse screech-owls foul shadows it allows,
Vultures and Furies nestled in the boughs.   20
To these my love I foolishly committed,
And then with sweet words to my mistress fitted;
More fitly had they wrangling bonds contained,
From barbarous lips of some attorney strained.
Among day-books and bills they had lain better
In which the merchant wails his bankrout debtor.
Your name approves you made for such like things,
The number two no good divining brings.
Angry, I pray that rotten age you wracks,
And sluttish white-mould overgrow the wax.

ELEGIA XIII
Ad Auroram, ne properet .
   Now o'er the sea from her old love comes she
That draws the day from heaven's cold axle-tree.
Aurora, whither slidest thou? down again,
And birds for Memnon yearly shall be slain.
Now in her tender arms I sweetly bide,
If ever, now well lies she by my side.
The air is cold, and sleep is sweetest now,
And birds send forth shrill notes from every bough:
Whither runn'st thou, that men and women love not?
Hold in thy rosy horses that they move not.   10
Ere thou rise, stars teach seamen where to sail,
But when thou comest, they of their courses fail.
Poor travellers, though tir'd, rise at thy sight,
And soldiers make them ready to the fight.
The painful hind by thee to field is sent,
Slow oxen early in the yoke are pent.
Thou coz'nest boys of sleep, and dost betray them
To pedants that with cruel lashes pay them.
Thou mak'st the surety to the lawyer run,
That with one word hath nigh himself undone.   20
The lawyer and the client hate thy view,
Both whom thou raisest up to toil anew.
By thy means women of their rest are barr'd,
Thou set'st their labouring hands to spin and card.
All could I bear; but that the wench should rise
Who can endure, save him with whom none lies?

How oft wish'd I night would not give thee place,
Nor morning stars shun thy uprising face.
How oft that either wind would break thy coach,
Or steeds might fall, forc'd with thick clouds' approach.   30
Whither goest thou, hateful nymph? Memnon the elf
Receiv'd his coal-black colour from thyself.
Say that thy love with Cephalus were not known,
Then thinkest thou thy loose life is not shown?
Would Tithon might but talk of thee awhile,
Not one in heaven should be more base and vile
Thou leav'st his bed because he's faint through age,
And early mount'st thy hateful carriage;
But held'st thou in thine arms some Cephalus,
Then wouldst thou cry, 'Stay night, and run not thus.'   40
Dost punish me, because years make him wane?
I did not bid thee wed an aged swain.
The moon sleeps with Endymion every day;
Thou art as fair as she, then kiss and play.
Jove, that thou shouldst not haste but wait his leisure,
Made two nights one to finish up his pleasure.
I chid no more; she blush'd, and therefore heard me,
Yet lingered not the day, but morning scar'd me.

ELEGIA XIV

Puellam consolatur cui prae nimia cura comae deciderant
   'Leave colouring thy tresses', I did cry;
Now hast thou left no hairs at all to dye.
But what had been more fair had they been kept?
Beyond thy robes thy dangling locks had swept.
Fear'dst thou to dress them being fine and thin,
Like to the silk the curious Seres spin,
Or threads which spider's slender foot draws out,
Fast'ning her light web some old beam about?
Not black nor golden were they to our view,
Yet although neither, mix'd of either's hue,   10
Such as in hilly Ida's wat'ry plains,
The cedar tall spoil'd of his bark retains.
Add, they were apt to curl an hundred ways,
And did to thee no cause of dolour raise.
Nor hath the needle, or the comb's teeth reft them,
The maid that kemb'd them ever safely left them.
Oft was she dress'd before mine eyes, yet never,
Snatching the comb to beat the wench, out drive her.
Oft in the morn, her hairs not yet digested,

[439]

Half-sleeping on a purple bed she rested;   20
Yet seemly, like a Thracian bacchanal,
That tir'd doth rashly on the green grass fall.
When they were slender, and like downy moss,
Thy troubled hairs, alas, endur'd great loss.
How patiently hot irons they did take,
In crooked trammels crispy curls to make.
I cried, ''Tis sin, 'tis sin, these hairs to burn,
They well become thee, then to spare them turn.
Far off be force, no fire to them may reach,
Thy very hairs will the hot bodkin teach.'   30
Lost are the goodly locks which from their crown
Phoebus and Bacchus wish'd were hanging down.
Such were they as Diana painted stands
All naked holding in her wave-moist hands.
Why dost thy ill-kemb'd tresses' loss lament?
Why in thy glass dost look being discontent?
Be not to see with wonted eyes inclin'd;
To please thyself, thyself put out of mind.
No charmed herbs of any harlot scath'd thee,
No faithless witch in Thessale waters bath'd thee.   40
No sickness harm'd thee (far be that away!),
No envious tongue wrought thy thick locks' decay.
By thine own hand and fault thy hurt doth grow,
Thou mad'st thy head with compound poison flow.
Now Germany shall captive hair-tires send thee,
And vanquish'd people curious dressings lend thee,
Which some admiring, O thou oft wilt blush,
And say, 'He likes me for my borrowed bush,
Praising for me some unknown Guelder dame,
But I remember when it was my fame.'   50
Alas she almost weeps, and her white cheeks,
Dy'd red with shame, to hide from shame she seeks.
She holds, and views her old locks in her lap;
Ay me, rare gifts unworthy such a hap.
Cheer up thyself, thy loss thou mayst repair,
And be hereafter seen with native hair.

ELEGIA XV
Ad invidos, quod fama poetarum sit perennis
   Envy, why carpest thou my time is spent so ill,
And terms my works fruits of an idle quill?
Or that unlike the line from whence I sprung,
War's dusty honours are refus'd, being young?

Nor that I study not the brawling laws,
Nor set my voice to sale in every cause?
Thy scope is mortal, mine eternal fame,
That all the world may ever chant my name.
Homer shall live while Tenedos stands and Ide,
Or into sea swift Simois doth slide.   10
Ascraeus lives while grapes with new wine swell,
Or men with crooked sickles corn down fell.
The world shall of Callimachus ever speak;
His art excell'd, although his wit was weak.
For ever lasts high Sophocles' proud vein,
With sun and moon Aratus shall remain.
While bondmen cheat, fathers be hard, bawds whorish,
And strumpets flatter, shall Menander flourish.
Rude Ennius and Plautus full of wit
Are both in fame's eternal legend writ.   20
What age of Varro's name shall not be told,
And Jason's Argos and the fleece of gold?
Lofty Lucretius shall live that hour
That nature shall dissolve this earthly bower.
Aeneas' war, and Tityrus shall be read,
While Rome of all the conquered world is head.
Till Cupid's bow and fiery shafts be broken,
Thy verses, sweet Tibullus, shall be spoken.
And Gallus shall be known from east to west;
So shall Lycoris whom he loved best.   30
Therefore when flint and iron wear away,
Verse is immortal, and shall ne'er decay.
To verse let kings give place, and kingly shows,
And banks o'er which gold-bearing Tagus flows.
Let base-conceited wits admire vilde things,
Fair Phoebus lead me to the Muses' springs.
About my head be quivering myrtle wound,
And in sad lovers' heads let me be found.
The living, not the dead, can envy bite,
For after death all men receive their right.   40
Then though death rakes my bones in funeral fire,
I'll live, and as he pulls me down mount higher.

P. Ovidii Nasonis Amorum, Liber Secundus

ELEGIA I

Quod pro gigantomachia amores scribere sit coactus

I, Ovid, poet of my wantonness,
Born at Peligny, to write more address.
So Cupid wills; far hence be the severe:
You are unapt my looser lines to hear.
Let maids whom hot desire to husbands lead,
And rude boys touch'd with unknown love, me read,
That some youth hurt as I am with Love's bow
His own flame's best acquainted signs may know,
And long admiring say, 'By what means learn'd
Hath this same poet my sad chance discern'd?'   10
I durst the great celestial battles tell,
Hundred-hand Gyges, and had done it well,
With Earth's revenge, and how Olympus' top
High Ossa bore, Mount Pelion up to prop.
Jove and Jove's thunderbolts I had in hand,
Which for his heaven fell on the Giants' band.
My wench her door shut, Jove's affairs I left,
Even Jove himself out of my wit was reft.
Pardon me, Jove, thy weapons aid me nought,
Her shut gates greater lightning than thine brought.   20
Toys and light elegies my darts I took,
Quickly soft words hard doors wide open strook.
Verses deduce the horned bloody moon,
And call the sun's white horses back at noon.
Snakes leap by verse from caves of broken mountains,
And turned streams run backward to their fountains.
Verses ope doors; and locks put in the post,
Although of oak, to yield to verses boast.
What helps it me of fierce Achill to sing?
What good to me will either Ajax bring?   30
Or he who warr'd and wand'red twenty year?
Or woeful Hector, whom wild jades did tear?
But when I praise a pretty wench's face,
She in requital doth me oft embrace.

[442]

A great reward: heroes, O famous names,
Farewell; your favour nought my mind inflames.
Wenches, apply your fair looks to my verse
Which golden Love doth unto me rehearse.

ELEGIA II

Ad Bagoum, ut custodiam puellae sibi commissae laxiorem habeat
  Bagous, whose care doth thy mistress bridle,
While I speak some few yet fit words, be idle.
I saw the damsel walking yesterday
There where the porch doth Danaus' fact display.
She pleas'd me soon, I sent, and her did woo,
Her trembling hand writ back she might not do.
And asking why, this answer she redoubled,
Because thy care too much thy mistress troubled.
Keeper, if thou be wise, cease hate to cherish;
Believe me, whom we fear, we wish to perish.   10
Nor is her husband wise; what needs defence
When unprotected there is no expense?
But furiously he follow his love's fire,
And think her chaste whom many do desire.
Stol'n liberty she may by thee obtain,
Which giving her, she may give thee again.
Wilt thou her fault learn, she may make thee tremble;
Fear to be guilty, then thou mayst dissemble.
Think when she reads, her mother letters sent her;
Let him go forth known, that unknown did enter;   20
Let him go see her though she do not languish,
And then report her sick and full of anguish.
If long she stays, to think the time more short
Lay down thy forehead in thy lap to snort.
Enquire not what with Isis may be done,
Nor fear lest she to the theatres run.
Knowing her scapes, thine honour shall increase,
And what less labour than to hold thy peace?
Let him please, haunt the house, be kindly us'd,
Enjoy the wench, let all else be refus'd.   30
Vain causes feign of him, the true to hide,
And what she likes let both hold ratified.
When most her husband bends the brows and frowns,
His fawning wench with her desire he crowns.
But yet sometimes to chide thee let her fall
Counterfeit tears, and thee lewd hangman call.
Object thou then what she may well excuse,

To stain all faith in truth, by false crimes' use.
Of wealth and honour so shall grow thy heap;
Do this and soon thou shalt thy freedom reap.   40
On tell-tales' necks thou seest the link-knit chains,
The filthy prison faithless breasts restrains.
Water in waters, and fruit flying touch
Tantalus seeks, his long tongue's gain is such;
While Juno's watchman Io too much ey'd,
Him timeless death took, she was deified.
I saw one's legs with fetters black and blue,
By whom the husband his wife's incest knew.
More he deserv'd; to both great harm he fram'd;
The man did grieve, the woman was defam'd.   50
Trust me, all husbands for such faults are sad,
Nor make they any man that hear them glad.
If he loves not, deaf ears thou dost importune;
Or if he loves, thy tale breeds his misfortune.
Nor is it easily prov'd, though manifest,
She safe by favour of her judge doth rest.
Though himself see, he'll credit her denial,
Condemn his eyes, and say there is no trial.
Spying his mistress' tears, he will lament
And say, 'This blab shall suffer punishment.'   60
Why fight'st 'gainst odds? To thee, being cast, do hap
Sharp stripes; she sitteth in the judge's lap.
To meet for poison or vilde facts we crave not,
My hands an unsheath'd shining weapon have not.
We seek that through thee safely love we may;
What can be easier than the thing we pray?

ELEGIA III
Ad Eunuchum servantem dominam
  Ay me, an eunuch keeps my mistress chaste,
That cannot Venus' mutual pleasure taste.
Who first depriv'd young boys of their best part,
With selfsame wounds he gave he ought to smart.
To kind requests thou wouldst more gentle prove,
If ever wench had made lukewarm thy love.
Thou wert not born to ride, or arms to bear,
Thy hands agree not with the warlike spear.
Men handle those; all manly hopes resign,
Thy mistress' ensigns must be likewise thine.   10
Please her, her hate makes others thee abhor;
If she discards thee, what use serv'st thou for?

[444]

Good form there is, years apt to play together,
Unmeet is beauty without use to wither.
She may deceive thee, though thou her protect,
What two determine never wants effect.
Our prayers move thee to assist our drift,
While thou hast time yet to bestow that gift.

ELEGIA IV
Quod amet mulieres, cuiuscunque formae sint
    I mean not to defend the scapes of any,
Or justify my vices being many.
For I confess, if that might merit favour,
Here I display my lewd and loose behaviour.
I loathe, yet after that I loathe I run;
O how the burden irks that we should shun.
I cannot rule myself, but where love please
Am driven like a ship upon rough seas.
No one face likes me best, all faces move,
A hundred reasons make me ever love.   10
If any eye me with a modest look,
I burn, and by that blushful glance am took.
And she that's coy I like for being no clown;
Methinks she should be nimble when she's down.
Though her sour looks a Sabine's brow resemble,
I think she'll do, but deeply can dissemble.
If she be learn'd, then for her skill I crave her;
If not, because she's simple I would have her.
Before Callimachus one prefers me far;
Seeing she likes my books, why should we jar?   20
Another rails at me, and that I write;
Yet would I lie with her if that I might.
Trips she, it likes me well; plods she, what than?
She would be nimbler, lying with a man.
And when one sweetly sings, then straight I long
To quaver on her lips even in her song.
Or if one touch the lute with art and cunning,
Who would not love those hands for their swift running?
And she I like that with a majesty
Folds up her arms and makes low courtesy.   30
To leave myself that am in love with all,
Some one of these might make the chastest fall.
If she be tall, she's like an Amazon,
And therefore fills the bed she lies upon;
If short, she lies the rounder; to speak troth,

Both short and long please me, for I love both.
I think what one undeck'd would be, being dress'd;
Is she attir'd? Then show her graces best.
A white wench thralls me, so doth golden yellow;
And nut-brown girls in doing have no fellow.   40
If her white neck be shadow'd with black hair,
Why, so was Leda's, yet was Leda fair.
Amber-tress'd is she, then on the morn think I;
My love alludes to every history.
A young wench pleaseth, and an old is good,
This for her looks, that for her womanhood.
Nay what is she that any Roman loves
But my ambitious ranging mind approves?

ELEGIA V
Ad amicam corruptam
   No love is so dear (quiver'd Cupid, fly)
That my chief wish should be so oft to die.
Minding thy fault, with death I wish to revel;
Alas, a wench is a perpetual evil.
No intercepted lines thy deeds display,
No gifts given secretly thy crime bewray:
O would my proofs as vain might be withstood,
Ay me, poor soul, why is my cause so good?
He's happy, that his love dares boldly credit,
To whom his wench can say, 'I never did it.'   10
He's cruel, and too much his grief doth favour,
That seeks the conquest by her loose behaviour.
Poor wretch I saw when thou didst think I slumb'red;
Not drunk, your faults in the split wine I numb'red.
I saw your nodding eyebrows much to speak,
Even from your cheeks part of a voice did break.
Not silent were thine eyes, the board with wine
Was scribbled, and thy fingers writ a line.
I knew your speech (what do not lovers see?)
And words that seem'd for certain marks to be.   20
Now many guests were gone, the feast being done,
The youthful sort to divers pastimes run.
I saw you then unlawful kisses join
(Such with my tongue it likes me to purloin).
None such the sister gives her brother grave,
But such kind wenches let their lovers have.
Phoebus gave not Diana such, 'tis thought,
But Venus often to her Mars such brought.

'What dost?' I cried, 'transport'st thou my delight?
My lordly hands I'll throw upon my right.   30
Such bliss is only common to us two,
In this sweet good why hath a third to do?'
This, and what grief enforc'd me say, I said;
A scarlet blush her guilty face array'd,
Even such as by Aurora hath the sky,
Or maids that their betrothed husbands spy;
Such as a rose mix'd with a lily breeds,
Or when the moon travails with charmed steeds,
Or such as, lest long years should turn the dye,
Arachne stains Assyrian ivory.   40
To these, or some of these, like was her colour,
By chance her beauty never shined fuller.
She view'd the earth: the earth to view beseem'd her.
She looked sad: sad, comely I esteem'd her.
Even kembed as they were, her locks to rend,
And scratch her fair soft cheeks I did intend.
Seeing her face, mine uprear'd arms descended,
With her own armour was my wench defended.
I that erewhile was fierce, now humbly sue,
Lest with worse kisses she should me endue.   50
She laugh'd, and kiss'd so sweetly as might make
Wrath-kindled Jove away his thunder shake.
I grieve lest others should such good perceive,
And wish hereby them all unknown to leave.
Also much better were they than I tell,
And ever seem'd as some new sweet befell.
'Tis ill they pleas'd so much, for in my lips
Lay her whole tongue hid, mine in hers she dips.
This grieves me not; no joined kisses spent
Bewail I only, though I them lament.   60
Nowhere can they be taught but in the bed;
I know no master of so great hire sped.

ELEGIA VI
In mortem psittaci
   The parrot, from east India to me sent,
Is dead; all fowls her exequies frequent!
Go, goodly birds, striking your breasts bewail,
And with rough claws your tender cheeks assail.
For woeful hairs let piece-torn plumes abound,
For long shrill'd trumpets let your notes resound.
Why, Philomel, dost Tereus' lewdness mourn?

[447]

All-wasting years have that complaint outworn.
Thy tunes let this rare bird's sad funeral borrow,
Itys is great but ancient cause of sorrow.   10
All you whose pinions in the clear air soar,
But most, thou friendly turtle-dove, deplore;
Full concord all your lives was you betwixt,
And to the end your constant faith stood fix'd.
What Pylades did to Orestes prove,
Such to the parrot was the turtle dove.
But what avail'd this faith? Her rarest hue?
Or voice that how to change the wild notes knew?
What helps it thou wert given to please my wench?
Birds' hapless glory, death thy life doth quench.   20
Thou with thy quills mightst make green emeralds dark,
And pass our scarlet of red saffron's mark;
No such voice-feigning bird was on the ground,
Thou spokest thy words so well with stammering sound.
Envy hath rapt thee, no fierce wars thou movedst,
Vain babbling speech and pleasant peace thou lovedst.
Behold how quails among their battles live,
·Which do perchance old age unto them give.
A little fill'd thee, and for love of talk,
Thy mouth to taste of many meats did balk.   30
Nuts were thy food, and poppy caus'd thee sleep,
Pure water's moisture thirst away did keep.
The ravenous vulture lives, the puttock hovers
Around the air, the caddesse rain discovers,
And crows survive arms-bearing Pallas' hate,
Whose life nine ages scarce bring out of date.
Dead is that speaking image of man's voice,
The parrot given me, the far world's best choice.
The greedy spirits take the best things first,
Supplying their void places with the worst.   40
Thersites did Protesilaus survive,
And Hector died, his brothers yet alive.
My wench's vows for thee what should I show,
Which stormy south winds into sea did blow?
The seventh day came, none following mightst thou see,
And the Fate's distaff empty stood to thee;
Yet words in thy benumbed palate rung:
'Farewell, Corinna', cried thy dying tongue.
Elysium hath a wood of holm-trees black,
Whose earth doth not perpetual green grass lack;   50
There good birds rest (if we believe things hidden)

Whence unclean fowls are said to be forbidden;
There harmless swans feed all abroad the river,
There lives the Phoenix one alone bird ever,
There Juno's bird displays his gorgeous feather,
And loving doves kiss eagerly together.
The parrot into wood receiv'd with these,
Turns all the goodly birds to what she please.
A grave her bones hides; on her corpse great grave
The little stones these little verses have: 60
'This tomb approves I pleas'd my mistress well,
My mouth in speaking did all birds excel.'

ELEGIA VII
Amicae se purgat quod ancillam non amet
      Dost me of new crimes always guilty frame?
To overcome, so oft to fight I shame.
If on the marble theatre I look,
One among many is to grieve thee took.
If some fair wench me secretly behold,
Thou arguest she doth secret marks unfold.
If I praise any, thy poor hairs thou tearest;
If blame, dissembling of my fault thou fearest.
If I look well, thou think'st thou dost not move;
If ill, thou say'st I die for others' love.   10
Would I were culpable of some offence,
They that deserve pain, bear't with patience.
Now rash accusing, and thy vain belief,
Forbid thine anger to procure my grief.
Lo how the miserable great-eared ass,
Dull'd with much beating, slowly forth doth pass.
Behold Cypassis, wont to dress thy head,
Is charg'd to violate her mistress' bed.
The gods from this sin rid me of suspicion,
To like a base wench of despis'd condition.   20
With Venus' game who will a servant grace?
Or any back made rough with stripes embrace?
Add she was diligent thy locks to braid,
And for her skill to thee a grateful maid,
Should I solicit her that is so just,
To take repulse, and cause her show my lust?
I swear by Venus, and the wing'd boy's bow,
Myself unguilty of this crime I know.

ELEGIA VIII
Ad Cypassim ancillam Corinnae

Cypassis, that a thousand ways trimm'st hair,
Worthy to kemb none but a goddess fair,
Our pleasant scapes show thee no clown to be,
Apt to thy mistress, but more apt to me.
Who that our bodies were compress'd bewray'd?
Whence knows Corinna that with thee I play'd?
Yet blush'd I not, nor us'd I any saying
That might be urg'd to witness our false playing.
What if a man with bondwomen offend,
To prove him foolish did I e'er contend?   10
Achilles burn'd with face of captive Briseis,
Great Agamemnon lov'd his servant Chryseis.
Greater than these myself I not esteem;
What graced kings, in me no shame I deem.
But when on thee her angry eyes did rush,
In both thy cheeks she did perceive thee blush.
But being present, might that work the best,
By Venus' deity how did I protest!
Thou, goddess, dost command a warm south blast
My false oaths in Carpathian seas to cast.   20
For which good turn my sweet reward repay,
Let me lie with thee, brown Cypass, today.
Ungrate, why feign'st new fears, and dost refuse?
Well mayst thou one thing for thy mistress use.
If thou deniest, fool, I'll our deeds express,
And as a traitor mine own fault confess,
Telling thy mistress where I was with thee,
How oft, and by what means we did agree.

ELEGIA IX
Ad Cupidinem

O Cupid, that dost never cease my smart,
O boy, that liest so slothful in my heart,
Why me that always was thy soldier found
Dost harm, and in thy tents why dost me wound?
Why burns thy brand, why strikes thy bow thy friends?
More glory by thy vanquish'd foes ascends.
Did not Pelides whom his spear did grieve,
Being requir'd, with speedy help relieve?
Hunters leave taken beasts, pursue the chase,
And than things found do ever further pace.   10
We people wholly given thee feel thine arms,

[450]

Thy dull hand stays thy striving enemies' harms.
Dost joy to have thy hooked arrows shaked
In naked bones? Love hath my bones left naked.
So many men and maidens without love;
Hence with great laud thou mayst a triumph move.
Rome, if her strength the huge world had not fill'd,
With strawy cabins now her courts should build.
The weary soldier hath the conquer'd fields,
His sword laid by, safe, though rude places yields.   20
The dock inharbours ships drawn from the floods,
Horse freed from service range abroad the woods.
And time it was for me to live in quiet
That have so oft serv'd pretty wenches' diet.
Yet should I curse a god, if he but said,
'Live without love', so sweet ill is a maid.
For when my loathing it of heat deprives me,
I know not whither my mind's whirlwind drives me.
Even as a headstrong courser bears away
His rider vainly striving him to stay,   30
Or as a sudden gale thrusts into sea
The haven-touching bark now near the lea,
So wavering Cupid brings me back amain,
And purple Love resumes his darts again.
Strike, boy, I offer thee my naked breast,
Here thou hast strength, here thy right hand doth rest.
Here of themselves thy shafts come, as if shot;
Better than I their quiver knows them not.
Hapless is he that all the night lies quiet,
And slumb'ring, thinks himself much blessed by it.   40
Fool, what is sleep but image of cold death?
Long shalt thou rest when Fates expire thy breath.
But me let crafty damsel's words deceive,
Great joys by hope I inly shall conceive.
Now let her flatter me, now chide me hard,
Let me enjoy her oft, oft be debarr'd.
Cupid, by thee Mars in great doubt doth trample,
And thy stepfather fights by thy example.
Light art thou, and more windy than thy wings;
Joys with uncertain faith thou tak'st and brings.   50
Yet, Love, if thou with thy fair mother hear,
Within my breast no desert empire bear;
Subdue the wand'ring wenches to thy reign,
So of both people shalt thou homage gain.

ELEGIA X
Ad Graecinum quod eodem tempore duas amet
  Graecinus (well I wot) thou told'st me once
I could not be in love with two at once.
By thee deceiv'd, by thee surpris'd am I,
For now I love two women equally.
Both are well favoured, both rich in array,
Which is the loveliest it is hard to say.
This seems the fairest, so doth that to me,
And this doth please me most, and so doth she.
Even as a boat toss'd by contrary wind,
So with this love and that, wavers my mind.   10
Venus, why doublest thou my endless smart?
Was not one wench enough to grieve my heart?
Why add'st thou stars to heaven, leaves to green woods,
And to the vast deep sea fresh water floods?
Yet this is better far than lie alone;
Let such as be mine enemies have none.
Yea, let my foes sleep in an empty bed,
And in the midst their bodies largely spread.
But may soft love rouse up my drowsy eyes,
And from my mistress' bosom let me rise.   20
Let one wench cloy me with sweet love's delight
If one can do't, if not, two every night.
Though I am slender, I have store of pith,
Nor want I strength, but weight, to press her with.
Pleasure adds fuel to my lustful fire,
I pay them home with that they most desire.
Oft have I spent the night in wantonness,
And in the morn been lively ne'er the less.
He's happy who love's mutual skirmish slays,
And to the gods for that death Ovid prays.   30
Let soldier chase his enemies amain,
And with his blood eternal honour gain;
Let merchants seek wealth and with perjur'd lips,
Being wrack'd, carouse the sea tir'd by their ships;
But when I die, would I might droop with doing,
And in the midst thereof, set my soul going,
That at my funerals some may weeping cry,
'Even as he led his life, so did he die.'

ELEGIA XI
Ad amicam navigantem
  The lofty pine, from high Mount Pelion raught,

Ill ways by rough seas wond'ring waves first taught,
Which rashly 'twixt the sharp rocks in the deep
Carried the famous golden-fleeced sheep.
O would that no oars might in seas have sunk,
The Argos wrack'd had deadly waters drunk.
Lo, country gods and known bed to forsake
Corinna means, and dangerous ways to take.
For thee the east and west winds make me pale,
With icy Boreas, and the southern gale. 10
Thou shalt admire no woods or cities there,
The unjust seas all bluish do appear.
The ocean hath no painted stones or shells,
The sucking shore with their abundance swells.
Maids, on the shore with marble-white feet tread,
So far 'tis safe; but to go farther dread.
Let others tell how winds fierce battles wage,
How Scylla's and Charybdis' waters rage,
And with what rocks the fear'd Cerannia threat,
In what gulf either Syrtes have their seat. 20
Let others tell this, and what each one speaks
Believe; no tempest the believer wreaks.
Too late you look back when with anchors weigh'd
The crooked bark hath her swift sails display'd.
The careful shipman now fears angry gusts,
And with the waters sees death near him thrusts.
But if that Triton toss the troubled flood,
In all thy face will be no crimson blood.
Then wilt thou Leda's noble twin-stars pray,
And 'he is happy whom the earth holds' say. 30
It is more safe to sleep, to read a book,
The Thracian harp with cunning to have strook;
But if my words with winged storms hence slip,
Yet, Galatea, favour thou her ship.
The loss of such a wench much blame will gather,
Both to the sea-nymphs and the sea-nymphs' father.
Go, minding to return with prosperous wind,
Whose blast may hither strongly be inclin'd,
Let Nereus bend the waves unto this shore,
Hither the winds blow, here the spring-tide roar. 40
Request mild Zephyr's help for thy avail,
And with thy hand assist the swelling sail.
I from the shore thy known ship first will see,
And say it brings her that preserveth me.
I'll clip and kiss thee with all contentation,

For thy return shall fall the vow'd oblation,
And in the form of beds we'll strew soft sand,
Each little hill shall for a table stand:
There wine being fill'd, thou many things shalt tell,
How almost wrack'd thy ship in main seas fell,   50
And hasting to me, neither darksome night
Nor violent south winds did thee aught affright.
I'll think all true, though it be feigned matter;
Mine own desires why should myself not flatter?
Let the bright day-star cause in heaven this day be,
To bring that happy time so soon as may be.

ELEGIA XII
Exultat, quod amica potitus sit
   About my temples go, triumphant bays;
Conquer'd Corinna in my bosom lays,
She whom her husband, guard, and gate, as foes,
Lest art should win her, firmly did enclose.
That victory doth chiefly triumph merit,
Which without bloodshed doth the prey inherit.
No little ditched towns, no lowly walls,
But to my share a captive damsel falls.
When Troy by ten years' battle tumbled down,
With the Atrides many gain'd renown: 10
But I no partner of my glory brook,
Nor can another say his help I took.
I, guide and soldier, won the field and wear her,
I was both horseman, footman, standard-bearer.
Nor in my act hath fortune mingled chance;
O care-got triumph, hitherwards advance.
Nor is my war's cause new; but for a queen
Europe and Asia in firm peace had been.
The Lapiths and the Centaurs, for a woman,
To cruel arms their drunken selves did summon.   20
A woman forc'd the Troyans new to enter
Wars, just Latinus, in thy kingdom's centre;
A woman against late-built Rome did send
The Sabine fathers, who sharp wars intend.
I saw how bulls for a white heifer strive,
She looking on them did more courage give.
And me with many, but yet me without murther,
Cupid commands to move his ensigns further.

ELEGIA XIII
Ad Isidem, ut parientem Corinnam iuvet

While rashly her womb's burden she casts out,
Weary Corinna hath her life in doubt.
She secretly with me such harm attempted,
Angry I was, but fear my wrath exempted.
But she conceiv'd of me, or I am sure
I oft have done what might as much procure.
Thou that frequents Canopus' pleasant fields,
Memphis, and Pharos that sweet date trees yields,
And where swift Nile in his large channel slipping,
By seven huge mouths into the sea is skipping,   10
By fear'd Anubis' visage I thee pray,
So in thy temples shall Osiris stay,
And the dull snake about thy off'rings creep,
And in thy pomp horn'd Apis with thee keep:
Turn thy looks hither, and in one spare twain:
Thou givest my mistress life, she mine again.
She oft hath serv'd thee upon certain days,
Where the French rout engirt themselves with bays.
On labouring women thou dost pity take,
Whose bodies with their heavy burdens ache.   20
My wench, Lucina, I entreat thee favour;
Worthy she is thou shouldst in mercy save her.
In white, with incense I'll thine altars greet,
Myself will bring vow'd gifts before thy feet,
Subscribing, 'Naso with Corinna sav'd.'
Do but deserve gifts with this title grav'd.
But if in so great fear I may advise thee,
To have this skirmish fought, let it suffice thee.

ELEGIA XIV
In amicam, quod abortivum ipsa fecerit

What helps it woman to be free from war,
Nor, being arm'd, fierce troops to follow far,
If without battle self-wrought wounds annoy them,
And their own privy-weapon'd hands destroy them?
Who unborn infants first to slay invented,
Deserv'd thereby with death to be tormented.
Because thy belly should rough wrinkles lack,
Wilt thou thy womb-inclosed offspring wrack?
Had ancient mothers this vile custom cherish'd,
All human kind by their default had perish'd;   10
Or stones, our stock's original, should be hurl'd

[455]

Again by some in this unpeopled world.
Who should have Priam's wealthy substance won,
If wat'ry Thetis had her child fordone?
In swelling womb her twins had Ilia killed,
He had not been that conquering Rome did build.
Had Venus spoil'd her belly's Troyan fruit,
The earth of Caesars had been destitute.
Thou also, that wert born fair, hadst decayed,
If such a work thy mother had assayed.   20
Myself, that better die with loving may,
Had seen, my mother killing me, no day.
Why tak'st increasing grapes from vine-trees full?
With cruel hand why dost green apples pull?
Fruits ripe will fall, let springing things increase,
Life is no light price of a small surcease.
Why with hid irons are your bowels torn?
And why dire poison give you babes unborn?
At Colchis stain'd with children's blood men rail,
And, mother-murder'd Itys, thee bewail;   30
Both unkind parents, but for causes sad,
Their wedlock's pledges veng'd their husbands bad.
What Tereus, what Jason you provokes
To plague your bodies with such harmful strokes?
Armenian tigers never did so ill,
Nor dares the lioness her young whelps kill.
But tender damsels do it, though with pain;
Oft dies she that her paunch-wrapp'd child hath slain;
She dies, and with loose hairs to grave is sent,
And whoe'er see her, worthily lament.   40
But in the air let these words come to nought,
And my presages of no weight be thought.
Forgive her, gracious gods, this one delict,
And on the next fault punishment inflict.

ELEGIA XV
Ad annulum, quem dono amicae dedit
    Thou ring that shalt my fair girl's finger bind,
Wherein is seen the giver's loving mind,
Be welcome to her, gladly let her take thee,
And her small joint's encircling round hoop make thee.
Fit her so well as she is fit for me,
And of just compass for her knuckles be.
Blest ring, thou in my mistress' hand shalt lie;
Myself, poor wretch, mine own gifts now envy.

O would that suddenly into my gift
I could myself by secret magic shift!   10
Then would I wish thee touch my mistress' pap,
And hide thy left hand underneath her lap;
I would get off though strait, and sticking fast,
And in her bosom strangely fall at last.
Then I, that I may seal her privy leaves,
Lest to the wax the hold-fast dry gem cleaves,
Would first my beauteous wench's moist lips touch,
Only I'll sign nought that may grieve me much.
I would not out, might I in one place hit,
But in less compass her small fingers knit.   20
My life, that I will shame thee never fear,
Or be a load thou shouldst refuse to bear.
Wear me, when warmest showers thy members wash,
And through the gem let thy lost waters pash.
But seeing thee, I think my thing will swell,
And even the ring perform a man's part well.
Vain things why wish I? Go, small gift from hand,
Let her my faith with thee given understand.

ELEGIA XVI
Ad amicam, ut ad rura sua veniat
　　Sulmo, Peligny's third part, me contains,
A small but wholesome soil with wat'ry veins.
Although the sun to rive the earth incline,
And the Icarian froward dog-star shine,
Pelignian fields with liquid rivers flow,
And on the soft ground fertile green grass grow.
With corn the earth abounds, with vines much more,
And some few pastures Pallas' olives bore.
And by the rising herbs, where clear springs slide,
A grassy turf the moistened earth doth hide.   10
But absent is my fire: lies I'll tell none,
My heat is here, what moves my heat is gone.
Pollux and Castor might I stand betwixt,
In heaven without thee would I not be fix'd.
Upon the cold earth pensive let them lay
That mean to travel some long irksome way,
Or else will maidens, young men's mates, to go
If they determine to persever so.
Then on the rough Alps should I tread aloft,
My hard way with my mistress would seem soft.   20
With her I durst the Libyan Syrtes break through,

And raging seas in boist'rous south winds plough.
No barking dogs that Scylla's entrails bear,
Nor thy gulfs, crooked Malea, would I fear;
No flowing waves with drowned ships forth-poured
By cloy'd Charybdis, and again devoured.
But if stern Neptune's windy power prevail,
And waters' force force helping gods to fail,
With thy white arms upon my shoulders seize,
So sweet a burden I will bear with ease.   30
The youth oft swimming to his Hero kind,
Had then swum over, but the way was blind.
But without thee, although vine-planted ground
Contains me, though the streams in fields surround,
Though hinds in brooks the running waters bring,
And cool gales shake the tall trees' leafy spring,
Healthful Peligny I esteem nought worth,
Nor do I like the country of my birth.
Scythia, Cilicia, Britain are as good,
And rocks dy'd crimson with Prometheus' blood.   40
Elms love the vines, the vines with elms abide,
Why doth my mistress from me oft divide?
Thou swarest division should not 'twixt us rise,
By me, and by my stars, thy radiant eyes.
Maids' words more vain and light than falling leaves,
Which, as it seems, hence wind and sea bereaves.
If any godly care of me thou hast,
Add deeds unto thy promises at last,
And with swift nags drawing thy little coach
(Their reins let loose), right soon my house approach.   50
But when she comes, you swelling mounts sink down,
And falling valleys be the smooth ways' crown.

ELEGIA XVII
Quod Corinnae soli sit serviturus
    To serve a wench if any think it shame,
He being judge, I am convinc'd of blame.
Let me be slandered, while my fire she hides,
That Paphos, and the flood-beat Cythera guides.
Would I had been my mistress' gentle prey,
Since some fair one I should of force obey.
Beauty gives heart; Corinna's looks excel;
Ay me, why is it known to her so well?
But by her glass disdainful pride she learns,
Nor she herself but first trimm'd up discerns.   10

[458]

Not though thy face in all things make thee reign
(O face most cunning mine eyes to detain),
Thou oughtst therefore to scorn me for thy mate:
Small things with greater may be copulate.
Love-snar'd Calypso is suppos'd to pray
A mortal nymph's refusing lord to stay.
Who doubts with Peleus Thetis did consort,
Egeria with just Numa had good sport,
Venus with Vulcan, though, smith's tools laid by,
With his stump foot he halts ill-favouredly.   20
This kind of verse is not alike, yet fit,
With shorter numbers the heroic sit.
And thou, my light, accept me howsoever,
Lay in the mid-bed, there be my lawgiver.
My stay no crime, my flight no joy shall breed,
Nor of our love to be asham'd we need.
For great revenues, I good verses have,
And many by me to get glory crave.
I know a wench reports herself Corinn:
What would not she give that fair name to win?   30
But sundry floods in one bank never go,
Eurotas cold, and poplar-bearing Po.
Nor in my books shall one but thou be writ,
Thou dost alone give matter to my wit.

ELEGIA XVIII
Ad Macrum, quod de amoribus scribat
   To tragic verse while thou Achilles train'st,
And new-sworn soldiers' maiden arms retain'st,
We, Macer, sit in Venus' slothful shade,
And tender love hath great things hateful made.
Often at length my wench depart I bid,
She in my lap sits still as erst she did.
I said, 'It irks me'; half to weeping framed,
'Ay me,' she cries, 'to love why art ashamed?'
Then wreathes about my neck her winding arms,
And thousand kisses gives that work my harms.   10
I yield, and back my wit from battles bring,
Domestic acts and mine own wars to sing.
Yet tragedies and sceptres fill'd my lines,
But though I apt were for such high designs,
Love laughed at my cloak and buskins painted,
And rule so soon with private hands acquainted.
My mistress' deity also drew me fro it,

[459]

And Love triumpheth o'er his buskin'd poet.
What lawful is, or we profess love's art,
(Alas, my precepts turn myself to smart!)   20
We write, or what Penelope sends Ulysses,
Or Phyllis' tears that her Demophöon misses,
What thankless Jason, Macareus, and Paris,
Phaedra, and Hippolyt may read, my care is,
And what poor Dido with her drawn sword sharp
Doth say, with her that lov'd the Aonian harp.
As soon as from strange lands Sabinus came,
And writings did from divers places frame,
White-cheek'd Penelope knew Ulysses' sign,
The stepdame read Hippolytus' lustless line,   30
Aeneas to Elisa answer gives,
And Phyllis hath to read, if now she lives.
Jason's sad letter doth Hypsipyle greet,
Sappho her vow'd harp lays at Phoebus' feet.
Nor of thee, Macer, that resound'st forth arms,
Is golden love hid in Mars' mid-alarms:
There Paris is, and Helen's crime's record,
With Laodamia, mate to her dead lord.
Unless I err, to these thou more incline
Than wars, and from thy tents wilt come to mine.   40

ELEGIA XIX
Ad rivalem, cui uxor curae non erat
  Fool, if to keep thy wife thou hast no need,
Keep her for me, my more desire to breed.
We scorn things lawful, stol'n sweets we affect,
Cruel is her that loves whom none protect.
Let us both lovers hope and fear alike,
And may repulse place for our wishes strike.
What should I do with fortune that ne'er fails me?
Nothing I love that at all times avails me.
Wily Corinna saw this blemish in me,
And craftily knows by what means to win me.   10
Ah, often, that her hale head ach'd, she lying,
Will'd me, whose slow feet sought delay, be flying;
Ah, oft, how much she might, she feign'd offence,
And doing wrong made show of innocence.
So having vex'd she nourish'd my warm fire,
And was again most apt to my desire.
To please me, what fair terms and sweet words has she!
Great gods, what kisses and how many gave she!

[460]

Thou also, that late took'st mine eyes away,
Oft cozen me, oft being woo'd, say nay;   20
And on thy threshold let me lie dispread,
Suff'ring much cold by hoary night's frost bred.
So shall my love continue many years;
This doth delight me, this my courage cheers.
Fat love, and too much fulsome, me annoys,
Even as sweet meat a glutted stomach cloys.
In brazen tower had not Danae dwelt,
A mother's joy by Jove she had not felt;
While Juno Io keeps, when horns she wore,
Jove lik'd her better than he did before.   30
Who covets lawful things takes leaves from woods,
And drinks stol'n waters in surrounding floods.
Her lover let her mock that long will reign;
Ay me, let not my warnings cause my pain.
Whatever haps, by suff'rance harm is done;
What flies I follow, what follows me I shun.
But thou, of thy fair damsel too secure,
Begin to shut thy house at evening sure.
Search at the door who knocks oft in the dark,
In night's deep silence why the ban-dogs bark.   40
Whether the subtle maid lines brings and carries,
Why she alone in empty bed oft tarries.
Let this care sometimes bite thee to the quick,
That to deceits it may me forward prick.
To steal sands from the shore he loves alife,
That can affect a foolish wittol's wife.
Now I forewarn, unless to keep her stronger
Thou dost begin, she shall be mine no longer.
Long have I borne much, hoping time would beat thee
To guard her well, that well I might entreat thee.   50
Thou suff'rest what no husband can endure,
But of my love it will an end procure.
Shall I, poor soul, be never interdicted,
Nor never with night's sharp revenge afflicted?
In sleeping shall I fearless draw my breath?
Wilt nothing do, why I should wish thy death?
Can I but loathe a husband grown a bawd?
By thy default thou dost our joys defraud.
Some other seek that may in patience strive with thee;
To pleasure me, forbid me to corrive with thee.   60

P. Ovidii Nasonis Amorum, Liber Tertius

ELEGIA I

Deliberatio poetae, utrum elegos pergat scribere an potius tragedias

An old wood stands uncut of long years' space,
'Tis credible some godhead haunts the place.
In midst thereof a stone-pav'd sacred spring,
Where round about small birds most sweetly sing.
Here while I walk, hid close in shady grove,
To find what work my muse might move, I strove.
Elegia came with hairs perfumed sweet,
And one, I think, was longer of her feet;
A decent form, thin robe, a lover's look,
By her foot's blemish greater grace she took.   10
Then with huge steps came violent Tragedy:
Stern was her front, her cloak on ground did lie;
Her left hand held abroad a regal sceptre,
The Lydian buskin in fit paces kept her.
And first she said, 'When will thy love be spent,
O poet careless of thy argument?
Wine-bibbing banquets tell thy naughtiness,
Each cross-way's corner doth as much express.
Oft some points at the prophet passing by,
And, "This is he whom fierce love burns", they cry.   20
A laughing-stock thou art to all the city,
While without shame thou sing'st thy lewdness' ditty.
'Tis time to move grave things in lofty style,
Long hast thou loiter'd; greater works compile.
The subject hides thy wit; men's acts resound;
This thou wilt say to be a worthy ground.
Thy muse hath play'd what may mild girls content,
And by those numbers is thy first youth spent.
Now give the Roman Tragedy a name,
To fill my laws thy wanton spirit frame.'   30
This said, she mov'd her buskins gaily varnish'd,
And seven times shook her head with thick locks garnish'd.
The other smil'd (I wot) with wanton eyes;
Err I? or myrtle in her right hand lies.

'With lofty words, stout Tragedy,' she said,
'Why tread'st me down? art thou aye gravely play'd?
Thou deign'st unequal lines should thee rehearse;
Thou fight'st against me using mine own verse;
Thy lofty style with mine I not compare,
Small doors unfitting for large houses are.   40
Light am I, and with me, my care, light Love;
Not stronger am I than the thing I move.
Venus without me should be rustical;
This goddess' company doth to me befall.
What gate thy stately words cannot unlock,
My flatt'ring speeches soon wide open knock.
And I deserve more than thou canst in verity,
By suff'ring much not borne by thy severity.
By me Corinna learns, cozening her guard,
To get the door with little noise unbarr'd;   50
And slipp'd from bed, cloth'd in a loose nightgown,
To move her feet unheard in setting down.
Ah, how oft on hard doors hung I engrav'd,
From no man's reading fearing to be sav'd!
But till the keeper went forth, I forget not,
The maid to hide me in her bosom let not.
What gift with me was on her birthday sent
But cruelly by her was drown'd and rent?
First of thy mind the happy seeds I knew,
Thou hast my gift, which she would from thee sue.'   60
She left; I said, 'You both I must beseech,
To empty air may go my fearful speech.
With sceptres and high buskins th'one would dress me,
So through the world should bright renown express me.
The other gives my love a conquering name;
Come therefore, and to long verse shorter frame.
Grant, Tragedy, thy poet time's least tittle,
Thy labour ever lasts, she asks but little.'
She gave me leave, soft loves in time make haste,
Some greater work will urge me on at last.   70

ELEGIA II
Ad amicam cursum equorum spectantem
  I sit not here the noble horse to see,
Yet whom thou favour'st, pray may conqueror be.
To sit and talk with thee I hither came,
That thou mayst know with love thou mak'st me flame.
Thou view'st the course, I thee: let either heed

[463]

What please them, and their eyes let either feed.
What horse-driver thou favour'st most is best,
Because on him thy care doth hap to rest.
Such chance let me have: I would bravely run,
On swift steeds mounted till the race were done.   10
Now would I slack the reins, now lash their hide,
With wheels bent inward now the ring-turn ride;
In running if I see thee, I shall stay,
And from my hands the reins will slip away.
Ah, Pelops from his coach was almost fell'd,
Hippodamia's looks while he beheld,
Yet he attain'd by her support to have her:
Let us all conquer by our mistress' favour.
In vain why fly'st back? Force conjoins us now:
The place's laws this benefit allow.   20
But spare my wench, thou, at her right hand seated,
By thy side's touching ill she is entreated.
And sit thou rounder, that behind us see;
For shame press not her back with thy hard knee.
But on the ground thy clothes too loosely lie;
Gather them up, or lift them, lo, will I.
Envious garments so good legs to hide!
The more thou look'st, the more the gown envied.
Swift Atalanta's flying legs, like these,
Wish in his hands grasp'd did Hippomenes.   30
Coat-tuck'd Diana's legs are painted like them,
When strong wild beasts she stronger hunts to strike them.
Ere these were seen, I burn'd; what will these do?
Flames into flame, floods thou pour'st seas into.
By these I judge delight me may the rest,
Which lie hid under her thin veil suppress'd.
Yet in the meantime wilt small winds bestow,
That from thy fan, mov'd by my hand, may blow?
Or is my heat of mind, not of the sky?
Is't women's love my captive breast doth fry?   40
While thus I speak, black dust her white robes ray;
Foul dust, from her fair body go away.
Now comes the pomp; themselves let all men cheer:
The shout is nigh, the golden pomp comes here.
First, Victory is brought with large spread wing:
Goddess, come here, make my love conquering.
Applaud you Neptune that dare trust his wave,
The sea I use not: me my earth must have.
Soldier, applaud thy Mars: no wars we move,

Peace pleaseth me, and in mid-peace is love.   50
With augurs Phoebus, Phoebe with hunters stands,
To thee, Minerva, turn the craftsmen's hands;
Ceres and Bacchus countrymen adore,
Champions please Pollux, Castor love horsemen more;
Thee, gentle Venus, and the boy that flies
We praise; great goddess, aid my enterprise.
Let my new mistress grant to be beloved;
She beck'd, and prosperous signs gave as she moved.
What Venus promis'd, promise thou we pray;
Greater than her, by her leave, th'art, I'll say.   60
The gods and their rich pomp witness with me,
For evermore thou shalt my mistress be.
Thy legs hang down, thou mayst, if that be best,
Awhile thy tiptoes on the footstool rest.
Now greatest spectacles the praetor sends,
Four-chariot horses from the lists' even ends.
I see whom thou affect'st: he shall subdue;
The horses seem as thy desire they knew.
Alas, he runs too far about the ring;
What dost? Thy wagon in less compass bring.   70
What dost, unhappy? Her good wishes fade,
Let with strong hand the rein to bend be made.
One slow we favour; Romans, him revoke,
And each give signs by casting up his cloak.
They call him back; lest their gowns toss thy hair,
To hide thee in my bosom straight repair.
But now again the barriers open lie,
And forth the gay troops on swift horses fly.
At least now conquer, and outrun the rest;
My mistress' wish confirm with my request.   80
My mistress hath her wish; my wish remain:
He holds the palm, my palm is yet to gain.
She smil'd, and with quick eyes behight some grace:
Pay it not here, but in another place.

ELEGIA III
De amica, quae periuraverat
    What, are these gods? Herself she hath forswore,
And yet remains the face she had before.
How long her locks were, ere her oath she took,
So long they be since she her faith forsook.
Fair white with rose red was before commix'd;
Now shine her looks pure white and red betwixt.

[465]

Her foot was small: her foot's form is most fit;
Comely tall was she: comely tall she's yet.
Sharp eyes she had: radiant like stars they be,
By which she perjur'd oft hath lied to me.   10
In sooth th'eternal powers grant maids' society
Falsely to swear, their beauty hath some deity.
By her eyes, I remember, late she swore,
And by mine eyes, and mine were pained sore.
Say, gods: if she unpunish'd you deceive,
For other's faults why do I loss receive?
But did you not so envy Cepheus' daughter,
For her ill-beauteous mother judg'd to slaughter?
'Tis not enough she shakes your record off,
And, unreveng'd, mock'd gods with me doth scoff.   20
But by my pain to purge her perjuries,
Cozen'd, I am the cozener's sacrifice.
God is a name, no substance, fear'd in vain,
And doth the world in fond belief detain,
Or if there be a God, he loves fine wenches,
And all things too much in their sole power drenches.
Mars girts his deadly sword on for my harm;
Pallas' lance strikes me with unconquer'd arm;
At me Apollo bends his pliant bow;
At me Jove's right hand lightning hath to throw.   30
The wronged gods dread fair ones to offend,
And fear those that to fear them least intend.
Who now will care the altars to perfume?
Tut, men should not their courage so consume.
Jove throws down woods and castles with his fire,
But bids his darts from perjur'd girls retire.
Poor Semele, among so many burn'd,
Her own request to her own torment turn'd;
But when her lover came, had she drawn back,
The father's thigh should unborn Bacchus lack.   40
Why grieve I? And of heaven reproaches pen?
The gods have eyes and breasts as well as men.
Were I a god, I should give women leave
With lying lips my godhead to deceive.
Myself would swear the wenches true did swear,
And I would be none of the gods severe.
But yet their gift more moderately use,
Or in mine eyes, good wench, no pain transfuse.

ELEGIA IV
Ad virum servantem coniugem
  Rude man, 'tis vain thy damsel to commend
To keeper's trust: their wits should them defend.
Who, without fear, is chaste, is chaste in sooth:
Who, because means want, doeth not, she doth.
Though thou her body guard, her mind is stain'd:
Nor, lest she will, can any be restrain'd.
Nor canst by watching keep her mind from sin;
All being shut out, th'adulterer is within.
Who may offend, sins least; power to do ill
The fainting seeds of naughtiness doth kill.   10
Forbear to kindle vice by prohibition,
Sooner shall kindness gain thy will's fruition.
I saw a horse against the bit stiff-neck'd
Like lightning go, his struggling mouth being check'd;
When he perceiv'd the reins let slack, he stay'd,
And on his loose mane the loose bridle laid.
How to attain what is denied we think,
Even as the sick desire forbidden drink.
Argus had either way an hundred eyes,
Yet by deceit love did them all surprise;   20
In stone and iron walls Danae shut,
Came forth a mother, though a maid there put.
Penelope, though no watch look'd unto her,
Was not defil'd by any gallant wooer.
What's kept, we covet more: the care makes theft;
Few love what others have unguarded left.
Nor doth her face please, but her husband's love;
I know not what men think should thee so move.
She is not chaste that's kept, but a dear whore;
Thy fear is than her body valued more.   30
Although thou chafe, stol'n pleasure is sweet play;
She pleaseth best, 'I fear' if any say.
A free-born wench no right 'tis up to lock,
So use we women of strange nations' stock.
Because the keeper may come say, 'I did it',
She must be honest to thy servant's credit.
He is too clownish whom a lewd wife grieves,
And this town's well-known custom not believes,
Where Mars his sons not without fault did breed,
Remus and Romulus, Ilia's twin-born seed.   40
Cannot a fair one, if not chaste, please thee?
Never can these by any means agree.

Kindly thy mistress use, if thou be wise;
Look gently, and rough husbands' laws despise.
Honour what friends thy wife gives, she'll give many;
Least labour so shall win great grace of any;
So shalt thou go with youths to feast together,
And see at home much that thou ne'er brought'st thither.

ELEGIA V
Ad amnem, dum iter faceret ad amicam
  Flood with reed-grown slime banks, till I be past
Thy waters stay; I to my mistress haste.
Thou hast no bridge, nor boat with ropes to throw,
That may transport me without oars to row.
Thee I have pass'd, and knew thy stream none such,
When thy wave's brim did scarce my ankles touch.
With snow thaw'd from the next hill now thou rushest,
And in thy foul deep waters thick thou gushest.
What helps my haste? What to have ta'en small rest?
What day and night to travel in her quest,   10
If standing here I can by no means get
My foot upon the further bank to set?
Now wish I those wings noble Perseus had,
Bearing the head with dreadful adders clad;
Now wish the chariot, whence corn seeds were found,
First to be thrown upon the untill'd ground.
I speak old poets' wonderful inventions,
Ne'er was, nor shall be, what my verse mentions.
Rather, thou large bank-overflowing river,
Slide in thy bounds, so shalt thou run for ever.   20
Trust me, land-stream, thou shalt no envy lack,
If I a lover be by thee held back.
Great floods ought to assist young men in love,
Great floods the force of it do often prove.
In mid-Bithynia, 'tis said, Inachus
Grew pale, and in cold fords hot lecherous.
Troy had not yet been ten years' siege outstander,
When nymph Neaera rapt thy looks, Scamander.
What, not Alpheus in strange lands to run
Th'Arcadian virgin's constant love hath won?   30
And Creusa unto Xanthus first affied,
They say Peneus near Phthia's town did hide.
What should I name Asop, that Thebe lov'd,
Thebe who mother of five daughters prov'd.
If, Achelous, I ask where thy horns stand,

Thou say'st, broke with Alcides' angry hand.
Not Calydon, nor Aetolia did please;
One Deianira was more worth than these.
Rich Nile by seven mouths to the vast sea flowing,
Who so well keeps his water's head from knowing,   40
Is by Evadne thought to take such flame
As his deep whirlpools could not quench the same.
Dry Enipeus, Tyro to embrace,
Fly back his stream charg'd; the stream charg'd, gave place.
Nor pass I thee, who hollow rocks down tumbling,
In Tibur's field with wat'ry foam art rumbling,
Whom Ilia pleas'd, though in her looks grief revell'd;
Her cheeks were scratch'd, her goodly hairs dishevell'd.
She, wailing Mars' sin and her uncle's crime,
Stray'd barefoot through sole places on a time.   50
Her from his swift waves the bold flood perceiv'd,
And from the mid-ford his hoarse voice upheav'd,
Saying, 'Why sadly tread'st my banks upon,
Ilia, sprung from Idaean Laomedon?
Where's thy attire? Why wand'rest here alone?
To stay thy tresses white veil hast thou none?
Why weep'st, and spoil'st with tears thy wat'ry eyes,
And fiercely knock'st thy breast that open lies?
His heart consists of flint and hardest steel
That seeing thy tears can any joy then feel.   60
Fear not: to thee our court stands open wide,
There shalt be lov'd: Ilia, lay fear aside.
Thou o'er a hundred nymphs or more shalt reign,
For five score nymphs or more our floods contain.
Nor, Roman stock, scorn me so much (I crave)
Gifts than my promise greater thou shalt have.'
This said he: she her modest eyes held down,
Her woeful bosom a warm shower did drown.
Thrice she prepar'd to fly, thrice she did stay,
By fear depriv'd of strength to run away.   70
Yet rending with enraged thumb her tresses,
Her trembling mouth these unmeet sounds expresses:
'O would in my forefathers' tomb deep laid
My bones had been, while yet I was a maid.
Why being a vestal am I woo'd to wed,
Deflower'd and stained in unlawful bed?
Why stay I? Men point at me for a whore,
Shame, that should make me blush, I have no more.'
This said, her coat hoodwinked her fearful eyes,

And into water desperately she flies.   80
'Tis said the slippery stream held up her breast,
And kindly gave her what she liked best.
And I believe some wench thou hast affected,
But woods and groves keep your faults undetected.
While thus I speak the waters more abounded,
And from the channel all abroad surrounded.
Mad stream, why dost our mutual joys defer?
Clown, from my journey why dost me deter?
How wouldst thou flow wert thou a noble flood,
If thy great fame in every region stood?   90
Thou hast no name, but com'st from snowy mountains;
No certain house thou hast, nor any fountains.
Thy springs are nought but rain and melted snow,
Which wealth cold winter doth on thee bestow.
Either th'art muddy in mid-winter tide,
Or full of dust dost on the dry earth slide.
What thirsty traveller ever drunk of thee?
Who said with grateful voice, 'Perpetual be'?
Harmful to beasts and to the fields thou proves;
Perchance these others, me mine own loss moves.   100
To this I fondly loves of floods told plainly,
I shame so great names to have used so vainly.
I know not what expecting, I erewhile
Named Achelous, Inachus, and Nile.
But for thy merits I wish thee, white stream,
Dry winters aye, and suns in heat extreme.

ELEGIA VI
Quod ab amica receptus cum ea coire non potuit, conqueritur
　　Either she was foul, or her attire was bad,
Or she was not the wench I wish'd t'have had.
Idly I lay with her, as if I lov'd not,
And like a burden griev'd the bed that mov'd not.
Though both of us perform'd our true intent,
Yet could I not cast anchor where I meant.
She on my neck her ivory arms did throw,
Her arms far whiter than the Scythian snow,
And eagerly she kiss'd me with her tongue,
And under mine her wanton thigh she flung.   10
Yea, and she sooth'd me up, and called me 'Sir',
And us'd all speech that might provoke and stir.
Yet like as if cold hemlock I had drunk,
It mocked me, hung down the head, and sunk.

Like a dull cipher or rude block I lay,
Or shade or body was I, who can say?
What will my age do, age I cannot shun,
Seeing in my prime my force is spent and done?
I blush, that being youthful, hot and lusty,
I prove neither youth nor man, but old and rusty.   20
Pure rose she, like a nun to sacrifice,
Or one that with her tender brother lies.
Yet boarded I the golden Chie twice,
And Libas, and the white-cheek'd Pitho thrice.
Corinna crav'd it in a summer's night,
And nine sweet bouts we had before daylight.
What, waste my limbs through some Thessalian charms?
May spells and drugs do silly souls such harms?
With virgin wax hath some imbas'd my joints,
And pierc'd my liver with sharp needle points?   30
Charms change corn to grass and make it die;
By charms are running springs and fountains dry.
By charms mast drops from oaks, from vines grapes fall,
And fruit from trees when there's no wind at all.
Why might not then my sinews be enchanted,
And I grow faint as with some spirit haunted?
To this add shame: shame to perform it quail'd me,
And was the second cause why vigour fail'd me.
My idle thoughts delighted her no more
Than did the robe or garment which she wore.   40
Yet might her touch make youthful Pylius' fire,
And Tithon livelier than his years require.
Even her I had and she had me in vain,
What might I crave more, if I ask again?
I think the great gods griev'd they had bestow'd
The benefit which lewdly I forslow'd.
I wish'd to be receiv'd in, in I get me;
To kiss, I kiss; to lie with her, she let me.
Why was I blest? Why made king to refuse it?
Chuff-like had I not gold and could not use it?   50
So in a spring thrives he that told so much,
And looks upon the fruits he cannot touch.
Hath any rose so from a fresh young maid
As she might straight have gone to church and pray'd?
Well, I believe she kiss'd not as she should,
Nor used the sleight and cunning which she could.
Huge oaks, hard adamants might she have moved,
And with sweet words cause deaf rocks to have loved.

Worthy she was to move both gods and men,
But neither was I man nor lived then.   60
Can deaf ears take delight when Phemius sings,
Or Thamyris in curious-painted things?
What sweet thought is there but I had the same?
And one gave place still as another came.
Yet notwithstanding, like one dead it lay,
Drooping more than a rose pull'd yesterday.
Now, when he should not jet, he bolts upright,
And craves his task, and seeks to be at fight.
Lie down with shame, and see thou stir no more,
Seeing now thou wouldst deceive me as before.   70
Thou cozen'st me: by thee surpris'd am I,
And bide sore loss with endless infamy.
Nay more, the wench did not disdain a whit
To take it in her hand and play with it,
But when she saw it would by no means stand,
But still droop'd down, regarding not her hand,
'Why mock'st thou me,' she cried, 'or being ill,
Who bade thee lie down here against thy will?
Either th'art witch'd with blood of frogs new dead,
Or jaded cam'st thou from some other's bed.'   80
With that, her loose gown on, from me she cast her;
In skipping out her naked feet much grac'd her.
And lest her maid should know of this disgrace,
To cover it, spilt water in the place.

ELEGIA VII
Quod ab amica non recipiatur, dolet
    What man will now take liberal arts in hand,
Or think soft verse in any stead to stand?
Wit was sometimes more precious than gold,
Now poverty great barbarism we hold.
When our books did my mistress fair content,
I might not go whither my papers went.
She prais'd me, yet the gate shut fast upon her,
I here and there go witty with dishonour.
See a rich chuff, whose wounds great wealth inferr'd,
For bloodshed knighted, before me preferr'd.   10
Fool, canst thou him in thy white arms embrace?
Fool, canst thou lie in his enfolding space?
Knowest not this head a helm was wont to bear?
This side that serves thee, a sharp sword did wear.
His left hand, whereon gold doth ill alight,

A target bore; blood-sprinkled was his right.
Canst touch that hand wherewith someone lie dead?
Ah, whither is thy breast's soft nature fled?
Behold the signs of ancient fight, his scars,
Whate'er he hath his body gain'd in wars.   20
Perhaps he'll tell how oft he slew a man,
Confessing this, why dost thou touch him than?
I, the pure priest of Phoebus and the Muses,
At thy deaf doors in verse sing my abuses.
Not what we slothful know, let wise men learn,
But follow trembling camps and battles stern,
And for a good verse draw the first dart forth:
Homer without this shall be nothing worth.
Jove, being admonish'd gold had sovereign power,
To win the maid came in a golden shower.   30
Till then, rough was her father, she severe,
The posts of brass, the walls of iron were;
But when in gifts the wise adulterer came,
She held her lap ope to receive the same.
Yet when old Saturn heaven's rule possess'd,
All gain in darkness the deep earth suppress'd.
Gold, silver, iron's heavy weight, and brass,
In hell were harbour'd; here was found no mass.
But better things it gave, corn without ploughs,
Apples, and honey in oaks' hollow boughs.   40
With strong ploughshares no man the earth did cleave,
The ditcher no marks on the ground did leave,
Nor hanging oars the troubled seas did sweep;
Men kept the shore, and sail'd not into deep.
Against thyself, man's nature, thou wert cunning,
And to thine own loss was thy wit swift running.
Why gird'st thy cities with a tow'red wall?
Why let'st discordant hands to armour fall?
What dost with seas? With th'earth thou wert content;
Why seek'st not heaven, the third realm, to frequent?   50
Heaven thou affects; with Romulus, temples brave
Bacchus, Alcides, and now Caesar have.
Gold from the earth instead of fruits we pluck;
Soldiers by blood to be enrich'd have luck.
Courts shut the poor out; wealth gives estimation;
Thence grows the judge and knight of reputation.
All they possess: they govern fields and laws,
They manage peace, and raw war's bloody jaws.
Only our loves let not such rich churls gain;

'Tis well if some wench for the poor remain.   60
Now, Sabine-like, though chaste she seems to live,
One her commands who many things can give.
For me, she doth keeper and husband fear;
If I should give, both would the house forbear.
If of scorn'd lovers god be venger just,
O let him change goods so ill got to dust.

ELEGIA VIII
Tibulli mortem deflet

If Thetis and the Morn their sons did wail,
And envious Fates great goddesses assail,
Sad Elegia, thy woeful hairs unbind:
Ah now a name too true thou hast, I find.
Tibullus, thy work's poet, and thy fame,
Burns his dead body in the funeral flame.
Lo Cupid brings his quiver spoiled quite,
His broken bow, his firebrand without light.
How piteously with drooping wings he stands,
And knocks his bare breast with self-angry hands.   10
The locks spread on his neck receive his tears,
And shaking sobs his mouth for speeches bears.
So at Aeneas' burial, men report,
Fair-fac'd Iulus, he went forth thy court.
And Venus grieves, Tibullus' life being spent,
As when the wild boar Adon's groin had rent.
The gods' care we are call'd, and men of piety,
And some there be that think we have a deity.
Outrageous death profanes all holy things,
And on all creatures obscure darkness brings.   20
To Thracian Orpheus what did parents good,
Or songs amazing wild beasts of the wood?
Where Linus by his father Phoebus layed
To sing with his unequall'd harp is sayed.
See Homer from whose fountain ever fill'd
Pierian dew to poets is distill'd:
Him the last day in black Avern hath drown'd;
Verses alone are with continuance crown'd.
The work of poets lasts Troy's labour's fame,
And that slow web night's falsehood did unframe.   30
So Nemesis, so Delia famous are:
The one his first love, th'other his new care.
What profit to us hath our pure life bred?
What to have lain alone in empty bed?

When bad fates take good men, I am forbod
By secret thoughts to think there is a god.
Live godly, thou shalt die; though honour heaven,
Yet shall thy life be forcibly bereaven.
Trust in good verse: Tibullus feels death's pains,
Scarce rests of all what a small urn contains.   40
Thee, sacred poet, could sad flames destroy?
Nor feared they thy body to annoy?
The holy gods' gilt temples they might fire
That durst to so great wickedness aspire.
Eryx' bright empress turn'd her looks aside,
And some that she refrain'd tears have denied.
Yet better is't, than if Corcyra's isle
Had thee unknown interr'd in ground most vile.
Thy dying eyes here did thy mother close,
Nor did thy ashes her last off'rings lose.   50
Part of her sorrow here thy sister bearing
Comes forth her unkemb'd locks asunder tearing.
Nemesis and thy first wench join their kisses
With thine, nor this last fire their presence misses.
Delia departing, 'Happier lov'd', she saith,
'Was I: thou liv'dst, while thou esteem'dst my faith.'
Nemesis answers, 'What's my loss to thee?
His fainting hand in death engrasped me.'
If aught remains of us but name and spirit,
Tibullus doth Elysium's joy inherit.   60
Your youthful brows with ivy girt to meet him,
With Calvus, learn'd Catullus, come and greet him,
And thou, if falsely charg'd to wrong thy friend,
Gallus, that car'st not blood and life to spend.
With these thy soul walks: souls if death release,
The godly sweet Tibullus doth increase.
Thy bones I pray may in the urn safe rest,
And may th'earth's weight thy ashes nought molest.

ELEGIA IX
*Ad Cererem, conquerens quod eius sacris cum amica concumbere non
permittatur*
      Come were the times of Ceres' sacrifice:
In empty bed alone my mistress lies.
Golden-haired Ceres, crown'd with ears of corn,
Why are our pleasures by thy means forborne?
Thee, goddess, bountiful all nations judge,
Nor less at man's prosperity any grudge.

Rude husbandmen bak'd not their corn before,
Nor on the earth was known the name of floor;
On mast of oaks, first oracles, men fed,
This was their meat, the soft grass was their bed.　10
First Ceres taught the seed in fields to swell,
And ripe-ear'd corn with sharp-edg'd scythes to fell;
She first constrain'd bulls' necks to bear the yoke,
And untill'd ground with crooked ploughshares broke.
Who thinks her to be glad at lovers' smart,
And worshipp'd by their pain and lying apart?
Nor is she, though she loves the fertile fields,
A clown, nor no love from her warm breast yields.
Be witness Crete (nor Crete doth all things feign),
Crete proud that Jove her nursery maintain.　20
There he who rules the world's star-spangled towers,
A little boy, drunk teat-distilling showers.
Faith to the witness Jove's praise doth apply;
Ceres, I think, no known fault will deny.
The goddess saw Iasion on Candian Ide,
With strong hand striking wild beasts' bristled hide;
She saw, and as her marrow took the flame,
Was divers ways distract with love and shame.
Love conquer'd shame, the furrows dry were burn'd,
And corn with least part of itself return'd.　30
When well-tossed mattocks did the ground prepare,
Being fit broken with the crooked share,
And seeds were equally in large fields cast,
The ploughman's hopes were frustrate at the last.
The grain-rich goddess in high woods did stray,
Her long hair's ear-wrought garland fell away.
Only was Crete fruitful that plenteous year;
Where Ceres went, each place was harvest there.
Ida, the seat of groves, did sing with corn,
Which by the wild boar in the woods was shorn.　40
Law-giving Minos did such years desire,
And wish'd the goddess long might feel love's fire.
Ceres, what sports to thee so grievous were,
As in thy sacrifice we them forbear?
Why am I sad, when Proserpine is found,
And Juno-like with Dis reigns underground?
Festival days ask Venus, songs and wine,
These gifts are meet to please the powers divine.

ELEGIA X
Ad amicam, a cuius amore discedere non potest
   Long have I borne much, mad thy faults me make:
Dishonest love, my wearied breast forsake.
Now have I freed myself, and fled the chain,
And what I have borne, shame to bear again.
We vanquish, and tread tam'd love under feet,
Victorious wreaths at length my temples greet.
Suffer, and harden: good grows by this grief,
Oft bitter juice brings to the sick relief.
I have sustain'd so oft thrust from the door
To lay my body on the hard moist floor.   10
I know not whom thou lewdly didst embrace,
When I to watch supplied a servant's place;
I saw when forth a tired lover went,
His side past service, and his courage spent.
Yet this is less than if he had seen me;
May that shame fall mine enemies' chance to be.
When have not I, fix'd to thy side, close layed?
I have thy husband, guard, and fellow played.
The people by my company she pleas'd;
My love was cause that more men's love she seiz'd.   20
What should I tell her vain tongue's filthy lies,
And, to my loss, god-wronging perjuries?
What secret becks in banquets with her youths,
With privy signs, and talk dissembling truths?
Hearing her to be sick, I thither ran,
But with my rival sick she was not than.
These hard'ned me, with what I keep obscure;
Some other seek, who will these things endure.
Now my ship in the wish'd haven crown'd,
With joy hears Neptune's swelling waters sound.   30
Leave thy once powerful words, and flatteries;
I am not as I was before, unwise.
Now love and hate my light breast each way move,
But victory, I think, will hap to love.
I'll hate, if I can; if not, love 'gainst my will:
Bulls hate the yoke, yet what they hate have still.
I fly her lust, but follow beauty's creature;
I loathe her manners, love her body's feature.
Nor with thee, nor without thee can I live,
And doubt to which desire the palm to give.   40
Or less fair, or less lewd would thou mightst be;
Beauty with lewdness doth right ill agree.

Her deeds gain hate, her face entreateth love;
Ah, she doth more worth than her vices prove.
Spare me, O by our fellow-bed, by all
The gods who by thee to be perjur'd fall,
And by thy face to me a pow'r divine,
And by thine eyes whose radiance burns out mine.
Whate'er thou art, mine art thou: choose this course,
Wilt have me willing, or to love by force?   50
Rather I'll hoist up sail, and use the wind,
That I may love yet, though against my mind.

ELEGIA XI
*Dolet amicam suam ita suis carminibus innotuisse ut rivales multos sibi
pararit*
  What day was that which, all sad haps to bring,
White birds to lovers did not always sing?
Or is I think my wish against the stars?
Or shall I plain some god against me wars?
Who mine was call'd, whom I lov'd more than any,
I fear with me is common now to many.
Err I? Or by my books is she so known?
'Tis so: by my wit her abuse is grown.
And justly: for her praise why did I tell?
The wench by my fault is set forth to sell.   10
The bawd I play, lovers to her I guide:
Her gate by my hands is set open wide.
'Tis doubtful whether verse avail or harm,
Against my good they were an envious charm.
When Thebes, when Troy, when Caesar should be writ,
Alone Corinna moves my wanton wit.
With Muse oppos'd would I my lines had done,
And Phoebus had forsook my work begun.
Nor, as use will not poets' record hear,
Would I my words would any credit bear.   20
Scylla by us her father's rich hair steals,
And Scylla's womb mad raging dogs conceals.
We cause feet fly, we mingle hairs with snakes,
Victorious Perseus a wing'd steed's back takes.
Our verse great Tityus a huge space outspreads,
And gives the viper-curled dog three heads.
We make Enceladus use a thousand arms,
And men enthrall'd by mermaids' singing charms.
The east winds in Ulysses' bags we shut,
And blabbing Tantalus in mid-waters put.   30

[478]

Niobe flint, Callist we make a bear,
Bird-changed Procne doth her Itys tear;
Jove turns himself into a swan, or gold,
Or his bull's horns Europa's hand doth hold.
Proteus what should I name? Teeth, Thebes' first seed?
Oxen in whose mouths burning flames did breed?
Heav'n star Electra, that bewail'd her sisters?
The ships whose godhead in the sea now glisters?
The sun turn'd back from Atreus' cursed table?
And sweet-touch'd harp that to move stones was able?   40
Poets' large power is boundless and immense,
Nor have their words true history's pretence.
And my wench ought to have seem'd falsely prais'd.
Now your credulity harm to me hath rais'd.

ELEGIA XII
De Iunonis festo

. When fruit-fill'd Tuscia should a wife give me,
We touch'd the walls, Camillus, won by thee.
The priests to Juno did prepare chaste feasts,
With famous pageants, and their home-bred beasts.
To know their rites well recompens'd my stay,
Though thither leads a rough steep hilly way.
There stands an old wood with thick trees dark clouded:
Who sees it grants some deity there is shrouded.
An altar takes men's incense and oblation,
An altar made after the ancient fashion.   10
Here, when the pipe with solemn tunes doth sound,
The annual pomp goes on the covered ground.
White heifers by glad people forth are led,
Which with the grass of Tuscan fields are fed,
And calves from whose fear'd front no threat'ning flies,
And little pigs, base hogsties' sacrifice,
And rams with horns their hard heads wreathed back;
Only the goddess-hated goat did lack,
By whom disclos'd, she in the high woods took
Is said to have attempted flight forsook.   20
Now is the goat brought through the boys with darts,
And give to him that the first wound imparts.
Where Juno comes, each youth and pretty maid
Show large ways, with their garments there display'd.
Jewels and gold their virgin tresses crown,
And stately robes to their gilt feet hang down.
As is the use, the nuns in white veils clad,

Upon their heads the holy mysteries had.
When the chief pomp comes, loud the people hollow,
And she her vestal virgin priests doth follow. 30
Such was the Greek pomp, Agamemnon dead,
Which fact and country wealth Halesus fled,
And having wand'red now through sea and land,
Built walls high tow'red with a prosperous hand.
He to th'Etrurians Juno's feast commended;
Let me, and them by it be aye befriended.

ELEGIA XIII
Ad amicam, si peccatura est, ut occulte peccet
Seeing thou art fair, I bar not thy false playing,
But let not me, poor soul, know of thy straying.
Nor do I give thee counsel to live chaste,
But that thou wouldst dissemble, when 'tis past.
She hath not trod awry that doth deny it;
Such as confess have lost their good names by it.
What madness is't to tell night pranks by day,
And hidden secrets openly to bewray?
The strumpet with the stranger will not do
Before the room be clear, and door put to. 10
Will you make shipwrack of your honest name,
And let the world be witness of the same?
Be more advis'd, walk as a puritan,
And I shall think you chaste, do what you can.
Slip still, only deny it when 'tis done,
And before folk immodest speeches shun.
The bed is for lascivious toyings meet;
There use all tricks, and tread shame under feet.
When you are up and dress'd, be sage and grave,
And in the bed hide all the faults you have. 20
Be not asham'd to strip you, being there,
And mingle thighs, yours ever mine to bear.
There in your rosy lips my tongue entomb,
Practise a thousand sports when there you come.
Forbear no wanton words you there would speak,
And with your pastime let the bedstead creak.
But with your robes put on an honest face,
And blush, and seem as you were full of grace.
Deceive all; let me err, and think I am right,
And like a wittol think thee void of sleight. 30
Why see I lines so oft receiv'd and given,
This bed and that by tumbling made uneven,

Like one start up, your hair toss'd and displac'd,
And with a wanton's tooth your neck new-rac'd?
Grant this, that what you do I may not see;
If you weigh not ill speeches, yet weigh me.
My soul fleets when I think what you have done,
And thorough every vein doth cold blood run.
Then thee whom I must love I hate in vain,
And would be dead, but dead with thee remain. 40
I'll not sift much, but hold thee soon excus'd,
Say but thou wert injuriously accus'd.
Though while the deed be doing you be took,
And I see when you ope the two-leav'd book,
Swear I was blind, deny, if you be wise,
And I will trust your words more than mine eyes.
From him that yields the palm is quickly got,
Teach but your tongue to say, 'I did it not',
And being justified by two words, think
The cause acquits you not, but I that wink. 50

ELEGIA XIV
Ad Venerem, quod elegis finem imponat
   Tender Love's mother, a new poet get;
This last end to my elegies is set,
Which I, Peligny's foster-child, have fram'd
(Nor am I by such wanton toys defam'd),
Heir of an ancient house, if help that can,
Not only by war's rage made gentleman.
In Virgil Mantua joys, in Catull Verone,
Of me Peligny's nation boasts alone,
Whom liberty to honest arms compell'd,
When careful Rome in doubt their prowess held. 10
And some guest, viewing wat'ry Sulmo's walls,
Where little ground to be enclos'd befalls,
'How such a poet could you bring forth?' says;
'How small soe'er, I'll you for greatest praise.'
Both loves to whom my heart long time did yield,
Your golden ensigns pluck out of my field.
Horn'd Bacchus greater fury doth distil,
A greater ground with great horse is to till.
Weak elegies, delightful Muse, farewell;
A work that after my death here shall dwell. 20

[481]

The Passionate Shepherd to His Love

'The Passionate Shepherd to his Love', which exists in a number of manuscripts, was first printed in *The Passionate Pilgrim*, probably in 1599, where it consists of four stanzas. A six-stanza version, attributed to '*Chr. Marlow*', was printed in *Englands Helicon* (1600). Izaak Walton finds a seventh stanza for the version he includes in the second edition of *The Compleat Angler* (1655).

Marlowe parodies himself in *The Jew of Malta* IV.ii.102. The date of composition is otherwise quite uncertain.

The Passionate Shepherd to His Love

Come live with me, and be my love,
And we will all the pleasures prove
That valleys, groves, hills and fields,
Woods, or steepy mountain yields.

And we will sit upon the rocks,
Seeing the shepherds feed their flocks
By shallow rivers, to whose falls
Melodious birds sing madrigals.

And I will make thee beds of roses,
And a thousand fragrant posies, 10
A cap of flowers, and a kirtle,
Embroid'red all with leaves of myrtle.

A gown made of the finest wool
Which from our pretty lambs we pull,
Fair-lined slippers for the cold,
With buckles of the purest gold.

A belt of straw and ivy-buds,
With coral clasps and amber studs,
And if these pleasures may thee move,
Come live with me, and be my love. 20

The shepherd swains shall dance and sing
For thy delight each May morning.
If these delights thy mind may move,
Then live with me, and be my love.

Lucan's First Book

Marlowe's translation of Lucan's *Pharsalia* Book I was entered
to John Wolf in the Stationers' Register on 28 September 1593
as 'Lucans *firste booke of the famous Civill warr betwixt POMPEY
and CESAR* Englished by Christopher Marlow'. This was
followed by the only edition, the (quarto-form) octavo of 1600,
published by Thomas Thorpe to be sold by Walter Burr.
Evidently Edward Blount had some right in the work. Thorpe
acknowledges this in the epistle. On 26 June 1600 '*HERO and
LEANDER* with *the .j. booke of* Lucan by MARLOWE' is mentioned amongst Paul Linley's books assigned to John Flasket.
The title-page of Flasket's 1600 edition of *Hero and Leander*
promises the Lucan, but the Chapman continuation of *Hero
and Leander* is included instead.

The date of composition is unknown. Marlowe's Latin text
for Lucan may have been that published in Frankfurt in
1551.

Blount: I purpose to be blunt with you, and out of my
dullness to encounter you with a dedication in the memory
of that pure elemental wit Chr. Marlowe, whose ghost or
genius is to be seen walk the churchyard in (at the least)
three or four sheets. Methinks you should presently look
wild now, and grow humorously frantic upon the taste of it.
Well, lest you should, let me tell you. This spirit was
sometime a familiar of your own, *Lucan's first book translated,*
which (in regard of your old right in it) I have rais'd in
the circle of your patronage. But stay now, Edward: if I   10
mistake not, you are to accommodate yourself with some
few instructions touching the property of a patron that you
are not yet possess'd of, and to study them for your better
grace as our gallants do fashions. First you must be proud
and think you have merit enough in you, though you are
ne'er so empty; then when I bring you the book take
physic, and keep state, assign me a time by your man to
come again, and afore the day be sure to have chang'd your
lodging; in the meantime sleep little, and sweat with the
invention of some pitiful dry jest or two which you may   20
happen to utter, with some little (or not at all) marking of
your friends, when you have found a place for them to come
in at; or if by chance something has dropp'd from you
worth the taking up, weary all that come to you with the
often repetition of it; censure scornfully enough, and somewhat like a traveller; commend nothing lest you discredit
your (that which you would seem to have) judgement.
These things if you can mould yourself to them, Ned, I
make no question but they will not become you. One
special virtue in our patrons of these days I have promis'd   30
myself you shall fit excellently, which is to give nothing; yes,
thy love I will challenge as my peculiar object, both in this,
and (I hope) many more succeeding offices. Farewell: I
affect not the world should measure my thoughts to thee by
a scale of this nature: leave to think good of me when I fall
from thee.

Thine in all rites of perfect friendship,

Thom. Thorpe

[488]

Lucan's First Book

Wars worse than civil on Thessalian plains,
And outrage strangling law, and people strong
We sing, whose conquering swords their own breasts launch'd,
Armies allied, the kingdom's league uprooted,
Th'affrighted world's force bent on public spoil,
Trumpets and drums like deadly threat'ning other,
Eagles alike display'd, darts answering darts.
　　Romans, what madness, what huge lust of war,
Hath made barbarians drunk with Latin blood?
Now Babylon, proud through our spoil, should stoop,   10
While slaught'red Crassus' ghost walks unreveng'd,
Will ye wage war, for which you shall not triumph?
Ay me, O what a world of land and sea
Might they have won whom civil broils have slain!
As far as Titan springs, where night dims heaven,
Ay to the torrid zone where mid-day burns,
And where stiff winter, whom no spring resolves,
Fetters the Euxine Sea with chains of ice;
Scythia and wild Armenia had been yok'd,
And they of Nilus' mouth, if there live any.   20
Rome, if thou take delight in impious war,
First conquer all the earth, then turn thy force
Against thyself: as yet thou wants not foes.
That now the walls of houses half-rear'd totter,
That rampires fallen down, huge heaps of stone
Lie in our towns, that houses are abandon'd,
And few live that behold their ancient seats,
Italy many years hath lien untill'd
And chok'd with thorns, that greedy earth wants hinds,
Fierce Pyrrhus, neither thou nor Hannibal   30
Art cause; no foreign foe could so afflict us;
These plagues arise from wreak of civil power.
But if for Nero (then unborn) the Fates
Would find no other means (and gods not slightly
Purchase immortal thrones, nor Jove joy'd heaven
Until the cruel Giants' war was done)
We plain not heavens, but gladly bear these evils
For Nero's sake: Pharsalia groan with slaughter,

And Carthage souls be glutted with our bloods;
At Munda let the dreadful battles join;   40
Add, Caesar, to these ills, Perusian famine,
The Mutin toils, the fleet at Leuca sunk,
And cruel field near burning Etna fought.
Yet Rome is much bound to these civil arms,
Which made thee emperor, thee (seeing thou, being old,
Must shine a star) shall heaven, whom thou lovest,
Receive with shouts, where thou wilt reign as king,
Or mount the sun's flame-bearing chariot,
And with bright restless fire compass the earth,
Undaunted though her former guide be chang'd;   50
Nature and every power shall give thee place,
What god it please thee be, or where to sway.
But neither choose the north t'erect thy seat,
Nor yet the adverse reeking southern pole,
Whence thou shouldst view thy Rome with squinting beams.
If any one part of vast heaven thou swayest,
The burdened axis with thy force will bend;
The midst is best; that place is pure and bright.
There, Caesar, mayst thou shine and no cloud dim thee,
Then men from war shall bide in league and ease,   60
Peace through the world from Janus' fane shall fly,
And bolt the brazen gates with bars of iron.
Thou, Caesar, at this instant art my god:
Thee if I invocate, I shall not need
To crave Apollo's aid or Bacchus' help,
Thy power inspires the Muse that sings this war.
The causes first I purpose to unfold
Of these garboils, whence springs a long discourse,
And what made madding people shake off peace.
The Fates are envious, high seats quickly perish,   70
Under great burdens falls are ever grievous;
Rome was so great it could not bear itself.
So when this world's compounded union breaks,
Time ends, and to old Chaos all things turn,
Confused stars shall meet, celestial fire
Fleet on the floods, the earth shoulder the sea,
Affording it no shore, and Phoebe's wain
Chase Phoebus, and enrag'd affect his place,
And strive to shine by day, and full of strife
Dissolve the engines of the broken world.   80
All great things crush themselves; such end the gods
Allot the height of honour, men so strong

By land and sea no foreign force could ruin.
O Rome, thyself art cause of all these evils,
Thyself thus shivered out to three men's shares:
Dire league of partners in a kingdom last not.
O faintly-join'd friends, with ambition blind,
Why join you force to share the world betwixt you?
While th'earth the sea, and air the earth sustains,
While Titan strives against the world's swift course,   90
Or Cynthia, night's queen, waits upon the day,
Shall never faith be found in fellow kings.
Dominion cannot suffer partnership;
This need no foreign proof nor far-fet story:
Rome's infant walls were steep'd in brother's blood;
Nor then was land, or sea, to breed such hate,
A town with one poor church set them at odds.
    Caesar's and Pompey's jarring love soon ended,
'Twas peace against their wills; betwixt them both
Stepp'd Crassus in, even as the slender Isthmus   100
Betwixt the Aegean and the Ionian sea
Keeps each from other, but being worn away,
They both burst out, and each encounter other:
So whenas Crassus' wretched death who stay'd them
Had fil'd Assyrian Carrha's walls with blood,
His loss made way for Roman outrages.
Parthians, y'afflict us more than ye suppose:
Being conquered, we are plagu'd with civil war.
Swords share our empire; Fortune, that made Rome
Govern the earth, the sea, the world itself,   110
Would not admit two lords; for Julia,
Snatch'd hence by cruel fates with ominous howls,
Bare down to hell her son, the pledge of peace,
And all bands of that death-presaging alliance.
Julia, had heaven given thee longer life,
Thou hadst restrain'd thy headstrong husband's rage,
Yea, and thy father too, and, swords thrown down,
Made all shake hands as once the Sabines did;
Thy death broke amity, and train'd to war
These captains emulous of each other's glory.   120
Thou fear'dst, great Pompey, that late deeds would dim
Old triumphs, and that Caesar's conquering France
Would dash the wreath thou war'st for pirates' wrack.
Thee war's use stirr'd, and thoughts that always scorn'd
A second place; Pompey could bide no equal,
Nor Caesar no superior: which of both

Had justest cause unlawful 'tis to judge.
Each side had great partakers: Caesar's cause
The gods abetted, Cato lik'd the other.
Both differ'd much: Pompey was strook in years,   130
And by long rest forgot to manage arms,
And being popular sought by liberal gifts
To gain the light unstable commons' love,
And joy'd to hear his theatre's applause;
He liv'd secure, boasting his former deeds,
And thought his name sufficient to uphold him,
Like to a tall oak in a fruitful field,
Bearing old spoils and conquerors' monuments,
Who though his root be weak, and his own weight
Keep him within the ground, his arms all bare,   140
His body (not his boughs) send forth a shade;
Though every blast it nod and seem to fall
When all the woods about stand bolt upright,
Yet he alone is held in reverence.
Caesar's renown for war was less, he restless,
Shaming to strive but where he did subdue;
When ire or hope provok'd, heady and bold,
At all times charging home, and making havoc;
Urging his fortune, trusting in the gods,
Destroying what withstood his proud desires,   150
And glad when blood and ruin made him way:
So thunder which the wind tears from the clouds,
With crack of riven air and hideous sound
Filling the world, leaps out and throws forth fire,
Affrights poor fearful men, and blasts their eyes
With overthwarting flames, and raging shoots
Alongst the air, and, nought resisting it,
Falls, and returns, and shivers where it lights.
Such humours stirr'd them up; but this war's seed
Was even the same that wracks all great dominions.   160
When Fortune made us lords of all, wealth flow'd,
And then we grew licentious and rude;
The soldiers' prey and rapine brought in riot;
Men took delight in jewels, houses, plate,
And scorn'd old sparing diet, and ware robes
Too light for women; Poverty, who hatched
Rome's greatest wits, was loath'd, and all the world
Ransack'd for gold, which breeds the world decay;
And then large limits had their butting lands,
The ground which Curius and Camillus till'd   170

Was stretch'd unto the fields of hinds unknown.
Again, this people could not brook calm peace,
Them freedom without war might not suffice;
Quarrels were rife, greedy desire, still poor,
Did vilde deeds; then 'twas worth the price of blood,
And deem'd renown to spoil their native town;
Force mastered right, the strongest govern'd all.
Hence came it that th'edicts were overrul'd,
That laws were broke, tribunes with consuls strove,
Sale made of offices, and people's voices   180
Bought by themselves and sold, and every year
Frauds and corruption in the field of Mars;
Hence interest and devouring usury sprang,
Faith's breach, and hence came war to most men welcome.
  Now Caesar overpass'd the snowy Alps;
His mind was troubled, and he aim'd at war,
And coming to the ford of Rubicon,
At night in dreadful vision fearful Rome
Mourning appear'd, whose hoary hairs were torn,
And on her turret-bearing head dispers'd,   190
And arms all naked, who with broken sighs,
And staring, thus bespoke: 'What mean'st thou, Caesar?
Whither goes my standard? Romans if ye be,
And bear true hearts, stay here!' This spectacle
Strook Caesar's heart with fear, his hair stood up,
And faintness numb'd his steps there on the brink.
He thus cried out: 'Thou thunderer that guard'st
Rome's mighty walls built on Tarpeian rock,
Ye gods of Phrygia and Iulus' line,
Quirinus' rites and Latian Jove advanc'd   200
On Alba hill, O vestal flames, O Rome,
My thought's sole goddess, aid mine enterprise.
I hate thee not, to thee my conquests stoop;
Caesar is thine, so please it thee, thy soldier;
He, he afflicts Rome that made me Rome's foe.'
This said, he laying aside all lets of war
Approach'd the swelling stream with drum and ensign;
Like to a lion of scorch'd desert Afric,
Who, seeing hunters, pauseth till fell wrath
And kingly rage increase, then having whisk'd   210
His tail athwart his back, and crest heav'd up,
With jaws wide open ghastly roaring out,
Albeit the Moor's light javelin or his spear
Sticks in his side, yet runs upon the hunter.

In summer time the purple Rubicon,
Which issues from a small spring, is but shallow,
And creeps along the vales dividing just
The bounds of Italy from Cisalpine France;
But now the winter's wrath, and wat'ry moon,
Being three days old, enforc'd the flood to swell,   220
And frozen Alps thaw'd with resolving winds.
The thunder-hoof'd horse, in a crooked line,
To scape the violence of the stream, first waded,
Which being broke the foot had easy passage.
As soon as Caesar got unto the bank
And bounds of Italy, 'Here, here,' saith he,
'An end of peace; here end polluted laws;
Hence, leagues and covenants; Fortune, thee I follow,
War and the Destinies shall try my cause.'
This said, the restless general through the dark,   230
Swifter than bullets thrown from Spanish slings,
Or darts which Parthians backward shoot, march'd on,
And then, when Lucifer did shine alone,
And some dim stars, he Ariminum enter'd.
Day rose, and view'd these tumults of the war;
Whether the gods or blust'ring south were cause
I know not, but the cloudy air did frown.
The soldiers, having won the market-place,
There spread the colours, with confused noise
Of trumpet's clang, shrill cornets, whistling fifes.   240
The people started; young men left their beds
And snatch'd arms near their household-gods hung up,
Such as peace yields: worm-eaten leathern targets
Through which the wood peer'd, headless darts, old swords
With ugly teeth of black rust foully scarr'd.
But seeing white eagles, and Rome's flags well known,
And lofty Caesar in the thickest throng,
They shook for fear, and cold benumb'd their limbs,
And muttering much, thus to themselves complain'd:
'O walls unfortunate, too near to France,   250
Predestinate to ruin; all lands else
Have stable peace, here war's rage first begins,
We bide the first brunt. Safer might we dwell
Under the frosty Bear, or parching East,
Wagons or tents, than in this frontier town.
We first sustain'd the uproars of the Gauls
And furious Cimbrians, and of Carthage Moors;
As oft as Rome was sack'd, here 'gan the spoil.'

Thus sighing whispered they, and none durst speak
And show their fear or grief; but as the fields,   260
When birds are silent thorough winter's rage,
Or sea far from the land, so all were whist.
Now light had quite dissolv'd the misty night,
And Caesar's mind unsettled musing stood;
But gods and Fortune prick'd him to this war,
Infringing all excuse of modest shame,
And labouring to approve his quarrel good.
The angry Senate, urging Gracchus' deeds,
From doubtful Rome wrongly expell'd the tribunes
That cross'd them; both which now approach'd the camp,   270
And with them Curio, sometime tribune too,
One that was fee'd for Caesar, and whose tongue
Could tune the people to the nobles' mind.
'Caesar,' said he, 'while eloquence prevail'd,
And I might plead, and draw the commons' minds
To favour thee, against the Senate's will
Five years I length'ned thy command in France;
But law being put to silence by the wars,
We, from our houses driven, most willingly
Suffered exile: let thy sword bring us home.   280
Now, while their part is weak and fears, march hence:
Where men are ready, lingering ever hurts.
In ten years wonn'st thou France; Rome may be won
With far less toil, and yet the honour's more;
Few battles fought with prosperous success
May bring her down, and with her all the world.
Nor shalt thou triumph when thou com'st to Rome,
Nor Capitol be adorn'd with sacred bays.
Envy denies all; with thy blood must thou
Aby thy conquest past: the son decrees   290
To expel the father; share the world thou canst not;
Enjoy it all thou mayst.' Thus Curio spake,
And therewith Caesar, prone enough to war,
Was so incens'd as are Eleius steeds
With clamours, who, though lock'd and chain'd in stalls,
Souse down the walls, and make a passage forth.
Straight summon'd he his several companies
Unto the standard; his grave look appeas'd
The wrestling tumult, and right hand made silence,
And thus he spake: 'You that with me have borne   300
A thousand brunts, and tried me full ten years,
See how they quit our blood shed in the north,

Our friends' death, and our wounds, our wintering
Under the Alps; Rome rageth now in arms
As if the Carthage Hannibal were near.
Cornets of horse are mustered for the field,
Woods turn'd to ships; both land and sea against us.
Had foreign wars ill-thriv'd, or wrathful France
Pursu'd us hither, how were we bested,
When, coming conqueror, Rome afflicts me thus?   310
Let come their leader whom long peace hath quail'd,
Raw soldiers lately press'd, and troops of gowns;
Brabbling Marcellus; Cato whom fools reverence;
Must Pompey's followers, with strangers' aid,
Whom from his youth he brib'd, needs make him king?
And shall he triumph long before his time,
And having once got head still shall he reign?
What should I talk of men's corn reap'd by force,
And by him kept of purpose for a dearth?
Who sees not war sit by the quivering judge,   320
And sentence given in rings of naked swords,
And laws assail'd, and arm'd men in the Senate?
'Twas his troop hemm'd in Milo being accus'd;
And now, lest age might wane his state, he casts
For civil war, wherein through use he's known
To exceed his master, that arch-traitor Sulla.
As brood of barbarous tigers, having lapp'd
The blood of many a herd, whilst with their dams
They kennell'd in Hyrcania, evermore
Will rage and prey: so, Pompey, thou having lick'd   330
Warm gore from Sulla's sword art yet athirst;
Jaws flesh'd with blood continue murderous.
Speak, when shall this thy long-usurp'd power end?
What end of mischief? Sulla teaching thee,
At last learn, wretch, to leave thy monarchy.
What, now Sicilian pirates are suppress'd,
And jaded king of Pontus poisoned slain,
Must Pompey as his last foe plume on me,
Because at his command I wound not up
My conquering eagles? Say I merit nought,   340
Yet, for long service done, reward these men,
And so they triumph, be't with whom ye will.
Whither now shall these old bloodless souls repair?
What seats for their deserts? What store of ground
For servitors to till? What colonies
To rest their bones? Say, Pompey, are these worse

Than pirates of Sicilia? They had houses.
Spread, spread these flags that ten years' space have
   conquer'd.
Let's use our tried force; they that now thwart right,
In wars will yield to wrong: the gods are with us.   350
Neither spoil nor kingdom seek we by these arms,
But Rome at thraldom's feet to rid from tyrants.'
This spoke, none answer'd; but a murmuring buzz
Th'unstable people made: their household gods
And love to Rome (though slaughter steel'd their hearts,
And minds were prone) restrain'd them; but war's love
And Caesar's awe dash'd all. Then Laelius,
The chief centurion, crown'd with oaken leaves
For saving of a Roman citizen,
Stepp'd forth and cried: 'Chief leader of Rome's force,   360
So be I may be bold to speak a truth,
We grieve at this thy patience and delay.
What doubt'st thou us? Even now when youthful blood
Pricks forth our lively bodies, and strong arms·
Can mainly throw the dart, wilt thou endure
These purple grooms, that Senate's tyranny?
Is conquest got by civil war so heinous?
Well, lead us then to Syrtes' desert shore,
Or Scythia, or hot Libya's thirsty sands.
This hand, that all behind us might be quail'd,   370
Hath with thee pass'd the swelling ocean,
And swept the foaming breast of Arctic Rhene.
Love overrules my will, I must obey thee,
Caesar; he whom I hear thy trumpets charge
I hold no Roman; by these ten blest ensigns
And all thy several triumphs, shouldst thou bid me
Entomb my sword within my brother's bowels,
Or father's throat, or women's groaning womb,
This hand, albeit unwilling, should perform it;
Or rob the gods, or sacred temples fire.   380
These troops should soon pull down the church of Jove.
If to encamp on Tuscan Tiber's streams,
I'll boldly quarter out the fields of Rome;
What walls thou wilt be levell'd with the ground,
These hands shall thrust the ram, and make them fly,
Albeit the city thou wouldst have so raz'd
Be Rome itself.' Here every band applauded,
And with their hands held up all jointly cried
They'll follow where he please. The shouts rent heaven,

As when against pine-bearing Ossa's rocks   390
Beats Thracian Boreas, or when trees bow down
And rustling swing up as the wind fets breath.
    When Caesar saw his army prone to war,
And Fates so bent, lest sloth and long delay
Might cross him, he withdrew his troops from France,
And in all quarters musters men for Rome.
They by Lemannus' nook forsook their tents;
They whom the Lingons foil'd with painted spears,
Under the rocks by crooked Vogesus;
And many came from shallow Isara,   400
Who, running long, falls in a greater flood,
And ere he sees the sea loseth his name;
The yellow Ruthens left their garrisons;
Mild Atax glad it bears not Roman boats,
And frontier Varus that the camp is far,
Sent aid; so did Alcides' port, whose seas
Eat hollow rocks, and where the north-west wind
Nor Zephyr rules not, but the north alone
Turmoils the coast, and enterance forbids;
And others came from that uncertain shore   410
Which is nor sea, nor land, but ofttimes both,
And changeth as the ocean ebbs and flows;
Whether the sea roll always from that point
Whence the wind blows, still forced to and fro,
Or that the wand'ring main follow the moon,
Or flaming Titan, feeding on the deep,
Pulls them aloft, and makes the surge kiss heaven,
Philosophers, look you, for unto me,
Thou cause, whate'er thou be whom God assigns
This great effect, art hid. They came that dwell   420
By Nemes' fields, and banks of Satirus,
Where Tarbel's winding shores embrace the sea;
The Santons that rejoice in Caesar's love,
Those of Bituriges and light Axon pikes;
And they of Rhene and Leuca, cunning darters,
And Sequana that well could manage steeds;
The Belgians apt to govern British cars;
Th'Averni too, which boldly feign themselves
The Romans' brethren, sprung of Ilian race;
The stubborn Nervians stain'd with Cotta's blood,   430
And Vangions who, like those of Sarmata,
Wear open slops; and fierce Batavians,
Whom trumpets' clang incites, and those that dwell

By Cinga's stream, and where swift Rhodanus
Drives Araris to sea; they near the hills
Under whose hoary rocks Gebenna hangs;
And Trevier, thou being glad that wars are past thee;
And you, late-shorn Ligurians, who were wont
In large-spread hair to exceed the rest of France;
And where to Hesus and fell Mercury   440
They offer human flesh, and where Jove seems
Bloody like Dian, whom the Scythians serve.
And you, French Bardi, whose immortal pens
Renown the valiant souls slain in your wars,
Sit safe at home and chant sweet poesy.
And, Druides, you now in peace renew
Your barbarous customs and sinister rites;
In unfell'd woods and sacred groves you dwell,
And only gods and heavenly powers you know,
Or only know you nothing. For you hold   450
That souls pass not to silent Erebus
Or Pluto's bloodless kingdom, but elsewhere
Resume a body: so, if truth you sing,
Death brings long life. Doubtless these northren men,
Whom death, the greatest of all fears, affright not,
Are blest by such sweet error; this makes them
Run on the sword's point and desire to die,
And shame to spare life which being lost is won.
You likewise that repuls'd the Cayc foe,
March towards Rome; and you, fierce men of Rhene,   460
Leaving your country open to the spoil.
These being come, their huge power made him bold
To manage greater deeds; the bordering towns
He garrison'd, and Italy he fill'd with soldiers.
Vain fame increas'd true fear, and did invade
The people's minds, and laid before their eyes
Slaughter to come, and swiftly bringing news
Of present war, made many lies and tales.
One swears his troops of daring horsemen fought
Upon Mevania's plain, where bulls are graz'd;   470
Other that Caesar's barbarous bands were spread
Along Nar flood that into Tiber falls,
And that his own ten ensigns and the rest
March'd not entirely, and yet hide the ground;
And that he's much chang'd, looking wild and big,
And far more barbarous than the French, his vassals,
And that he lags behind with them, of purpose,

Born 'twixt the Alps and Rhene, which he hath brought
From out their northren parts, and that Rome,
He looking on, by these men should be sack'd.   480
Thus in his fright did each man strengthen Fame,
And, without ground, fear'd what themselves had feign'd.
Nor were the commons only strook to heart
With this vain terror, but the Court, the Senate:
The fathers' selves leap'd from their seats, and, flying,
Left hateful war decreed to both the consuls.
Then, with their fear and danger all distract,
Their sway of flight carries the heavy rout
That in chain'd troops break forth at every port;
You would have thought their houses had been fir'd,   490
Or, dropping-ripe, ready to fall with ruin;
So rush'd the inconsiderate multitude
Thorough the city, hurried headlong on,
As if the only hope that did remain
To their afflictions were t'abandon Rome.
Look how when stormy Auster from the breach
Of Libyan Syrtes rolls a monstrous wave
Which makes the mainsail fall with hideous sound,
The pilot from the helm leaps in the sea,
And mariners, albeit the keel be sound,   500
Shipwrack themselves: even so, the city left,
All rise in arms, nor could the bedrid parents
Keep back their sons, or women's tears their husbands;
They stay'd not either to pray or sacrifice,
Their household gods restrain them not, none lingered
As loth to leave Rome whom they held so dear;
Th'irrevocable people fly in troops.
O gods, that easy grant men great estates,
But hardly grace to keep them: Rome, that flows
With citizens and captives, and would hold   510
The world (were it together) is by cowards
Left as a prey now Caesar doth approach.
When Romans are besieg'd by foreign foes,
With slender trench they escape night stratagems,
And sudden rampire rais'd of turf snatch'd up
Would make them sleep securely in their tents.
Thou, Rome, at name of war runn'st from thyself,
And wilt not trust thy city walls one night:
Well might these fear, when Pompey fear'd and fled.
Now evermore, lest some one hope might ease   520
The commons' jangling minds, apparent signs arose,

Strange sights appear'd, the angry threat'ning gods
Fill'd both the earth and seas with prodigies;
Great store of strange and unknown stars were seen
Wandering about the north, and rings of fire
Fly in the air, and dreadful bearded stars,
And comets that presage the fall of kingdoms;
The flattering sky glitter'd in often flames,
And sundry fiery meteors blaz'd in heaven,
Now spear-like, long, now like a spreading torch;   530
Lightning in silence stole forth without clouds,
And from the northren climate snatching fire
Blasted the Capitol; the lesser stars
Which wont to run their course through empty night,
At noonday mustered; Phoebe, having fill'd
Her meeting horns to match her brother's light,
Strook with th'earth's sudden shadow, waxed pale;
Titan himself thron'd in the midst of heaven
His burning chariot plung'd in sable clouds
And whelm'd the world in darkness, making men   540
Despair of day, as did Thyestes' town,
Mycenae, Phoebus flying through the east.
Fierce Mulciber unbarred Etna's gate,
Which flamed not on high, but headlong pitch'd
Her burning head on bending Hespery.
Coal-black Charybdis whirl'd a sea of blood;
Fierce mastiffs howl'd; the vestal fires went out;
The flame in Alba, consecrate to Jove,
Parted in twain, and with a double point
Rose like the Theban brothers' funeral fire;   550
The earth went off her hinges, and the Alps
Shook the old snow from off their trembling laps.
The ocean swell'd as high as Spanish Calpe,
Or Atlas' head. Their saints and household gods
Sweat tears to show the travails of their city.
Crowns fell from holy statues, ominous birds
Defil'd the day; at night wild beasts were seen,
Leaving the woods, lodge in the streets of Rome.
Cattle were seen that muttered human speech;
Prodigious births with more and ugly joints   560
Than nature gives, whose sight appals the mother;
And dismal prophecies were spread abroad;
And they whom fierce Bellona's fury moves
To wound their arms, sing vengeance; Cybel's priests,
Curling their bloody locks, howl dreadful things;

Souls quiet and appeas'd sigh'd from their graves;
Clashing of arms was heard; in untrod woods
Shrill voices shright, and ghosts encounter men.
Those that inhabited the suburb fields
Fled; foul Erinnys stalk'd about the walls,   570
Shaking her snaky hair and crooked pine
With flaming top, much like that hellish fiend
Which made the stern Lycurgus wound his thigh,
Or fierce Agave mad; or like Megaera
That scar'd Alcides, when by Juno's task
He had before look'd Pluto in the face.
Trumpets were heard to sound; and with what noise
An armed battle joins, such and more strange
Black night brought forth in secret: Sulla's ghost
Was seen to walk, singing sad oracles;   580
And Marius' head above cold Tav'ron peering,
His grave broke open, did affright the boors.
To these ostents, as their old custom was,
They call th'Etrurian augurs, amongst whom
The gravest, Arruns, dwelt in forsaken *Luca,   *or Luna
Well skill'd in pyromancy, one that knew
The hearts of beasts, and flight of wand'ring fowls.
First he commands such monsters Nature hatch'd
Against her kind, the barren mule's loath'd issue,
To be cut forth and cast in dismal fires;   590
Then, that the trembling citizens should walk
About the city; then the sacred priests
That with divine lustration purg'd the walls,
And went the round, in and without the town.
Next, an inferior troop, in tuck'd-up vestures,
After the Gabine manner; then the nuns
And their veil'd matron who alone might view
Minerva's statue; then, they that keep and read
Sibylla's secret works, and wash their saint
In Almo's flood; next, learned augurs follow,   600
Apollo's soothsayers, and Jove's feasting priests,
The skipping Salii with shields like wedges,
And flamens last, with network woollen veils.
While these thus in and out had circled Rome,
Look what the lightning blasted Arruns takes,
And it inters with murmurs dolorous,
And calls the place bidental; on the altar
He lays a ne'er-yok'd bull, and pours down wine,
Then crams salt leaven on his crooked knife;

The beast long struggled, as being like to prove   610
An awkward sacrifice, but by the horns
The quick priest pull'd him on his knees and slew him.
No vein sprung out, but from the yawning gash,
Instead of red blood, wallowed venomous gore.
These direful signs made Arruns stand amaz'd,
And searching farther for the gods' displeasure,
The very colour scar'd him; a dead blackness
Ran through the blood, that turn'd it all to jelly,
And stain'd the bowels with dark loathsome spots;
The liver swell'd with filth, and every vein   620
Did threaten horror from the host of Caesar:
A small thin skin contain'd the vital parts;
The heart stirr'd not, and from the gaping liver
Squeez'd matter through the caul the entrails pour'd;
And which (ay me) ever pretendeth ill,
At that bunch where the liver is, appear'd
A knob of flesh, whereof one half did look
Dead and discolour'd, th'other lean and thin.
By these he seeing what mischiefs must ensue
Cried out, 'O gods! I tremble to unfold   630
What you intend: great Jove is now displeas'd,
And in the breast of this slain bull are crept
Th'infernal powers. My fear transcends my words,
Yet more will happen than I can unfold.
Turn all to good, be augury vain, and Tages,
Th'art's master, false.' Thus in ambiguous terms
Involving all, did Arruns darkly sing.
But Figulus, more seen in heavenly mysteries,
Whose like Egyptian Memphis never had
For skill in stars and tuneful planeting,   640
In this sort spake: 'The world's swift course is lawless
And casual; all the stars at random range;
Or if Fate rule them, Rome, thy citizens
Are near some plague. What mischief shall ensue?
Shall towns be swallowed? Shall the thick'ned air
Become intemperate? Shall the earth be barren?
Shall water be congeal'd and turn'd to ice?
O gods, what death prepare ye? With what plague
Mean ye to rage? The death of many men
Meets in one period. If cold noisome Saturn   650
Were now exalted, and with blue beams shin'd,
Then Ganymede would renew Deucalion's flood,
And in the fleeting sea the earth be drench'd.

[503]

O Phoebus, shouldst thou with thy rays now singe
The fell Nemean beast, th'earth would be fir'd,
And heaven tormented with thy chafing heat;
But thy fires hurt not. Mars, 'tis thou inflam'st
The threat'ning Scorpion with the burning tail,
And fir'st his cleyes. Why art thou thus enrag'd?
Kind Jupiter hath low declin'd himself;   660
Venus is faint; swift Hermes retrograde;
Mars only rules the heaven. Why do the planets
Alter their course, and vainly dim their virtue?
sword-girt Orion's side glisters too bright:
War's rage draws near, and to the sword's strong hand
Let all laws yield, sin bear the name of virtue.
Many a year these furious broils let last;
Why should we wish the gods should ever end them?
War only gives us peace. O Rome, continue
The course of mischief, and stretch out the date   670
Of slaughter; only civil broils make peace.'
These sad presages were enough to scare
The quivering Romans, but worse things affright them.
As Maenas full of wine on Pindus raves,
So runs a matron through th'amazed streets,
Disclosing Phoebus' fury in this sort:
'Paean, whither am I hal'd? Where shall I fall,
Thus borne aloft? I see Pangaeus' hill
With hoary top, and under Haemus' mount
Philippi plains. Phoebus, what rage is this?   680
Why grapples Rome, and makes war, having no foes?
Whither turn I now? Thou lead'st me toward th'east,
Where Nile augmenteth the Pelusian sea;
This headless trunk that lies on Nilus' sand
I know. Now throughout the air I fly
To doubtful Syrtes and dry Afric, where
A fury leads the Emathian bands; from thence
To the pine-bearing hills, hence to the mounts
Pyrene, and so back to Rome again.
See, impious war defiles the Senate-house,   690
New factions rise; now through the world again
I go; O Phoebus, show me Neptune's shore
And other regions; I have seen Philippi.'
This said, being tir'd with fury she sunk down.

FINIS.

In Obitum Rogeri Manwood

The epitaph on Sir Roger Manwood is found twice in a manuscript commonplace-book which is now in the Folger Library but which was once kept by Henry Oxinden (1609–70), a country gentleman in Kent, a Marlowe enthusiast who copied out extracts from his works and hearsay about his life. Manwood, born in 1525, had had a distinguished legal career before his death on 14 December 1592; he was one of the judges before whom Marlowe appeared in December 1589 at the Old Bailey. He is known to have been a benefactor to his birthplace Sandwich and to his later parish of St Stephen's, Canterbury, where he is buried; and his son Sir Peter followed in his footsteps as a patron of letters.

At the foot of one version of the epitaph there is the note 'C. Marlo. Auth: Hero. & Lean', and in the margin are translations, taken from Thomas Cooper's *Thesaurus Linguae Romanae & Britannicae*, of *ganeonis, †Nepotes and ‡effœtas, each being underlined and marked with conventional signs (here modernized) in the text: '* a hanter of baudrie & riotous houses, a ruffian, a ravener of a dilicate meates a gluttoun. † riotous persons ‡ with much bear⟨i⟩ng spent'. At the foot of the other version of the epitaph there is the longer note: '* These verses above written were made by Christopher Marlo, who was a Shomakers son of Canterbury; it was that Marlo, who made the 2 first bookes of Hero & Leander, witnes Mr Alderich.' Simon Aldrich, who came of another Canterbury family, entered Trinity College, Cambridge, about 1593, graduated B.A. in 1596 or 1597, and was a fellow by 1599; he proceeded M.A. 1600, B.D. 1607, and was a vicar in Sussex 1611–26; up to the time of his death in 1655 he was Oxinden's tenant and neighbour, and is cited as the authority for several statements in the commonplace-books about Marlowe's art, learning, atheism, and death.

On the Death of Sir Roger Manwood

In obitum honoratissimi viri Rogeri Manwood
militis quaestorii Reginalis Capitalis
Baronis

Noctivagi terror, ganeonis triste flagellum,
Et Jovis Alcides, rigido vulturque latroni,
Urna subtegitur. Scelerum gaudete nepotes.
Insons, luctifica sparsis cervice capillis
Plange; fori lumen, venerandae gloria legis,
Occidit: heu, secum effetas Acherontis ad oras
Multa abiit virtus. Pro tot virtutibus uni,
Livor, parce viro; non audacissimus esto
Illius in cineres, cuius tot milia vultus
Mortalium attonuit: sic cum te nuntia Ditis   10
Vulneret exsanguis, feliciter ossa quiescant,
Famaque marmorei superet monumenta sepulchri.

ON THE DEATH OF THE MOST NOBLE GENTLEMAN, SIR ROGER
MANWOOD, LORD CHIEF BARON OF THE QUEEN'S EXCHEQUER.

The terror of the night-prowler, the grim scourge of the
profligate, Jove's Hercules, a vulture to the rough highway-
man, lies within an urn. Rejoice, you sons of crime; you who
are innocent, mourn, with hair flowing over your pitiable
neck; the light of the courts, the glory of the venerable law,
is dead. Alas, much virtue has departed with him to the
unfruitful shores of Acheron. Because of his many virtues,
Envy, spare this man alone. Do not vent your insolence on
the ashes of him whose countenance awed so many thousands
of mortals. So may your bones lie happily at rest, and may
your fame outlive the memorials on your marble tomb, when
the bloodless messenger of Pluto wounds you.

Appendix

The Baines Note

There are two copies of the Baines Note among the Harleian Manuscripts in the British Library, Harl. 6848 fol. 185-6 and Harl. 6853 fol. 307-8. The relation between them is uncertain, but the former appears to go back to an earlier state of the text, and so it is given here. On the back there is a largely obliterated endorsement with a hand pointing at it: it concludes with 'of his blasphemies', and traces of what may be the name 'Richard Baines' are discernible above this. The other manuscript of the Note is endorsed 'Copy of Marloe's blasphemies as sent to her H[ighness]', i.e. to the Queen. There are a number of differences in the two texts, some of them no doubt due to the carelessness of the scribe. But an editor has also been at work. In the 6853 text, the reference to Sir Walter Raleigh as Hariot's master does not appear at all; nor does the unbiblical sister of the woman of Samaria. The heading first written (which was originally much the same as in 6848) is scored through and a new one interlined: 'A note delivered on Whitsun Eve last of the most horrible blasphemies and damnable opinions uttered by Christofer Marly, who within 3 days after came to a sudden and fearful end of his life.' Even so, the latter part is a second thought: the editor first wrote 'who since Whit-Sunday died a sudden and violent death', but then scrapped it. Marlowe was in any case killed on 30 May, some three days *before* Whitsun Eve, which fell on 2 June 1593. The editor also marks material to be cut: the shaven crowns in the list of papistical ceremonies, the article on boys and tobacco, the article on coining, and the rambling peroration beginning 'These things, with many other' and concluding with a veiled reference to 'some great men'. Then there are a few tinkerings: oddly, 'the woman of Samaria' becomes 'the women of Samaria' to suit the plurals that linger in the article; the spelling 'Barabas' that has crept once into the text is corrected (with an interesting punctiliousness); and in the margin, against the name of Richard Chomley, stands the ominous jotting, 'He is laid for'.

The allegations of the Note are consistent with other evidence as to Marlowe's expressed opinions, including letters written by Thomas Kyd, the playwright and former friend of

[511]

Marlowe's. There was a Richard Baines, a merchant's son born in St Peter's, Cornhill, in 1566, who in 1582 was formally admitted to the Middle Temple but took up residence at St John's College, Oxford. On his father's death in 1588 he came to the notice of the Privy Council for attempting to defraud a creditor, a merchant stranger. Thomas Hariot (1560–1621) was an outstanding mathematician and scientist (with the inevitable reputation for sorcery) in the service of Sir Walter Raleigh. John Poole was a coiner in Newgate Prison when Marlowe was held there in 1589. Richard Chomley was a government agent who was in the personal service of the Earl of Essex. Information laid against him which is also preserved in the Harleian Manuscripts alleges opinions, including atheism, similar to those alleged to be Marlowe's. He is reported to have said that 'Marlowe told him that he hath read the atheist lecture to Sir Walter Raleigh and others'.

A note containing the opinion of one Christopher Marly concerning his damnable judgment of religion and scorn of God's word

That the Indians and many authors of antiquity have assuredly written of above sixteen thousand years agone, whereas Adam is proved to have lived within six thousand years.

He affirmeth that Moses was but a juggler and that one Heriots, being Sir W. Raleigh's man, can do more than he.

That Moses made the Jews to travel forty years in the wilderness, which journey might have been done in less than one year, ere they came to the Promised Land, to the intent that those who were privy to most of his subtleties might perish, and so an everlasting superstition remain in the hearts of the people.

That the first beginning of religion was only to keep men in awe.

That it was an easy matter for Moses, being brought up in all the arts of the Egyptians, to abuse the Jews, being a rude and gross people.

That Christ was a bastard and his mother dishonest.

That he was the son of a carpenter and that, if the Jews among whom he was born did crucify him, they best knew him and whence he came.

That Christ deserved better to die than Barabbas and that the Jews made a good choice though Barabbas were both a thief and a murderer.

That if there be any God or any good religion, then it is in the papists', because the service of God is performed with more ceremonies, as elevation of the mass, organs, singing-men, shaven crowns, etc. That all protestants are hypocritical asses.

That if he were put to write a new religion, he would undertake both a more excellent and admirable method; and that all the New Testament is filthily written.

That the woman of Samaria and her sister were whores; and that Christ knew them dishonestly.

That St John the Evangelist was bed-fellow to Christ and leaned always in his bosom; that he used him as the sinners of Sodoma.

That all they that love not tobacco and boys were fools.

That all the apostles were fishermen and base fellows,

neither of wit nor worth; that Paul only had wit, but he was a timorous fellow in bidding men to be subject to magistrates against his conscience.

That he had as good right to coin as the Queen of England, and that he was acquainted with one Poole, a prisoner in Newgate, who hath great skill in mixture of metals; and, having learned some things of him, he meant through help of a cunning stamp-maker to coin French crowns, pistolets and English shillings.

That if Christ would have instituted the sacrament with more ceremonial reverence, it would have been had in more admiration; that it would have been much better being administered in a tobacco-pipe.

That the angel Gabriel was bawd to the Holy Ghost, because he brought the salutation to Mary.

That one Ric Cholmley hath confessed that he was persuaded by Marloe's reasons to become an atheist.

These things, with many other, shall by good and honest witness be approved to be his opinions and common speeches; and that this Marlow doth not only hold them himself but, almost into every company he cometh, he persuades men to atheism, willing them not to be afeared of bugbears and hobgoblins, and utterly scorning both God and his ministers; as I Richard Baines will justify and approve, both by mine oath and the testimony of many honest men, and almost all men with whom he hath conversed any time will testify the same. And, as I think, all men in Christianity ought to endeavour that the mouth of so dangerous a member may be stopped. He saith likewise that he hath quoted a number of contrarieties out of the Scripture, which he hath given to some great men who in convenient time shall be named. When these things shall be called in question the witness shall be produced.

Richard Baines

Glossary

Explanations to be found in *The Concise Oxford Dictionary* are not usually repeated here. Several special conventional signs have been adopted:
* usage earlier than any recorded in *The New English Dictionary*;
† usage recorded in the *N.E.D.* as first occurring in Marlowe's works;
comb combination of distinct senses; + lesser connotation; → see;
(→) see the preceding; × error, e.g. mistranslation, misreading.

A per se a, t.h.e. the, o per se o, deny orgon, gorgon, i.e. he spells out the words like a child learning to read: *per se* = 'on its own', e.g. article 'a', interjection 'o'. He garbles 'demogorgon', 293.

Abanus, i.e. Pietro d'Abano (1250?–1316?), famous Italian physician academic suspected of magic, 279.

* *abortive*, misborn, 106.

Abram's happiness, old, i.e. as in Gen. xii.2, xiii.2, etc. [but Christians applied promise to themselves, Rom. iv.13, Gal. iii.14–16, 29], 336.

Acantha, Acanta, town in C. Turkey, 77.

accident, incident, 60. *accidental*, inessential, abnormal, 117.

Achelous → *Hercules*.

Acheron, river of underworld (Hades), 405.

Achilles, Pelides (son of Peleus), handsome Greek hero, friend of Patroclus (who was killed in Trojan War), 141; withdrew forces in rage at Agamemnon's claiming his captive *Briseis*, 435; wounded Telephus and cured him with rust from the spear, 450.

Actaeon, huntsman saw Diana bathing naked; changed by her into a stag, torn to pieces by his own hounds, 126.

Ad amicam, 'To his mistress', 425.

Ad amicam, a cuius amore, etc., 'To his mistress, whom he cannot leave loving', 477.

Ad amicam corruptam, 'To his unfaithful mistress', 446.

Ad amicam cursum equorum spectantem, 'To his mistress watching horse-racing', 463.

Ad amicam navigantem, 'To his mistress going to sea', 452.

Ad amicam, si peccatura est, etc., 'To his mistress, that if she sin, she sin in secret', 480.

Ad amicam, ut ad rura sua veniat, 'To his mistress, that she should come to his country place', 457.

Ad amnem, dum iter faceret ad amicam, 'To the river, while he travels to his mistress', 468.

Ad annulum, quem dono amicae dedit, 'To the ring which he has given as a present to his mistress', 456.

Ad Atticum, etc., 'To Atticus, that a lover ought not to be lazy any more than a soldier', 434.

Ad Auroram, ne properet, 'To Aurora, not to hurry', 438. → *Morn*.

Ad Bagoum, etc., 'To Bagous, that he should keep watch with greater laxity over the girl committed to his charge', 443.

Ad Cererem, etc., 'To Ceres, complaining that he is not allowed to sleep with his mistress because of her sacraments', 475.

Ad Cupidinem, 'To Cupid', 450.

Ad Cypassim, etc., 'To Cypassis, Corinna's maid', 450.

Ad Eunuchum servantem dominam, 'To the eunuch protecting his mistress', 444.

Ad Graecinum, etc., 'To Graecinus, that he loves two at the same time' [consul A.D. 16], 452.

Ad invidos, quod fama poetarum sit

[515]

perennis, 'To the envious, that the fame of poets lasts forever', 440.

Ad Isidem, etc., 'To Isis, to help Corinna give birth', 455.

Ad Janitorem, etc., 'To the porter, to open the door for him', 428.

Ad Macrum, quod de amoribus scribat, 'To Macer, that he is writing of love', 459.

Ad pacandam amicam, etc., 'To placate his mistress, whom he had beaten', 430.

Ad puellam, etc., 'To his mistress, not to ask reward for love', 435.

Ad rivalem, etc., 'To his rival, whose wife was of no concern to him', 460.

Ad Venerem, etc., 'To Venus, that he is bringing the elegies to an end', 481.

Ad virum servantem coniugem, 'To the husband keeping a watch on his wife', 467.

Adon, Adonis → *Venus*.

advance, elevate; exalt, 493.

Aegeus → *Hercules*.

Aeneas, ancestral hero of Rome, 432.

Aeolus, god of winds [which were kept in a cave on *Aeolia*, floating Aeolian island near Sicily], 194.

Aeque tandem, ? 'equally at last' [? eminence and decay both shared in the end], 145.

Aesop's cock, i.e. in fable attributed to Aesop, it rejected a precious stone, not knowing what it was, for a barleycorn [? + 'cock' = * 'penis'; 'jewel' = 'virginity', 'genitals'], 414.

Aetolia, part of Greece N. of Corinthian Gulf, 469. → *Hercules*.

affect, aspire to, 13; fancy, 129; love, 217; prefer, 405. *affection*, feeling; inclination [? Tamburlaine's towards Theridamas], 15.

affied, betrothed, 413.

Africa, ? i.e. (full extent of) Turkish Empire, 12.

again, back, 443.

Agamemnon, commander of Greek forces besieging Troy, (reluctantly) tried to sacrifice daughter *Iphigenia* to obtain wind for fleet, 337; prisoner *Chryseis* (a priest's daughter) became his mistress

[×], 450; murdered on return home, 480.

Agave, tore her son, King of Thebes, to pieces in Bacchic frenzy, 502.

Agenor, King of Phoenicia, ancestor of Dido. Hence *Agenor's stately town*, Carthage, 198.

Agrippa, Heinrich Cornelius (1486–1535), scholar and magician, raised likenesses of dead, 278.

air → *element, region, sphere*. * *airy*, ? effervescent [the *element* (→) air is the equivalent of the 'humour' blood, both being hot and moist], 88; † heavenly, etherial, 278.

Ajax, Greek hero, son of Telamon [in madness killed sheep believing them enemies. His mighty shield was made of seven hides], 430. *either Ajax*, e.g. the Greek hero son of Oïleus [also at Troy], 442.

Alba → *Jove*.

Albania, S.E. Georgia, 11. *Albanese*, ? Georgians; ? Albanians; ? people of the Morea, 66.

Alcibiades, debauched young Athenian taken up by Socrates, 141.

Alcides → *Hercules*.

Alcinous, island king with fairest of orchards, bearing fruit twice a year [plenty where that came from], 436.

Aldebaran, bright red star, eye of Taurus, 106.

Alexander died, Alexander's love → *Helen, Paris. Great Alexander lov'd Hephaestion*, i.e. his boyhood friend and comrade, 141; *Alexander and his beauteous paramour*, ? i.e. Thaïs [induced him to burn down Persepolis]; ? Campaspe [in play by Lyly], 304; he fell fatally ill after drinking-bout [said to have been poisoned], 366. *Pope Alexander*, i.e. in this way Alexander III (1159–81) humbled Emperor Frederick, who had set up a rival pope, 298.

* *alife*, dearly, 461.

Alleyn, Edward (1566–1626), eminent actor for Admiral's Men; played Tamburlaine, Barabas, Faustus, 329.

Almain, German, 65.

Almo, (tiny) tributary of Tiber

[where statues of Cybele = *Ops* (→), the Great Mother (*their saint*), were washed], 502.

Alpheus → *Arethusa.*

Amasia, province of N. Turkey, 80.

Amazonia, approx. Zambia, 67.

Amicae se purgat, etc., 'He clears himself from his mistress's accusation that he loves her maid', 449.

Amicam, qua arte, etc., 'He advises his mistress what stratagem or nods she should employ at dinner in her husband's presence', 425.

Amymone, sent by her father *Danaus* (→) in search of water, attracted Neptune, 435.

Analytics, works of Aristotle on logic, about scientific proof and cognition [but the Latin is from *Ramus* (→)], 276.

Anchises, father of Aeneas, 215.

Antarctic Pole, ? i.e. in S. hemisphere, 119. *antarctic world*, ? i.e. night comes from the south [? = winter's night], 280.

Antenor, Trojan prince, 202.

Antwerp bridge, i.e. fire-ship smashed Parma's bridge made for siege of Antwerp in 1585, 278.

Anubis, dog-headed Egyptian god, 455.

Aonia, district round *Thebes* (→) [Muses' Mt Helicon was in Aonia: lyre attribute of *Apollo* (→)], 45, 423. *her that lov'd the Aonian harp*, i.e. *Sappho* (→), 460.

Apelles, great Greek painter, 331.

aphorism, (scientific, esp. medical) precept [+Hippocrates' *Aphorisms*: first one is 'Life is short, and Art is long; the occasion fleeting, experience deceitful, and judgment difficult'], 276.

Apis, Osiris incarnate in sacred bull [at Memphis], 455.

Apollo, god of prophecy, 16; of song and music [born on Delos, hence *Delian music*, 217]; and of the sun, 420, [hair as sun's rays], 401; father of *Linus*, personification of the lament, 474. Temple at Delphi, on Parnassus, celebrated for oracle, hence *Delphian oracle*, 279. *Apollo's laurel bough*, i.e. highly gifted in (poetic) arts

[? + laurel symbolic of expiation], 326.

* *appetence*, feeling of attraction, affinity [e.g. in gravity, magnetism], 414.

appointed, equipped, 166.

approve, try by experience, 21.

apt, like, just as well adapted, 428.

Arachne, famous dyer in purple, 447.

Araris, ? Araxes [? river in Armenia emptying into Caspian], 19; × [? river on which Persepolis stood; ? tributary of Euphrates in Mesopotamia; ? Oxus], 21; the Saône, tributary of Rhône, 499.

Aratus (*c.* 270 B.C.), popular Greek astronomer poet, 441.

Arethusa, nymph turned into fountain on island near Syracuse; pursued there by Alpheus, partly underground river of Peloponnesus, 468; [no myth connects her with sun. But → *Thetis*], 320.

Argier, Algiers, 6.

argin, rampart outside ditch, 87.

Argolian, ? * Greek [= Argive], 45.

Argos = Argo, ship built of pines from *Pelion* (→) in which Jason fetched the Golden Fleece from *Colchis* (→), 453.

argument, concerns, 100.

Argumentum testimonii, etc., i.e. argument by authority is not of its own nature conclusive [Guise literally proves the force of his own assertion], 247.

Argus → *Hermes, Jove.*

Ariadan, Saudi-Arabian town on Red Sea, 96.

Ariadne, i.e. Theseus deserted her on island, 430; married by Bacchus, who placed her bridal crown among stars, 396.

Arion, Greek musician saved from drowning by dolphins captivated by his playing, 232.

Aristarchus (*c.* 217–145 B.C.), exacting Alexandrian scholar, 183.

array, arrangement (in lines), 254.

artier, channel carrying the 'vital spirits' (*lively spirits*) in the bloodstream from the heart to promote animal functions [veins proper carry 'natural spirits' from liver to promote growth and lower bodily functions, incl. that of heart], 102. 'Spirits' are † *organons*, refined substances by which the mind operates the body [imprecise], 117.

arts, strange, ? i.e. Aeneas invented fire-making from flint [×], 197.

asafoetida, foul-smelling medicinal gum extracted from an Asiatic plant, 113.

Ascanius, Iulus, son of Aeneas [beauty's masterpiece, as radiant as the sun], 195. *Ascanius' prophecy*, i.e. his destiny to found Rome, lasting a thousand years, and the Julian line (incl. Julius Caesar), 227.

Ascraeus, Hesiod (*fl.* 700 B.C.), born in Ascra [wrote about corn and wine], 441.

† *aspect*, face, expression, 15; astrological position, favourable or otherwise, of a heavenly body [pun], 43.

Asphaltis, ? somewhere near Aleppo, 105; artificial bituminous lake near Babylon, 112.

Asteroth, Belimoth, devils, 308, 310.

astonied, stunned, amazed, 32.

† *astracism*, constellation; ? division of cosmos into earth, planets and stars, 106.

Astraeus, father of stars, 194.

Atalanta, virgin huntress, 430; won by Hippomenes in foot-race, 464.

Atax, modern R. Aude, rising in Pyrenees, 498.

Atreus, king of Mycenae, tricked his brother *Thyestes* into eating his own children [the sun recoiled, was eclipsed, in horror], 479.

Atrides, Agamemnon (→), son of Atreus, 203.

* *attract*, take in, 196.

Aulis, harbour where Greek fleet assembled for attack on Troy, 231.

Aurora → *Morn*.

Auster and Aquilon, South Wind and North Wind, 32.

Avern, Avernus, classical hell [guarded by Cerberus: → *Hercules*], 15; infernal lake, 47.

Averni, for Arverni, tribe in Auvergne, 498.

avoid, quit, 162.

axle-tree, axle of a vehicle; axis or pole of heaven, sky [? comb], 43; [earthquake], 67.

Axon, of R. Axona, modern Aisne, in N.E. Gaul, 498.

Azamor, Azimur, town on Atlantic coast of Morocco, 74.

Bacchus, Horn'd, i.e. god of tragic inspiration, 481.

Bacon, Roger (1214?–94), experimental scientist with reputation as magician, 279.

bacon, i.e. country fare commonly begged at door, 373.

Bagdet, Baghdad [equated with Babylon], 112.

Balaam, i.e. in Numbers xxii–iv, xxxi [× : kept faith with God in *not* cursing Israelites, who killed him], 77.

† *balance*, compensate for; equal, 217.

Balsera, ? i.e. Passera in Anatolia [×], 89.

banco, bank, 371.

band, little, small ruff [mark of an academic (? and Puritan)], 143.

banquet, dessert course of delicacies and wine, 47. *running banquet*, snack, 376.

Bardi, order of sacred poets in Gaul, 499.

barely, i.e. on its own, 335.

base, bid a, challenge [to a race, in the game 'prisoner's base'], 166. *base-conceited* → *conceit*.

basilisk, heavy cannon, 40.

basso, pasha, (Turkish) general, 29.

bastone, cudgel, 35.

battle, battle array; main body, 85, 502.

Baucis, old peasant-woman who was hospitable to Jupiter and Mercury [in Ovid], 199.

beat on, impinge, batter, 54. *beaten*, embroidered [pun], 283.

bed, (dinner) couch, 426.

behight, promise, 465.

Belcher, devil, 303.

Belgasar, Beglasar, town near modern Ankara [×], 77.

Belimoth, Argiron, Asteroth, devils, 308.

Belus, Assyrian god-king, founder of Babylon, 110.

bend, ? tighten, 465. *bending*, ? exposed; ? quailing [×], 501.

Berkeley, castle in Gloucestershire, 177.

bested, in a plight, 496.

bever, snack, 292.

bewray, reveal, 71; betray, 364.

bickering, skirmishing, 29.

* *bidental*, holy [and requiring sacrifice because of the thunderbolt], 502.

Bien para todos mi ganado no es, 'My flock is not good for everybody' (Spanish), 349.

Biledull, town (Biled) or province (Biledulgerid) in S. Algeria, 74.

bill, axe-headed spear [*brown* = 'rusty' or 'painted'], 157; prescription, 276; deed, 286. * *bill of entry*, note of goods entered at custom-house, 335.

Bithynia, region of Asia Minor opposite Constantinople, 33.

Bituriges, Celtic tribe in C. and S. Gaul, 498.

blind, unlighted [by Hero's lantern], 458.

blood, kin; life [+ blood conveys emotion such as rebelliousness], 52. *bloodless*, pale-faced, 139.

Blount, Edward, London bookseller 1594–1632; play publisher, 400.

blue, *bluish sulphur*, i.e. the colour of burning brimstone, hellish, 300; discoloration from despondency, debility, etc. [comb], 204.

boast, i.e. are only too pleased, flattered, 442.

bodkin, frizzling-iron [less curved than the curls], 440.

boist'rous, unyielding, 426.

bolt, leg-iron, 129.

bombard, large cannon, 387.

* *Böotes*, N. constellation at tail of Great Bear, 16.

Boreas, North Wind [carried off *Oreithyia* by violence], 429; [*Thracian* because northerly], 498.

Borgia, Cesare (1475–1507), son of Pope Alexander VI, who was reputed to have been poisoned by him, 366.

Borno, town by Lake Chad (*Borno lake*, 118), 76.

boss, fat woman, 37.

bough, gallows, 154.

bounce, knock, 315.

* *Bourbon*, i.e. Navarre, 266.

brabble, babble, 496.

* *breach*, breaking waves; gulf, 500.

breathe, long, 153.

breeching, flogging, 183.

brent, burnt, 43.

brigandine, small, fast and manœuvrable ship suitable for raiding, 39.

† *brisk*, smartly turned out, 142.

Bristow, Bristol, 170.

brother, Dearly beloved, i.e. Puritan style of address [and in e.g. Anglican Prayer Book], 246 → Wagner, 280. *my fair brother*, i.e. Cupid, 217. *brothers of the earth*, armed men who grew from a dragon's teeth sowed by Cadmus and killed all but five of each other, 20.

brunt, assault, onset, 15.

buckle, close, engage, 199.

bug, bogy, 97.

bulk, body, 245.

bull → *Jove*.

burst, cause to burst out, 239.

butt, shoot, 217. *butting*, (having a) boundary, adjoining [? + 'pushing and shoving'], 492.

buzz, whisper, 187.

Byather, Biafar = ? Biafra, 75.

Byron, town near Babylon, 65.

* *cabinet*, private council-chamber, 262.

caddesse, jackdaw, 448.

Caesar, Augustus [descendant of Venus], 425; Nero, 490. *Caesar shall go forth*, i.e. as Julius Caesar went to his death [→ Shakespeare's *J.C.* II.ii.28], 263.

Callimachus (3rd cent. B.C.), Alexandrian grammarian and poet, 441.

Callist, Callisto, Arcadian nymph [changed into the Great Bear], 479.

Calpe, Gibraltar, 501.

Calvus (82–?47 B.C.), orator and poet, friend of Catullus, 475.

Calypso, island nymph who detained Ulysses [? ×], 459.

Glossary

Camillus, M. Furius, national hero of 4th cent. B.C. [victorious against Faliscans, captured Falerii], 479.

camp, (campaigning) army, 25.

Cancer's line, the midst of, i.e. where the meridian intersects the tropic, close to Canary Islands [on Ortelius' map], 118.

Candia, Candy, Crete, 335.

Canopus, city at mouth of Nile, 455.

Capys, Aeneas' grandfather, 217.

† *carbonado*, grilled meat, 48.

Carmonia, Carmania, S.E. province in Asia Minor, 84.

Carolus the Fifth, Charles V (1500–1558), King of Spain (with Sicily and Malta) and Emperor of Germany, 355; [court at Innsbruck in *Faustbook*], 304.

carouse the sea, i.e. drown, 452.

Carthage souls be glutted, i.e. at Thapsus, 490. → *Emathian*.

case, pair, 292.

Cassandra, Trojan prophetess dragged from sanctuary of *Minerva* (→) by Greeks [×], 206; [i.e. apart from being violated. ×], 430.

cast, predict, 151; scheme, 179; defeat; throw in wrestling [+ 'throw (animal) on back'], 427.

Catholic, i.e. King Philip of Spain, 240.

Catiline (d. 62 B.C.), Roman politician infamous for cruelty, extortion, intrigue, depravity [sought to plunder public treasures], 170.

† *catzery*, roguery, pimping [→ *Cazzo*], 378.

caul, membrane, 503.

cavaliero, artillery platform, 83.

Cayc foe, Cayci, Chauci, Cauci, tribe of N.W. Germany, 499.

Cazates, town on great lake (the Zaire), source of Congo and Nile, 75.

* *Cazzo diabole*, 'Cock, the Devil' (Italian and Spanish), 370.

censure, criticism, judgment, 5; (vb) judge [i.e. the appearance instantly determines our preference], 405.

centaurs, i.e. they carried off Hippodamia, beautiful bride of the King of the Lapiths in Thessaly, and thus started a famous war, 426.

centre, earth [comb], 82; * midst, 156. *centre's latitude*, equator, 86.

centronel, sentinel, 207.

Cephalus, beautiful Athenian youth abducted against his will by Aurora (→ *Morn*), 439; with wonderful hound, joined hunt of monstrous vixen [×], sent by *Themis*, goddess of sexual propriety, to ravage the *Thebes* (→) of Oedipus, 45.

Cepheus' daughter, Andromeda [given up to monster, sent by Neptune because her mother declared herself more beautiful than Nereids], 466.

Cerania, Cerannia, Ceraunia, stormy coastal range in Epirus, 196, 453.

chafer of fire, chafing-dish, 286.

chain'd troops, unbroken columns, 500.

Cham, Emperor of Tartary, 12.

champion, open and level country [suitable for a battlefield], 20.

channel, throat, ? gullet, 73; gutter, 129.

character, distinctive mark, stamp [? * pun], 15. *characters of signs*, graphic symbols of planetary forces, 281.

charge, entrust, commission, 8; (sb) orders, 8; office, 22.

chariot, whence corn, etc., i.e. given by Ceres to Triptolemus to introduce agriculture, 468. *chariots* [pl. for sing.], 108.

Charles the Fifth → *Carolus, Dionysius*.

Charybdis, monster swallowing and regurgitating sea; dangerous whirlpool in Straits of Messina, 458.

check, stamp [+ pun 'revile'], 416.

chief, best part, 69.

chimney-sweeper and an oyster-wife, ? i.e. black and stinking; ? the lowliest, 292.

Chio, Chia, town in N. Asia Minor, 85.

Chirk, town in Clwyd (Denbighshire) in border-country [lordship awarded Mortimer Senior about 1282; built his castle there], 140.

chuff, miser, 471.

churchyard, i.e. St Paul's Churchyard, centre of retail book-trade [pun], 488.

Cilicia, rugged district in S.E. Asia Minor [of brigands and pirates], 458.

Cimbrian, of savage Celtic tribe of 2nd cent. B.C., from Jutland [victorious against Romans at first, and settled in Spain], 102.

* *Cimmerian*, black, hellish, 32.

Cinga, modern Spanish R. Cinca rising in Pyrenees, 499.

Circes, island enchantress [transformed Ulysses' comrades into swine with her wand], 136.

circle, full extent of time [? + weary, changeless repetition; confinement], 27; where spirits are raised by a sorcerer, 488. *two circles over the whole world*, i.e. × [seasons confused with hours of daylight in account of hemispheres], 315. → *antarctic world*.

circuit, *Keeping his*, i.e. sitting as a judge [? + swinging sword-stroke], 53.

clap, get in (with), make up (to), 164; * throw oneself; shut up [+ *under hatches* = 'humiliated, dejected'], 232.

cleye, claw [Mars in Scorpio portends war], 504.

climate, latitudes [lightning comes like Caesar], 501.

* *cloak, velvet-cap'd*, i.e. clerical gown, 143.

clog, fetter [like a ball and chain], 95.

Clymen → *Phaeton*.

coat, skirt, tunic [× ; ? + discharging (liveried servant) from service], 431.

Cock-pit, theatre by Drury Lane, opened in 1617, 329.

Cocytus, river of Hades, 55.

Codemia, town on R. Bug, 76.

coelum igneum, and cristallinum → *sphere*.

Colchis, Colchos, country S. of Caucasus [Medea, king's daughter, murdered her children by Jason when he deserted her], 456. → *Argos*.

coll, embrace, 221.

collier, coalman, 248.

colossus, i.e. Colossus of Rhodes, astride harbour entrance, 317.

comfort, brace up, 117.

commence, take doctorate (of divinity) [comb], 275.

* *comment*, expound [? passes numerous judgments, prompted by Zenocrate's reactions], 54.

commit, imprison; copulate [pun], 316.

compass, range [? pun (with *points*) on geometrical and/or navigational senses; + *compass* = 'spherical shape' of bullet], 19; (vb) encompass, 196; win, 211.

competitor, partner, 16.

conceit, device; fanciful expression or action, 7; imagination, 13; fancy, notion, 31; mental capacity, 263; conception, thought, 277. *with thy conceit*, in your estimation, 108. *base-conceited*, vulgar, 441. *dull-conceited*, dull-witted, 210. *(of a) self-conceit*, (made possible by; ? proper to) self-regard, 275. † *vain-conceited*, empty-headed, 5.

conceive, become possessed with, 10; make pregnant [*hell-born* = 'infernal', but this confuses image], 196.

concoct, digest, 88.

condition, social position, 355.

conduct, command, 16.

* *coney*, cunt, 435.

congé, bow, 183.

consort, † harmony; orchestra, 48.

conster, construe, 185.

Consummatum est, 'It is finished' [Christ's dying words: John xix.30], 286.

content, pleasure, 193; peace of mind [she will become restless again], 216; contents [? comb], 217.

continent, solid land, 67; container, 79; (adj.) continuous (with), 10.

convinced, convicted, 458.

cope (with), join battle (with); exchange (for); * make contact (with) [? comb], 168.

Corcyra, Corfu [where Tibullus was taken ill], 475.

Corinn, Corinna, mistress celebrated by Ovid, 83. *Corinnae concubitus*,

'Going to bed with Corinna', 427.

corn with least part of itself return'd, i.e. a poor return on the grain, 476.

cornet, company of cavalry, 496.

Corpo di Dio, 'Body of God' (Italian) [Christian oath], 340.

corps-du-gard, picket, 434.

corpse great grave, on her, i.e. big in proportion to the body; ? made grand by (tiny) body, 449.

corpus naturale, 'natural body', physically a real human being [? pun on sense 'matter', the subject of physics], 280.

Corrive with, rival, 461.

Corsic, i.e. Corsican honey was notoriously bitter, 437.

countenance, good standing, 171; favour and support, 400.

counterbuff, rebuff, 157.

covent, convent, monastery, 372.

Crassus, defeated and killed by Parthians at Carrhae in Mesopotamia 53 B.C. [*Babylon* = 'Parthia'], 489, 491.

Crete, i.e. birthplace of Jupiter [Cretans a byword for lying], 476.

* *crisis*, ? conjunction of planets on particular days [determining course of illness, etc.], 117.

crooked, curving [→ *Arion*], 418.

cross, i.e. coin with cross stamped on it, 358. *cross-bite*, blackmail, doublecross, 378.

crown'd, garlanded at safe conclusion of voyage, 477.

crownet, coronet, 126.

cruel, savage; ? insensitive, 460.

Cubar, Guber, region S. of Timbuktu, 75.

cullions, riff-raff, 142.

cum ceteris, etc., 156.

Curius, M. Curius Dentatus, 3rd-cent. B.C. national hero [byword for oldfashioned frugality; refused more acres than others had], 492.

curse, first, ? guilt for crucifixion [→ Mat. xxvii.25]; ? unredeemed original sin, 341.

cursen, Christian, 314.

curstly, sharply, harshly, 179.

curtle-axe, cutlass, 12.

Cutheia, modern Kütahya, capital of Natolia, 77.

Cybel, Rhea = *Ops* (→), mother of the gods, 501.

Cyclops, giant smiths, native to Sicily and neighbouring islands, assistants of Vulcan, 196. *Cyclopian wars*, i.e. Titans, the old gods, fought unsuccessfully against Jupiter and the new gods [Cyclops provided Jupiter with thunderbolts], 22.

Cymodoce, sea-goddess, 196.

* *Cynthia*, moon. *Cynthia with Saturn join'd*, i.e. in astrology, this conjunction makes men ill-looking, foolish, vacillating, timid, little regarded, unhappy and unfortunate, 7. *shining veil of Cynthia*, moonlit sky [? barrier to (mortal) perception], 79. → *region*.

Cyrus, ? × for *Darius* (→).

Cytherea, Venus [cult assoc. with island by Crete, *Cythera* = modern Cerigo, 458], 195, [?+ Proserpine legend], 347.

Damon, Syracusan, risked his life as hostage for Pythias (Phintias) [proverbial for devoted friend], 8.

Danae → *Jove*.

Danaus, King of Libya and Argos [required his fifty daughters to murder their bridegrooms], 443.

dang, fling, hurl, 420.

Daphne, daughter of river-god Peneus, escaped Apollo by turning into a laurel [Apollo's favourite tree], 397.

Dardania, district around Troy, 318, named after *Dardanus*, legendary ancestor of Trojans, 230.

Darius III (*c.* 380–330 B.C.), King of Persia [defeated and plundered by Alexander the Great of Macedonia], 11. *Darius I* (521–486 B.C.), whose campaigns in Greece ended at Marathon, is probably meant by *Cyrus*, 10.

Darote, town in Nile delta, 69.

De amica, quae periuraverat, 'Concerning his mistress's perjury', 465.

De Iunonis festo, 'On the festival of Juno', 479.

* *deduce*, bring down, 442.

Deiphobus → *Helen*.

Delia, mistress of Tibullus, 474; ? and of Samuel Daniel's sonnets, 396. *Delian* → *Apollo*.

Deliberatio poetae, etc., 'The poet's deliberation, whether he should continue to write elegies, or tragedies instead', 462.

Delphian → *Apollo*.

Destinies → *Fates*.

Desunt nonnulla, 'Some things are lacking', 420.

Deucalion, Noah of classical mythology [earth was repeopled after Flood by animating stones], 75.

diameter, i.e. line passing through centre of earth, 82; i.e. perpendicular at noon, when more distant than if horizontal (*lateral*) near horizon, 415.

Diana painted, i.e. Dione = Venus (by Apelles) [×], 440. *Diana's name*, i.e. some have slandered the virgin goddess herself, 407. *Diana's shrouds*, i.e. hunting costume [? + irony on death of virginity], 214.

† *dichotomist*, logician who proceeds by dividing every class into two, 247.

Dido, i.e. wrote suicidal letter in Ovid's *Heroides*, 460.

* *digested*, disposed in order, 439.

dignity, great honour [? + 'astrological influence', i.e. of Mars], 195.

Diomede → *Tydides*.

Dionysius, ? tyrant of Syracuse (*c.* 430–367 B.C.) [fortified and defended Sicily against Carthage: ? Barabas's Malta might be so *back'd* against Turks by King of Spain and Sicily, the overlord of Malta. → *Carolus*], 387.

Dipsas = 'thirsty' [drunken], 431.

Dis, (Pluto, god of) underworld, 28; god of underground wealth, 420. *Dis above*, ? celestial Devil [blunder, on model of *infernal Jove* for 'Dis'], 376.

discoloured, variegated, 404.

disparagement, dishonour from social inequality of marriage partners, 42.

† *dispensive*, subject to dispensation, 77.

distain, make pale, 32; sully, 429.

Dolet amicam, etc., 'He grieves that his mistress has been given so much publicity by his poems that he has provided himself with many rivals', 478.

Dolon, Trojan spy caught by Ulysses, betrayed *Rhesus* (→), 194.

dominion or intelligentia, guardian angel, 290.

Doric music, i.e. simple and solemn and martial [? × for 'Lydian' = 'effeminate'], 408.

Douai, i.e. where English college trained priests for English mission [1578–93 at Rheims, where Marlowe may have attended], 264.

doubtless, fearless, 27. *doubtful*, treacherous, 504.

Draco, 7th-cent. B.C. Athenian legislator, advocate of death penalty for most crimes, 333.

dragon, shooting star with tail, 86.

drawn, ? i.e. as in drawn-work, 401.

dreary, bloody; cruel, 419.

drench, overwhelm, 466.

drunk overnight, if a man be, etc., ? i.e. God takes care of fools and drunken men [proverbial], 305.

dry, dull, 488.

dull-conceited → *conceit*.

eagle → *Jove*.

* *earn*, grieve, 172.

Ebena, i.e. darkness personified [Marlowe's coinage], 54.

* *écu*, French crown, 240.

Egeria, nymph, mistress and counsellor of Numa, legendary second King of Rome, 459.

Ego mihimet sum semper proximus, 'I am always my own nearest and dearest' (after Terence), 338.

Electra, one of Pleiades, daughters of Atlas; killed themselves and became stars [×], 479.

Elegia, elegian → *verse*.

Eleius, for *Eleus* = 'Elean', of Elis in W. Peloponnesus [where Olympics held], 495.

element, one of four constituents of matter, i.e. earth, water, air, fire; the proportions of each in man determine temperament, 28. Hence *elements*, the world of nature beneath the moon (each element having a region or layer proper to it: water above earth, air above water, fire above air. → *region*); alternatively, the *spheres* (→), 287. *same proportion of elements*, the same physical make-up and hence likemindedness [? comb idea of body returning to earth in death], 27. *watches of the element*, i.e. of the sky: *watches* = 'planets' seen as timepieces and/or watchmen; and/or = the divisions of the night [comb], 175. *Water and air, being symboliz'd in one*, a merging of phlegmatic and sanguine temperaments [the first dull, cowardly, white, and the second sensual, pleasure-loving], 71. *humidum and calor*, normal moisture and heat, ordinarily constituents of air, blood and the sanguine temperament; working with 'spirits' (→ *artier*) and essential to life [believed by some to be etherial substances], 117. *elemental*, ? simple, ? unadulterated; ? of the sky [? + 'earthly' with ref. to ghost], 488.

Elisa, Eliza, for Elissa = 'Dido' [+ Queen Elizabeth], 219.

Emathian, from Emathia, part of Macedonia; for 'Thessalian' [i.e. veterans of Pharsalia at Caesar's victory at Thapsus (46 B.C.), in Tunisia], 504.

Emden, the signory of, i.e. the lordship of a great prosperous port, 285.

empale, encircle (and beautify), 161.

Enceladus → *Giants*.

endure, strengthen, harden, 118.

Endymion, beautiful youth, perpetually asleep on Mt *Latmus* in Asia Minor, beloved by moon, 439.

engines, i.e. eyes, 56; ? i.e. hoisting tackle; ? scales [attribute of Fate Atropos and of (Judaeo-) Christian Creator. comb], 411; universal structure, 490; siege engines, 278.

Enipeus, (god of) river in Thessaly; loved Tyro, 469.

Ennius (239–169 B.C.), father of Latin poetry, 441.

Epeus, builder of Trojan horse, 194.

† *equivalent*, equal part, 295.

Eryx, mountain in W. Sicily with temple to Venus. Hence *Erycina*, *Erycine*, Venus (→), 108, 420.

essence, something that exists, 407. → *form*.

Ethiopian Sea, S. Atlantic, 75.

Etna, i.e. war in Sicily between Agrippa and Pompey, 36 B.C., 490.

Europa, Europe → *Jove*.

Eurotas, river by Sparta, 459.

Euxine Sea, Black Sea, 11.

Evadne, for 'Evanthe', daughter of river-god [× in Ovid text], 469.

event, outcome, consequence, 51.

excrement, ? hair [? comb], 181.

Execratur lenam, etc., 'He curses the bawd who has been instructing his mistress in the arts of the whore', 431.

Exhaereditare filium, etc., 'The father may not disinherit the son, unless . . .' (Justinian's *Institutes*), 276.

exhalation, exhale → *region*.

Exultat, quod amica potitus sit, 'He boasts that he has conquered his mistress', 454.

eye, by the, without limit, 366. * *eyeball*, pupil [evil eye], 432.

fact, (course of) action, 443; crime, 480.

faith evasion, made thy, has your fidelity swerved, 437. *Faith to the witness Jove's praise doth apply*, Jove's approval confirms the credibility of the witness, 476.

falling valleys, etc., ? may smooth roads have the supreme advantage of (or have no harder slope than) downward-sloping valleys [×; comb], 458.

Famastro, town in Asia Minor, 85.

far-fet, far-fetched ['Far fetched and dear bought is good for ladies' proverbial. → 315], 216.

fashion-sake, for, as a formality, 338.

* *Fates*, Destinies, three goddesses determining the course of human

life, 16. Hence *Fatal Sisters*, 83.
hand of Fate, [pun on clock], 216.
Fate's distaff, i.e. from which the
Fates spun earthly life, 448. *fatal*,
fated [for him to die in], 120.
fatally enrich'd, ? endowed with
good fortune, 59.

fear, frighten, 66. *Fear to be guilty*,
etc., be afraid to be implicated,
pretend ignorance [×], 443.

feet fly, We cause, e.g. of *Hermes*,
Perseus (→), 478.

fet, fetch(ed) [as by Prometheus],
418.

fig = modern 'nuts (to)' [pun on
'raisin', pron. 'reason'], 315.

Figulus (d. 44 B.C.), senator, philosopher, astrologer, augur, sup-
porter of Pompey, 503.

figure, appearance; ? mark; ? prefiguration (acc. Islamic belief)
[? + 'horoscope'. → Rev. vii.3],
18; [? i.e. his whip], 105; diagram
of (? fixed) stars, 281; (vb) repre-
sent, * prefigure, 18.

file, defile, 265.

*Finis Actus Quinti, et Ultimi huius
Primae Partis*, 'The end of the
fifth and last act of this first part',
63.

fire, celestial, i.e. stars, 490.

Flanders mares, i.e. famous breed of
heavy horses [? + 'whores'], 367.

* *flaring*, gaudy, 406.

flattering, i.e. delusively clear, 501.

Fleet, London prison for people of
rank, 129.

foil, deflower [pun], 352.

following, of their, i.e. from chasing
after the females, 102.

fondling, fool, 5.

for to end his life, i.e. with the opposite
effect that the King will himself
be killed, 266.

forehead → *horns*.

forestall his market, i.e. corner his
goods beforehand, 258.

† *forfeiting*, exacting penalty on over-
due payments, 355.

form, informing principle, (inward)
nature, 104. *good form*, beauty,
445. *form not meet to give that subject
essence*, i.e. his character is not fit
to give life and individuality to
that substance, 100.

forslow, lose by neglect or slowness,
152.

fortune, i.e. such fortune as you
enjoy, 14. *Fortune's wheel*, i.e. the
emblem of the goddess of chance
[the prosperous rise on one side
but are flung down on the other],
179.

four-chariot, i.e. in teams of four,
465.

fowl, princely, ? i.e. spread-eagle,
emblem of (Holy) Roman
Empire, 67.

fray, frighten, 52.

free, unrestrained, ? * forward, 258;
generous; unpaid [pun + 'set
free'], 428.

frequent, throng; ? celebrate, 447.

friends, kinsfolk, 49.

Furies, Tisiphone, Alecto and
Megaera; infernal goddesses,
terrifying avengers of crimes
against family and society [with
snake-entwined hair], 300.

furniture, equipment, 15.

Gabine manner, i.e. ceremonial way of
wearing toga [after town of
Gabii], 502.

gabion, wicker basket filled with
earth, 91.

Gaetulia, Biledulgerid, 209. → *Biledull*.

Galatea, sea-nymph, 453.

Galen (129-199 ?), very influential
Greek physician, 276.

Gallus (c. 69-26 B.C.), elegiac poet
[non-extant poems to his mistress
Lycoris; lost friendship of Augustus after military success in
Egypt], 475.

gambols, sports [? crude satires], 308.

Ganymede → *Jove*.

garboil, turmoil, 490.

gaudy, brightly coloured, 403.

gear, affair, business, 19; * genitals,
429. *if this gear hold*, if this arrangement does the trick [and/or *gear*
= 'weapon'], 258.

Gebenna, the Cevennes [whole sentence ×], 499.

gem, this fair, i.e. virginity, 406.

gentle, maggot [puns on 'well-bred'
and 'gentile'], 358.

Giants, i.e. monstrous rebels (incl.

Enceladus, 478) against the Olympian gods; they hurled crags, piled up mountains (→ *Pelion*) to reach heaven; were buried under Etna and other volcanoes, 62.

Gihon, river out of Eden encompassing Ethiopia; Nile [→ Gen. ii.13 : but it was Pison assoc. with gold], 53.

glaive, axe-headed spear [? assoc. with peasantry], 168.

glorious, boastful, vainglorious, 42.

goings out, i.e. holes in his clothes [pun], 283.

gold doth ill alight, i.e. the gold ring of knighthood [? ×], 472.

gown, i.e. 'civvies', 496.

Gracchus, 2nd-cent. B.C. brothers Gracchus, tribunes of plebs, agrarian reformers [bitterly opposed by Senate], 495.

* *grace*, credit, honour, 77. *graced*, well-received; well presented, 5; given clearance for degree at Cambridge [pun], 275.

Greekish strumpet → *Helen*.

groat, grey, i.e. like 'brass farthing', 377.

groom, inferior, underling, 134.

Gruntland, Greenland, 66.

Guallatia, Gualata, province in Mauritania, 75.

Guise, Henry, Duke of (1550–88), eminent French aristocrat, persecutor of Protestants [→ *Massacre at Paris*], 333.

Guyron, town N.E. of Aleppo; ? × for a river [? reached by forward troops only], 65.

Gyges, one of three hundred-armed monsters, sons of Tellus, the Earth, inveterate enemy of Jove [joined the rebellion of the *Giants* (→)], 442.

habit, bearing, 15.

Haemus, mountain range in Thrace above *Philippi* (→) and Pharsalia, 504.

Hainault, S. Belgian province, 124.

hairs, *loose*, i.e. sign of mourning, 456.

halcyon, kingfisher [hung up by beak, showed direction of wind], 334.

Halesus, son of *Agamemnon* (→);

founder of Etruscan town Falerii, 480.

Halla, town S.E. of Aleppo, 94.

hand, (solemn) word; friendship, 351. *in hand withal*, busy about it, 158. *hold in hand*, keep in suspense; ? delude, 362. *kiss my hand*, ? i.e. like cringing, polite Italian gesture [? expressive of indifference], 351.

happily, haply, 388.

harp, sweet-touch'd, → *Orpheus*.

head, (position of) power, 496. *gather head*, gather forces, 147. *hold my head*, wager my head, 365.

hearse, (trapping of) bier; * coffin, 189.

heartless, disheartened, 355.

heat, vigour, 196. *heat and moisture* → *element*.

Hebe → *Jove*.

hebon, ? some poisonous plant, 366.

Hecat, Titaness, threefold deity of underworld, teacher of magic and witchcraft [worshipped at crossroads with pole or statue; or *Hecat's tree* may be the yew], 300.

Hector, Trojan hero [married to Andromache], 435. *Hector's race*, Trojans, ancestors of Romans, 195. *woeful Hector*, i.e. corpse dragged behind Achilles' chariot, 442.

Hecuba, Queen of Troy, 200.

Helen, Helena → *Paris*. On death of Paris (= *Alexander*) she married the Trojan *Deiphobus*, who was later killed by her former husband *Menelaus*, 207. *Helen's brother*, ? Pollux, son of Jupiter by Leda [? he was supposedly hostile to Juno], 193; → *Jove*.

Helle, i.e. drowned in Hellespont, named after her [beloved by Neptune], 417.

hempen tippet, i.e. noose, 375.

Hercules (*Alcides*). In his labours he tamed the man-eating horses of Diomedes (*Aegeus*) [whom they ate], 105; slew dragon and stole apples in paradise garden of nymphs *Hesperides* [image of deflowerment], 419; fetched Cerberus from Hades, his arch-enemy Juno sending him mad by

Megaera, one of *Furies* (→) [×], 502. In rivalry for *Deianira*, daughter of King of Calydon, chief town of *Aetolia*, defeated *Achelous* (god of river on border) who took form of a bull; Hercules broke off horn, 468. Loved *Hylas*, beautiful youth whom, to his distress, he lost on the Argonautic expedition, 128. *Alcides' port*, modern Monaco, 498. *Alcides' post*, doorpost of Hercules' temple, 63. *Alcides-like*, etc., ? i.e. just as Hercules rescued Hesione from the sea-monster, 415.

Hermes, Mercury, Jupiter's messenger and so god of oratory, 16; [with wings on head and feet], 194; [lulled the hundred-eyed guard *Argus* asleep with his flute], 203.

Hermoso placer de los dineros, 'Beautiful pleasure of money' (Spanish), 349.

Hero, i.e. Leander drowned when her lantern went out, 458.

Hesperia, Hespery, western land = Italy, 199. *Hesperides* → *Hercules*. *Hesperus*, properly, evening-star [= Venus, which is also morning-star Lucifer, Phosphorus]; grandfather of Hesperides, 420.

Hesus, Gallic god equated with Mars, 499.

† *hey-pass* (*and re-pass*), allez-oop, hey presto, 317.

Heywood, Thomas (c. 1574–1641), actor, playwright and pamphleteer, 329.

hide, ancient measure of land sufficient for one household [pun. Dido bought as much land as might be enclosed with a bull's hide, which was then cut into thin strips], 219.

Hippolyt, Hippolytus, son of Theseus; dedicated to Diana, torn to pieces by frightened horses after refusing advances of stepmother *Phaedra*, 121; [*wild* = 'unruly', 'untamed' (by love); ? 'wild driving'; ? 'crazy'], 402; [recipient of letter from Phaedra in Ovid's *Heroides*], 460.

Hodie tibi, cras mihi, 'Your turn today, mine tomorrow' (from Apocrypha: about dying), 374.

hold, stronghold, 89.

Homo fuge, 'fly, man', 286.

horns, make, i.e. indecent gesture with forked fingers, indicating a cuckold, 257.

horse-courser, horse-dealer [with reputation of a used-car salesman], 312. *horse-pestilence* i.e. with play on 'with a pestilence' = 'with a vengeance', 367.

hostry, hostelry, 293.

hue, appearance [? + sunburnt], 425.

humidum and calor → *element*.

humour, bloody, i.e. fluid which fuels the body through the veins, producing in the brain the spirits (→ *artier*) which control the sinews, 49. *mares' rank humour*, i.e. menstrual discharge, 431. *humorously*, fantastically, 488.

hundred for a hundred, i.e. 100% interest, 370.

Hyades, stars presaging rain, 32.

Hybla, Sicilian town proverbial for honey, 227.

Hydra → *Lerna*.

hypostasis, sediment, 117.

Hyrcania, rugged N. part of Persia, 230.

Iasion, lover of Ceres [in ploughed field], 476.

Icarian, of constellation Little Dog [after Maera, faithful dog of Icarius], 457.

Icarus, i.e. drowned when artificial wings fell off in sun's heat, 232.

Ida, Ide, mountain range in Asia Minor [assoc. with Trojan war], 93; [? × for Idalium, town in Cyprus sacred to *Venus* (→)], 214; mountain in Crete [assoc. with Jupiter's upbringing], 476. *Idalian*, of Trojan Ida, Ganymede's birthplace [? × for *Idaean* (→ 469)], 404.

Ilia, Rhea Silvia, vestal virgin (with white fillet), mother by Mars of Romulus and Remus [her uncle ordered them to be drowned in Tiber], 456.

illustrate, make illustrious, 99.

Illyrian, of country on Adriatic, 66.

* *imbase*, impair, 471.

imbecility, weakness, ? disqualification, 184.

imprecation, prayer, 51.

In amicam, quod abortivum ipsa fecerit, 'Against his mistress because she has herself procured an abortion', 455.

In mortem psittaci, 'On the death of her parrot', 447.

Inachus, Greek river-god [loved sister, ocean-nymph *Melia*], 468.

incens'd, inflamed [with lust], 403.

* *incest*, adultery, 444.

inch of raw mutton, etc., ? i.e. genitals, 293.

incony, sweet [+ *coney* (→)], 380.

Inde, India, America(s) or Far East, 133. *Indian mines*, ? i.e. in Kashmir, 25. *Indian Moors*, American slaves, 278.

index, table of contents, 416.

infer, confer, bring in, 472.

Io → *Jove*.

io, i.e. exclamation of joy, 424.

ipse dixi, 'I have spoken', 247.

Iris, gods' messenger, 141.

Irus, a beggar [in *Odyssey*], 202.

Isara, tributary of Rhône, 498.

Isis, (Egyptian) moon-goddess [worshipped by Romans with annual period of continence]; ? i.e. menstruation, 433.

Isle Asant, Zante, Ionian island, 39. *late-discovered isles*, West Indies, 11. *Western Isles*, ? West Indies, 8.

Italia, i.e. after legendary king Italus, 199.

Itys → *Procne*.

Iulus, Ascanius (→), 227.

ivy, i.e. sacred to Bacchus, 475.

Ixion, father of the (lustful) centaurs [wretched in Hades for trying to seduce Juno], 403.

Jaertis, R. Jaxartes [Samarkand is near by], 100.

Jairim, Kirriah, ? Kirjath-jearim [? × for town in I Chron. ii.50–53], 337.

Jason, i.e. in Ovid's *Heroides*, receives letter from *Hypsipyle*, Queen of Lemnos, his deserted mistress, 460. → *Colchis*.

Jebusite, one of Canaanites dispossessed of Jerusalem by David; one who is not of children of Israel (→ Judges xix.11–12), 358.

Jerome's Bible, Vulgate [Rom. vi.23, quoted incompletely, I John i.8 out of context: neither is in words of Vulgate], 276.

jet, swagger, 142; stick out, 472.

jig, mocking ballad; musical farce at end of a play, 149. † *jigging*, jig-making; sportive; jogging, 7.

John the Great, Prester John, 75.

J[ones], R[ichard], London bookseller 1564–1602, printer of popular literature, 5.

Jove, Jupiter, i.e. supplanted his father, the old god Saturn, with aid of his mother *Ops* (→), 28. *black, infernal Jove* → *Dis. force of angry Jupiter* → *Giants. Latian Jove*, i.e. of Latium, the 'home county' of Rome, where the ancient Roman capital Alba Longa stood on Mt Albanus [*flame in Alba* is ritual fire, 501], 493. *Jove's huge tree*, oak, 188. *Jove, the Sun, and Mercury*, i.e. in astrology, Jupiter promotes ideal qualities of leadership; Sun confers energy, majesty, impressive speech; and Mercury eloquence and intelligence, 7. In his amours, Jupiter *Made two nights one* with Alcmene, 439; became a shower of gold to take *Danae* in a tower, 145, [inept image for bribery], 163; a bull to carry off *Europa (Europe)* to Crete, 66; an eagle to carry off the beautiful Trojan boy *Ganymede* (Aquarius, 503), whom he made his cupbearer in place of *Hebe*, Jupiter's daughter by his sister and wife *Juno*, 136; a swan to couple with *Leda* and sire *Helen* [she also bore *Castor*, famous for breaking horses, *Pollux* for boxing, 465; they became stars and were protectors of sailors, 453], 435; a shepherd to court Mnemosyne, 16; turned *Io* into a white heifer [Juno set the hundred-eyed Argus to guard her, but *Hermes* (→) killed him],

70; *his adulterous child*, Venus [by Titaness Dione], 212.

Julia, daughter of Julius Caesar, and wife of Pompey [died with baby 54 B.C.], 491.

Julius, Pope, ? for Pope John XXIII, deposed in 1415, 298.

Juno, sister and wife of Jupiter (→ *Jove*), 32. *Juno's bird*, peacock, 193. *Juno's town*, Carthage, 217.

Jupiter → *Jove*.

Justinian (*c.* 482–565), Emperor of Constantinople [drew up *Corpus Juris Civilis*, the body of (Roman) civil law, incl. *Institutiones*], 276.

Killingworth, Kenilworth, 173.

Lacedaemon, Sparta [home of Helen (→ *Paris*)], 224.

lake, dungeon; channel of water, 186.

Lantchidol, further part of Indian Ocean, 67.

Laocöon, Trojan priest [Minerva sent serpents to kill him for distrusting the horse, at which he threw spear], 204.

Laodamia, faithful wife of *Protesilaus* [brought him back from underworld], 460. → *Thersites*.

Laomedon, King of Troy, father of *Priam*, 469.

Larissa, modern El Arîsh, S. of Gaza, 71.

Latinus → *Turnus*.

Latmus mount → *Endymion*.

Latona's daughter, Diana, 62.

launch, pierce, 489.

Lavinia → *Turnus*.

lavish, squandering, 75.

lawnd, glade, 198.

League, Holy, association to promote Catholic interests, formed in 1576, 259. *leaguer*, camp, 75.

Leda → *Jove*.

Lemannus, Lake of Geneva, 498.

Lerna, district in N. E. Peloponnesus where Hercules killed Hydra, many-headed water-snake [spitting venom], 47; its blood was deadly poison, 366.

Lesbia, mistress celebrated by Catullus, 83.

let not, did not omit, 463.

letter of my name, etc., i.e. to give the whole name instead of the initial was a common joke, 293.

Leuca, Leucas, Ionian island [near Actium, where Augustus defeated Antony], 490; Leuci, tribe in N.E. Gaul [×], 498.

Levi, tribe of, i.e. priests who gave refuge to slayers, Josh. xxi. [? pun on 'levy'], 351.

Libya, N. Africa [*southern* = 'southward'], 198.

lift upwards, drawn upright; elevated; proud and presumptuous, 18.

Ligurian, of Liguria, region in N.W. Italy and in Gaul, 499.

Limnasphaltis → *Asphaltis*.

Lingons, Gallic tribe round modern Langres, 498.

Linus → *Apollo*.

lists' even ends, i.e. the starting-chambers on the course are level, 465.

Litora litoribus contraria, etc., 'Let your shores oppose their shores, your waves their waves, your arms their arms. That is my imprecation. Let them fight, they, and their sons' sons, for ever' (Virgil), 234.

load of logs, one that has eat a, ? i.e. financed his high living by selling his woods, 314.

Longshanks, Edward, Edward I, 157.

loves, Both, i.e. Venus and Cupid, 481. *love's art*, ? i.e. in Ovid's *Ars Amatoria*, 460.

lown, (low-born) rogue, 134.

Luca, modern Lucca [*Luna* is distinct town], 502.

Lucina, (surname of) goddess of childbirth, 455.

Lutetia, Paris, 267.

Lycurgus, Thracian King [Bacchus sent him mad for his hostility, and he maimed himself trying to cut down vines], 502.

Macareus, incestuous lover [recipient of letter in Ovid's *Heroides*], 460.

Maccabees, books in Apocrypha, 355.

Machda, Ethiopian town on tributary of Blue Nile, 75.

Maenas, priestess of Bacchus, 504.

maids' society, maids as a class, 466.

Maior sum, etc., 'I am too great for Fortune to harm' (Ovid), 184.

Malea, promontory, S.E. Peloponnesus, 458.

Maledicat Dominus, 'May the Lord curse him', 302.

† *malgrado*, in (downright) defiance of, 153.

Manent, remain, 9.

Manico, Manicongo, i.e. the Congo, 75.

Marcellus, i.e. consul and Caesar's enemy [there are three of this name], 496.

March-beer, strong beer [brewed in March], 292.

Mare Majore, Black Sea, 76. *Mare Rosso*, Red Sea, 96.

Marius, C. (*c.* 157–86 B.C.), consul and military leader [Sulla, his enemy, had his body disinterred and thrown into R. Anio], 502.

mark, sign, 446; quality, 448. *marking*, notice, 488.

Maro, Virgil, buried near Naples [regarded as magician in Middle Ages], 295.

Mars → *Venus*. *field of Mars*, Campus Martius outside Rome [where popular assembly voted], 493. *opposed star of Mars*, i.e. unfortunate circumstances [+ effect of wars], 432.

Martlemas-beef, i.e. old salt beef [at Martinmas, 11 November, cattle were slaughtered for the winter], 292.

mask, disguise oneself, dress up for fun, 16.

mass, treasure; (precious) metal in lump, 473.

masty, ? swinish; like a fat pig, 381.

mate, confound, 9; abash [? with *Mars* as object]; defeat [? × in history], 275.

Mauritania, Morocco and Fez (= Barbary), 34.

Mausolus, king in Asia Minor commemorated by the famous mausoleum, 83.

meaning has a meaning, i.e. the allusion serves a purpose, 381.

meanly, appropriately, 211.

Media, country on Caspian bordering Persia [assoc. with luxury], 11.

Megaera → *Furies, Hercules*.

Meleager, Argonaut; led heroes to slay boar devastating Calydon in *Aetolia* (→) [with fatal consequences], 45.

Memnon → *Morn*.

Memphis, once Egyptian capital, 12, [assoc. with occult], 455.

Menelaus → *Helen*.

meridian line, where the sun reaches its height, 43.

meteor, atmospheric phenomenon [cloud = airy meteor, rain = watery meteor], 61. *fiery meteors*, lightning, shooting stars, etc., 43. *freezing meteors*, frosts, 7.

Mevania, modern Beragna [famous for oxen], 499.

Midas, i.e. valued only gold, and preferred Pan's music to Apollo's, 411.

Milo Papinianus, T. Annius, i.e. when he was convicted in 52 B.C. of killing political rival, Pompey's troops intimidated his counsel, Cicero, 496.

Minerva, Pallas Athena, virgin goddess of wisdom, arts and crafts, incl. war [allegedly offended by Greek sacrilege], 203; [incensed with crow for telling tales], 448; [giver of olive to man], 457.

minion, 3-inch cannon, 90.

Minos, King and legislator of Crete, 476.

miss, loss, 102.

mithridate, universal antidote to poison [? × for poison itself], 53.

mo, more, 408.

mobile, able to move [pun on 'liable to change', a property of matter. Like Faustus, no matter stays forever in one place or state], 280.

Monsieur, Duc d'Alençon, younger brother of the King, 254. *Monsieur of Lorraine*, Guise, 264.

moon travails with charmed steeds, i.e. witchcraft causes an eclipse, 447.

Morn, Aurora, married to *Tithonus* [gods granted him immortality but not eternal youth, hence *old love*, 438]; their son *Memnon* was black King of Ethiopia [thus herself black-hearted], 439; killed by Achilles, he was commemorated by yearly battle of birds sprung from his ashes, 438. Marlowe has Apollo her lover, 415.

mortify, make oneself dead to the world, 346.

Mortimer, i.e. from *Mortuum Mare*, 'Dead Sea' [fanciful derivation, from Crusading], 151.

† *mother-wit*, one of untutored intelligence, 7. *he who on his mother veng'd his sire*, Orestes [*Destinies* × for *Furies* (→)], 430.

motion, emotion, 58; proposal, suggestion [pun], 221; [pun], 237.

mought, might, 215.

mount, rise up [i.e. pump out], 88; * go up into, 262. *Mount Faucon*, gibbet hill outside Paris, 245.

mountains of my breast, etc., ? i.e. vindictive enemies oppress Navarre's proud heart [+ as though on his lofty native mountains] but their arrogance will wither [? comb: *power of vengeance* also being Navarre's], 256.

† *Muff*, German or Swiss [probably derogatory], 65.

Mulciber, Vulcan, 501.

Munda, S. Spanish town [where Julius Caesar defeated sons of Pompey 45 B.C.], 490.

Musaeus, legendary Greek poet related to Orpheus; centre of a throng in Virgil's Hades (where the dead swarm like bees to return to earthly life) [confused in Renaissance with 5th-cent. A.D. grammarian, author of *Hero and Leander*], 278.

muschatoes, moustache, 375.

mushrump, mushroom, 139.

Mutin, Mutina, modern Modena [Antony besieged Brutus there 44–43 B.C.: two consuls were killed], 490.

Mycenae, ancient Greek city, E. Peloponnesus, 501.

Napen alloquitur, etc., 'He tells Nape to carry a letter to Corinna', 436.

napkin, ? handkerchief, 143.

Nar, modern R. Nera, 499.

Naso, Ovid, 455.

Natolia, Anatolia, i.e. Asia Minor, 64; ? a city [×], 93.

near . . . driven, reduced to sorry straits, 197.

nego argumentum, 'I deny the argument', 247.

Nemean beast, monstrous lion slain by Hercules in S.E. Peloponnesus; Leo [Sun is in Leo July–August, not winter], 504.

Nemes, i.e. the Nemetes, tribe once on Rhine, 498.

Nemesis, mistress celebrated by Tibullus, 474.

Neoptolemus, Pyrrhus, son of Achilles, 204.

* *nephew*, kinsman, 207.

Neptune's shore, ? i.e. to get away from it all, 504.

Nereus, old man of sea, father of 50 sea-nymphs, 453.

Nervians, Nervii, tribe in N.E. Gaul [defeated legion under L. Aurunculeius Cotta 54 B.C.], 498.

net, veil; snare [+ 'march in a net' = 'fail to escape notice'], 99.

never-singling, never separating [Hymen makes one flesh], 407.

New Temple, headquarters of Knights Templars [later seized by Edward and given to Earl of Lancaster], 131.

new-rac'd, newly scratched, 481.

Nigra Silva, 'Black Forest' S. of Kiev, 76.

Nilus' mouth, source of Nile, 489.

nine daughters, the Muses, 193.

Ninus, legendary Assyrian conqueror, founder of Nineveh, husband of *Semiramis* (→) [first ever to wage war], 110.

Nubia, region between L. Chad and Nile, 75.

number two no good divining brings, i.e. it was a bad omen that the tables were double (two-faced), 438.

O lente, lente, currite noctis equi, 'O, horses of the night, run slow, run slow' (Ovid) [spoken by lover to his mistress: *Amores* I.xiii.40], 324.

O per se o → *A per se a.*

Oblia, Olbia, town on Dnieper [×], 76.

Occasion's bald behind, i.e. time can be taken only by the forelock, 385.

Oceanus, sea god [Venus arose from the sea foam], 196.

Oenon → *Paris.*

on kai me on, 'existence and non-existence' (? attributed to Aristotle), 276.

One is no number, i.e. according to Aristotle, 406. *One among many is to grieve thee took*, i.e. she picks on some girl in the audience to resent as imaginary rival, 449.

onus quam gravissimum, 'the heaviest of burdens', 184.

Ops, goddess of (earthly) plenty, wife of Saturn and mother of *Jove* (→) [*heavenly* is ironical or inept], 28.

Orcus gulf, abyss of Hades, hell-mouth, 31.

order, row (of horns); (in this) manner [? pun], 308.

organon → *artier. Organon*, title of Aristotle's logical treatises, 247.

oriental sea, Pacific, 40.

† *orifex*, mouth of wound [blood was produced in liver], 91.

Orion, constellation assoc. with storms and rain [visible at beginning of winter], 199.

Orminius mount, modern Ala Dagh, range of mountains near Ankara, 77.

Ormus, trading centre or region at mouth of Persian Gulf, 356.

Orpheus, i.e. son of Apollo (Phoebus) and Muse Calliope, 474; rocks followed sound of his harp, 479.

Ossa, mountain in N. Thessaly, by Pelion, Tempe and Olympus, 498. → *Giants.*

ostent, portent, 502.

overthwarting, criss-crossing, 492.

overwatch'd, exhausted from lack of sleep, 187.

† *overweighing*, tipping the balance, overriding [the next decision may be God's], 51.

Ovid's flea, i.e. in *Elegia de Pulice*, 'Elegy on a Flea', poem attributed to Ovid, 292.

Oxen in whose mouths, etc., i.e. the oxen Jason ploughed with to win the Golden Fleece, 479. → *Argos.*

pack, conspire [+ 'be off' and 'hoist all possible sail'], 224.

Padalia, region between Dniester and Bug, 76.

Paean, the sun-god *Apollo* (→), 217.

painted, colourful, 145.

pais'd, weighed, 413.

Pallas → *Minerva.*

Pampelonia, Pamplona, capital of Navarre [now in Spain], 252.

Pangaeus, mountain in Thrace [overlooking Philippi], 504.

Paphos, town on Cyprus, centre of Venus cult, 217.

Par la mort Dieu, il mourra, 'God's death, he dies', 257.

paragon, consort, equal, 36.

parbreak, vomit, 56.

Paris (= *Alexander*), Trojan who abducted the Greek Helen [and so provoked the (disastrous) Trojan wars], 8. He had awarded a golden apple (*ball*) to Venus rather than Juno or Minerva as the most beautiful goddess, thus winning Helen in place of his wife, the nymph *Oenone* [? pun on ball-game], 212; [in Ovid's *Heroides*], 460.

Parma, Duke of (1545–92), Spanish governor of Netherlands, 263.

pash, crush, 36; splash, gush [× : does Marlowe mean in urinating? Also + *gem* = 'genitals'], 457.

pass, care, 9. *as't passes*, as beats everything, 293.

passion, painful attack, 241.

pathetical, stirring, 16.

patience of another sort, etc., i.e. my Protestant enemies, though persecuted, would not do such a thing, 251.

peacock → *Juno.*

Peleus → *Thetis.*

Pelides → *Achilles.*

Peligny = the Peligni, a tribe of C. Italy [× : not a town], 442.

Pelion, mountain range in *Thessaly* (→); provided timber for *Argo* (→), 452.

Pelops, served up as meal to gods by father *Tantalus* (→) [but reconstituted with artificial shoulder of ivory; loved and carried off by

Neptune], 402; won Hippodamia in chariot-race, 464.

Pelusian, of Pelusium, town in Lower Egypt [near where Pompey was killed and beheaded], 504.

Penelope, faithful wife of absent Ulysses [put off suitors on pretext of finishing robe, but secretly unpicked it at night], 467, → 474; [challenged suitors to string Ulysses' bow only to assess them as lovers: → *horn*], 432; [writes letter in Ovid's *Heroides*], 460.

Peneus, river in Thessaly, 468. *Nymphaeque Peneiae*, Daphne (→), 396.

per accidens, 'by accident', i.e. 'incidentally', 281.

Per inaequalem motum respectu totius, 'Through the unequal motion in respect of the whole' [the speed and direction of individual planets vary], 290.

Pereat iste, 'Let the fellow die', 186.

Pergama, Troy, 196.

period, sentence, 103; † accomplishment; ? * limited scope, 54.

Perkins, Richard (1585?–1650?), leading actor in 17th-cent. companies, probably playing e.g. Flamineo in Webster [friend of *Heywood* (→)] 331.

perpendicular, ? i.e. vertical bar representing Mediterranean in medieval T-in-O maps centred on Jerusalem [? + 'dependent' (province)], 49.

Persepolis, former capital of Persian Empire [actually ruins], 8.

Perseus, i.e. wore winged sandals to kill Medusa; Pegasus rose from her blood, 468.

Perusia, Perugia [starved out by Augustus 41–40 B.C.], 490.

Peter's chair, Saint, papal throne, 297. *holy Peter's feast*, i.e. on 29 June, 294.

Phaedra → *Hippolyt*.

Phaeton, son of the Sun by Clymene; lost control of his father's chariot and almost burnt the earth [Jupiter killed him with a flash of lightning], 121.

Phalaris, 6th-cent. B.C. Sicilian tyrant, overthrown by populace and burnt in his own brazen *bull* [+ ? pun on 'bull' = 'edict', another form of *letters*]. *Letters of Phalaris*, once attributed to him, have the penetrating candour of Machiavelli [but rather than write letters, or frame laws, or commission an ingenious instrument of torture, he would have done better to build a fort]. The *great ones* suffer the *envy* of the *petty*, 333.

Pharsalia, territory in Thessaly [where Caesar defeated Pompey, 48 B.C.], 489.

Phemius, musician [in Odyssey], 472.

Philip, King of Spain, 263.

Philippi, city in Macedonia [where Antony and Octavianus defeated Brutus and Cassius, 42 B.C.]; for 'Pharsalus' [where Caesar defeated Pompey], 504.

Philomel → *Procne*.

Phlegethon, river of Hades, 296.

Phoebe, moon, 31.

Phoebus, Apollo (→), 12.

Phoenissa, 'Phoenician woman', i.e. Dido, 220.

Phrygian, Trojan, 198.

Phthia, city and region in Thessaly, 468.

Phyllis, daughter of Thracian king; killed herself when her betrothed Demophöon was too slow returning [letter-writer in Ovid's *Heroides*], 460.

physic, take, i.e. plead indisposition, 488.

Phyteus, Pythius = *Apollo* (→), 121.

pickadevant, short pointed beard, 283.

Pierides, daughters of Pierus defeated in singing contest by Muses, 32.

pillar, i.e. a kind of mace, 297.

Pindus, mountain in Thrace [centre of Bacchus cult], 504.

piper, i.e. who leads the procession, 293.

pirates' wrack, i.e. victory over the pirates, 491.

† *pitch*, ? shoulders, 18.

place, topic, head; ground of proof, 247. *one place*, ? private parts [×], 457. *rude places yields*, ? withdraws from barbaric regions [×], 451.

place's laws, seating arrangements, 464.

plage, region, 67. *frozen plage of heaven*, ? i.e. the *zona frigida*, the Arctic, 49.

planet, moving several ways, i.e. being carried round by its own *sphere* (→) and the system as a whole, 409. *wand'ring planet*, moving heavenly body [as distinct from a fixed star], 28.

* *planeting*, * *tuneful*, (studying the) harmonies of the cosmos [×], 503.

plat, coin, piece of silver [? worth ⅜ crown], 353.

platform, draw a, lay a, make a map, design, 226.

Plato's wondrous year, i.e. according to *Timaeus*, the long period needed for the whole system of heavenly bodies to come full circle [later supposed to end in cosmic cataclysm or to be a particular year of disaster. *wondrous* = 'astonishing, prodigious'], 44.

plaud, appeal our, ? direct our plea for applause, 275.

pleasance, fine linen, 193.

plume (on), pluck out the feathers (of), 496.

poet's god, i.e. *Apollo* (→) [the gold of poetry is not the clever transferable sort], 432.

pointed, appointed [pun], 352.

poles → *sphere*.

Pollux and Castor → *Helen, Jove*.

* *Polony*, Poland, 252.

Polypheme, Cyclops outwitted by Ulysses, 66.

Polyxena, daughter of *Priam* (→), 206.

Pontus, district in N.E. Asia Minor, famous under aggressive King Mithridates [only when demoralized was he defeated by Pompey; took poison, 63 B.C.], 496.

porpentine, porcupine [believed to throw its spines as darts], 126.

port, gateway [echoes Matt. vii.14], 19.

portague, Portuguese coin worth £3 or so, 344.

Portingale, Portugal. *Bay of Portingale*, Bay of Biscay, 40.

* *powder, with a*, 'with a vengeance'; in a rush, ? gallop [pun], 367.

prefer, recommend, 106.

prest, ready for action, 68.

pretend, portend, 503; intend, signify, 364; offer, 386.

Priam, Priamus, King of Troy at its fall, 196, [depicted in Carthaginian temple], 200. *Priam's loose-tress'd daughter*, Cassandra (→), 435.

Primum Mobile, Primus Motor → *sphere*.

princess-priest conceiv'd by Mars → *Ilia*.

Prior, i.e. Ferneze, Grand Master of the Order [supposed to be celibate], 363.

privy ditch, i.e. along centre of main ditch, as defence against infantry and mining, 87.

prize was play'd, part was taken in (an acting) competition, 331.

problem, (question proposed for) academic discussion, 278.

proceed, make progress, 373.

Procne, served her husband *Tereus*, King of Thrace, with the flesh of their son *Itys*, in revenge for his adultery with her sister *Philomel* [the sisters were metamorphosed into a swallow and nightingale], 47.

prolocutor, spokesman, 16.

promise → *Abram's happiness*.

proof, for, in practice, 240. *to the proof*, to (good) effect, 127.

propterea quod, quandoquidem, i.e. both words = 'because', but the point of the variation is obscure. Baldock seems to mean that he does not *naturally* search his conscience; and Spencer's reply may play on far-fetched indecencies in *quando* and *conjugate*, 143.

† *prorex*, viceroy, 9.

prove, experience, 33.

provinces, i.e. of Holy Roman Empire, 278.

psalm, let me begin the, ? i.e. the Puritans were assoc. with psalm-singing, 246.

Puellam consolatur, etc., 'He comforts his mistress, whose hair has fallen out from too much care and attention', 439.

purchase, endeavour; what is at stake [? + 'loot'], 26.

purple, ? i.e. dressed in the purple-edged toga of the consul [×], 497.

puttock, kite, 448.

Pygmalion, King of Cyprus [Venus answered his prayer to animate a statue he had made], 200.

Pylades and Orestes, i.e. prepared to take each other's place as human sacrifice in Crimea (part of Scythia) [proverbial for their friendship], 17.

Pylius, Nestor, King of Pylos, elderly Greek at Troy, 471.

pyramides, pyramids; tapering shapes, 211; obelisk [actually brought by Caligula], 296.

Pyrene, Pyrenees, 504. → *Munda*.

pyromancy, divination by fire, 502.

Pyrrhus (319–272 B.C.), King of Epirus, victorious invader of Italy, 489. → *Neoptolemus* (his alleged ancestor).

Quam male conveniunt, 'How ill-suited they are' [i.e. to share one throne (or abode), as Ovid says of Majesty and Love], 132.

quarters, divisions of (celestial) *sphere* (→), incl. earth, 294.

quasi vestigiis nostris insistere, 'as if to tread in our footsteps', 284.

queen, but for a, i.e. Helen (→ *Paris*), 454.

quem dies vidit, etc., 'He whom the dawning day has seen exalted in his pride, the departing day has seen downfallen' (Seneca), 172.

Quemadmodum a Cupidine, etc., 'How he is obliged by Cupid to write of love instead of war', 423.

Qui mihi discipulus, 'Who (are) my pupil' [from a poem familiar in schools], 283.

Quin redis, Mephostophilis, etc., 'Why do you not come back, Mephostophilis, in the likeness of a friar?', 281.

quinque-angle, five-sided [one is free (on a dry plain?) to site the less defensible salient angles towards the enemy's most difficult approach], 87.

Quirinus, Romulus as god, 493.

quite, repay, 26; clear, rid [of suspecting or being suspected], 260.

Quod ab amica non recipiatur, dolet, 'He is grieved that he is not entertained by his mistress', 472.

Quod ab amica receptus, etc., 'He complains that, being admitted by his mistress, he could not copulate', 470.

Quod amet mulieres, etc., 'That he loves women whatever their looks', 445.

Quod Corinnae soli sit serviturus, 'That he is going to serve Corinna alone', 458.

Quod primo amore, etc., 'That, being carried away by first love, he suffers himself to be led in triumph by Cupid', 424.

Quod pro gigantomachia, etc., 'That he is obliged to write of love-affairs instead of the battle of the Giants', 442.

rabbi, scholar, 104.

Rainbow, Iris, 404.

rake up, cover (a fire) with ashes [so it smoulders unseen], 125.

Ramus, Petrus (1515–72), famous controversial philosopher; rejected argument by authority, esp. Aristotle; reformed logic, 246.

raught, carried off [lit. = 'reached'], 452.

ray, array [pun], 423; (vb) soil, 464.

record, witness, 466; † (vb) call to witness, 62; recall, consider, 114. *use will not poets' record hear*, poets' claims are not usually believed, 478.

redouble, return, 443.

reduce, set down, record; subjugate [pun], 48.

reflect, reflex, shine, 193, † 30.

region of the air, triple, i.e. the air was divided into three layers, 43; between these and the moon lay pure, invisible fire, *the fiery element* [? i.e. a barrier to mortals], 82. → *Cynthia*. Fumes (*exhalations*) were drawn up by the sun and stars, 193, 270, and might catch fire in the uppermost layer of the air, causing a fiery *meteor* (→), 110, [man-made], 86. *windy exhalations*, fumes and vapours struggling to break free from the interior of the earth and causing earthquakes, 13. *exiled air* is such pent-up air striving to return to its native place (→ *element*), 415. *exhaled sweets*, fragrance given off, 227. *build up nests/So high within the region of the air*, ? remain conspicuously and proudly alive; ? subsist on insubstantial hopes, 56. *triple region in the world*, ? i.e. medieval geography of Europe, Asia, Africa [but → Rev. vii.1], 48. *regions far*, ? i.e. the disaffected go abroad, 412.

renied, renegade, 29.

respect, end in view [with following quibble], 138.

† *retorqued*, recoiling, 56.

revoke, i.e. the crowd signal that the race is to be re-started, 465.

Rhadamanth and Aeacus, judges in Hades, 101.

Rhamnus, town in Attica where Nemesis, goddess of good and ill fortune, and vengeance, had a sanctuary, 22, hence surnamed *Rhamnusia*, 92.

Rhene, Rhine [× in Lucan text], 498. *Arctic Rhene*, Rhine to the north, 497.

Rhesus, Thracian ally of Troy whose magnificent horses were captured by Ulysses in a night attack, 194.

Rhodanus, Rhône, 499.

Rhode, modern Stadtroda, near Jena, 275.

Rhodope, (snowy) mountains in Thrace [called 'mounts of silver' because of silver mines], 13.

ringled, with rings on, 416.

Riso, Rize, coastal town in N.E. Turkey, 85.

† *rivell'd*, twisted, 210.

Rivo Castiliano, i.e. a drinker's salutation [obscure mock-Spanish], 379.

rombelow, i.e. meaningless refrain [? drum roll], 149.

Rome, ? Constantinople; ? × for 'Roma-nia' on map, 76. *Rome's infant walls*, etc., i.e. Romulus killed Remus, 491.

room, office, post, 22.

round, ring-dance, 167. *rounder*, more neatly, trimly, readily [pun], 445. *roundly*, briskly, 386; flatly, 163.

rout, rabble, 9. *Where the French rout*, etc., ? i.e. in some ceremony [× in Ovid text], 455.

† *royalize*, celebrate, make famous, 21.

ruffs, smooth faces and small, i.e. plausible (? young) university men, 308. → *band*.

rule . . . with private hands acquainted, ? i.e. grand political subject handled by an inexperienced private citizen, 459.

run, play, 380. *run division*, play melodic variations [pun], 377.

Ruthens, Ruthenians, tribe in S.W. Gaul, 498.

Rutter, (German) cavalryman, 65.

Saba, (Queen of) Sheba, country in S. Arabia, 288.

Sabines, ancient C. Italian people of simple virtue [war broke out when the Romans abducted their women, but under their king *Tatius* they amalgamated with Romans under Romulus], 432, [the Sabine women reconciled fathers and new husbands], 491. *Sabine gauntlets*, i.e. as the price of her treachery, the Roman Tarpeia asked for what was on the Sabines' left arms, meaning armlets, and was crushed beneath their shields instead, 436.

Sabinus, Ovid's friend [wrote replies to his *Heroides*, imaginary letters from famous women], 460.

sadness, seriousness, 294.

Saint Jacques' Even, 24 July, 366.

Salii, priests of Mars, 502.

Salmacis, nymph who threw herself at Hermaphroditus [and merged with him into a bisexual being], 414.

Samnites, ancient people of C. Italy, offshoot of *Sabines* (→), 334.

Sancina, Santina, town at E. end of Black Sea, 85.

Sanctus Jacobus, 'Saint James' (patron saint of Spain), 246.

Santons, Santones, tribe in W. Gaul [×: they actually rejoiced to see him go], 498.

Sappho, 7th-cent. B.C. poetess [letter-writer in Ovid's *Heroides*, vowing her harp to Phoebus if she freed herself from love-longing], 460.

sarell, harem, 35.

Sarmata, Sarmatia, i.e. E. Europe, 498.

Satirus, i.e. × in Ovid text for Atur = modern R. Adour in S.W. France, 498.

Saturn's royal son, Jove (→), 108.

Saturnia, Juno (→), 110.

Saul, offended God by sparing the Amalekites from total annihilation (I Sam. xv), 77.

Saving your reverence, i.e. 'Excuse the liberty' [pun], 129.

scald, contemptible, 'rotten', 19.

Scalonia, Ascalon in Palestine, 85.

Scamander, Xanthus (→), 468.

scamble up, scrape together, 336.

scape, escapade, 443.

Scheckius, Jacobus, philosopher of Tübingen; engaged in (published) debate with Ramus, 247.

* *scheme*, astrological diagram; horoscope, 277.

schools, public, lecture rooms, 277.

Scylla, betrayed her father, Nisus King of Megara, to Minos, by cutting off lock of his hair, 478; Minos deserted her and she swam after his ship, 232; sea-monster, a pack of barking dogs below the waist, 458; rock dangerous to seafarers between Italy and Sicily, 196.

† *'sdain'st*, i.e. disdainest, 180.

sea, into, i.e. into thin air, to no avail, 448. *purple sea* → *Oceanus*. *sea agate*, ? i.e. with wavy markings, 404.

seal, broad, Great Seal [on 'brief', royal mandate for charitable appeal, e.g. for captives of infidel], 148. *town seal*, i.e. stolen, to authenticate protection from arrest, 353.

sect, religious order; sex, 344.

See how he comes, i.e. he has not shown up, 33. *seen*, well versed, informed, 247.

seem, think fit, 252.

Selinus, hill city in Sicily, with great temple of Jupiter [destroyed by Carthage], 108.

Semele, i.e. requested her lover Jupiter to appear in his true form and was burned up; Jupiter then bore their child *Bacchus* in his *thigh*, 466.

Semiramis, legendary Empress of Nineveh [assoc. with hanging gardens of Babylon], 94, [voluptuous], 427.

Sequana, Seine [× for 'Sequani' tribe in E. Gaul], 498.

Seres, Chinese, 439.

serpent's head, i.e. (like 'serpent's tail') point where moon's path crosses sun's [in eclipse of the moon], 82.

servitor, veteran, 496.

set, beset, 243.

* *shade*, disguise, insubstantial shape, 198.

shadow, version, 44; spectral form, 278; (vb) screen, 51. *shadowing*, giving expression to, 62.

† *shag-rag*, ragged; rascally, 379.

shake off love with her heels, spurn love; copulate [pun], 257.

Shatillian, Chatillon, i.e. Admiral's family name, 245.

shine, shining, 423.

ships whose godhead, etc., i.e. Aeneas's ships, turned into goddesses of the sea, 479.

Show large ways, ? exhibit * grand manners, 479.

shright, shrieked; ? shriek, 502.

shroud, (vb) harbour, 100; (sb) garment, 214.

Si bene quid de te merui, etc., 'If I was ever kind to you, or if anything about me made you happy, please, please, if it is not too late to beg you, have pity for the ruin of a home, and change your mind. . . . Cease to upset yourself, and me also, with these protests. It is not by my own choice that I voyage onward to Italy' (Virgil), 230.

Si una, etc., 'If one and the same object is left to two people, one (is to have) the object, the other the value of the object, etc.' (after Justinian), 276.

ic probo, 'thus I prove (my point)', 279.

Sic, sic juvat ire sub umbras, 'Yes, yes; it pleases me to go into the dark' (Virgil), 234.

Sichaeus, Dido's dead husband, 202.

side, flanks, loins, 432.

Sidonian, from Sidon = Phoenician, Carthaginian, 198.

sign, seal, 460. *to give signs dull wit to thee is odious*, maladroitness in giving signals is contemptible to you, 437.

silly, pitiful, defenceless, 12; feeble, insignificant, 30; rustic, humble, 199; simple, 471.

Silvanus, god of fields and forests [loved *Cyparissus*, who was metamorphosed into a *cypress* owing to grief for a pet stag accidentally killed], 404.

silverling, shekel, 334.

Simois, river near Troy, 441.

sinew, nerve, 251. † *sinewy*, strung with sinew [×], 423.

Sinon, Greek who talked Trojans into admitting horse, 202.

Sint mihi dei Acherontis, etc., 'May the gods of Hades be favourable to me; farewell to the threefold godhead of Jehovah; hail, spirits of fire, air, water and earth! Prince of the East, Beelzebub, monarch of burning hell, and Demogorgon, we beseech you that Mephostophilis may rise into view. Why do you delay? By Jehovah, hell, and the holy water which I now sprinkle; and the sign of the cross which now I make; and by our vows, may Mephostophilis himself now rise to serve us', 281.

Sinus Arabicus, Red Sea, 107.

situ et tempore, 'in position and in time', i.e. direction and speed round the earth, 290.

Sixtus, Pope (1521–90), 263.

Slavonian, Yugoslav, 65.

smack, smattering, 247.

'Snails, God's nails [oath], 293.

snake, i.e. sacred to Isis, it shows goddess is gratified, 455. *mingle hairs with snakes* → *Furies*.

snicle, ? snare [crux. Does Ithamore describe or demonstrate a cat's cradle?], 380.

snort, snore, 443.

soil, plain; the refuge of a hunted animal, 216.

Solamen miseris socios habuisse doloris, 'It is a comfort to the wretched to have had companions in suffering', 285.

Soldino, Levantine town, 85.

sollar, loft, 371.

son slew her, etc., i.e. Alcmaeon killed his mother because she sent his father to his death in return for a necklace [×], 436. *son decrees*, etc. → *Julia*.

Sorbonnist, theologian of Sorbonne [? i.e. to be so self-opinionated is to miss the (divine) truth of Aristotle], 247.

Soria, Syria, 77.

sound, signal [by blowing, as on a trumpet], 194.

souse, knock, 495.

sparrow, i.e. sacred to Venus, 401.

sped, provided (with); well served (by), 427; done down, 311. *of so great hire sped*, so well paid, 447.

sphere, a heaven, one of the series of transparent globes, set one inside another, carrying the heavenly bodies (incl. the sun and moon, 16) in their orbits round the earth. An outer sphere, the *firmament*, 294, holding the *fixed stars*, is turned by the *Primum Mobile*, believed by some (incl. Marlowe's revisers in *Faustus*, if not by him) to be a separate sphere, surrounded by the abode of God (*the empyreal heaven*) and actuated by Him (as *Primus Motor*, 'first mover', 342); motion is thus imparted to the entire system, 42, which revolves round the axis of the *world's wide pole*, *the poles of the world*, every 24 hours, 290, [the poles remaining motionless, ? and not contributing to the music of the spheres], 277, while on the off-centre *poles of the zodiac* the sun and planets follow their seasonal courses, 290. *coelum cristallinum* and *coelum igneum* were spheres without heavenly bodies believed by some to lie between the firmament and empyreal heaven (or *Primum Mobile*), 290, [*fiery circles* suggest empyreal heaven or *coelum igneum*; and his eyes (or head) direct him just as the stars (or God) direct human affairs. → Chapman's tribute to Hariot], 18, → 82.

spial, spy, scout, 20.

spite of thee, in, involuntarily, 425.

spring, shoots, growth, 458. *in a spring thrives*, etc. → *Tantalus*.

Spurca, 'Filthy' (Italian), 364.

stale, accomplice, tool [? + * 'prostitute'], 436.

stall, ? licensed pitch, e.g. bench, 351.

standing, (military) position, 15; booth; erection [pun], 258.

star, erring, planet, 281. *fixed star* → *sphere*. *stars that shall be opposite*, i.e. there will never be another such horoscope, 95. *starry towers*, heavens, 195, → 476.

start up, Like one, i.e. who has started out of sleep, 481. *starting-hole*, bolting-hole, 160.

state, condition of life; high office; dignity, pomp; throne, 9; lord, 10; commonweal, 11; † (vb) station, set up, 350. *to our state*, as our rank, 16. * *keep state*, be dignified, haughty, 488.

stature of their feathered bird, statue of a golden eagle with eyes of precious stones, set on a tower in Damascus, 44.

stay, stop, 10; await, 33; wait, tarry, 374. *thereon do they stay*, they are awaiting the outcome; they are much concerned with it, 256.

steel, † strike; ? * sharpen, 157.

stepfather → *Venus*.

stern, rudder, 210.

stilt, crutch, 356.

Stoka, town on Dniester, 76.

stomach, appetite; ill-will; courage, spirits [pun], 47; (vb) resent, 130.

stones, our stock's original → *Deucalion*.

strait, tight-fitting, 457. *Straits*, ? i.e. of Otranto, 39; of Gibraltar, 40.

strike, ? produce (suddenly and violently), 460.

stripp'd, i.e. for a race (*course*) [? + sexual overtone], 405.

strive, strove, 454.

stuff'd, richly supplied, 19.

stump foot, club foot, 459.

Styx, (poisonous) river of Hades, 61; a mighty goddess of the underworld [with her children Zeal, Victory, Strength and Force, assisted Jupiter to overthrow the Titans, and was empowered to judge and punish perjury among the gods], 56.

subject → *form*.

* *suck*, breathe [we have been given the same healthy upbringing (in our home country)], 27.

Sulla, L. Cornelius (*c.* 138–78 B.C.), dictator [successful (with Pompey) in civil war against popular party led by Caesar's uncle, C. *Marius*; resigned before death], 496.

Sulmo, modern Sulmona, town of Ovid's birth, 457.

sum, high-point; totality, 55. *summ'd and satisfied*, ? fully accounted for and settled [he would break even on the investment with only a third of his return], 334.

Sun's bright sister, Diana, 197.

supply, reinforcement, provision, 242; (vb) * fill, * tenant, 82; * replace, 214.

sure, make, betroth, 141.

surprise, captivate, 412.

Suscepi . . . provinciam, 'I accepted the appointment' [as Protector], 184.

sway, impetus, impulse, 500.

Switzer, Swiss mercenary, 244.

symboliz'd, combined, 71.

synagogue, ? i.e. contemptuous, for 'Puritan assembly', 250.

Syrtes, Gulf of Sidra and Gulf of Gabès, off N. Africa [infamous hazards to shipping], 453.

Tabellas quas miserat, etc., 'He curses the letter which he had sent, because his mistress refused him the night', 437.

Tages, Etruscan founder of divination, 503.

taint, make a hit upon, 72.

talent, talon [? + 'appetite', 'anger'], 28.

tall, brave, 258.

Tanaïs, the Don [boundary of Europe], 165.

Tantalus, i.e. punished for divulging secrets of Jupiter: *tantalized* by water and branches of fruit receding from his reach as he stands in water, 414.

Tanti, i.e. (I rate them) no higher, 125.

taratantara, trumpet call, 99.

Tarbel, Tarbelli, coastal tribe in S.W. Gaul [? ×], 498.

Tarpeian rock, i.e. Capitol [with temple of Jupiter], 493.

tartar, dregs [? pun], 100.

Tartarian, of Tartary; * of hell (Tartarus) [pun], 9.

Tav'ron, R. Anio, tributary of Tiber, 502. → *Marius.*

temper, concoct, 80; melt; make well-disposed [comb], 81.

temple, *sumptuous*, St Mark's, Venice, 295.

Tenedos, island, Greek base by Troy, 82.

Tereus → *Procne.*

term, terminal figure [pun], 39; condition, 411. *stand upon terms*, make difficulties, 68. *terms of life*, lively terms, ? * lifelike terms, 18.

Terminat hora diem, terminat Author opus, 'The hour concludes the day, the author his work' [found on MS in library of Corpus Christi, Cambridge], 326.

termine, extremity, 290.

Terrene, Mediterranean, 29.

Tesella, town just S. of Oran, 74.

Thamyris, (blinded) Thracian musician [in *Iliad*], 472.

than, then, 445.

Thebe, wife of river-god Asopus, 468.

Thebes, Greek city famous in legend, site of great heroic war [ancestors sprang from dragon's teeth], 479. *he that built the walls of Thebes*, Amphion [played his lyre and the stones moved to build the walls], 289. *Theban brothers*, Eteocles and Polynices [the flames of their single pyre separated, from their undying enmity], 501.

† *theoria*, ? contemplation; ? scheme, 104.

Thersites, foul-mouthed and deformed Greek at Troy [*Protesilaus* was the first Greek killed], 448.

Thessale, Thessalia, Thessaly, flat N. region of Greece [→ *Pharsalia*, where relative fought relative], 489; [famous for sorcery and poison], 53, 431.

Thetis, (kindly-disposed) sea-goddess, mother of Achilles by *Peleus*, a mortal king in *Thessaly* (→) [? no known myth with Apollo. But → *Arethusa*], 75.

thirl, whirl, spin, 403.

Thracian, i.e. savage and rapacious, licentious, 403. Thrace home of Orpheus, inventor of lyre, and other early poets, 453.

Thrasimene, Trasimenus Lacus = modern Lago Trasimeno [where Carthaginians won great victory, 217 B.C.], 275.

thrust, make one, make one press forward [to join such a circle of comrades], 22.

Thyestes → *Atreus.*

Tibullus, love-poet, d. 19 B.C., 441. *Tibulli mortem deflet*, 'He grieves for the death of Tibullus', 474.

tilt, strive, clash, 13; charge, 33.

tire (on), tear (at) [like a hawk]; prey on, 28.

Tisiphon, one of *Furies* (→), 175.

Titan, sun [course appears counter to that of the *world* (= 'stars'). ×], 491.

Tithon → *Morn.*

Titus and Vespasian, father and son, Roman emperors (A.D. 9–79 and 39–81), conquerors of Judaea, 351.

Tityrus, shepherd in Virgil's Eclogues, 441.

Tityus, giant in Hades, covering 9 acres, 478.

toils, troubles, 490.

topless, lofty [? comb], 320.

totter'd, tattered, 377.

toward, promising, 98.

toy, antic, 'bit of fun', amusing pastime, triviality, trifle, 20; caresses, dallying, 426.

trace, traverse; chart, 48.

trade, habitual course of action, 42.

train, armed band, supporting troops, entourage, 8; tail, 82; treachery, 162; (vb) induce, entice [pun], 153.

tralucent, translucent, 407.

trammel, braid, 440.

trample, march along, 451.

transfuse, transfer, 466.

trapp'd, adorned [pun], 66.

Trebizon, town in N.E. Turkey [assoc. with chivalry], 66.

Trevier, (one of) Treveri, tribe in N.E. Gaul based on modern Trier, Trèves, 499.

Triton, son of Neptune, controlling waves with conch trumpet [? sounding fame of Troy], 196. *Triton's niece*, Scylla (→), 232.

triumph, i.e. Pompey had been below legal age (in 81 B.C.), 496.

trot, 'bag', hag, 431.

Troyans new, Romans under Aeneas, 454.

Tue, tue, tue, 'Kill, kill, kill' (French), 245.

Tuissimus, entirely yours, 329.

Tully, Cicero, 141.

Turk of tenpence, ? i.e. (cheap) archery target; aunt-sally, scarecrow, 375.

turns (up), disorders, 139. *Turns all the goodly birds to what she please*, ? i.e. they pay attention to what she wants, 449.

Turnus, in legendary Italy, King of the Rutuli, with Ardea as capital [Latinus, King of Latium, promised him his daughter Lavinia, but gave her in marriage to Aeneas. Hence Turnus fought and was defeated by Aeneas], 195.

Tuscia, ? Tuscany [×], 479.

twigger, lusty lad, 226.

Tydides, Diomedes [in Homer, wounded Venus in Trojan wars], 430.

Typhoeus, * *Typhon*, dragon who rebelled against Jupiter and stole his thunderbolts [monstrous progeny incl. destructive winds], 36. *Typhoeus' den*, ? Tarsus in Asia Minor; ? Etna, Jupiter's armoury [Typhoeus buried beneath by Jove], 218.

Tyrian, Phoenician, 197.

Tyros, Dniester, 76.

ubi desinit philosophus, ibi incipit medicus, 'where the (natural) philosopher ends, the doctor begins' (after Aristotle), 276.

uncertain shore, tidal coast [? of Belgium], 498.

Undique mors est, 'Death on all sides', 145.

unresisted, irresistible, 213.

† *unvalued*, priceless, 12.

uplandish, inland [+ 'rustic'], 402.

up-staring, ? with hair standing on end, 417.

ure, use, 355.

use, patient, habit of patience, 433.

Uz, modern Jordan [assoc. with godly Job (i.1)], 334.

vain name, i.e. no matter what the stigma, 433.

Valois, royal family [× : Isabella's brothers were Kings of France, but not of house of Valois], 148; [× : Guise belonged to house of Lorraine], 259.

value, valour, 50.

† *valurous*, valuable, 14.

Vangions, Vangiones, tribe on Rhine, 498.

Vanholt, Anhalt, region in which Wittenberg stands, 313.

Vanity, Lady, character in morality-play [not to be espoused by the hero Youth], 354.

Varna, Bulgarian seaport, 76.

Varro Atacinus (b. 82 B.C.), author of lost *Argonautae*, 441.

Varus, modern R. Var [boundary of Italy], 498.

vault, sewer, 185.

* *vein*, stream (of blood), 503.

Veni, veni, Mephostophile, 'Come, come, Mephostophilis', 285.

Venus, i.e. Vulcan, lame god of fire, caught his wife Venus and her lover Mars (who was thus Cupid's *stepfather*, 451) in a bronze net [and humiliated them], 216; mother of Aeneas, 456; her loved one *Adonis* was killed by a boar, and scarlet anemones sprang rom his life-blood [cult in Cyprus], 214. → *Oceanus*.

verse, line of verse [epic was written in hexameters, love-poetry in the alternating hexameter and pentameter lines of elegiac verse], 423, 459.

viper-curled, i.e. with mane of snakes [Cerberus], 478.

Virgo, salve, 'Hail, maiden', 363.

virtue, force, power, 24; property [as e.g. in medicine], 25; personal merit, manly excellence, 50. *With virtue of*, by virtue of, by means of [? + 'by moral endeavour of'], 60. *virtuous*, potent, life-giving, 30.

Vive la messe, 'Long live the mass', 263.

Vogesus, for Vosegus = the Vosges [× as river], 498.

Vulcan → *Venus*.

wall'd-in with eagle's wings → *Jove*.

Walsingham, Sir Thomas (1568–1630), country gentleman, courtier; cousin of the statesman Sir Francis; patron of Thomas Watson, George Chapman and Marlowe (who stayed at his house at Scadbury), 400.

war, two husbands', i.e. Trojan war, caused by *Helen* (→), wife of Menelaus and *Paris* (→), 435. *War only gives us peace*, ? i.e. saves us from worse disorders (i.e. tyranny) [? ×], 504. *wars 'twixt France and Germany*, i.e. mainly between Francis I of France (1494–1547) and Charles V of Spain (1500–58) [latter gave Malta to Knights of St John in 1530], 355. *he who warr'd and wand'red*, Ulysses, 442.

watch, look for an opportunity (to attack) [i.e. stalk], 156. *watch and ward*, armed guard, 80. *watches of the element* → *element. watchword*, signal for attack, 243.

water and air → *element*.

way, out of the, off course; out of his depth, 375. *covered way*, walk-way in cover behind *argin* (→), 87.

wear, enjoy as one's own [as in proverb 'win her and wear her' = woo successfully], 454.

web, slow, → *Penelope*.

weed(s), clothes, 12; herb, 54.

Welsh hook, bill-hook, 172.

wen, blemish, 428.

what, why, 448.

When, i.e. get on with it [stop bobbing up and down], 363.

whereas, where, 87.

while, until, 48.

whippincrust, hippocras [garbled], 294.

Wigmore, Mortimers' castle in County of Hereford and Worcester [might be sold], 149.

wind up, i.e. furl (the flags), 496.

windy, changeable, 451.

* *wings*, ? finger-guards [? pun: his lieutenants commanding the wings of the army], 22.

winter's tale, yarn, 216.

wis, I, indeed, 160.

'wist, had I', 'if I had known, [i.e. a thoughtless impulse, to be regretted later], 155.

wonted eyes inclin'd, Be not to see with, do not expect to see your familiar self, 440.

wood, senseless [pun], 225.

work the best, might that, i. in the hope that my protestations on the spot would do the trick [×], 450.

world, threefold, triple, → *region*.

wreak, vindictive injury, 489; (vb) harm, 453.

wrong wheels, i.e. (magic) spinning-wheel [? + 'wrung' = 'twisted (to do harm)'], 431. *as first wrong'd the wronged sometimes banish*, sometimes reject your wronged lover as though he had wronged you first, 433.

wrought, embroidered, 292.

Xanthus, Scamander, river by Troy, 200; Xuthus, king of Peloponnesus, husband of *Creusa*, daughter of Athenian king [Ovid's ×], 468.

Xerxes, King of Persia (486–465 B.C.), led two million soldiers against Greece, drinking rivers dry [campaign failed], 21.

y-sprung, issued, born [decoratively archaic form], 36.

Zanzibar, approx. S. Angola; S.W. and S. of Africa, 75.

* *zenith*, point of dominant (astrological) influence, 86.

Zoacum, tree in Turkish hell with beguiling bitter fruit, 80.

Zona Mundi, N. range of Urals, 98. *zone*, lateral division of (celestial) sphere, 294, incl. earth, e.g. *torrid zone*, tropics, 50.

Zula, town in Hungary, 76.

Everyman
A selection of titles

*indicates volumes available in paperback

Complete lists of Everyman's Library and Everyman Paperbacks
are available from the Sales Department, J.M. Dent and Sons Ltd,
Aldine House, 33 Welbeck Street, London WIM 8LX.

BIOGRAPHY

Bligh, William. *A Book of the 'Bounty'*
Boswell, James. *The Life of Samuel Johnson*
Byron, Lord. *Letters*
Cibber, Colley. *An Apology for the Life of Colley Cibber*
*De Quincey, Thomas. *Confessions of an English Opium-Eater*
Forster, John. *Life of Charles Dickens* (2 vols)
*Gaskell, Elizabeth. *The Life of Charlotte Brontë*
*Gilchrist, Alexander. *The Life of William Blake*
Houghton, Lord. *The Life and Letters of John Keats*
*Johnson, Samuel. *Lives of the English Poets: a selection*
Pepys, Samuel. *Diary* (3 vols)
Thomas, Dylan
   Adventures in the Skin Trade
   Portrait of the Artist as a Young Dog
Tolstoy. *Childhood, Boyhood and Youth*
*Vasari, Giorgio. *Lives of the Painters, Sculptors, and Architects*
   (4 vols)

ESSAYS AND CRITICISM

Arnold, Matthew. *On the Study of Celtic Literature*
*Bacon, Francis. *Essays*
Coleridge, Samuel Taylor
   Biographia Literaria
   Shakespearean Criticism (2 vols)
Dryden, John. *Of Dramatic Poesy and other critical essays*
   (2 vols)

*Lawrence, D.H. *Stories, Essays and Poems*
*Milton, John. *Prose Writings*
Montaigne, Michel Eyquem de. *Essays* (3 vols)
Paine, Thomas. *The Rights of Man*
Pater, Walter. *Essays on Literature and Art*
Spencer, Herbert. *Essays on Education and Kindred Subjects*

FICTION

---

*American Short Stories of the Nineteenth Century
Austen, Jane
    Emma
    Mansfield Park
    Northanger Abbey
    Persuasion
    Pride and Prejudice
    Sense and Sensibility
*Bennett, Arnold. *The Old Wives' Tale*
Boccaccio, Giovanni. *The Decameron*
Brontë, Anne
    Agnes Grey
    The Tenant of Wildfell Hall
Brontë, Charlotte
    Jane Eyre
    The Professor and *Emma* (a fragment)
    Shirley
    Villette
Brontë, Emily. *Wuthering Heights* and *Poems*
*Bunyan, John. *Pilgrim's Progress*
Butler, Samuel.
    Erewhon and *Erewhon Revisited*
    The Way of All Flesh
Collins, Wilkie
    The Moonstone
    The Woman in White
Conrad, Joseph
    *The Nigger of the 'Narcissus', Typhoon, Falk and other
       stories*
    Nostromo

*Stowe, Harriet Beecher. *Uncle Tom's Cabin*
Stevenson, R.L.
    Dr Jekyll and Mr Hyde, The Merry Men and other tales
    Kidnapped
    The Master of Ballantrae and *Weir of Hermiston*
    Treasure Island
Swift, Jonathan
    Gulliver's Travels
    A Tale of a Tub and other satires
Thackeray, W.M.
    Henry Esmond
    Vanity Fair
Thomas, Dylan
    Miscellany 1
    Miscellany 2
    Miscellany 3
*Tolstoy, Leo. *Master and Man and other parables and tales*
Trollope, Anthony
    The Warden
    Barchester Towers
    Dr Thorne
    Framley Parsonage
    Small House at Allington
    Last Chronicle of Barset
*Voltaire, *Candide and other tales*
*Wilde, Oscar. *The Picture of Dorian Gray*
Woolf, Virginia. *To the Lighthouse*

HISTORY

*The Anglo-Saxon Chronicle
Burnet, Gilbert. *History of His Own Time*
*Crèvecoeur. *Letters from an American Farmer*
Gibbon, Edward. *The Decline and Fall of the Roman Empire*
    (6 vols)
Macaulay, T.B. *The History of England* (4 vols)
Machiavelli, Niccolò. *Florentine History*
Prescott, W.H. *History of the Conquest of Mexico*

LEGENDS AND SAGAS

*Beowulf and Its Analogues
*Chrétien de Troyes. *Arthurian Romances*
 Egils Saga
 Holinshed, Raphael. *Chronicle*
*Layamon and Wace. *Arthurian Chronicles*
*The Mabinogion
*The Saga of Gisli
*The Saga of Grettir the Strong
 Snorri Sturluson. *Heimskringla* (3 vols)
*The Story of Burnt Njal

POETRY AND DRAMA

*Anglo-Saxon Poetry
*American Verse of the Nineteenth Century
*Arnold, Matthew. *Selected Poems and Prose*
*Blake, William. *Selected Poems*
*Browning, Robert. *Men and Women and other poems*
 Chaucer, Geoffrey
        **Canterbury Tales*
        **Troilus and Criseyde*
*Clare, John. *Selected Poems*
*Coleridge, Samuel Taylor. *Poems*
*Elizabethan Sonnets
*English Moral Interludes
*Everyman and Medieval Miracle Plays
*Everyman's Book of Evergreen Verse
*Gay, John. *The Beggar's Opera and other eighteenth-century plays*
*The Golden Treasury of Longer Poems
 Goldsmith, Oliver. *Poems and Plays*
*Hardy, Thomas. *Selected Poems*
*Herbert, George. *The English Poems*
*Hopkins, Gerard Manley. *The Major Poems*
 Ibsen, Henrik
        **A Doll's House; The Wild Dick; The Lady from the Sea*
        **Hedda Gabler; The Master Builder; John Gabriel Borkman*

*Keats, John. *Poems*
*Langland, William. *The Vision of Piers Plowman*
  Marlowe, Christopher. *Complete Plays and Poems*
*Milton, John. *Complete Poems*
*Middleton, Thomas. *Three Plays*
Palgrave's Golden Treasury
*Pearl, Patience, Cleanness, and Sir Gawain and the Green Knight
*Pope, Alexander. *Collected Poems*
*Restoration Plays
*The Rubáiyát of Omar Khayyám and other Persian poems
*Shelley, Percy Bysshe. *Selected Poems*
*Six Middle English Romances
*Spenser, Edmund. *The Faerie Queene: a selection*
  The Stuffed Owl
*Synge, J.M. *Plays, Poems and Prose*
*Tennyson, Alfred. *In Memoriam, Maud and other poems*
  Thomas, Dylan
        Collected Poems, 1934–1952
        Under Milk Wood
*Wilde, Oscar. *Plays, Prose Writings and Poems*
*Wordsworth, William. *Selected Poems*

RELIGION AND PHILOSOPHY

  Aristotle. *Metaphysics*
*Bacon, Francis. *The Advancement of Learning*
*Berkeley, George. *Philosophical Works including the works on
        vision*
*The Buddha's Philosophy of Man
*Chinese Philosophy in Classical Times
*Descartes, René. *A Discourse on Method*
*Hindu Scriptures
  Hume, David. *A Treatise of Human Nature*
*Kant, Immanuel. *A Critique of Pure Reason*
*The Koran
*Leibniz, Gottfried Wilhelm. *Philosophical Writings*
*Locke, John. *An Essay Concerning Human Understanding
        (abridgment)*
*Moore, Thomas. *Utopia*

Pascal, Blaise. *Pensées*
Plato. *The Trial and Death of Socrates*
*The Ramayana and Mahábhárata

SCIENCES: POLITICAL AND GENERAL

Aristotle. *Ethics*
*Castiglione, Baldassare. *The Book of the Courtier*
*Coleridge, Samuel Taylor. *On the Constitution of the Church and State*
*Darwin, Charles. *The Origin of Species*
George, Henry. *Progress and Poverty*
Harvey, William. *The Circulation of the Blood and other writings*
*Hobbes, Thomas. *Leviathan*
*Locke, John. *Two Treatises of Government*
*Machiavelli, Niccolò. *The Prince and other political writings*
Marx, Karl. *Capital. Volume 1*
*Mill, J.S. *Utilitarianism; On Liberty; Representative Government*
Owen, Robert. *A New View of Society and other writings*
*Plato. *The Republic*
*Ricardo, David. *The Principles of Political Economy and Taxation*
Rousseau, J.-J.
   *Emile
   *The Social Contract *and Discourses*
Smith, Adam. *The Wealth of Nations*
*Wollstonecraft, Mary. *A Vindication of the Rights of Woman*

TRAVEL AND TOPOGRAPHY

Boswell, James. *The Journal of a Tour to the Hebrides*
*Darwin, Charles. *The Voyage of the 'Beagle'*
Giraldus Cambrensis. *Itinerary through Wales* and *Description of Wales*
Stevenson, R.L. *An Inland Voyage; Travels with a Donkey; The Silverado Squatters*
Stow, John. *The Survey of London*
*White, Gilbert. *The Natural History of Selborne*